William Austen (1701–1737)
Surgeon of Tonbridge

Cassandra Leigh (1739–1827)

= Revd George Austen (1731–1805) *Rector of Steventon and Deane*

Philadelphia Austen (1730–1792) *m. Tysoe Saul Hancock Their supposed daughter (actually the daughter of Warren Hastings) was*

Leonora Austen (1732–*post* 1769)

Edward Austen (1767–1852) *known as Edward Knight after 1812 m. Elizabeth Bridges, and had eleven children, of whom the eldest, Fanny-Catherine (b.1793) was a favourite with Jane Austen*

4. Henry-Thomas Austen (1771–1850) *bankrupt in 1816 and subsequently curate of Chawton*

= Eliza Hancock (1761–1813) *m. (1) Jean de Feullide (guillotined in 1794), and had one son, Hastings, (1786–1801); (2) Henry Austen, and had no further children*

JANE AUSTEN

A LIFE

David Nokes

FOURTH ESTATE · *London*

First published in Great Britain in 1997 by
Fourth Estate Limited
6 Salem Road
London W2 4BU

A catalogue record for this book is available from the British Library.

ISBN 1–85702–419–2

Typeset by
Rowland Phototypesetting Limited, Bury St Edmunds, Suffolk
Printed in Great Britain by
Clays Ltd, St Ives plc

To the Memory of
ETHEL MURRAY NOKES
1919–1996

I have . . . endeavoured to give something like the truth with as little incivility as I could . . .

Jane Austen, Letter to Cassandra, January 1807

Contents

Contents

PART IV *Chawton*

Illustrations

1. Jane Austen (reproduced by kind permission of A Austen Esq)
2. The Reverend George Austen (reproduced by kind permission of Mrs E Fowler)
3. Mrs George Austen (reproduced by kind permission of Mrs E Fowler)
4. Cassandra Austen (reproduced by kind permission of A Austen Esq)
5. Illustrations from *History of England* (The British Library)
6. Eliza Hancock (Geoff Goode Pictures)
7. Thomas Lefroy (reproduced by kind permission of J G Lefroy)
8. The Adoption of Edward Austen (reproduced by kind permission of R Knight Esq)
9. Edward Austen (reproduced by kind permission of the Jane Austen Memorial Trust)
10. Jane Austen (National Portrait Gallery)

Acknowledgements

In my researches for this book I have received much valuable assistance and inspiration from several members of the Jane Austen Society, in particular from the Chairman, Mr Brian Southam, and from the Honorary Secretary, Mrs Susan McCartan. Considerable useful information has been supplied by local residents in the area of Monk Sherborne, Hampshire, and in this connection I should especially like to thank Mr Alan Albery, Mr Eric Ford, Mr Wyndham Knight and Mrs Pope. I should also like to thank the helpful and efficient staffs of the Hampshire Record Office in Winchester, of the Centre for Kentish Studies in Maidstone, and of the India Office, Newspaper Library and Manuscript Department of the British Library.

Any new biographer of Jane Austen must acknowledge one scholarly debt above all others, and that is to the work of Miss Deirdre Le Faye. With her extensive revision and enlargement of the work of William and Richard Arthur Austen-Leigh in *Jane Austen: A Family Record* (1989) and her revision of the work of R.W. Chambers to produce a new edition of *Jane Austen's Letters* (1995), Deirdre Le Faye has presented us with authoritative scholarly texts upon which to base any new interpretations. Though I am conscious that Miss Le Faye will not always agree with the conclusions I have drawn in this biography, I trust that even disagreements, perhaps *especially* disagreements, may prove illuminating in the study of Jane Austen's elusive personality.

Among others whose help and inspiration, of various kinds, I should like to acknowledge are the following: Janet Bately, Jane Bradish-Ellames, Terry Castle, Tom Deveson, Peter Kemp, Adam Phillips, Christopher Potter and Randall Wright. I owe a special debt of gratitude to Petonelle Archer for her magnificent work as my research assistant on this book. Above all, my thanks are due to my wife, Marie, for her constant encouragement and advice, for her careful reading of early drafts of this book, and for much, much else.

David Noke
London, 1997

Introduction

And, after all, we have lives enough of Jane Austen . . .

Virginia Woolf, A ROOM OF ONE'S OWN, 1928

'To be burned', Cassandra Austen wrote in 1843 on a bundle of letters sent between Jane and herself over many years. She later told her niece Caroline that she had indeed burnt 'the greater part' of her sister's letters. Even among those letters which remained, as Caroline Austen noted, several 'had portions cut out'. What dark secrets of Jane Austen's life were lost forever on Cassandra's bonfire? What shocking admissions or scandalous remarks could have been thought so discreditable that they must be consumed in the flames? None at all, we are assured by later members of the Austen family. There was nothing in the least shameful in any of the letters which Cassandra chose to burn. It was merely that aunt Jane was given to expressing herself in rather too 'open and confidential' a manner. After all, had not aunt Jane herself written in *Persuasion* that 'no private correspondence could bear the eye of others'? Cassandra had merely been acting in a spirit of sisterly tact when she chose to suppress some of Jane's private confidences.

Tact was the polite term which the Austens often invoked to justify their habit of suppressing awkward or embarrassing facts.

It was tactful to make no mention of Jane's 'mad' brother George, sent away from home as an infant and never afterwards referred to. It was tactful to pass over the details of Jane's aunt Leigh-Perrot's trial for grand larceny at Taunton assizes. Above all, it was tactful to censor the evidence of Jane Austen's scabrous and invective wit. Three days before she died, Jane Austen wrote a short satiric poem. She had been unwell for several months, confined to her bed with fevers and frequent backache, and had been recently moved from her home at Chawton to lodgings in Winchester, where she could be attended by Mr Lyford, the Surgeon-in-Ordinary at the County Hospital. It was St Swithin's day – 15 July – and the Winchester races had just begun. St Swithin was buried in Winchester and the coincidence of these two facts – the races and the saint's shrine – provided her with comic material. But the real themes of this curious little six-stanza poem are death and immortality. Jane Austen pictured the saint leaping from his shrine to curse the depraved subjects of Winchester for idling their time away at the races. 'When once we are buried you think we are dead/But behold me immortal!' Three days later, in the early hours of 18 July 1817, Jane Austen died, aged forty-one. Cassandra copied out this last poem and even underlined those words, 'When once we are buried you think we are dead/But behold me immortal!' But the version of immortality which this poem represented was not of a kind that recommended itself to later members of the Austen family. Knowing that she was about to die, having made out her will and taken Holy Communion with her brothers, Jane Austen had spent her last conscious hours dictating a satiric incantation which took the form of a malediction. 'By vice you're enslaved/You have sinned and must suffer . . ./You shall meet with your curse in your pleasures.' The last words she ever wrote took the form of a curse.

The fate of this last poem is indicative of how the family dedicated themselves to idealizing Jane Austen's posthumous reputation. Her brother Henry had the bad taste to mention it in the 'Biographical Notice' which he published shortly after her death, even exaggerating the poem's proximity to the hour of her demise. 'The day preceding her death she composed some stanzas replete with fancy and vigour,' he wrote. But Jane's niece Caroline Austen and nephew James Edward Austen-Leigh were horrified that such 'light and playful' verses should be remembered as the last things their aunt had composed. Caroline protested that 'the joke about the dead saint, & the Winchester races, all jumbled up together, would read badly as amongst the few details given, of the closing scene'. Accordingly, all references to the poem were deleted from subsequent editions of Henry's 'Biographical Notice'. James Edward Austen-Leigh made no mention of it in his *Memoir of Jane Austen* (1870), and it was omitted by William and Richard Arthur Austen-Leigh from their book *Jane Austen: Her Life and Letters*, published in 1913.

Instead, the family preferred to cherish the memory of Jane celebrated in some elegiac verses composed by her eldest brother James. '. . . Not a word she ever penn'd / Which hurt the feelings of a friend,' he wrote (this of the woman who had once exhorted Cassandra to 'Abuse everybody but me'). James went on: 'And not a line she ever wrote / Which dying she would wish to blot.' This claim was true, though hardly in the way that James Austen intended it. It was not Jane Austen who wished to blot out scandalous lines or censor satirical thoughts. But there were many other Austens who *did* wish to blot them out. Caroline Austen disapproved of the notion that any of Jane's early satirical writing should be published; 'one knows not how it might be taken by the public,' she wrote. She similarly deplored the thought of publicizing anything about Jane Austen's emotional life. 'I should not mind *telling* any body, at this distance of time,' she wrote to her brother, James Edward Austen-Leigh, in 1867, 'but printing and publishing seem to me very different from *talking* about the past.' In his *Memoir* of 1870, Austen-Leigh was accordingly discreet: 'I have no reason to think that she ever felt any attachment by which the happiness of her life was at all affected,' he wrote. Jane Austen's great-nephew, Lord Brabourne, was inspired by similar feelings of family delicacy when he published the first bowdlerized edition of Jane Austen's *Letters* in 1884. 'No malice,' he insisted, ever 'lurked beneath' Jane Austen's wit. Where this was not the case, Brabourne sought to make it so by carefully omitting from his edition any malicious reflections that Cassandra had allowed to escape the flames. Henry Austen's unfortunate reference to his sister's final poem was carefully censored, but another sentence from his 'Biographical Notice' was widely proclaimed: 'Faultless herself, as nearly as human nature can be, she always sought in the faults of others, something to excuse, to forgive or forget.' That was how the Austen family were determined to remember her. Discreetly, they adjusted the records of her life in efforts to ensure that that was how the world should remember her too.

This family tradition of producing censored versions of Jane Austen's life and works has had its inevitable effect on subsequent biographies, most of which have been based upon the tactful memoirs of later Austens. 'Family disagreements, to say nothing of family quarrels, were unknown to them,' wrote Elizabeth Jenkins in *Jane Austen: A Biography* (1938), exactly as the Austens themselves would have wished. 'They were a devoted family,' wrote David Cecil in *A Portrait of Jane Austen* (1978), preferring to gloss over the fact that one Austen son was excluded from the family entirely, while another son was sent away for adoption by wealthier relations. Tact is a commendable quality, and a biographer who insists on challenging such benign assertions may risk appearing as not merely tact*less* but as impertinent and prurient. But there are more important qualities than delicacy, as Jane Austen's own writings suggest. Much as she may admire a proper sense of discretion, her strongest commendations are always bestowed on frankness and openness. Yet it is these very qualities that have been chiefly absent from traditional accounts of her life. What is a biographer to make of the strange silences created by the family policy of censorship: blank years, for which no letters exist; mysterious gaps in the family record? How should we interpret these enigmatic *lacunae*? In *Mansfield Park*, Jane Austen comments on the joy with which Fanny Price seizes upon a 'scrap of paper' containing a brief message from Edmund Bertram. 'Two lines more prized had never fallen from the pen of the most distinguished author – never more completely blessed the researches of the fondest biographer. The enthusiasm of a woman's love is even beyond the biographer's. To her, the hand-writing itself, independent of anything it may convey, is a blessedness.' The distinguished author of these lines would understand the frustrations of a biographer who well knows that so many of his subject's most revealing letters have been deliberately destroyed.

During my researches for this book, I made several discoveries concerning the circumstances of the Austen family which may help to piece together some of the missing elements in Jane Austen's life and work. If the portrait which emerges is less saintly and serene than the one with which most readers are familiar, it has at least, I hope, the virtue of greater authenticity. I have, as Jane Austen once wrote, 'endeavoured to give something like the truth with as little incivility as I could'. Often the most beguiling of literary forms, biography may also be the most complacent. Unlike a novel, which relies upon the arts of invention and surprise to tease our expectations with a narrative whose conclusion is unknown, a biography is a story whose plot and characters are often disconcertingly familiar. In a sense, a biography is like a novel written backwards; taking as its starting point the well-known achievements of its subject's maturity and tracing back the hints of inspiration which brought those great works into being. Blessed with the comfortable benefits of hindsight, a biographer may be tempted to describe the steady progress of genius from earliest childhood glimmerings to full adult brilliancy. Awkward gaps in the record may be invisibly repaired in the interests of a seamless narrative; discordant notes may be ignored as irrelevant to the central themes. Yet life itself is not lived backwards, but forwards, with no foreknowledge of what the next day, or the next year, may bring. The girl of fifteen, whatever her dreams or fantasies may be, has no predestined sense that she is to become a famous author. Her mind is filled only with the thoughts and imaginings of a girl of fifteen. Accordingly, in this biography I have sought, as far as possible, to present each moment of Jane Austen's life as it was experienced *at the time*, not with the detached knowingness of hindsight.

This is a biography written *forwards*. In formal terms, it does not adopt the 'objective' view of a modern biographer but, like a novel, presents events through the perceptions of its principal characters (with only such occasional authorial interventions as might be permitted to the 'omniscient narrator' of a fictional work). In *Northanger Abbey*, Catherine Morland protests against history for being dull and tiresome. 'Yet I often think it odd,' she adds, 'that it should be so dull, for a great deal of it must be invention. The speeches that are put into the heroes' mouths, their thoughts and designs – the chief of all this must be invention, and invention is what delights me in other books.' In this biography, the speeches put into people's mouths are *not* invention, and those who wish to verify their accuracy may find the sources in the footnotes. Nothing is spoken which cannot be authenticated, and no incident presented for which there is not documentary evidence. But in the disposition of a character's thoughts, as in the interpretation of his or her actions, there is some degree of invention. The novels *Sense and Sensibility* and *Pride and Prejudice* were not published until 1811 and 1813 respectively but had existed in draft forms (as 'Elinor and Marianne' and 'First Impressions') for some fifteen years before they appeared in print. In this biography I have drawn quotations from the later published works as indications of earlier unpublished preoccupations. This may be called 'invention', but I hope the insights thus obtained may justify the liberty I have taken. Similarly, the discoveries I have made are not marked out for special attention in the text since, though they may be new to us, they were not so to the Austens, whose lives I present from their own perspectives. These 'new' facts are therefore silently introduced through the consciousness of whichever character they most directly concern. Most readers, I believe, will not wish to have their reading interrupted by obtrusive scholarly claims. For those who are more inquisitive about such matters, the footnotes will supply all the necessary information.

During the time that I have been writing this book, Jane Austen has rarely been out of the news. When I began it, the newspapers were filled with angry reactions to the suggestion, first published in the *London Review of Books*, that she might have had lesbian feelings towards her sister Cassandra. Shortly afterwards, my own researches into Austen family dealings with the East India Company provoked a lurid headline: '*Jane Austen's father was an opium smuggler.*' Since then, there have been various film and television adaptations of Jane Austen's works as well as innumerable literary sequels. Jane Austen has never been more popular, yet it is surprising how little we really know about her, and what fierce reactions are produced by any attempt to question that benign view of her character which her family were so anxious to perpetuate. Writing in the *Athenaeum* in December 1923, Virginia Woolf declared: 'Anybody who has the temerity to write about Jane Austen is aware of [two] facts: first, that of all great writers she is the most difficult to catch in the act of greatness; second, that there are twenty-five elderly gentlemen living in the neighbourhood of London who resent any slight upon her genius as if it were an insult to the chastity of their aunts.' I have had the temerity not only to write about Jane Austen, but to do so in a manner which challenges the familiar image of her as a literary maiden aunt. This is not because I wish to offer any slight to her genius. It is because I prefer to present her *not* in the modest pose which her family determined for her, but rather, as she most frequently presented herself, as rebellious, satirical and wild. 'Pictures of perfection as you know,' she wrote to her niece Fanny Knight in 1817, 'make me sick & wicked.'

PART I

Family Secrets

There are secrets in all families, you know.

Mr Weston, EMMA, I, xiv

CHAPTER I

Family Secrets

Bengal, 1773

It is the rainy season in the Sunderbunds. Inside his lonely make-shift hut the Surgeon-Extraordinary sits writing a letter home to his wife in England. The livid orange sun is sinking over this dismal region of fetid salt-flats, swamp and jungle, and he writes by the light of a reading-lamp she sent him in the last consignment from England. But the lamp has no glass shade, and without this it is practically useless, like the religious books she also sent him, which he has neither time nor inclination to read. It is three years since he last saw his wife, and he knows now that he will never see her again. Toil and disease have wasted his body and depressed his spirits. The richly embroidered waistcoat she made and sent to him hangs unworn in the wardrobe of his garrison lodgings at Calcutta. 'I should be the most ridiculous animal upon earth,' he writes, 'could I put any finery upon such a carcass as mine, worn out with age and diseases.'[1]

He keeps her miniature portrait on the folding-table in front of him. It shows a slim, elegant woman, with large dark eyes and flowing lustrous hair, dressed in her favourite turquoise gown, with a pearl choker at her neck. The portrait was done for him by Smart in the months before he left England in the autumn of '68. It was encircled by diamonds and meant as a keepsake that he could have by him constantly during his years of lonely exile. But already the fierce Indian climate is fading its subtle colours and smudging its delicate outlines. Before long, he knows, he must send it back to her to preserve it from utter extinction. Then his loneliness will be complete. Beside it, on the table, stands another portrait, of the girl he calls his daughter, made up of clippings from her own hair. But her lovely, smiling features are quite unrecognizable in this clumsy daub. He received it only weeks before and his dismay at seeing it was indescribable. Where were the bright eyes he loved, the soft pink girlish cheeks? All vanished. In this ugly misshapen caricature her face is broader than her breast, and her head far bigger than her body. He turns away from it in anguish. 'Pray endeavour to keep Betsy's recollection of me alive,' he writes. 'I fear she will only remember me by the name of father.'

Outside, the sky is dark with clouds and the foul stench from the salt-flats fills his nostrils. Tysoe Saul Hancock, Surgeon-Extraordinary to the garrison at Calcutta, has been in the Sunderbunds for over a month, overseeing his contract to supply *chunam* to the East India Company. The work is not going well. The Sunderbunds are a vast, desolate region of muddy estuaries and island jungles extending over an area the size of England, southward from below Culpee towards Luckypore in the east. The jungle is so thick it is impossible to see more than a few feet in any direction, except where the salt-makers have laboured to make a clearing. There is an absence of fresh water, save in those island hollows where tigers, wild hogs and rhinoceroses abound. In the Sunderbunds there are neither houses nor huts, and the labourers who work there making salt or *chunam* are obliged before sunset to remove in their boats from the shore into the middle of the rivers. Even here they are not perfectly safe, for the tigers sometimes swim out and take them from their boats.

Tysoe Saul Hancock's thoughts turn once again to England, and to the Hampshire rectory of Steventon where his wife, Philadelphia, may, even now, be making one of her frequent visits to her brother, George Austen, the rector. How Hancock envies Austen's peaceful life in his sturdy whitewashed rectory surrounded by lofty English elms and orderly rows of spruce firs! How he covets George's sequestered hours of reading and meditation; his daily visits to see his infant sons, James and George and

Edward, at their nurse's cottage on Cheesedown farm; his life of rural contentment, disturbed only by an occasional dispute about a boundary wall between a Harwood and a Hillman. George is an honest man, unlike the coxcombs, politicians and cheats who make up the majority of the English colony in Bengal. In despatching consignments of diamonds back to his wife in England, Hancock has adopted a practice of addressing them to her brother George Austen, 'to guard against accidents', as he puts it. Among the accidents he has in mind are the machinations of their old uncle Frank. Frank Austen is supposed to be Hancock's attorney in England, but it is months since Hancock has heard from him, or had any statement of accounts. Money sent to Frank Austen at Sevenoaks has an unfortunate habit of disappearing, he finds, whereas money or diamonds despatched to George Austen of Steventon are sure to reach Philadelphia safely.

Hancock turns once again to the columns of figures in his account book. The loss of the *Aurora* the previous year was a blow from which he fears he may never recover. Yet still Philadelphia complains at being obliged to apply 'for every farthing' to old uncle Frank. How many times must he write to her that he dare not confront Frank Austen directly, for 'he has it in his power to hurt me'. Philadelphia's extravagance is a constant anxiety to him. For three years in London they had lived the fashionable life in their handsome apartment off the Strand; for three glorious years there had been splendid parties, elegant balls and spending at the rate of £1,500 a year, which was double their actual income. But at last all the money was gone. And now here he is, back in the pestilential Sunderbunds in a forlorn attempt to regain his fortune selling *chunam* to the Company. 'How heartily sorry I am,' he writes to her, 'that you do not understand accounts.' Yet all his exhortations to thrift fall on deaf ears. When he tells Philadelphia of the resourceful Mrs Taylor, who 'keeps her chariot and pays the schooling of her two children with every expense of housekeeping etc. with only five hundred pound a year', even he cannot restrain a mocking aside: 'Surely she must be a great economist!' Economy, he knows, is not in Philadelphia's nature, and in truth it is her extravagance that he loves. With every shipment home he sends her exotic gifts. He sends her the spicy Indian foods she had grown to love in their early married years together at Fort St David's: pickled limes, pickled chillies, balychong spice and cassondy sauce. He sends her favourite rare perfume, the precious attar of roses from Echarabad. He sends her rich Indian fabrics: soosy quilts and palampores for bed-linen, Malda silks, flowered muslin, seersuckers, atlas, doreas and sannow to be made up into gowns and shawls and underwear. He sends rich silks from Cossimbazar and muslin neck-cloths from Pullicat. Although living a life of monastic frugality himself, he cannot bring himself to reprove his wife's fondness for luxury. For Hancock knows if he should ever fail to provide for Philadelphia's desires, however whimsical, there is another who will cheerfully do so; and if he should omit the tender duties of a father towards his darling girl Betsy, there is always a rival father ready to assume his place. Before Hancock finishes his letter, fresh news arrives of further tiger attacks on the *chunam* workers on the river. 'We have unfortunately lost eight men by these terrible beasts,' he tells his wife. But there is other news which may be of greater interest to her. 'Mr Hastings is expected here the beginning of March,' he writes, and adds: 'his government will prove to him a crown of thorns.'

Deane parsonage, Hampshire, February 1764

It is nearly midnight in Deane parsonage, a damp, dilapidated building of small, dark, inconvenient rooms, scarcely any two of them on a level. George Austen sits at his desk by candlelight, laboriously rewriting the cramped and jumbled entries in the register of the adjoining parish of Steventon. He has had care of the parish for three years now, since his cousin Henry Austen resigned it in favour of the richer living of West Wickham, which lay in the gift of old Frank Austen of Sevenoaks. But George has only recently moved into the neighbourhood; for most of the past three years he has found it more agreeable to remain in Oxford, supported by his life fellowship at St John's. Though the revenues of the Steventon parish have, in the meanwhile, provided a welcome addition to his stipend, he has been quite content to leave the duties of preaching, along with other parochial chores, in the capable hands of another cousin, Thomas Bathurst, the curate. Only the imminent prospect of marriage has finally prompted him to resign from the comforts of St John's and retreat to the isolation of rural Hampshire. Now, as he toils over the parish records, he has reason to doubt the wisdom of that choice.

Torrential rain beats down heavily on the roof, and the uneven rectory floors are muddied with puddles of floodwater. For more than six months there has been unceasing rain in these parts; the river burst its banks in the first week of January, and since then there has been no passage on foot through the village. Several graves in the churchyard have fallen in, and there is no way of getting to church but through neighbour Harwood's garden or yard. The parish well has overflowed and a constant stream of water runs through the village from Shepherd's Pond by Hall Gate, through the common field and down to the parsonage meadow. There have even been small boys in the parsonage yard, catching fish from George Austen's back garden.[2]

As he labours at his self-imposed task of rewriting the parish records, he ponders over the secret histories of the lives whose details are now freshly memorialized in his neat clerical hand. He marvels at the promiscuous career of Mary Bennett, with her three bastard children: Rachel, baptized in July 1742; Hannah, baptized in February 1747; and John, baptized on 23 June 1753 and buried just nine days later. He laments the short, sad life of William Collins, son of Jeremiah and Ann Collins, baptized on 13 April 1749 and buried eight weeks later.[3] How silently these official records reduce the private joys and agonies of this secluded rural world to a few brief categories. How, he wonders, would the lives of his own Austen ancestors appear, abbreviated to such a bald summary? John Austen of Horsmonden in Kent (1560–1620); his son, John Austen II (1585–1650); and his grandson, John Austen III (1629–1705).[4] These Austens had flourished during that fortunate period when the family was included among the wealthiest wool merchants in the county. Power-brokers at county elections, and owners of substantial manor-house properties, their names were proudly enrolled, alongside the Bathursts and Courthorpes, in the annals of that prosperous company of woollen traders known as 'the Grey Coats of Kent'.[5] No simple parish record could ever disclose the disreputable details of that reversal of fortunes which his own branch of the Austen family had subsequently endured, and from whose painful consequences George himself still suffered. For that he must turn to a more eloquent document. Reaching inside a drawer, he takes out a sheaf of yellowed papers, loosely bound together by an unpractised hand. This is the private memorandum which his grandmother Elizabeth Austen had set down 'for mine and my children's reading', one bleak evening more than fifty years ago, when she found herself widowed, embattled and alone with seven impoverished children to support.[6] Elizabeth's husband – George's grandfather – had been a reckless, improvident man, who left many debts behind him when he died suddenly of a consumption in September 1704. Yet at first his widow was not greatly concerned by financial anxieties. Her father-in-law, John Austen, was still living, and was a very rich man, though, as she wrote, known to be 'loath to part with anything'. On his deathbed, her husband had begged his father to 'consider one child was dear to him as another' and besought him to take care of all seven Austen children. And his father had reassured him, though 'by a second hand', that he 'would not have him troubled about his debts', that he 'would see all should be paid' and that he would 'consider all his children'. But once her husband was dead, Elizabeth was quickly to learn how little such promises signified. John Austen now said the funeral should be as private as possible, and refused to allow even expenses of £10 to provide mourning clothes for the widow and children. As to his son's debts, he haggled, disputed and delayed, and at one point flatly refused to pay them. At last, after much argument, he was persuaded to part with £200; but on the day before the money was due to be paid, John Austen's brain was seized by a sudden fever and he too died. This was in July 1705, less than a year after the death of his son. The reading of John Austen's will had been a terrible shock to Elizabeth. Even as she recalled it, two years later, the memory of that day could still bring fresh tears to her eyes. She herself was never mentioned in it 'unless as it seem'd necessitated to make me appear as no friend, nay rather an enemy to ye family'. But the heaviest blow was 'to see my children so unkindly, nay I may say unnaturally dealt with'. For, in defiance of his promise, John Austen had singled out his eldest grandson (also called John) for special favour, but utterly neglected the rest. Grandson John Austen would inherit lands and estates; grandson John would be sent for education to Pembroke College, Cambridge; grandson John would ensure the survival and success of the Austen family line. What happened to his other grandchildren seemed not to concern him at all. Elizabeth had wept to see one child rewarded with a large estate, and 'ye others but as if servants'. When she saw how her daughter Betty was to be 'cut off from any prospect of future hopes', she could 'not forbear saying "Sure my father takes her for a bastard"'. Even the promised £200 to pay off her husband's debts was now denied, since, it was said, 'it was not specified in his will'. Nor was there anything she could do to challenge such cruelty. 'I had no pocket to know ye opinion of my Lord Chancellor in these cases.'

Reading again the severe terms of his own great-grandfather's will, George Austen was compelled to recognize in them an enduring Austen family trait. They were a family who had never scrupled to place sense above sentiment, and the calculations of prudence above mere affections of kinship. For a trading family in adverse circumstances, it was a matter of simple prudence to concentrate its resources, rather than parcel out lands and properties among a numerous progeny. But George's grandmother Elizabeth had thought less of land and chattels than of love and charity. Trusting to God's providence ('I hope He will give a blessing to all honest endeavours'), she had sold off all her household silver, together with her best bed and hangings, to pay off her husband's debts. She then let out the family home and moved to nearby Sevenoaks, where, as housekeeper at the grammar school, she got free schooling for her sons. 'It seemed to me,' she wrote, 'as if I could not do a better thing for my children's good, their education being my great care, and indeed all I think I was capable of doing for 'em.'

As he read through his grandmother's meticulous household accounts ('1708–9: For books, wax candle, school-firing and school-sweeping, 14s 6d'), George Austen wondered at the spirit of a woman whose resilience had rescued her children from the life of poverty to which their grandfather's will had seemed to condemn them. Elizabeth's dedication to the virtues of a sound education was something George Austen warmly approved. 'I always thought,' she wrote, 'if they had learning they might get better shift in ye world, with yt small fortune was alloted 'em.' With all the benefits of his own education at Tonbridge School and Oxford, George could not have expressed it better. By the time she died in 1721, his grandmother had the gratification of seeing all her children (save Robert who had died young) safely embarked on their chosen courses towards financial security. Betty was married to Mr Hooper of Tonbridge, and her four dispossessed sons were all apprenticed: Frank to an attorney, Thomas to a haberdasher, Stephen to a stationer, and William to a surgeon in Tonbridge. William Austen was George's father, though his memories of him were slight. He had risen to take up his own practice in Tonbridge, where he married George's mother, Rebecca Walter, the daughter of one physician and widow of another. George himself had been born in 1731, the third child of his parents' marriage and their only son.

George Austen had never known his mother. She had died shortly after the birth of George's sister Leonora, when George was barely a year old. But he did know his stepmother, Susannah Kelk, a selfish, unaffectionate old woman who, even now, continued to reside in their family home at Tonbridge, from which George and his sisters had been banished shortly after their father's death. Naturally, there had been a will to justify his stepmother's ways. George's father had drawn up his will after the death of Rebecca, but before his marriage to Miss Kelk.[7] Accordingly, no provision was made, or thought of, for any duties that a second wife might be expected to undertake on behalf of the children of a first. It was George's uncles, Frank and Stephen, who were nominated to act as guardians in the unhappy event of William Austen's death. Sadly, barely a year after making this second marriage, William Austen did die, quite suddenly, at the early age of thirty-six. His widow quickly left the children in no doubt that, since she was under no legal obligation to care for them, she wanted nothing so much as to be rid of them out of *her* house.

His uncle Stephen and uncle Frank had also proved themselves to be Austens of the severe and calculating kind. Whether it was that their own early education in the virtues of self-reliance and thrift had marked their characters with a zealous regard for economic self-interest, or whether it was an enduring jealousy of their wealthy eldest brother John, they had no time for any compassion which might interfere with trade. Both uncle Frank and uncle Stephen Austen had made it a point of principle to be rigorously unsentimental in the discharge of their avuncular obligations. Uncle Frank was then unmarried, and had neither the time nor the inclination to attend to the needs of a tribe of young nephews and nieces. He had set himself up in Sevenoaks, 'with £800 & a bundle of pens', close to the manor-house home of his brother John, where he contrived to amass 'a very large fortune'.[8] Uncle Stephen was married and had a son only one year younger than George. So the three Austen children, George, Philadelphia and Leonora, were sent off to his bookseller's shop by St Paul's Churchyard in London, at the sign of the 'Angel and Bible'. But uncle Stephen had not taken kindly to receiving these three infant charges into his home. For him, as young George Austen quickly learnt, the business sign which swung and creaked in the high winds that blew along Ludgate Hill was little more than a colourful trademark; it carried no promise of Christian charity. How well George remembered the day when he and his sisters presented themselves at their uncle's door, to be received 'with neglect, if not with positive unkindness'.[9] Everything that uncle Stephen had done for them had been done out of duty only, and with an undisguised ill will. His sole idea of education had seemed to consist in a settled determination to thwart every natural taste or inclination of his brother's children.[10] And, as soon as he had found a method to contrive it, he had despatched them on their travels once more, with no thought for their own wishes. George and his sisters had been cruelly separated and billeted out, one by one, in the homes of such relatives as could be prevailed upon to accept such an unwelcome burden. George himself was packed off to live with aunt Hooper at Tonbridge, where uncle Frank paid for tuition at Tonbridge School. Philadelphia was sent to their cousins, the Freemans, whence she had long since taken flight to Mr Hancock in Bengal; Leonora was despatched to begin that long, lonely existence as an object of family charity from which she had still not escaped.[11]

George Austen remembered Tonbridge School with a good deal of affection. It was there he had learnt to thrive under the patient discipline and sound instruction of his masters. The consciousness of his own impoverished circumstances had spurred him on to seize every opportunity for advancement. At the age of sixteen, he had gone up to St John's College, Oxford, on a fellowship reserved for boys from the school. Oxford had been his salvation. How he had loved the rituals and traditions of its collegiate life! Thereafter, his progress had been swift: a College Exhibition in 1751; ordination as a deacon in Christ Church Cathedral three years later; a period of schoolmastering at Tonbridge School, then a happy return to St John's as assistant chaplain and junior proctor. Oxford had always been good to him. Now, as he contemplated the uncertainties of married life in this damp corner of Hampshire, he was less sanguine about the future.

George Austen took out the miniature portrait that Cassandra Leigh had given him on their engagement two years earlier and contemplated the face of his future bride. Cassandra's features were aristocratic; her hair was dark and her eyes an unusual tint of grey.[12] She had an instinctive tendency to depreciate her own appearance; it was her elder sister Jane, she always insisted, who was the beauty of the family. But Cassandra did admit to a certain vanity concerning her fine patrician blade of a nose. She was amusingly particular about people's noses, he remembered, like one of the characters in the Reverend Laurence Sterne's strange new novel, *Tristram Shandy*. In the portrait, she wore an elegant blue gown which set off the slenderness of her face and her slight, spare figure. They had met first in Oxford, where the Leigh family had some very grand connections. Her uncle Theophilus had been Master of Balliol for almost forty years and was one of the university's celebrated wits. Cassandra loved to boast how as a six-year-old girl she had entertained this august figure with some smart nursery charades of her own devising. The old man, she said, had been greatly amused and had immediately pronounced her 'the poet of the family'.[13] Praise indeed from a man whose own *bons mots* were applauded by no less an authority than Samuel 'Diction-ary' Johnson! Cassandra's father, Thomas Leigh, had also been an Oxford man, elected into a fellowship at All Souls at so young an age that he was always known as 'Chick Leigh'. Cassandra had inherited much of her family's formidable quickness of wit and sharpness of memory. Though she was much given to regrets that her education had been 'not ... much attended to', it was her lively intelligence (what she called her 'sprack wit') that particularly endeared her to him. He did, though, experience a certain diffid-ence when she spoke, as she loved to do, of her family back-ground.[14] For the Leighs had rather more to boast of than mere academic honours. They were an aristocratic family with a distin-guished pedigree stretching back to the Reformation. Cassandra was never happier than when rehearsing the stories of her noble ancestors. There was Sir Thomas Leigh, who as Lord Mayor of London had conducted Queen Elizabeth on her coronation ride to St Paul's Cross in 1558. There was William Leigh of Adlestrop, who had forfeited his estates, and endured incarceration in Glou-cester prison, in the cause of his sovereign, Charles I. And there was Sir Thomas Leigh of Stoneleigh, who had sheltered Charles against his Roundhead enemies when the gates of Coventry were shut against him.[15] Cassandra's grandmother, Mary Brydges, was the sister of the Duke of Chandos, and the name Cassandra, which she shared with her aunt, was a Leigh family tribute to the Duke's wife, who bore the same name. All this was rather daunting for an orphaned boy whose own grandmother had been a school housekeeper. As he contemplated Cassandra Leigh's slender, aristocratic features, George wondered how a woman from such a family would take to the unglamorous life of a country vicar's wife in a humble rural rectory.

It was not that she was unfamiliar with the life of a country clergyman. Her own father had for twenty years been rector of

Harpsden in Oxfordshire until ill health had latterly forced him to retire to Bath. But Steventon was not Harpsden. Cassandra had been visibly discouraged by her first sight of the countryside surrounding her future Steventon home. She had been unable to disguise her dismay at the low, undulating Hampshire landscape when compared with the broad river, the rich valley and the noble hills she had been accustomed to behold at her native home near Henley.[16] Since their first meeting, George Austen had constantly striven to maintain a genteel air of confident prosperity. Their courtship had taken place in the fashionable squares and elegant crescents of Bath, or among the ancient quadrangles and sequestered college gardens of Oxford. Now, rather than dismay his future bride by disclosing the true privations of Steventon rectory (a small, dilapidated house of the most miserable description), he had hit upon a bold expedient. The rector of Deane, Mr Hillman, was a wealthy man who chose to inhabit the nearby mansion of Ashe Park rather than his own parish parsonage. Anxious to maintain appearances, George Austen had thought it a prudent investment to pay Hillman £20 a year in rent to live at Deane parsonage, rather than shock Cassandra with the prospect of Steventon's narrow rooms.[17] But he had reckoned without the rain and the floods. These recent inundations had reduced the parsonage to a state of waterlogged squalor, less prepossessing even than the rectory at Steventon. It was a useful lesson to him. He turned back to the parish records and resumed his work of patient transcription. 'John Cooper, the bastard son of Elizabeth Payne, privately baptised Feb 23, 1762.' Hereafter he would never seek to hide from his wife the realities of life in a rural parish.

Walcot church, Bath, February 1764

Away in Bath, Cassandra Leigh was leaving St Swithin's church in Walcot parish, where her father Thomas had been buried a few days earlier. His death, after a protracted illness, must put an end to any further delays in her proposed marriage to George Austen of Steventon. She reflected on what a mighty change in her circumstances this marriage must entail. It was not, perhaps, the kind of match that might once have been thought of. In terms of character Mr Austen was all that she could wish. He was blessed with a bright and hopeful disposition, combined with a mildness of temper and steadiness of principle. In appearance, too, he was more than satisfactory. At Oxford he had been known as 'the Handsome Proctor' on account of his commanding height and distinguished features. His eyes were not large, but of a peculiarly bright hazel; his complexion was clear, his countenance animated and his whole appearance striking.[18] Even in the miniature portrait which he had exchanged for hers at the time of their engagement, and in which he wore a pompous powdered wig with four sausage curls over each ear, the eyes retained their dark luminosity.[19] But in material terms it was hardly a match from which she could anticipate much ease, far less riches. There was, apparently, the prospect of some freehold properties in Tonbridge which he would inherit on his stepmother's death. That apart, they would be required to support themselves on Mr Austen's clerical income, which her father had reckoned at no more than £100 *per annum*, together with whatever produce might be yielded from the use of nearby farmland. Then there was Mr Austen's uncle Frank. Cassandra had heard a good deal about wealthy Frank Austen of Kent and what he might do to assist them. In recent years, it seems, Frank Austen had been busily buying up all the valuable land around Sevenoaks. Having remained thriftily single until he was nearly fifty, he had then married two wealthy wives. By the first, who died in childbirth, he had acquired some modest lands and properties; by the second wife, he had become a very wealthy man. She was a widow, left a great estate by her husband's will. But the man's family – the Lennards of West Wickham – had chosen to contest the will. The widow Lennard had then 'flung her cause into the hands of . . . old Frank Austen'.[20] Old Frank Austen had not only won the case, but won the wealthy widow as well. He had also persuaded the rich old Lady Falkland to act as godmother to his son, Francis-Motley. According to Mr Austen, this might easily produce a legacy to the boy worth £100,000. Cassandra knew that Frank Austen had recently purchased, on Mr Austen's behalf, the livings of the two adjacent parishes to Steventon, Ashe and Deane, so that Mr Austen might enjoy the revenues of whichever fell vacant first. But she drew little consolation from the thought that her best prospect of material comfort must depend on some neighbouring clergyman's death.

Yet, reflecting on her past experience (she was already nearly twenty-five!) and maturely considering with herself her best hopes of future happiness, Cassandra had decided that he must be the one. Many sensible men, she acknowledged, including perhaps her own dear Tom Lybbe-Powys, were somewhat alarmed by her habit of expressing *opinions* and her fondness for scribbling irreverent rhymes. She readily conceded that she was no great beauty. And of course, there was no question of anything that one could call a dowry. According to the terms of her father's will, she would inherit some leasehold properties in Oxford and the sum of £1,000 on the death of her mother. But that, she hoped, would be many years off. Her aunt Cassandra had received a £3,000 dowry from the Duke of Chandos, in part on account of sharing his wife's Christian name; but sadly, this tradition had not been continued to the next generation.[21] Of course, things were very different for her brother James. He already enjoyed the life of a landed gentleman, thanks to the intervention of great-aunt Anne Perrot, who used to read them nursery stories, and taught fine needlework to herself and Jane.[22] Great-aunt Anne had persuaded her childless brother Thomas to bequeath his estate at Northleigh to James. All that James had had to do was change his name from Leigh to Leigh-Perrot. James had then sold Northleigh to the Duke of Marlborough, and bought the charming Berkshire property of Scarlets, between Maidenhead and Reading. And now, it seemed, James was in the way to acquire yet more desirable properties. A marriage was in prospect with Miss Jane Cholmeley of Lincolnshire, who was heiress, as Cassandra heard, to grand estates in the Barbadoes.

Cassandra did not begrudge her brother his good fortune. Not herself romantic, her highest aspiration in matrimony was for kindness rather than wealth; her fondest hope was to emulate the contentment of her own parents' marriage. Her father had been widely known as one of the most sweet-tempered and cheerful of men. Their family life together in the old red-brick rectory at Harpsden might have been a period of happiness without alloy, had it not been for poor Thomas. It was several years since Cassandra had last seen her younger brother. In the family, his name was seldom mentioned. But she could still vividly recall his unavailing infant struggles to form a syllable or pronounce even the simplest of words. No one seemed to know the precise nature of his affliction. The physicians had many names for it, but were unequal to finding a cure. And then one day, when Cassandra herself was barely ten years old, little Thomas had been taken from the rectory, never to return. It was, undoubtedly, the only wise solution. She understood that Thomas was boarded out at the little village of Monk Sherborne, near Basingstoke, by a kindly couple called Cullum. He must now be sixteen years old.

It was only natural that Cassandra should have some misgivings at the momentous step she was about to take. Her first view of Mr Austen's Steventon parish had not greatly endeared the place to her. The landscape was low and undistinguished by any striking natural features; the rectory was mean and in a state of disrepair. But most of all she felt a lingering regret about severing her ties of affection with Tom Lybbe-Powys. The two of them had been friends since infancy, when they had played together at Hardwick Hall, or with the Cooper children at Phyllis Court. At last, the time had come for Tom to tell her that childhood friendship had matured into adult affection; but he had then no income to support a wife, nor any prospect of obtaining one. Whereas Mr Austen was the rector of one parish with the promise of another. She remembered the day, more than a year ago now, that had brought the news of Tom's appointment as rector of Fawley parish in Buckingham. By then she had engaged herself to Mr Austen, and the letter she had sent to Tom was filled with a tender regret. None of his friends, she wrote, could feel more real joy at this good fortune than she did herself. 'I am infinitely happy to know you Rector of Fawley as I well remember to have heard you wish for that appellation at a time when there was little probability of our living to see the day.' As she went on, she had allowed herself to indulge a brief fantasy of what might have been. 'May every wish of your heart meet with the same success,' she had written. 'May every blessing attend you, for no one more deserves to be blessed; &, (as the greatest felicity on earth) may you soon be in the possession of some Fair one, who must be one of the very best of her sex, or she will not merit the good fortune that awaits her. If her heart is as full of love & tenderness towards you, as mine is –' There she had paused. For a moment she had let the phrase stand as it was, as if complete: 'as mine is'. Then she had forced herself to supply the obligatory closing cadence: 'as mine is of esteem & friendship, you will have no cause to complain . . .'[23] Cassandra Leigh was too rational a person to dwell in a world of what might have been. Her future lay at Steventon in Hampshire and she resolved to accept it. She hoped that neither she nor Tom would ever have cause to complain.

George Austen completed his revision of the Steventon parish register on 11 March 1764. Four days later, the marriage settlement between himself and Cassandra Leigh was signed. They were married by licence on 26 April 1764 at St Swithin's church in Bath, where the marriage service was conducted by the rector of Fawley, Tom Lybbe-Powys. It was not an elaborate wedding. There was no money to waste on an extravagant bridal gown and, instead of virginal white silks, Cassandra wore a sensible travelling dress of hard-wearing red woollen fabric, cut in the style of a riding habit. The newly-wed pair set out straightaway for Hampshire, and their only honeymoon was a single night spent at Andover *en route*. Even that was hardly a romantic interlude. They were accompanied on their journey by a sickly seven-year-old boy – George Hastings.[24]

Hertford Street, London, June 1773

Philadelphia Hancock took a brief survey of the drawing-room of her new home in Hertford Street. For a modest house even here, in the most fashionable part of town, the rent still seemed excessive. But at last she need have no more worries on that score.

She and Betsy need never worry about money again. The letter that had come from Calcutta that morning had filled her with sheer delight. Hancock had always said the girl was to have the very best music-masters, but had despaired of finding the money to pay for them. He had often decreed that Betsy should learn 'to sit gracefully on a horse & ride without fear' (for her health only; Hancock called fox-hunting 'an indecent amusement for a lady'), but had lamented that he could not afford riding lessons. Now they could pay for everything – music-masters, riding-masters, dressmakers, even (if necessary) teachers of arithmetic. Philadelphia took up the letter once more, which trembled in her hand as she read it. 'A few days ago Mr Hastings, under the polite term of making his god-daughter a present, made over to me a *Respondentia* bond for 40,000 rupees to be paid in China. I have given directions for the amount, which will be about £5,000 to be immediately remitted home to my attorneys.'[25] Even Hancock, though he might regret the source of this sudden wealth, could not repine at its consequences. Betsy would now have a chance to become the fine young lady he had always wanted her to be. Philadelphia called out to Clarinda, her Indian maid, to make the girl ready for the first visit of Mr Berg, who was to instruct her in playing the guitar.[26]

Philadelphia Austen had first met Tysoe Saul Hancock at Fort St David twenty years earlier, in the late summer of 1752. She was then barely twenty-two years old, and had ventured all the little wealth she possessed on this daring voyage to India. For her, the choice had been stark and clear: either to live, like her sister Leonora, as a penniless dependent relative; or to find herself a husband as soon as possible. But, in the competition for eligible bachelors, Philadelphia had found herself at a serious disadvantage. Beauty and wit alone, she quickly found, were no substitute for a substantial dowry; and while her natural endowments might have proved sufficient to gain her any number of gentlemen admirers, they were not calculated to engage the serious attentions of sober men intent on matrimony.

An expedient had then presented itself. For several years, her uncle Frank Austen had acted as financial agent to a Surgeon Hancock of the East India Company, from which Mr Austen derived a useful profit by the investment of Mr Hancock's private shipments of diamonds and gold. The surgeon, though no longer young, was in search of an English wife. He let it be known that he was not particular about a dowry, so long as his bride should be young and of a good family. Voyaging halfway round the world in pursuit of a husband of whose personal qualities she could frame no adequate notion, save that his character was generally declared to be 'respectable', was hardly an amiable prospect. Yet something about the boldness of it appealed to her love of adventure. And so, with Frank Austen's assistance, she had petitioned the court of the East India Company for leave to travel to India aboard the *Bombay Castle*. The ostensible purpose of her journey was to visit friends at Fort St David, though no one was deceived by that claim. It had become quite a fashionable thing among young English ladies of great daring but small dowries to try the same experiment. Philadelphia found she was not alone on her voyage in search of a husband. The *Bombay Castle* carried eleven such hopeful ladies on its outward journey that January. 'I would advise you to guard your heart well against them,' a friend wrote to Robert Clive in Calcutta; 'these beauties will have a wonderful effect upon you.'[27] This was advice which Clive chose to ignore. He married one of the 'beauties', Miss Maskelayne, at Fort St David the following February. Four days later, Philadelphia Austen married the Surgeon-Extraordinary, Tysoe Saul Hancock, at the same place. She had been in India for just six months.

It had never been a perfect match. When Philadelphia arrived at Fort St David in 1752, her romantic inclinations were sadly unfulfilled by the elderly fiancé who greeted her. Mr Hancock was a man twenty years her senior, and quite the antithesis to her in most aspects of personal character. Mr Hancock was earnest, meticulous, hard-working and thrifty, whereas she was flirtatious and impetuous. From the first there was no great bond of intimacy between them. Philadelphia's daughter Betsy was not born until nine years later. For much of their married life, the Hancocks lived apart; he up-country about Company business, she sharing the diversions of the English Bengal community with the other Company wives. Mary Buchanan was a particular favourite; Philadelphia had formed an acquaintance with her years before, and it was a pleasure to renew such an agreeable friendship. When Mary married Warren Hastings after the loss of her first husband (trampled to death in the terrible Black Hole of Calcutta), Philadelphia was among the first to offer her congratulations.

Hastings was an altogether more charming figure than her own husband. He was bold and witty and generous, whereas Hancock was often dull and mean. Hastings loved poetry and classical literature, but Hancock took little pleasure in reading, and if he did sometimes take up a book, it would be some earnest treatise on trade. Warren and Mary Hastings quickly had two children, while the Hancocks still had none. Little George was born in December 1757 and Elizabeth only ten months later, but the poor girl survived just a few weeks. When she died, Philadelphia had cried almost as much as Mary herself. Hancock and Hastings were often together, business partners in a host of private ventures, trading in salt and timber and carpets, Bihar opium and rice. But it was after Mary's sudden death at Cossimbazar in the summer of '59 that things began to change.

Elizabeth Hancock was born in the December of '61, two years and a half after the death of Mary Hastings. She was named in memory of Mr Hastings's own dead little daughter, and Mr Hastings himself agreed to act as her godfather. There was some gossip among the English colony at the time, but Philadelphia preferred to ignore it, and even Hancock chose to pay it little heed. In the spring of '65 they had all returned to England, the Hancocks, little Betsy and Mr Hastings. Their voyage on the *Medway* cost the Hancocks all of £1,500, but the two men were flush with all the money they had made from their trading ventures and even that did not seem such a mighty sum. They had taken houses off the Strand, Mr Hastings in Essex Street and the Hancocks in Norfolk Street, where it had given Philadelphia great pleasure to boast to her brother George (still a penniless clergyman in his damp country parsonage) how vastly she had risen in the world. It was still unaccountable to her how the money had all disappeared so quickly. They had not lived so *very* extravagant a life; a carriage and servants and some small entertainments must surely be reckoned among the *necessities* of a London life. Still, she had reluctantly resigned herself, three years later, to her husband's return to India, where he might accumulate a new fortune on their behalf. She and Betsy, she said, would endeavour to support his absence with equanimity.

Since his return to Bengal, however, Hancock's letters, although regular (one every six months, aboard the Company ships), made depressing reading. His enterprises met with no success; he was gloomy and often unwell. He constantly hinted at conspiracies designed to thwart and defraud him, and she did not care for his hints and asides about the characters of the English women there. Most of these were women who had arrived in India, like herself, in hopes of finding a husband. She did not need him to remind her of the perils of such an adventure. Even when, as in her case, such matches had been arranged by relatives in England, she knew it was not unknown for a contract to be cancelled, and the poor girl left alone, cheated and utterly without friends. Hancock had written of the plight of one of them. 'The motive of [her] coming hither,' he wrote, 'was an engagement of being married to a Major Blair,' but 'he died the day that she arrived here.' The girl said Blair had 'promised to leave her a thousand rupees, but that she had got nothing but two or three old trunks with some old clothes worth very little'. The consequence was easy to guess. On Christmas Day, sick with fever, she had come to Hancock and begged him to give her money. 'I did so,' he wrote; 'but I am sorry to find that she has got with a set of people who, I believe, intend to make a market of her.' The girl, he said 'seemed not pleased at my enquiring so strictly into her situation'.[28]

This was not the only girl he told her about. He said much the same about two of her own former friends: 'Liliana has two children, is very seldom sober and is quite common in the barrack at Madras,' he wrote. As to her friend Diana, he had heard she was 'in keeping with a young fellow who will probably leave her in the town very soon'.[29] It had probably been a mistake on her part to suggest that Betsy might be sent to India when she was a little older.

Hancock had seemed quite furious at that idea. 'No argument can ever induce me to give my consent to the introduction of my daughter to so lewd a place as Bengal now is,' he wrote.[30] The girl, he said, would be arriving 'at that period of life when she will naturally form to herself false notions of happiness, most probably very romantick, the disappointment of which may greatly embitter the rest of her days'. He then added: 'Debauchery under the polite name of gallantry is the reigning vice of the settlement.' But the sentence which had impressed itself most forcibly on her mind was one in which he seemed to hint plainly at her own former conduct. 'You yourself,' he wrote, 'know how impossible it is for a young girl to avoid being attracted to a young handsome man whose address is agreable to her.'

Hancock was wrong to say 'impossible'. It would not have been *impossible* for Philadelphia to have resisted Mr Hastings's advances. It would, though, have been unfeeling, she believed, and even, perhaps, inhuman. The fidelity which depended upon insensitivity was not of a kind to which she had ever aspired. She remembered how utterly broken Hastings had been by the deaths, one after the other, of his daughter and his wife in the years '57 and '58. He had told his friends how he must 'submit to ye will of providence'. But privately he had said he believed it had 'fallen to the lot of very few men so early in life to be forced to so cruel a trial'.[31] For all his brave words, it had not been the spirit of Christian resignation which had yielded him his greatest solace during that lonely time. The gossip had begun soon after Betsy's birth. Philadelphia had heard of a letter from Lord to Lady Clive: 'In no circumstances whatever keep company with Mrs Hancock,' the Governor had told her; 'for it is beyond a doubt that she abandoned herself to Mr Hastings.'[32]

Even now, poor Hancock, who had saved that vain woman's life, was still excluded and despised by the Governor's inner circle. In one recent letter he had written: 'I am much mistaken if Lady Clive's most extraordinary coolness be not owing to the pride of that woman. Surely I did enough for her when I saved her life; her return for which was the basest ingratitude to you.'[33] There was such a strange, old-fashioned sense of dignity about the way he wrote that; as if he truly did not know the reason for Lady Clive's coolness. How strange too his love for Betsy, even when he guessed the girl was not his own. In letter after letter he pleaded to be remembered to the girl he always called his beloved daughter. In one: 'It affords me comfort that Betsy remembers me, poor child!' In another: 'She will find many three years pass before she will see me again, if ever she may.'[34] And yet, however affectionate his words might be, Hancock could never match the warmth, the generosity of the man who contented himself with the title of Betsy's godfather. Even when he was far away on Company duties, she remembered how Hastings would write constantly to the Reverend Stavely ('Old Rattle', they called him) for news of the baby's progress. 'Little Betsy is very fond of Miss Ironside & her guitar, she is a sweet little girl,' Stavely had told him when the girl was just a few months old.[35] Whereupon Hastings had tried to teach himself the guitar in order to amuse her. And now, thanks to Hastings, the girl was learning the guitar herself.

For years, Hastings had sent private letters to Philadelphia, which arrived quite separately from the public letters between them. 'Kiss my dear Betsy for me,' he wrote in one, 'and assure her of my tenderest affection. May the God of blessedness bless you both.'[36] Hastings had always been generous with presents and little gifts of money, and Hancock was always telling her how grateful she should be. Here, in a letter sent three years ago, he wrote: 'Mr Hastings was very kind in leaving you money. I am greatly in his debt.' Now that Hastings had given Betsy a fortune of £5,000, it was clear to her that Hancock felt humiliated by such an extravagant bounty, and anxious at the gossip it must inevitably provoke. 'Let me caution you not to acquaint even the dearest friend you have with this circumstance,' he wrote. 'Tell Betsy only that her godfather has made her a great present, but not the particulars; let her write a proper letter on the occasion.'[37] Did that mean, Philadelphia wondered, that she should not even tell her brother George about it? Her visit to Steventon was already planned for the time of Cassandra's next confinement. Surely Hancock would want them to know the good news? Rereading that morning's letter she was struck by a familiar phrase. 'Mr Hastings, under the polite term of making his god-daughter a present, made over to me a *Respondentia* bond for 40,000 rupees . . .' Stepping to her writing-desk, she took out a letter sent by Hancock the previous September. 'Debauchery *under the polite name* of gallantry, is the reigning vice of the settlement.' *Politeness*, evidently, had acquired a somewhat equivocal significance in Hancock's vocabulary. She had never suspected her husband to be guilty of anything so fashionable as *irony*. Could he *really* have intended a satirical reflection by that coincidence of phrase? She noticed, in Hancock's most recent letter, that he had been careful to include details of Mr Hastings's polite attentions to a pretty German lady, Marian von Imhoff, the wife of a painter of miniatures lately arrived at Madras.[38]

Deane and Steventon

The parsonage at Deane was damp and dark and made an inauspicious marital home. The parish itself was small, and offered few of the genteel amusements or lively companions to which Cassandra had become accustomed. Most of the surrounding land and property was owned by the Harwood family, who occupied Deane House, a handsome red-brick mansion next door to the church. The Harwoods had run the village for several generations, and the current squire, John Harwood, like so many other rural squires, was reputed to have been the model for Squire Western in Fielding's *Tom Jones*. Harwood's chief amusement lay in feuding with Hillman, the rector who lived at Ashe Park; together the pair of them engaged in protracted territorial disputes, providing much gossip for their neighbours and 'good sport for the lawyers'. At first, Squire Harwood made a game of deferring to the formidable learning of his clerical neighbours, the Austens; but his boorish attempts at wit were a poor substitute for the urbane company of Oxford or Bath. 'Do tell us,' he begged George Austen on one occasion, 'is Paris in France, or France in Paris? for my wife has been disputing with me about it.'[39] With only the stimulation of

such sparkling conversational gambits, Cassandra Austen felt herself truly isolated.

The principal landowning family in Mr Austen's own parish
of Steventon were the Knights, who preferred to reside in their
handsome Palladian mansion at Godmersham in Kent and spent
little time in Hampshire. Yet even they could not boast a family
pedigree to match that of the Leighs. Mr Thomas Knight was not
really a Knight at all. He had been born Thomas *Brodnax*, but
had changed that name to Thomas *May*, in order to inherit a
relative's estate. He had then changed *May* into *Knight* a few years
later to inherit the Chawton and Steventon estates. Since each
change of name had required a separate private Act of Parliament,
such rapid transformations had not passed without comment. As
one honourable member was heard to remark: 'This gentleman
gives us so much trouble, that the best way would be to pass
an Act for him to use whatever name he pleases.'[40] Cassandra
acknowledged that her own brother James had similarly altered his
name; but she was pleased that James had not entirely renounced
the aristocratic associations of *Leigh* in order to enjoy the wealth
of a *Perrot*. It was a characteristic, she observed, of such new-
minted gentry to wish to invest themselves with instant traditions.
The wife of Mr Brodnax, alias May, alias Knight, was an Austen
descendant, and it was thanks to her that a whole generation of
young Austen clergyman cousins (Thomas Bathurst, Henry
Austen and now Mr Austen himself) had benefited from the living
at Steventon. Such a continuity evidently gratified the new Mr
Knight's desire to view himself as at the heart of a network of
established family ties. It also, as Cassandra noticed, made plain
the precise terms of relationship between the landowning 'Knights'
and their dependent relatives, the Austens.

Money was a constant problem. For two years after her marriage
Cassandra had no new clothes, but was reduced to wearing her
red woollen wedding-dress as her constant daytime costume. Mr
Austen did not spare efforts to augment his modest clerical income.
The Steventon glebe was only a little over three acres, but Mr
Knight kindly allowed them to sell produce from the 200-acre
Cheesedown farm in the north of the parish. Mr Austen drew

up a careful list of all the tithe-paying parishioners of Deane, though as yet their payments went to Mr Hillman, not to him. Save for the Harwood estates, the receipts from such properties as William Small's, James Long's or George Roberts's were meagre and promised no substantial change to their circumstances.[41]

The boy George Hastings, who lived with them in the parsonage, was a sickly delicate child. His father was well known to the Leigh family as well as to the Austens, and the boy had lived at Adlestrop from his first arrival in England until Cassandra's marriage to George Austen. In the interests of the boy's education, however, it was then agreed that he should be accommodated at Deane, where he could be taught by Mr Austen. Had more consideration been given to his health than to his education, Cassandra thought he might more happily have remained in Gloucestershire, than in this damp and chilly house. Instead, the boy's condition worsened, and in the autumn he died, the victim of a putrid sore throat. Cassandra mourned deeply over his death. She had grown so attached to him that his death, she said, caused her 'as great a grief as if he had been a child of her own'.[42]

There was no time to write to the boy's father, who had already sailed for England, with his friends the Hancocks, aboard the *Medway*. Mr Hastings was back in London by June, where he took a house off the Strand, close to the home of his sister Anne and her husband John Woodman in Cleveland Row. It was there that George Austen went to see him to explain the dismal circumstances of his son's death. To Hastings, the blow was almost too much to bear. He had lost his daughter, then his wife, and now his son. Yet he attached no blame to George Austen, who, as the brother of his dear friend Mrs Hancock, and uncle of his beloved goddaughter Betsy, remained a trusted friend. The two men talked of literature and poetry. As a boy himself, Hastings had been a classical scholar at Westminster, and it had been a severe disappointment to him when, instead of proceeding to Oxford, he had been sent out to earn his living with the East India Company. He still liked to turn his hand to Latin versification, and George

Austen knew that a judicious flattery of Hastings's poetical achievements was the surest way to earn his favour or deflect his wrath.

The Austens' first child was born at Deane that February and
given the name James. He was followed by George in August 1766
and Edward in October the following year. It seemed a little strange
to set down so many Austen names, one after the other, in the
parish register, but no other children were born at Deane during
these years. Mrs Austen made it a point of principle that her infant
boys should spend as little time as possible in the parsonage itself.
She was content to nurse them, but as soon as they were weaned,
they were sent out to be raised by John and Bessy Littleworth at
their cottage on Cheesedown farm.[43] This was not entirely, or even
mainly, on account of the dampness of the parsonage. It might
perhaps be called a matter of pride, that the boys should be treated
not with that domestic intimacy which characterized the family
life of the lower gentry, but rather with the detachment which
belonged to the Leigh family's aristocratic traditions.

Cassandra took every reasonable care to see that the boys were
not neglected. The infant boys were visited every day by one or
sometimes both of their parents; or, just as frequently, were
brought to see their parents at the parsonage. But the cottage was
their home and would remain so until each boy was old enough
to run about and talk. For a family of such modest means, it might
appear a kind of extravagance to insist upon putting out the infant
boys to be fostered in this way. But Cassandra was resolved that
it would breed a healthy independence in her sons and Mr Austen
did not care to contradict her in a matter upon which she seemed
so determined. Considerable care was exercised over the choice
of the boys' godparents. James's godparents included his grandmother, Mrs Leigh, and Mr Nibbs, a wealthy young man whom
George Austen had tutored at Oxford, and who was heir to an
extensive West Indian estate. George's godparents included the
surgeon Mr Hancock and Edward's included Cassandra's fortunate brother, Mr James Leigh-Perrot. Though the Austens were
themselves quite poor, they could boast several very wealthy connections; it was a matter of simple prudence to furnish their sons

with godparents who might provide for their hopes and expectations in future years.

Mr Austen laid out what small sums he could command for improvements and alterations at Steventon rectory, to house their growing family there and leave off paying rent at Deane to Mr Hillman. His financial worries were further eased in the summer by the sale of the Tonbridge family home. Miss Kelk had died that January, and Mr Austen was not such a hypocrite as to mourn the death of his hard-hearted stepmother, particularly when it brought him a sum approaching £1,200 as his share from the sale of the old house. Cassandra, too, received money, though for her it was an unwished-for gift, since it came in the form of a legacy from her mother, who died at the end of August.[44] Jane Leigh was buried at Steventon on 1 September, and Cassandra watched her mother's body being lowered into the chancel of St Nicholas's church with a deep sense of loss and desolation. Mr Austen wrote on her behalf to the family at Adlestrop to discuss the details of Mrs Leigh's estate and learnt that Cassandra's portion would amount to some £1,000. This money, they both agreed, should not be laid out upon such ephemeral items as new clothes or personal adornments, but prudently invested for the future. Accordingly, a quantity of Old South Sea Annuities, amounting to a nominal value of £3,350, was purchased in Mrs Austen's name. Mr Austen had permitted himself to spend some portion of his own new money on completing the improvements at Steventon rectory, which was now ready to receive them. The distance from Deane to Steventon was very short, not more than two miles at most, yet the journey there proved inconvenient and distressful. The summer had again been very wet, and the narrow lane become so rutted and muddy as to be impassable for a light carriage. Cassandra was expecting another child and found herself compelled to perform the journey perched awkwardly upon a feather-bed, placed across several pieces of soft furniture in the wagon which held their household goods. Despite all their best precautions, the joltings of the wagon proved too much for her constitution to bear. Almost her first experience upon entering her new home was to lose her baby.[45]

★　　★　　★

'I cannot help wishing ... that you would pass the time ... at Steventon,' Mr Austen wrote in the spring of 1770 to his 'dear sister' Susanna Walter.[46] Although she was not in fact his sister, but the wife of his half-brother William Walter, Mr Austen did not feel such terms of family endearment at all misplaced. He felt quite as much kinship with Susanna as he did with his actual sister, Philadelphia, and eagerly invited her to come to Steventon, with her little daughter Phylly, while her husband was away. 'I need not say you will make your sister Austen and myself very happy by such a visit, and I hope the change of air and place may be of some little service to you.' George Austen and his wife had been living at Steventon a year and several months, and he was keen to demonstrate what mighty improvements he had made about the place. The boys were strong and healthy, though little George was often subject to alarming fits, but Mr Austen was assured that these were not uncommon in infants of his age. 'You must not refuse my request,' he told Susanna, 'and I dare say you will not.'

He wrote this letter from Bolton Street in London, where he was visiting Philadelphia. Her husband, too, was away from home, not like Walter for several weeks but for several years. Yet Philadelphia appeared to view Mr Hancock's absence with a certain equanimity. She had her daughter Betsy, now aged eight and full of mischief, for company; she had her Indian maid, Clarinda, her English servant, Peter, and a wide circle of fashionable friends. Although there was much talk of economy and poverty, Philadelphia always seemed to live in quite a style. *Her* visits to Steventon were very grand affairs. She would arrive in all her plumage, like some exotic bird of paradise, wafting a scent of attar of roses and wearing a diamond necklace. She had promised her assistance at Cassandra's next confinement, though whether her presence would help much on such an occasion Mr Austen rather doubted. Yet he found it pleasant to observe how all the sisters discovered a companionship in mothering. Cassandra had volunteered to act in the same office of 'nurse in ordinary' to her sister Jane that summer, though her services had not in fact been needed on account of the baby boy presenting himself some weeks before his time.[47] It was perhaps a little strange that Jane Leigh had not married earlier, being always reckoned the 'acknowledged beauty' of the family. Thirty-three was quite an advanced age for a lady of her rank in the world to be embarking on matrimony. But Dr Cooper was an agreeable man, who had cheerfully resigned his All Souls fellowship in favour of married life with Jane at Southcote manor. Their son, evidently, was more impatient for family life than his mother had ever been. Baby Edward Cooper was 'of course, a small one,' Mr Austen wrote to Susanna, 'but however very like to live.'

It was during Susanna's visit that the Austens were forced to acknowledge what they had previously preferred to ignore in the sickliness of their own son George. Though she said nothing to the boy's disadvantage, it was obvious to all of them that he did not thrive. Already four years old, he struggled to form a syllable and was still subject to strange fits. Cassandra scarcely dared to voice the fear that troubled her, that her son might have inherited the same mental infirmity that afflicted her young brother Tom. 'I am much obliged to you for your kind wish of George's improvement,' Mr Austen wrote to Susanna after her return home to Tonbridge. 'God knows only how far it will come to pass,' he added; 'but from the best judgement I can form at present we must not be too sanguine on this head; be it as it may, we have this comfort, he cannot be a bad or wicked child.'[48] More cheerfully, he told Susanna that she might 'depend upon it' that, 'if it is tolerably convenient, we will return your visit another summer'. He emphasized his use of the word *we*: 'for I certainly shall not let my wife come alone, and I dare say she will not leave her children behind her.' What he meant was that he certainly *hoped* Cassandra would not leave her children behind her *again*, since at the time of writing Cassandra was on her own in London, visiting Philadelphia.

Mr Austen did not greatly care for his wife venturing on such a solo expedition. He did not care for London, and he distrusted the influence of Philadelphia. 'I don't much like this lonely kind of life,' he told Susanna frankly; 'you know I have not been much used to it, and yet I must bear with it about three weeks longer, at which time I expect my housekeeper's return, and to make it the more welcome she will bring my sister Hancock and Bessy along with her.'[49] Of course, it was a little joke of his to describe Cassandra as his 'housekeeper'. But, at the same time, it did vex him to suffer the multiplicity of domestic inconveniencies and privations entailed by Cassandra's absence. It disturbed him that his wife might discover a taste for the expensive style of London life, in preference to the daily chores of a thrifty rural existence. His distress was all the greater from observing that his sons seemed to share none of his dismay at their mother's absence. 'My James . . . and his brothers are both well,' he told Susanna, 'and what will surprise you, bear their mother's absence with great philosophy; as I doubt not they would mine.' It was not upon their mother that the young boys doted, he discovered, but upon Bessy Littleworth, their foster-mother, whom they all called 'Movie'.[50] Mr Austen now found himself protesting against that very instinct of detachment which his own (and Cassandra's) rational policy had been calculated to instil. The boys 'turn all their little affections towards those who were about them and good to them,' he complained. He attempted to console himself by viewing such insensitivity as a form of disguised blessing. 'This may not be a pleasing reflection to a fond parent,' he wrote, 'but is certainly wisely designed by Providence for the happiness of the child.' Yet it was a form of providential wisdom that distressed him, all the same.

On her return from London, Cassandra was quickly made aware of how Mr Austen had fretted during her absence. There should have been no cause for anxiety, she assured him. London was not the place for her. She wrote to Susanna Walter to insist how little pleasure she found in the 'hurry' of London life. 'Tis a sad place,' she said. 'I would not live in it on any account; one has not time to do one's duty either to God or man.'[51] She was careful to fill her letter with details of the butter-yield of her little Alderney cows, as if determined to show that her own housekeeperly sense of duty extended not only to God and man, but even to domestic animals. That August, it was not the Austens who went to London, but London which came to them, in the shape of Philadelphia and her daughter Betsy. There was such a hectic bustle of self-importance about everything that Philadelphia did. She was like a *grande dame* of the stage whose every action hovered between tragedy and farce. Quite at a loss without her servants, her exit from Steventon had been like a piece of theatrical comedy.[52] She had set out with little Betsy in a post-chaise, and they had got as far as Bagshot Heath when 'the postillion discovered he had dropped the trunk from off the chaise'. Philadelphia had immediately sent the man back with the horses to find it, 'intending to sit in the chaise till he returned'. But she was soon out of patience 'and began to be pretty much frighted, so began her walk to the "Golden Farmer" about two miles off, where she arrived half dead with fatigue, it being in the middle of a very hot day'. That had not been the end of her misadventures. 'When she was a little recovered she recollected she had left all the rest of her things (amongst which were a large parcel of India letters which she had received the night before, and some of them she had not read) in the chaise with the door open.' So another man was sent to retrieve them. Miraculously, neither the trunk nor letters had been stolen, and Mrs Hancock and her daughter at last reached Bolton Street 'about nine o'clock'. This was the same Philadelphia who now declared that she intended to exchange the vanities of London life for the quiet pleasures of a rural cottage in Surrey. Cassandra did not disguise her scepticism about that pronouncement. It came as no surprise to her when, only three months later, Philadelphia was complaining about the rain and solitude of autumn in the country. Byfleet was such a damp and dismal sort of place, she said, that she could hardly wait to return to town.[53]

Had Cassandra harboured any secret hankerings of her own for London life, they were quickly extinguished in the most effective manner possible. Barely nine months after her return to Steventon, she gave birth to her fourth son. Henry-Thomas Austen was baptized on 8 June; Philadelphia was chosen as one godparent and Tom Lybbe-Powys as another. Six weeks later, she told Susanna that she was 'got quite stout again, had an extraordinary good time and lying in, and am bless'd with as fine a boy as perhaps you ever saw; he is much the largest I ever had, and thrives very fast'.[54] This new birth must put an end to any thoughts of further gadding. 'It is not in my power to take any journeys at present, my little family grows so numerous, there is no taking them abroad, nor can

I leave them with an easy mind.' This time Mr Austen determined against allowing his new son to think of Cheesedown farm as his true home and Bessy Littleworth as his true mother. Baby Henry was brought back to the rectory when only six months old, and Cassandra found herself much occupied with maternal duties. In November, she wrote again to Susanna: 'As to my travelling into Kent it is not to be thought of with such a young family as I have around me. My little boy is come home from nurse, and a fine stout little fellow he is, and can run anywhere, so now I have all four at home, and some time in January I expect a fifth . . .'[55] George Austen viewed his growing family of boys with some contentment. Though the expense of keeping them was by no means inconsiderable, he had at least ensured that his beloved 'housekeeper' would remain safely at home.

Little George was still a problem. Some time after his fourth birthday, Cassandra told Susanna: 'My poor little George is come to see me today. He seems pretty well, tho' he had a fit lately; it was near a twelve-month since he had one before, so was in hopes they had left him, but must not flatter myself so now.'[56] Away in India, Mr Hancock, the boy's godfather, seemed much concerned for George's welfare, though Cassandra thought he might have been less peremptory in the expression of his concern. On receiving news of Henry's birth he had written back to Philadelphia: 'That my brother and sister Austen are well I heartily rejoice, but I cannot say that the news of the violently rapid increase of their family gives me much pleasure; especially when I consider the state of my godson who must be provided for without the least hopes of his being able to assist himself.'[57]

Four children in six years hardly seemed to Cassandra to constitute a *violently* rapid increase, nor a sign of reckless profligacy, as Mr Hancock appeared to believe. The poor man was no doubt very solitary, and much inclined to view himself as a victim of others' self-indulgence. It suited him, apparently, to see his little godson as a fellow victim with himself. In her November letter to Susanna she wrote: 'Thank God we are all well in health', and said how glad she was to have all her four boys at home. But by the time of George's sixth birthday, all her flattering hopes of him had gone. The malady could no longer be disguised, nor the resolution longer delayed. Madness, or mental infirmity, in a family was a sickness which afflicted not only the sufferer but also those who were compelled to be the daily witnesses of its melancholy effects. For the sake of the other children it was agreed that little George should be sent away from home. The Cullums, who had charge of the boy's unhappy uncle, had proved themselves quite equal to such a task. Cassandra made no protest as the solemn edict was pronounced, and the boy removed into safe-keeping with his uncle at Monk Sherborne. There were to be no visits, no letters, no family memorials or family records beyond what was necessary for the maintenance of the poor child's life. It would be almost as if the boy had never existed.

Despite Mr Hancock's melancholy warnings, Cassandra was soon 'heavy & bundling as usual' and in January 1773 her first daughter, baptized Cassandra-Elizabeth, was born. Philadelphia was on hand to assist at this birth, and she promptly wrote to Hancock to acquaint him with the news. His reply was predictably gloomy. 'I must own myself sorry to hear of you going to Steventon, & for the occasion of it,' he wrote back to her. 'I fear George will find it easier to get a family than to provide for them.'[58] Sadly, it was true that the rectory finances had reached a parlous state. Despite the most rigorous economies, the sale of crops from Cheesedown farm, and their own most frugal husbandry of vegetables from the rectory garden, poultry from the yard and the produce of Cassandra's domestic dairy, the Austens had been living well beyond their means. Mr Austen had been reduced to selling off his £800 holding of Old South Sea Annuities, until even that stock was now exhausted. Had it not been for a payment of £300 from Cassandra's brother James that February, they might have been entirely destitute.[59] Mr Hancock, though, had schemes to assist them. Despite frequently protesting against Mr Austen's improvidence in fathering such a numerous progeny (here was yet another letter in which he declared: 'I think he will find it difficult to provide for so numerous a family as his will probably be'), he always treated the Steventon family with great kindness. He sent

Mr Austen gifts of neck-cloths woven from Indian muslin, and gave Cassandra a handkerchief of Pullicat silk. His suspicions of old Frank Austen were well known to them, and he now seemed convinced that George Austen and Mr Woodman would be more trustworthy and diligent agents in preserving the interests of his wife and child.

That December, Mr Hancock drew up letters of attorney enabling George to act on Philadelphia's behalf in the confidential handling of receipts from India. Invoices for consignments of diamonds shipped to England were now made out in Mr Austen's name, as well as Mrs Hancock's, and he sent money-bills made payable either to Philadelphia herself 'or to your brother George'.[60] The precise legality of the many clandestine transactions in opium and gold and precious jewels in which both Mr Hancock and Mr Hastings were so deeply involved was something about which Cassandra preferred not to enquire. Susanna's family, she knew, derived some wealth from the West Indian trade, as did her brother's wife, Jane. The rich bounties which derived from such far-flung colonies were too considerable to warrant nice enquiries into the manner of their acquisition. Mr Hastings's generous gift to Betsy, of which Philadelphia had informed them as a most solemn secret, was but one instance of those riches. The reasons for *his* generosity were not hard to fathom, and no doubt accounted in large part for that note of asperity which so frequently characterized Mr Hancock's letters to his wife.

Happily, no such hints of scandal attended another increase in their income that year, which occurred when the living of Deane fell vacant on the death of Mr Hillman. Mr Austen assumed the care of both parishes, with additional annual revenues amounting to some £110. Their income might now be considered tolerably sufficient to support a family with no fear of insolvency; yet it amounted to no more than a modest competency. There was no surplus to guard against unforeseen disasters, nor to allow them even the most inferior of luxuries. Mr Austen, not wishing to subject himself and his family to a lifetime of mean economies, now resorted to that familiar expedient of impecunious but scholarly clerics – teaching. He proposed to take in boys to prepare them for university by schooling them, alongside his own sons, in classical studies. He had not taken any such pupils since the death of poor George Hastings. But his own son James was eight years old, and he reasoned that it would take no more time or effort to teach three boys than might be expended on one.

The first batch of new boarders arrived at the rectory that summer, and included the young Lord Lymington, Lord Portsmouth's eldest son. 'Jemmy and Neddy are very happy in [their] new playfellow,' Cassandra told Susanna in June.[61] Though the young lord was 'very backward of his age' ('between five and six'), he was 'good tempered and orderly'. She earnestly hoped that Susanna and her husband would come and visit them at Steventon soon. Mr Austen wanted to show Mr W. 'his lands & his cattle & many other matters' while Cassandra was equally keen to show Susanna 'my Henry & my Cassy, who are both reckoned fine children. I suckled my little girl thro' the first quarter; she has been wean'd and settled at a good woman's at Deane just eight weeks; she is very healthy and lively, and puts on her short petticoats today.' Her dairy, she boasted, was quite fitted up 'and [I] am now worth a bull and six cows, and you would laugh to see them; for they are not much bigger than Jack-asses – and here I have got Jackies & ducks and chickens for Phylly's amusement. In short, you must come, and, like Hezekiah, I will shew you all my riches.'

To his dismay, Mr Austen soon found that the young Lord Lymington, for all his wealth and title, was not much of a scholar. The boy stammered and shook and showed scarcely more signs of reason than poor George, his own son. Neither was he himself the ideal tutor for such a nervous boy, having, as he would acknowledge, 'little toleration for want of capacity in man or woman'.[62] Before long, the boy's mother became alarmed at the hesitation in his speech, which grew worse, Cassandra observed, during his time at the rectory. She removed the boy from Mr Austen, and resolved to place him under the care of a Mr Angier in London, who professed to specialize in the cure of such disorders. In his place came Master Vanderstegen: 'very good temper'd and well-disposed', said Cassandra. This was more than she could say for her baby daughter Cassy, who was 'almost ready to run away'.[63] Cassandra was interested to hear of Susanna's nephew George going to Jamaica that spring. It was 'high time', she said, for the young man to have some employment, and, by all she could learn, there were no better opportunities to be had than in the East or West Indies.

Calcutta, October 1775

It is evening in Calcutta, and a warm, dry wind flutters the coloured awnings of the street bazaars and sways the branches of the toddy palms and pepul trees. Away to the north, on the plains of Oudh, there are wars between the Rohillas and the Marathas. Inside the garrison, and throughout the Company offices, there are conflicts of another kind. Warrants have arrived from India House in London for the dismissal of officials accused of maintaining a corrupt monopoly in the trade in salt and betel-nut and tobacco. There are even rumours of accusations and cabals against Governor Hastings himself.

Inside his dingy rooms, the Surgeon-Extraordinary sits writing out his will. For him, the struggle is nearly over; on the desk before him is a pile of papers, the evidence of a life of blasted hopes and vanished opportunities. By now, all his fond dreams of gaining a fortune in India have long since been rudely shattered. He had foolishly hoped his post as surgeon to the garrison would be a sinecure; but instead it had involved him in endless toil. His return to Bengal had coincided with a terrible famine which half depopulated the province. He remembers the stench of dead and dying bodies lying in every street. 'You know how much I hate the practice of physick,' he had written to Philadelphia; 'yet I am obliged to take it up again: nothing could have induced me to do so, but the hope of thereby providing for my family.'[64] In return, she had sent him jars of currant jelly and raspberry jam which arrived full of maggots; a copy of Goldsmith's *History of England* with almost half its pages missing. And she had continued to send him hand-embroidered waistcoats despite his repeated protests that he was too old for finery. 'It is fully sufficient to have been a coxcomb in my younger years,' he had told her, but she had taken no heed.[65]

His trading ventures had all been dismal failures. Once, he remembered, he had boasted to her that 'the Gentlemen of the Council' had made him manager of 'a joint trade on a very large stock . . . with the compliment of my being the most capable person in India'. Yet only a few months later he had been forced to confess: 'my hopes are totally frustrated by the gentlemen having entirely given up the scheme. All my expectations are vanished like a dream & have left me astonished how I could, against all experience, imagine that fortune would be long kind to me.'[66] For years he had lived a life of monastic frugality, totally without company, seldom going abroad, and never inviting a single person to his table, on which, at his insistence, 'was never placed more than a fowl or a bit of mutton, & that only at noon'. Yet even this resolution had misfired, as he had explained to Philadelphia: 'I was given to understand that I was looked upon as one whose misfortunes had sour'd his temper and made him unsociable; accordingly I was shunned by almost everybody. This had a bad effect on my affairs.'[67] Looking back over his career, it seemed to Hancock that almost everything he had touched had turned to disaster. His scheme to supply the Company with *chunam* had failed when his labourers were killed by tigers and his business partner reneged on the contract, leaving Hancock with a heavy loss. Then there had been his plan to turn 'carpenter and blacksmith', with a contract to provide the Company with gun carriages and carpentry work at the New Fort. Hardly had the contract been signed, when the Company reversed its policy and announced an entire stop to all such work. To Hancock, all such reverses are evident manifestation of a malign destiny. 'You see how little industry and application can avail when Fortune or whatever else you please to call it is against a man.'

Fortune is not the only name that Hancock gives to the insidious forces which have thwarted his hopes at every turn. Conspiracy is another. He knows he is a victim of conspiracies both within the Company and beyond it. Frank Austen is a man whom he particularly distrusts. More than a year ago, he had taken a firm resolution to take all his affairs out of Frank Austen's hands. Turning over his papers, he finds a copy of his angry letter, sent to Philadelphia at that time.

> Your uncle has used me extremely ill in not having followed my directions to discharge my bonds with the first sufficient cash. Not having given me the least account of the sums you mention his having received, and not having answered one of my letters, nor written to me one single line. I know you are anxious not to disoblige him, but you are to consider he will soon have in his possession the whole of my fortune, and should any accident happen to him before he has settled my account and given proper vouchers for what he has received, you and the child may be left entirely destitute.[68]

For all the time that Hancock's bonds had lain uncashed in Frank Austen's hands, Philadelphia and Betsy had been supported not by Hancock's hard-earned revenues but by Hastings's easy philanthropy. Hancock reflects bitterly upon the contrast between the Governor's flourishing schemes for self-enrichment and his own frustrated efforts. It was said that in the first year of his Governorship alone, Hastings had shipped out some fifty-two chests of opium, not to mention the handsome profits from his trade in rubies, emeralds and diamonds. 'It is almost a moral impossibility,' Hancock wrote to Philadelphia, 'that anyone should get money here who is not in high station or a very great favourite with the Government.'[69]

Hancock's body is racked with pain from gravel and the gout, and he no longer harbours expectations of any personal favours from the Governor or his staff. 'I must own myself much hurt by my disappointment,' he confides to Philadelphia: 'it has cured me of vanity, and sunk me very low in my opinion, for I am convinced that Mr Hastings did not forget me, but was determined by my incapacity.' Slowly, and with frail, painstaking hand, he begins the inventory of his obligations. 'Item: To my sister Olivia Hancock of Canterbury, £30 *per annum* . . .' There he pauses. Foremost among the heap of documents spread out before him on the desk is a copy of the Governor's latest ostentatious deed of gift to Hancock's own wife and daughter. Two years ago, Hastings had promised them a bond of £5,000, which was generous enough. Now he has gone even further. Hancock takes up the document and reads. 'Indenture: Between Warren Hastings, Governor General of Fort William of Bengal, and John Woodman Esquire of London and the Revd. Mr George Austen of Steventon in Hampshire, two trustees nominated and appointed by the said Warren Hastings . . .' His eye skips down the pompous terms of the preamble:

. . . as well for the love and affection he hath and beareth unto Tysoe Saul Hancock, merchant of Calcutta and Philadelphia Hancock his wife and unto Elizabeth Hancock their daughter . . . and for diverse other causes and valuable considerations him thereunto especially moving . . . he hath given and granted . . . the full and entire sum of Ten Thousand Pound sterling lawful money of Great Britain.[70]

Hancock puts down the document. Ten thousand pounds, he knows, is more than the entirety of his own stock will yield. Even in death, it seems, the Governor is determined to outdo him. He turns once more to the terms of his own bequests and thinks again about his spinster sister Olivia in Canterbury. He writes: 'in case my estate shall not amount to eleven thousand pounds sterling . . . then this legacy to my sister is to be totally null & void and I can only recommend her to such assistance as my wife and daughter can afford to give her'.[71] There is a meanness in this gesture, he knows, but it is a meanness which the humiliation of circumstances has forced upon him. Only the week before, in the business of the Persian cat, there was yet another instance of the way the Governor seemed determined to humiliate him. Returning to the pile of documents, Hancock retrieves from it the only letter his beloved Betsy has sent to him all year. The girl has all but forgotten him, despite his pleas to Philadelphia that she should teach her to retain 'some small notion of a father who went to India'. To Betsy herself, now almost fourteen, he writes:

My dear child,

... The Governor, your godfather, desired me to send a
very fine white Persian cat of mine to you as a present from
him, which I would have done with pleasure. But your cousin
Stanhope, having quarrelled with a gentleman who lives at a
house next to mine, & the cat having strayed into his house,
this gentleman, or some of his people, shot her; I suppose to
be revenged on Mr Stanhope . . .[72]

Revenge, he thinks of adding, is a very powerful human emotion,
but she is probably too young to understand. Instead, he contents
himself by adding: 'If I should be so fortunate as to procure
another, I will send it next year.' Together with this letter he sends
her four strings of pearls 'exceeding even' and a filigree bottle
sewn into a bag. But for his final bequest he has another thought
in mind. Returning to his will, he adds this clause.

To my daughter Elizabeth I bequeath the miniature picture of
her mother painted by Smart and set in a ring with diamonds
around it which I request she will never part with, as I intend
it to remind her of her mother's virtues as well as of her
person.

He hesitates over the final words. How will Philadelphia understand this reference to her 'virtues'? As a final gesture of forgiveness, or as a last mocking rebuke? The word has a pleasing
ambiguity. For fifteen years he has lived the shadow life of a
cuckold, and for seven years the solitary existence of an exile. But
it affords him some satisfaction that Betsy Hancock should know
he was not entirely a fool.

Steventon

Late in the summer of 1775, George Austen received the revised
terms of Warren Hastings's trust fund on behalf of Philadelphia
and Betsy. It came with an accompanying letter from Hancock,

which Philadelphia brought down to show him. The letter was written with Hancock's usual despondent fussiness and peremptory obsession with detail. 'You must get your brother to come to town & with Mr Woodman to sign the deed,' Hancock instructed her, but then, with his constant concern for the state of the Steventon family budget, he had added this note: 'It ought not to occasion any expense to your brother, therefore you must repay what his journey to London may cost.'[73]

Cassandra was expecting her seventh child to be born some time in November. 'I am more nimble and active than I was last time,' she wrote to Susanna.[74] Happily, the rest of the family were all doing well: baby Frank 'very stout' and already running about on his own; little Cassandra 'talks all day long' and proving herself a very entertaining companion. Four-year-old Henry had been in breeches some months and 'thinks himself near as good a man as his bror Neddy'. Indeed, she wrote: 'no-one would judge by their looks that there was above three years and a half difference in their ages, one is so little and the other so great.' Master Vanderstegen had departed for his holidays earlier that morning, leaving the Austens to enjoy the late summer together.

Tysoe Saul Hancock died in Calcutta in November 1775 at the age of sixty-four and was buried in the Great Burying-ground at Chowringhee. A few weeks later, on 17 December, Mrs Austen gave birth to a baby daughter at Steventon. It had been an unusually protracted pregnancy, as George Austen explained to Susanna.

You have doubtless been for some time in expectation of hearing from Hampshire, and perhaps wondered a little we were in our old age grown such bad reckoners but so it was for Cassy certainly expected to have been brought to bed a month ago. However, last night the time came, and without a great deal of warning, everything was soon happily over. We have now another girl, a present plaything for her sister Cassy and a future companion. She is to be Jenny, and seems to me as if she would be as like Henry as Cassy is to Neddy.[75]

It would indeed be pleasant, he thought, for Cassy, who showed every sign of being a very lively girl, to have this little sister as a playfellow. Jane Austen's birth occasioned no great excitement at the rectory, beyond some natural concern at the inordinate length of her gestation. Her mother quickly resumed her domestic duties among her galiny hens and dairy cattle, while her father's thoughts soon ran upon more masculine diversions. As long as the present severe frosts did not continue, there would be a ploughing-match the following Tuesday, 'Kent against Hampshire, for a rump of beef'.

PART II

Steventon

People get so horridly poor & economical in this part of the world, that I have no patience with them.

Jane Austen, Letter to Cassandra, December 1798

CHAPTER 2

Noisy and Wild

> ... *she was moreover noisy and wild, hated con-*
> *finement and cleanliness, and loved nothing so well*
> *in the world as rolling down the green slope at the*
> *back of the house.*

NORTHANGER ABBEY, I, i

The cradle of genius

But the severe weather did continue. The winter of 1775–6 was among the harshest in living memory. Roads were blocked with snow and ice; the local post-chaise, Collyer's 'Flying Machine', was out of service for the whole of January, and the Austens' baby girl did not receive her formal baptism in St Nicholas's church till early April. All winter, the newspapers carried regular reports of the revolt of the American colonists. Two days after Jane Austen's birth, the 36th regiment marched into Portsmouth from Fareham, Waltham and Wickham and embarked from South Sea beach to strengthen the British forces in New England. Throughout the year, the *Hampshire Chronicle* reported the arrival of further regiments of foot at Portsmouth and Winchester, where they beat up for recruits in the market-place, offering great encouragements 'during the present trouble'. The local Hampshire militia was placed in a state of readiness with regular training exercises and drilling. 'All Militia men who shall absent themselves,' the *Chronicle* warned, 'will be fined and punished.'[1] Before long, the columns of the paper were filled with lists of casualties from the American war, details of the latest military manoeuvres and information on the fitting-out, fire-power and commanders of war-fighting ships-of-the-line.

For most of Jane Austen's life, England was a country at war. Yet, famously, her novels rarely hint at this fact. Her characters may include several handsome officers, but they appear less as fighting men than as gentlemen in uniform whose principal manoeuvres concern the capture of female hearts, not the storming of French garrisons. Absence of war is a condition of Jane Austen's fiction much prized by modern readers, who find great charm in her apparent depiction of a tranquil realm of domestic harmony and rural peace. The temptation to view Jane Austen's chosen fictional milieu ('3 or 4 families in a country village')[2] as an accurate social microcosm of Regency England has proved irresistibly beguiling to readers wishing to discover, in the pages of her novels, a lost England of innocent pride and faintly comic prejudices.

Steventon plays a vital part in the familiar Austen myth. In this secluded Hampshire village, deep in a curving valley some seven miles from Basingstoke, Jane Austen spent the first twenty-five years of her existence, or rather more than half her total life-span. The rectory itself no longer exists, demolished soon after her death to make way for a new parsonage on the opposite side of the valley. In its place, all we have are nostalgic family memories of the house, its gardens and surrounding countryside, the flowering hedgerows and winding lanes; memories which unconsciously refashion the landscape into a topographical metaphor for Austen's art. Here are 'no grand or extensive views . . . the hills are not bold, nor the valleys deep'. The beauties of the place are all small and unassuming; small winding lanes 'fringed with irregular borders of native turf, [that] lead to pleasant nooks and corners'; a small village of cottages 'scattered about prettily on either side of the road'; gently sloping meadows 'well sprinkled with elm trees'.[3] Steventon, wrote Jane Austen's nephew, James Edward Austen-Leigh, was, 'the cradle of her genius'.

Generations of later Austens have embowered that cradle in the nursery landscape of a vanished pastoral arcadia. There are loving descriptions of the rectory's old-fashioned gardens, 'in which vegetables and flowers . . . combined, flanked and protected on the east by one of the thatched mud walls common in that country and over-shadowed by fine elms'. There are picturesque evocations of the village lanes with their flowering hedgerows, under whose shelter 'the earliest primroses, anemones and wild hyacinths were to be found'. For Jane Austen's niece Anna Lefroy (*née* Austen), who spent two years of her infancy at Steventon after her mother's sudden death, this beloved place with its enclosed garden, its row of spruce firs and its romantic 'Wood Walk', had the magical quality of a childhood paradise.

> . . . near the Wood Walk gate, and garden bench adjoining, was placed a tall white pole surmounted by a weathercock. How pleasant to childish ears was the scrooping sound of that weathercock, moved by the summer breeze! How tall its stem! And yet how much more stupendous was the height of the solitary silver fir that grew at the opposite end of the terrace, and near the church road door! How exquisitely sweet too the honeysuckle, which climbed a little way up its lofty stem! . . . Oh me! we never saw the like again.[4]

Other family members and friends have embellished the arcadian scene with the depiction of smiling peasants dotted among the landscape. We are invited to picture the village wives spinning flax or wool in their thatched and whitewashed cottages scattered round the green. We are encouraged to imagine the flowering shrubs extending their tendrils across each little casement window. We are assured that on Sunday afternoons this village green became the village playground, where cottagers would laugh and gossip beneath the old maple tree.[5]

Such images of Steventon as an English bucolic paradise form an essential part of the Austen myth. Yet Jane Austen's own silence on the subject of her native landscape (save for complaining, now and then, about the dirtiness of the lanes) is eloquent. Unlike her niece Anna, Jane Austen has left us no delicious Proustian memories of the rectory's magical garden, with its fragrant honeysuckle, its sunny cucumber-frames, its abundance of pot-herbs and marigolds. Unlike her nephew James Edward, she was not inspired to graveyard meditations on the centuries of 'sweet violets, both purple and white' nestled in their 'sunny nook' beneath the south wall of the church.[6] For her, the rural isolation of Steventon implied privation rather than pastoral contentment. 'People get so horridly poor & economical in this part of the world,' she wrote, 'that I have no patience with them.'[7] Frustrated by the cramped rooms, low ceilings and limited horizons of Steventon, she longed for the elegant drawing-rooms and fine company of the Knights' magnificent Godmersham mansion in Kent. 'Kent is the only place for happiness. Everybody is rich there.' 'To sit in idleness over a good fire in a well-proportioned room,' she wrote in 1800, 'is a luxurious sensation.'[8]

By contrast, the rectory was busy, noisy and overcrowded. On the ground floor there were three rooms at the front of the house, the best parlour, the common parlour and the kitchen. Behind these were Mr Austen's study, the back kitchen and the stairs. Upstairs there were seven bedrooms and three attics, 'low-pitched but not otherwise bad'. Even to a Victorian sensibility, anxious to discover quaint charms in Steventon's rural simplicity, there was a distressing lack of elegance about the property: 'No cornice marked the junction of wall and ceiling; while the beams which supported the upper floors projected into the rooms below in all their naked simplicity, covered only by a coat of paint or whitewash.'[9] Despite George Austen's improvements and extensions to the property, Steventon remained a homely place with few pretensions to architectural refinement, and even less to genteel leisure. Visitors to the rectory would find Mrs Austen busy with her darning-needle in the parlour, or supervising her poultry and dairy cattle in the yard. Lodged in their attic dormitory, George Austen's pupils were rather less enchanted than Anna Lefroy at the perpetual 'scrooping', creaking and groaning of the rectory weathercock.

Beyond the rectory's garden walls, village life in rural Hampshire, especially in wartime, was rarely tranquil or untroubled. Hardship and illness, harsh weather and poor harvests, rural poverty and rural crime were as much a part of everyday life as the sound of the weathercock creaking in the wind. A typical charge-list for the county assizes reveals cases of highway-robbery near Wickham, attempted murder at Bedhampton, rape at Fareham, burglaries at Froyle, house-breaking at Alverstoke, sodomy in Winchester and bestiality on the Isle of Wight.[10] The murder of illegitimate children was a disturbingly frequent offence. In July 1773, the *Chronicle* reported the case of Jane Goodall, charged with murdering her bastard child by drowning it in a ditch. 'It is become a melancholy reflection,' the paper noted, 'that so many infants should be unfairly made away with, at a time when our country is greatly depopulated.'[11] Infant mortality at this period was always high, but reading through the Steventon parish register, it is noticeable how many of the village's illegitimate babies met early deaths: John, the bastard child of Mary Bennett, privately baptized on 23 June 1753 and buried nine days later; William-Jolliffe, the bastard child of Christian Collins, baptized in May 1774 and buried the following August; William Edmund, the 'base-born' son of Sarah Tilbury, baptized in January 1789 and buried in May.

The proximity of several large army camps, with other wartime establishments, brought further social disturbances. In 1778, a thousand French prisoners of war were imprisoned in the King's House at Winchester, and their frequent escape attempts caused alarm throughout the neighbourhood. The following year, two new military encampments for some eight thousand men were established on either side of Steventon, at Andover and Basingstoke, as increasingly large tracts of the Hampshire countryside came to assume the character of an armed camp. Inevitably, the arrival of so many military in the area had profound effects on local life. Some of these, undoubtedly, were welcome, as when the officers of the 25th regiment, quartered in Winchester, sponsored balls and assemblies in the city. Others were less so. The courts were frequently required to deal with cases of rape, burglary and murder committed by drunken troops, though some of the soldiers' violence was self-inflicted. In July 1776, the *Hampshire Chronicle* reported on a sergeant in the 25th who hanged himself in his room. 'It appeared the poor man had lately turned methodist,' it noted, 'and was assured by his teacher that faith alone would carry him to Heaven.'[12]

The two principal families in Steventon were the Austens at the rectory and their neighbours, the Digweeds, who rented the Tudor manor house, opposite St Nicholas's church, from the Knights. The rectory stood at one end of the village, at the corner of the lane leading up to the church. The manor house was an altogether more handsome edifice of flint and stone, with mullioned windows and generously proportioned rooms, standing in a grove of elms and sycamores. In addition, there were some thirty other families living in the parish. They included shepherds, who tended their flocks on the chalky downs, and labourers, who worked the surrounding fields, producing wheat and sainfoin, turnips, peas and beans. Wives and children worked in the fields, or at home, spinning flax or wool, or were employed as servants by the Austens, the Digweeds, or James Holder at Ashe Park. We find their names in the parish register, inscribed in George Austen's clear and formal hand: the Adams family and the Tilburys, the Lovells and the Armstrongs. The Staples, with their nine children, received charity from the Austens and were employed as servants at the rectory. Mary Steeves did the rectory washing; the Littleworths nursed the infant Austens at Cheesedown farm. From time to time their numbers were swelled by travellers and vagrants, who would spend a season in the neighbourhood, cutting peat and furze. In December 1766, Francis, 'the bastard son of Sarah Eyles, a vagrant', was baptized in the parish church.

Of love and friendship

Such alarming reports as one read in the newspapers concerning the depopulation of our rural villages did not ring true to Philadelphia Hancock's ears. Whenever she visited Steventon she found the rectory filled with all the noise and hubbub of young children and, as like as not, her sister Austen already pregnant with the next. Now, at the age of forty, Cassandra had just given birth to her eighth child, a baby boy called Charles. It was quite a blessing that poor George had been sent away or where would they have found the space to keep him? James, the eldest, had been packed off just a week after this latest little brother's arrival. Only fourteen, he was gone up to Oxford – to his father's college, St John's – with the grand title and privileges of 'Founder's Kin', thanks to his mother's Perrot family connections. James Austen always struck Philadelphia as a solemn, studious boy, already full of high ambitions. He was going to be a poet, he said; not a mere scribbler of comic verses like his mother, but something in the high romantic vein. Of course, he was still very raw. There was a story of how, soon after arriving at the university, he had been honoured by a dinner invitation from Cassandra's uncle, the Master of Balliol. Being unaccustomed to the habits of the place, James had been about to remove his academic gown, quite as if it were a great-coat, when the old man, who was considerably turned eighty, said to him with a smile, 'Young man, you need not strip, we are not going to fight.'[13]

The necessary economies attending such a life of domestic duties were no doubt less irksome to those who were long accustomed to endure them; but the life of rural virtue held little appeal for Philadelphia. George Austen's income she reckoned might amount to some £300 *per annum*. She herself was condemned to subsist in London on an annual income barely twice that sum, which she considered a state of virtual pauperdom. It was impossible, she told Cassandra, to maintain herself and Betsy (who was now quite a young lady, and had a young lady's taste) in any degree of *style* in London on such a beggarly amount. She had heard that the living in Brussels was somewhat more reasonable, and just as fashionable as London. Accordingly, she set out with Betsy and Clarinda to seek their fortune on the Continent. They went first to Germany, passed a summer at Brussels, but eventually settled in Paris. Mr Hancock had always wanted his daughter to acquire some of the tasteful refinements of French culture; but Eliza (as Betsy now called herself) moved in a more exalted company than he could ever have dreamed of. Philadelphia encouraged the girl to write home to her cousins in Hampshire and Kent to boast of her present good fortune. 'We were a few days ago at Versailles,' she wrote, '& had the honor of seeing their majesties & all the royal family dine & sup.'[14]

At Steventon, Cassandra Austen sat nursing her baby son Charles, and watching, from the corner of an eye, as his little sisters, Jane and Cassy, made searches through her work-bag for ends of colourful threads. Cassandra was relieved to know the rectory finances seemed in a tolerable way to improvement. Mr Austen enjoyed a high reputation as a teacher, and there was scarcely a wealthy family in the neighbourhood that would hesitate to place their hopeful sons under his care. At present he had four pupils, each paying £35 *per annum* for their tuition, board and lodging. Master East was Sir William East's son, of Hall Place in Berkshire, and Master Fowle the son of George's university friend, Thomas Fowle.[15] Frank Stuart's father was godfather to their own son Charles, and Master Deane came of a most respectable family at Reading. East was the least scholarly of the company. His youthful spirit seemed to find it quite mortifying to grind through his two lessons daily from Virgil's *Aeneid*, however often Cassandra might twit him (in verse) that the story, though in Latin, was 'quite entertaining'.[16] It often fell to her part to encourage the boys with little comic rhymes in this way. Her style of poetical coaxing, the Austens had discovered, frequently proved more effective with recalcitrant minds than her husband's more severe manner. When young Buller and Goodenough would complain at the noise of the weathercock over their heads, it was she who pacified them by mimicking their protests in rhyme. She penned some doggerel verses on their behalf which she grandly entitled: 'The humble petition of R. Buller and William Goodenough'.

> *Dear Sir: We beseech and entreat and request*
> *You'd remove a sad nuisance that breaks our night's rest.*
> *That creaking old weathercock o'er our heads*
> *Will scarcely permit us to sleep in our beds.*

It whines and it groans and makes such a noise
That it greatly disturbs two unfortunate boys
Who hope you will not be displeased when they say,
If they don't sleep by night, they can't study by day.[17]

Similarly, when East delayed returning to the rectory that summer, it was she who sent polite reminders in the form of some whimsical verses.

Your Steventon friends
Are at their wits' ends
To know what is become of Squire East.
They very much fear
He'll never come here
Having left them nine weeks at the least . . .

Then pray thee, dear Sir,
No longer defer
Your return to the mansion of learning;
For we study all day,
(Except when we play)
And eke when the candles are burning.

Gilbert East's inclinations tended rather more in the direction of dances and balls than towards classical learning. But would an accomplished skill in dance steps, she wondered, really be sufficient to equip him for the demands of adult life?

That you dance very well
All beholders can tell,
Tis lightly and nimbly you tread,
But pray, is it meet
To indulge thus your feet
And neglect all the while your poor head?

Cassandra took pleasure in dreaming up such light-hearted verses for the diversion of their children and pupils alike. She raised all her children with a fondness for rhyming-games, songs and charades, and would teach them to write their own answers in rhyme to the riddles she set them. But, with the pupils especially, there was always the danger of jealousy, if she seemed to devote more of her rhymes to one boy than another. James Stuart's boy Frank once accused her of favouritism 'in writing verses for F.C. Fowle & not for him'. Naturally such a charge required an immediate response; though Cassandra took care to remind young Master Stuart that her literary favours were not his to command but to earn.

> *But do dismiss*
> *a thought like this*
> *which does me such injustice:*
> *I mind always*
> *That rule which says*
> *Serve that man first who first is.*[18]

Much as she loved such poetical *jeux d'esprit*, Cassandra did not disguise from herself that her verses were not entirely devoid of serious purpose. Not to be too delicate about the matter, these boys were their bread and butter, and it was her part to defuse their adolescent grumbles by deflecting the spirit of youthful rebellion into outbursts of a purely poetical kind. She had quickly discovered that there was no domestic accident, inconvenience or misadventure which could not be embellished into mock-epic verses and then solemnly declaimed for the whole household's amusement. If only she had thought to comfort little Lord Lymington with more nursery rhymes, he too might have stayed with them longer.

Moreover, since there was little money to spare for more extravagant diversions, the family's amusements must perforce be home-made. At Mr Delatouche's ball in Winchester in November 1775, an allemande by Miss Hancock was among the dances 'most applauded'. But the Austens were rarely at liberty to attend such events. Cassandra was gratified that her Leigh family's Perrot connections had enabled James to proceed to St John's with a scholarship as 'Founder's Kin'. Sadly, she acknowledged that the Leigh family's Chandos connections were not now of a kind to warrant similar favours in their social activities. The Duke of Chandos was patron of the great musical festival held every summer at Winchester. But the Austens' name was never included among the published list of the 'first families in the county' attending that event.[19] Cassandra's life of domestic duties as dairy-maid, housekeeper, school-matron and mother was perhaps rather less than a woman of her rank might have hoped for. But as baby Charles slept in her lap and little Jane played around her chair she felt no envy for Philadelphia and the high life of Brussels and Paris.

From her mother's apartment high above the boulevard, in what was then the most fashionable part of Paris, Miss Eliza Hancock wrote to her cousin Phylly Walter at Ightham parsonage in Kent. Her letter was so written (or, to use her own modish term, *griffonée*) as to convey the notion of the most sublime contentment. No other place on earth, she believed, could be quite so delightful as Paris. It was 'the city in the world best calculated to spend the whole year in'; not like London, where the summer months were quite 'insupportable'.[20] Here the walks, the rides, the amusements and the fashionable company continued the whole year round. Everything in Paris was completely *comme il faut*. 'There is perhaps no place in the world where dress is so well understood & carried to so great a perfection as in Paris,' she declared. Powder was universally worn '& in very large quantities; no-one would dare to appear in public without it'. Yet Eliza could not entirely suppress her English sense of the ridiculous when she added that 'the heads in general look as if they had been dipped in a meal-tub'. Of course, the most fashionable creature of all was the French Queen, Marie Antoinette. Watching the exquisite monarch as she made her splendid progress through the state rooms of Versailles, Eliza took careful note of every item of her elaborate costume and coiffure: 'a corset & petticoat of pale green lutestring, covered with a transparent silver gauze, the petticoat & sleeves puckered & confined in different places with large bunches of roses, & an amazing large bouquet of white lilac'. More roses adorned the Queen's hair, 'together with gauze, feathers, ribbon & diamonds . . . Her neck was entirely uncovered & ornamented by a most beautiful chain of diamonds, of which she had likewise very fine bracelets.'

Eliza was determined her English cousins must see how far she herself had proceeded in the acquisition of an elegant continental style. She included with her letter 'my picture in miniature done here', which she directed 'to my Uncle G. Austen'. 'It is reckoned here like what I am at present,' she added. 'The dress is quite the present fashion & what I usually wear.'[21] Mr Austen, though, was rather less impressed by the receipt of this miniature than his niece might have hoped. For all the affectation of sophistication, what he saw was a small, pointed girlish face with large dark eyes and a sad mouth. Blue ribbons trimmed her dress and were entwined among her artfully dishevelled curls. Yet the bare neck and slender shoulders seemed to him more waif-like than alluring. Nor was he entirely content that his niece and sister should find so much to admire in the monarchs of an enemy country. Militiamen still patrolled the southern shores of England to guard against a French invasion, while the two countries' navies fought each other in Caribbean waters. They were all alarmed at the French threat to plunder the West Indies islands, where Mr Austen's friend James Nibbs had extensive sugar plantations. King George had said that the sugar islands must be defended at all costs, even at the risk of an invasion of Britain itself. 'If we lose our sugar islands,' he declared, 'it will be impossible to raise money to continue the war.'[22] Neither Mr Austen nor the boy George Nibbs, who was now a pupil at Steventon, felt much inclined to indulge that fondness towards the French monarchs and their powdered entourage expressed by the bare-necked young lady in the miniature, with blue ribbons in her hair.

Eliza did not greatly trouble herself with thoughts of naval battles, or sugar islands or any such unfashionable topics. It was bothersome and unnecessary, she thought, that there should be such rivalries between the English and the French. She made a point of assuring all her English relations that it was 'not at all likely' she would settle permanently in France. Yet she lost no opportunity of demonstrating her sophisticated superiority to any narrow national prejudice. 'Worth,' she proclaimed, 'is confined to no country or nation, & equally to be found in Germany, Flanders or France.'[23] She was particularly critical of the 'tiresome' rules of English ballroom etiquette, which decreed that her poor provincial cousins must 'have the same partner (& maybe a bad one) the whole evening, while perhaps there are twenty others in the room whom you would have preferred'. Such a thing would never happen in France, she assured Phylly; 'on the contrary, you have generally more on your hands than you know what to do with. I have frequently been engaged for more than 15 dances the same evening,' she boasted, '& for 8 or 10 for the next ball.'[24]

In reality, the prospects for the Hancock household were rather less rosy than Eliza claimed in her letters. As usual, they were living well beyond their means. The endless afflictions of Clarinda's damaged hand (for five months she had been quite helpless) had cost them more than they had ever reckoned on. Three surgeons, three severe operations, and a physician who now came to dress her arm twice daily, and still the poor woman had not recovered the full use of her fingers. That spring, after a silence of many years, Eliza's mother had even ventured to write to Mr Hastings enquiring about funds. 'Has my uncle given you any account of the money left in his hands?' she asked; 'about two thousand pounds, I imagine.'[25] It had been a difficult letter to write. Mr Hastings was seen everywhere with the von Imhoff woman, who, it was said, had obtained 'a fixed ascendancy' over his mind since her divorce from her portrait-painter husband. The fund which Mr Hastings had established in Eliza's name, and which had seemed so generous at the time, now appeared less so, as it was clearly designed as a final settlement of all responsibilities in that direction. Mr Hastings had let it be known that he would not welcome any further communications from Mrs Hancock on this or any other matter. Philadelphia had written to remind him of the 'many mortifying and disagreeable events' she had suffered in her life, and to beg him 'not to refuse me this request – the last perhaps I shall ever make you . . .' But as far as Eliza knew, Mr Hastings had never replied.

There was, of course, an obvious solution to their financial difficulties. Eliza must find herself a rich husband. There was no disgrace, her mother assured her, for a young lady of a pleasing disposition to seize her earliest opportunity for securing a wealthy mate. And how fortunate Eliza was! There would be no need for her to voyage halfway round the world in pursuit of a man she had never met. Eliza might have her pick among the handsome chevaliers and eligible noblemen who frequented the ballrooms and ante-chambers of Paris and Versailles. So long as the man she fixed on should have at least as much money as other attractions, Philadelphia would make no difficulties about her choice. Eliza, whilst admitting the wisdom of her mother's advice, was not entirely reconciled to such a calculating view of matrimony. Foolish as it might seem, she still hankered after romance. That May, she wrote to Phylly Walter to assure her that she had not lost her heart to any foreign beau: 'You may be certain I never was more mistress of it than at this moment, & that I do not doubt keeping it *whole* for many years to come.'[26] Yet barely a month later she wrote again, enquiring: 'How should you like it, my dear, was I to introduce *un cousin françois* to your acquaintance? Should you receive him very cordially, or are you persuaded like most of our nation that nothing good can come from France?' She hastened to add: 'I only joke & am far from having any serious thoughts of marrying in this country. No, no,' she went on, 'you will most likely see me return to England without having changed my name.'[27] That was just before she met the Comte de Feuillide.

Captain Jean-François Capot de Feuillide was a handsome officer in the Queen's regiment of dragoons, just ten years older than herself. Whether he was *really* a Count was something Eliza could never entirely determine; what was certain was that his family owned substantial estates at Nerac in Guienne in the south-west of France. Not to be outdone, Philadelphia gave out to all their Paris friends that she and Eliza were also '*immensement riche*', exactly as might be expected of ladies so well connected with the '*fameux* lord Hastings, *gouverneur de l'Inde*'.[28] The Comte de Feuillide had left his family home some years before to join the regiment of dragoons, and now enjoyed a reputation, among his intimates at least, as one of France's finest officers. In short, he was handsome, he was dashing, and he was rich. Within the year he and Eliza Hancock were engaged to be married. Eliza's mother promptly wrote to her brother Austen at Steventon demanding the immediate release of all remaining moneys in Mr Hastings's trust fund. The Comte, she said, was 'of good family with expectation of good fortune', though at present, she conceded, he had 'but little'. Nevertheless, she was willing 'to give up . . . the sum which was settled on her for life', in order that the money might be 'transferred into the French Funds' and put at the disposal of the Count and his future bride.[29]

George Austen was embarrassed by Philadelphia's letter. Although long used to indulging his sister's volatile eccentricities, he strongly disapproved of this impulsive marriage to a foreigner, a self-styled aristocrat and a Catholic. As a trustee of the Hastings fund, it was his duty to act not merely as Philadelphia might require or demand, but in the long-term interests of Eliza. He conferred with his fellow trustee, Mr Woodman, and together they concluded it was 'prudent for her sake to decline' Philadelphia's request. Inevitably, George Austen felt some awkwardness at communicating to his sister a reply which she would find most unwelcome. Accordingly, it fell to Woodman to acquaint Mr Hastings with Mr Austen's disquiet at a marriage which, he feared, must mean 'giving up all their friends, their country, and . . . their religion'. Yet, despite all George Austen's cautions, the wedding went ahead. In December, Woodman wrote again to Hastings, with gloomy predictions of its likely consequences.

> I wrote Mrs Hancock . . . who is in France, where I believe she intends to end her days, having married her daughter there to a gentleman of that country, I am afraid not very advantageously, although she says it is entirely to her satisfaction, the gentleman having great connections and expectations. Her uncle Mr Austen, and brother don't approve of the match, the latter is much concern'd at it; they seem already desirous of draining the mother of every shilling she has.[30]

A few months later, Eliza wrote again from Paris to Phylly Walter in Kent. She was flattered by Phylly's request for another portrait of herself, and promptly sent a newly painted miniature, in the back of which she enclosed a lock of her dark-brown hair with the motto *Amoris et Amicitiae* – 'Of Love and Friendship'. The phrase recalled the lines she had written to Phylly two years earlier, when she confided that her heart was 'entirely insensible to any *tender sentiments* but those of friendship'. Now that she was married, Phylly would no doubt expect the tender sentiment of *love* to have become the predominant emotion in the young bride's heart. 'My uncle Austen acquainted you with my marriage, soon after its taking place,' Eliza wrote tersely. She did not need to dwell upon her uncle Austen's opinion of the marriage. His refusal of the trust fund money had made *that* all too clear. But she felt herself bound to offer, if not a defence, at least an explanation of a decision which her English friends considered rash and foolish, but which she herself described as 'the most important . . . of my life'. She had not embarked upon this marriage, she said, without 'mature deliberation'. 'It was a step I took much less from my own judgement than that of those whose councils [*sic*] & opinions I am the most bound to follow.' She meant, of course, her mother, but refrained from saying so in as many words. 'I trust I shall never have any reason to repent it.'[31]

For Phylly's benefit, she set herself upon itemizing de Feuillide's many qualities. 'The man to whom I have given my hand,' she wrote, 'is everyways amiable both in mind & person. It is too little to say he loves, since he literally adores me; entirely devoted to me, & making my inclinations the guide of all his actions . . .' What she did *not* say was that she loved him. However much she might respect him, she did not, and could not, love him. It vexed Eliza that she must pass at Steventon for a giddy, thoughtless girl who had plunged hopelessly in love with a dashing French officer when, in reality, the motives for her marriage had been entirely selfless, prompted, as Phylly told her brother James, by 'the highest duty, love and respect for her mother, for whom there is not any sacrifice she would not make . . .'[32] *Amoris et Amicitiae* was the tender message which Eliza bound about her token braid of hair. Though love must always be granted an ostensible priority of place, it was in the friendship of women who understood her sacrifice that Eliza found her greatest comfort.

'I could die of laughter'

George Austen felt a deep dismay when he discovered how his niece's future prospects of happiness had all been put at risk not, as he first imagined, through her own romantic foolishness, but merely to satisfy the vanity of a mother who loved nothing more than the flourish of an aristocratic title. Stratagems of this kind were quite repugnant to him; yet he might have allowed the cynicism of Philadelphia's manoeuvre to pass with only a modest reflection on the sad ways of the world, had he not formed a settled conviction that the man himself, upon whom all their hopes were now irrevocably fixed, was a fool and a fraud. His disapproval was not lessened by the consciousness that he too must soon confront the problem of furnishing his numerous children with the wherewithal to flourish in the wider world. Hancock's laconic words would often return to haunt him: 'I fear George will find it easier to get a family than to provide for them.' And, whilst he deplored the cold-heartedness of his sister's calculating policy, he still made sure to school his own children in all those charming infant ways of modest courtesy and obedience that might recommend them to the indulgent attention of their more affluent relations. Mrs Austen's cousin, the Reverend Thomas Leigh, would often visit Steventon on his way between Adlestrop and London, and never failed in giving some small sum to one or all of the Austen children. The money was distributed with a mighty flourish of generosity and much scribbling in his notebook to record the precise amount. One year it might be half a guinea to 'Jemmy Austen'; another year, ten shillings for all 'the Masters Austen' to share among them.[33]

Other relatives, George hoped, might be more generous in their benefactions. On a visit to old uncle Frank at Sevenoaks, Mr and Mrs Austen took little Henry with them. Henry well recalled that day when, as a small boy of nine, he had been taken in to see the ancient figure, well past his eightieth year. 'He wore a wig like a bishop, & a suit of light gray ditto, coat, vest & hose.'[34] How strange it was, he remembered, to see the great man in the flesh, and then to see, behind his head, a portrait of the same great man, hanging above the chimney-piece, dressed in the very same clothes. And yet not quite the same. Peering closely at the portrait, the boy could see the coat and vest were edged with gold. But the man himself had no gold edges, only grey. It was the absence of gold edges which remained most vividly in Henry's mind. How often they had all been told the stories of this great-uncle Frank. He was a mighty lawyer, a 'smart man' from the era of George the First, a man of vast riches from whom great things might be hoped. So why had he left off the gold edgings from his clothes? When old Frank Austen died at last, at the great age of ninety-three, Henry was up at Oxford. He received the news that the great man had left £500 apiece to each of his nephews with something less than rapture. Five hundred pounds must undoubtedly be reckoned a generous bequest, though it was rather less than Henry had once hoped for. 'It is a sort of privilege,' he remarked, 'to have seen and conversed with such a model of a hundred years since.' But it would have been an even greater privilege to have benefited more handsomely from old Frank Austen's gold.

Edward ('Neddy') was always the charmer among the Austen children. It was Neddy whom visiting relations loved especially, and it was not unusual for Neddy to be singled out for favour. That April, after Henry's trip to Sevenoaks, the Reverend Leigh had given the Austen boys 10s 6d to share among them; but, when he returned the following month, it was only 'Neddy Austen' who was given money. Neddy had 5s all to himself. When Mr Knight (the son of Mr Knight of Godmersham) was married to Miss Knatchbull of Chilham in Kent, the couple made a wedding tour of all the family estates. Calling in at Steventon, they were both so greatly entertained by Neddy, who was then just twelve years old, that they asked if he might be permitted to accompany them 'by way of amusement' for the rest of their honeymoon tour. 'It may be supposed,' wrote Henry, recalling that fateful day, 'that they were first attracted by his personal beauty, but no particular consequences at that time ensued, or seem to have been expected from this mark of preference for one little boy.'[35] Neddy returned home to Steventon a few weeks later and settled back to his daily lessons with Frank and Henry, East, Fowle, Stuart and Deane. But the Knights, it seemed, had not forgotten their favourite little Neddy. The following summer a letter arrived from Godmersham, 'begging that little Edward might be allowed to spend his holidays' with the Knight family in Kent. Henry remembered that his father was 'not . . . inclined to consent' to this request. Mr Austen disliked the prospect of 'so many weeks idleness, and a probable falling behind in the Latin grammar'. It would be Gilbert East all over again, he thought; a summer wasted in idleness and dancing instead of studying for Oxford. But their mother had thought otherwise. 'I think, my dear,' she said, 'you had better oblige your cousins and let the child go.' 'And accordingly go he did,' Henry recalled, 'riding all the way on the pony which Mr Knight's coachman, himself on horseback, had led from Godmersham for his use.'

Henry felt some sadness, and not a little jealousy, as he watched his brother ride away. From their earliest boyhood years Henry had always reckoned himself as good a man as Neddy. Even by the age of four he had grown so tall that 'no one would judge . . . there was above three years and a half difference in their ages'.[36] Why should it always be Edward, and not him, whom their rich relations doted on? Henry had heard all about Godmersham, how like a palace it was, with its Temple Walk and River Walk, its summerhouses and Hermitage. At Godmersham, Edward would be living the life of a young nobleman, while Henry would be left at Steventon to drudge through more pages of Virgil.

Life was not all drudgery, however. When not studying at their Latin exercises, young Frank and Henry Austen loved nothing better than to go pony-riding, or even hunting, after their own childish fashion. Though Frank was only seven, he had already a passion for riding after hounds. As an infant, Jane found it strange to be often told how afraid Frank used to be of the Digweeds' braying donkey. Now, he was always rushing to get astride any donkey or pony he could find. Frank had become so reckless and scurrying a little fellow that the family all called him 'Fly'. Early in the morning, Henry and Fly would scramble across the fields with the Digweed boys from the manor house, and take turns riding their steeds. But Fly was not satisfied with that. He must have a mount of his own. He took all the money he had – the grand sum of £1 11s 6d – and spent it all on a bright chestnut pony.[37] He called the pony 'Squirrel', but Henry, to plague him, called it 'Scug'. Where Fly had got the money from to pay for such a nag was a mystery to him; Henry could never lay his hands on more than a few pennies. 'Here comes Fly on his Scug,' he would shout, as his little brother came galloping down the lane. Their mother took the last of the red woollen dress she had worn as a wedding-gown and cut it up into a hunting-jacket for Fly to wear in the field. Fly was like Neddy in this respect at least; they both seemed to possess a magical skill in obtaining money. It was mortifying to Henry when, after two years' riding, Fly eventually sold the nag and made a guinea profit.

When Edward returned at last from Godmersham, the other Austen children were required to hear how splendid *his* summer had been. The Knights, it appeared, had been so captivated by his lively, amiable spirit that they could scarcely bear to part with him. They had, as yet, no children of their own, and all that fondness which might naturally have been devoted to a son and heir had been lavished upon Edward. Gradually, Henry began to detect changes, not only in his brother's manner, but in the way that Edward was treated in the rectory. 'Edward Austen returned from Godmersham ostensibly as much Edward Austen as ever, & remained for some years as such under the care of his natural parents.' However, as he recalled, 'by degrees ... it came to be understood in the family that Edward was selected amongst themselves as the adopted son & heir of Mr Knight'. It was only a matter of time before Edward 'was taken more entire possession of, & sent to study in some German university'.[38]

The adoption of Edward Austen by his wealthy relations, the Knights, did not happen all at once. For several years the Knights clung to the hope of producing an heir of their own. During this period they maintained, as it were, an option on Edward's future. He was their bespoken heir, should their own efforts prove unavailing. Meanwhile, Edward was groomed for future greatness by his Austen parents, in the hopes (at first) and subsequently the expectation of his elevation to higher things. At last, in 1783, the Knights abandoned hope of begetting children of their own and Edward Austen was removed from Steventon to live in wealth and splendour at Godmersham.

It is remarkable how little disturbance this dynastic transfer has caused to subsequent biographers and family historians. For Elizabeth Jenkins, Edward's removal from the Steventon family circle was 'a stroke of fantastical good fortune'. According to William and Richard Arthur Austen-Leigh, it was 'a compliment to the Austen family in general, whose early promise their cousins had probably observed'. Such remarks implicitly acknowledge the Austens' status as poor relations, whose best hope of prospering was, in Mrs Austen's phrase, to 'oblige' their wealthy Kentish cousins. As if in formal recognition of this dynastic 'compliment', a silhouette by William Wellings was commissioned to commemorate the moment of Edward's handover to the Knights.[39] The iconography of this silhouette is revealing; although not done until 1783, when Edward was sixteen years old, the boy who stretches out his arms towards his new parents in this image is a diminutive childlike figure, not yet into his teens. Behind him, Mr Austen stands in an upright but clearly deferential pose, with his hands on the boy's shoulders, as if offering his son for approval. In the opposite corner, Mr Knight adopts an altogether more aristocratic stance, legs crossed, leaning casually on the back of his wife's chair, surveying the boy with a connoisseur's eye. Between them, their wives sit at a table playing chess. As a composition, this silhouette is as much about power as about family feelings. By visually antedating the time of Edward's adoption, the Knights effectively reduce the role of the natural parents, while the game of chess, which occupies the centre of the picture, transforms the boy into a pawn in a game of dynastic manoeuvres. One of the first things the Knights did after taking possession of their new heir, was to have his portrait done by the society painter George Romney in a manner to confirm his new identity. Edward appears as a solemn-faced boy, with a pinched mouth and long flowing curls, somewhat ill at ease in his expensive blue jacket and large frilly white shirt. But by the time he was doing the Grand Tour at the age of twenty-one, Edward had fully relaxed into the pose of the young English milord. A portrait of him then shows him effortlessly affecting an aristocratic cross-legged pose, leaning nonchalantly on his walking-cane with a classical carving at his feet.[40]

Such singular good fortune could not but inspire some jealous feelings among Edward's less-favoured siblings. Henry would never admit to harbouring any ungenerous sentiments towards his elder brother. Yet his account of how Edward was 'selected from amongst themselves', to be taken 'entire possession of' by the Knights, is not without a certain edge of asperity, most obvious in the casual comment that Edward was sent abroad to study 'in some German university'. Jane, who was only eight at the time of Neddy's removal, felt saddened and disturbed by his sudden disappearance from the Austen family home. Years later, when Edward finally relinquished the Austen name in favour of the name Knight, she wrote drily: 'I must learn to make a better K.' Her niece Fanny was less restrained in expressing her disapproval. 'We are therefore all *Knights* instead of dear old *Austens*,' she wrote. 'How I hate it!!!!!!' 'There is something so shocking in a child's being taken away from his parents and natural home,' Jane wrote in *Emma*, concerning young Frank Weston's similar adoption by his wealthy relatives, the Churchills.[41]

To a child of eight, this sudden loss of yet another brother confirmed how much the home she lived in resembled the strange enchanted lands she read about in fairy tales. One brother, whom she had never known, had been mysteriously banished and locked away like a prisoner in some dark and lonely dungeon, his name never mentioned and his affliction unknown. Another brother, whom she knew and loved, was now mysteriously singled out for glory and riches, like a foundling prince in disguise who had been reclaimed by his true royal parents and taken to a palace in some faraway country. Where would she be taken? What would these people, who called themselves her mother and her father, do with her? As soon as Jane began to write, she filled her notebook with dreamy stories of families who were strangers to each other. She imagined a mother who discovered a baby girl beneath a haycock, and did not remember, till more than twenty years had passed, that it was her own daughter, whom she herself had placed there. She imagined a young man, travelling in a stage-coach beside a strange and beautiful young woman, who did not know the woman was his wife whom he had married that same year. She herself would marry a prince, she had already decided, and his name would be Edmund, or Fitzwilliam.[42] Or perhaps she would be beheaded as a martyr to some noble cause. Or perhaps both. But what would happen to Cassandra? Jane would only marry a prince if Cassandra could marry a prince too. The previous summer, Cassandra had been sent to Bath to stay with her aunt and uncle Cooper, and Jane had been quite wretched and moping all the time she was away. She remembered the fine summer evening her father had set out in a hack-chaise to meet Cassandra at Andover and bring her home. She and Charles had run all the way to New Down to meet them, and to have the pleasure of riding home.[43] But the pleasure of riding in a hack-chaise was nothing to the pleasure of having Cassandra safely home again. It would be too terrible, she thought, if Cassandra were ever sent away.

When James returned from Oxford that Christmas, his head was filled with ideas about acting. Nothing would do but they must have their very own play here at the rectory. He would hear no dissuasion; there need be no inconvenience to anyone, he was sure. It would be the easiest thing in the world to fit up the barn to make a theatre. Nothing grand or extravagant was required, he insisted. It would be a return to the original simplicity of the Greek tragedians. He had already penned a prologue to that effect: 'When Thespis first professed the mimic's art,/Rude were his Actors, & his stage a cart . . .' Here at Steventon there would be none of the histrionic affectations of the London stage, where each frantic actress 'her beauteous tresses tears,/By different fits scolds, freezes, cries, raves and swears . . .' Here they would pursue a simpler and more noble aim:

> *To speak with elegance, & act with ease,*
> *To fill the softened soul with grief sincere*
> *And draw from Pity's eye the tender tear.*[44]

James had already hit upon the perfect play for them to perform. It was Dr Thomas Franklin's blank-verse play *Matilda*, 'A Tragic Tale from Norman William's Age'.[45] When Edward, for whom this would be the last Christmas at the rectory, took a survey of the play, he could not see why a tragedy whose plot turned upon the bitter struggle of two brothers, one of whom was called Edwin, should be thought such a perfect choice. In the drama, the two brothers, Edwin and Morcar, were pitched on opposite sides in a bloody civil war and were rivals in love for the same woman, Matilda. Having captured Matilda and Edwin, Morcar soon discovered that Matilda loved Edwin not him. In a jealous rage, Morcar despatched his henchman Siward to murder his brother. But Siward disobeyed his master's orders, and the play ended in scenes of mutual forgiveness, from which Edwin emerged with victorious felicity, having gained both the castle and the girl, while Morcar retired to some 'deep distant solitude', pledging to dedicate his life to 'pious sorrow'. Edward must play Edwin, of course; that was quickly decided. James rather inclined to keep the part of Morcar for himself. He had already conned by heart the villain's soliloquies in which, like Macbeth, he suffered the agonies of conscience in bad dreams and guilty visions.

> MORCAR *Methought*
> *I heard a voice cry – stop – it is thy brother;*
> *We lov'd each other well; our early years*
> *Were spent in mutual happiness together . . .*

It was objected by Henry, who was wont to vow that he could easily undertake any character that ever was written, from Shylock or Richard III down to the singing hero of a farce in his scarlet coat and cocked hat, that he, not James, should play the part of Morcar. After all, a fellowship at St John's College, such as James now enjoyed, hardly represented a 'deep, distant solitude'. But it was the character of Siward, said James, upon which the whole *dénouement* of the play depended; and it was Siward who had some fine touches of Machiavelli about his scheming, that Henry must surely relish. The wrangling over parts continued for some days; everybody had a part which was either too long or too short, too solemn or too dull. But at last all was resolved. Edward spoke the words of the prologue ('We . . . fondly hope from your applause to gain / A great reward for all our care & pain'). But there remained a general rivalry amongst all the family (including Jane) to pronounce the final words of the epilogue, denouncing that reptile character, the critic. 'Death is his trade and damning his profession . . . / Like fabled giants here they roam for food, / And Fe! Fa! Fum! snuff up an author's blood.'

All this time, while the Austen boys had laboured at their Latin grammar, or preened themselves in tragic dramas, the education of the Austen girls had not been much attended to. Classical learning was deemed too rigorous an exercise for feminine minds (though Jane had learnt enough to write '*Ex dono mei Patris*' in a notebook that her father gave her).[46] Save for what their mother taught them, and for what knowledge of the world might be gained from fairy tales and such nursery classics as *The History of Goody Two Shoes*, they were innocent of all formal instruction.[47] However, on learning that Mr Cooper's sister, Mrs Cawley, ran a school for girls at Oxford, the Austens decided that this might be the very place for Cassandra and Jane. There were many advantages to recommend the school. Mrs Cawley was the widow of a former principal of Brasenose College; James was on hand to ensure his little sisters came to no harm; and their cousin, Jane Cooper, would be included among their classmates.

For Jane, it was not a happy experience to exchange the freedom of Steventon for the petty rules and regulations of Mrs Cawley's academy. Mrs Cawley was stiff in manner and solemn in her mode of instruction. Even Oxford itself seemed gloomy and forbidding.

At the age of thirteen, Jane admitted her dismay at having been 'dragged', as a child, through numerous 'dismal chapels, dusty libraries and greasy halls'. 'It gave me the vapours for two days afterwards,' she declared.[48] 'The vapours' might be thought a somewhat modish indisposition to afflict a girl of only seven. Yet Jane Austen had no hesitation in ascribing to her infant self such early indications of fashionable feelings and a superior sensibility. It would be altogether too dull and common to confess to mere girlish sulks and homesickness.

When Mrs Cawley chose to move her school from Oxford to Southampton, the prospects seemed at first a little brighter. South-ampton was a great port, busy with military activity. Instead of dull scholars in black and greasy gowns, here would be handsome officers in splendid uniforms. Jane Cooper, now aged twelve, already had an eye for a fine uniform, and the three girls were content to follow their teacher to her new south coast location. But the move was less fortunate than at first appeared. There was a sickness in the town. People said it was the typhoid fever, brought into Southampton by troops returned from Gibraltar. But Mrs Cawley paid no heed to rumours like that. Even when the number of deaths started to multiply, Mrs Cawley saw no cause for alarm.[49] Cassandra caught the infection, and shortly afterwards Jane; but still Mrs Cawley did not believe their illness sufficiently serious to warrant mentioning it to their parents. At last, it was Jane Cooper herself who wrote to her mother to tell her they were all sick and like to die.

How daring that rescue had been! Quite like an episode from a Gothic romance. Mrs Cooper and Mrs Austen had rushed to the school and removed their daughters immediately.[50] But how tragic the consequence! For it was not the girls who perished – but their bold rescuer. Jane Austen was ill for several weeks and often appeared on the brink of death, but at last grew well and strong again. Her aunt Cooper was less fortunate and suffered a severe bout of the infection. For three weeks she lay a victim of feverish attacks at her home in Bath, until her body at last proved unequal to the struggle. She died on 25 October and was buried in her husband's church a few days later. 'Her form the beauties of her

mind express'd,/Her mind was Virtue by the Graces dress'd.'[51]
Dr Cooper, heartbroken at his wife's sudden death, immediately
resigned his living, left his home in Bath and retreated to his
beloved Thames Valley as vicar of Sonning in Berkshire. From
there, he sent small tokens to the Austen girls by which to remember their courageous aunt. To Cassandra he sent a ring 'representing a sprig of diamonds, with one emerald'; to Jane he sent
a headband, which she was often proud to wear at balls in later
years when the romantic reminder of a tragic death was most
appealing to her sensibility.[52]

The return to Steventon that autumn brought a welcome sense
of security. Even the newspapers agreed in regarding their own
tranquil neighbourhood as a haven of calm in a dangerous world.
Reading through the *Hampshire Chronicle*'s gloomy reports of war
casualties, street robberies, suicides and scandals, the Austens were
pleased to find this cheerful note: 'There is at this time in the
garden of John Harwood Esq of Deane, Berks, two rooks' nests;
one containing five young almost fledged; and the other with several eggs.'[53] For Jane, the shocking threat of death, and the actual
death of her brave aunt, were too painful to recall without the
saving disguise of comic fiction. The perils of her own dramatic
rescue from a place of life-threatening contagions were quickly
assimilated into her private chronicle of comic misadventures
which flattered her self-conceit as a hapless romantic heroine.
'Beware of the unmeaning luxuries of Bath,' she made Isabel warn
Laura in her youthful novel *Love and Freindship*, 'and of the stinking fish of Southampton.' Typhoid fever was neither sufficiently
romantic, nor sufficiently tragic, to be mentioned as a heroine's
affliction; but 'stinking fish' had at least the virtue of mock-heroic
comedy.

Making light of her own sufferings (except in so far as might
be strictly required by her status as a romantic heroine), Jane was
pleased to allow that her brothers might have endured almost
equivalent tortures during their sisters' absence. Frank and Henry
told her of a visit to their uncle Henry Austen at Tonbridge. Uncle
Henry had three children, including a boy, Frank, who was the
same age as Fly. Frank of Tonbridge had challenged Frank of

Steventon to say if he knew what 'wiring' was. When Fly said that he didn't, his cousin had deliberately run a pin a considerable way into his leg.[54] That was 'wiring', he said. Jane always loved stories like that. She was soon writing comic sketches about neighbours who did not hesitate 'to kick one another out of the window on the slightest provocation' or a pastoral nymph with her leg 'caught in one of the steel traps so common in gentlemen's grounds'.[55]

Having once determined to give his daughters the benefits of formal instruction, Mr Austen resolved to continue that process at home. For the sum of £11 9s the watercolour artist Mr Claude Nattes was engaged to instruct them in the ladylike accomplishment of pencil portraiture.[56] Cassandra showed some aptitude for this activity, but Jane had little patience with it. Henry often liked to flatter her by pretending that she showed 'great power of hand in the management of the pencil'.[57] But Jane's own view of her attainments in this discipline was rather different. It was of herself she was thinking when she wrote of little Catherine Morland that 'her taste for drawing was not superior'.[58] She well knew the like frustration of seizing upon any odd pieces of paper, and doing what she could with them by way of drawing houses and trees, hens and chickens, only to find her houses and her chickens looked very much the same. Like Catherine, she would far rather play at boys' games with her brothers, than settle to the female repertoire of accomplishments recommended by her drawing-master or music-master. She, too, 'greatly preferred cricket not merely to dolls, but to the more heroic enjoyments of infancy, nursing a dormouse, feeding a canary-bird, or watering a rose-bush'. She, too, 'was noisy and wild, hated confinement and cleanliness, and loved nothing so well in the world as rolling down the green slope at the back of the house'. The only symptom of a preference for any of the diversions common to her own sex lay in her love for historical romance.

In the spring, it was decided that Cassandra should be sent away to continue her instruction at the Abbey School in Reading. But Jane could not bear the idea of being separated from her sister. She protested to her parents, who told her she was still too young to benefit from the Abbey School's curriculum. Still, she insisted that she *would*, she *must*, go with Cassandra, until her mother concluded that it was useless to argue with her further. 'If Cassandra's head had been going to be cut off,' Mrs Austen said, 'she believed that Jane would insist on having hers cut off too.'[59] Decapitation was indeed a favourite theme of Jane Austen's childish imagination. The romance of martyrdom had a strong hold on her mind, and she proclaimed a fierce attachment to the sacred memory of such beheaded monarchs as Mary Queen of Scots ('bewitching princess') and Charles I ('amiable monarch').[60] In Southampton, the two Austen sisters had faced death together, not from decapitation but from the rather less glamorous typhoid fever. When she heard the plan to send Cassandra to the Abbey School, whose premises included the romantic ruins of a twelfth-century Cluniac monastery, Jane was determined that she should not be sent upon such a perilous adventure without the faithful companionship of her loving sister. Reluctantly, Mr Austen acquiesced to his younger daughter's demands, and found the necessary £37 19s to send both girls to the Abbey School in the summer of 1785.[61]

Jane Austen was not disappointed in her romantic expectation of this new school. The ruined abbey had more than its full complement of ghosts. The eyeless corpse of King Henry I had been buried nearby, and it was said his coffin had been opened and his skeleton scattered when the abbey was destroyed. The pale spectres of Isabella and John, ill-fated grandchildren of King John, were rumoured to haunt the grounds. A shrivelled human hand, said to be that of St James the Apostle, was discovered in the abbey ruins during her first year at the school; and, shortly afterwards, a 'perfect skeleton' unearthed beneath the Abbey walls.[62] All this provided gory subject-matter for lurid late-night stories among the girls who slept two to a bed in their turret rooms.

The school's headmistress, Mrs La Tournelle, was herself a character from Gothic fiction. Although this lady had not lost her head, she had lost a leg, and clumped about the school on a leg made out of cork. How she had lost her real leg was a solemn secret. Perhaps it had been caught in one of the steel traps so common in gentlemen's grounds. All morning the girls would hear her heavy uneven tread up and down the school's grand staircase, with its chipped gilt balustrades.[63] Everything about 'Mrs La Tournelle' was an elaborate mystery. Jane quickly learnt that the woman was not French at all, nor a widow, as she pretended. Her real name was Miss Sarah Hackett, and she came from London, but her employers had thought it right to introduce her under a foreign name to suggest her expertise in languages. This stratagem seemed of somewhat limited effect, however, since it was the common gossip among all the girls that 'Mrs La Tournelle' could not speak a word of her 'native' tongue. Other rumours surrounded her strange absences after lunch, when the girls were left entirely to their own amusements. No human being took trouble to consider where the girls might spend the rest of the day, whether gossiping in one turret or another.

It soon became apparent to the Austen sisters that Mrs La Tournelle was entirely lacking in even the most rudimentary of learned qualifications, and that she preferred to confine herself to such domestic matters as 'giving out clothes for the wash, making tea, ordering dinner'. What she lacked in scholarly skills, she made up for by the cultivation of solemn mysteries. Her little wainscoted parlour was done out as a private shrine, 'hung round with chenille pieces representing tombs and weeping willows'. Her unchanging form of dress, winter and summer alike, had the austere ritual solemnity of a nun's habit: 'her white muslin handkerchief was always pinned with the same number of pins, her muslin apron always hung in the same form; she always wore the same short sleeves, cuffs and ruffles . . .' During morning prayers she would sometimes break into urgent whispers: 'Make haste, make haste', and seemed to view herself as an actress-*manquée*, still acting out the part of the tragic heroine of some lofty romantic drama. Mrs La Tournelle, they found, was never happier than when holding forth on plays and play-acting, stage anecdotes and the private life of actors.

Such formal instruction as was attempted at the school was in the hands of Miss Pitts and her two assistants. Together these ladies offered the full female repertoire of French, music, drawing, writing and dancing. Needlework and spelling were alternatives; Jane was always skilled at the first and lamentable at the second, though whether as a result of the Abbey School curriculum seems very doubtful. More masculine subjects, such as history, mathematics and geography, might be taken by the older girls, under the tuition of masters from Dr Valpy's school for boys across the meadow. 'Play-acting' was also available at Dr Valpy's school, whose pupils were invited to dances at the Abbey School in return. 'A real honest, old-fashioned Boarding school' was how Jane Austen later described Mrs Goddard's school in *Emma*, 'where a reasonable quantity of accomplishments were sold at a reasonable price, and where girls might be sent to be out of the way and scramble themselves into a little education, without any danger of coming back prodigies'.[64] That was just how she remembered the Abbey School, from which she and Cassandra were certainly in no danger 'of coming back prodigies'. Even at the age of ten, she suspected the chief purpose of such schools was as places where girls might be 'sent to be out of the way'. While she and Cassandra 'scrambled themselves' into a little education at Reading, their places at the rectory were usurped by male pupils like John Willing Warren and Charles Fowle, who were allowed to benefit from Mr Austen's instruction in an altogether more serious syllabus designed to equip them for university or the gentlemanly professions. Girls, of course (or idiots, like their poor brother George), must be sent 'out of the way', in order that this more serious masculine project might be accomplished.

Jane and Cassandra took full advantage of the Abbey School's indolent atmosphere. They spent their idle afternoons gossiping and laughing with the other girls; 'I could die of laughter at it,' Jane wrote once to Cassandra, 'as they used to say at school.'[65] In October, Thomas Leigh paid them a visit and gave them exactly half a guinea apiece. But it was far more exciting when their glamorous brother Edward and cousin Edward Cooper called at the school and insisted on taking them out to dine in high style at the smartest inn in the town. Even this modest example of youthful self-indulgence seemed rather shocking to later members of the family. 'It is true that Edward Cooper was Jane Cooper's brother, and Edward Austen was brother to our aunts, but it was a strange thing to allow.'[66] The Victorian generation of Austens were never happy with the notion that aunt Jane should ever have taken pleasure in spontaneous acts of exuberance.

Towards the end of 1786, Mr Austen recalculated the equation between the 'reasonable quantity of accomplishments' provided by the Abbey School and the 'reasonable price' he was paying for them, and concluded, reasonably enough, that the figures did not balance. Those idle afternoons, he reckoned, could be better spent helping Mrs Austen with the dairy, or mending clothes, or reading books in the rectory library. Extravagant dinner-parties at the Bear hotel might only give his daughters a taste for the kind of dissipated diversions that their cousin Eliza had always favoured. Midway through the Michaelmas term, he abruptly removed both girls from the school, and Jane was back at Steventon in time for her eleventh birthday. It was to be her last independent adventure in the outside world. Thereafter, for the rest of her life, she never strayed outside the enclosure of her family circle.

CHAPTER 3

Growing Up

One does not care for girls till they are grown up.

Jane Austen, Letter to Anna Austen, September 1814

'Whimsical & affected'

Christmas at Steventon was more than usually lively that year. On 21 December, Eliza Hancock, under her grand new style of the Comtesse de Feuillide, made her long-anticipated entrance, accompanied by her noisy baby, Hastings, and her irrepressible mother, Philadelphia. The baby was immediately pronounced 'very fair & very pretty' and declared to be growing visibly fatter every day.[1] A pianoforte was promptly borrowed, on which the Comtesse charmed them all with daily recitals. A few days later, the 'two little Coopers' came over to swell the party, and there were snug little dances in the parlour for all the sisters and brothers, nephews and nieces. As a birthday gift, Eliza presented her cousin Jane with a set of M. Berquin's *L'Ami des Enfans*. But what Jane chiefly loved was to sit by the fireside and listen to the Comtesse's own romantic tales of the beautiful French Queen,

Marie Antoinette, and of the daring M. Blanchard, who ascended a full fifteen hundred fathoms over Paris in a hot-air balloon.[2]

Sadly, there were no theatricals at the rectory that Christmas. Wind-bound on the island of Jersey, on his way to visit the Comtesse's husband in Guienne, James Austen was inspired to the production of tender love lyrics instead of tragic dramas. Lady Catherine Powlett of Hackwood Park was the latest object of his affections, and he occupied himself in penning earnest love sonnets to his beautiful, absent sweetheart. James's business at the time should have been to prepare himself for ordination, but his principal devotions were of a more pagan kind. Lady Catherine in his verses appeared as the reincarnated Venus, transposed from 'fair Idalia's love-devoted shades' to the sunny woodlands of Hampshire.[3] Edward, too, was absent from the rectory. The adoptive heir of Godmersham had spurned the domes and spires of Oxford in favour of the mountains of Switzerland, preferring to complete his education in a truly aristocratic style by doing the Grand Tour. In Switzerland, he affected the company of the fashionable 'Neufchâtel Set' of young English milords; in Dresden (where he idled a whole year away), he was received at the court of the Elector of Saxony; in Rome, he did as the English do: had himself painted as an elegant dilettante, casually surveying the classical ruins.

Henry was still at home at Steventon. A handsome young man of fifteen, and already as tall as his father, he had need of his sunny disposition not to resent his brother Edward's good fortune. For Henry, there seemed little prospect of foreign adventures. He was obliged to satisfy his own impetuous love of travel by careering recklessly down the narrow Hampshire lanes as if they were the pathways of some Alpine ravine. Once, impatient at the slow pace of the post-chaise carrying him back to Steventon, he protested to the postillion: 'Get on boy! Get on, will you?' 'I *do* get on, sir, where I can!' the insulted 'boy' replied. 'You stupid fellow!' said Henry. 'Any fool can do that. I want you to get on *where you can't!*'[4]

Even Fly had dreams of foreign travel. Only twelve years old, Fly was the most daring of all the Austen brothers ('Fearless of danger, braving pain,' wrote Jane), and had already set his heart upon a glorious naval career.[5] Looking back on these childhood years, Fly disavowed all hint of youthful bravado. His memoirs, written in the colourless, impersonal third-person style of an official report, remembered only a boyhood of diligent attention to duty ('He was educated at home under the immediate superintendance of his father who was admirably calculated to the instruction of youth . . . Under his paternal roof he made considerable progress in the usual scholastic exercises . . .').[6] But that was not at all how he appeared to his sister Jane. She loved Fly's 'saucy words and fiery ways', his 'warmth' and 'insolence of spirit'. She hated to think of that fiery independence being tamed by the severe discipline of the Portsmouth Naval Academy. The place had a fearsome reputation for bullying and flogging, and Orchard, who was master there, was said 'to flourish with direful sway an infernal horsewhip'.[7] Mr Austen, too, was somewhat surprised by his young son's choice of profession. Theirs was not a family with any naval traditions, and consequently without those connections which might further the boy's career. But Frank was firm in his resolution, and, since both board and tuition at the Academy were free, Mr Austen saw no reason to deny his wishes. Fly enrolled at the Portsmouth Academy some days short of his twelfth birthday and returned to Steventon that Christmas with many tales of his life there: tales of how his schoolfellows Baber and Colepepper had got Dashwood dead drunk at the Sun Tavern; of gunnery training on the hulks moored in Portsmouth harbour; and of hours spent studying Robertson's *Elements of Navigation*.[8]

The fireside gossip at the rectory that Christmas ranged widely from India to America, from the court at Versailles to the boulevards of Brussels, and from the snowy mountains of Switzerland to the fertile plains of south-west France. The Comtesse enthralled her young Hampshire cousins with her magical descriptions of the splendours of Versailles, like the Arabian Nights entertainments of enchanted palaces. She recalled balls in noble salons, lit by eight thousand shimmering lights, where there were gold and silver and diamonds to be seen on every side, and the French Queen, presiding over it all, like some exotic goddess in her Turkish dress of silver gauze. She described the night sky over Paris illumined by a thousand fireworks, and operas at the Tuileries where a troop of five hundred horse appeared on stage.[9] Philadelphia recalled the far-away mysteries of Bengal; tigers that prowled on the edge of the jungle; the scent of attar of roses from Echarabad and the perils of a six-month sea journey to meet a strange husband in a stranger land. Frank drew charts of American enemy positions in Louisiana, Maryland, Pennsylvania, the Jerseys and New England. Mrs Austen wrote to her niece Phylly Walter, chiding her for not joining their family party. Phylly 'might as well be in Jamaica keeping your brother's house,' she wrote, 'for anything that we see of you.'[10]

Mrs Austen also loved to recite the heroic tales of Leigh family history, recently recorded in verse by her cousin Mary Leigh of Adlestrop. Once again they heard about Sir Thomas Leigh:

> *When great Elizabeth ruled this realm,*
> *(And a mighty Queen was she)*
> *To be proclaim'd at St Paul's she rode,*
> *Behind Sir Thomas Leigh.*

With her romantic attachment to Mary Queen of Scots, Jane was unimpressed by such devotion to 'wicked' Queen Elizabeth. She far preferred to hear the story of Sir William Leigh, ruined and imprisoned for his loyalty to her Stuart favourite, Charles I.

> *But it was not the custom of Leighs to flinch*
> *From their sovereign in times of need.*
> *So William lost both house and land,*
> *And did everything but bleed . . .*[11]

And when at last all the company were gone, the stories they had told remained in Jane's imagination. For her, a year among the abbey ruins at Reading had seemed a heroic adventure. But here, in that Steventon Christmas company, had been others whose imaginations and memories travelled the trade routes of ambition from the southern oceans to the capitals of Europe. It was the stories of Eliza – the Countess – that made the strongest impression on her mind. She had long heard about her scandalous cousin, and often wondered what such a person might be like. The woman herself was a kind of revelation. There was nothing of impropriety in her manner, and yet she had a kind of shocking frankness; a beguiling manner which permitted all sorts of free-doms that could only be admired. What would it have been like, she wondered, to have lived a life of such bold adventures? How must such a worldly woman regard her provincial female cousins, who had never ventured more than fifty miles from home?

Eliza, Countess de Feuillide, returned to her smart house in Orchard Street, delighted by her winter sojourn among her Hampshire cousins, and refreshed for the forthcoming London season. She had achieved just the exact combination of maternal devotion and worldly *savoir faire* that she had striven for. Not that she acknowledged ever *striving* for particular effect. Her style was quite instinctive. Little Hastings had been a perfect ally, charming his Austen aunts and uncles with his happy gurglings and innocent grin. Even Mr Austen had been quite disarmed by those. As for the boy Henry, the poor youth was quite smitten, she could tell. Only sixteen, but already taller than his father and with those soft hazel eyes. How he had blushed when she invited him to stay with her in London that April, before he was *obliged* to take up residence in Oxford. Oh, she was certainly become the greatest rake imagin-able. She often wondered how such a meagre creature as she was could support the fatigue of this racketing London life. Standing for two long hours in the King's drawing-room, loaded with a great hoop of no inconsiderable weight; then on to the Duchess of Cumberland's in the evening, and thence to Almack's till five in the morning.[12] She regretted that Henry's visit must inevitably postpone her promised reunion with her Kentish cousin Phylly Walter. It was really quite provoking to have been so long in England without seeing her. But some sacrifices must be endured for the pleasure of entertaining such a young and handsome cousin.

In September, the Countess had her wish. She and her mother at last prevailed upon Phylly Walter to accompany them on a visit to Tunbridge Wells. But how quaint and awkward the dear creature had become. Although the same age as the Countess, Phylly had become quite an old maid, rarely venturing beyond the safety of her home in Kent. During their first few days at Tunbridge she seemed quite determined to be miserable, affecting to be shocked at what she called the 'dissipations' of Eliza's way of living, and forever seeking to shrink herself into some corner. Imagine, to be always travelling in a coach and four with a coronet on the door! It afforded Eliza the greatest pleasure imaginable to tease and shock her timid cousin.[13] The very first evening she dragged her to the Assembly Rooms to hear two celebrated Italian singers, and then insisted on her dancing, which they kept up till after midnight. The next morning it was a hunt through all the milliners' shops for hats. 'Why is the taste for all the most frightful colours?' poor Phylly had complained. Whereupon the Countess presented her with a fancy hat of the most frightful colours of all, a mixture of green and pink with a wreath of pink roses and feathers. That night they danced till past two o'clock, concluding with a cotillon that Phylly called 'The Baker's Wife' because she could not pronounce the French name. The next day it was off to the races, to see Mr Cumberland's horse beat Lord Sackville's. They paid visits and left their cards; they strolled on the Pantiles, rambled on the rocks. And every night there were balls and dances or visits to the playhouse. They saw *The Drummer* and *Robinson Crusoe*, *Percy* and *The Maid of the Oaks*. But the best evening was when the Countess bespoke a special performance of Mrs Cowley's *Which is the Man?* and Garrick's *Bon Ton* for their very own amusement. The house was crowded for both plays, and even Phylly seemed content to join in the general approbation.

By the end of the visit, Phylly had decided that Eliza's mother was quite without fault, almost a model of perfection. But as to Eliza herself, she seemed less sure. Between them there existed a kind of rivalry which provoked some lively disputes. Phylly professed herself shocked that Eliza, while expressing the highest degree of respect and esteem for her husband's undoubted merits, could not bring herself to say she loved him. But, since Eliza had been brought up to know no other life than this dissipated existence, Phylly supposed her addiction to it was hardly to be wondered at.

Before they parted, Eliza obtained Phylly's reluctant consent that together they should petition their Austen cousins to perform at the rectory that Christmas the same double-bill that had proved such a triumph at Tunbridge. Thanks to James, the barn at Steventon was fitted up quite like a theatre, and Eliza could already picture herself in the leading roles, Lady Bob Lardoon in *Which is the Man?* and Miss Tittup in *Bon Ton*. All the young folks would have parts, James, Henry and Francis, Cassandra and Jane; and, of course, Phylly herself. But Phylly was less enthusiastic. 'I should like to be a spectator,' she wrote, 'but am sure I should not have courage to act a part.'[14] Such bashfulness was extremely provoking. Eliza had already obtained her aunt Austen's consent to their Christmas arrangements, who waited only to be assured of Phylly's plans to join them. Eliza dashed off an urgent letter. 'Indeed my dear cousin,' she wrote, 'your compliance will highly oblige me and your declining my proposal as cruelly mortify me.' She begged Phylly to consider that this would be 'the only Christmas we may pass together for many, many years', since she must certainly return to France before another year was out. As to Phylly's diffidence about her acting abilities, Eliza begged that that might be 'sent to *Coventry*'.[15] The parts allotted to her were neither long nor difficult, and she was certain to succeed in them perfectly.

It vexed Eliza to the heart that people must make such difficulties about the simplest of arrangements. Mrs Austen was uneasy about accommodation for such a numerous Christmas company and could only promise Phylly 'a place to hide your head in'. But what did that matter? And if she was worried about costumes, the 'Green Room' – by which grand term Eliza designated the seamstress skills of her cousins Jane and Cassandra – would supply all her needs. 'We shall have a most brilliant party & a great deal of amusement,' she assured her, 'the house full of company & frequent balls. You cannot possibly resist so many temptations, especially when I tell you your old friend James is returned from France & is to be of the acting party.'

But Phylly *could* resist even these temptations. Imagine the Countess's mortification when she received, by return of post, a letter from her cousin expressing a strong reluctance against 'appearing in public'. She wrote back immediately. A performance in Steventon barn, she protested, could hardly be called a *public* show, since only a select group of friends would be present. Her Austen cousins were all agreed in urging her to act with them, and aunt Austen had declared she had 'no room for any *idle young people*'.[16] But Phylly was deaf to all persuasion. She sent kind wishes to baby Hastings, who was suffering the agonies of teething.

The Countess, her mother and baby Hastings reached Steventon a week before Christmas that year. A few days later they were joined by James Austen, who had just been ordained deacon in St David's cathedral. Eliza's first duty was to hear from James the latest news from her husband's estate at Guienne. He was happy to confirm what Eliza already knew; that de Feuillide had at last completed his 'important work' of draining the marshlands at Ga-barret; that the area was now freed of all 'pernicious exhalations' and transformed into a fertile plain; and that the Count himself was now regarded as the general benefactor of the whole province. The entire Austen family joined together in proposing remedies for Eliza's 'wonderful brat' Hastings, whose teeth still plagued him a good deal, and she herself was required to assume her best matronly manner in acknowledging their kind attentions.

It was not until Boxing Day that the long-anticipated theatricals took place, by which time Eliza had graciously withdrawn her own darling scheme of staging *Which is the Man?* and *Bon Ton* in favour of James Austen's choice of Mrs Centlivre's *The Wonder: A Woman Keeps a Secret*. James Austen, whom she had not seen for ten years, now fancied himself as something of a poet. He addressed sonnets to his latest lady-love, the 'sweet enchantress' Charlotte Brydges at Deane parsonage (the Hampshire Venus, Lady Catherine Powlett, was apparently quite forgotten). Actually, James Austen seemed rather eclectic in his amorous devotion and was scarcely less flattering to Eliza herself, composing a verse epilogue to *The*

Wonder especially for her to speak. Almost as handsome as Henry, and six years older, here was another eligible young bachelor with whom it was fun to flirt. The play, in which Eliza played the heroine, Donna Violante, was filled with the most glorious opportunities for coquettish innuendoes. Set in Portugal, it was one of those old-fashioned comedies in which miserly fathers threaten their daughters with arranged marriages or banishment to a nunnery, while the daughters elope and conspire with handsome young lovers. Eliza loved the lascivious officer, Colonel Britton, who lusted after a nunnery full of 'soft, plump, tender, melting, wishing, nay, willing girls'.[17] She made sure to give full force to Donna Violante's lines proclaiming the sovereignty of love over all financial interests. But most of all she loved the epilogue, in which James allowed her to voice a mischievous female polemic. 'In barbarous times,' it began, 'ere learning's sacred light / Rose to disperse the shades of Gothic night', women had been treated as 'the light playthings' of men's 'idle hours'. But not now.

> *But thank our happier stars, those days are o'er,*
> *And woman holds a second place no more.*
> *Now forced to quit their long held usurpation,*
> *These men all wise, these Lords of the Creation!*
> *To our superior rule themselves submit,*
> *Slaves to our charms, & vassals to our wit;*
> *We can with ease their every sense beguile,*
> *And melt their resolutions with a smile.*[18]

Smiling appropriately as she delivered this final line, Eliza permitted herself to wonder what would happen if James ever came to believe the things he had set down for her so cleverly. A week later, James was even bolder with his prologue to their second theatrical offering, Garrick's *The Chances*. It amused Eliza to watch this future parson striving so hard to impress her with his modish pose as a would-be rake. He loved to give her vivid descriptions of the bull-run he had witnessed at Pamplona during the festival of St Fermin,[19] and in his prologue affected an equally worldly tone, with his mockery of puritan piety.

In those sad times, which once Britannia knew,
When few gave balls & no-one played at loo;
When children loved their parents, men their wives
And spent in dull domestic joys their lives . . .

James pretended to proclaim a new age of libertinism.

No more shall prudence with her chilling powers
Blast every joy that blooms in youth's gay bowers;
Duty no more 'gainst pleasure war shall wage,
Nor indiscretion fear the frown of age . . .

But James Austen, she suspected, was a libertine only in rhyme. His indiscretions were purely verbal and he would soon enough settle, like the rest of the Steventon clan, for a life of dull domestic joys.

It was James's younger sister Jane who gave most signs of a truly rebellious spirit. The girl was forever scribbling cruel and witty stories about people who shot each other, committed suicide or lost several of their limbs. And, of course, the girl was in love (what girl of twelve is not?), or at least, as was usually the case, in love with the idea of *being* in love. She had inscribed her name, and that of her future husband, in the page of marriage entries in her father's parish register.[20] Nor had she confined herself to one husband only, but prudently, or wickedly, enough, had already married herself to *three*. The first entry read: 'The banns of marriage between *Henry Frederic Howard Fitzwilliam* of *London* and *Jane Austen* of *Steventon*'. She had taken particular care with the names. 'Fitz' always signified the illegitimate offspring of a king, she explained. She thought it was particularly romantic for someone to be the *unacknowledged* child of a monarch or great man. Romantic possibly, thought Eliza, but not always convenient or easy. A little lower down the page, Jane had imagined for herself a different husband: '*Edmund Arthur William Mortimer* of *Liverpool* and *Jane Austen* of *Steventon* were married in this church . . .' Mortimer was the name of a deposed royal house, and Jane felt a peculiar fondness for deposed and displaced monarchs like Mortimer, or Charles I or Mary Queen of Scots. Of course, Edmund, Arthur and William were all the names of legendary kings. There was a particular nobleness in the name of Edmund, she thought. 'It is a name of heroism and renown; of kings, princes, and knights; and seems to breathe the spirit of chivalry and warm affections.'[21] But why from Liverpool? Liverpool hardly had the sound of heroism and chivalry. Liverpool was an upstart city of merchants and traders growing rich on the slave trade to the Americas. But he would be a prince *in disguise*, said Jane. No one could tell what poor or sordid profession a deposed or displaced prince might be obliged to maintain. And was 'Jack Smith' a prince too? Eliza wanted to know, reading Jane's final entry in the register. 'This marriage was solemnized between us, *Jack Smith & Jane Smith late Austen.*' It seemed to her that here was a deposition indeed. Her cousin's romantic dream of marrying a latter-day chivalric king – a Fitzwilliam or a Mortimer – banished and replaced by the sober dread of yielding her maiden identity to some local rural nonentity. ('Mrs Smith, such a name! . . . A mere Mrs Smith, an every day Mrs Smith . . . who was her husband? One of the five thousand Mr Smiths whose names are to be met with every where.')[22] Of course, it was only fantasy, like the stories that she wrote. But if the girl were ever to write about a truly aristocratic and romantic hero she would be sure to call him Fitzwilliam; and if she were ever to describe a poor, unacknowledged female, she would certainly call her Smith.

That Christmas, the Countess was especially conscious of her own status as the unacknowledged daughter of a great man. While they acted out their comic dramas in the barn, or played charades around the fireside, the man whom she believed to be her father awaited trial on twenty-two charges of 'high crimes and misdemeanours'. Proceedings against Warren Hastings had begun more than a year before, when Edmund Burke first published his list of accusations. On 1 May 1786, Hastings had been summoned to appear in person before the most crowded House of Commons that the reporter from the *Morning Chronicle* had ever seen. At first, his friends and relatives, among whom the Austens were included, had not been unduly dismayed. Neither the King nor

Prime Minister Pitt, they knew, was any friend to Hastings's accusers. All that had changed in June, when the Benares charge came before the House. Hastings was accused of attempting to exact a fine of £500,000 from Chait Singh.[23] The evidence seemed damning, and even Pitt declared that Mr Hastings had acted in a 'manner repugnant to motives of principle'. There followed months of bitter argument and debate, but the votes went against Hastings. In May 1787, the House voted by a large majority for his impeachment. Warren Hastings was taken into custody by the Sergeant-at-Arms and released again on bail of £40,000. Little was said about the matter at Steventon, though whether the Austens' reticence on this subject proceeded from delicacy or shame was something which Eliza could not precisely determine. It seemed strange to her that they could express so much solicitude for her baby Hastings's teeth, while maintaining such a steadfast silence on the far greater sufferings of the child's grandfather and namesake.

For the Countess, it soon became a point of honour to demonstrate her feelings by publicly befriending the second Mrs Hastings, the former Marian von Imhoff. She and her mother took tea with Mrs Hastings at her town house in St James's Place. Accompanied by Phylly Walter, these ladies were to be seen together at the opera, where they sat in Hastings's private box. And of course, they attended the trial when it began that February at Westminster Hall. Phylly Walter, though, seemed strangely insensitive to the seriousness of the proceedings. To her, the trial was merely another of the diversions of this 'racketing' London life. 'I have once been to the trial,' she wrote to her brother James in Lincolnshire, 'which, because an uncommon sight, we fancied worth going to.' She found it rather fatiguing that Eliza and her aunt insisted on staying there the whole day, from ten in the morning to four in the afternoon. For want of other amusement, she sketched a brisk review of the star performances in this piece of political theatre.[24] Mr Sheridan, the dramatist, spoke so low that they could hardly hear him; Mr Burke was so hot and hasty that they could not understand him. But Mr Fox, though superior in his oratory, afforded them even less satisfaction; 'he is so much against Mr Hastings whom we all here wish so well'. For Eliza, it was quite a relief when her cousin's visit ended. She had grown weary of Phylly's endless sniping comments at the 'ridiculous' ways of London life, and her want of natural feeling for the man on trial at Westminster Hall.

Throughout the summer, the Countess continued her visits to Mrs Hastings, both in London and at her country estate of Beaumont Lodge. But as the days lengthened, fresh troubles seemed to assail her on every side. Her boy, Hastings, suffered an alarming series of fits, and within the family there were already dark suggestions of his being 'like poor George Austen'.[25] Eliza hardly took it kindly when they said he had the appearance of a weak head, and remarked on the peculiar squint of his eyes. To her, the boy showed every outward symptom of good health, yet it was a mystery why he could not yet make use of his feet, nor talk, but only make a great noise continually. Then there was the alarming news from France of riots and turmoil in every part of the country. De Feuillide sent hints that he might be called upon to rejoin his regiment, which would be a fearful duty, to bear arms against his own countrymen. The Countess consulted the French ambassador, who advised a brief delay in returning to Guienne.

None but those who had experienced it could form a just idea of the plague and fatigue of mind and body which Eliza felt in planning her removal to a country which seemed scarcely less ungovernable than life at Orchard Street. There were articles of every kind to purchase, furniture to bespeak, and the packing of the whole to attend to.[26] And then, amid all the hurry and the worry and confusion, the Austens chose to pay a call, on their way back to Hampshire after visiting old Frank Austen at Sevenoaks in Kent. Eliza found it mortifying that they should thus encounter her, amid all the dust and litter of trunks and packing-chests rather than among her usual elegant surroundings. But any initial awkwardness that she experienced quickly passed. Mr Austen appeared to her more amiable than ever. Phylly Walter, who had dined with the Austens at Sevenoaks, had been surprised by his white hair, but Eliza thought it gave him an additional air of kindliness. What an excellent and pleasing man he was. She loved him most sincerely, as she did the whole Austen family. Young Jane had delighted her by writing a fantastical tale, all made up of chapter headings, called 'The Beautiful Cassandra'. It was all about a wild girl (surely *not* her virtuous sister) who went on a riot through the London streets. The girl devoured six ices, refused to pay for them, knocked down the pastrycook and walked away. She then drove all round London in a hackney-coach, but when the coachman asked for money, pushed her bonnet down on his head and ran away. When she got home, the girl smiled and whispered to herself: 'This is a day well spent.' Jane seemed mighty proud of that story. Eliza would miss her sorely when she returned to France.

The Countess was not at all surprised to learn that Phylly took an altogether different view of Jane's character. Phylly had never met the Austen girls before, and after she had seen them she immediately pronounced Cassandra the handsomer and more congenial of the two. *She* might be reckoned 'very pretty', said Phylly, and able to keep up an excellent conversation in a sensible and pleasing fashion. (Phylly did admit that her admiration for Cassandra might be influenced by her discovery of a striking resemblance between Cassandra's features and her own – which resemblance Cassandra herself could not distinguish, and seemed hardly gratified to have it generally acknowledged.) Jane, though, was a disappointment. Phylly found her 'very like her brother Henry, not at all pretty & very prim, unlike a girl of twelve . . . whimsical & affected'.[27] Eliza could not help smiling when she read this. To her, it seemed a curious notion of prettiness that could prefer a girl who might resemble the homely Phylly Walter to one who took after the lively Henry Austen. It was the whimsicality of the younger Austen daughter that Eliza loved. But she was not surprised that Phylly had failed to appreciate the twelve-year-old's wit. The girl had a dry manner that delighted in confounding the prejudices of those whose only idea of praise was to discover a conformity with their own supposed virtues.

Before leaving England in September, the Countess took a final tour of some of her favourite English places. She spent some time at Beaumont Lodge, where she found her (god)father less cast down by the indictments of his enemies than she could ever have hoped. He was busily planning improvements to the Daylesford estate, near Adlestrop, sold by his ancestors a century ago but recently repurchased by him. Then it was on to Ramsgate, where little Hastings could benefit from the sea-bathing. She was pleased to be able to boast to her cousins that her little hero was now acquiring some new accomplishment every day. 'His last is a very elegant one,' she wrote: 'he doubles his *prodigious* fists & boxes quite in the English style.'[28] Finally, she went to Oxford, to visit her two young Austen admirers, James and Henry. Poor Henry had been in hopes of accompanying her to France, and was cruelly mortified at one of the fellows of St John's choosing that exact moment to marry or to die (he was unsure which; to him they seemed almost equivalent fates). This had created a vacancy which he was reluctantly *obliged* to fill. How the two of them had harped on that relentless word *obliged*; they were neither of them free creatures. She must apply herself to her conjugal duties in France, he to his scholarly ones in Oxford. But how handsome he looked in his fellow's robes, taller than ever, and with his hair powdered and dressed in a very *ton*-ish style. The two Austen brothers took her on trips to see the lions, the colleges, the museum, vying with each other in the elegance of the entertainments they could propose. They spent a day at Blenheim, where the Countess was delighted with the park but was surprised to discover the inside of the palace so very old-fashioned and shabby. They were meant to have seen Nuneham too, but were prevented because His Majesty, without consulting them, had most unkindly chosen to breakfast there on the very day of their intended visit. Altogether she pronounced herself mightily taken by Oxford. The college garden was so very splendid. She teased Henry by telling him how she longed to be a fellow herself, that she might walk in it every day. And besides, she said, parading before him in his long black gown and neat square cap, did he not think the academic costume was really mighty becoming?

The two Austen brothers were full of literary schemes. In the New Year, they told her, they meant to publish their very own literary review. The *Gentleman's Magazine* and the *Monthly Review* would be as nothing beside *The Loiterer*. It was designed to be quite a family enterprise, with the two brothers writing most of the issues between them. Even Jane, who was grown to be a prodigious reader, was eager to contribute. She had devoted her past two summers to reading through bound copies of the *Tatler* and the *Spectator* that she found on her father's shelves.[29] It was Jane's whimsical manner of pronouncing opinions in the august tones of a female Addison that Phylly Walter found so very disconcerting.

Travelling back to London, the Countess and her mother endured the most dreadful storm of thunder and lightning that either of them could ever remember as they crossed Hounslow Heath. But at least the terrible weather saved them from a worse misadventure. She afterwards learnt that two highwaymen had been waiting for their prey, and only the violence of the storm prevented them from stopping the coach.[30] As Eliza contemplated the worse perils that might await her in France, she thought with envy of the life of an Oxford fellow, composing witty essays in the gentle bowers of a college garden, or of a young girl, scribbling fantastical adventures in the security of an English country rectory.

'Nice affecting stories'

Girl children in Jane Austen's fiction are chiefly recommended by their lack of conspicuous qualities. They gain approval not for what they are, but for what they are *not*. At the age of ten, Fanny Price was 'not vulgar'; she displayed 'no glow of complexion, nor any other striking beauty'. The best that could be said of her was that her character contained 'nothing to disgust her relations'. Catherine Morland at the same age had 'nothing heroic about her'; her taste was 'not superior' and she 'never could learn or understand anything before she was taught'. The girls who attended Mrs Goddard's school were in no danger of 'coming back prodigies'. At the age of ten, Jane Austen herself was no prodigy; her appearance (at least to Phylly Walter's eyes) displayed no very striking signs of beauty, nor did her actions evince any early symptoms of heroism. But already she was learning to distinguish between that docility of temperament which might fix a young female in the affections of her family, and that inner conviction of superior gifts which, at the risk of alienating some family affections, might lead on to greater things. 'Imbecility in females,' she once wrote, 'is a great enhancement to their personal charms.'[31] By the time that her bold cousin, the Countess Eliza de Feuillide, was preparing to set sail for France, Jane had determined that, whatever else might be her fate, she would *not* indulge the role of a charming female imbecile.

Jane Austen's education began the day that she left school. Unlike Mrs Cawley's school at Southampton and Madame La Tournelle's school at Reading, Mr Austen's library at Steventon opened out to her a whole world of intellectual adventures. Browsing among the several hundred volumes on her father's shelves, she fed her youthful imagination with works of history and poetry, essays, sermons, plays, and, above all, novels. The family were all 'great novel-readers & not ashamed of being so',[32] and she readily pounced on volumes of Fielding and Richardson, Goldsmith, Swift and Defoe. Inspired by Eliza's recommendation, *The Arabian Nights* was another early favourite, together with Johnson's *Rasselas*. Jean-Jacques Rousseau liked to boast that he had read all the major modern novels by the time he was seven years old. The adolescent Byron felt it barely worth mentioning the 'above four thousand novels' (including 'the works of Cervantes, Fielding, Smollett, Richardson, Mackenzie, Sterne, Rabelais & Rousseau') that he had read before going up to Harrow at the age of fifteen.[33] Jane Austen never presented herself as such a prodigy of bookishness. In later years, she would describe herself as 'the most unlearned, & uninformed female who ever dared to be an authoress'.[34] But this coy denial of intellectual pretensions is as revealing in its own way as Byron's literary boastfulness. And, at the age of thirteen, she was less modest in her claims. 'You must know, sir,' she declared in an essay for her brothers' Oxford magazine, 'I am a great reader, and not to mention some hundred volumes of novels and plays, have in the past two summers, actually got through all the entertaining papers of our most celebrated periodical writers, from the *Tatler* and *Spectator* to the *Microcosm* and the *Olla Podrida*.'[35] Her brother Henry agreed. 'Her reading was very extensive in history and belles lettres,' he recalled, 'and her memory extremely tenacious.' But Henry was anxious to insist that his sister's reading was not merely extensive, but guided by sound moral principles. 'Her favourite moral writers,' he insisted,

> were Johnson in prose and, Cowper in verse. It is difficult to say at what age she was not intimately acquainted with the merits and defects of the best essays and novels in the English language. Richardson's power of creating, and preserving the consistency of his characters, as particularly exemplified in *Sir Charles Grandison*, gratified the natural discrimination of her mind, whilst her taste secured her from the errors of his prolix style and tedious narrative. She did not rank any work of Fielding quite so high. Without the slightest affectation she recoiled from everything gross. Neither nature, wit, nor humour could make her amends for so very low a scale of morals.[36]

Actually it was Henry, rather than Jane, whose mind 'recoiled from anything gross'. By the time he wrote these words in 1817, Henry had transformed himself into an evangelical preacher and had become as keen as all the others in the Austen family to emphasize the strict piety of his dead sister's character. In fact, what is most striking about Jane Austen's reading is the unprudish eclecticism of her literary tastes. Fielding's *Tom Jones* (which Dr Johnson considered 'vicious' and 'shocking') was an early favourite, as was Sterne's *Tristram Shandy* (another work denounced by Johnson). She was an avid connoisseur of Gothic shockers like *The Castle of Otranto*, *The Castle of Wolfenbach*, *Mysterious Warnings*, *The Necromancer of the Black Forest* and *Horrid Mysteries*. She loved to read the novels of Ann Radcliffe, like *The Mysteries of Udolpho* and *The Italian*, which she borrowed from the library of Anne Lefroy at Ashe rectory. The 'grossness' of a book was never any bar to her reading it. She read and seemingly enjoyed Matthew Lewis's lurid tale of rape, incest and necrophilia, *The Monk*. This, despite the fact that one shocked reader described the book as 'a romance which, if a parent saw it in the hands of a son or daughter, he might reasonably turn pale', and even Byron found in it 'the philtered ideas of a jaded voluptuary'.[37] Nor did Mr Austen once attempt to censor his daughters' literary tastes; rather the opposite. It was he who insisted on buying *Fitz-Albini*, a novel written by their former neighbour at Deane parsonage, Sir Samuel Egerton Brydges, even though Jane expressed uneasiness 'that we should purchase the only one of Egerton's works of which his family are ashamed'. But, she quickly assured her sister: 'That these scruples, however, do not at all interfere with my reading it, you will easily believe.'[38] Henry's lofty insistence that his sister preferred the more respectable genres of 'history and belles lettres' to vulgar novels is flatly contradicted by the very novel to which his comments served as a preface.

Let us leave it to the Reviewers to abuse such effusions of fancy at their leisure, and over every new novel to talk in threadbare strains of the trash with which the press now groans ... Although our productions have afforded more extensive and unaffected pleasure than those of any other literary corporation in the world, no species of composition has been so much decried. From pride, ignorance, or fashion, our foes are almost as many as our readers. And while the abilities of the nine-hundredth abridger of the History of England, or of the man who collects and publishes in a volume some dozen lines of Milton, Pope, and Prior, with a paper from the Spectator, and a chapter from Sterne, are eulogized by a thousand pens, – there seems almost a general wish of decrying the capacity and under-valuing the labour of the novelist, and of slighting the performances which have only genius, wit and taste to recommend them. 'I am no novel reader – I seldom look into novels – Do not imagine that *I* often read novels – It is really very well for a novel'. – Such is the common cant. – 'And what are you reading, Miss –?' 'Oh, it is only a novel!' replies the young lady; while she lays down her book with affected indifference, or momentary shame. – 'It is only *Cecilia* or *Camilla*, or *Belinda*'; or, in short, only some work in which the greatest powers of the mind are displayed, in which the most thorough knowledge of human nature, the happiest delineation of its varieties, the liveliest effusions of wit and humour are conveyed to the world in the best chosen language.[39]

Even at the age of thirteen, Jane rejected Henry's brand of moralistic masculine literary snobbery. Under the pseudonym of 'Sophia Sentiment' she haughtily dismissed the first few issues of *The Loiterer* ('I think it is the stupidest work of the kind I ever saw'), and begged to tell the authors the error of their ways. 'Only conceive, in eight papers, not one sentimental story about love and honour and all that.' 'Let us hear no more of your Oxford journals,' she warns them; 'let us see some nice affecting stories, relating the misfortunes of two lovers . . .' Henry Tilney mocks the word 'nice' when Catherine Morland voices a similar protest and declares *The Mysteries of Udolpho* 'the nicest book in the world'.[40] 'But it *is* a nice book,' she insists, 'and why should not I call it so?' 'And this is a very nice day, and we are taking a very nice walk, and you are two very nice young ladies,' says Henry, instinctively deflecting an argument about literary judgements into a homily on diction. 'Sophia Sentiment' is a self-caricature; the young Jane Austen made sure she invested her comic persona with a girlish longing for Eastern tales 'full of bashas and hermits, pyramids and mosques', or for affecting romances in which star-crossed lovers with 'very pretty names' are lost at sea, run mad or shoot themselves. But this precocious piece of self-parody in fact disguised an awkward moment of self-discovery when, for the first time, she was forced to recognize what might be lost, as well as gained, by the fulfilment of her secret desire to be an author.

The New Year had begun with the appearance in the heavens of 'the long expected comet', and, in Oxford, of *The Loiterer*. All through the Christmas vacation James and Henry had been making preparations for their first public appearance as literary men. Their new periodical boldly promised 'a regular succession of moral lectures, critical remarks and elegant humour', but soon settled for a less demanding programme of stock comic vignettes. They drew characters like Sir Dilatory Doubtful of Dubious Hall, who could never make up his mind about anything, and Edmund Escutcheon, who deplored the modern vogue for pompous coats of arms. 'Luke Lickspittle' was just one among several hard-drinking, fox-hunting Oxford bucks reduced to the wretched condition of country curates, and eking out a miserable existence on £50 a year. By this time, James himself was enduring his own first curacy, at Stoke Charity near Steventon. Life there was very different from the hedonistic fantasies he had once indulged with Eliza. One issue of *The Loiterer* compared the curate's melancholy diversions ('cribbage . . . picquet and back-gammon') with those of a prisoner in the Bastille. Another issue contained a spoof advertisement: 'Wanted – a curacy in a good sporting country, near a pack of fox-hounds, and in a sociable neighbourhood . . . The advertiser has no objection to undertaking three, four or five churches of a Sunday . . . Direct to the Turf coffee-house, or Tattersall's Betting Room.'[41]

It was not long before James had his wish. Within the year he was curate at Overton, near Steventon; shortly afterwards, courtesy of the Leighs, he added the parishes of Cubbington and Hunningham in Warwickshire to his haul of ecclesiastical livings. James did not trouble himself to visit these remote Midland parishes, but the income he derived from them enabled him to indulge his love of hunting. He rode to hounds with the Kempshott pack (whose members included the Prince of Wales) and at the Vyne, near Basingstoke. Hunting was more than a passion; it was also a convenient means of self-promotion. It was thanks to their bond as fellow sportsmen that William Chute of the Vyne presented James to the nearby vicarage of Sherborne St John. 'Nothing is more certain,' *The Loiterer* observed, 'than that a good shot has often brought down a comfortable vicarage, and many a bold rider leaped into a snug rectory.'[42]

Jane Austen was both shocked and disappointed when she read the first issues of *The Loiterer*. Until that moment she had naively cherished a thrill of pleasure at her brothers' literary aspirations. As a child she had always loved their quick-wittedness at family charades, Henry's impromptu jokes and James's theatrical improvisations. But when she read *The Loiterer*, with its laboured facetiousness, its well-worn formulas and self-important Oxford jokes, she experienced a bewildering disillusionment. Denied any training in the classical languages and literature on account of her sex, she had hitherto instinctively deferred to her brothers' supposed superiority in literary matters. It came as a shock to discover, at the age of thirteen, that her own gift for literary invention might actually *exceed* theirs. The tone of her 'Sophia Sentiment' piece is a kind of comic exultation; in reality, the sensations which this discovery provoked were rather more confused: a thrilling, but also guilty, awareness of a talent which she scarcely dared acknowledge. Henceforward, much of her life would be spent devising strategies to disguise, by self-mockery and sometimes by silence, her own extraordinary abilities. It became a habit with her to insist on the superior literary talents of her brothers and her sister while diminishing her own. She told Cassandra: 'You are indeed the finest comic writer of the present age',[43] and dedicated one of her short burlesque novels ('Lesley Castle') to Henry under the pretence of returning an honour he had 'frequently' paid to her. This fantasy, that Henry, James and Cassandra were the *real* writers, and she herself was merely an inferior imitator, became an instinctive defence against any consciousness of pre-eminence. She would happily submit to her brothers' strictures on her own woeful diction ('nice') and erratic spelling ('freindship') as a deserved punishment for the guilt of superior talents. 'A woman especially, if she have the misfortune of knowing anything,' she wrote in *Northanger Abbey*, 'should conceal it as well as she can.'[44] It was a lesson she learnt early and never forgot.

Henry's insistence on his sister's special fondness for Richardson's sober and voluminous work *Sir Charles Grandison* has often been claimed as proof of her moral preoccupations. 'Every circumstance narrated in *Sir Charles Grandison*, all that was ever said or done in the cedar parlour, was familiar to her; and the wedding days of Lady L. and Lady G. were as well remembered as if they had been living friends.'[45] Certainly *Sir Charles Grandison* was a work Jane Austen knew well, and from an early age. As a child she was presented with her own copy of the first edition, and carefully inscribed her name on the title-page of each of its seven volumes in a stiff copperplate hand.[46] Echoes of the book pervade her writing, from her earliest juvenilia to her final novels. Yet it has puzzled even her most ardent admirers that such a witty and incisive writer should give her preference to a tedious, didactic work which is 'now and again absurd and at all times long-winded'.[47] *Sir Charles Grandison* was precisely the kind of sober, didactic conduct-book that well-intentioned parents would present to their daughters. But modern readers tend to agree with Isabella Tilney in *Northanger Abbey*, who thought it 'an amazing horrid book', or with Miss Andrews, who 'could not get through the first volume'.[48]

In fact, what she loved was to make *fun* of Richardson's book, turning its sententious moral episodes into brisk comic sketches. When little Anna Austen came to the rectory in the summer of 1795, she too came to love this game of making up mock 'Grandison' scenes to be acted out at family gatherings, amid the charades and comic recitations. Between them, Jane and Anna succeeded in reducing Richardson's million-word, moralizing epic to a ten-minute stage lampoon. Richardson's villain, the rakish Sir Hargrave Pollexfen, was transformed into a ludicrous figure of knockabout farce; Richardson's heroine, the virtuous Harriet Byron, was made ridiculous by her constant habit of fainting. Henry liked to pretend that his sister found Fielding's writings 'low' and 'gross', but Jane Austen's 'Grandison' bears much the same relation to Richardson's *Grandison* as Fielding's *Shamela* does to Richardson's *Pamela*. Like Fielding, the young Jane Austen had an irresistible impulse to deflate the solemn wind-baggery of Richardson's style. In her story 'Jack and Alice', she transformed the fragrant Italian orange-grove in *Grandison* into a rather less sweet-smelling citron-grove situated between 'her ladyship's pig-sty' and 'Charles Adams's horsepond'. In 'Frederic and Elfrida', she ridiculed Harriet Byron's frequent fainting fits by describing a heroine who 'was in such a hurry to have a succession of fainting fits, that she had scarcely patience enough to recover from one before she fell into another'.[49]

Jane was delighted when, in March, her brother James decided to perform Fielding's burlesque comedy *Tom Thumb* in the Steventon barn for 'a small circle of select friends'. At twelve, she considered herself quite old enough to play the part of the diminutive hero Tom Thumb, though perhaps not that of the giant princess Huncamunca, with her 'pouting breasts like kettle-drums of brass'. James composed a prologue to the play which showed his thoughts were with the absent Eliza, soon to depart for France. Despite its 'private poverty' and 'public debts', France was still a land of pleasure, he wrote, where 'the merry beggars dance'. He advised his cousin: '. . . in scenes of mirth your time employ / Practise your steps & halloo *Vive le Roi*'.[50] Jane took more pleasure in the play than in the prologue. She loved all the outrageous parodies (like Huncamunca's lament: 'O, Tom Thumb! Tom Thumb! wherefore art thou Tom Thumb?'). But most of all she relished the absurd climax, in which all the characters, the pathetic king, the drunken queen, the Noodles and the Doodles and *even the ghost* were killed, one after the other, in a kind of frenzied dance.

This kind of slapstick massacre appealed to her macabre imagination, and she loved to fill her sketches with similar arbitrary killings. In 'Sir William Mountague', her hero won his lady-love by simply killing his rival; 'She preferred a Mr Stanhope: Sir William shot Mr Stanhope; the lady had then no reason to refuse him . . .' In 'Jack and Alice', the jealous Sukey murdered her rival, Lucy: 'She . . . took her by poison from an admiring world at the age of seventeen.' Comic mutilations were another favourite theme. In 'Henry and Eliza', the heroine's starving children relieved their hunger 'by biting off two of her fingers'. Jane liked to dedicate these scenes of comic carnage and casual cruelty to various members of the family. She 'humbly dedicated' 'Sir William Mountague' (one murder and several violent passions) to her younger brother Charles, and 'respectfully inscribed' 'Jack and Alice' (one murder, one mutilation, an elopement and several persons 'dead drunk') to her elder brother Frank. Of course, 'The Beautiful Cassandra', with its delinquent heroine who assaults a pastrycook and bilks a coachman, was dedicated to Cassandra, in terms of fulsome flattery that parodied Phylly Walter's praise. 'You are a phoenix,' she told Cassandra: 'Your taste is refined, your sentiments are noble and your virtues innumerable. Your person is lovely, your figure elegant and your form, magestic [*sic*]. Your manners are polished, your conversation is rational and your appearance singular.' Like Fielding, Jane had already learnt that flattery could be a most deadly form of satire.

By Christmas-time, Eliza and her mother were back in Paris, where all their careful plans were thrown into a sudden disarray. De Feuillide was ill; a malignant fever raged through their estate at Nerac, and Eliza herself was so very thin and feverish 'as hardly to admit of my quitting my fireside'. 'Do not laugh,' she wrote to Phylly Walter, 'when I tell you, my *nerves* are still most exceedingly disordered.' Worst of all, Eliza's former acquaintances among the gay world of Paris found her sadly dull and old-fashioned after her prolonged stay in England. She had become so *matronly* in her concerns, and such a solemn family creature. 'Family news & family parties,' declared one of her witty friends, 'would have exhausted the patience of Job himself.'[51] At that moment, though, Eliza would gladly have exchanged her lonely Paris fireside for the pleasures of a family party at Steventon. How she envied the fortunate Jane Cooper in her starring role opposite Henry in James Austen's Christmas double-bill, *The Sultan* and *High Life Below Stairs*. 'Miss Cooper performed the part of Roxalana, & Henry the Sultan,' she wrote gloomily to Phylly Walter. 'I hear that Henry is taller than ever . . .' Secretly, the Countess was already hoping for a speedy return to England. In February, Philadelphia sent John Woodman a tentative enquiry about the possibility of summer lodgings at Cleveland Row: 'We shall want only two beds, and one of them for our maid Rosalie, the only person we shall bring with us . . .'[52] At least little Hastings was in better spirits. 'Comfortably rude and riotous', he would chatter away happily in a mixture of English and French, while generously handing round his half-munched apples to any visitors who could endure such a *matronly* ménage.

Eliza was not the only absentee from that year's Steventon festivities. Just two days before Christmas, young Frank Austen, still only fourteen, sailed for the East Indies as a 'Volunteer' aboard HMS *Perseverance*. The boy had completed his studies at

Portsmouth with unusual diligence and speed, and his headmaster sent a glowing report to the Lords of the Admiralty commending his 'uncommon assiduity' and irreproachable conduct.[53] Before he sailed, Mr Austen sent Frank a letter full of sober fatherly advice. Now that he was going from them, prudence must be his watchword. 'Never any action of your life in which it will not be your interest to consider what she directs! She will teach you the proper disposal of your time and the careful management of your money, – two very important trusts.'[54] Above all, he urged him: 'Keep an exact account of all the money you receive or spend, lend none but where you are sure of an early repayment, and on no account whatever be persuaded to risk it by gaming.' The older Austen sons were well used to receiving such homilies. One issue of *The Loiterer* included a 'Diary of a Modern Oxford Man', which contained this comment. 'Saturday. Found a letter from my father, no money and a great deal of advice – wants to know how my last quarter's allowance went – how the devil should I know? He knows I keep no accounts. Do think fathers are the greatest *bores* in nature . . .'[55] But Frank Austen did not consider his father a bore. At Frank's death, at the age of ninety-one, his father's letter was found, frayed, water-stained and dog-eared from much rereading, among his private papers. Nor were Mr Austen's lessons of financial prudence lost on his son, who put to sea not merely in a glamorous pursuit of maritime glories and heroic adventures, but also with a sober eye to trading opportunities overseas. Frank Austen embarked on the *Perseverance* carrying secret instructions from Warren Hastings, still on trial at Westminster Hall, who advised Frank to make contact with Hastings's remaining friends in the East India Company.[56] For a young, ambitious naval officer, the opportunities for enrichment by colluding with the unofficial traffic in precious Company commodities were considerable. Another issue of *The Loiterer* satirized an idle Oxford toff who witnessed a coach crash in which a man's leg was broken: ' "Oh Lord," says Ned Easy, "It's of no consequence, the fellow *was only a tradesman.*" ' But for the Austens, trade was a patriotic duty. 'England is a trading nation, commerce is our distinguishing characteristic, a characteristic that . . . has made us the most flourishing people of the most flourishing quarter of the globe.'[57] Jane Austen was brought up in a world of commodities and prices. When in 'Sir William Mountague' a bereaved sister is asked what recompense she requires for her murdered brother, her reply is prompt and precise. 'She fixed on 14s.'

While the Countess languished, a virtual prisoner, by her own Paris fireside, the barn at Steventon rang with proud boasts of British liberty. 'You are the great Sultan; I am your slave,' Jane Cooper declaimed in the role of Roxalana. 'But I am also a free-born woman, prouder of that than all the pomp and splendour Eastern monarchs can bestow.'[58] Jane Austen loved to parody this kind of heady rhetoric. Roxalana challenged her royal captor: 'Let your window-bars be taken down; let the doors of the seraglio be thrown open.' Similarly, in her story 'Henry and Eliza', Jane imagined a romantic pick-pocket heroine locked in a private dungeon ('She went to the door; but it was locked. She looked at the window, but it was barred with iron').

The other play chosen for their Christmas theatricals that year provided Jane with even more glorious opportunities for parody. The Reverend Townley's farce *High Life Below Stairs* presented a ridiculous topsy-turvy world in which servants took over their masters' houses, assumed their titles, copied their speech, affected their connoisseurship of fine wines and delighted in all the fashionable diversions of gambling, horse-racing and visiting theatres. Jane immediately designed a comic counterpart to this fantasy of social disruption. The servants in *High Life Below Stairs* feed on the most delicious French dainties, and drink the finest wines ('claret, burgundy and champagne, and a bottle of tokay for the ladies').[59] But in her own short play, *The Visit*, Jane imagined the exact opposite, a dinner-party of elegant aristocrats consuming the meanest labourer's food: cowheel, tripe and suet pudding, washed down with home-made elderberry and gooseberry wines. Something about the anarchy of such incongruous social reversals appealed to her sense of fictional adventure. Turning over the pages in the Steventon parish register, she dreamt of elevating the promiscuous illiterate peasant girl Mary Bennett into the prim and bookish daughter of a respectable county family. She imagined resurrecting the dead infant William Collins into a pompous clergyman devoted to an aristocratic Lady Catherine de Bourgh. (The name of Lady Augusta De Burgh made quite a splash in the gossip columns in the summer of 1787.)[60] At the age of thirteen, Jane Austen took great delight in such bold egalitarian gestures. 'How much are the poor to be pitied, & the rich to be blamed!' she scribbled in the margin of the family's copy of Goldsmith's *History of England*.[61]

In France that summer, the language of equality took on a rather more dramatic significance. As the people of Paris stormed the Bastille, the Comtesse Eliza de Feuillide soon found herself fleeing before the chants of the revolutionary crowds. In Hampshire, the same chants were used for more homely purposes when a Mr Malkin of Winchester put up a heroic defence of an Englishman's right to adorn his house with bow windows. After the county hangman had refused a bribe to demolish the offending windows, Malkin's victory was celebrated with fireworks and banners proclaiming 'Liberty and Property to the Inhabitants of Winchester'. The triumphant Malkin decorated his windows with the sword of justice, the cap of liberty and the inscription '*Maintain your Rights*'.[62]

Stories of mob violence in Paris soon filled the columns of English newspapers, but in *The Loiterer* James Austen attacked the fashion for sneering at all French 'mounseers' as 'half-starved, lousy devils' wearing wooden shoes and eating 'fricasseed frogs'. Such mean prejudices, *The Loiterer* loftily maintained, were 'inconsistent with the liberality of the human mind'.[63] As for violence, there was no shortage of examples much nearer home. At Chawton that January, John Gellet had been beaten to death by Henry Miller with a heavy iron-tipped cudgel. At Steventon, the Digweeds' carter, Thomas Gilbert, was kicked to death by his horse. And an unknown body, thought to be that of an escaped lunatic, was dragged 'in a state of putrefaction' from the river near Upper Mill in Long Parish.[64]

For Jane Austen, death was quite romantic. She loved to read affecting stories of doomed sweethearts who 'died suddenly, just as they were going to church'. She sent *The Loiterer* her own prescription for the most diverting kinds of fictional death. 'Let the lover be killed in a duel, or lost at sea, or you may make him shoot himself, just as you please; and as for his mistress, she will of course go mad; or if you will, you may kill the lady, and let the lover run mad; only remember, whatever you do, that your hero and heroine must possess a great deal of feeling, and have very pretty names.'[65] Following her own advice, she made sure to include in her next story, 'Frederic and Elfrida', the affecting suicide of the lovely Charlotte, who 'threw herself into a deep stream which ran thro' her aunt's pleasure grounds in Portland Place'. For her, the true consummation of love must be represented as either death or madness, or possibly a combination of the two. She dedicated 'Frederic and Elfrida' to Martha Lloyd, whose family had recently come to live at Deane parsonage, thanking Martha for her generosity 'in finishing my muslin cloak'. In the story too, Jane's heroine greeted a new neighbour with praise for her understanding of 'the different excellencies of Indian and English muslins'. But if she meant this as a compliment, she disguised it by Elfrida's savage comments on the 'horror' of her new friend's appearance (her 'forbidding squint', 'greasy tresses' and 'swelling back'). Poor Martha Lloyd, like her younger sister Mary, had recently suffered a severe bout of smallpox which left them both scarred for life. It can hardly be doubted that she was shocked by the Austen girl's cruel humour.

Jane Austen always loved to shock people, and took a wicked girlish delight in saying the unsayable. There is a restless, reckless undercurrent of frustration in all her early sketches; a violent fantasizing energy, which uses the disguise of fiction to subvert the careful rules and reticences of polite rectory life. She filled her stories with wild elopements and improbable misalliances: 'the eldest Miss Fitzroy ran off with the coachman'; the 'excellent' governess, Miss Dickins, 'eloped with the butler'; Eliza and Henry run off together, leaving only the curtest of notes: 'Madam, We are married and gone.' She made respectable people behave in the most disreputable way; the Johnson family, described (in another parody of *Grandison*) as 'a family of love', are 'carried home dead drunk'; the Drummonds and the Falknors like to 'kick one another out of the window'. Children steal from their parents, lovers murder their rivals, and neighbours rejoice in abusing one another to their faces.

Yet running through all this fictional anarchy, Jane loved to include direct and topical allusions to family and friends. Early in 1791, Edward Austen became engaged to Elizabeth Bridges, one of the thirteen children of Sir Brook Bridges of Goodnestone Park in Kent. Among the Bridges girls there was something of a competition to see which of them might first attract an eligible suitor; Jane parodied their matrimonial rivalries in her story 'The Three Sisters'. In this story, Mary Stanhope, courted by Mr Watts, savours a prospective triumph 'to be married before Sophy [or] Georgiana'. This despite the fact that she finds Mr Watts 'extremely disagreable' and '*so* plain that I cannot bear to look at him'. Mrs Stanhope does not mind which of her daughters Mr Watts marries. 'If Mary won't have him, Sophy must, and if Sophy won't, Georgiana *shall*.' Mr Watts is equally unfussy about his choice and assures his fiancée that 'it is equally the same to me which I marry of the three'. One sister regards him as 'extremely vulgar', another finds him 'hideous in his person', yet all seem to regard the prospect of marriage with equanimity. One thing they are agreed about: Mr Watts is *old*. Indeed, at 'two and thirty' he was a full eight years older than Edward Austen, to whom Jane 'respectfully inscribed' her mischievous tale. In the event, it was Fanny Bridges who was married first; but Elizabeth and Sophia would be worthy runners-up. They planned to share a double wedding after Christmas, to Edward Austen and William Deedes.

A recurring motif in these early sketches is the evocation of a strange kind of emotional inadvertency, in which people fail to remember, or recognize, their own closest relatives. In 'The Adventures of Mr Harley', the hero fails to recognize his own wife, or to remember that he has a wife at all. In 'Henry and Eliza', Lady Harcourt, having abandoned her baby in a haycock, 'soon forgot I had one'. The most curious of all these dream-like confusions is at the start of 'Frederic and Elfrida'. In the manuscript, the first line reads: 'The uncle of Elfrida was the mother of Frederic.' The subsequent clause only adds to the mystery: 'in other words, they were first cousins by the father's side.' Jane Austen has created a nonsensical family riddle in which the roles of uncle, mother and father were all strangely jumbled. Often, the parentage of her heroines is mysterious or doubtful. In *Love and Freindship*, Laura's mother is 'the natural daughter of a Scotch peer by an Italian opera-girl'; the beautiful Cassandra's father is 'of noble birth, being the near relation of the Duchess of —'s butler'. She loved to imagine wild, irreverent heroines pursuing their impulsive pleasures free from all parental restraints. The foundling, Eliza, of 'Henry and Eliza', begins her career by stealing a £50 bank-note; she elopes with her lover, endures exile in France, lives beyond her means, suffers imprisonment, and is partly eaten alive by her young sons. Yet she emerges triumphant from all her trials, acknowledged by her rightful parents, demolishes the prison of her enemies, and gains 'the blessings of thousands and the applause of her own heart'.

CHAPTER 4

Partial, Prejudiced
& Ignorant

*The History of England from the reign of Henry
4th to the death of Charles the 1st. By a partial,
prejudiced & ignorant Historian*

'I have often felt myself extremely satirical'

Margate beach was cold and grey under a louring January sky. A
few seagulls circled and squawked, swooping down to a rocky
outcrop where they ruffled their feathers against the chill east wind.
Watched by his mother, a lonely naked boy stepped down from
a bathing machine and dipped his toe into the icy waters. He
shivered. 'Go on,' she called to him, pulling her scarf of Pullicat
silk tight around her neck. 'Quickly.' Reluctantly, the boy lowered
himself into the sea, first to his knees, then to his waist. He felt
once again the painful sensation of breathlessness as his chest
tightened with the cold. He called out to her in a strange mixture
of French and English. But she shook her head. 'Further,' she
said. 'Swim. *C'est pour la santé.*' The Countess had been assured
by her personal physician that one month's bathing at this time
of the year was worth six at any other. Why else would she be

subjecting herself to such a dismal solitude? Margate was dull even in midsummer. Now, in the depth of winter, its few diversions – the assembly rooms, balls and occasional plays – were long since closed down, and the only tolerable companions had almost all departed. But sacrifices had to be made, and little Hastings did seem to derive great benefit from his daily sea-bathing. Resignedly, Eliza and Philadelphia put off all thoughts of further jaunting. 'Like a most *exemplary parent*,' she wrote to Phylly Walter, she had resolved on forgoing the fascinating delights of London for one month longer. 'Was not this heroic?'[1]

Hardly as heroic as her son, his body blue with cold, returning to the bathing-machine, where Clarinda wrapped him in a warm towel. Together the little party made their way back to the house. For the rest of the day Eliza contrived to fill her tedious hours, like a lonely schoolgirl, with reading, music, drawing and different kinds of study. In the evenings there was still a small circle left of people whom she referred to as her *agreeables*. But already she was counting the days till her return to Orchard Street, which she had fixed on for the 28th of February.

At her first return from France, the previous summer, Eliza had thrown herself on the hospitality of her Steventon relations. The Austens were welcoming, as always, especially Jane, who delighted her with the gift of a curious short novel entitled *Love and Freindship*, written in parody of the vogue for sentimental fictions. The title, as Eliza affectionately noted, was an echo of words she herself had inscribed on the back of the miniature portrait she had once sent to Phylly Walter with a lock of hair: *Amoris et Amicitiae*. But Henry insisted on claiming the credit for the title to himself, pointing to his *Loiterer* essay which declared: 'Let every girl who seeks for happiness conquer both her feelings and her passions. Let her avoid love and friendship.'[2] These were sentiments which, as it seemed to Eliza, Henry might do well to remember himself. She could not fail to notice a certain coldness in his behaviour towards her, as if resentful of some supposed slight. But she had more problems on her mind than the sulkiness of an infatuated nineteen-year-old. The shocking affairs in France had quite dashed any hopes she had of de Feuillide's joining her in England. A strong *Aristocrate*, as the royalist party now styled themselves, he had hastened to Turin, where the French princes of the blood were assembled, watching for some favourable opportunity to reinstate themselves in power. To Eliza, in her mood of pessimism, their cause seemed almost hopeless. 'I am no politician,' she told Phylly Walter, 'but think they will not easily accomplish their purpose.' With her destiny in the balance, she took a certain masochistic pleasure in subjecting herself to the same Spartan regimen as her son. 'I still continue bathing,' she boasted, 'notwithstanding the severity of the weather & frost & snow, which is I think somewhat courageous.'[3]

The Countess found a more agreeable diversion in reading her cousin's little *jeu d'esprit* of a novel. By common consent, the two Austen girls were on the way to becoming two of the prettiest girls in England, though there was always something teasing about the way Jane drew attention to her new-found passions for dancing and curling her hair. It was as if she were playing the part of the frivolous young flirt, as a defence against becoming one. Her writing was full of such coy play-acting. She loved to poke fun at friends and relations, and thought nothing of sending a favourite jest halfway round the globe to her midshipman brother on HMS *Perseverance*. Eliza could not even be sure that *Love and Freindship* did not poke fun at her. The story was full of high-flown characters of the most exalted minds and most delicate sensibilities, who made a conspicuous virtue of defying the cruel and mercenary shackles of parental authority. She wondered if her young cousin had ever caught sight of the letter in which she had confessed that her own marriage to de Feuillide was 'much less from my own judgement than that of those whose councils and opinions I am most bound to follow'. As to the exalted feelings, she was, she acknowledged, given to expressing her *mortification* at dull companions, and had drawn laughter from Phylly Walter when she complained of her *nerves*. But if her young cousin designed a satire of her in this book, it only increased Eliza's fondness for the girl. There were few things she liked better than a bold wit; Swift and Sterne were her favourite authors, and any girl who could combine the satire of the one with the sentiment of the other was sure of her applause. She particularly relished the comical death scenes: the exalted Edward and Augustus tumbling to their deaths from their fashionably high phaeton, while the tender Sophia fell in refined fainting fits, and the melancholy Laura ran modishly mad. Visions of one's dead husband as a mutton-leg or a cucumber were a gloriously comic moment, and Sterne had nothing to outdo Sophia's affecting death-bed speech to her friend. 'One fatal swoon has cost me my life . . . Beware of swoons, dear Laura . . . A frenzy fit is not one quarter so pernicious; it is an exercise to the body and if not too violent is, I dare say, conducive to health in its consequences. Run mad as often as you choose, but do not faint.' It occurred to her that she might perhaps try running mad during her next icy plunge off Margate beach.

Eliza, Philadelphia and Hastings returned to Orchard Street in March as planned, but change of location brought little relief from anxiety. Philadelphia continued to suffer severe pains in her chest; the news from France grew worse and worse; money was a constant problem and the trial of Warren Hastings, now entering its fourth year, seemed no nearer a resolution. 'Never will the year 1791 be effaced from my memory,' Eliza wrote to Phylly Walter in June; 'for from the first month of its commencement to the present period, my feelings have constantly been exposed to some fresh trial.'[4] In such low spirits, Eliza found little occasion and less desire for mixing with the gay world of London society. 'I find infinitely more satisfaction,' she wrote, in her most sober, matronly manner, 'in endeavouring to amuse my mother, & if possible render her present situation less irksome.' All this while, the family at Steventon were perfectly unacquainted with her troubles, until at last she could bear it no longer, and wrote them a letter in anything but exalted feelings. The response was immediate. Within days, Edward Austen called at Orchard Street and was all solicitude for their situation. This young man, so much the grandest of the Austen brothers, was so very considerate in his enquiries after their health that Eliza quite found her spirits rally, and she even began to tease him about his fiancée, Miss Elizabeth Bridges. Was it not true, as she had heard, that he was about to embark on a visit to the lakes with Mr and Mrs Knight, but that his beloved was not to be one of their party? 'Alas,' he replied, it was true that they were not to be blessed with her presence on this occasion. 'But how would he be able to exist without her?' The gentleman's only reply was a calm smile of such benign resignation that Eliza was left to wonder whether his sister Jane were not telling the truth when she hinted that it might be a matter of indifference to her brother which of the Bridges girls he married.

The Austen girls were also at the seaside that summer. When twelve-year-old Charles Austen chose to follow his brother Frank as a pupil at the Naval Academy, Mr Austen brought the family to Portsmouth for a holiday by the coast. The presence of so many eligible young naval officers in the vicinity must furnish many glorious opportunities for flirtation, Eliza thought. She was full of envy, imagining the extravagant expressions of devotion which two such pretty girls must inevitably inspire among those 'very gallant gentlemen'. 'They are perfect beauties,' she wrote to Phylly Walter, '& of course gain hearts by dozens.' How Eliza longed to be eighteen again, and attracting the admiring glances of every handsome young man in uniform. The merest hint that reached her of the girls' amatory adventures was sufficient to provoke delicious memories of her own youthful conquests. Without a doubt, she fancied, Cassandra had already broken the heart of at least one 'Son of Neptune' in the course of her aquatic excursions.[5]

The Countess experienced less agreeable emotions when she received the news of old Frank Austen's death. The old man's estate was reckoned to be worth a cool £6,000 *per annum*, but there was nothing in his will for Philadelphia. 'Extremely unkind' was the politest term that Eliza could find to describe such mean injustice. Poor Philadelphia herself, now a frequent martyr to violent chest pains, was more philosophical about her uncle's neglect. After all, he had left nothing to his niece Elizabeth Fermor either, and she had kept house for him for several years. Justice had nothing to do with it. The old man had simply excluded females from his list of beneficiaries. The bulk of his estate passed to his elder son, 'who was immensely rich before', as Eliza sourly noted.[6] His younger son, John Austen, received £12,000 and there was £500 for each of his nephews. To George Austen such a sum was quite a fortune. He not only took his family to the seaside but even indulged himself to the extent of risking £26 4s on government lottery tickets. The gamble was not a success; he won a quarter-prize, worth just £5, but lost the rest of his stake. He would have done better, as he ruefully acknowledged, to have remembered the advice he had given his son Frank: 'Keep an exact account of all [your] money . . . and on no account whatever be persuaded to risk it by gaming.'

Returning from her seaside excursions, Jane Austen set about her most ambitious literary parody to date. Now that all her brothers were embarked on their chosen careers, she found herself increasingly vexed at the notion that all the most serious worldly activities belonged, like legacies, exclusively to men. Away in the East Indies, Frank was transferring from HMS *Perseverance* to HMS *Minerva*; James was regularly hunting with the Prince of Wales at Kempshott Park; Edward was setting himself up as a great landowner in Kent; Henry was at Oxford, and even little Charles was placing his first foot on the ladder of naval command. Her brothers lived in the public world of history, politics and global affairs, but Jane was confined to the domestic world of female preoccupations, a world quite invisible to the eye of history, where a confidence in pronouncing the superiority of an Indian muslin over an English one must be reckoned a very great accomplishment. It dismayed her how these busy men would all affect to despise mere *novels* as ephemeral female diversions; *their* only reading must be in more weighty subjects: history, political economy and the more sententious kind of moral essays.[7] Her brother James rigorously excluded any hint of mere *romance* from the pages of *The Loiterer*, but devoted one whole issue to the manly virtues of history. No wise statesman, he wrote, should ever ignore the sober lessons of history, which all pointed to the necessity of tolerance:

The Great have learned that all unnecessary exertions of power are productive of discontent, murmurs and insurrections; and their inferiors will readily allow that confusions, disorder and anarchy are as certainly attendant on groundless disaffection and rebellion without cause – Thus each party, by

mutually receding from the rigid inflexibility of their favourite
opinion, and partially relinquishing their separate rights, prevent the collision of jarring principles, and secure the general
happiness of the whole on a firm foundation.[8]

Such lofty enunciations of pious Whiggish principles were rather
too much for James's whimsical Tory sister to bear. In *The History
of England*, which she set about writing that autumn, Jane defiantly
championed her own favourite opinions in all their most rigid
inflexibility. Happily proclaiming herself a 'partial, prejudiced &
ignorant Historian', she mocked all suggestion of tolerance or
compromise. For her, history was a grand comic romance; not a
solemn lesson in political statecraft, but a glorious costume-farce,
filled with heroes and villains, treachery and murder. 'But history,
real solemn history, I cannot be interested in,' Catherine Morland
complained in *Northanger Abbey*. 'I read it a little as a duty, but it
tells me nothing that does not either vex or weary me. The quarrels
of popes and kings, with wars or pestilences, in every page; the
men all so good for nothing, and hardly any women at all – it is
very tiresome.'[9] These were Jane's thoughts too. Forced to toil
through the four volumes of Goldsmith's *History of England*, she
peppered the margins with pert asides. She would mock Goldsmith's solemn conclusions ('My dear Dr G – I have lived long
enough in the world to know that it is always so'). She would flatly
deny any facts she disliked ('Anne should not have done so –
indeed I do not believe she did'). Above all, she would boldly reject
Goldsmith's Whiggish principles in favour of her own romantic
attachment to the ill-fated house of Stuart ('A family who were
always ill-used Betrayed or Neglected – whose virtues are seldom
allowed while their errors are never forgotten').[10]

Catherine Morland thought it odd that history should be so dull,
'for a great deal of it must be invention . . . and invention is what
delights me in other books . . .' Jane Austen's *History* is full of
comic invention ('like my dear Dr Johnson,' she once wrote to
Cassandra, 'I believe I have dealt more in Notions than Facts').[11]
She always preferred fictional sources to factual ones, and
borrowed favourite 'historical' stories from Shakespeare's plays,

Sheridan's *The Critic* and the romances of Charlotte Smith and Sophia Lee. Monarchs and warriors appear like quarrelsome neighbours; Joan of Arc 'made such a *row* among the English', Henry Tudor 'made a great fuss about getting the crown', Henry VIII's dissolution of the monasteries was 'of infinite use to the landscape'. Real neighbours and friends are dragged in as impromptu witnesses; 'Mr Whitaker, Mrs Lefroy, Mrs Knight & myself' are produced as particular friends to Mary Queen of Scots, and Jane's brother Frank proclaimed as a future Sir Francis Drake. Jane was particularly comical on the subject of heroic deaths. 'Lord Cobham was burnt alive,' she wrote, 'but I forget what for'; Richard II 'happened to be murdered'; Lord Protector Somerset was beheaded, though 'it does not appear that he felt particularly delighted with the manner of it'. Real solemn history books must include plenty of dates, but not Jane's: 'NB. There will be very few Dates in this History,' she declared on her title-page. The dates that she did include were splendidly arbitrary. Writing of Henry VIII, she explained: 'Tho' I do not profess giving many dates, yet . . . I think it proper to give some & shall of course make choice of those which it is most necessary for the Reader to know.' Thus she thought it right to inform the reader that Anne Boleyn's solemn letter to King Henry 'was dated on the 6th of May'.

While Jane parodied the text of Goldsmith's *History*, Cassandra made fun of its illustrations, decorating her sister's manuscript with miniature medallion-shaped caricatures. Edward IV 'was famous only for his beauty & his courage,' Jane wrote; so naturally Cassandra took delight in portraying him with an ugly porcine face, wide snout, flabby cheeks and double chin. For the portrait of Henry V, who won 'the famous battle of Agincourt', Cassandra chose to depict the heroic monarch in modern naval uniform, just like their brother Frank.[12]

Catherine Morland objected that there were 'hardly any women' in history, but Jane's *History* is full of women. There is Joan of Arc ('They should not have burnt her – but they did'). There is Lady Jane Grey ('an amiable young woman & famous for reading Greek while other people were hunting'). And there is Jane Shore, who 'has had a play written about her, but it is a tragedy & therefore not worth reading'. Though professing disdain for tragedy, Jane took great delight in fairy tales, and the three women who dominate her *History*, Mary, Elizabeth and Mary Queen of Scots, are presented like Cinderella and her ugly sisters. Mary is the first ugly sister, blamed for assuming the throne 'in spite of the superior pretensions, merit & beauty' of her cousin, the Queen of Scots. Elizabeth is even uglier: that 'disgrace to humanity', that 'pest of society', that 'deceitful betrayer' and 'wicked murderess'. This is a *History* which delights in perverse and outrageous judgements (there are kind words for Richard III, whom Jane is 'rather inclined to suppose . . . a very respectable man'). But the depiction of Elizabeth is the most outrageous of all. At a time when the country once again faced the threat of foreign invasion, it was customary to portray Elizabeth as a chaste Protestant heroine, the valiant champion of English liberty against Catholic tyranny. But Jane transforms Elizabeth into a cruel-hearted monster of Machiavellian duplicity, while Mary Queen of Scots appears as an innocent victim and romantic martyr. As a 'partial, prejudiced' historian, she boasts her intention 'to vent my spleen *against*, & shew my hatred *to* all those people whose parties or principles do not suit with mine, & not to give information'. In her romantic attachment to the glamour of lost causes, she refuses to contaminate her prejudices with any taint of proof. Airily disdaining to specify the crimes of which the Queen of Scots was accused, she 'most seriously' assures her reader 'that she was entirely innocent'. Similarly, she asserts, there is 'one argument' which must certainly convince 'every sensible & well disposed person' that Charles I was never guilty of 'arbitrary & tyrannical government' – '& this argument is that he was a *Stuart.*'

Splendidly arbitrary and opinionated, Jane Austen's *History of England* was written, like the rest of her sketches, with a desire to mock and shock. She even ventured to hint at King James I's perverse amorous inclinations by including a charade on the word 'carpet'. 'My first is what my second was to King James the 1st, and you tread on my whole.' Robert *Carr* was indeed James's *pet*, and Jane was bold enough to emphasize the point with another *double-entendre*. 'His majesty,' she wrote, 'was of that amiable disposition which inclines to freindship, & in such points was possessed of a keener *penetration* in discovering merit than many other people.'[13] She loved it when relations were scandalized by her wicked innuendoes. Years later, her niece Caroline thought it 'remarkable' that the early workings of Jane's mind 'should have been in burlesque, and comic exaggeration, setting at nought all rules of probable or possible'. All of aunt Jane's 'finished and later writings' were so very much the contrary, she said, so polished and correct.[14] But Jane's rebellious instinct for comic subversion remained unextinguished beneath the surface of even her most polished works. Just a few months before she died, she told Fanny Knight: 'Pictures of perfection, as you know, make me sick & wicked.'[15] It made little difference whether that picture of perfection was the virtuous Sir Charles Grandison or the Virgin Queen Elizabeth, her irresistible instinct was to mock it. For her brother James, history offered a didactic model of human progress, and a lesson in enlightened patriotism. This is how he liked to picture the studies of the young (and of course *male*) historian.

He will view [science] with pleasure, rising after a long night of Gothic darkness, and dispersing by degrees the clouds of ignorance, and the mists of superstition; and he will boast, with a pardonable partiality, that if she has chosen Europe for her temple, she has also selected England for her shrine.[16]

Jane preferred to present herself as a young historian whose partiality was deliberately *un*pardonable, and who gloried in a Gothic ignorance she had no wish to disperse. In refusing to submit her own lofty prejudices to the parliament of proof, she imagined herself as another of the arbitrary monarchs whose wilful powers she loved to praise. Her *History* was a form of secret biography, and her proud knock-down argument ('he was a *Stuart*') has the same peremptory finality as her own boast: 'the recital of any events (except what I make myself) is uninteresting to me.' Her principal reason for writing the *History*, she concluded, was 'to prove the innocence of the Queen of Scotland, which I flatter myself with having effectively done, and to abuse Elizabeth'. It appealed to her vanity, at the age of fifteen, to vilify the sensible, dutiful Virgin Queen, and praise her impulsive, wayward, murderous and promiscuous cousin.

Jane finished the *History* on 26 November and dedicated it to Cassandra. Almost immediately, as if playing a part, she made a point of assuming her most obedient and dutiful manner. James had at last decided to marry. His bride was Anne Mathew of Laverstoke, six years older than him (and, as Jane noted, with 'a good deal of nose'). Anne's mother was the daughter of the Duke of Ancaster, and her father, General Mathew, had been for ten years Governor of Grenada. Altogether it seemed a highly satisfactory match – to the Austens at least – though to begin with, there was no great superfluity of money. The Mathews made Anne an allowance of £100 a year and Mr Austen made James his curate at Deane. It was, of course, a sadness that the Lloyds should be thus required to vacate Deane parsonage to make way for James and his new bride, and the Austens were at pains to mitigate the distress of this enforced removal. As the family prepared to leave for Ibthorpe, some eighteen miles away, Jane embroidered a little cotton bag as a farewell present for Mary Lloyd, and placed inside a little needlework 'housewife', together with some dainty verses:

> *This little bag I hope will prove*
> *To be not vainly made –*
> *For if you thread and needle want*
> *It will afford you aid.*
> *And as we are about to part*
> *'Twill serve another end,*
> *For when you look upon the bag*
> *You'll recollect your friend – Jany 1792.*

Nothing could be more modest or demure than this gift of a pretty bag and girlish verses. It is as if, in offering this embroidered bag as a memento of herself, Jane was endeavouring to disguise the wayward would-be monarch of her private imagination in the appearance of a little domestic 'housewife'. Jane also dedicated her latest little 'novel', 'Evelyn', to Mary Lloyd. 'Evelyn' is a curious dream-like tale, an *Arabian Nights* fantasy transposed to the Sussex countryside. Amid a landscape of gloomy Gothic castles and sunny Arcadian vales, a traveller enters the charming house of a family of total strangers and is overwhelmed by their benevolent hospitality. He has only to make a wish and it is instantly granted. When he asks them to give him their house, they immediately agree. When he demands their daughter's hand in marriage, they agree again, only apologizing that 'her fortune is but ten thousand pounds'. Lovers marry within hours of first meeting, perish equally suddenly and then reappear, as it seems, from the dead. A wife dies of a broken heart after being separated from her husband for just three hours. It might perhaps have appeared less than tactful to give Mary a story about a miraculously donated house just at a time when her family were being politely ejected from Deane parsonage. But the symbolism of this dream-like fable suggests a subconscious attempt at restitution or atonement. In May, Jane Austen acquired a new manuscript book, and her father wrote inside the front cover: 'Effusions of Fancy by a very Young Lady consisting of Tales in a Style entirely new.'[17] 'Evelyn' was the first of the 'effusions' which she transcribed into the book.

Phylly Walter took a rather different view of the impulsiveness of wayward women from her cousin Jane at Steventon. As Phylly read Eliza's melancholy letters, describing her lonely vigil by her mother's sick-bed, she experienced the smug self-satisfaction of the righteous. 'Poor Eliza must be left at last friendless and alone,' she wrote to her brother James:

> The gay and dissipated life she has so long had so plentiful a share of has not ensur'd her friends among the worthy: on the contrary, many who otherwise have regarded her have blamed her conduct and will now resign her acquaintance. I always felt concerned and pitied her thoughtlessness. I have frequently looked forwards to the approaching awful period, and regretted the manner of her life, & the mistaken results of my poor aunt's intended, well-meant kindness: she will

soon feel the loss & her want of domestic knowledge. I have wrote to assure her she may command my services.[18]

The Countess knew only too well how frequently Phylly had 'looked forwards' to this moment of sanctimonious triumph, and it was a temporary comfort when de Feuillide was finally able to join her in England just before her mother's death on 26 February. Philadelphia had suffered violently during those final months, and Eliza's heart was ready to burst with grief and vexation. Following the funeral in Hampstead, de Feuillide took his wife to Bath for a fortnight's recuperation. Even little Hastings now cut a more manly appearance in his jacket and trousers, having laid aside his babyish feminine garb. 'I think it will make him hold himself more upright & walk better,' Eliza noted, 'now he has got rid of that terrible incumbrance called petticoats.' But the relief was sadly brief. Within weeks of their return to London, de Feuillide received an urgent message from France which peremptorily informed him 'that already having exceeded his leave of absence, if he still continued in England he would be considered as one of the emigrants, & consequently his whole property forfeited to the nation'.[19] Such a summons was not to be ignored, and de Feuillide promptly prepared for his departure to Paris. Before he left, he gave Eliza his solemn promise that he would do everything in his power to return to her within the year. Whether she believed him or not is uncertain. After so many torments, her health at last gave way and throughout June she suffered a severe bout of the chicken-pox. But Phylly Walter was wrong to assume the Countess would now find herself 'friendless and alone'. The Woodmans offered her a refuge at their charming country place near Epsom, where she made a slow recovery. By August, she was well enough to travel to Hampshire for a long-anticipated visit to the Austens. It pleased her to be able to thank Phylly Walter for her proffered 'services' but assure her that she stood in no immediate need of them. 'I mean to make [Steventon] my resting-place for the remainder of the year.'

Steventon in August was a truly delightful place, with the elm trees in full leaf, the Wood Walk dappled all shades of green, and in the evening the sweet smell of honeysuckle twining around the doors. The tranquillity of the place filled Eliza's heart with many tender emotions. Mr Austen looked uncommonly well, and his likeness to her beloved mother struck her more strongly than ever. Often she would sit, tracing her features in his, till her heart overflowed at her eyes. She had always loved her uncle, but now he was dearer to her than ever. Simply to be in his presence brought an inexpressible comfort.[20] He was the nearest and most beloved relative of the parent she had lost. Together, in those first warm summer evenings, they would share their reminiscences, and George Austen allowed his mind to travel back to those early days of hardship, when Philadelphia had made her bold resolve to sail halfway round the globe to marry a man she had never met. Jane listened, and found inspiration in this story of another reckless and determined woman. In her new 'novel', *Catharine,* she set herself to understand her aunt's thoughts and feelings.

> The eldest daughter had been obliged to accept the offer of one of her cousins to equip her for the East Indies, and tho' infinitely against her inclinations had been necessitated to embrace the only possibility that was offered to her of a maintenance. Yet it was *one,* so opposite to all her ideas of propriety, so contrary to her wishes, so repugnant to her feelings, that she would almost have preferred servitude to it, had choice been allowed her – Her personal attractions had gained her a husband as soon as she had arrived at Bengal, and she had now been married nearly a twelve month. Splendidly, yet unhappily married. United to a man of double her own age, whose disposition was not amiable, and whose manners were unpleasing, though his character was respectable.

Of course, Hastings was the general favourite at the rectory; chattering away in French and English, he was the plaything of the whole family. 'On every formal visit,' as Jane drily observed, 'a child ought to be of the party, by way of provision for discourse.'[21] Eliza was relieved to find that the coolness between Henry and herself was now happily a thing of the past. For his part, Henry was gracious enough to make due acknowledgement of his former silliness, which she, for her part, was pleased to accept. They were now on very proper cousin-like terms, and she did not even embarrass him by smiling when she learnt that the family now designed him for the church.

But the chief pleasure of the visit was the company of Jane and Cassandra, both very lively and accomplished young ladies, though Eliza could not disguise a preference for Jane, which was only natural, considering the kind partiality which Jane demonstrated towards her. Now that all the Austen boys, bar Henry, were away from home, one of the bedchambers over the dining-room had been fitted up into a sort of drawing-room for the girls' own private use. The walls were cheaply papered and the chocolate-coloured carpet covering the floor had a rather common look; but the room was brightened with the signs of the girls' exuberant native wit. Cassandra's drawings were affixed to the wall; Jane's pianoforte occupied the middle of the room, and a painted press with shelves above for books stood opposite the fireplace.[22] Here were kept Casssandra's pencil sketches and Jane's literary skits, filled with all her clever fun and nonsense.

When Eliza first arrived, Cassandra was away visiting Edward at Rowling, his country mansion in Kent, and for some weeks she and Jane shared a delicious intimacy in that little drawing-room retreat. Jane listened eagerly as Eliza relived the terrifying London riots that summer, in Mount Street, not half a mile from her own home. She vividly recalled how she had suddenly found herself surrounded by an immense angry mob, armed with bricks and staves, fighting against a party of guards on horseback. She described in detail the noise of the crowd, the drawn swords and pointed bayonets of the soldiers, the fragments of bricks and mortar thrown on every side, one of which had nearly killed her own coachman, the sounds of rifle-fire echoing all along the street.[23] Nothing like that ever happened in Hampshire, her young cousin observed with something like regret. The most dangerous incident in their neighbourhood, she declared, had been when a mad dog got into the Prince of Wales's kennels at Kempshott and bit eighteen couple of his highness's hounds.[24]

The girl had a wicked sense of humour that Eliza loved. Her latest novel, called 'Lesley Castle' and set in some gloriously gloomy Scottish ruin, was full of mocking echoes of people they both knew. She had caught Phylly Walter exactly in the prim tones of Margaret Lesley, forever harping on about other people's 'gay and dissipated way of life'. Reading the passage where Margaret denounced her mother, who 'had so openly violated the conjugal duties', Eliza laughed out loud at Jane's wonderful talent for mimicry. She herself often loved to tease their spinster cousin about her elevated opinion of 'conjugal duties'. Together they took turns in reading parts, practising their voices and expressions in the looking-glass that hung between the windows. 'How often have I wished that I possessed as little personal beauty as you do; that my figure were as inelegant; my face as unlovely; and my appearance as unpleasing as yours!' declared Eliza, in the role of the ineffable Margaret. 'I hate scandal and detest children,' proclaimed Jane, in the role of selfish Susan, before breaking off for some new piece of gossip about the 'fat girls with short noses' whom she met at a Hurstbourne Park ball, or to play at skittles with little Hastings.

Eliza was constantly intrigued by her young cousin's gift for disguising her own voice among the characters she created. In *Love and Freindship*, Jane had briefly sketched a flattering self-portrait in the character of the fifteen-year-old Janetta: 'naturally well disposed, endowed with a susceptible heart, and a sympathetic disposition', who 'might have been an ornament to human nature . . . had these amiable qualities been properly encouraged'. But then, of course, she exploded the whole thing by turning Janetta's father into a comical ogre of insensitivity, who had never even read *The Sorrows of Young Werther*. Naturally, the tender-hearted young creature had no other option but to fall violently in love with the first handsome captain she met, and elope with him to Gretna Green. Jane hardly struck Eliza as the eloping kind, though she was full of a secret mischievous spirit of adventure. Her voice was clearly detectable in some words she gave to Charlotte in 'Lesley Castle': 'I have often felt myself extremely satirical, but [this] was the only time I ever made my feelings public.' If Jane ever caught the habit of making her feelings public, she might become a very satirical young lady indeed. As it was, she had an irrepressible instinct for transforming every tiny incident into a little comic sketch. When Cassandra returned from Rowling, Eliza could not help observing how very much both sisters had grown, and that even Jane was now taller than herself.[25] In the novel, this was turned into Susan's protest at the Lesley sisters as 'two great, tall, out of the way, overgrown . . . Scotch giants'.

Apparently Henry, too, now fancied himself as something of a novelist, though of an altogether more rational kind than his sister. One of his *Loiterer* essays ridiculed the 'degenerate and sickly refinement' of sentimental novels and their lady readers, who 'tortured by the poignant delicacy of their own feelings . . . fall martyrs to their own susceptibility'. Inevitably, Jane had responded by describing her own Janetta as 'endowed with a susceptible heart'. Eliza loved the to-and-fro of this in-house authorial rivalry and applauded Jane's decision to dedicate her latest fiction to Henry with a little mocking flourish: 'Sir, I am now availing myself of the liberty you have frequently honoured me with of dedicating one of my novels to you.' Henry was gallant enough to reply in kind, repaying this compliment to his fantasy fiction with a handsome cheque drawn on a fantasy bank: 'Messrs Demand & Co – please to pay Jane Austen spinster the sum of one hundred guineas on account of your humble servant.' At the time, Eliza was charmed by Henry's playful riposte, though in later years she reflected that a whimsical fondness for issuing fantasy cheques was perhaps an unhappy omen for a future banker.

At the end of August, there came news of the death of old Dr Cooper at Sonning vicarage. The family had recently returned from the Isle of Wight, where Jane Cooper had fallen as violently and precipitately in love as any of her cousin's most susceptible young heroines. The family had first met Captain Thomas Williams, RN, Commander of HMS *Lizard*, at a dinner-party on 2 July.[26] By the end of the month, everything was settled; Jane and the captain were engaged to be married and even their wedding day fixed. Only the melancholy death of Jane's father interrupted their impetuous rush into wedlock. After his burial, at Whaddon,

Jane came immediately to Steventon to spend a respectable period in mourning with her Austen cousins before a new wedding day could be arranged. Eliza, who recalled Jane Cooper only dimly as 'one of the theatrical troop', was hardly impressed by the young lady's latest performance, as the pale bereaved maiden, trembling at the brink of matrimony. 'I never was but at one wedding in my life,' she wrote drily to Phylly Walter; '& that appeared a very stupid business to me.'[27] She referred, of course, to her own wedding; so much for 'conjugal duties'.

Mrs Austen was more sympathetic. She too had been married within months of her father's death and now hastened to make all the necessary arrangements. Jane Cooper would be married from Steventon, and a date in December was fixed upon for the ceremony. Jane and Cassandra would serve as witnesses and they would make quite a little party of it. 'I suppose we are to be mighty gay,' noted Eliza with some weariness. She herself was feeling anything but gay. The three young cousins now seemed in a constant flutter of excitement about wedding-clothes and parties, dances and balls; and even Jane seemed at times 'seized with that desperation of sixteen and a half, of ever seeing a man who could satisfy her ideas of perfection'.[28] There was a club ball at Basingstoke and a private ball at Enham House, both of which Jane and Cassandra declared to be 'very agreable'. But Eliza decided she was too ill to attend such things, and took to her bed with a feverish attack. Her only pleasure was in hearing Jane's malicious descriptions of the 'vulgar, broad-featured' Miss Coxes whom she met at the Enham House ball.[29]

In October, Jane and Cassandra went to visit the Lloyds at Ibthorpe and, deprived of other female company – save that of the susceptible Miss Cooper – Eliza wrote once again to Phylly Walter. Phylly, she knew, would be pleased to hear that the new Mrs James and Mrs Edward Austen were faithfully fulfilling their conjugal duties and were both 'in the increasing way'. She herself, though, was decidedly on the wane. 'There is to be another ball the 4th of Novr,' she wrote, 'which I shall go to if I am able, but I do not think I shall dance; see how staid & sober I grow!' The news from France remained dismal. 'My private letters confirm the intelligence afforded by the public prints & assure me that nothing we there read is exaggerated.'[30] De Feuillide was still making efforts to return to England, 'but finds it impossible to get away'. With her (god)father on trial for treason in England and her husband under suspicion as an aristocrat in France, Eliza felt herself increasingly threatened. She concluded her letter with an ominous note: 'Pray do not neglect burning this.'

In her cousins' absence, Eliza spent some evenings reading through the most recent of Jane's comic fictions. *Catharine* was not only longer than anything she had attempted before, it was also far more accomplished. There was, it was true, the same ostentatious fondness for literary chatter, the same lively parody of girlish gossip, the same irresistible urge to pillory Queen Elizabeth. But there was also something deeper; her cousin seemed less impatient to produce facetious effects, less tempted to dismiss her creations with a sharp epigram or sudden death. There was a maturity of observation and a measured quality of sympathy quite remarkable in a girl who was still not yet seventeen. Perhaps the most tender passages were those which seemed to allude to their own parents' early hardships. Jane wrote with feeling of the 'dispersion' of a family 'left in great distress' by the death of their father and 'reduced to a state of absolute dependance on some relations, who though very opulent and very nearly connected with them, had with difficulty been prevailed on to contribute anything to their support'. Eliza found herself moved to tears by the sympathetic portrayal of her own mother's painful circumstances. 'They are the luckiest creatures in the world!' declares the vain Miss Stanley on the subject of poor orphans fortunate enough to be patronized by their wealthy relations. 'Do you call it lucky, for a girl of genius and feeling to be sent in quest of a husband to Bengal?' Catharine demands in reply. 'To be married there to a man of whose disposition she has no opportunity of judging till her judgement is of no use to her, who may be a tyrant or a fool or both for what she knows to the contrary. Do you call *that* fortunate?' Miss Stanley's retort, that she thought such a voyage must be 'very good fun' for a poor girl, was exactly the kind of casual indignity that Philadel-

phia had been long used to endure. Less frequently heard was
Catharine's eloquent rebuke: 'To a girl of any delicacy, the voyage
in itself, since the object of it is so universally known, is a punishment that needs no other to make it very severe.' There was something in Miss Stanley's chatter to make Eliza wince; all that
empty-headed rattle about Regency walking-dresses and gold net
caps was uncomfortably close to her own adolescent gush. But
what most fascinated her was Jane's talent for presenting her heroine's private satirical thoughts. '"She *must* write well," thought
Kitty, "to make a long letter upon a bonnet and pelisse."' How
often, Eliza wondered, was her young cousin revolving such sharp
asides in her head while she eavesdropped on the general conversation? She loved the Cinderella moment when poor lonely Kitty,
unable to go to the ball with her fashionable friends, was suddenly
and unexpectedly burst in upon by her unknown Prince Charming.
And what poise she achieved in the presentation of that first
encounter between Kitty and Mr Percival. Really, there was such
subtlety in the feelings and such a confident sparkle to the repartee
that she could think of nothing to better it in Miss Burney or Miss
Smith. Her cousin's description of a country-house ball had all
the sophistication of an habituée, rather than of a girl who had
only come out that season. And her portrayal of the charming Mr
Stanley was so well drawn and imbued with such lively feelings
that Eliza could never believe it was not taken from life. But how
typical of Jane that the passionate conversation which provoked
the young man to kiss the heroine should concern the character
of King Richard III! If her young cousin really believed that history
was the way to a man's heart, she still had a lot to learn.

One thing puzzled Eliza about this story. In all her comic tales,
her cousin constantly presented parents and guardians as insensitive tyrants, forever determined upon extinguishing the tender
sensibilities of their offspring and thwarting their most cherished
inclinations. In the short burlesque sketches, this worked well
enough as a comic motif (like the incessant gibes at *Sir Charles
Grandison* which Jane seemed to find so endlessly amusing). But
in this more rational comedy, it seemed to strike a disturbing note.
The jealous caution of Kitty's aunt Percival seemed the more

repressive because it proceeded from a genuine, if misplaced, solicitude on behalf of her niece. 'Her aunt was most excessively fond of her, and miserable if she saw her for a moment out of spirits; Yet she lived in such constant apprehension of her [niece] marrying imprudently' that she strictly forbade her all contact with young men whatsoever. The result of this 'scrutinizing severity' was not merely to deprive Kitty of many innocent pleasures, but to make her question 'whether [her aunt] loved her or not'. Inevitably, after rashly kissing Kitty in her garden bower, the handsome young Mr Percival was immediately sent abroad by his parents before he had a chance to declare his love. The girl was left alone in her beloved bower, built for her by two childhood friends who had also been sent away, reflecting sadly on her isolation. Eliza found it hard to believe her young cousin experienced comparable feelings of repression from such amiable and sensible parents as the Austens. From all that she discerned, Mrs Austen betrayed no very violent signs of apprehension at allowing her daughters to scramble for handsome partners with the Misses Cox or other fat girls with short noses at neighbourhood balls. Yet, for all that, there remained the unmistakable trace of some unfulfilled craving for adventure and mischief which escaped from Jane in her self-willed heroines and their satirical asides.

When Jane returned, Eliza begged her to point out the bower in the garden which had inspired her. To which her cousin replied that it was all a fiction; there were several bowers in the garden, and none to which she attached any special affection. The marriage of Jane Cooper to her naval captain took place on 11 December, with Mr Austen's former pupil Tom Fowle officiating. The Leighs of Adlestrop gave the bride a cloak worth £5 16s 8d and the happy pair set off for the Isle of Wight, with a pressing invitation to Eliza to visit them there. 'If I am alive next summer,' she commented, 'I may possibly accept.'[31] The following week brought Jane's seventeenth birthday. In the fulsome dedication to Cassandra which preceded the text of *Catharine*, she had written: 'the following novel, . . . I humbly flatter myself, possesses merit beyond any already published, or any that will ever in future appear, except such as may proceed from the pen of your most grateful, humble servt., The Author.' The tone was, as always, self-mocking; but the boast was not entirely in jest. Like her heroine, Jane Austen 'possessed such a fund of vivacity and good humour as could only be damped by some very serious vexation'. As she prepared herself for the minor vexations of a winter season as Mrs Egerton's guest at Bath, Eliza entreated her young cousin to persevere in that vein of deliciously subversive humour. The family was much taken up by the news from the East Indies, where Frank was promoted to the rank of lieutenant; but among all their chorus of farewells and good wishes, Eliza would always remember Jane's voice, with its sparkle of gaiety and depth of sense.

'I am now going to murder my sister'

The Fowles of Kintbury had been friendly with the Austens ever since Thomas Fowle had first encountered George Austen as an undergraduate at Oxford. All four of Tom Fowle's sons had been taught by Mr Austen at the rectory and had taken it in turns to play and tease and flirt with the young Austen girls. Fulwar was the serious one, full of high ambitions. When not studying his Latin texts he would ramble the fields with James, and the two of them would discuss what great things they would do.[32] William was rather quiet, but Charles had always been Jane's favourite, so full of wild and wonderful schemes. Cassandra, though, had tended to find young Tom Fowle the most congenial of the brothers. Now that Tom was staying at the rectory once more, preparing for Jane Cooper's wedding, the two of them would often take a walk together, around the garden, beneath the elms. A handsome clergyman of twenty-eight must be reckoned, even by the least susceptible of young ladies, a most eligible prospect, and accordingly, before the end of his visit, he and Cassandra became engaged. Tom had obtained the rectory of Allington from his kinsman, the Earl of Craven. But though the situation, near Amesbury, was most convenient, they both agreed the living there was scarcely sufficient to support a family. Prudently, they decided to postpone all thought of matrimony until the Earl's further promise, of the next vacant living among his Shropshire estates, might be fulfilled.

Jane Cooper's brother Edward was more fortunate, and obtained the curacy of Harpsden upon his marriage to Caroline Lybbe-Powys.[33] The couple quickly took up residence in the house that once had been Mrs Austen's childhood home, where, they insisted, she was always welcome to visit. Such familial alliances were highly satisfactory, and James Austen loved to tease his sister with hints of his impatience to perform the wedding ceremony between herself and his own dear friend, Tom Fowle. Jane likewise did her best to demonstrate enthusiasm for her sister's forthcoming nuptials and set herself to compose a poem for Cassandra in the high romantic style. But instead of writing an ode to wedded joys, she produced an 'Ode to Pity', full of moonlight and nightingales, myrtle groves and ancient grottoes. It was the dark romance of love's lonely disappointments, rather than the bright prospect of marital bliss, that inspired her verses. 'The pale moon her beams doth shed/On disappointed love', she wrote, imagining a landscape of picturesque dilapidation, with the 'mouldering heap' of an ancient abbey just glimpsed between the aged pines.

In January, a baby girl, christened Fanny-Catherine, was born at Rowling, the first child of Edward and his wife Elizabeth. Jane was now an aunt, a fact which stimulated her to further serious reflections on the lives and destinies of females. She promptly sent the baby girl a miscellany of her 'opinions & admonitions on the conduct of young women'. From these, baby Fanny might learn that a young woman who murdered both her parents might easily be forgiven, and even rewarded by marriage to a millionaire colonel of horse-guards. All she had to do was forge a will and promise to reform. For a polite young lady, murder and forgery were negligible crimes; the only cardinal female sin was wit. A murderess, particularly one who was orphaned (even if by her own hand), might easily become an object of compassion. But a young woman who was vain enough to boast of her own cleverness was certain to bear an evil reputation for 'peevishness, envy and spite' till the end of her days.

At Deane parsonage, James Austen's wife Anne suffered a more difficult pregnancy. Late one night, in the middle of April, Mrs Austen was suddenly called from her bed to assist at her daughter-in-law's painful labour. Walking by the dim light of a solitary lantern, she negotiated the mile and a half of muddy country lanes from Steventon to Deane, and was just in time to help with the birth of her new grandchild, Anna.[34] Jane Austen promptly sent the baby girl two more of her literary 'morsels' from which, as she solemnly pretended, little Anna might derive 'very important instructions with regard to your conduct in life'. One morsel instructed her in such pretty diversions as flinging stones at ducks, and putting brickbats into people's beds. The other coached her in the art of exhibiting an affecting style of permanent indisposition, sighing, fainting, keeping to her bed and only resisting the temptation to think of dying by contriving never to think at all.

Jane also tried her hand at a little one-act drama. Set in several taverns, it contained a comic bridal-song which might do well enough, she thought, to amuse her affianced sister. 'I shall be married to Strephon,' sings Chloe, 'And that to me will be fun.' A ploughboy chorus then repeats her line:

CHORUS *Be fun, be fun, be fun,*
And that to me will be fun.

Jane imagined Chloe settling down to a leg of beef and a tough old partridge, with the ploughboys all still singing: 'Tough one, tough one, tough one'. Somehow she could not rid her mind of a most unfortunate association between husbands and butcher's meat. Chloe's problems with her leg of beef were not far removed, she knew, from Laura's vision, in *Love and Freindship*, of her dead husband as a leg of mutton. She hoped Cassandra would not take the song as any ill reflection on her own impending assumption of 'conjugal duties'. Still, she could not resist concluding another of her comic sketches with the line: 'I am now going to murder my sister.'

Little Anna Austen's baptismal party at Laverstoke that May was a very grand affair. The godparents were the Duke and Duchess of Ancaster, and her grandfather, General Mathew, 'a very generous

and free-handed man who carried his money literally and meta-
phorically loose in his pocket and gave to everyone that asked
without deigning to look whether the coin bestowed was a guinea
or a shilling'.[35] The General's largesse in giving twenty guineas to
be divided between the nurse and maidservants was exactly the
kind of careless generosity which provoked ill feeling: 'the nurse
was very dissatisfied that she had not more – had five only been
given she would have been thankful.'[36] His manner was entirely
opposite to that of the Reverend Thomas Leigh of Adlestrop, who
accounted exactly for every penny given as a gratuity or gift, and
noted in his private account book the sum of £1 16s 6d given to
Cassandra in July the following year, which he no doubt considered
a generous contribution to her trousseau.

In February, revolutionary France declared war on Britain, ending
ten years of uneasy peace. This event was hardly unexpected, and
among the Austens its effects were not entirely unwelcome. General Mathew further displayed his generosity by purchasing a chap-
laincy in a newly raised regiment of foot on behalf of his son-in-law
James Austen.[37] Of course, James never actually intended to go to
war; the post was another welcome sinecure, like his parishes in
Warwickshire. Even after paying for a deputy to discharge his
duties, the salary provided a useful supplement to his income,
enabling him to keep his horses, his carriage and his pack of har-
riers. Nearly every Sunday, after preaching at Sherborne St John,
James would dine at the Vyne and share hunting stories with Mr
Chute; about the Prince of Wales's dismal attempts to make his
heavy old staghounds chase after foxes; about Henry Digweed's
imprisonment for removing posts and rails from a neighbour's
estate; or about the impoverished émigré German prince who stole
a hare from Mr Digweed's hounds, only to lose it again to Mr
Chute's beagles.[38] A less congenial duty associated with these visits
to his parish was the obligation to call in from time to time on the
Cullums at Monk Sherborne, who had charge of his brother
George. James did not linger on these occasions, but restricted
himself to ensuring that George, now into his twenty-eighth year,
should not want for bodily comforts. It was a sad fact, but a fact

nonetheless, that there was nothing that could be done to recover his nobler faculties.

The war also allowed Henry to postpone the uncongenial prospect of ordination by taking a lieutenant's commission in the Oxford militia. Being an officer in the militia provided all the glamour of a title and handsome uniform with few of the attendant dangers and discomforts of military life. Militia regiments were not expected to fight overseas, but were designed as a home defence against the threat of French invasion. During the next few years, the Oxford militia was conveniently quartered in East Anglia, and Henry found little difficulty in making regular visits to London, Steventon and Kent, and even managed to retain his fellowship at St John's.

The war hastened the return to England of Frank Austen from the Far East, where he had spent the past five years. Promoted to lieutenant the previous year, when still only eighteen, Frank's activities in the China seas had successfully combined naval duties with lucrative trading ventures on behalf of the East India Company. Now summoned back by the Lords of the Admiralty to assume war duties in home waters, he made sure to load his ship, the *Minerva*, with a rich cargo for the homeward trip. But the directors of the East India Company, shrewd judges of their own commercial interests, declined to defray the expenses of a voyage undertaken on Admiralty orders. Eight years later, Frank was still petitioning the Company 'for an allowance to indemnify him for his expenses in returning from India to Europe in the year 1793'.[39]

Arriving back at Steventon that winter, Frank enjoyed a few months' shore leave before taking up his posting to the sloop HMS *Lark* in March 1794. Together he and Henry had great fun escorting their sisters to balls and country-house parties throughout the county. In December, they visited their relatives, the Butler-Harrisons, at Southampton. As a young woman in Tonbridge, Elizabeth Butler-Harrison (*née* Austen) had enjoyed a reputation as 'one of the most beautiful women in Kent' (but then, as Jane observed, 'the sweetest girls in the world were to be met with in every part of England').[40] Now pregnant with her third child, Mrs Butler-Harrison was one of the leading ladies in Southampton society, with a husband who had already been sheriff and had ambitions to be mayor. At their invitation, Jane and Cassandra danced at an assembly ball in the Dolphin Inn among all the newly commissioned young officers. Jane stayed on to be godmother to the Butler-Harrisons' new-born daughter, and thus missed attending another ball at Basingstoke in January, at which Cassandra was greatly admired, and Henry danced with the shy young Mrs Chute. Mrs Austen was so vexed that her younger daughter should have been deprived of such a convivial occasion that she promptly despatched a rhyming letter to her, itemizing all the company.

> *Miss Eyre of Sherfield and her Mother;*
> *One Miss from Dummer and her brother . . .*
> *Charles Powlett and his pupils twain;*
> *Small parson Hasker, great Squire Lane . . .* [41]

Reading her mother's verses, Jane was reminded of that narrow world of Hampshire society from which, before long, she must be expected to select an eligible husband. Lord Portsmouth's family was rich, but afflicted by madness, and while madness was diverting to write about, it might be less agreeable to live with. Then there were the baronets, like Sir Alexander Grant from Malshanger House and Sir William Heathcote of Hursley Park. There were the Jervoises of Herriard (members of parliament), and the Bigg-Withers of Manydown Park. There were the Mildmays of Dogmersfield, the Powletts of Hackwood, the Portals of Freefolk, the Harwoods of Deane, the Holders, Lefroys, Bramstons, Williamsons and Hickses. Most of the men were parsons or squires, indigent curates or indolent landowners, who clubbed together for philanthropic purposes or to demonstrate their defiance of French threats of invasion. That summer, Mr Austen and James had joined Squire Harwood, Wither Bramston, the Reverend Lefroy, and several other worthy citizens of the neighbourhood to contribute a guinea each for the victims of a terrible fire at Barton Stacey. James was also happy to have his name included alongside those of Lord Bolton, Colonel Lefroy, John Harwood, the Reverend

Lefroy and Charles Powlett as founders of the North Hants Association, pledging themselves 'to be trained to the use of arms in our neighbourhood, once in every week, and that in the case of an actual invasion, [to] . . . perform such military duties as shall be required'.[42] They were practical men, staunch in defence of their property, and no doubt quite fond of their wives. But Jane had never yet discerned among them any signs of a romantic Fitzwilliam.

If the Austens had harboured any doubts concerning the dangers of the revolutionary government in France, these were quickly dispersed by the sudden reappearance of Eliza at Steventon that summer as a widowed and penniless refugee. Pregnant, impoverished, and threatened with arrest by the Committee of Public Safety, the Countess had gambled everything on a desperate flight to England. She told of her terrifying journey from Paris to Calais, accompanied only by an Englishwoman whose inability to speak French placed them both in constant peril. At Calais there had been worse miseries and more delays. The hardships of the journey had brought on Eliza's labour, and in a cramped rented room she underwent the agonies of childbirth, followed by the anguish of watching her baby son die within days of drawing breath. But there had been no time for grieving or recovery. Three days later, she crossed over to Dover and came immediately to Steventon to seek the consolation and comfort of her Austen cousins.

The stories that Eliza told left Jane with a loathing for republican France which endured for the rest of her life. Eliza's return to Paris, the previous year, had coincided with the start of the Terror. Suddenly, the Marquise de Marboeuf, widow of de Feuillide's friend and former commander, was accused of conspiring against the republic. Naturally, de Feuillide insisted on coming to the Marquise's defence, though he had quickly realized that her case was not a strong one. Accordingly, he had attempted to bribe one of the secretaries of the Committee of Public Safety, a man named Morel, to destroy the evidence against her. Of course, it was a foolish thing to have done; but it was what everyone else was doing. It was even more foolish to think of obtaining justice from the sort of court which now existed in France. The man Morel was a true Machiavelli. At first, he had pretended to acquiesce to de Feuillide's scheme. He agreed to meet a man named Cordier, sent by de Feuillide, in a café at the Palais d'Egalité, where Cordier had offered Morel 15,000 livres to set the Marquise free.[43] But Morel had said he would not deal with any go-between and insisted on meeting de Feuillide himself. So de Feuillide had met him and repeated the offer of 15,000 livres. Morel said it was not enough. De Feuillide then offered 20,000, but Morel said that was still not enough. At last, de Feuillide had offered 24,000 livres and told Morel it was his final offer. Morel must take it or leave it, he said. Morel said he would take it. The two men had gone at midnight to see Predicant, the Marquise's man of business, and Predicant had given Morel 6,000 livres. The next day, the three men had met again and Predicant had given Morel another 4,000 livres. The rest of the money, he said, would be paid once the Marquise was set free. And so they had parted.

But Morel was a villain. He had betrayed de Feuillide and reported all their meetings back to the Committee of Public Safety. They had come for de Feuillide at midnight, ransacking their lodgings in the Rue Grenelle et St Honoré. Eliza had been forced to watch in horror as the agents of the Committee pawed through all their household belongings. In a pocket of de Feuillide's trousers they had found a receipt for 14,000 livres payable to the bearer and signed by Morel. Documents were impounded; money was confiscated; and as to what remained, the Committee decreed that everything else in the house should be left in the charge of Eliza's illiterate black servant girl, *la citoyenne* Rose Clarisse. In these revolutionary times, only servants and the labouring poor were trusted to be loyal to the new republic. At his trial a few weeks later, de Feuillide had even tried to pretend that he was really a servant himself, a poor patriotic valet who had murdered his master, the real Comte de Feuillide. But this desperate stratagem had been easily confounded by Rose Clarisse and by their housekeeper, *la citoyenne* Joubert. Eliza had even had to endure the mortification of hearing de Feuillide's former mistress, *la citoyenne* Grandville, testifying against him.

To Jane, this whole ghastly pantomime of aristocrats pretending to be menials sounded like a grotesque parody of the farce *High Life Below Stairs*, in which Jane Cooper had performed with Henry all those years before. It had been a terrible shock, Eliza agreed, to see loyal servants, whom they had always trusted, turning against them in open defiance. On 22 February (or 4th Ventose, as they styled it), de Feuillide had been taken to the guillotine, where his head had been struck from his body.

The Austens showed every kindness to Eliza, and Henry seemed particularly at pains to comfort her. But whilst his attentions were flattering, Eliza was in no mood for flirtations and found greater solace in the sensible conversation of Jane and Cassandra, and the ever benevolent care of Mr Austen. In July, she travelled north to stay with friends near Durham. It was there that she received a kindly letter of condolence and concern from Warren Hastings, who was not so taken up with his own affairs that he could not spare a paternal thought for his (god)daughter's sufferings. 'I find myself much the better for the northern air,' she assured him, thanking him sincerely for all the 'many favours' he had shown her throughout her life.[44] There were also regular letters from Jane, who kept Eliza informed of her various summer excursions.

In England at least, that summer, there was still time for such frivolously girlish diversions as tea-parties and balls. In July, as Robespierre himself finally mounted the scaffold of the guillotine in the Place de la Révolution, Jane and Cassandra Austen paid a visit to their Leigh cousins at Adlestrop, where they had the gratification of being generally admired as two 'very charming young women'.[45] To Jane, this was praise indeed. To appear *charming* was a very great improvement on Phylly Walter's dismissal of her as 'not at all pretty'. 'To look *almost* pretty,' as she once observed, 'is an acquisition of higher delight to a girl who has been looking plain the first fifteen years of her life, than a beauty from her cradle can ever receive.'[46]

Later that summer, as the gaols in Paris were thrown open and thousands of prisoners released, the Austen sisters were on their travels again, journeying down to Rowling in Kent, where little Fanny Austen now had a new baby brother, Edward. The weather for the journey was hot and Jane always remembered the bad butter they were served at their first staging-post, the Bull Inn at Dartford. Hot weather was her aversion: 'It keeps one in a continual state of inelegance.'[47] But she was evidently not too inelegant to attract the notice of her brother's eligible neighbour, Mr Edward Taylor of Bifrons. For several weeks she imagined herself passionately in love with this handsome young man. She confessed to Cassandra how much she 'fondly doated' on his beautiful dark eyes.[48]

But dark eyes and bad butter proved an inadequate literary inspiration and, away from Steventon, Jane Austen found little inclination to write. From fifteen to seventeen she had been in training for a literary heroine; now aged eighteen, she was determined upon making her entrance as a character of romance. Her imagination was no longer satisfied by the ironic triumphs of the solitary authoress; and the desire to tease and shock, which had formerly animated the pages of her notebooks, was now transposed to assembly-room balls and country-house parties. Dancing and flirting were all her passion now, as she set herself to attract suitors at least as eligible as Cassandra's Tom Fowle. Her behaviour was of a kind to attract comment – not all of it favourable. Mrs Mitford, mother of one of the short, fat girls at a Basingstoke ball, described Jane as 'the prettiest, silliest, most affected husband-hunting butterfly she ever remembered'.[49] There was a kind of whimsical mock-urgency about Jane's sudden passion for marrying herself off, which suggests less emotional conviction than sisterly rivalry. 'If Cassandra were to have her head cut off,' their mother had once said, 'Jane would insist on having hers cut off too.' If Cassandra were determined to be married, it seemed that Jane could envisage no better fate than to emulate her in that sacrifice. Her fantasies of a sudden betrothal received an unexpected boost from the death of Mr Knight at his Chawton estate that October. In his will, Mr Knight left Jane and Cassandra £50 apiece – hardly enough to qualify them as heiresses, but almost certainly the largest sum that either of them had yet possessed.[50] Their father allowed them only a meagre £20 a year each for their personal expenses, and even that was prudently paid out in quarterly instalments.

With this unlooked-for legacy Jane could imagine herself, for a brief instant, as a young woman of means. But Mr Taylor had ambitions for parliament, and had set his dark eyes somewhat above the pretensions of a clergyman's daughter, even with £50 to her name. Marriage notices in the *Hampshire Chronicle* were unsentimentally frank in itemizing a bride's assets, witness the announcement of the marriage of Mrs Mitford herself (*née* Russell): 'Miss Russell, only daughter of the late Revd. Dr Russell, Rector of Ashe . . . a most amiable young lady, and possessed of a fortune of £20,000.'[51]

The Austen males received more substantial benefits from Mr Knight's will. Although Godmersham, and all the other estates, were left to his widow for her lifetime, the will confirmed Edward Austen as Mr Knight's adopted heir, and further provided that, should Edward's line fail, these properties should descend to each of the other Austen sons in succession. Edward offered Henry £1,200 to purchase the succession to the rectorship at Chawton, whenever it should fall vacant; but John Papillon, who held the right to the Chawton parish, refused to sell.

In September, Charles Austen, now aged fifteen, left the Naval Academy at Portsmouth and went to take up war-fighting duties as a midshipman aboard HMS *Daedalus*, under the command of Jane Cooper's husband, Captain Williams. Even with the benefit of such a friendly commander, the life he was now set to endure was hardly enviable. Young midshipmen were generally disliked by the older sailors (many of them criminals, others press-ganged into service) under their command. It was not unknown for a midshipman, suspected of reporting on the men to superior officers, to be knifed in his hammock. Many of the ships were old and rotting, and his quarters would be damp, cramped and fetid with the stench of excrement and sweat. Away from land for months at a time, he would eat dry salt beef and maggoty biscuits, washed down with a sour white wine called *mistella* but known to the men as Miss Taylor.[52] His brother Frank, still vexed at the Company's delay in settling his expenses for the voyage back to England, and angered by the Admiralty's refusal to promote him, now asked his father to see if Mr Hastings's influence might be used on his behalf. This was a dangerous strategy. Although much of the urgency had gone out of the proceedings against Hastings (during 1791 the court sat for only five days), the trial itself was not concluded and the outcome still in doubt. Yet Mr Austen had always remained in contact with his beleaguered friend, and now thanked him for 'the friendly manner in which you have undertaken our cause, & the application you have made in behalf of my son'. As to the efficacy of such applications, Mr Austen pronounced himself 'not very sanguine, convinced as I am that all patronage in the navy rests with Lord Chatham'. But he was sincerely grateful for Hastings's efforts in procuring one 'warm friend' at the Admiralty Board, in the form of Admiral Affleck, whose influence might be 'of material service to us'. Nor did he feel any diffidence in indicating clearly the precise 'service' he had in mind. 'Should we not succeed in our first object of getting him promoted, it might forward his views to have him removed to a flag-ship on a more probable station; & this is a circumstance you might, if you had no objection, mention to the Admiral when you meet him [in] town.'[53] While such lobbying proceeded on his behalf, Frank was recalled to his ship, HMS *Lark*, as part of a fleet sent to evacuate British troops from Ostend and Nieuwpoort in the bitter winter of 1794–5. A few months later, the *Lark* returned across the North Sea as part of a squadron sent to ferry the Princess Caroline of Brunswick to England for her marriage to the Prince of Wales. It was not a happy assignment. The Princess came as a considerable disappointment to her future husband ('swears like an ostler and smells like a farmyard' was one unkind courtier's remark).[54]

For her nineteenth birthday, Mr Austen bought Jane 'a small mahogany writing desk with 1 long drawer and glass ink stand compleat', which he purchased from Ring's of Basingstoke for 12s.[55] Mr Austen had long observed with approval his younger daughter's facility for literary composition, and 12s seemed to him a modest enough sum to invest in a talent which might prove, after all, to be nothing more than a source of ephemeral diversions. For Cassandra, there was a dowry to be provided; for Frank, there were Admiralty Lords to be lobbied; but to satisfy Jane's desires at present all that seemed needful was a writing-desk. He had noted with some disquiet Jane's recent fondness for flirting in a most immoderate fashion at recent balls. And, whilst he would have not the least objection to her making a sensible match, he considered it highly desirable that what he called her 'effusions of fancy' (which tended invariably to elopements and similar reckless adventures) should be confined to the pages of her manuscript book, and not acted out in real life.

Jane's reaction to this gift was a spirited piece of literary defiance. The first thing that she wrote at her new desk only confirmed her fascination with the disruptive powers of flirtation. Lady Susan Vernon, the heroine of her next and most ambitious work so far, was to be an incorrigible flirt, a cheerful home-wrecker and unashamed adulteress, who boasted of her reputation as 'the most accomplished coquette in England'. Later members of the Austen family regarded Lady Susan with horror, and found it hard to reconcile themselves to the idea that aunt Jane could ever have imagined herself into the mind of such a 'vicious woman' and 'wholly sinister figure'.[56] Yet the witty, energetic and charming Lady Susan was merely the latest in Jane Austen's youthful repertoire of wild and wayward women who find a malicious delight in wreaking havoc among their more respectable friends. 'No house was ever more altered,' she comments, taking satisfaction in the results of her diverting autumn campaign of flirtations at a relative's country house; 'the whole family are at war . . . It is time for me to be gone.' Like a female Lovelace, Lady Susan takes a connoisseur's delight in the artistry of her intrigues. 'There is exquisite pleasure in subduing an insolent spirit,' she writes; 'in making a person pre-determined to dislike, acknowledge one's superiority.' Sexually confident and unashamedly selfish, there is a cool manipulative finesse in the way she plays with her victims. Reginald De Courcy has been explicitly forewarned of her deceitful ways, which makes her more determined than ever to deceive him. Sure enough, within days of meeting her, he falls hopelessly under her spell. 'I have subdued him entirely by sentiment and serious conversation,' she boasts, 'and made him I may venture to say *half* in love with me, without the semblance of the most common-place flirtation.' 'There is something agreable,' she adds, 'in feelings so easily worked on.' Lady Susan is irresistible, and her power derives not merely from her physical beauty, for, as several characters observe, at thirty-five she is 'no longer young', but equally from her seductive verbal skill. 'If I am vain of anything,' she confides to a female friend, 'it is of my eloquence. Consideration and esteem as surely follow command of language as admiration waits on beauty.' For Jane Austen, still polishing her own verbal skills, there was an unmistakable thrill in creating a character whose command of language could have such devastating effects.

For the plot of *Lady Susan*, Jane borrowed hints from the career of the Lloyds' tyrannical grandmother, Mrs Craven, a woman of such unfeeling selfishness in her dealings with her children that three of her daughters had fled from home to escape her despotic rule.[57] In the novel, Lady Susan is determined to push her 'stupid', 'horrid', 'tiresome' daughter Frederica into a marriage with the weak-headed Sir James Martin, whom the girl despises. Lady Susan likes to protest that, of course, she would not 'force Frederica into a marriage from which her heart revolted'. Instead, she adopts the more subtle policy of merely 'rendering her life thoroughly uncomfortable' until she submits to her mother's wishes. But if the plot of *Lady Susan* owes something to the conduct of Mrs Craven, the seductive language of worldly intrigue suggests the influence of the Countess de Feuillide. It was from Eliza that Jane had learnt the racy idioms of society flirtation. It was from Eliza that she heard of the dangerous excitement of sexual deceit. The language of Lady Susan is the language of Eliza. Recently widowed, Lady Susan 'cannot easily resolve on anything so serious as marriage, especially as I am not at present in want of money . . .' Now widowed herself, Eliza had similar doubts about a second marriage ('I have an aversion to the word *husband*'). Lady Susan recommends adultery as the best policy to the wife of an elderly, gouty husband ('it is undoubtedly better to deceive him entirely; since he will be stubborn, he must be tricked'). Even after her second marriage, Eliza still liked to hint at her fascination with the amorous '*trade*'.[58]

Even if Jane Austen did not *approve* of Lady Susan, she could at least imagine the excitement of this uncowed, irresistible female power. Lady Susan sneers at 'that insupportable spot, a country village', and longs instead for London, where there 'will be always the fairest field of action'. At the time Jane wrote this, two of her brothers were engaged in warfare at sea; but, for a woman, the only possible forms of heroic combat and conquest were of the kind that Lady Susan dealt in. Imagining such reckless characters as Lady Susan and Mary Queen of Scots was an exciting fantasy which filled Jane's mind with the suggestion of dangerous adventures. And, having written out her stories, or read sections of them aloud to Cassandra, she would come downstairs to her satin stitch, or give orders in the kitchen for boiled chicken or haricot mutton.[59]

CHAPTER 5

Profligate and Shocking

*I am almost afraid to tell you how my Irish friend
and I behaved. Imagine to yourself everything most
profligate and shocking in the way of dancing and
sitting down together.*

Jane Austen, Letter to Cassandra, January 1796

'I write only for fame'

On 23 April 1795, final verdicts were delivered in the trial of
Warren Hastings. One-third of the members of the House of Lords
had died during the nine years of the trial's proceedings, and only
twenty-nine were left who were qualified to pass judgement. They
found Hastings 'not guilty' on every one of the charges against
him.[1] At last the ordeal was over, and Henry Austen lost no time
in sending the great man his warmest felicitations. 'Permit me to
congratulate my country & myself as an Englishman,' he wrote;
'for right dear to every Englishman must it be to behold the issue
of a contest where forms of judicature threatened to annihilate the
essence of justice.'[2] Henry was now very keen in his affections for
the widowed Eliza de Feuillide and eager to cultivate the good
opinion of the Countess's (god)father. Thomas Leigh was equally
prompt in sending his warmest wishes. 'We beg you to be assur'd

that amist [*sic*] the flood of congratulations flowing in upon you, none will be accompanied with more heartfelt sincerity than those which you receive from Adlestrop . . .'[3] The trial had been an anxious time for all the Austens, and there were rejoicings at Mr Hastings's acquittal from Adlestrop to Godmersham and from Steventon to Portsmouth dock. With the clearing of Hastings's name, his friends and allies in the Admiralty could more openly accede to honouring his solicitations. In May, Frank Austen was transferred to the thirty-two-gun HMS *Andromeda*, presumably through the influence of Hastings's friends, Admiral Affleck and Mr Pybus. In the autumn he was moved again, this time to the ninety-eight-gun flag-ship HMS *Glory*, just as his father had requested. But there was soon more solemn news to quell the sense of exultation at Steventon. On 3 May, just as Frank was receiving his commission for *Andromeda*, James's wife Anne died suddenly at Deane. She was thirty-six years old, and left a baby daughter, Anna, who was only two.

Frank's new ship, the *Glory*, was intended to lead a troop convoy of 19,000 men to the West Indies, where the French were inciting the slaves to rebel against British rule. Amongst the troops to sail were the 3rd regiment of foot ('The Buffs'), of which Lord Craven, Tom Fowle's patron, had recently purchased the colonelcy. Craven invited Fowle to accompany him on the voyage as his private chaplain. For the young clergyman, dependent as he was on Craven's favour, it was a difficult decision. His marriage to Cassandra Austen had already been postponed, and this expedition must entail further delays. Yet together he and Cassandra reasoned themselves into an acceptance of what must be. Disagreeable as it was, they assured each other, this interruption need not prove such a disadvantage as he feared. As Craven's private chaplain, Fowle would be often in the Earl's company, and it was not unknown for such intimacy to lead on to greater things. As a prudent precaution, and as an earnest of his future intentions, Fowle hurriedly made out his will on 10 October, before joining the Earl's entourage. In it he left £1,000 to Cassandra and the rest of his property to his father.[4] The Buffs sailed out of Portsmouth with the main fleet in early November, and were immediately battered by fierce storms in the Channel which caused several casualties to ships and men. Fortunately, Lord Craven and his chaplain did not sail with the rest of the regiment, but followed behind in Craven's own private yacht and thus missed the worst of the storms. Fowle wrote to Cassandra and Jane in early January from Falmouth, where they awaited a favourable wind. 'By this time . . . they are at the Barbadoes, I suppose,' Jane wrote cheerfully to her sister a week later, adding, with a more waspish note: 'I am very glad . . . that Mr & Mrs Fowle are pleased with you. I hope you will continue to give satisfaction.'[5]

Jane Austen liked Tom Fowle, and of course she wished her sister every happiness. But she did wish there were something more romantic about him. He had become such a *very* prudent young man. How like him to have missed all the storms in the Channel! Of course it was very sensible to delay marriage until there was money enough to support a family; and of course it was the height of prudence and rational good sense to make out his will in Cassandra's behalf before he sailed away. But all the same, there was something so very sober about it. Perhaps the West Indies would put more fire in him. At present she was writing another novel – her longest yet – about two sisters, one of whom, the elder, was rational, prudent and full of good sense, while the other was impatient, impulsive and full of wild, romantic notions. Elinor, the elder, was in love with such a sensible, modest, prudent young man, who wanted only to be a rural clergyman, but his family – who thought themselves very grand – would not countenance anything so low, even for a younger son. And of course they would not even *dream* of allowing him to marry anyone so low as Elinor, from a family without money or a title. Poor Elinor not only endured such slights without protest; she even seemed to approve of the insensitivity, disguised as prudence, which provoked them. For Marianne, the younger sister, love was all that mattered (though how Elinor could really be in love with a man who read Cowper with such hideous insensibility was beyond her). She was impatient at all this talk of legacies and great estates, annuities and parish livings. 'What have wealth and grandeur to do with happiness?' she demanded. Elinor's response – like Cassandra's – was eminently sensible. 'Grandeur has but little,' she agreed; 'but wealth has much to do with it.' 'Elinor, for shame!' cried Marianne, indignant at such mercenary considerations. Jane Austen, in her high romantic vein, had convinced herself that she cared nothing for money either. 'I write only for fame,' she declared loftily, 'and without any view to pecuniary emolument.'[6] 'Elinor and Marianne' was her most ambitious novel yet, and she was determined that this would be the one that would announce to an admiring world the emergence of a new literary star.

However, her diversions at the time were not entirely literary. She was already greatly admired among the young gentlemen of the neighbourhood, and it was become a moot point with her whether flirtation or novel-writing afforded her the greater delight. On the whole, she rather inclined to believe that it must be flirtation; there was something so delicious about teasing Charles Fowle about the silk stockings he offered to buy for her; or flattering rich Mr Heartley; or cheating Charles Powlett of a kiss and dancing with John Warren, whom she remembered as an ugly, clumsy boy when he used to be one of her father's pupils at the rectory. Warren's middle name was 'Willing', which he was, but Jane was not. The young man took his disappointment stoically enough. When she commanded him to draw a portrait of his more fortunate rival, Tom Lefroy, he did so and delivered it to her, as she reported gleefully, 'without a sigh'.[7] Yes, decidedly, flirtation was by far the greater pleasure. She was long accustomed to receiving applause as a wit; but never before now had the gentlemen competed with each other in complimenting the fineness of her bright hazel eyes; or remarked upon her beautiful light brunette curls, or admired the sweet musicality of her voice. Sometimes, it was true, these same gentlemen were disconcerted when she turned on them, as she loved to do, the smart phrases she had practised in the voices of her heroines. Such a one, she would declare, had no soul, for he had not read *The Mysteries of Udolpho*. Such another was no better than a brute for preferring a snug farmhouse to an ancient picturesque ruin. But far above the rest of them, it was Tom Lefroy that she loved. Though he did not have the beautiful dark eyes of Mr Taylor or the extensive estates of Mr Heartley, this young Irishman had something about him that was worth infinitely more; a sense of wit and fun and daring that could match her own repartee. On his birthday, on 8 January, there was a splendid ball at the Bigg-Withers' house at Manydown, where the greenhouse was magically illuminated with several hundred candles. Everyone was there, except only her dear Cassandra, who was still at Kintbury with the Fowles, taking leave of her own Tom before his voyage to the West Indies. Jane danced with Willing Warren (twice!) and once with Charles Watkins, and entirely escaped from dancing with John Lyford at all. But it was Tom Lefroy who entirely engrossed her affections. 'I am almost afraid to tell you how my Irish friend and I behaved,' she wrote excitedly to Cassandra the next morning. 'Imagine to yourself everything most profligate and shocking in the way of dancing and sitting down together.'[8]

Cassandra had been at Kintbury for such an *age* that she and Tom had never met, for he had only recently come to the neighbourhood and was staying with his uncle George at Ashe. Jane offered a brief description: 'He is a very gentlemanlike, good-looking, pleasant young man, I assure you.' Although she had known Tom Lefroy for barely a few weeks, their intimacy was already the talk of the neighbourhood. 'But as to our having met, except at the three last balls, I cannot say much; for he is so excessively laughed at about me at Ashe, that he is ashamed of coming to Steventon.' They both knew that Tom's time in Hampshire was strictly limited. His family in Ireland had great ambitions for him as a lawyer, and his visit to Ashe was designed merely as a short holiday, for the good of his health, before he resumed his legal studies. Embarrassed by the teasing that his attentions to Jane provoked, the young man had actually run away when the Austens paid a visit to his aunt Lefroy a few days earlier. But the previous night's ball had changed everything, it seemed. Before she could finish her letter, Jane heard a knock at the rectory door. There was Tom Lefroy, accompanied by his cousin George. Her pleasure at seeing him was so great that she could only control it by recourse to her familiar defence of literary mockery. His coat was a great deal too light in colour, she complained. But then, what could one expect of a man who was such a professed admirer of *Tom Jones*? Was he, she wondered, attempting to copy the sartorial style of his wounded hero?[9] It was such a delight to be with a man who not only understood, but responded to, such allusions. And it was an even more tempting delight to be admired by a man whose notion of manly heroism was drawn from *Tom Jones* rather than *Sir Charles Grandison*.

Every day for the following week she sent excited bulletins to Cassandra on the progress of this *grand amour*, disguising it, with coy propriety, among gossip about Charles Fowle's silk stockings, Benjamin Portal's handsome eyes, and Henry's latest scheme for joining up with the Regulars and getting himself posted to the Cape of Good Hope. Poor Henry was suffering from Eliza's latest switch of affection, for, now that James was single again, she did rather seem to be inclining towards him. Eliza was incorrigible, but would a parson – even a parson who rode to hounds with the Prince of Wales – really be to her taste? Jane had been pleased to see James dancing with Alethea Bigg at the Manydown ball. Really, she thought, he deserved encouragement for 'the very great improvement' which had lately taken place in his dancing. But Friday was to be the great day. That evening there was to be a ball at Ashe, one last wonderful party before Tom Lefroy was packed off to Lincoln's Inn. In her imagination, she had already acted out the scene. 'I look forward with great impatience to it,' she confided eagerly to Cassandra, 'as I rather expect to receive an offer from my friend in the course of the evening.' Naturally, she would refuse him, she wrote with a smile, 'unless he promises to give away his white coat'. Already she was imperiously discarding all her other beaux. 'Tell Mary that I make over Mr Heartley & all his estate to her for her sole use and benefit in future, & not only him, but all my other admirers into the bargain ... as I mean to confine myself to Mr Tom Lefroy, for whom,' she added, teasingly, 'I do not care sixpence.'[10]

But by Friday morning all her hopes had turned to ashes. The ball, to which she had looked forward with such eager anticipation, would be a penance, not a pleasure. There was to be no proposal from Tom Lefroy, no delicious *tête-à-tête* or secret understanding.

His family, taking sudden fright at the prospect of an engagement between this young and penniless couple, had stepped in to prohibit any further contact between them. That morning, she sent Cassandra a very different bulletin: 'At last the day is come on which I am to flirt my last with Tom Lefroy . . .' The young man was to be sent away immediately to London, in virtual disgrace, and never allowed to return. Of course, she should have realized this disappointment was entirely predictable; had she not, indeed, predicted it in the concluding pages of *Catharine*, where Mr Stanley, equally careless as her own dear Tom about his coat, was suddenly dispatched to France by his father the very morning he might have proposed to the heroine? Like Catharine, Jane Austen resolved to let her disappointment be 'of service' to her; 'it will teach me in future *not* to think everybody is in love with me.' Turning herself into a character provided some refuge from her pain. 'When you receive this it will be over,' she wrote to Cassandra, then added in the voice of a literary heroine: 'My tears flow as I write, at the melancholy idea.'[11] What was it, after all, but another case of 'the old, well established grievance of duty against will, parent against child'? But the bitterness she felt escaped her in sharp asides directed at the clumsy solicitude of those who tried to humour her. William Chute paid a call: 'I wonder what he means by being so civil,' she demanded tartly. There was a report that another Tom – Tom Chute – was to marry a Lichfield lass. She no doubt had rather more than £50 for her dowry. Even John Lyford came to visit them as Edward's guest. 'We shall all go together to Ashe,' she wrote, adding, with weary irony, 'I understand we are to draw for partners.' She had thought that she had found her partner, and it pained her to find herself once more back in the pack.

That Friday night, at Ashe, she and Tom Lefroy danced together for the last time, savouring the sweet melancholy of a final embrace. It was the last time that she ever saw him. Mrs Lefroy was so deeply disturbed by her nephew's indiscreet conduct towards Jane Austen, she could never afterwards bring herself to mention his name in her presence. It was nearly three years before Jane heard any further news of the man she had once fondly dreamt of as her own picaresque hero. 'I was too proud to make any enquiries,' she wrote to Cassandra; 'but on my father's afterwards asking where he was, I learn that he was gone back to London in his way to Ireland, where he is called to the bar and means to practise.'[12] Shortly afterwards, Tom Lefroy married the sister of a college friend, and together they raised a family on their rich estate in County Longford. As a barrister he was very successful and eventually rose to become Lord Chief Justice of Ireland. But he never forgot Jane Austen and the snow on the trees as they walked together from Steventon to Ashe. 'To the last year of his life, she was remembered as the object of his youthful admiration.'[13]

For Jane, the pain of losing Tom Lefroy was real enough, though mitigated, as she must privately concede, by the status that this episode had conferred on her of being a woman who had loved and lost. It was no small consolation to her wounded pride to be able to view herself in the tradition of romantic heroines. She studied, by her manner and address (a brave smile, a low voice, a hint of moisture in the eyes as she revisited the places where *he* had lately walked with her), to live up to the dignity of such a role. There was no lack of well-wishers, both male and female, determined to rally her back to cheerfulness. But strangely, the most invigorating counsel came from the person least sympathetic to her suffering. Now back in London, her cousin Eliza declared herself far happier as a widow than she had ever been as a wife. The loss of a husband, she insisted, whether by the barbarity of the guillotine or the tyranny of jealous parents, was no very great disaster. 'Independence and the homage of half a dozen,' she wrote, 'are preferable to subjection and the attachment of a single individual.'[14] Between them there soon existed a regular correspondence, and Jane found a constant stimulation in the bold and worldly tone of Eliza's letters, as she boasted of her amorous intrigues. By rights, Jane knew, it ought to trouble her that the two men whom Eliza most loved to flirt with were Jane's own brothers, James and Henry. But secretly she found a kind of fascination in observing how Eliza toyed with them. Sometimes it was James she seemed to favour, and sometimes it was Henry, until the two men were driven almost to distraction by her coquetry.

Often it appeared as if Eliza were intent upon causing as much havoc among the Austens of Steventon as Lady Susan Vernon had done among the De Courcys of Langford. For a brief period in the early part of the year, while Eliza had been staying at the rectory, she had seemed quite resolved upon marrying James. There was something so beguiling about the Hampshire country-side in the spring, when the hedgerows were full of early primroses and the elm trees were in bud, that made matrimony seem the most natural thing in the world. In Phylly Walter's mind, the thing was as good as settled. On a summer trip to Brighton, the two women chattered happily over the prospect of life in a country parsonage and Phylly said how greatly she looked forward to visiting Steventon for the wedding. Henry, at least, believed that his own cause was lost and promptly got himself engaged to a Miss Mary Pearson, daughter of Captain Richard Pearson of the Greenwich Hospital for Seamen. He obtained a miniature of Miss Pearson and showed it proudly to his parents. Mrs Austen was pleased to see that Miss Pearson was such a pretty girl. Eliza, though, had heard a rather different report. 'She is a pretty wicked looking girl with bright black eyes which pierce through & through,' she told Phylly Walter. 'No wonder this poor young man's heart could not withstand them.'[15] Throughout the summer, Eliza indulged a pleasant fantasy of exchanging her hectic London life for the tranquillity of the country. 'When I am quietly settled in that said domestic retreat,' she wrote to Phylly, 'you must charit-ably come & prevent my spouse & self from going to sleep or quarrelling for want of other amusement.'[16] But when Jane Austen visited London in late August, with her brothers Edward and Frank, she found Eliza back in her natural element. 'Here I am once more in this scene of dissipation & vice,' Jane wrote jokily to Cassandra from Cork Street, 'and I begin already to find my morals corrupted.'[17] There was not much corruption to be feared from her evening excursion to Astley's equestrian circus. But Eliza's elaborate levée every morning at nearby Durweston Street was a rather different matter; she boasted of entertaining as 'reasonable quantity of beaux' as the 'present hard times' allowed.[18]

Travelling on from London down to Rowling, Jane was compelled, by Henry's urgent request, to stop *en route* at Greenwich, to meet her future sister-in-law, Miss Pearson. Henry was most particularly anxious that Jane should bring Miss Pearson back to Steventon with her when she returned from visiting Edward. Indeed, he made such a *thing* about it, forever changing his plans, marching about from Kent to Yarmouth, and always complaining about his health, that it quite spoiled her own arrangements. She was at a loss to know whether she would be returning to Steventon with Frank in a week, with Henry and Miss Pearson in a month, or with Edward the Lord knew when. And, having once met this alleged beauty, she passed on a warning to Cassandra. 'If Miss Pearson should return with me, pray be careful not to expect too much beauty. I will not pretend to say that on a *first view*, she quite answered the opinion I had formed of her. My mother I am sure will be disappointed, if she does not take great care. From what I remember of her picture, it is no great resemblance.'[19]

Miss Pearson notwithstanding, Jane's stay in Kent that September was a period of great happiness. She took pleasure in playing with her newest baby nephew, George, born the previous November, and with his three-year-old sister Fanny, who was given a little butter-churn by Frank that he had carved for her himself. There were visits to Edward's in-laws, the innumerable Bridges of Goodnestone, including an impromptu ball ('two country dances & the boulangeries') after which they all walked home at night under the shade of two umbrellas. Her brothers were determined to take advantage of the excellent local shooting ('they say there are a prodigious number of birds hereabouts this year'), though their first efforts were undistinguished. 'Edward & Fly went out yesterday very early in a couple of shooting jackets, and came home like a couple of bad shots, for they killed nothing at all.' The next day they had better luck ('Edward with his two brace, Frank with his two and a half. What amiable young men!'), and Jane felt almost tempted to join them – 'perhaps *I* may kill a few'.[20] But for the most part she practised her piano, sewed shirts, read *Camilla* and gossiped. Of course, there were all the usual topics: 'Mr Richard Harvey is going to be married; but . . . it is a great secret, & only known to half the neighbourhood.' Cassandra's own forthcoming match was a subject of much interest: 'I took an opportunity of assuring Mr J.T. that neither he nor his father need longer keep themselves single for you.' And there was always the ineffable Miss Pearson.

The sudden death of a local farmer, Mr Claringbould, provoked Edward to some devious speculations: 'I fancy Edward means to get some of his farm,' Jane noted, 'if he can cheat Sir Brook [Bridges] enough in the agreement.' Her brother's constant readiness to trade identity for property rather shocked her, though she disguised her shock as praise. 'Edward had some idea of taking the name of Claringbould,' she solemnly informed Cassandra, 'but that scheme is over, tho' it would be a very eligible as well as a very pleasant plan, would anyone advance him money enough to begin on.'[21] Even that great name-changer Thomas Brodnax/May/ Knight would hardly have changed his name for half a mortgaged farm. Name changes, though, were very much on her mind, as, driving through Bifrons and 'the abode of him on whom I once fondly doated', she mused on how her life might have altered had her name been now changed to Taylor or Lefroy. 'Mr Richard Harvey's match is put off,' she noted, 'till he has got a better Christian name, of which he has great hopes.'[22]

Not the least of the pleasures of being away from Steventon was the sheer delight of receiving regular letters from Cassandra. The first letter which reached Jane at Rowling was a perfect joy. '[It] diverted me beyond moderation,' she wrote back. 'I could die of laughter at it, as they used to say at school. You are indeed the finest comic writer of the present age.'[23] The prospect of marriage had clearly brought Cassandra none of those gloomy apprehensions of domestic dullness and 'conjugal duties' that Eliza so dreaded. Fired up with a spirit of sisterly rivalry, Jane sent letters back full of sharp social comedy and epigrammatic wit. 'Mr Children's two sons are both going to be married, John & George,' she wrote: 'They are to have one wife between them; a Miss Holwell, who belongs to the Black Hole at Calcutta.' 'Miss Fletcher and I were very thick,' she noted in another letter. 'There are two traits in her character which are pleasing; namely, she admires Camilla, & drinks no cream in her tea.'

Jane and Cassandra took a shared delight in these little bookish allusions. It was like a kind of private shorthand, or secret code, between them. Fanny Burney's *Camilla* was their current favourite; Jane had subscribed to the first edition, published earlier that year, and now her letters were peppered with cryptic references to the book. 'Tomorrow I shall be just like Camilla in Mr Dubster's summer-house,' she wrote soon after her arrival; 'for my Lionel will have taken away the ladder by which I came here, or at least by which I intended to get away.' Two weeks later she wrote again: 'Give my love to Mary Harrison, & tell her I wish whenever she is attached to a young man, some *respectable* Dr Marchmont may keep them apart for five volumes.'[24] Burney's novel provided a ready fund of those little comic vexations – like a missing ladder, or a sententious Dr Marchmont – which could be relied upon to impede the smooth progress of young romantic love. After all, what was an elopement without a ladder? Jane herself had had great fun with a rope-ladder in 'Henry and Eliza'. And of course, in a novel, unlike life, everything would come right at the end of the fifth volume. Burney's earlier novel, *Evelina*, was another part of their code. When she visited Bath three years later, Jane told Cassandra of her encounter with an earnest young Oxford freshman who 'wears spectacles, & has heard that *Evelina* was written by Dr Johnson'.[25] Jane also loved to imitate and parody other authors' styles. She could work up a tolerable imitation of Mrs Piozzi, and when one of Edward's friends, a Mr Evelyn, recommended him a pair of coach horses, she was ready with the appropriate literary quip: 'If the judgement of a Yahoo can ever be depended on, I suppose it may now, for I believe Mr Evelyn has all his life thought more of horses than of anything else.'[26]

The pleasant family gathering at Rowling was brought to a sudden end on 18 September, when Frank received news of his latest posting, to HMS *Triton*, a new thirty-two-gun frigate just launched at Deptford. He was to join his ship immediately, and, as a consequence, Jane's own plans were thrown into a sudden disarray which extended even to her prose. Frank was expected 'on board the Captn John Gore,' she told Cassandra, 'commanded by the Triton'.[27] Her inclination was to travel to London with

Frank, but that still left the problem of Miss Pearson. 'I wrote to Miss P on Friday, & hoped to receive an answer from her this morning.' But no answer was received. Why not travel to London anyway, she thought, and take her chances when she got there? The whole family was united in dissuading her from 'so rash a step'. What if the Pearsons were not at home? For Jane to be alone in London was an eventuality too perilous to be contemplated. 'I should inevitably fall a sacrifice to the arts of some fat woman who would make me drunk with small beer.'[28] Cassandra would easily recognize this allusion to Hogarth's *The Harlot's Progress*. But what the family really feared, Jane knew, was that she might fall a sacrifice to the equally worldly arts of her London cousin, Eliza. Mr Austen was at least determined to prevent *that*: 'My father will be so good as to fetch home his prodigal daughter from town.'

Miss Pearson duly came to Steventon, where the disappointment was mutual. Within weeks the engagement was broken off, and it was Henry's turn to go to London, where he sought sympathy from Eliza. 'He looks thin & ill,' she told Phylly Walter, adding that poor Henry's 'late intended' was well known as 'a most intolerable flirt, & reckoned to give herself great airs'.[29] This was in November, by which time James, disturbed by his brother's renewed interest in Eliza, and vexed by her constant prevarications and delays, was pressing hard for a decision. But Eliza, newly removed into a most agreeable mansion in one of her favourite streets, just off Manchester Square, was still in no hurry to give him the answer he required. Phylly Walter was at a loss to account for such hesitation, and wrote frequently to urge her friend not to lose such a worthy opportunity. But Phylly Walter always did take such a sanguine view of 'conjugal duties'. Phylly must by no means anticipate an early wedding, she warned; and quite possibly there would be no wedding at all. 'Preliminaries are so far from settled that I do not believe the parties ever will come together.' It was not that she and James had quarrelled; rather that 'one of [the parties] . . . cannot bring her mind to give up dear liberty, & yet dearer flirtation'.[30] During her sojourn in the Hampshire countryside, she had indeed been tempted to believe that 'sober matrimony' might be possible. But, back in London, Eliza was forced to recognize 'how little the state suits [my] taste'. The more James pressed her for a decision, the more recalcitrant she became. At last, on the very day in late November when she was due to deliver him her answer, she indulged herself instead in a gloriously defiant bout of flirtation. 'The last day of my liberty, mind, I do not say widowhood, . . . Mrs Stevenson & myself did our best to entertain eleven beaux,' she told Phylly Walter, adding slyly: 'I thought the party remarkably pleasant.' Even as she wrote these words, the visiting-card of her newest aristocratic admirer was delivered at her door, 'which I think very ominous, considering I was talking of matrimony; but it does not signify. I shall certainly escape both peer & parson . . .'[31]

At Steventon, Eliza's failure to accept James's proposal was met with something like relief. Even Jane, much as she savoured her bold cousin's wit, was forced to acknowledge doubts as to her suitability as a country parson's wife. Not that James himself was entirely averse to flirtation. For some months he had been dividing his attention between Eliza and two Marys – Mary Harrison, of Andover, and Mary Lloyd, formerly of Deane. 'Let me know . . . which of the Marys will carry the day with my brother James,' Jane joked to Cassandra in September.[32] Indeed, it seemed to her quite possible that James had deliberately provoked Eliza's rejection, for no sooner had he heard from her than he proposed to Mary Lloyd, who had conveniently been staying at Steventon for several weeks. Mary Lloyd accepted him immediately. Naturally, Mrs Austen was delighted at the news and wrote at once to send Mary her 'best love' and assure her of her 'heartfelt satisfaction at the prospect . . . of adding you to the number of our very good children'. 'Had the election been mine,' she added, 'you, my dear Mary, are the person I should have chosen for James's wife, Anna's mother, and my daughter, being as certain, as I can be of anything in this uncertain world, that you will greatly increase and promote the happiness of each of the three.'[33] She could hardly have said the same for Eliza, and Mrs Austen was not ashamed to acknowledge a selfish motive in her preference for Mary. 'I look forward to you as a real comfort in my old age, when Cassandra is gone into Shropshire & Jane – the Lord knows where.' Jane's potential waywardness was something that caused Mrs Austen some misgivings, but at least there was no immediate prospect of Eliza being permanently in the neighbourhood to entice her younger daughter into scandalous adventures.

Phylly Walter was shocked to hear this latest news. She sent Eliza a stern letter, chiding her for missing the opportunity of such a perfect match. 'Be satisfied my dear Phillida,' Eliza wrote back to her, 'that I am fully sensible of the truth & justice of the observations in your last, but my impulse in favour of liberty, & disfavour of a lord & master is . . . irresistible.'[34] Eliza felt a certain grudging respect for the way James had out-manoeuvred her, and could not resist noting that the woman he had now chosen was 'not either rich or handsome' though 'very sensible' (a damning word, in her vocabulary) and 'good-natured'. More importantly, she added, 'Jane seems much pleased with the match, and it is natural she should be, having long known & liked the lady.' Part of the reason for Jane's satisfaction, she suspected, was the knowledge that her mother regarded Mary as a potential source of comfort in old age. Having such a sensible – if scar-faced – sister-in-law might allow her to escape the burden of domestic duties once Cassandra had left home. But enough of such matrimonial matters; Eliza had more important things on her mind: 'wigs such as mine are all the rage . . .'

James and Mary were married at Hurstbourne Tarrant on 17 January 1797, and James recalled the occasion in some anniversary verses.

> *Cold was the morn, & all around*
> *Whitened with new fallen snow the ground,*
> *Yet still the sun with cheering beam,*
> *Played on the hill, & vale, & stream,*
> *And almost gave to winter's face*
> *Spring's pleasing cheerfulness and grace.*[35]

Having been forced to leave Deane parsonage to make room for James's first wife, it gave Mary considerable satisfaction to return there as his second. In the neighbourhood, people were polite about her in public, but privately expressed severe misgivings. Mrs Chute was dismayed by the marks of the smallpox, 'which has scarred and seamed her face dreadfully'.[36] Even the Austens, who genuinely liked Mary, recognized that this marriage was 'more imprudent . . . than the first, for the very small fortune the lady possessed she insisted should be spent in paying the gentleman's debts, and he had nothing to settle on her to provide for a second family'.[37] It was generally thought at Steventon that the marriage could not have taken place at all had it not been for General Mathew, who continued to contribute £100 per year for the maintenance of his granddaughter Anna. Little Caroline Austen, who was born eight years later, always feared the general as a man 'whose word was undisputed law to his whole family'.[38]

'First Impressions'

None of Jane Austen's private letters survives for the following two years. From the time that she returned home to Steventon in September 1796, till the time she visited Kent in the autumn of 1798, we have only silence. That silence is broken only once: for a single, brief and formal message of condolence sent to Phylly Walter, in the spring of 1798, on the occasion of Phylly's father's death. But there is nothing personal about this letter, whose pious sentiments ('the goodness which made him valuable on earth will make him blessed in heaven') are expressed in solemn Christian formulas from which all hint of individuality has been drained.[39] It fell to Jane to write this letter because Cassandra was away from home at the time. But it is written in the role of family amanuensis, rather than as an expression of personal feelings, and its abstract formal tones merely draw attention to a strange absence of identity.

However, silence itself can be eloquent. Why do we have no letters from this period? It can hardly be because Jane Austen did not write any, since letter-writing had now become one of her favourite diversions. It can only be that Cassandra, to whom most of her letters were addressed, and in whose custody they remained after Jane Austen's death, chose to destroy them. For Cassandra, 1797 was one of the most painful years of her existence, and she preferred to obliterate the memory of a period of such distress.

Throughout the winter months, Cassandra had been adding to her trousseau in preparation for her wedding which, she hoped, would take place that spring. 'Fanny [Cage] enquired very much after you,' Jane reported from Rowling, 'whom she supposed to be making your wedding-clothes.' The whole family at Steventon were eagerly awaiting Tom Fowle's promised return from the West Indies by Easter at the latest. Instead, one day in April, they received a devastating message. On 3 May, Eliza wrote to Phylly: 'I have just received a letter from Steventon where they are all in great affliction (as I suppose you have heard) for the death of Mr Fowle, the gentleman to whom our cousin Cassandra was engaged. He was expected home this month from St Domingo, where he had accompanied Lord Craven, but alas, instead of his arrival, news were received of his death.'[40] Details were sparse, but there was no doubt in the case. Fowle had died of yellow fever, and been buried at sea. 'This is a very severe stroke to the whole family,' Eliza went on, '& particularly to poor Cassandra for whom I feel more than I can express. Indeed I am most sincerely grieved at this event & the pain which it must occasion our worthy relations.'

Cassandra received the news with a kind of numbness. Outwardly, she was strangely calm. 'Jane says that her sister behaves with a degree of resolution & propriety which no common mind could evince in so trying a situation,' said Eliza. Inwardly too, Cassandra allowed herself no obvious relief from the pain she felt. There was to be no ritual of grieving for a body buried several thousand miles away at sea. Lord Craven protested that, had he known of Tom's engagement, he would never have allowed him to travel to so dangerous a climate. But that was little consolation now. On 2 June, Tom Fowle's will was proved. 'Have you heard?' Eliza wrote to Phylly, 'Cassandra's intended has left her a thousand pounds. I was extremely glad to learn it and thought you would be equally so, but as it is perhaps a secret, do not mention it when you write to Steventon.'[41] Such a generous gesture was a further touching proof of the young man's infallibly kind instincts. Invested in government stocks, this money would yield Cassandra an income of some £35 a year; hardly enough to live on, but sufficient to make her slightly less dependent on family charity. Of course, there was no reason why a handsome young woman of twenty-four should not, after a respectable period of mourning, form a second attachment every bit as sincere as the first. Marianne, the younger sister in 'Elinor and Marianne', might disapprove of such second attachments but, as her elder sister observed: 'Her opinions are all romantic . . . A few years however will settle her opinions on the reasonable basis of common sense and observation.' In this case, however, it was Cassandra who seemed determined to play the romantic. Towards the end of the year, Eliza picked up some whisper of a new engagement, and eagerly passed on the gossip to Phylly. 'Mr Hampson . . . told me he had heard Cassandra was going to be married, but Jane says not a word of it.'[42] But the rumour proved to be groundless. Gradually, as the months went by, Cassandra discovered within herself no inclination for new attachments. Instead, she quietly resigned herself to a life of spinsterhood, taking over more of the household duties from her mother, and patiently devoting herself to her role of godmother and maiden aunt to the children of her brothers.

Only Jane was privy to the emotions which led Cassandra to choose withdrawal in this manner, rather than renewal. Between them there developed an intimacy far closer than the usual bond between sisters. 'They seemed to lead a life to themselves within the general family life which was shared only by each other. I will not say their true, but their *full* feelings and opinions were known only to themselves. They alone fully understood what each had suffered and felt and thought.'[43] Upon Jane the influence of this change in her sister's disposition was no less profound for being, at first at least, unacknowledged and unperceived. She did not suddenly relinquish her love of balls or abandon her delight in flirtation. But there was, perhaps, a little more play-acting, a little less earnestness in her endeavour to discover a bold Tom Jones or a chivalrous Prince Fitzwilliam among the local parsons and squires. There was, for her, every difference in the world between finding a husband for herself after Cassandra had been carried away to conjugal duties in Shropshire, and being the one to initiate such a separation. He would need to be an entirely remarkable suitor who could persuade her willingly to remove herself from a closeness with her sister which she had little hopes of matching in a marital union.

However, if Jane allowed herself a certain capriciousness with respect to gentlemen admirers, she was increasingly inclined to take her writing seriously. No sooner had she returned from Rowling than she set about a new full-length novel, which she called 'First Impressions'. The theme of the book was simple enough. An intelligent young woman, with rather too high an opinion of her own wit and perspicacity, develops a settled prejudice against an apparently arrogant young man, based on her first impression of a snub he has directed against her family. At the heart of this book, as of 'Elinor and Marianne', was a study of two sisters in their hesitant progress towards matrimony. This time she called the elder sister Jane, but put more of her own character into the younger sister, Elizabeth. For the family name, she chose Bennet, from the parish register, naming the bookish youngest Bennet daughter Mary, after the promiscuous peasant girl who figured so prominently in the local bastardy records. Serious as she was, she could still not resist such little private jokes and continued to regard her writing first and foremost as a form of family entertainment. She loved reading passages aloud to the family after dinner, playing all the parts, and assuming all the voices. Little Anna Austen, now aged three and a half, listened so attentively and was so taken up by all the family talk about 'Jane & Elizabeth', that it was soon resolved 'for prudence sake' to read no more of the story in her hearing.[44] Childish chatter about how Jane loved Mr Bingley or Jane's sister loved Mr Darcy could easily be misconstrued into gossip, even by those less eager for scandalous tit-bits than Eliza de Feuillide.

By the spring, the story was nearly finished, but then came the news of Tom Fowle's death and Jane was prevented from completing it by her solicitude for her sister's distress. It was not until August that she felt sufficiently satisfied with the story to present it to her father for his amusement. His reaction came as something of a shock. Quite unlike the barbarous fathers whom she so loved to ridicule in all her juvenile sketches, Mr Austen did not demand of her what she meant by idling her time away on such ephemeral nonsense. On the contrary, he pronounced himself so pleased with the story that he thought it should be published. Jane might protest, in an affectation of exalted sensibility, that she wrote 'only for fame, and without any view to pecuniary emolument', but her father took a more worldly view. Mr Austen had a shrewd view of his younger daughter's literary talents, and had invested in them to the extent of allowing her the run of his library as a child, encouraging her to subscribe to the latest works of Miss Burney and Miss Radcliffe, and expending all of 12s on a writing-desk. Now that he had ceased taking pupils, Mr Austen's income had dwindled to rather less than £100 a year, made up from dividends and a small pension from the Hand-in-Hand Society. Any other monies, from the sale of produce from Cheesedown farm, were quite undependable and fluctuated from year to year. He therefore took the view that girls who could not, or would not, find husbands to provide for them, must find ways of providing for themselves. He had read sufficient of the contemporary kind of comical romance to feel confident that Jane was equal to the task. Accordingly, on 1 November, he wrote to the London publisher Thomas Cadell:

I have in my possession a manuscript novel, comprised in three vols about the length of Miss Burney's *Evelina*. As I am well aware of what consequence it is that a work of this sort should make its first appearance under a respectable name, I apply to you. Shall be much obliged therefore if you will inform me whether you chuse to be concerned in it. What will be the expense of publishing at the author's risk; & what will you venture to advance for the property of it, if on a perusal, it is approved of? Should your answer give me encouragement I will send you the work.[45]

At the London offices of Thomas Cadell the letter caused little excitement. It was perhaps Mr Austen's mention of *Evelina,* which he thought such a hopeful hint, that discouraged them. Miss Burney's little book had been published all of nineteen years ago and seemed almost to belong to a different age. Although Miss Burney's (now Madame D'Arblay's) writings continued to have their devoted admirers, the public taste was quite altered: 1797 was the year of Mrs Radcliffe's *The Italian,* following on the triumph of *The Mysteries of Udolpho* three years earlier. Publishers' lists were filled with titles like *Horrid Mysteries* or *The Necromancer of the Black Forest.* There was little enthusiasm for a slight, ironic tale with such an unassuming title as 'First Impressions' from a clergyman's daughter in Hampshire. Across the top of Mr Austen's letter someone in the office scrawled 'declined by return of post'.

To Jane, it seemed oddly appropriate that the first impression of 'First Impressions' should be so misguided. Was that not, after all, what the novel was about? There were, of course, other publishers, but for the present she was content to continue writing for her own and for the family's amusement. It was her father who was keen, in his prudent way, to turn her private diversion into a source of income. But, whilst she felt no dislike of the idea of publication, she was more intent upon satisfying her own sense of literary form than in striving to meet the popular taste. For the present, 'First Impressions' was put to one side and she embarked upon rewriting 'Elinor and Marianne', for which she had now determined on a more abstract, even philosophical, title. Her mother had lately subscribed to a new journal, the *Lady's Monthly Museum,* filled with little moralizing essays, in one of which she encountered the bold headline 'Sense and Sensibility'. Henceforth, she decided, that was what her novel would be called.

Jane's work on this revision was not very far advanced when her uncle, Mr Leigh-Perrot, arrived at Steventon to conduct the whole Austen family to Bath. Mrs Austen's health had recently been causing her some distress, and she believed her constitution might benefit from a regimen of taking the waters. The Leigh-Perrots had lodgings in Paragon Buildings, where the Austens arrived one gloomy November afternoon and remained for about

a month. Jane Austen was not greatly impressed by Bath. It rained
a lot and the streets were wet and dirty. But at least she was pleased
to tell Eliza that her mother's health had greatly improved. Mr
Leigh-Perrot had an excellent library, and when they left he gave
her, for her birthday, Hume's *History of England*, in belated hopes,
it seemed, of making her less 'partial, prejudiced and ignorant' in
her historical opinions.[46]

Meanwhile, Eliza had resumed her flirtation with Henry, but
was coyly evasive on this subject when questioned about it by
Phylly. Captain Austen had recently spent a few days in town, she
acknowledged in May, though she seemed more interested in the
details of Miss Farren's forthcoming union with Lord Derby ('her
wedding night-cap is the same as the Princess Royal's & costs
eighty guineas') than in discussing her own matrimonial prospects.
Now loaded with the dignities of captain, paymaster and adjutant,
Henry Austen was indeed 'a very lucky young man,' she conceded;
'& bids fair to possess a considerable share of riches & honours'.
She was particularly pleased that he had 'given up all thoughts of
the Church'. 'He certainly is not so fit for a parson as a soldier,'
she told Phylly.[47] The following month she dined with Mr Austen,
who looked as young and well as he had done ten years before,
and discussed with him the technical arrangements for dissolving
the trust which Warren Hastings had set up for her all those years
before. Now that her father, mother and husband were all dead,
it seemed high time, she thought (and Mr Austen agreed), for the
sum that remained to be made over entirely to her.[48] There was
no explicit mention of Henry, who was away in Norwich at the
time, but young Charles Austen also dined with them ('really a
fine youth,' she told Phylly), to remind her of the eligibility of all
the Austen males. But when Phylly asked her a direct question,
the Countess resorted to her most delphic manner. 'As to your
enquiry concerning another youth I have to say that I believe his
match with a certain friend of ours, which I know you looked upon
as fixed, will never take place. For my own part, I think this
young man ill-used but the lady is so well-pleased with her present
situation that she cannot find it in her heart to change it.'[49] Indeed,
she added, she was 'more & more convinced' that 'the lady' in

question (meaning herself) 'is not at all calculated for sober matrimony'.

Even when she visited Lowestoft in September, Eliza insisted it was entirely on her son Hastings's account ('Sir Walter Farquhar has declared that sea-bathing & sea air are more likely to be of service to him than anything else') and had nothing to do with Henry's presence in the area. Phylly was unconvinced by this subterfuge and Eliza protested vainly against her friend's suspicions. 'You are . . . mistaken in the motives which you have so cunningly found out for my visiting . . . *now*,' she wrote. 'Indeed, had you known that Lowestoft is no less than 28 miles from Norwich, you would probably have dismissed all your *wicked* surmises, for you must allow that a person who cannot absent himself from his corps for more than a few hours at a time, cannot very conveniently travel 56 miles to pay a visit.'[50] Rather than acknowledging any special preference for Henry Austen, Eliza insisted on presenting herself still as a carefree flirt. She and her latest friend, Miss Payne, were having great fun with the 'pretty plentiful crop' of local beaux, she wrote. 'Miss P & myself gather hearts by dozens . . . I have made one conquest, who has between thirty & forty thousand pr annum, but unfortunately he has also a wife . . .'

Now aged thirty-six, however, even Eliza was forced to recognize an element of fantasy in her pose as a bewitching spa-town Cleopatra. Before travelling to Lowestoft she had spent some time at Daylesford, the country home of her (god)father, Warren Hastings. The place filled her with a sense of longing for a tranquillity and status that had always eluded her. It was truly one of the most beautiful places she had ever seen. The park and grounds were 'a little paradise' and the house itself 'fitted up with a degree of taste & magnificence seldom to be met with'. In the parlour hung a vast painting of Mrs Hastings's heroic voyage down the stormy Ganges to nurse her sick husband.[51] How Eliza longed to have been able to call this place home! But instead, all she had was the tiny, dwindling residue of the trust fund that her unacknowledged father had set up for her as a child. When she returned home to London, the sense of her impoverishment, emotional and financial, struck her with full force. Despite the benefits of his sea-bathing, her son's health remained precarious. In December, he suffered one of his worst fits for many years, and for some days Eliza feared that she would lose him. Then there were the bills. Her landlord was talking of increasing her rent by £32 a year to pay for the new window tax; her manservant wanted an extra four guineas. There were the costs of her carriage, her food, her clothes. 'These new taxes will drive me out of London,' she wrote to Phylly, '& make me give up my carriage.'[52] Amid all the gloom there was one kindly light, and his name was Henry Austen. Henry had always loved her, she knew; he was lively; he was young; he was an officer (if only in the militia); he was an Austen; he seemed to be lucky; and above all, he had been very *patient*.

At last, that Christmas, Eliza consented to become Henry's wife, though not without a list of provisos and conditions which might have daunted a less amiable man. To Mr Hastings, Eliza described the motives, including Henry's 'possession of a comfortable income', which had at last 'induced me to an acquiescence which I have withheld for more than two years'. To Phylly, she was more explicit. She had insisted on 'having my own way in everything,' she boasted. 'Henry well knows that I have not been much accustomed to control & should probably behave rather awkwardly under it; and therefore, like a wise man, he has no will but mine, which to be sure some people would call spoiling me, but I know it is the best way of managing me . . .'[53] The ceremony took place promptly on the last day of the year, not at Steventon, but at Marylebone parish church in London, a place well known for hasty weddings. None of the family attended, and within days Henry had rejoined his regiment at Ipswich, accompanied by his new wife.

Apart from having the convenience of someone else to pay her bills, Eliza acknowledged no other change to her chosen manner of life from her new marital status. She still rattled on to Phylly about all her gentlemen admirers, like the colonel of the regiment, Lord Charles Spencer. 'If I was married to my third husband instead of my second, I should still be in love with him,' she wrote. 'He is a most charming creature, so mild, so well bred, so good, but alas! he is married as well as myself.' In fact, she was delighted to find the militia camp full of handsome young officers. 'The inhabitants of this place are much more fashionable people than I had expected,' she wrote. Captain Tilson was 'remarkably handsome', and Messrs Perrott and Edwardes 'may be chatted with very satisfactorily', though of course, she hastened to reassure Phylly, 'I have . . . *entirely* left off *trade*'.[54] But it was gratifying the way all the handsome officers made a point of calling her *Comtesse*, and of granting her the precedence that such a title implied. Henry, too, was conscientious about deferring to her in matters of title, and the two of them continued to address each other as 'cousin' in preference to any more intimate term. 'I have an aversion to the word *husband*,' she confessed, '& never make use of it.'[55]

At Steventon, there were mixed feelings about the marriage. After so many years of on–off flirtation it could hardly be called a surprise; but the suddenness of the wedding itself carried with it some unwelcome sense of impetuosity. And there was always the fact that Eliza was so much *older* than Henry – a full ten years – and so much more experienced than him in the ways of the world. Mrs Austen promptly suffered a return of her old complaint, undoing the improvement that had been achieved at Bath. Throughout the neighbourhood there had always been some merriment at the way their London cousin Eliza liked to insist on her aristocratic title. And it happened that, shortly after the marriage, Mr Austen purchased a carriage which had, painted on its panels, the family crest of a stag on a crown mural. 'Mr Austen has put a coronet on his carriage,' remarked one of the local squires, 'because of his son's being married to a French countess.'[56]

Jane herself was neither surprised nor disappointed by the match. Though she hoped, for Henry's sake, that Eliza would now restrain her flirtatious instincts within the bounds of what was proper for the wife of an officer and an Austen, she had no very great misgivings on that account. It was remarkable, in her experience, how frequently those deemed too bold or rakish to accommodate themselves to the dull domestic joys of matrimony, confuted their detractors by making excellent wives; while those who seemed destined for no other blessedness than that of wife and mother, proved sadly disappointing. Mary Lloyd was a case in point. How they had all rejoiced – Mrs Austen in particular – when she became James's second wife. But now, how different it all seemed. Poor Mary never could forgive James for marrying Anne *first*; and, worse still, for proposing to Eliza. She had made herself quite a scold, forever passing ill-natured comments about Eliza, and chiding James for the time he spent away from her at Steventon. But it was the way she treated little Anna that most distressed the family at the rectory. Mary did not love her step-daughter, and seemed to take a pride in slighting her, treating her harshly, and often bringing tears to the little girl's eyes.[57] It became a habit with Jane and Cassandra to take the little girl for walks, even in the wintry weather, through the sloppy lane from Steventon to Deane. Anna always remembered their bonnets, 'precisely alike in colour, shape & material', and how she used to guess at which belonged to which. And she remembered too how Mr Austen used to call after them, 'Where are the girls?', 'Are the girls gone out?'[58] That was very odd, she thought, for her aunts were not girls at all, but women, quite as old as her stepmother. It was their kindness, and their playfulness, she thought, that made them seem like girls.

Before long, Jane found herself receiving the attentions of another self-styled suitor. For this she had to thank Madam Lefroy at Ashe. Though she would never admit to it in so many words, Anne Lefroy felt qualms of conscience at the way she had so abruptly terminated the friendship between Jane Austen and her nephew Tom. As a kind of reparation, she felt it was her duty to provide Jane with a more suitable replacement, and at Christmas she invited the Reverend Samuel Blackall, a tall and erudite fellow of Emmanuel College, Cambridge, to stay with her at Ashe. Soon the Reverend Blackall was paying his visits to the rectory at Steventon, where he was entertained by Jane playing the pianoforte pieces she had practised for her music-master Mr Chard. He, in turn, sought to impress the Austen ladies with lengthy homilies on college fellowships and college livings, and on all kinds of virtue, from the virtue of Christian piety to the virtues of green tea and cold veal pies.

The Reverend Blackall was not a disagreeable young man,

though somewhat humourless and self-satisfied for a lover. He put Jane in mind of a character she had created in one of her earliest fictions. *That* self-assured young man, not content with describing himself as 'a perfect beauty', had gone on: 'Partiality aside, I am certainly more accomplished in every language, every science, every art and every thing than any other person in Europe.' The Reverend Blackall struck her, similarly, as 'a piece of perfection, *noisy* perfection'.[59] Blackall's Christmas visit was quite brief but Madam Lefroy, in her role as match-maker, urged him to return for Christmas the following year. 'It would give me particular pleasure,' he replied, 'to have an opportunity of improving my acquaintance with that family [the Austens] – with a hope of creating to myself a nearer interest. But at present I cannot indulge any expectation of it.' Jane was amused by such a tactful reply. 'This is rational enough,' she remarked to Cassandra; 'there is less love and more sense in it than sometimes appeared before, and I am very well satisfied. It will all go on exceedingly well, and decline away in a very reasonable manner.'[60] For Jane, who had no intention of allowing Madam Lefroy to determine whom she might or might not marry, part of the appeal of the noisily perfect Mr Blackall was the opportunity he afforded for private sisterly jokes. 'There seems no likelihood of his coming into Hampshire this Christmas,' she reported to Cassandra at Godmersham; 'and it is therefore most probable that our indifference will soon be mutual, unless his regard, which appeared to spring from knowing nothing of me at first, is best supported by never seeing me. Mrs Lefroy,' she added, 'made no remarks on the letter, nor did she indeed say anything about him as relative to me. Perhaps she thinks she has said too much already.'

Late in the summer, Jane herself paid a visit to Godmersham in company with her parents and Cassandra. Soon after Mr Knight's death, old Mrs Knight had decided it would be better for Edward and his young family to take possession of the place immediately, rather than wait for her to die and then inherit. This, it was generally agreed, was a very gracious gesture, though Edward was at first a little nervous of taking his adoptive mother at her word. He wrote to her to declare that he 'should never be happy' at

Godmersham whilst she was living in a 'smaller and less comfortable house'. How often he had heard her say that her 'whole happiness' was centred on that dear place, and he could never endure to think that she should retire from her 'favourite mansion' merely 'to enrich us'.[61] Such a modest demurral was nicely calculated to soften further the heart of a woman already well disposed towards him, and Mrs Knight wrote back to Edward in her most affectionate vein.

> From the time that my partiality for you induced Mr Knight to treat you as our adopted child I have felt for you the tenderness of a mother, and never have you appeared more deserving of affection than at this time; to reward your merit, therefore, and place you in a situation where your many excellent qualities will be call'd forth and render'd useful to the neighbourhood, is the fondest wish of my heart. Many circumstances attached to large landed possessions, highly gratifying to a man, are entirely lost on me at present; but when I see you in the enjoyment of them, I shall, if possible, feel my gratitude to my beloved husband redoubled, for having placed in my hands the power of bestowing happiness on one so very dear to me.[62]

Accordingly, Mrs Knight retired to White Friars, a house in Canterbury, while Edward and his family quitted Rowling to take up residence at Godmersham. When the Austens came to visit him in late August 1798, he showed them round his new palatial home with all the pride of a great landowner. Here were the new east and west wings that Mr Thomas Knight had built not long before his death in 1781. Here was the excellent library, and please to observe, from the upper storey, the delightful prospect of the hill, with its fine summerhouse in the form of a Doric temple, and the pleasure-grounds where the children loved to play. Edward conducted them along the Temple Walk, where stood another summerhouse in the style of a Gothic hermitage, down to the River Walk, a narrow pathway sheltered by lime trees, that led to the little Norman church of St Lawrence. He pointed out the

splendidly decorated plaster-work, the fine carvings and the magnificent marble chimney-pieces. Everything, they agreed, was quite
as delightful as one might hope to find in the grandest house in
the land.[63]

To Jane, Godmersham was like a dream of elegant living, and
whilst her mother might take a private pleasure in finding fault
with this or that detail of Mrs Edward Knight's domestic economy,
Jane found nothing that did not fill her with a kind of wistful
longing. What books one might aspire to write in such a handsome
library as this one, with its view over the beautiful parkland! As
Elizabeth, her heroine in 'First Impressions', expressed it, on catching her first sight of Mr Darcy's mansion, Pemberley: 'She had
never seen a place for which nature had done more, or where
natural beauty had been so little counteracted by an awkward
taste.'[64] Nor could Jane quite suppress the thought that sprang
unprompted to her heroine's mind 'that to be mistress of Pemberley [or Godmersham] might be something!' But there, alas, was
the difference between novels and real life. As an author, she
had the power to make Elizabeth mistress of Pemberley. But as a
younger, impoverished sister, there was nothing she could do to
make her stay at Godmersham anything but a brief interlude. Once
again she was compelled to acknowledge that mighty part that
money must always play in the establishment of human happiness.
Here was a style of living to which her father, for all his kindliness
of temper, might never aspire. Even their little vanity, the private
carriage with its coat of arms, had had to be given up. They would
return to Steventon, as they had arrived, by the public coach, with
her mother complaining, all the journey, about the uncomfortable
swaying and jolting.

During those long sunny days at Godmersham, Jane loved to
play with her favourite nephew, little George (or 'itty Dordy' as
he pronounced it), making up little songs for the boy to sing to
her. At other times she would sit in the library, reading, or finishing
her revisions of the book she now called *Sense and Sensibility*.
Already she had the idea for a new novel, to be called 'Susan',
inspired by her recent visit to Bath; but as yet the shape of the
work was unclear. It would concern a lively girl who had read too

many Gothic romances. Henry would no doubt find it amusing, if he were not too engrossed by conjugal duties, and the serious business of defending the coastline from foreign invaders, to find time for comic fiction. In the evenings there were balls at Ashford, which might have been amusing had it not been for the over-crowded rooms and hot weather. Edward's wife did not attend, of course, as she was expecting their fifth child. By the time the baby was born (a boy, William, on 10 October), the Austens were already planning their return to Steventon, but Edward invited Cassandra to stay longer. She might help to nurse Elizabeth, he suggested, and assist in running the household until she recovered from the birth. Eventually it was agreed. Daniel, Edward's own coachman, carried the Austens as far as Sittingbourne, from where they travelled on, by stages, first to Rochester and thence to the Bull and George Inn at Dartford, where they all sat down, a little after five, to a dinner of beef-steak and boiled fowl, but, as Jane noted, 'no oyster sauce'.[65] On the whole, Mrs Austen bore the journey tolerably well, complaining only of a slight fatigue. After dinner, Jane intended writing to Cassandra, as she always did when they were separated, for however short a period. But she discovered, to her horror, that her writing-box, containing 'all my worldly wealth' – the magnificent sum of £7 – had been packed off into a Gravesend coach, and was already, no doubt, *en route* to the West Indies. A horseman was immediately sent off to the rescue, and returned within the hour, with the box safely in his hands. 'I [have] the pleasure of being as rich as ever,' she observed wryly to Cassandra. The evening ended with Mrs Austen nodding off by the fireside, Jane writing her letter, and Mr Austen reading a copy of Francis Lathom's new Gothic shocker, *The Midnight Bell*, one of the novels which Jane intended as a favourite with her latest heroine, Susan.

By the time they reached home, Mrs Austen's health had deteri-orated. There had been signs of distress and a sore throat at Staines and by Basingstoke she was vomiting bile. Fortunately, Lyford was on hand to see to her there, and he prescribed twelve drops of laud-anum in a soothing dandelion tea. He called on her again at Steventon, by which time Mrs Austen had taken to her bed, and would take no further part in household duties than to discuss with Lyford some slight alteration to the dandelion tea regimen which might be better adapted to her constitution. Jane was in hopes that her mother's health might recover in 'a few days', but Mrs Austen had evidently determined on being a proper invalid.

In Cassandra's absence, Jane found herself entrusted with the household keys, and with responsibilities for giving orders in the kitchen. 'Our dinner was very good yesterday, & the chicken boiled perfectly tender; therefore I shall not be obliged to dismiss Nanny on that account,' she reported to Cassandra after her first day of household management.[66] For a few days it was quite fun to be in charge of all the menus and to spend one's time deciding between ragout veal or haricot mutton. 'I am very fond of experimental housekeeping,' she told Cassandra in November, 'such as having an ox-cheek now and then; I shall have one next week, and I mean to have some little dumplings put into it, that I may fancy myself at Godmersham.' Up in her sick-room, Mrs Austen seemed as highly delighted by this new arrangement as was consistent with preserving the melancholy demeanour of an invalid. 'My mother desires me to tell you that I am a very good housekeeper,' Jane wrote, adding, with some irony, 'which I have no reluctance in doing, because I really think it my peculiar excellence.'[67] Mrs Austen's cousin, Mrs Cooke of Great Bookham, was about to publish an historical romance called *Battleridge*. Egerton Brydges, who used to live at Deane, had brought out a scandalous novel called *Fitz-Albini*, which Mr Austen found disappointing, though Jane did not because she expected nothing better. But for Jane herself there was now no time for writing. Her own 'peculiar excellence', it seemed, was not to be in the novel-writing line at all; it was to be in ordering pease-soup, spare-rib and pudding. 'I always take care to provide such things as please my own appetite, which I consider as the chief merit in housekeeping,' she told Cassandra, affecting to take as much pleasure in composing menus as she found in composing plots.

For five weeks Mrs Austen kept to her room, and Jane had 'the dignity' of measuring out her nightly drops of laudanum. How strange it was to be dining alone with her father, in her mother's place! The two of them would sit together and talk of books: Boswell's *Tour to the Hebrides*, his *Life of Johnson* and Cowper's poetry. Suddenly, Jane found that all the servants came to her to supervise their duties. Mrs Steevens would take over from Mrs Bushell in seeing to their laundry; Mrs Staples would do very well as a maid, but Jane was less sure about the young girl from Ashe they had lately hired as a scrub. Outside, the village lanes were dirty with the persistent rain. She envied Cassandra the elegance of Godmersham with its spacious rooms and handsome park. The closest that she could come to such a style of gracious living was in ordering little dumplings to accompany their ox-cheek dinner, quite in the Godmersham manner. How eagerly she waited for Cassandra's letters from Godmersham, telling her that 'itty Dordy' still thought fondly of her. 'I shall think with tenderness & delight on his beautiful and smiling countenance,' she replied. Cassandra's letters were not only witty, but neat, and Jane quite despaired of matching their sophisticated style. 'I am quite angry with myself,' she confessed; 'why is my alphabet so much more sprawly than yours?'

She did her best to entertain her sister with all the local gossip, and it mortified her severely when Cassandra was slow to reply. In one letter she announced the birth of James's new son, James Edward. But instead of replying, Cassandra wrote directly to James to congratulate him. Jane was furious. 'I shall not take the trouble of announcing to you any more of Mary's children,' she wrote, 'if, instead of thanking me for the intelligence, you always sit down and write to James. I am sure nobody can desire your letters as I do, and I don't think anybody deserves them so well.'[68] After this little outburst of what she called 'malevolence', Jane attempted to resume her customary humdrum tone in reporting all the local gossip. But malevolent was how she felt, and she could not, or would not, disguise it. 'Mrs Hall of Sherbourn was brought to bed yesterday of a dead child, some weeks before she expected,' she wrote, 'owing to a fright – I suppose she happened unawares to look at her husband.' Two other ladies, Mrs Coulthard and Anne 'late of Manydown', were said to have died in childbed. 'We have not regaled Mary with this news,' she wryly remarked.[69] Mary herself was still 'in raptures' over her baby son, but Jane disliked all the effusive display of maternal bliss. Something about it struck her as rather vulgar. 'Mary does not manage things in such a way as to make me want to lay in myself. She is not tidy enough in her appearance; she has no dressing-gown to sit up in; her curtains are all too thin, and things are not in that comfort and style about her which are necessary to make such a situation an enviable one.'[70] It was all so very different from the style and elegance of Elizabeth's lying-in at Godmersham. 'Elizabeth was really a pretty object with her nice clean cap put on so tidily and her dress so uniformly white and orderly.' At Godmersham, Jane was quite prepared to make all the appropriate noises of admiration in respect of both mother and baby. But really, she could not find it in herself to assume quite the same nonsensical attitude of flattery towards Mary Lloyd at Deane. Women with husbands and babies had a habit of assuming such a smug, condescending way towards their spinster cousins. It suited Jane's gloomy mood to disclaim all desire to undergo such an inelegant experience herself, rather than acknowledge that, as a younger daughter with a worldly wealth of precisely £7, she was scarcely likely to be given that opportunity.

As she busied herself about her household tasks that wet November, Jane had an unmistakable sense of narrowing horizons. The days of admiring young gentlemen and grand country balls seemed to be over. Even had there been balls to go to, without a carriage she must be reduced once more to soliciting the kindness of neighbours to attend them. 'Our assemblies have very kindly declined ever since we laid down the carriage,' she noted, 'so that dis-convenience and dis-inclination to go have kept pace together.' Charles Powlett insisted on giving a dance at the end of the month, for which he was much ridiculed by his neighbours, 'who, you know, take a most lively interest in the state of his finances, and live in hopes of his being soon ruined'.[71] That apart, Mrs Leigh-Perrot had kindly invited the Austens to join her again in Bath, a prospect which Jane found less than inspiring. It was a kindness, she suggested, 'that deserves a better return than to profit by it'.[72]

On the last day of the month, Mrs Austen finally rose from her sick-bed. 'My mother made her *entree* into the dressing-room through crowds of admiring spectators yesterday afternoon,' Jane wrote with some sarcasm, 'and we all drank tea together for the first time these five weeks.' She found something faintly irritating, and even a little absurd, about her mother's affectation of such a regal manner. 'She . . . bids fair for a continuance in the same brilliant course of action today.'[73] With Mary posing as the Madonna with her child at Deane, and her mother acting like a tragic heroine at home, Jane felt increasingly irritable. Almost her only pleasure was in reading Cassandra's wonderful letters. 'You must read your letters over *five* times before you send them,' she told her, '& then perhaps you may find them as entertaining as I do.' They made her laugh out loud and she treasured up her sister's jokes for retelling to all her acquaintance. She longed to hear every detail about life at Godmersham. 'How do you spend your evenings? I guess that Eliz:th works, that you read to her, & that Edward goes to sleep.' It was all so different from Steventon, where Mr Lyford's praise of a mutton dinner was the high point of the week. 'People get so horridly poor & economical in this part of the world,' she protested, 'that I have no patience with them. Kent is the only place for happiness. Everybody is rich there.'[74] It irked her to be reduced to haggling over sheets of drawing-paper. 'I have been forced to let James & Miss Debarry have two sheets . . . but they shan't have any more. There are not above 3 or 4 left, besides one of a smaller & richer sort.' She felt ashamed of their homely routines ('we dine now at half after three, & have done dinner I suppose before you begin . . . I am afraid you will despise us'); and she despaired of her humdrum companions: 'we are to have company to dinner on Friday; the three Digweeds & James. We shall be a nice silent party, I suppose.' By contrast, everything about Godmersham fascinated her – even the pigs. 'Lord Bolton is particularly curious in *his* pigs,' she remarked; 'has had pigstyes of a most elegant construction built for them, and visits them every morning as soon as he rises.'[75] In Hampshire, it seemed, the pigs maintained a more aristocratic and elegant style of life than the people. Yet she promised not to pester Cassandra with impatient demands for more letters. 'I have made it a rule not to expect them till they come, in which I think I consult the ease of us both.'

Mrs Martin from Basingstoke wrote, inviting Jane to subscribe to a new library. '[She] tells us that her collection is not to consist only of novels, but of every kind of literature &c &c. She might have spared this pretension to *our* family, who are great novel-readers & not ashamed of being so; but it was necessary I suppose to the self-consequence of half her subscribers.'[76] Yet even in this simple matter, Jane could not act independently. The subscription was taken out in Cassandra's name, not hers, and it was her mother who put up the money. For her birthday that December, Jane had £10 from Mrs Knight, but that was sensibly put aside for winter clothes, not books. She found it wearisome to take many pains about her appearance when there was no one to see her, and made simple mob-caps to wear in the evenings over her plaited hair, to save herself 'a world of torment as to hair-dressing'.

When she could not be reading Cassandra's letters, Jane's greatest pleasure was to be entirely alone. One day in mid-December, when the air was still and frozen, and the country lanes icy with a hard black frost, she walked to Deane all by herself. It was a delicious sensation of freedom. 'I do not know that I ever did such a thing in my life before.'[77] Quite suddenly, she found her mood began to change. The remedy for her own low spirits, she decided, must be in her own hands. It would not do to wait for someone else to rescue her from depression. 'I do not think it worth while to wait for enjoyment until there is some real opportunity for it,' she wrote to Cassandra. She would find enjoyment where she could. Returning home, she fished out an old black velvet bonnet of Cassandra's, which she had always previously found 'too *nidgetty*' to please her. Now she set about adorning it with coquelicot feathers ('all the fashion this winter') and a narrow silver band. There was to be a Christmas ball at Manydown. No doubt it would be 'a very stupid ball' and there would be 'nobody worth dancing with', but *she* at least was determined to enjoy it. In her newly adorned bonnet, she fancied that she looked a little like Lady Conyngham, who was reckoned to have such influence over the Prince of Wales, 'which is all that one lives for now,' she remarked in a worldly tone to Cassandra.[78] If a comment like that made her sound a little like cousin Eliza, that too was part of the fun.

CHAPTER 6

I Say Nothing

I say nothing, & am ready to agree with anybody.

Jane Austen, Letter to Cassandra, November 1800

'I do not want people to be very agreable'

Actually, the Manydown ball was rather fun. Very thin (only thirty-one people, but of those, only eleven were ladies, and of *those* only five were *single* ladies), so it was really not at all unpleasant. Jane danced every one of the twenty dances, without any fatigue at all. She danced with Mr Wood and Mr Rice, with Mr Lefroy and Mr Butcher, with Mr Orde, Mr Temple (not the horrid one) and Mr Harwood. But, best of all, she danced with Mr Calland, who protested that he wouldn't dance with any one at all, but she soon teased him out of that. Indeed, Mr Calland was altogether the genius and flirt of the evening. 'I fancy I could just as well dance for a week together as for half an hour,' she told Cassandra, greatly pleased by the whole event. 'My black cap was openly admired by Mrs Lefroy, & secretly I imagine by everybody else in the room.'[1] All her mischievous wit returned in a sudden revival of good spirits, and she was satirical without ill humour. Among the ladies at the dance, Miss Blatchford, she observed, was agreeable enough. 'I do not want people to be very agreable, as it saves me the trouble of liking them a great deal.' As to the Miss Blackstones, she *did* dislike them, but 'I was always determined not to like them, so there is the less merit in it.' Yet, for all the pleasure she took in the Manydown ball, it was nothing compared with the grand ball at Ashford that Cassandra had attended. *She* had danced and supped with a prince! Imagine, the joy of it, to sup with Prince William-Frederick and all the grandest people of Kent. Mr John Calland would hardly appear such a genius among that exalted company. But the really important news that Christmas season concerned their sailor brothers, Frank and Charles.

Frank was now at Cadiz, from where he continued to petition the East India directors about reimbursing his expenses from Asia, while pressing their Lordships of the Admiralty for promotion to a superior command. Charles, too, was in hopes of promotion; he was tired of being kept on the tiny sixteen-gun *Scorpion*, and hankered after a frigate. Mr Austen lobbied energetically on his sons' behalf, contacting Admiral Gambier, a relative of General Mathew. On Christmas Eve, he received a very welcome reply. 'With regard to your son,' the Admiral assured him, 'his promotion is likely to take place very soon.'[2] Sure enough, four days later, Jane was able to write to Cassandra: 'Frank is made. He was yesterday raised to the rank of Commander, & appointed to the Petterel Sloop, now at Gibraltar.'[3] In addition, not only had India House 'taken Captn Austen's petition into consideration', but it was also officially announced that Lieutenant Charles Austen was promoted to a frigate, HMS *Tamer*. 'We cannot find out where the *Tamer* is,' Jane admitted, but they had ever hope of seeing him soon. She even procured Charles an invitation to Lady Dorchester's New Year ball at Kempshott, 'though I have not been so considerate as to get him a *partner*'.

Set beside such grand successes as these, her own ballroom triumphs seemed pretty inconsequential. 'I am sure I can neither write nor do anything which will not appear insipid to you after this.' Yet she was determined to make a success of every opportunity. For the Kempshott ball she would wear a new Egyptian mamalouc cap ('it is all the fashion now, worn at the opera, & by Lady Mildmays at Hackwood balls'), and a new short-sleeved gown. Dressed in this exotic costume, she might think of herself once more in the role of a romantic heroine. It vexed her when Cassandra displayed scant concern for her truly heroic adventures. 'You express so little anxiety about my being murdered under Ashe Park copse by Mrs Hulbert's servant,' she wrote in mock-Gothic indignation, 'that I have a great mind not to tell you whether I was or not.'[4] The ball itself was generally reckoned a success, chiefly, she thought, on account of the smallness of the room. 'There were more dancers than the room could conveniently hold, which is enough to constitute a good ball at any time.' Success of all kinds was relative, and, despite the mamalouc cap, she found herself 'not very much in request' by partners. 'People were rather apt not to ask me till they could not help it,' she frankly admitted. 'One's consequence you know varies so much at times without any particular reason.' So, instead of dancing, she found amusement in observing her fellow guests. 'There was one gentleman, an officer of the Cheshire, a very good looking young man, who I was told wanted very much to be introduced to me. But as he did not want it quite enough to take much trouble in effecting it, we never could bring it about.'[5] Her greatest disappointment though was the absence of her younger brother. 'Charles never came! Naughty Charles.'

Jane spent most of the evening with the Manydown party, who had constituted themselves into quite a little set. There was Catherine Bigg and her stuttering brother Harris Bigg-Wither (it was confusing how the men added 'Wither' to their surnames, while the ladies did not); also Catherine's sisters, Alethea and Elizabeth, and their cousins, Anne and Winifred. During Cassandra's absence, this group had grown very close and Jane would sometimes stay overnight at Manydown after one of their agreeable dinner-parties. She also spent two pleasant nights with Martha Lloyd at Ashe Park, sharing a bed with her in the old nursery. The two of them lay awake, talking and laughing till two in the morning before drifting off to sleep. 'I love Martha better than ever,' she told Cassandra. She was even tempted to think better of Martha's sister Mary, now that she was becoming 'rather more reasonable' about her new baby's charms, '& says that she does not think him really handsome'.[6]

While enjoying the hospitality of Ashe Park, Manydown or the Harwoods' home at Deane House, she felt less envious for Godmersham and was even tempted to hint at faults in Edward's Kentish arcadia. When she heard that Edward was unwell, she could not entirely resist a hint of mockery. 'Poor Edward! It is very hard that he who has everything else in the world that he can wish for, should not have good health too.' She hoped that 'with the assistance of bowel complaints' her brother would 'soon be restored to that blessing likewise', speculating that his 'nervous complaint' might proceed from 'a suppression of something that ought to be thrown out'.[7] Privately, it occurred to her to wonder whether the easeful evacuation that her brother required might not be financial. 'I am tolerably glad to hear that Edward's income is so good a one,' she wrote to Cassandra in another letter; 'as glad as I can at anybody's being rich besides you & me.' From what she heard, Edward's retentiveness was further proof of his loyal adherence to Knight family values. 'Mrs Knight's giving up the Godmersham estate to Edward was no such prodigious act of generosity after all, it seems,' she remarked to Cassandra. 'For she has reserved herself an income out of it still; this ought to be known, that her conduct may not be over-rated.' Nevertheless, she was still rather taken with the notion of travelling down to Kent with Charles when he went to join his new ship at Deal, and surprising them all with an impromptu visit. But she rather feared Edward might not approve of Charles's modish style of wearing his hair unpowdered and cut in a crop, even though short hair was all the fashion now, following the severe new tax on hair powder. Almost the only ones exempt from the new tax were clergymen whose income amounted to less than £100 *per annum*. It was amusing to think that reverend gentlemen like their father would be the only bewigged dandies left. She sent love to 'itty Dordy' and commended him for his new skill in face-making.

Much as she enjoyed visiting, Jane was always sensitive to any hint of condescension on the part of those whose houses she stayed in. An invitation to stay with their Cooke cousins at Bookham was received with dismay. 'I assure you that I dread the idea of going to Bookham as much as you can do,' she told Cassandra; 'but I am not without hopes that something may happen to prevent it.'[8] The Cookes talked of going on to Bath in the spring; 'perhaps they may be overturned in their way down,' Jane fantasized, '& all laid up for the summer.' The fact that Mrs Cooke was always going on about her great friend and neighbour Madame D'Arblay, and boasting about how she would soon be publishing a novel herself, did nothing to endear her to an aspiring literary rival. Yet the sad truth was that, for the present, Jane found herself in considerably better spirits at Manydown or Ashe Park than she did at home, where her mother continued to vex her with her constant affectations of illness. 'I [have] been somewhat silent as to my mother's health,' she admitted to Cassandra at the end of January; 'but I thought you could have no difficulty in divining its exact state – you, who have guessed so much stranger things.'[9] As far as Jane was concerned, her mother was 'tolerably well', though naturally, Mrs Austen would never admit it. 'She would tell you herself that she has a dreadful cold in her head at present.' Some people's illnesses provided a valuable topic of general discussion. When poor Mr Wither suffered a seizure which prevented his family from attending a ball, 'it was a fine thing for conversation at the ball'. Jane Austen regarded her own indispositions, like the eye-strain she suffered at the start of the year, as merely a 'sad bore' for preventing her reading and writing as she wished. Only her mother had the talent for turning a mild head cold into a major domestic drama. 'I have not much compassion for colds in the head, without fever or sore throat,' she observed tersely.

At last, in early March, Cassandra came back from Godmersham and it was Jane's turn to be the one gadding from home, while her sister took up domestic duties. It was Jane, not Cassandra, who dined with the Chutes at the Vyne in April; and when Edward decided that his illness was serious enough to warrant a remedial visit to Bath, it was Jane who accompanied him, together with her parents and Edward's whole family, while Cassandra remained at

Steventon. They arrived at Bath on a wet Friday afternoon in the middle of May, and at first the place looked just as gloomy as it had done last November twelvemonth, with all the umbrellas up, and the pavements black and dirty. But Jane cheered up immensely when she saw the house in Queen Square that Edward had rented for them. She rushed to tell Cassandra all about it. 'We are exceedingly pleased with the house; the rooms are quite as large as we expected, Mrs Bromley is a fat woman in mourning, & a little black kitten runs about the staircase . . . I like our situation very much – it is far more cheerful than Paragon.'[10]

As usual, her mother made a fuss about who should have which room, but Jane was highly delighted with her bedroom, with its 'very nice chest of drawers & a closet full of shelves'. The view from the drawing-room where she sat writing her letter was particularly picturesque, commanding 'a perspective view of the left side of Brock Street, broken by three lombardy poplars in the garden of the last house in Queen's Parade'. They had called in briefly on the Leigh-Perrots in Paragon, but the place was too wet and dirty to allow for getting out. Living in Bath, she decided, was all a matter of the right location and the right company. Casting her eye over the columns of the *Bath Chronicle*, she was gratified to find the names of Mr and Mrs E. Austen included among a long list of new arrivals in the city, 'so that we need not immediately dread absolute solitude'; nor, as she privately thought, dread what was worse, confinement to the company of aunt Leigh-Perrot and her friends.[11] To be without fashionable acquaintances in a place like Bath would be a far more mortifying condition, she knew, than to be solitary in the country. It was exactly the fate that she imagined for her latest heroine, Susan, sitting alone and unregarded in the crowded Upper Rooms, with only her vain neighbour, Mrs Allen, for company. 'How uncomfortable it is,' whispered Susan, 'not to have a single acquaintance here . . . What shall we do? The gentlemen and ladies at this table look as if they wondered why we came here – we seem forcing ourselves into their party.'[12]

Fortunately for the Austens, escorted as they were by the squire of Godmersham, there was no danger of seeming to force themselves into anybody's party. Jane looked forward to a period of elegant diversions. There was a fashionable public breakfast every morning in Sydney Gardens 'so that we shall not be wholly starved', and on Tuesday evening, a grand gala concert in the same gardens, with illuminations and fireworks. This was the kind of concert she liked best, she noted wryly, 'as the gardens are large enough for me to get pretty well beyond the reach of its sound'.[13] At the theatre, to mark the King's birthday, there was a performance of *The Birth-Day* by the German playwright Kotzebue, while Lady Willoughby presented colours to 'some corps of yeomanry or other' in the Crescent. Reading an adjacent column of the *Chronicle*, she found something which amused her. 'Travellers should be very careful to deliver their luggage to the proper coachman or porter,' it warned. 'A lady was on Monday robbed of her trunkfull of wearing apparel by a man who *voluntarily* assisted in receiving it from a stage-coach in this city, with which he got clear off.'[14] Jane had insisted on packing so many indispensable items into her own trunk that it had proved too heavy for the coach to take it. 'I have some hopes of being plagued about my trunk,' she teased, having eventually entrusted it to a wagoner who promised faithfully to deliver it the next day, but 'who knows what may not happen?' Mindful of the oversight at Dartford which had almost sent her writing-box off to the West Indies, she found something hugely diverting about the fantasy of some Somersetshire highwayman making off with all her gowns and lace.

For Edward, the trip to Bath was essentially of a remedial nature. He had not come to amuse himself, but to subject himself to a rigorous medical regime. His bowel complaints had not lessened, but rather intensified to include faintnesses, sicknesses and loss of appetite. He had hardly touched the delicious dinner of asparagus and lobster procured for them at Devizes; nor the savoury cheesecakes 'on which the children made so delightful a supper as to endear the town of Devizes to them for a long time'. Really, he seemed well on his way to becoming as much a hypochondriac as his mother. 'What must I tell you of Edward?' Jane wrote to Cassandra. 'Truth or falsehood? I will try the former, & you may chuse for yourself another time . . . He drinks at the Hetling pump, is to bathe tomorrow, & try electricity on Tuesday.'[15] Electricity was Edward's own idea. It was the very latest thing, and he proposed it himself to Dr Fellowes, his physician. Fellowes was tactful enough to voice no objection, though the Austens were sceptical. 'I fancy we are all unanimous in expecting no advantage from it.' By the end of a week, Edward was feeling 'pretty well'; but by the end of a fortnight, all the old symptoms had returned, and he now believed himself to be suffering from gout. There was general dismay among the Austens and the Leigh-Perrots that Edward should feel himself 'tied down' to follow Fellowes' opinions when it was well known in Bath that Dr Mapleton was the only man to consult. 'There is not a physician in the place who writes so many prescriptions as he does.' As a fellow sufferer from the gout, Mr Leigh-Perrot was eloquent in his views on medical men. Now mostly house-bound, with his feet wrapped in flannels, he earnestly recommended Mapleton, or possibly Millman, as they drank tea together one Sunday in No. 1 Paragon Buildings. Millman sent Edward to an apothecary who ridiculed the idea that he was afflicted by gout. He had merely eaten 'something unsuited to his stomach', the apothecary declared, nothing more. 'A sensible, intelligent man,' commented Jane.[16]

Once her trunk was safely arrived, Jane began replenishing it with all sorts of new fabrics and gauzes from the less expensive shops near Walcot church. She was highly amused by the latest fashion for hats extravagantly adorned with fake vegetation. 'Flowers are very much worn, & fruit is still more the thing – Eliz: has a bunch of strawberries, & I have seen grapes, cherries, plumbs & apricots.' Ever since her mamalouc cap, she had rather taken a fancy to exotic headgear. 'Eliz: has given me a hat,' she told Cassandra, '& it is not only a pretty hat, but a pretty *stile* of hat too.' But, much as the idea of walking about with a bunch of cherries on her head appealed to her sense of the bizarre, there was always the tiresome matter of money to consider. Four or five 'very pretty sprigs' of floral decoration might be had 'for the same money which would procure only one Orleans plumb'. 'Besides,' she wrote to Cassandra, 'I cannot help thinking that it is more natural to have flowers grow out of the head than fruit. What do you think on that subject?'[17] She went to the gala concert and enjoyed the fireworks, 'which were really beautiful, & surpassing my expectations'; she took a 'charming walk' up Beacon Hill and across the fields to the village of Charlcombe. She attended plays at the theatre and perambulated in the Pump Room. How strange it was, she remarked to Cassandra, 'I have never seen an old woman at the Pump Room.'

Altogether, despite the valetudinarian grumbles of her mother, brother and uncle Leigh-Perrot, Jane was determined to enjoy herself. She loved to send back teasing hints and innuendoes to Cassandra at home. How to convince Martha Lloyd that 'fair men are preferable to black', she wondered. 'For I mean to take every opportunity of rooting out her prejudices. – Benjamin Portal is here. How charming that is! – I do not exactly know why, but the phrase followed so naturally that I could not help putting it down.' That was a pretty broad hint to Cassandra, with whom she had often shared coy remarks on the Reverend Portal's handsome eyes. And while she was delighted that Martha and Mrs Lefroy wanted the pattern of her elegant Bath headgear, she was less pleased with Cassandra for giving it to them. 'Some wish, some prevailing wish is necessary to the animation of everybody's mind,' she reflected, '& in gratifying this, you leave them to form some other which will not probably be half so innocent.'[18] Better for Martha (and perhaps herself) to dream of straw bonnets festooned with cherries than to long for clergymen with handsome eyes. But what of Cassandra's own innuendoes? Why had she been so anxious that their stay in Bath should be 'lengthened beyond last Thursday'? 'There is some mystery in this,' Jane declared. 'What have you going on in Hampshire besides the *Itch* from which you want to keep us?' She let Edward's children fill up the end of her letter with wishes of their own to be gratified: 'We like gooseberry pie & gooseberry pudding very much.' 'We shall be with you on Thursday to a very late dinner,' Jane told Cassandra on 19 June. Pleased for once to be able to play the part of the *grande dame* accustomed to lobster and asparagus, rather than the Steventon housekeeper, she took the liberty of adding: 'You must give us something very nice, for we are used to live well.'[19]

All that summer there were more visits. The Cookes at Bookham could not be entirely avoided, then it was quickly on to the Leighs at Adlestrop and the Coopers at Harpsden. This final visit to Mrs Austen's childhood home was a sad leave-taking, for the Coopers were about to move to Staffordshire. Their sister Jane, Lady Williams, had been killed in a road accident at Newport in the Isle of Wight the previous summer, when the light gig she was driving herself was crashed into by a runaway dray-horse. Now Mary Leigh of Stoneleigh had offered them the chance of a lucrative northern living. 'Yesterday came a letter to my mother from Edward Cooper to announce not the birth of a child but of a living,' Jane wrote to Cassandra in January, 'for Mrs Leigh has begged his acceptance of the rectory of Hamstall-Ridware in Staffordshire.' 'Staffordshire is a good way off,' she added, with her usual vagueness as to geography, 'so we shall see nothing more of them till, some fifteen years hence, the Miss Coopers are presented to us, fine, jolly, handsome ignorant girls.'[20] This from a young woman who was barely past her own twenty-fourth birthday. At home in the rectory, where she wrote this letter, Jane was always expected to demonstrate the maturity of a respectable adult. In her imagination though, her life was rather different. Nearly all her heroines were younger than herself. The Bennet sisters were aged from fifteen upwards; 'Susan' was just seventeen, as was Marianne Dashwood from *Sense and Sensibility*. These were young women for whom all the hopes and vanities of the world were still fresh and vivid. Dancing at Manydown, or walking alone in the icy lanes, or writing her comic novels, Jane loved to indulge fond thoughts of how 'young ladies of 17 ought to "go on"', enjoying a life of 'admiring and [being] admired', which was (she wrote) such 'a much more rational' way of living than the rectitude of those prematurely middle-aged ladies who 'had so little of that kind of youth'.

By the time she returned to the rectory that summer, Jane Austen had completed three full-length novels, 'First Impressions', *Sense and Sensibility* and now 'Susan'. Among family and friends, 'First Impressions' was the clear favourite, with its sparkling dialogue and comic scenes. 'I do not wonder at your wanting to read *First Impressions* again,' Jane wrote to Cassandra on her birthday the previous year; 'so seldom as you have gone through it, and that so long ago.' But when Martha Lloyd demanded another look at it, she was rather less keen. 'I would not let Martha read *First Impressions* again upon any account, & am very glad that I did not leave it in your power. She is very cunning, but I see through her design; she means to publish it from memory, & one more perusal must enable her to do it.'[21] The question of publishing did rather trouble her. It was not that she had been too terribly cast down by the curt rejection from Messrs Thomas Cadell. It was rather that she lacked the confidence to take such a very public step. In some ways, she wished that some kindly intermediary, her father, her brother Henry, or even Martha Lloyd, might take it upon themselves to bring about the public recognition that she craved, but had not confidence to solicit. However, it was not Jane, but her aunt Leigh-Perrot who was to experience the rude assault of sudden public attention in the months ahead.

Grand larceny

Returning from an evening party to her home at No. 1 Paragon on 12 August 1799, Jane Leigh-Perrot was astonished to find a mysterious note addressed to her as 'Mrs Leigh Perrot, Lace Dealer'. The note was anonymous, but its threat was clear. It read: 'Your many visiting Acquaintance, before they again admit you into their houses, will think it right to know how you came by the piece of lace *stolen from Bath St.*, a few days ago. Your husband is said to be privy to it!' Alarmed, she showed the note to her husband, James, who was already weary from the exertion of their outing, having been confined to bed with his wretched gout for several weeks.[22] The accusation was preposterous, of course. It was some stratagem of the shop-woman Gregory, they both agreed, who seemed determined to plague and threaten them. Mrs Leigh-Perrot still remembered, with some indignation, the disagreeable little incident the woman had contrived at Smith's shop in Bath Street a few days before. (It was still *called* Smith's shop, though everybody knew the man Smith had absconded and been declared a bankrupt many months ago. The woman Gregory now had the shop, which she managed with Charles Filby; of course, Gregory and Filby were lovers; that was the kind of thing one had come to expect among people of their sort.) Mrs Leigh-Perrot had visited the shop the previous Thursday in order to buy some black lace to trim a cloak. Actually, she had *first* visited the shop on Wednesday, but Gregory had told her she was expecting some new lace from London and would have a much better selection the following day. That was her mistake, said Mr Leigh-Perrot. That had given Gregory and Filby time to lay their trap. It was a common thing, he said; he had heard of the same contrivance being attempted with other customers. If it was such a common thing, his wife replied, she would have been grateful if he had told her so beforehand, rather than allow her to become the innocent victim of a pack of villainous cheats and liars. As it was, she returned to Smith's shop the following afternoon and enquired if the new lace had arrived from London. Miss Gregory was all apologies. Sadly, she said, the delivery had been delayed, but she still had some excellent black lace which she hoped Mrs Leigh-Perrot might approve. This was indeed the case, and Mrs Leigh-Perrot bought a length of black lace for £1 9s which she paid for with a £5 note. Even at the time, she was a little surprised at the way the shopman Filby had taken the lace to the back part of the shop to put up into a parcel. The man then brought her the parcel, together with her change, and she left the shop. She had met her husband near the Cross Bath, where they stopped to pay a tradesman's bill and put a letter into the post office. It was shortly after this, as they were returning through Bath Street, that the woman Gregory had come across the street and accosted her. 'I beg pardon, madam,' she said; 'but was there by mistake a card of white lace put up with the black you bought?' Mrs Leigh-Perrot had told her that she did not know, as she had not opened the parcel, but she gave the parcel to Gregory to satisfy herself. Gregory opened the parcel and quickly found a card of white edging. 'Oh here it is,' she said, taking it up and returning to the shop. Mrs Leigh-Perrot had thought no more about the matter, until, as they got towards the Abbey Church Yard, they found the man Filby was following them. He came up to them and told them, in a surly manner, that he had *not* put up the card of white edging, and demanded to know her name and place of abode. That had indeed alarmed her, but Leigh-Perrot had known how to deal with such insolence. He told the man curtly that he lived at No. 1 Paragon and that his name was on the brass plate on the door.

Worse was to follow. Two days after receiving the anonymous note, Jane was sitting by her husband's bedside when her maid came up to tell her that a gentleman was in the parlour and wished to speak to her. Descending, she was horrified to find a constable, with a warrant from the mayor demanding her immediate appearance before the city magistrates. She went back to Perrot, still sick in bed and in a profuse perspiration, and told him the terrible news. The dear man, forgetting everything but her danger, refused to let her go alone. Supported on two sticks, and with his foot still swathed in flannel, he insisted on accompanying his wife to the Town Hall. The mayor and magistrates were all kindness. The Leigh-Perrots were well known to them and they lamented greatly subjecting such well-respected persons to this hideous indignity. But in this matter they had no choice. The two wretches, Gregory and Filby, had sworn a solemn oath that Mrs Leigh-Perrot had stolen the white lace. The one swore to having seen her take it; the other to finding it in her possession. 'Which she certainly did,' said Mrs Leigh-Perrot, 'though how it came there, they best can tell.' The lace was valued at twenty shillings, the magistrates said. It was not worth half that much, said Mrs Leigh-Perrot. But it was at least worth more than one shilling, said the mayor, which made it a matter of grand larceny. The pronouncement of those terrible words made Mr Leigh-Perrot perspire even more profusely. Grand larceny, he knew, was punishable by death.

The next few months were the most wretched of Jane Leigh-Perrot's existence. She was sent to the County Gaol at Ilchester to await trial at Taunton assizes. At first, she lived in hopes that her imprisonment there would be only brief – perhaps ten days at most – while her husband arranged bail for her. During this time she made every endeavour to ingratiate herself with her gaoler (or *Governor*, as he was grandly styled), Mr Scadding, who was one of those venal mortals not averse to pecuniary inducements. In return for a little money, she was spared the indignity of wearing the filthy coarse brown-and-yellow striped prison costume. She was also saved from living in the prison building itself, where she would be compelled to sleep in straw and share a cell with some murderous drab. Instead, Mr Scadding allowed her and her dear husband (who remained by her constantly, with the fortitude and sweet serenity of a guardian angel) to live with him in his own house. Mr Scadding even accompanied them to London, keeping guard over Mrs Leigh-Perrot in a noisome house called the Angel, behind St Clements, while her husband sought to obtain an order for bail from a judge in King's Bench. Imagine her horror when she was told that judges 'were only occasionally in London' during the summer season. And when at last a judge had been found, there were then 'no persons of our acquaintance' in town to assist them. Eventually, four sureties were obtained; from tradespeople, certainly, but from *substantial* tradespeople, '*ready* and *happy*' to show their best services in bailing her. But the wretches Gregory and Filby objected to sureties from rival traders. The Leigh-Perrots' lawyer insisted that some fifty sureties might be easily obtained from persons in Hampshire, but the judge was now deaf to all such pleas. Bail was refused and Mr Scadding conducted them back to Ilchester Gaol.

There was no way that the shame of such a terrible business could be kept secret. 'Although the newspapers have only reached as yet the *initials* of my name,' Mrs Leigh-Perrot wrote to her cousin Mountague Cholmeley in October, 'they consider me now as fair game, and I shall travel for the future at full length, I daresay.'[23] Her relatives were all very kind, but even their kindness was a sort of humiliation. Mrs Austen wrote from Steventon offering to send Jane, or Cassandra, or both, to stay with their aunt throughout her imprisonment. But Mrs Leigh-Perrot declined this magnanimous offer. She could not procure them accommodation in Mr Scadding's house, she explained; and she would not permit such elegant young women to become inmates of a prison and suffer the many unspeakable indignities of that vile place which she was obliged to endure.[24]

After seven weeks of incarceration, Jane Leigh-Perrot was close to despair. 'Had the choice of death or such a 7 weeks as the last been left to me,' she wrote to her cousin, 'I should not have hesitated one moment in determining on the first.'[25] In addition to his slatternly wife, 'Governor' Scadding had five young children, and the house was filthy, noisy and cramped. 'This room joins to a room where the children all lie, and not Bedlam itself can be half so noisy; besides which, as not one particule of smoke goes up the chimney, except you leave the door or window open, I leave you to judge of the comfort I can enjoy.' It was on behalf of her dear husband, in particular, that she most resented these vile conditions. 'Cleanliness has ever been his greatest delight and yet he sees the greasy toast laid by the dirty children on his knees, and feels the small beer trickle down his sleeves on its way across the table unmoved . . . *Mrs Scadding's* knife *well licked to clean it from fried onions* helps me now and then – you may believe how the mess I am helped to is disposed of – here are *two dogs and three cats* always *full as hungry* as myself.'[26] Yet she dared not voice her complaints to 'Governor' Scadding. However much the vulgar man would swear and shout, she must 'keep very fair with him, because I hear, and indeed sometimes from his own mouth, that he has a number of relatives and dependents who are always on the petty jury, and may do me favour or otherwise if he pleases'. 'Good God!' she wrote, to think that she should be reduced to depending on such people's good opinion!

It was very clear to her that she had been the victim of a vile conspiracy. The whole thing had been made plain in two more anonymous letters sent to Leigh-Perrot.[27] The first was from an employee of William Gye, the printer, who was a trustee for the creditors of Smith's shop. It told of a blackmail plot laid against the Leigh-Perrots by Gye and Filby. The two men, it said, were 'disappointed' that no offer had yet been made to them by Leigh-Perrot 'to buy off the witnesses against your innocent and highly injured lady'. Now they were 'circulating the most false and injurious calumnies to prejudice Mrs Perrot in the eye of the world; but they find she has too many friends for this purpose to succeed to their utmost wish . . .' The other letter was from a servant at the Greyhound Inn, where Gye and Filby had done much of their plotting, and said more to the same effect. The girls at the Bath Street shop had been 'tampered with', it said, '& such promises made them, if they would appear as witnesses against her, and such threats if they would not, that they have been drawn in . . .' Both letters were full of colourful details of the plotters' evil schemes. 'If Mrs P should not offer some considerable remuneration,' one of them explained, Gye would 'publish a ludicrous print of your crest, with a card of lace, & other articles in the parrot's [i.e. *Perrot*'s] bill'. 'But be firm sir,' the letters counselled; 'give the rogue rope enough & he will hang himself.'

Mrs Leigh-Perrot found it some gratification at least to learn that her friends refused to believe the vile slanders against her, though her husband cautioned her against placing any faith in such sneaking testimonies as these. It was beyond a doubt, he said, that the letters were themselves part of the plot they purported to reveal. It was those wretches' way of demanding money to withdraw their accusations. As to the calumnies themselves, they were real enough; and it was hardly to be expected that they would entirely pass without credit. Already it was widely rumoured, not only that *she* had done the thing of which she stood accused, but that *he* had sought to buy off her accusers. There was a lawyer, Symes, who made it his business to repeat such things. Already, as Leigh-Perrot was reliably informed, the vicar of Over Stowey had said it was a pity that money should be able to screen a person from justice in a kingdom so remarkable for good laws and uncorrupted judges. The same vicar had also had the goodness to describe Jane as 'a person of considerable fortune' and Leigh-Perrot himself as 'a poor Jerry Sneak of a husband who adheres to her through all difficulties'.[28]

Mrs Leigh-Perrot dreaded the thought of a whole winter spent in prison. Apart from the degradation of the place itself, she feared 'that my being so long imprisoned would prejudice a future jury against me'. In January, her husband's illness grew worse. He lay awake for the whole of one night in an agony of pain and Mrs

Leigh-Perrot was almost forced to the desperate expedient of summoning the Ilchester medical man. Since the man in question advertised his various trades as *Apothecary, Surgeon, Coal dealer, Brick and Tile Maker &c.*, her heart ached at the thought of it.[29] After all their careful discussions of the rival merits of Dr Mapleton and Dr Fellowes, it was a dreadful thought to be reduced to the remedial expertise of a coal-man and brick-maker. Fortunately, her husband recovered in the following days, with the aid of opiate drops and James's powders. He presented his wife with a seed-pearl necklet as a token of his undying affection, together with a little poem.

> *With thee no days can winter seem,*
> *Nor frost nor blast can chill;*
> *Thou the soft breeze, the cheering beam,*
> *That keeps it summer still.*[30]

As the date of the trial approached, Mrs Austen wrote again from Steventon and, though hardly in a good state of health herself, repeated her offer to come to Ilchester. Mrs Leigh-Perrot was distressed to hear that poor James Austen had broken his leg in falling from a horse. The young man had been 'a perfect son' to her through all her troubles, and she had hoped to have his friendship and support during the trial.[31] But now, of course, she found she could ask neither James's mother, nor his wife, to leave him. 'Nor could I accept the offer of my nieces,' she wrote to Cholmeley in early March. 'To have two young creatures gazed at in a public court would cut one to the very heart.' Jane Austen was relieved to be spared once again the humiliation of attending her aunt in such wretched circumstances. Even in her moments of utmost self-abasement, she could not truthfully present herself as one who would readily volunteer for such a penitential role.

The trial of Jane Leigh-Perrot took place at Taunton assizes on Saturday 29 March 1800, in the Great Hall of the castle where, many years before, the fearsome Judge Jeffreys had held his Bloody Assize.[32] The case had attracted great attention and the court was excessively crowded. Looking round her, Mrs Leigh-Perrot could see row upon row of eager, leering faces, and, here and there, the paler countenances of well-wishers and friends. 'No fewer than 2,000 persons could be present,' reported the *Bath Chronicle*; 'the throng, tumult and confusion' of this 'vast, promiscuous multitude was so great that at least half an hour elapsed before any proceedings could be heard'. In his wife's defence Mr Leigh-Perrot had engaged four of the finest lawyers from London: Mr Bond and Mr Dallas, Mr Jekyll and Mr Pell. These counsel, Mrs Leigh-Perrot knew, were the very best that money could buy; and there were powerful friends who would swear to her character. And yet she was fearful. 'I can only think with . . . horror of what *Art* may do against *Innocence*,' she wrote.

Mr Vicary Gibbs opened the case for the prosecution a little after half past eight. He was a short man of meagre frame, not more than five feet four inches in height. He was also a man so wholly devoid of humour, and so sour in his manner, that he had earned the nickname 'Sir Vinegar'. After making his opening remarks, Mr Gibbs called Miss Gregory to give her evidence. Miss Gregory was very precise. She remembered exactly where each box of black lace and white lace had been placed. She also remembered the prisoner asking change for a £5 bank-note. But unfortunately she had gone downstairs for her dinner at the time when the theft must have occurred. It was her absence downstairs, she said, which had given the prisoner the opportunity for the theft. Miss Gregory then recalled the incident some time later when she spoke to the prisoner in the street. The prisoner had trembled very much when she was stopped, Miss Gregory said; she was 'much frightened, and coloured as red as scarlet'. Upon opening the parcel, Miss Gregory immediately saw the card of white lace concealed beneath the black lace, and with their own shop-mark clearly visible. The prisoner then said that the man must have given it to her by mistake, but Miss Gregory said to her: "'Tis no such thing, 'tis no such thing; you stole it, you are guilty.'

The next witness was Filby. With him, Gibbs adopted a bold strategy. Knowing that the defence would seek to discredit the man's character, he began by anticipating their principal charges.

Yes, Filby boldly admitted, he had lived with Miss Gregory – outside wedlock – for six months. Yes, he had twice been declared bankrupt in London. Once these facts had been disposed of, in such a manner as to make them appear of little consequence, Mr Gibbs asked Filby to state the main substance of his charge. The villain then described in detail how he had seen the prisoner take the card of white lace in her left hand and hide it under her cloak, while she thought he could not see her. He was busy in the back shop at the time, finding change for her £5 note. But he had seen her clearly drawing her left hand, with the card of lace in it, under her cloak. Mr Gibbs asked him again if he had any doubt about having seen the prisoner take the card of lace, and the man swore positively that he had seen her take the white lace out of the box and conceal it under her left arm. It then fell to Mr Bond to cross-examine the witness.

Had it ever happened before, Mr Bond wanted to know, that the witness had, by accident, put up more goods into a customer's parcel than the customer had purchased? Witness did not recollect that it ever had. Had the witness ever heard of a lady of the name of Blagrave? No, the witness never had. Mrs Blagrave had bought a black veil at the witness's shop but when she got the parcel home she found *two* veils instead of one. Did the witness not remember that Mrs Blagrave had brought back the second veil and delivered it into his hand? The witness thought perhaps he did recall an incident of this kind. The witness was reminded that he had said he never put up more things than had been purchased. The witness replied that he did not *know* this to be the case with Mrs Blagrave. He had received the veil brought back, but was not obliged to believe this had been the case just because the lady said so. He did *not* believe he had put up the extra veil. Witness was then asked if he would have received back the veil if he had not believed it belonged to the shop. Witness said he would not, and that he knew the veil did belong to the shop. Witness had not told the lady he had not put it up. Witness did not recollect exactly what he had said. Thought he recollected saying he did not *know* of having put it up. Witness did not know of any other instance of the same occurring. Witness asked if he remembered several persons called Kent. Witness did not. Witness reminded of a lady of that name who had bought some gloves, a few days before Mrs Leigh-Perrot came to the shop, who returned to complain there were more gloves in her parcel than she purchased. Witness had no recollection of any such circumstance. Very few customers that time of year. Witness could not swear *positively* that it had not occurred. So many customers in general that he could not recall it. Witness taxed with contradicting himself. Were there *very few* customers, or *so many*? Witness said that though there were not a *great* many customers at that time of year, yet there were *so* many as for him not to be able to recollect every circumstance. Mrs Leigh-Perrot was much encouraged by the way in which Bond trapped the villainous fellow into these stupid contradictions. But she was mortified when the judge, Mr Justice Lawrence, intervened to say that *he* thought the testimony was clear enough and if Mr Bond had no more questions it might be time to hear the next witness.

Sarah Raines was the last witness to give evidence for the prosecution. Raines was Miss Gregory's shop-girl and had been present in the shop at the time of the events in dispute. Questioned by Mr Burroughs, Raines said she had seen Filby wrap up the parcel of black lace, and was sure there was nothing else in the parcel. Raines was then cross-examined by Mr Jekyll. He put it to Raines that at the time when Filby was making up Mrs Leigh-Perrot's parcel, Raines herself was principally engaged in putting away the box of black lace. Raines agreed that this was the case. Mr Jekyll suggested that there was nothing particular to draw her attention to Filby's manner of making up the parcel; that she saw Filby making up parcels every day; that she did not pay any special attention to this particular parcel and that she had not even observed where Filby had got the paper to wrap it in. Raines seemed to have difficulty with these questions. Though in general she was clear enough in what she wanted to say, when it came to details she relapsed into silence. Mrs Leigh-Perrot observed the girl's silence with relief. She was clearly a worthless witness. But her relief turned to dismay when the judge intervened once again to come to the girl's assistance. *He* put the questions to her in such a simple manner that the girl returned brightly to her memorized script. 'You say he did not put any white lace in the parcel with the black; how could you know that, not being particularly observant?' he asked. 'I saw that he put in the black lace only,' said Raines. 'Are you certain of that?' the judge asked her. 'Yes, my lord, I am,' said Raines.

Mrs Leigh-Perrot was at a loss to account for the judge's conduct. At first, he had behaved quite handsomely to her, wished her to be seated and sent several times to signify such wishes. But he did not let enough be said of Filby's villainy – such a vile character, so adept at swearing *black was white*. And why had he helped the Raines girl, in such a deliberate way?

Now it was her turn to speak. She could not give evidence under oath – that was forbidden – nor be cross-examined, else she could have disproved having on *any* cloak at all, despite the villain swearing she had concealed the lace under her *black cloak*. But she could read a short statement in her own defence. She rose and, in a faltering voice, began to address the court.

My Lord and Gentlemen of the Jury . . . Placed in a situation the most eligible that any woman could desire, with supplies so ample that I was rich after every wish was gratified – blessed with the affections of the most generous man as a husband, what could induce me to commit such a crime?

She was so agitated she could barely read the words before her. Her voice failed and she stopped. Her junior counsel, Mr Pell, she noticed, was sobbing most eloquently on her behalf. Mr Jekyll was requested to repeat her words to the court, since her own voice was too faint for the jury to hear them. She resumed reading her statement, slowly, with pauses between each phrase, so that Mr Jekyll could repeat them.

You will hear from my noble and truly respectable friends what has been my conduct and character for a long series of years; you will hear what has been, and what is now their opinion of me. Can you suppose that disposition so totally altered, as to lose all recollection of the situation I held in society – to hazard for this meanness my character and reputation, or to endanger the health and peace of mind of a husband whom I would die for?

(Mr Pell sobbed loudly at that.)

You have heard their evidence against me, I shall make no comment upon it – I shall leave that task where I am certain it will be executed with justice and mercy. I know my own oath in this case is inadmissible, but I call upon that God whom we all adore to attest that I am innocent of this charge, and may he reward or punish me as I speak true or false in denying it. I call that God to witness that I did not know that I had the lace in my possession, nor did I know it when Miss Gregory accosted me in the street. I have nothing more to add.

Now it was not only Mr Pell who was sobbing. Indeed, as she later recalled, 'I never saw so many men weep.'[33] The agitation of her husband was so truly distressing that it drew down the sympathy of almost all who were present. Now it was the turn of Mrs Leigh-Perrot's witnesses to give their evidence. Mrs Blagrave confirmed that she had bought and paid for one veil at Miss Gregory's shop, but when she got home she had found two veils in the parcel. When she returned the veil to Filby, he took it and said he was obliged to her and that he had not missed it. Mrs Kent said she had bought four pair of gloves at Miss Gregory's shop, but when she got home she found there were five pair of gloves in the parcel. She had returned the fifth pair to the shop. The witnesses to Mrs Leigh-Perrot's character were then called to give evidence. George Vansittart MP said she was a person of honourable and religious principles, incapable of any act of dishonesty. Lord Braybroke swore that she was honourable and unimpeachable, and that he knew no family in the neighbourhood of Berkshire that was more respected. Francis Annesley MP said she was much beloved and no one who knew her supposed she could do anything dishonourable. Mr John Grant, the Reverend Mr Nind, the Reverend Mr Wake, Dr Mapleton, Mr Baldwin, Mr Winstone and several others all spoke to the same effect. All agreed that Mrs Leigh-Perrot was a woman of the highest honour and most respectable character. It was then time for Mr Justice Lawrence to sum up the evidence to the jury. On the good character of Filby, his Lordship observed, there hung some doubt; yet his evidence stood uncontradicted in any material point, and was corroborated by the testimony of Gregory and Raines. On the other hand, he said, it was impossible that any person could have a higher character than was given to the prisoner by Lord Braybroke, Mr Vansittart, Mr Annesley and several other persons of the greatest respectability. But that if the jury were satisfied with the evidence, and believed the witnesses for the prosecution, that character ought not to avail her; and however exemplary her former conduct might have been, they were bound to pronounce her guilty. On the part of the prisoner, his Lordship observed that her returning and passing by Miss Gregory's shop, with the parcel still in her hand, so soon after leaving it, certainly did not appear to be the conduct of a guilty person. Thieves, he said, were wont to hide away and conceal the property they had stolen. Nor should the prisoner's agitation, 'turning as red as scarlet' when accosted by Miss Gregory, be construed as an indication of guilt. Any person, he suggested, stopped in the public street and taxed with so heinous a crime, might, in all probability, display similar signs of agitation. In conclusion, Mr Lawrence said that if, upon taking all the circumstances of the case into consideration, the jury should see any reason to disbelieve the witnesses, or which led them to doubt of the prisoner's guilt, they should recollect the very excellent character which had been given to her. In that case, he said, such a character ought to have great weight with them towards an acquittal.

The jury retired and, having consulted for less than ten minutes, returned a verdict of *Not Guilty*. Immediately, there was a loud clapping of hands all round the court, which the judge struggled to silence as inappropriate to the dignity of the proceedings.

Mrs Leigh-Perrot was naturally delighted both with the verdict and with the speed of the jury's deliberations ('7 *minutes and a half*,' she boasted). Clearly, they had not had the slightest doubt of her innocence.[34] She and her husband hastened back to Bath the following day and reached home a little before midnight. The next day was filled with friends and well-wishers. From ten in the morning till late at night, it was all '*kissing and crying*'. The following morning she wrote to her dear cousin Cholmeley. 'Once more I address you *unprison'd*, but oh! how I have been wrung! – to the very quick, believe me.'[35] She railed against the villain Filby and his vile accomplices, but no praise was high enough for the jurymen who acquitted her, so 'much more enlightened than petty jurors generally are'. Now she was only left with frightful expense of it all. 'I am told it will be nearer *two* than one thousand pounds and from the large demands already made only for conveying the witnesses (and the *two* days expenses for the *house* and *eating* at Taunton which alone amounted to £93 odd money), I can easily suppose it will be full that sum.' And all for a 20s piece of lace! 'What a comfort that we have no children!'[36]

Every day brought letters of congratulation; there were callers from morning till night, friends 'old and new' constantly seeking their company. 'To be sure,' she told Cholmeley, 'I stand some chance of being killed by popularity – tho' I have escaped from villainy.' There was even a letter from Mrs Scadding, who declared she could not have been happier 'if it had been . . . my own family' that had been acquitted. Mrs Scadding did not omit to mention the several ailments afflicting her family, which Mrs Leigh-Perrot did not resent, being in a most charitable mood. Even 'Governor' Scadding now struck her as quite a fine fellow. 'Indeed,' she told Cholmeley, 'when I saw the man weep like a child at my distress in court, I *almost* loved him.' Instead of merely paying off the two guineas that were due on her prison account, Mrs Leigh-Perrot sent the Scaddings a draft for £25. 'Believe me,' Mrs Scadding wrote back in reply, 'it was not in hopes of any reward, or owing to your rank in life, that induced me to behave with . . . attention to you.' She offered a few words of homely advice. 'Wrap yourself up warm,' she wrote, and 'take a few glasses of port wine every day.'[37]

Yet, despite her acquittal, Mrs Leigh-Perrot soon found that her enemies had not entirely done with her. An anonymous letter repeated the threat of printing the 'parrot's bill' lampoon unless the Leigh-Perrots paid a hundred guineas to the city's general hospital. A newspaper claimed that the trial jury had never come to a verdict; that Mrs Leigh-Perrot had staged a faint and been carried out of court; and that when she was brought back to court she was tried 'by a fresh jury which had all been bribed with a guinea each'. How could such vile lies be allowed to circulate? 'Surely our boasted laws are strangely defective,' she complained, which allowed such 'abominable falsehoods' by Filby's 'diabolical set' to be published with perfect impunity.[38] But at least the horror of imprisonment was over, and her family and friends offered every possible comfort. 'My dear and affectionate sister Austen is impatient for our getting into Hampshire,' she told Cholmeley on 14 April, 'but I cannot go just yet. I shall not feel quite easy till our heavy charges are *known* and *paid*.'[39]

Jane Austen made no comment, or none that has survived, on the subject of her aunt's imprisonment and trial. Like the rest of the family, she was vastly relieved to receive the news of Mrs Leigh-Perrot's acquittal. The thought of her aunt as a convicted criminal, transported to Botany Bay (the death penalty would surely have been commuted in her case), was too terrible to contemplate. It was said that if that had happened, Mr Leigh-Perrot would have sold his properties and followed his wife to Australia. The loneliness and humiliation of remaining in England without her would have been too much to bear. Though Jane could pretend to no great enthusiasm for sharing her aunt's Ilchester prison room, she would have gone there had Mrs Leigh-Perrot desired it. And though she could hardly endorse the glowing accounts of her aunt's character that had been offered in court by Lord Braybroke, Mr Vansittart, Mr Ayling *et al.*, she could not conceive of her as a criminal. Snobbery and peevishness did not yet appear on the statute as capital crimes.

'I hope to be disappointed again'

In October, Jane's brother Edward paid a visit to the rectory, bringing his young son, Edward, with him. This time there were no more grumbles about gout, Jane noticed, pleased to recall the terse diagnosis of that eminently sensible apothecary in Bath. But Edward had lost none of his imperious manner. Before she knew it, it was quite a settled matter that Edward would be taking Cassandra back with him to Godmersham, and then, perhaps, to London. How long would she be away from Steventon? Who could tell? Until Christmas, certainly. It vexed Jane how casually her brother would bring about these lengthy separations, including, almost at a whim it seemed, sometimes one sister, and sometimes the other, as part of his entourage. It particularly vexed her that Cassandra was the one more usually singled out to share in the high life of Godmersham, where there were princes to dine with, carriages to travel in, spacious rooms and witty conversation. To be separated from her sister was bad enough; but to be excluded from the refinements of Kent – 'the only place for happiness' – was quite mortifying. The fortunate party was in such a hurry to depart that young Edward quite forgot the fine Steventon chestnuts he had made such a boast of transplanting to Godmersham, and even the drawing he had laboured at for 'itty Dordy'. The chestnuts 'will therefore be deposited in the soil of Hampshire instead of Kent,' Jane wrote to Cassandra. As to the drawing: 'I have already consigned [it] to another element.'[40] She felt no sentimental compunctions about burning the child's sketch. It was like a little token of that style of easy promises, carelessly made and quickly forgotten, with which the fortunate rich beguiled their poorer relations.

Alone in the rectory, with only her parents for companions, Jane felt inclined to be cynical. No doubt Cassandra, too, would quickly catch the grand Godmersham style of promising. Had she not already promised to send Jane a parcel of shoes, stockings and combs directly from London? What a sly pleasure it gave her when no such parcel arrived. 'I was a little disappointed,' she wrote, 'but not more than is perfectly agreable; & I hope to be disappointed again tomorrow.' *Hoping* to be disappointed saved her the mortification of actually being so. Indeed, she determined to take a martyr's pleasure in her lack of pleasures, arranging her observations into a pretty little essay in self-denial. '*You* have had a very pleasant journey, of course,' she remarked sardonically; 'I congratulate you on it.' '*We* have had to rejoice two or three times at *your* having such very delightful weather . . .' Had it been possible, she would have boasted of having endured rainstorms in Hampshire while Cassandra basked in the sunshine of Kent. But sadly, the October sun shone as brightly at Steventon as at Godmersham; still, with only a little ingenuity, that too might be represented as a hardship. 'We have been obliged to take advantage of the delightful weather ourselves by going to see almost all our neighbours,' she wrote. Oh what a treat it was to eat sandwiches 'all over mustard' at Oakley Hall. They would know little of such delicate rural cuisine at Godmersham. And why should she envy Cassandra the chance of visiting all the fashionable London shops, when she could buy 'ten pair of worsted stockings & a shift' in Oakley village? One day they were threatened with a visit by Mrs Bramston and Mrs Chute, 'but we knew a trick worth two of that'.[41] Had she thought of it, she might have taken pleasure in disabusing Mrs Chute of her fond notion that Edward had ever intended visiting *her*; 'but unluckily it did not occur to me'. She found a grim amusement in the news of local bankruptcies; the bailiffs were in at Mrs Martin's house (the library venture, evidently, had not been a success); and, from what they heard, at Wilson's too. That provoked her to a wicked thought. 'My hearing nothing of you,' she wrote, 'makes me apprehensive that you, your fellow travellers & all your effects might be seized by the bailiffs when you stopped at the Crown.' She found it a diverting fantasy to imagine what kind of sorry figure Edward would make, stripped of the trappings of Knight family wealth and privilege by hosts of angry creditors.

So taken was she with this self-denying role that her only disappointment came in *not* being disappointed. When Cassandra's parcel promptly arrived, followed by Cassandra's letter, it quite spoiled a little epistolary gambit that she had been dreaming up all night. Rather than waste this *bon mot*, she chose to use it, notwithstanding. 'Tho' I have received no letter from you since your leaving London,' she boldly began her next letter, 'the post, & not yourself must have been unpunctual.' Only later did she confess: 'Your letter is come; it came indeed twelve lines ago, but ... I am glad it did not arrive till I had completed my first sentence, because the sentence had been made ever since yesterday, & I think forms a very good beginning.'[42] Increasingly, the pose which Jane adopted, like the sentences she penned, was carefully pre-composed. She scarcely welcomed those unexpected contingencies – particularly contingencies of an ostensibly pleasurable kind – which might disturb the literary effect.

She found amusement in studying to compose herself like a character from one of her own fictions. She was to be one of those clever satirical ladies, neither severe, nor given to insipid loquacity; an observer, reserved in company, yet confiding all her brilliant remarks to her correspondence like the heroine of an epistolary romance. Such a woman might determine to find her chief pleasure in not being pleased at all; or, rather, in only acknowledging those pleasures which others chose to deprecate. 'I like the gown very much,' she told Cassandra, as she examined the parcel of clothes from London, then added, wryly: 'Mother thinks it very ugly.'[43] The pink shoes were perfectly to her taste, since 'they are not particularly beautiful'. But the cloak was a different matter. 'It is too handsome to be worn, almost too handsome to be looked at.' In fact, of course, she affected a perfect unconcern as to her appearance. Whatever did it matter, the figure she created at a mere country ball? 'My hair ... I fancy looked very indifferent,' she remarked complacently; 'nobody abused it however.' Or again: 'my hair was at least tidy, which was all my ambition'. She found it droll to observe how her neighbours seemed so anxious to encourage her diversions. No fewer than *three* neighbouring families offered their carriages to convey her to one October ball. But when she arrived, she was met with a familiar scene: 'there was a scarcity of men in general, & a still greater scarcity of any that were good for much.'[44]

Such a woman was cursed with dreams and aspirations which soared far beyond the homely routines of a handful of Hampshire rural villages; yet with a sensibility too rational for romantic fantasies of escape. It was only to be expected that her frustrations should break out at the end of a pen. As she sat among the other superfluous ladies at the November ball, wondering which, if any, of the male Hoopers, Holders or Harwoods might eventually invite her to dance, she cast her eyes around the room and practised brilliant phrases for the letter she would write that night. There was Mrs Warren, expecting her first child. 'Mrs Warren I was constrained to think a very fine young woman,' she noted; 'which I much regret.' It was not her way to think of any of the ladies in the room as 'very fine', and presently hit upon an agreeably indelicate afterthought to qualify such flattery: 'She has got rid of some part of her child, & danced away with great activity, looking by no means very large.' Mr Warren she found 'ugly enough', uglier even than his cousin, the Willing Warren she had rejected four years before. There were the Miss Maitlands ('with brown skins ... & a good deal of nose'); the Miss Debarries ('I was as civil to them as their bad breath would allow me'); the Miss Atkinsons ('fat girls with short noses'); Miss Cox ('vulgar, broad-featured'); and Miss Champneys ('a queer animal with a white neck'). Whatever did Cassandra mean by hinting that Jane had a fondness for disliking people? 'It was *you* that always disliked Mr N. Toke so much, not *I*.'[45] She was perfectly disposed to think well of people who did not trouble her with unwanted effusions of congeniality. Mr Austen's former pupil, the Reverend Buller of Colyton, was a good example. On receiving his recent letter, Jane had at first dreaded that 'he would oppress me by his felicity & love for his wife' (he was newly married). But the man was quite pleasantly rational; 'he calls her simply Anna without any angelic embellishments', unlike Charles Powlett's silly wife, who insisted on calling her husband '*caro sposo*'. For that reason, if no other, Jane wished him well, and was inclined to welcome Buller's invitation to the Austens to visit them in Devon that summer.[46]

The winter's crop of illnesses, like the autumn's spate of bankruptcies, provided an invaluable source of whimsical reflections. Earle Harwood of Deane, now a lieutenant of marines, had an unfortunate accident with a pistol which kept the neighbourhood in gossip for more than a week. Cocking the said pistol in the guard room, he somehow contrived to shoot himself in the thigh. Whereupon two young Scotch surgeons 'were polite enough to propose taking off the thigh at once'. Mr Heathcote met with 'a genteel little accident' out hunting one day, when his horse trod on his ankle and broke a bone. And poor Harris Bigg-Wither was a frequent invalid 'from his bad habit of body'. Naturally, Jane did try to be sympathetic to their various sufferings; but, all the same, to have three young men languishing simultaneously did seem a little excessive, rather like having three carriages to choose from to take her to the ball. 'It would really be too much,' she wrote to Cassandra, 'to have three people to care for!'[47] At home, there were the usual elegant diversions. One evening might be spent playing whist and casino with the Bramstons and Clarkes, while James and Mrs Bramston read to each other from Dr Jenner's pamphlet on the cow-pox. Another time, the three Digweeds would come over to play a pool at commerce. 'James Digweed left Hampshire today,' she told Cassandra; 'I think he must be in love with you,' she added, judging from the young man's earnest fascination with all Cassandra's doings at the Faversham balls.

The great storm of the night of 9 November supplied more agreeably dismal news. The storm brought down all three of the great elms in Hall's meadow and tore up chestnut trees and firs. At the rectory a chimney was brought down and the maypole with the weathercock was broken in two (Richard Buller would be pleased at that). Even two weeks later, the dining-room was still quite unusable from all the clutter of the broken chimney. But luckily there were no human casualties; 'we grieve therefore in some comfort,' Jane remarked.[48] Inevitably, James Digweed affected to be waggish on the subject of the fallen elms, pretending to suppose that they had succumbed from grief at Cassandra's absence. 'Was not it a gallant idea?' she commented drily to her sister. 'It never occurred to me before, but I dare say it was so.' The man Hacker had been there from Basingstoke, putting in new fruit trees. There were all sorts of plans for new plantations beside the old Elm Walk; Hacker favoured a little orchard, with apples, cherries and pears; but there were other voices in favour of larch, mountain-ash and acacia. 'I say nothing, & am ready to agree with anybody,' said Jane.[49] She really could not bring herself to arbitrate in these back-garden disputations concerning the relative merits of apples or acacia blooms.

Whenever she could, she stole away to grander houses, where the apartments at least had some pretensions to elegance, even if the conversation left much to be desired. 'To sit in idleness over a good fire in a well-proportioned room is a luxurious sensation,' she wrote to Cassandra after an evening spent at Ashe Park listening to James Holder's infamous puns.[50] He was not so outrageous in his puns, though, as Martha's friend Mrs Stent, with her farmyard ribaldry about ejaculating cocks.

One evening at Hurstbourne, Jane allowed herself to get drunk on the wine, and in the morning her hand shook so much she could hardly hold a pen. 'You will kindly make allowance therefore for any indistinctness of writing,' she scrawled.[51] In Cassandra's continuing absence, she found a most serviceable companion in Martha Lloyd. Together, the two of them worked at cultivating each other's refined appetite for disappointment. 'Our merit in that respect is much upon a par,' Jane wrote to Martha one November evening, 'our self-denial mutually strong.' A visit to Ibthorpe was much talked of but, with perseverance, Jane suggested, they might even 'have tired ourselves with the very idea of my visit, before my visit begins'. They planned long walks for themselves (they were both 'desperate walkers') through a 'nice black frost' and Martha suggested books they might read together. But Jane had no patience with that. 'I come to you ... not to read or hear reading,' she wrote back; 'I can do *that* at home.'[52] Her mind was full of more daring adventures; she indulged vivid fantasies of abandonment and escape, imagining wild coach rides, when they could throw themselves into a post-chaise, 'one upon the other, our heads hanging out at one door, & our feet at the opposite'. But, true to their shared dedication to the spirit of self-denial, she also enclosed a suitably solemn prospectus for a week of drearily improving lectures from Mr Robert Henry's six-volume *History of England*; 'for every evening ... there will be a different subject – Arts & Sciences – Commerce, Coins & Shipping – &

Manners . . .' In the event, the Ibthorpe visit lasted for over a week at the end of November and the two women returned together to Steventon early the following month. They were met in the rectory hall by Mrs Austen, who is said to have greeted them with these words: 'Well, girls, it is all settled, we have decided to leave Steventon in such a week and go to Bath.' To Jane, we are told, the shock of this news was so great that she immediately fainted.

'Beware of swoons'

Jane Austen's fainting fit appears as a crucial traumatic event in all the traditional accounts of her life. Yet the authority for this story is not strong, and we might pause to query why it has found such widespread acceptance. It derives, in the main, from a letter written almost seventy years later by her niece Caroline Austen. 'My aunt was very sorry to leave her native home, as I have heard my mother relate. My aunts had been away a little while, and were met in the hall on their return by their mother who told them it was all settled, and they were going to live at Bath. My mother who was present said my aunt was greatly distressed.'[53] Not only was this account written many years after the events it purports to describe; it also seems rather confused about who exactly witnessed this painful scene. Remember, it was Martha Lloyd, not Cassandra, who accompanied Jane back from Ibthorpe to Steventon that December. Caroline's reference to these two women as 'my aunts' could therefore be accurate enough. But her later use of the term 'their mother' creates a confusion. Calling Mrs Austen 'their mother' strongly suggests that Caroline believed it was *Cassandra* who returned with Jane to the rectory. But we know that Cassandra remained at Godmersham until February, and then travelled on to London, where she stayed for three weeks. Moreover, Caroline's letter makes no mention whatsoever of Jane Austen *fainting*. She merely states that, according to Mary Austen, she was 'greatly distressed'. The detail about the 'fainting fit' was not published until 1913, when it appeared in *Jane Austen: Her Life and Letters*, by William and Richard Arthur Austen-Leigh.

'The shock of the intelligence was so great to Jane,' they assert, 'that she fainted away.' Subsequent biographers have been eager to accept this account. 'Jane fainted . . . the shock was too much for her,' writes Elizabeth Jenkins; 'Overcome by shock, Jane fainted dead away,' writes Lord David Cecil; 'At this news Jane fainted,' writes Park Honan, though he does at least acknowledge the original hearsay source for this additional detail: 'so Anna Lefroy heard'.[54]

Austen's biographers have been happy to repeat a story which accords so well with their own views of how she *ought* to have reacted. Imagine her anguish! To be torn away from the native Hampshire village that she loved and dragged away, against her will, to Bath, that fashionably soulless resort of quacks, hacks, thieves, conspirators and hypochondriacs. There is a tendency for them to wax indignant on her behalf at such a forced removal. 'To exchange permanently the homely but comfortable rectory and the fields and woodlands of Hampshire for a tall narrow terrace house in one of Bath's stone-paved streets must have been nearly as dismaying a prospect to Jane as that of incarceration in the Ilchester gaoler's house had been to Mrs Leigh-Perrot,' writes Deirdre Le Faye. 'In leaving Steventon she was being uprooted and crushed,' writes Honan. 'She was being taken from a small community, which she knew well, from people whose words, actions and looks in repose or at work she cherished. There could be no compensation in a jangling, noisy town.' 'We cannot doubt that the loss of her native county . . . was exquisitely painful,' writes R.W. Chapman.[55]

All these biographers note a significant gap in the sequence of letters between Jane and Cassandra at this time, and draw similar conclusions from it. 'No letters to Cassandra survive for the month of December 1800,' writes Le Faye; 'which suggests that she destroyed those in which Jane gave vent to feelings of grief and perhaps even resentment at being so suddenly uprooted from her childhood home . . .'[56] Perhaps. But quite possibly the inadmissible sentiments which Cassandra chose to suppress were those of an unseemly excitement. In the next letter which does survive, written on 9 January, we find Jane confessing the need to conceal her true feelings in this respect. 'It must not be generally known,' she writes, 'that I am not sacrificing a great deal in quitting the country – or I can expect to inspire no tenderness, no interest in those we leave behind . . .'[57] In the same letter she also admits: 'We have lived long enough in this neighbourhood, the Basingstoke balls are certainly on the decline, there is something interesting in the bustle of going away, & the prospect of spending future summers by the sea or in Wales is very delightful . . .' This is not the language of someone who feels crushed, grief-stricken or incarcerated. Honan writes of the neighbourhood of Steventon as a 'community . . . of people whose words, actions and looks . . . she cherished'. Yet in her letters she hardly seems to cherish this world of queer ugly animals with their fat necks, pink husbands, short noses and bad breath.

For years, Jane had dreamt of a larger world, where she might savour the luxury of well-proportioned rooms, or indulge a taste for wild coach-rides. On her visit to Bath two summers earlier, she had thrown herself with some energy into the excitement of gala concerts, fireworks, shopping and scandal. 'I do not think it worthwhile to wait for enjoyment until there is some real opportunity for it,' she declared, plunging into this mad world where ladies went about in extravagant hats adorned with bunches of wild cherries or pyramids of Orleans plums. It was the potential *energy* of Bath which excited her. 'There is nothing that energy will not bring one to.' Aunt Leigh-Perrot's terrifying ordeal was, of course, a cautionary lesson; yet even *she* chose to remain living in Bath for part of the year, rather than retire permanently to her country home at Scarlets. Her cousin Cholmeley might denounce *Infernal Bath* as 'a den of villains and a harbour for all sorts of swindlers', but Mrs Leigh-Perrot still seemed to prefer the company of villains in Bath to complete seclusion in rural Berkshire.[58]

In Jane Austen's brief comic novel *Love and Freindship*, written ten years before, the tragic heroine Sophia, expiring from a fainting fit, utters these words to her friend Laura: 'Beware of swoons, dear Laura . . . Run mad as often as you chuse, but do not faint.' Later members of the Austen family preferred to remember Jane Austen as a woman of affecting swoons and tactful silences. But the evidence of her writing suggests a stronger instinct for running mad than for fainting. As she wrote on another occasion: 'If I *am* a wild beast, I cannot help it. It is not my own fault.'[59]

Once the idea of the removal to Bath was established as a fact, Jane determined to adopt a resolutely practical attitude towards it. Among the many enjoyments which might be anticipated from such a move, there remained one principal source of anxiety. This concerned the likely figure which the family might be expected to assume in the city. Living in reduced circumstances on her father's income would be a very different matter from enjoying the luxury of a house in Queen Square as the guests of Mr Edward Austen of Godmersham. Her father, she knew, was doing all in his power to increase his income by raising his tithes and other revenues, and she did not despair of his 'getting very nearly six hundred a year'.[60] But Bath was an expensive place, and the height of their social ambitions, she feared, might be to be included among the Leigh-Perrots' circle. When she thought of the Leigh-Perrots, she thought of her aunt's endless complaints about how the man Jekyll had charged such an exorbitant fee to bungle her case; and how the judge had let off the villain Filby scot-free. She thought, too, of her gouty uncle, with his feet permanently swathed in flannel ('with me a flannel waistcoat is invariably connected with aches, cramps, rheumatisms, and every species of ailment that can afflict the old and the feeble,' Marianne protested in *Sense and Sensibility*). Jane rather feared that she might be reduced to the flannel-waistcoated company of elderly, impoverished relatives. To be poor in the country was one thing; to be poor in a place like Bath, where an unfashionable address might mean all the difference between acceptability and exclusion, was quite a different matter.

As soon as Mrs Leigh-Perrot heard of their proposed move she wrote to express her 'greatest pleasure' that they would all soon be settled in Bath together. It was an event which, she said, would 'attach her to the place more than anything else could do'. She offered her own advice on likely properties. Axford Buildings, she declared, would be the perfect place for them; 'but we all unite in particular dislike of that part of the town,' Jane wrote to Cassandra,

'& therefore hope to escape.'[61] In this delicate matter of house-hunting, Jane once again professed to have no opinion at all. If Mrs Austen fixed her wishes on the corner house in Chapel Row, Jane was happy to agree with that. If Cassandra expressed an aversion to Trim Street, she was content to agree with that too. And if Mr Austen expressed particular favour for the streets near Laura Place, Jane did not offer to contradict him, though privately she feared they might prove to be 'above our price'. She did confess a sneaking preference for Charles Street; 'the buildings are new, & its nearness to Kingsmead fields would be a pleasant circum-stance'. Failing that, she thought it might be 'very pleasant' to be near Sydney Gardens: 'We might go into the labyrinth every day.'[62] As the family argued and debated over town maps of Bath, the whole place seemed a little like a labyrinth to her.

Then there was the question of servants. Mrs Austen was deter-mined on keeping at least two maids: 'my father is the only one not in the secret,' Jane remarked to Cassandra. Pleased with this whimsical thought, she developed it into a little comic fantasy. 'We plan having a steady cook, & a young giddy housemaid, with a sedate middle-aged man, who is to undertake the double office of husband to the former & sweetheart to the latter. No children of course to be allowed on either side.' Furniture was another subject of debate. Her father, it seemed, was determined upon selling everything. Only the beds would be spared ('My father & mother, wisely aware of the difficulty of finding in all Bath such a bed as their own, have resolved on taking it with them').[63] Every-thing else was to go. Her own chest of drawers, and even the pembroke table, so universally admired when it was bought only months before, were to be sold ('the trouble & risk of the removal would be more than the advantage of having them at a place where everything may be purchased'). Within days, the rectory with its broken chimney was transformed into a kind of public auction-room. Neighbours, ostensibly calling to express regrets at their departure, pored over the household furniture in hopes of securing a bargain. Mr Bayle, the auctioneer from Winchester, stalked through the sitting-rooms, filling out an inventory. Two hundred pounds, he thought, might be a reasonable estimate. Several ladies from the neighbourhood arrived in a commodious green vehicle to appraise Mrs Austen's poultry, and made off with her stock of bantam-cocks and galinies. 'Hardly a day passes,' Jane noted, 'in which we do not have some visitor or another.'[64]

It was already agreed that James and Mary would move into the rectory as soon as the Austens had left it. That was only sensible. It meant that James could act as his father's curate in the parish after Mr Austen had left. But was it not a strange coincidence, Jane thought, that all these arrangements had been made when, for once, she and Cassandra had *both* been away from Steventon, and could raise no objections? Cassandra was still away and would take no part in the move. Since she was not to be consulted about the disposal of her home and belongings, she preferred to absent herself entirely from the dismal scene. Instead, she planned a spring visit to Henry's new home in London after her winter diversions with Edward at Godmersham.

Jane wrote to her from the plundered rectory to express her dark suspicions of the stratagems which must have provoked their father's sudden resolution. Ever since the great storm, she had noticed how James and Mary had been continually lamenting the terrible expense and inconvenience that the Austens must undergo to set everything to rights at the rectory. They had dropped hints about Mrs Austen's continuing ill health, and Mr Austen's advancing years. Bath, said Mary, would exactly suit Mrs Austen's case, and besides, 'it was a place that she liked'. Now it appeared that all those family possessions which were not sold off would pass directly to James. He would possess their various pictures ('the battlepiece, Mr Nibbs, Sir Wm East &c'), together with the sketches and 'all the old heterogenous, miscellany, manuscript, scriptoral pieces' dispersed about the house. However, she wrote to Cassandra: 'Your own drawings will not cease to be your own', as if her sister should be deeply grateful for this magnanimous concession.[65] Above all, Jane regretted the loss of her father's fine library – some five hundred volumes – which were all to be sold. If her brother wanted these, she thought, he ought at least to pay for them. 'I want James to take them at a venture at half a guinea a volume.' Even before they had left the rectory, James seemed to treat the place as his own. 'My father's old ministers are already deserting him to pay their court to his son,' Jane wrote. The animals were just as bad. 'The brown mare, which as well as the black was to devolve on James at our removal, has not had patience to wait for that, & has settled herself even now at Deane.'[66]

For his part, James was left with the task of finding a curate to replace him at Deane. Jane took some pleasure in observing the difficulties that this caused him. The tedious Mr Debarry turned it down because, he said, he wished 'to be settled somewhere nearer London'. 'A foolish reason!' said Jane; 'that Deane should not be universally allowed to be as near the metropolis as any other country village.'[67] Mr Austen himself then offered the curacy to James Digweed, though Jane hardly imagined he would be tempted. 'Unless he is very much in love with [Miss Lyford], he is not likely to think a salary of £50 equal in value or efficacy to one of £75.' On the other hand, she teased Cassandra, 'were *you* indeed to be considered as one of the fixtures of the house!' *That* might be a very different matter! She continued to insist on her amiable fantasy that Digweed was desperately in love with her sister. 'Why did not J.D. make his proposals to you?' she wrote to her a fortnight later. 'I suppose he went to see the Cathedral that he might know how he should like to be married in it.' Eventually, James settled for his curate on Henry Rice, who was engaged to Madam Lefroy's daughter. It amused Jane to wonder how her interfering sister-in-law Mary would compete with Mr Rice's 'perverse and narrow-minded' mother-in-law, Madam Lefroy, for influence over the young couple's domestic arrangements: 'It will be an amusement to Mary,' she wrote, 'to superintend their household management & abuse them for expense, especially as Mrs L means to advise them to put their washing out.'[68]

One by one, all of the Austen family's possessions were snapped up by obliging neighbours. Mr Holder of Ashe Park agreed to take over Cheesedown farm, as well as the services of John Bond, the Austens' farm bailiff. But when Mr Holder then made a show of extending his acquisitive instincts in *her* direction, Jane was forced to remind him that she, like Cassandra, was *not* included among the rectory's fixtures and fittings. The man's boorishness was well known to her, but even she had not anticipated quite such a display of ill breeding. 'Your unfortunate sister was betrayed last Thursday into a situation of the utmost cruelty,' she told Cassandra. Naturally, she contrived to turn the whole painful incident into a mock-*Grandison* parody. 'I arrived at Ashe Park before the party from Deane, and was shut up in the drawing-room with Mr Holder alone for ten minutes. I had some thoughts of insisting on the housekeeper or Mary Corbett being sent for, and nothing could prevail on me to move two steps from the door, on the lock of which I kept one hand constantly fixed.'[69] In retrospect it all seemed quite comical; but at the time she had not found it so. It was one of those unpleasant reminders of how defenceless one might become when placed in a position of dependency.

As her father's books were inventoried for sale, Jane was left with only her own native wit to inspire her. Like everything else about this sudden move, this provoked in her ambiguous feelings, at once of loss, but also of liberation. 'I have now attained the true art of letter-writing,' she boasted to Cassandra, 'which, we are always told, is to express on paper exactly what one would say . . . by word of mouth.'[70] 'Not being overburdened with subject,' she added, 'I shall have no check on my genius.' Yet 'genius' was something she would never claim without irony. As if to puncture her own self-esteem, she filled her letters not with examples of genius but with vulgar exclamation marks and modish French banalities, quite in the manner of Mr Holder's niece, whose notion of a 'lively' style consisted of plenty of adverbs '& due scraps of Italian & French'.[71] 'Our visit to Ashe Park . . . went off in a *comme-ca* way,' she began one letter, and ended another – '*voila tout*'. Throughout the winter, the two sisters sought to divert each other with snippets of scandalous gossip, as if practising the Bath style of worldly repartee. Cassandra sent wicked hints from Godmersham about old Mrs Knight's latest indisposition. 'I cannot think so ill of her,' Jane replied, 'in spite of your insinuations, as to suspect her of having lain in. I do not think she would be betrayed beyond an *accident* at the utmost.'[72] She ridiculed Charles Powlett's empty-headed wife, who liked to display herself 'at once expensively & nakedly dressed', and remarked, in her best *ton*-ish manner, on Lord Craven's irregular ménage at Ashdown Park: 'The little flaw of having a mistress now living with him . . . seems to be the only unpleasing circumstance about him.'[73]

Having made up her mind to leaving Hampshire, Jane was now impatient to be gone. 'There is no place here or hereabouts that I shall want to be staying at.' Aunt Leigh-Perrot was most pressing with invitations for the Austens to lodge with them in Bath while seeking their new home. 'She is . . . very urgent with my mother not to delay her visit in Paragon if she should continue unwell.' Jane, though, was rather more excited about a proposed seaside trip to visit the Bullers at Dawlish; 'we greatly prefer the sea to all our relations,' she wrote.[74] The one relation she *did* want to see was Cassandra. '*Your* going I consider indispensably necessary,' she told her sister, and added, firmly: '& I shall not like being left behind.' Jane did not conceal her jealousy that, after three months at Godmersham, Cassandra was now to have three weeks in London, 'in the regions of wit, elegance, fashion, elephants & kangaroos'. She was almost tempted to stop writing to her sister out of spite. 'For a three months' absence I can be a very loving relation and a very excellent correspondent,' she said; 'but beyond that I degenerate into negligence and indifference.'[75] Jane had grown tired of Mary's self-importance, her mother's illness, Madam Lefroy's interference and Mr Holder's impertinence. She wanted her sister to come home. Wherever she might be constrained to live, whether at Steventon, in Bath, by the seaside or in London, it would only seem like home when Cassandra was with her.

PART III

Labyrinths

It would be very pleasant to be near Sidney Gardens! We might go into the labyrinth every day.

Jane Austen, Letter to Cassandra, January 1801

CHAPTER 7

Conspiracy

—∎—

The whole world is in a conspiracy to enrich one part of our family at the expence of another.

Jane Austen, Letter to Cassandra, May 1801

'Constant exertion'

The Countess de Feuillide looked out from her windows in Upper Berkeley Street towards Portman Square, waiting for her cousin Cassandra to arrive. It still pleased the Countess to be known by her former title rather than as plain 'Mrs Austen', and she was always gratified by tradespeople and others who thought to humour her vanity in this matter. Eliza had gradually accustomed herself to signing her letters with the simple initials 'E.A.', but she still avoided anything more explicit in the way of wifely submission. She had been greatly relieved when Henry finally resigned his commission in the militia and they had been able to move to London. All those months of being sequestered alone in Surrey, with only poor Hastings for company, while Austen was away on army business in Dublin, dancing attendance on the Lord Lieutenant, had been really rather trying. Of course, they both made a great show of enjoying it.[1] She would be forever agreeing with Lady Burrell, Lady Talbot and all the other great dames in the Dorking neighbourhood, how greatly they all preferred to shun smart society. For herself, she would tell them, she was never so happy as when enjoying a perfect solitude, with her books, her harp and her pianoforte. And Henry would play his part in the pretty fiction, writing to assure her how much he hankered after her little rural hermitage, and how much he regretted being forced to spend his evenings with such dull fellows as Lord Charles Spencer. Naturally, it was all a perfect deception. Eliza had thought she might be quite contented to live in Dublin, especially with the company of such a man as the charming Lord Charles Spencer! Failing that, she fancied that she might perhaps retire to Wales. Wales seemed so romantic. The people in cousin Jane's youthful scribblings were always retiring to Wales. It was, Eliza wrote to Phylly Walter, the perfect place for 'resigning from the world'. But it had come as something of a shock when Henry said that he agreed with her.[2] No, no, that was not what she had meant at all. Wales was not really somewhere that one *lived*; it was somewhere to have sublime feelings about, like a Gothic ruin or mountain crag.

Eventually, Austen had done just as she desired; resigned his commission and set up as a banker in London. He had handsome offices in Cleveland Court, which he shared with his partner Henry Maunde. Their house in Upper Berkeley Street was sufficiently spacious to allow them to live, if not in splendour, at least in style. Having a French chef was one of those little comforts of London life which counted hardly as a luxury, almost as a necessity with her. And M. Halavant was universally acknowledged as one of the best. Naturally, they kept a carriage for paying visits around town; there were servants, there was finery, there was money. It was the life that she had been bred to. It was curious, she thought, how things worked out. She recalled a phrase from Jane's amusing little tale, *Lady Susan*: 'When a man has once got his name in a banking house, he rolls in money.' Eliza rather hoped it would prove prophetic.

When Cassandra was eventually shown up into the elegant drawing-room of No. 24 Upper Berkeley Street, she came charged with strict instructions from her sister to observe 'everything worthy notice' and thereby 'lay in a stock of intelligence' that might provide Jane with amusement 'for a twelvemonth to come'.[3] She did as she was bid, carefully admiring all the furnishings and hangings, and marvelling at the number of exquisite dishes into which M. Halavant was capable of transforming a humble Steventon turkey. Henry had invited his friend Mr Smithson, and together they made plans for seeing Mrs Jordan at the opera house and for visits to the menagerie at Exeter Change (though Henry was good enough to warn his sister privately that Smithson was a great miser).[4] But for all the appearance of elegance and gaiety, Cassandra could not fail to notice some more disquieting signs. The boy Hastings was still subject to frequent alarming fits, which Eliza believed to be epilepsy but which had hitherto defeated all the aid of medicine. Henry, too, was prone to sudden bouts of coughing, and suffered the most hectic pains in the side, all of which, they agreed, denoted a galloping consumption. In short, it seemed that Dr Baillie was a constant visitor to the house, and Eliza's appearance of high spirits was achieved only at a considerable effort of will.

In her more reflective moments, Eliza acknowledged regrets at having felt obliged to refuse Phylly Walter's brother's request for a favour from Warren Hastings; but then, she said, she 'knew how much Mr H, was teased with requests and solicitations' and had long since mentally bound herself 'never to add to their number'.[5] Henry agreed. Warren Hastings he pronounced 'the special saviour of the British Empire'. He could 'never forgive', he said, the ingratitude of a kingdom which had prevented 'the powers of that worthy man's benevolence from equalling the wishes of his heart'.[6] (Henry was rather prone to such grandiloquent outbursts after one of M. Halavant's dinners.) There were toasts to the system of English justice, which had (eventually) acquitted Mr Hastings and Mrs Leigh-Perrot. There were execrations for the barbarity of the villainous French courts, which had condemned the innocent Comte de Feuillide to death.

Of course, Eliza said, the French had still not abandoned the idea of an invasion. Had Cassandra seen prints of the rafts on which they meant to reach us? Look, she said, when Henry had fished one out of a cupboard drawer; they are to be worked with wheels which have the effects of oars, can you believe it? They are to be bordered with cannon and support a tower filled with soldiers. 'I can hardly believe that they seriously mean to trust to such a contrivance.'[7] 'The Government appears convinced of it,' said Henry. Eliza smiled. 'When *we* were in the militia,' she said, '*we* received orders to add one hundred and fifty men to *our* regiment, and hold ourselves in readiness to march at the shortest notice. I went out to bespeak my regimentals and be *drilled* without delay.'

There were toasts to the exploits of their naval brothers. According to the public prints, Captain Frank Austen of the *Peterel* had been involved in all kinds of heroic activities. Lucrative ones, too, said Henry. Patrolling the coastline between Marseilles and Genoa, the *Peterel* had captured some forty vessels on their way back to French ports. One fishing boat carried enemy officers and $9,000 in specie; from which, said Henry, Captain Austen must have pocketed $750 in prize money. Another time, intercepting three French ships within point-blank range of the shore batteries at Marseilles, Captain Austen drove two of them on to the rocks, and captured the third, the brig *La Ligurienne*, without the loss of a single man of his crew. And, in the blockade of Alexandria, Captain Austen captured and burned an eighty-gun Turkish warship, to prevent it falling into French hands. Cassandra had heard that the Turkish captain was so grateful, he had presented Frank with a sabre and pelisse. The Admiralty were even more grateful, said Henry, and promoted him to post-captain.[8] As his brother's rank and prize money both continued to rise, Henry even wondered whether the military life might not have been more lucrative than the life of a banker. Second Lieutenant Charles Austen, back on board the *Endymion*, was also capturing enemy ships, including one, *La Furie*, off Algeciras, from which his share of the prize money was £40. And when the *Scipio*, with a crew of over one hundred, was captured in a storm, Charles, with no more than four of his crew to assist him, took control of this prize. After all this excitement, said Cassandra, Jane thought it almost a blessing that *Endymion* had not been *plagued* with any more prizes. Even now, Jane was back at Steventon making shirts for their homecoming hero.[9]

During her last days at the rectory, Jane spent some time inscribing the records of recent baptisms and burials in the parish registers of Steventon and Deane. It was a satisfyingly solemn occupation, marking these mortal entrances and exits: 'Joseph, son of John Lovell & Anne his wife, privately baptised August 12 1800.'[10] Meanwhile, through the house, the auctioneer's men completed their inventories of household goods. 'Joshua Wakeford, buried Octr. 30th, 1800.' It quite put the loss of a piano, or pembroke table, in its proper context. Towards the end, she sensed a desire among the family to gather together at Steventon for one last time. Cassandra returned from London at the end of February; Edward and Elizabeth paid a farewell visit in April. Even Post-Captain Frank Austen returned home on shore leave, fresh from his Mediterranean triumphs, and resplendent in his new Turkish sabre and pelisse. Charles, too, having spent three pleasant days in Lisbon in the company of his 'fat, jolly and affable' royal passenger, Prince Augustus, was sailing back towards Portsmouth, with the intention of coming 'to Steventon once more, while Steventon is ours'.[11] But there was to be no grand family reunion. At the beginning of May, Mrs Austen and her daughters left their old home for Ibthorpe, while Frank and his father went to London on business matters and thence to Godmersham. 'Nathaniel Martel Junior, kill'd by a waggon going over him, buried March 22, 1801.' That was the last sad entry Jane noted in the register. Two days later, leaving Cassandra behind them at Ibthorpe, Jane and her mother travelled to Bath in a single day.

Jane Austen was determined to like Bath, and was at pains to note all the most promising omens. The journey from Ibthorpe was 'exceedingly agreable' and 'perfectly free from accident or event'. The weather was 'charming', and their tavern meal 'magnificent . . . we could not with the utmost exertion consume the twentieth part of the beef'.[12] Once arrived at the Leigh-Perrots' home at No. 1 Paragon, she was delighted to find that she had her *own* room, 'with everything very comfortable about me'. The weather remained fine; 'I am warmer here without any fire than I have been lately with an excellent one', and her mother had borne the journey 'without any fatigue'. It was true that her aunt had a violent cough ('do not forget to have heard about *that* when you come,' she warned Cassandra) and was now deafer than ever. But her uncle had quite got the better of his lameness, and was happy to accompany her on nocturnal rambles by the canal with only his stick to assist him.

Such a determined policy to see only the bright side of Bath could not be long sustained. Soon she was forced to confess that her first view of Bath *in fine weather* did not entirely answer her expectations: 'I think I see more distinctly thro' rain.'[13] Having once abandoned the endeavour to maintain a mood of perpetual sunny cheerfulness, she settled easily into a more conveniently cloudy tone. 'I cannot anyhow continue to find people agreable,' she grumbled to Cassandra. Among her new acquaintances, Miss Langley was 'like any other short girl with a broad nose & wide mouth, fashionable dress & exposed bosom'. Admiral Stanhope was 'a gentlemanlike man' though 'his legs are too short, & his tail too long'. And while Jane respected Mrs Chamberlayne 'for doing her hair well', she was forced to confess '[I] cannot feel a more tender sentiment.' Bath, she found, was depressingly like Basingstoke, full of dull people attending each other's dull parties. 'Another stupid party last night,' she complained.[14] She had hoped at least that the parties would be larger here, but there were 'only enough to make one card table, with six people to look over & talk nonsense to each other'. 'We are to have a tiny party here tonight,' she wrote the following week. 'I hate tiny parties – they force one into constant exertion.'

What she found chiefly depressing was a constant preoccupation with money. As they trudged along the dusty streets of Bath, through all the shadows, smoke and confusion, in search of their new home, it was impossible to ignore the reality of their strict financial constraints. Her uncle took her to view a property in Green Park Buildings; the dining-room seemed comfortable enough, but there were symptoms of dampness in 'the offices', and the surrounding families were all plagued by 'putrid fevers'.

'When you arrive,' Jane commented to Cassandra, 'we will . . . have the pleasure of examining some of these putrifying houses again.'[15] They tried Seymour Street, but found the largest room downstairs was no more than fourteen feet square; even that was preferable to a house she went to look at with her mother in New King Street – 'quite monstrously little'.

From Steventon came dismal news of the auction of their goods, as cows and bacon, hay and hops, the piano and the tables all went under the hammer. Only £11 for their pembroke tables! And £8 for her piano! It was, she told Cassandra, 'about what I really expected to get', though she had hoped for a great deal more. Sixty-one and a half guineas for the three cows was some compensation, but the real insult was the wretched figure that Bent, the auctioneer, had put on her father's books. 'Mr Bent seems *bent* upon being very detestable,' she wrote, 'for he values the books at only £70.'[16] When she thought of Edward, with all the wealth of Godmersham at his disposal, and James and Mary benefiting from their move to the rectory, she was disposed to be bitter. 'Mary is more minute in her account of their own gains than in ours,' she noted sourly. Away in London, Eliza was soon hearing rumours of the grand style that was now being affected by the new curate of Steventon. 'He has made such alterations and embellishments,' she told Phylly, 'that it is *almost* a pretty place.'[17] 'The whole world is in a conspiracy,' Jane wrote bitterly to Cassandra, 'to enrich one part of our family at the expence of another.'

Every day, she found herself compelled to devise yet more thrifty economies. Meat was reasonable at only 8d a pound; and butter at 12d and cheese 9½d. But the price of fish was quite exorbitant. 'A salmon has been sold at 2s 9d pr pound the whole fish,' she protested, but hoped that 'the Duchess of York's removal' would make that article 'more reasonable'. Her uncle was pleased by the gift of a cucumber (1s each). But imagine, 1s 1½d for a box of lozenges! How it depressed her to be reduced to these penny-pinching concerns. And what a relief it was to receive Charles's letter, which proved he at least was not part of the family conspiracy to ruin them. The generous, foolish youth had spent the whole of his £40 prize money on gold chains and topaz crosses for Cassandra and herself. It was reckless of him, quite reckless. 'What avail is it to take prizes if he lays out the produce in presents to his sisters?' Jane demanded in mock indignation. 'He must be well scolded . . . We shall be unbearably fine.'[18]

At least walking was an inexpensive pleasure, and when she learnt that Mrs Chamberlayne not only did her hair well, but was also a prodigious walker, Jane could not help feeling 'a regard' for her, though 'as to agreableness,' she insisted, 'she is much like other people'. The two of them were soon shaking hands whenever they met and, one sunny Wednesday, they set out together up Sion Hill to walk to the nearby village of Weston. 'It would have amused you to see our progress,' Jane wrote to Cassandra. 'In climbing a hill Mrs Chamberlayne is very capital; I could with difficulty keep pace with her – yet would not flinch for the world. On plain ground I was quite her equal – and so we posted away under a fine hot sun, *she* without any parasol or any shade to her hat, stopping for nothing, & crossing the church yard at Weston with as much expedition as if we were afraid of being buried alive.'[19] Striding out across Sion Hill did much to revive her spirits, which had indeed felt in danger of being buried alive, not in the churchyard of Weston, but in the putrefying houses of Bath. Mr Philips, the proprietor of No. 12 Green Park Buildings, signified a willingness to raise the kitchen floor, but such efforts, she wrote, would be 'fruitless'. 'Tho' the water may be kept out of sight, it cannot be sent away, nor the ill effects of its nearness be excluded.' The subject depressed her, so she avoided it: 'I have nothing more to say on the subject of houses.'[20]

Jane was also somewhat disappointed by the quality of Bath gossip. Surely this was a place of scandal and intrigue? But when she did take the trouble to dress herself in all her inexpensive finery for the penultimate ball of the season, she found the Upper Rooms sadly lacking in dangerous characters. She did manage to spy out one (mildly) scandalous figure, Miss Twistleton, mistress of Charles Taylor, the MP for Wells. 'I am proud to say I have a very good eye at an adulteress,' she boasted; for, despite being assured that another lady 'was the *she*, I fixed upon the right one from the first.' She added, mischievously: 'A resemblance to Mrs

Leigh was my guide.'[21] There was also the raffish Mr Pickford, the boorish Mr Holder and the drunken Mr Badcock, whose equally drunken wife, running all round the Rooms in search of her husband, made 'an amusing scene'. But for all that, the company seemed 'shockingly and inhumanly thin for this place'.

In desperation, she did what she could to create little scandals of her own. She spread a rumour that the innocuous young Mr Busby had fathered ten children instead of three, and even invented a completely fictitious flirtation between herself and old Mr Evelyn, with whom she would sometimes walk in Sydney Gardens. She teased Cassandra with coy hints of their secret trysts and intimate conversations. After all, in Bath it did not do for a single lady to be without *any* admirers, and Mr Evelyn, although possessed of a wife, was also possessed of a 'very bewitching' phaeton. 'There is now something like an engagement between us,' she hinted, then added, '& the phaeton – which, to confess my frailty I have a great desire to go out in.' The following morning, the promised outing took place. 'We went to the top of Kingsdown – & had a very pleasant drive.' But if Jane had nursed a secret hankering to emulate Catherine Morland's wild ride in Mr Thorpe's gig over Claverton Down, she was sadly disappointed. 'I really believe he is very harmless,' she admitted; 'people do not seem afraid of him here, and he gets groundsel for his birds & all that.'[22] Jane looked forward to the end of the month when her father, travelling back from Godmersham, would collect Cassandra from Kintbury and bring her at last to Bath. Writing to her sister on 27 May, she signed off with these words: 'Unless anything particular occurs, I shall not write again.'[23]

Her words were curiously prophetic.

Missing person

In June 1801, Jane Austen went missing. Not in the *physical* sense, of course; physically, we know she remained in Bath with her family, or took holidays with them on the Devonshire coast. But as to her thoughts and emotions, her experiences and her words, we know nothing at all. It is almost as if she had disappeared. A writer's life exists in words; not in the haphazard recollections of indifferent observers, nor in the selective anecdotes of admiring friends, but in the words with which she herself constructs the constant dialogue between private feelings and public events. And for the next three and a half years we have none of Jane Austen's words. For those three crucial years, from the spring of her twenty-sixth year, till the late summer of her twenty-ninth, we know nothing of her mind, her sensibility or her actions. It is not that she did not 'write again'; but that what she wrote has been destroyed by Cassandra, who evidently did not wish the Jane Austen of those years to be publicly known or recognized. Others have been happy enough to supply this gap in our knowledge with their own partial or hearsay accounts. But what they can offer is, at best, a hazy reconstruction, made up of rumour, speculation and surmise.

Tracing the life of Jane Austen between June 1801 and September 1804 is like searching for a missing person. We know, or like to think we know, her voice, her character and appearance, though even here we are heavily dependent on the flawed testimony of relatives and friends. What did our missing person look like? 'She was pretty – certainly pretty,' says one witness. 'She was not, I believe, an absolute beauty,' says another. 'Her complexion was of the finest texture,' said Jane's brother Henry. 'It might with truth be said, that her eloquent blood spoke through her modest cheek.' But Anna Lefroy remembered her 'mottled skin, not fair, but perfectly clear & healthy in hue'. 'She had a bright, but not a pink colour – a clear brown complexion,' Caroline Austen recalled. Her face had 'a good deal of colour,' said Fulwar-William Fowle, 'like a doll – no . . . like a child – quite a child very lively and full of humor'. She had 'bright hazel eyes,' says one; 'very good hazel eyes,' agrees another; 'she had large dark eyes,' says a third; her eyes were '*not* large but joyous & intelligent,' says another. Her cheeks were 'a little too full' according to one former neighbour; 'her face was rather round than long,' Caroline agreed. But 'by *no means so broad* & plump as represented,' said another neighbour, remembering her 'very high cheek bones'. Her hair was a 'light brunette', says one. She had 'fine naturally curling hair, neither light nor dark,' says another. Her hair was 'a darkish brown' and 'curled naturally . . . in short curls round her face,' says a third. But Louisa Knight vividly recalled her aunt Jane's 'long, long black hair down to her knees'.[24]

About her character there is more agreement. 'Faultless herself . . . she never uttered either a hasty, a silly, or a severe expression,' wrote her brother Henry. 'She was as far as possible from being either censorious or critical,' wrote her niece Caroline. 'Her sweetness of temper never failed,' wrote her nephew James Edward Austen-Leigh: 'There was in her nothing eccentric or angular; no ruggedness of temper; no singularity of manner; none of the morbid sensibility or exaggeration of feeling, which not unfrequently accompanies great talents.'[25] Yet can this really be the same woman who ridiculed the 'queer animals' with bad breath at a Hampshire ball? Can these descriptions really help us to identify the person who once confessed she was 'forced to be abusive for want of subject'?[26] Even the evidence of Jane Austen's earlier letters may be of only limited value in assessing the feelings of our missing person; for the identity which they disclose is that of a woman circumscribed by the familiar world of her childhood home. But the woman we are seeking was a virtual stranger in a new world of fashionable diversions at Bath and Sidmouth, Dawlish and Teignmouth. What we *do* know is that the emotions and experiences of this person were such that her sister Cassandra chose to destroy all record of them.

In the *Bath Chronicle* for 21 May this advertisement appeared.

The lease of No. 4 Sydney Place, 3 years and a quarter of which are unexpired at Midsummer. The situation is desirable, the rent very low, and the landlord is bound by contract to paint the first two floors this summer. A premium will therefore be expected. Apply Messrs. Watson and Foreman, Cornwall Buildings, Bath.

The same issue of the *Chronicle* announced the arrival in the city of the Reverend Mr Austen. He immediately applied to Messrs Watson and Foreman, inspected the property and agreed to take on the lease. The house overlooked Sydney Gardens, just as Jane had always wished ('We might go into the labyrinth every day'). For the next three years, Jane Austen disappeared into a labyrinth of rumours.

From time to time, we catch elusive and indistinct sightings of her, a distant fugitive creature caught in a sudden sunburst of chatter. One such sighting, the most tantalizing, occurs in the summer of 1801. While their new landlord busied himself with redecorating No. 4 Sydney Place, the Austens took their long-promised holiday on the Devonshire coast. 'You know of our uncle & aunt Austen & their daughters having spent the summer in Devonshire,' Eliza wrote to Phylly in October.[27] Where exactly in Devonshire is uncertain. Jane had long cherished a 'scheme' for Dawlish, but more recently Sidmouth, near to the Bullers, with their handsome Tudor vicarage at Colyton, had been spoken of as their summer abode. When Caroline Austen heard the story from Cassandra, many years later, the precise location was unclear. 'I think she said in Devonshire; I don't think she named the place, and I am sure she did not say Lyme, for that I should have remembered.'[28] The exact location would hardly matter, were it not for the tradition that this was the place where Jane Austen fell suddenly in love. 'Teignmouth, Starcross, Sidmouth etc.,' suggested Louisa Lefroy, who had her own version of the story; '*I* believe it was at the last named place that they made acquaintance with a young clergyman when visiting his brother, who was one of the young doctors of the town . . .'[29] Caroline said nothing about the young man being a clergyman. What she remembered was how her aunt Cassandra had been so very struck by a similarity between a certain Mr Henry Edridge of the Engineers whom she met at Newtown in the summer of 1828, and 'a gentlemen whom they had met one summer when they were by the sea'.[30] Cassandra was not even sure about the year. 'It was the summer of 1801,' said Louisa, firmly. 'He was very pleasing and very good-looking,' Cassandra remembered (thinking of Mr Edridge). Caroline was surprised by such strong expressions of commendation; her aunt so rarely admired strangers. 'I suppose it was an intercourse of some weeks,' Caroline went on, 'and that when they had to part

... he was so urgent to know where they would be the next summer ...'; '... he asked permission to join them again further on in their tour,' said Louisa; 'implying or perhaps saying that he should be there also, wherever it might be,' said Caroline; 'permission was given,' said Louisa. 'I can only say,' said Caroline, 'that the impression left on Aunt Cassandra was that he had fallen in love with her sister.' 'He and Jane fell in love with each other,' said Louisa, 'but instead of his arriving as expected, they received a letter announcing his death.' 'Mr Henry Edridge also died of a sudden illness soon after we had seen him at Newtown,' said Caroline. 'I suppose it was that coincidence of early death that led my aunt to speak of him – the unknown – at all.'

The hazy details and occasional contradictions of these two narrations, both recounted so many years after the event, reinforce the dream-like quality of this mysterious seaside encounter. The name of the man himself – Jane's supposed lover, who may, or may not have been a clergyman – remained a secret. Cassandra once hinted at having met his brother on a later occasion, but gave no indication of where or when. Caroline refers to him, appropriately, as 'the unknown'. Everything about the story is wreathed in romantic mysteries; the place and date unknown, the man himself a beguiling stranger; the love so brief, the death so sudden and unexplained. Instead of factual details, what we have are the sublime shadows of romantic myth. Cassandra's recollections of Jane's unknown lover are intermingled, in an almost dream-like confusion, with memories of Mr Henry Edridge (so 'very pleasing and very good-looking'). The result is to create the impression of a kind of masculine ideal, combining the sensibility of a clergyman with the manliness of an officer in the Royal Engineers. '[I]t was,' Caroline supposed, 'that coincidence of early death' (between Mr Edridge and Jane's unknown lover) 'that led my aunt to speak of him'. What she does not point out is the even stronger coincidence that lurks as a ghostly presence behind Cassandra's account. For Cassandra, too, had been loved by a clergyman who met an early death when, like an army officer, he had gone off to war.

What is most remarkable about Cassandra's account of Jane's unknown lover is the emotional symmetry that it suggests between the two sisters' lives. Fanny Lefroy made the obvious connection. 'The similarity of their fates,' she wrote, 'endeared the two sisters to each other and made other sympathy unnecessary to each. No one was equal to Jane in Cassandra's eyes. And Jane looked up to Cassandra as one far wiser and better than herself. They were as their mother said "wedded to each other".'[31] It was the role of this mysterious stranger to establish such a coincidence of marital misfortune between the sisters, that might explain the strange intensity of their shared emotional bond. Just as she had been engaged to Tom Fowle, so Cassandra was in no doubt that, despite the brevity of their seaside encounter, Jane and her 'unknown' would have been married; 'she thought he was worthy of her sister . . . and . . . she did not doubt either, that he would have been a successful suitor.' What is strange, though, is that there was never any hint of this important Devonshire *amour* until Cassandra's meeting with Henry Edridge in 1828 provoked these fond recollections. This was a year *after* the death of Mrs Austen, the only other person who might have known something of the matter. Is it significant that Cassandra waited for her mother's death before alluding to the episode? And if so, was her silence dictated by delicacy, or fear of contradiction?

It would seem fanciful to suspect Cassandra of inventing the story of Jane's mysterious Devonshire lover; Deirdre Le Faye loyally describes her authority as 'unimpeachable'.[32] Yet it was Cassandra who destroyed Jane's own records of these years, and the *suggestio falsi* is only one small step beyond the *suppressio veri*. This is not to suggest that Jane did *not* meet a handsome clergyman at Sidmouth, Teignmouth, Dawlish or wherever. Such encounters were an inevitable consequence of visiting sea-bathing resorts. 'Sidmouth on the coast is disgraced if its young ladies fail to strike love in clerical hearts.'[33] But it may reasonably be questioned whether the nature of that encounter conformed quite so strikingly to the pattern of Cassandra's own earlier disappointment. Psychologically, the appeal of such a romantic tale of sudden love and sudden death is irresistible. Casting her mind back half a lifetime, at the age of fifty-five, it would hardly seem surprising if Cassandra allowed her recollections of this incident to become coloured by unconscious associations with her own emotional loss. For her nieces, too, the story was irresistible; they loved to imagine this secret romantic tragedy in aunt Jane's life. But these are *their* stories, not Jane Austen's. They are stories which, moreover, with their seductive blend of wistful longing and mysterious make-believe, belong to a genre that she herself never indulged in, but only parodied. It is worth reminding ourselves that we do not possess a single word from Jane Austen herself on this matter. There are no slight hints or sly allusions in any of her letters that survive; there are no fond references to the sudden deaths of eligible clergymen in any of the novels. She was not usually so secretive about her *amours*. She was happy enough to recall the pale coat of Tom Lefroy, the dark eyes of Mr Taylor and the 'noisy perfection' of Mr Blackall. Why should she make such a mystery about her unknown admirer in Devonshire? Either Cassandra was particularly thorough about expunging all such references from her sister's letters, or we must be allowed to have some doubts, not merely about this unknown lover's identity, but about his existence at all.

Though we know nothing of Jane Austen's thoughts or feelings at this time, we are paradoxically well informed about her activities. As we plot her movements from week to week, she appears as a mute, elusive figure, moving silently across southern England like a shadow. At the end of September we know that the Austens returned briefly from Devonshire to Hampshire, where they stayed with James and Mary at Steventon. We know that Jane and Cassandra spent the day with Madam Lefroy at Ashe rectory on 29 September, and that the Lefroys dined with the Austens at Steventon on Saturday 3 October. Two days later we know that the Austens returned to Bath, where Eliza heard they were soon 'superintending the fitting up of their new house' in Sydney Place.[34] Later that autumn, Napoleon sued for peace at the Treaty of Amiens. In Bath, *The Phantasmagoria, or Wonderful Display of Optical Illusions* was the hit of the winter season at the Theatre Royal.[35] Cynical people were inclined to regard the peace treaty itself as just such another kind of optical illusion; for while the

British government quickly set about demobilizing its troops, Napoleon was recruiting reinforcements. Charles Austen was paid off from the *Endymion* in the spring, and came to join the family in Sydney Place. In April, James and Mary paid a visit, bringing with them James's nine-year-old daughter Anna. After they had gone, the Austens spent part of the summer with Charles in Devonshire (Jane found the library at Dawlish 'particularly pitiful and wretched') and the rest of it in Wales, travelling as far west as Tenby and as far north as Barmouth.[36]

Somewhere on this trip, Cassandra made a watercolour sketch of her sister – one of only two authenticated portraits of Jane Austen, both done by Cassandra, that we have. 'I would give a good deal, that is as much as I could afford,' Anna Lefroy later commented, 'for a sketch which Aunt Cassandra made of her in one of their expeditions – sitting down out of doors, on a hot day with her bonnet strings untied.'[37] Yet this curious, unprepossessing sketch only reinforces the strange, enigmatic image of her sister which Cassandra seemed determined to present. The sketch offers a rear view of a plump, dumpy woman seated on a tuft or stool, gazing away from us into a white vacant blankness. The woman's face and expression are completely hidden, for not only is the head turned away, but even the back of the head is concealed by a large blue bonnet which, though its strings are untied, remains very firmly in place. All that we can glimpse is the merest hint of a plump, pink child-like curve of cheek. The woman's body is enveloped in a long blue gown whose generous folds unflatteringly suggest a somewhat ample figure beneath. Although in some ways charmingly informal, what this sketch does is to depersonalize Jane Austen, rendering her not as a character, but as a shape. Seated beneath a tree, it is a shape which suggests nursery associations; this blue-bonneted female hardly seems adult at all; she is an innocent childlike Miss Muffet sitting on her tuffet. By destroying her sister's letters, and refusing to draw her adult facial expression, it is Cassandra who most contrived to make a mystery of Jane Austen. 'There is such a sweet serene air over her countenance as is quite pleasant to contemplate,' she wrote of her sister's face in death. She found it less easy to remember or record Jane's face when it was animated by something more dangerous than serenity.

The Austen family travelled back to Hampshire in early August. We know that Mr and Mrs Austen and Charles arrived at Steventon on 14 August, but there is no word of Jane or Cassandra. Perhaps they spent some time with the Fowles at Kintbury, or possibly with the Lefroys at Ashe. Yet it seems strange that they did not join the family party, including James and Mary, which went to visit Frank at Portsmouth, where he was waiting for his ship, the ninety-eight-gun HMS *Neptune*, to be paid off. In fact, Jane and Cassandra did not arrive at Steventon until 1 September. Two days later, they were on their travels again, joining Charles on a visit to Godmersham, where they remained for several weeks. Charles brought his sisters back to Steventon on 28 October.[38] A month later, on 25 November, Jane and Cassandra went to visit their old friends Catherine and Alethea Bigg at Manydown, promising themselves two or three agreeable weeks of 'candour & comfort & coffee & cribbage'. Within the week they had returned, in a state of some distress.

'Horrible eligibilities'

On the morning of Friday 3 December, as Mary Austen looked out from the windows of Steventon rectory, she was surprised to see a carriage from Manydown draw up outside. Inside she saw Jane and Cassandra together with Alethea and Catherine. Hurrying down to greet them, Mary found a tense and awkward scene. The Bigg girls insisted that they could not stay, and returned, with apologies, to the carriage which had brought them. Once they had departed, Jane and Cassandra likewise declared that it was absolutely necessary for them to return to Bath the very next day. James, they insisted, must take them there. James protested that that was quite impossible. They must know that Saturday was not a day when a single-handed parson could take leave of his parish. He had his sermon to write, and there was no time to arrange for a substitute at such short notice. They must wait till Monday, he told them; Monday would be quite soon enough. But the sisters were utterly determined. They must leave the neighbourhood the very next day. No reason was given, but their insistence was absolute, and James was eventually compelled to yield to their demands. Mary had never seen Jane in such a state of distress. What catastrophe, she wondered, could have rendered this self-possessed woman so overwrought? But her questions were met only by silence and evasions. As James conveyed his sisters away from Steventon that Saturday morning, Mary was left to puzzle over the strange scene she had witnessd.

What happened at Manydown Park on the night of 2 December 1802 was to prove a decisive moment in Jane Austen's life. Yet we can only guess at what really occurred. Once, it seems, there may have been letters in which Jane Austen set down her own account of the night's events. But those letters, if they ever existed, have been long since destroyed. Frank Austen's daughter Catherine said there were letters, and that she had read them. She was one of the ones who later claimed to know the secret of that night at Manydown Park. Mary Austen herself passed on some gossip that she heard about it to her daughter Caroline; Fanny Lefroy picked up some family rumours that she recorded several years later. From all these various sources some hazy details emerge that might deceive us into believing that we truly understood what happened that night at Manydown. But in reality, all we have are legends, anecdotes and rumours. None of these women actually witnessed what occurred, and their hints and whispers, so often reproduced as facts, are little more than conjectures. Cassandra ensured that no faithful record of the events of 2 December 1802 should be preserved among her sister's papers. It is part of the Austen enigma that the most difficult decision of her life should be a mystery to us.[39]

Manydown was a house where Jane Austen had enjoyed some of her happiest hours. It was here that she had danced in such a profligate and shocking manner with Tom Lefroy; here that she shared girlish confidences with Catherine Bigg or laughed and teased with Alethea over glasses of an excellent wine made from Seville oranges. Set in its ancient green park of cedars and beech trees just six miles east of Steventon, this old mansion, built around a square courtyard, was full of pleasant memories. She loved the history and tranquillity of the place. There had been Withers at Manydown for more than four centuries; one of them, the poet George Wither, twice imprisoned for his scandalous satires, had also written beautiful lyrics.

> *Shall I, wasting in despair,*
> *Die because a woman's fair?*
> *Or make pale my cheek with care*
> *'Cause another's rosy are?*
>
> *Be she fairer than the day,*
> *Or the flow'ry meads in May,*
>   *If she be not fair to me,*
>   *What care I how fair she be?*
>
> *I will ne'er the more despair;*
> *If she love me, this believe,*
> *I will die ere she shall grieve.*[40]

Timber from Manydown Park had been used to construct the roof and nave of Winchester Cathedral, and Jane Austen loved to sit in the old wainscoted room where for over four hundred years Withers had held their Court Leet to settle disputes among their tenants. Over the centuries, some of the family lands had been lost. The Bighton estate, bought from Shakespeare's patron, the Earl of Southampton, had been sold off. When Lovelace Bigg-Wither had come to the house thirteen years earlier, he had disposed of property at Chilton Foliat, but used the income to extend Manydown Park itself, adding over a thousand new acres with arable farms at Monk and West Sherborne, Basing and Wortley, Bramley, Pamber and Up Nately.[41] 'I grow and wither both together' was the appropriate family motto, under a curious coat of arms of a field argent surmounted by a hare with three wheat ears in its mouth. Lovelace longed to buy back the adjacent Tangier Park estate, with its bowling green and wilderness of eight acres, that had once belonged to the family. But Tangier was now owned by the unyielding Mrs Penelope Sclater. 'Kill poor Mrs

Sclater if you like it, while you are at Manydown,' was Jane Austen's kindly hint to Cassandra some years later.[42]

Lovelace Bigg-Wither was a genial, heavy-jowled widower with two sons and seven daughters. A cousin to the great lawyer Sir William Blackstone, he was an able magistrate, a member of the Winchester Grand Jury and Deputy Lieutenant for the county. At Basingstoke he founded an association to assist the labouring poor, and established a poorhouse for the district of Wooton. 'His life is so useful,' Jane Austen remarked, 'his character so respectable and worthy.' For once, she believed, 'there was a good deal of sincerity' in the concern expressed for Mr Bigg-Wither's illness in the early months of 1799.

Despite the presence of so many daughters (most of whom were now safely married off), Manydown preserved an essentially masculine character. The dusty tomes in the breakfast parlour were solemn and worthy treatises on law and history and military strategy. 'Ladies who read those enormous great stupid thick quarto volumes,' Jane remarked to Cassandra, 'must be acquainted with everything in the world.'[43] Actually, neither Catherine nor Alethea Bigg betrayed any inclination to set themselves up as prodigies of learning. Catherine's disposition lay in another direction entirely; she it was who advised Jane on the most economical means of achieving a fashionable appearance. 'A round gown, with a jacket, & a frock front, like Cath Bigg's' was what she had recently ordered from Mrs Mussell, her dressmaker in Bath.[44] It was Catherine that Jane chose to dance with at neighbourhood balls when a shortage of men threatened her with a lack of partners. Between the Austen girls it had become a habit to tease and mimic the speech of their Manydown friends. When she first met Mrs Evelyn in Bath, Jane remarked on her pleasing manners: 'The Biggs would call her *a nice woman*.' With her long thin face, Catherine always put Jane strongly in mind of Marianne Bridges of Goodnestone, while Alethea bore such a striking resemblance to Marianne's sister Harriot that, on a recent visit to Kent, Jane had been more than once on the point of calling Harriot 'Alethea'. Both girls had the same pleasant and cheerful manner, interested in everything, and yet 'thoughtful' and 'considerate' with a 'decided turn of mind'.

Married or unmarried, the Bigg girls remained very close, and during Cassandra's lengthy absences from home, Jane would often tease her with sly comparisons. 'There is no denying that they are very capricious!' she wrote: 'For they like to enjoy their elder sisters company when they can.'[45]

Harris Bigg-Wither was a less amiable companion. Tall, clumsy and awkward, he would shamble through the house, or lounge on a sofa, adding little to the general conversation. His presence would cast something of a blight over the high spirits of his sisters. It was not just his stutter which made him taciturn; he was silent by nature and avoided much society. Brought up as a younger son, with six elder sisters, he was accustomed to amuse himself by tormenting his sisters with boyish pranks. On the death of his elder brother, Harris had become the heir to Manydown at the age of just thirteen. A tutor, Mr Wallington, prepared him for entry to Worcester College, Oxford, but Harris returned from the university with few signs of learning or other accomplishments. Wit was never a strong point with him. On one occasion, having ordered his butler to serve his guests a punch of ill-assorted wines, Harris rose to make a speech. 'Gentlemen,' he said, 'my punch is like you. In your individual capacity you are all very good fellows, but in your corporate capacity you are very disagreeable.'[46] That was Harris Bigg-Wither's idea of a *bon mot*. There were frequent rows with his father and even more frequent bouts of illness. His hand bled, his tongue stuttered and he walked in a clumsy, stumbling fashion. Jane Austen sympathized with the poor man's 'bad habit of body'; at twenty-one Harris was six years younger than her, but seemed even younger, almost like an overgrown schoolboy. To her amazement, on the night of 2 December, just one week after her arrival at Manydown, the schoolboy asked her to marry him.

His proposal came as a complete shock, but, once he had uttered it, she was forced to think very seriously about her reply. One thing she knew for certain: she did not love Harris Bigg-Wither, yet that fact in itself need not be decisive. She was within a fortnight of her twenty-seventh birthday, and she had long thought of twenty-seven as a critical age. 'A woman of seven and twenty,' Marianne Dashwood declares, 'can never hope to feel or inspire affection again.' Charlotte Lucas was twenty-seven when she accepted Mr Collins, explaining her decision to Elizabeth Bennet in these terms: 'I am not romantic you know. I never was. I ask only a comfortable home.'[47] Jane Austen, too, had ceased to think of herself as 'romantic'. Romantic love as the basis of a happy marriage was, she believed, a principle more fondly adhered to in a certain kind of fiction than in real life. And Manydown would be a very comfortable home indeed. In real life, a desirable match was one in which both parties – and their relations – found something to their mutual advantage. Her own advantage from these proposals was something which no sensible person could doubt. To be removed from a situation of relative poverty in rented lodgings at Bath and transformed into the mistress of such a magnificent estate as Manydown; an estate, moreover, within a few miles of the scenes of her childhood, surrounded by family and friends. This was an opportunity which she might well have believed to exceed her wildest aspirations. It was more difficult for her to conceive wherein Mr Wither found his own advantage from this proposal. His evident affection for her was something she had never expected, and was certainly very flattering: 'It is something for a woman to be assured, in her eight-and-twentieth year, that she has not lost one charm of earlier youth.'[48] And, even if she could not *love* him, she could at least like him. He was young and, with guidance, it was not impossible to imagine that he might improve. In the circumstances, it might almost be argued that it would be a piece of recklessness *not* to marry him. 'You know we must marry,' Miss Watson reminds her younger sister Emma in *The Watsons*. 'I could do very well single for my own part. A little company, and a pleasant ball now and then, would be enough for me, if one could be young forever; but my father cannot provide for us, and it is very bad to grow old and be poor and laughed at.' Jane Austen already felt the same fear of growing old to be poor and laughed at. 'A single woman, with a very narrow income, must be a ridiculous, disagreeable old maid!'[49] Accordingly, late in the evening of 2 December, she informed Mr Bigg-Wither that she accepted his proposal and agreed to marry him.

Almost as soon as she had given him her word, it seems that

she regretted it. Whether it was his manner of receiving her assent which gave her warning how widely their sensibilities differed; or whether it was the terrible finality of such an irrevocable choice, she was plunged into a sudden melancholy. According to Fanny Lefroy, she felt 'a revulsion of feeling'. Caroline Austen agrees: 'She found she was miserable & that the place & fortune which would certainly be *his*, could not alter the *man*.' After the initial excitement of saying 'yes' it was only natural that there should be some anxious moments of nocturnal reflections. Inevitably, at some point during the night, Jane must have consulted her sister Cassandra. Whether she did so before giving her answer, or afterwards, we cannot tell; nor can we know the nature of Cassandra's advice. Did she, in the words of Marianne Dashwood, condemn it as a 'compact of convenience', a 'commercial exchange in which each wished to be benefited at the expense of the other'? Or did she remind Jane of all the 'horrible eligibilities and proprieties of the match', and the pleasure it would give to all her family and his?[50]

Although we can never know the precise answers to such questions, we may perhaps glean some clues from fictional scenes which Jane Austen wrote shortly after this awkward episode. Such 'clues', if they may be dignified by such a term, must be treated with extreme circumspection. Jane Austen is not, in any obvious way, an autobiographical writer. Her sources are literary, rather than personal, and her ironic tone is notable for the manner in which it contrives to conceal all traces of private emotion in its detached and urbane style. Yet *The Watsons*, which she began barely a year after the events at Manydown, may be more revealing in this respect than most of her other writings. For *The Watsons* exists as a fragment only, unfinished and unrevised; something about the hard, cynical tone of the piece deterred her from ever returning to it. That fragment focuses, clearly and painfully, on some unenviable choices in the marital prospects of the Watson sisters. Its lack of conclusion suggests some diffidence in achieving a satisfying narrative resolution to the dilemmas which it presents.

From the start, one important character is missing. Emma Watson's elder sister Penelope is someone we never meet; like Jane's own

elder sister Cassandra, she is a powerful off-stage presence, ma-
nipulating the fates and prospects of others, but never visible in her
own terms. It was Penelope, we learn, who had destroyed her sister's
chance of marriage. 'Yes, Emma, Penelope was at the bottom of it.
She thinks everything fair for a husband; I trusted her, she set him
against me, with a view of gaining him herself, and it ended in his
discontinuing his visits and soon after marrying someone else.' 'You
quite shock me,' Emma replies. 'Could a sister do such a thing?
Rivalry, treachery between sisters!' 'You do not know Penelope,'
says Miss Watson. 'There is nothing she would not do to get married
. . . Do not trust her with any secrets of your own . . .'

There is no reason to suspect Cassandra of having attempted,
in this way, to supplant Jane in Harris Bigg-Wither's affections.
What is interesting about this exchange (and about several similar
passages in *The Watsons*), is less the narrative detail than the under-
lying sense of uncertainty and distrust. It is the emphasis on
'rivalry, treachery between sisters' that strikes a disturbing note.
Could there have been rivalry – even treachery – between the
Austen sisters?

We have grown used to regarding Jane and Cassandra as virtually identical in all their thoughts and feelings. It was Jane's constant instinct, we are told, to defer to Cassandra's opinions: 'the
habit of looking up to her begun in childhood, seemed always to
continue.' 'I truly believe' (wrote Caroline) 'she did always *really*
think of her sister, as the superior to herself.'[51] Though it was Jane
who wrote some of the greatest novels in the English language
(novels moreover which are remarkable for their quality of intellectual discrimination), we have continued to accept this notion of
her instinctive deference to Cassandra's supposed 'superiority'.
The traditional image of these two inseparable sisters as a like-
minded pair has had such a powerful hold on the imagination of
later generations, that we have scarcely observed some contrary
indications. It has hardly been noticed, for example, how, in Jane
Austen's later novels, there is little of the affectionate closeness
between sisters that we find in *Pride and Prejudice* and *Sense and
Sensibility*. In *Persuasion*, Anne Elliot's sisters are described as
'repulsive and unsisterly'; in *Mansfield Park*, the Bertram sisters

are described as 'alienated from each other'; and in *Emma*, the friendship between Emma and Isabella is chiefly maintained by the fact that they live sixteen miles apart.[52] Part of the appeal of the story of the mysterious gentleman of Sidmouth was to reinforce the symmetry of the Austen sisters' fates. But Harris Bigg-Wither's proposal did something entirely different. It marked a clear distinction between them. On this occasion, Jane was clearly singled out. Had she married Harris Bigg-Wither it must have put an end to the special closeness between her sister and herself. Cassandra and her parents would, of course, have been welcome to visit Jane at Manydown; but they would have been there as guests of Jane's husband. Just as, when staying at Godmersham, they were beneficiaries of Edward's Knight family fortune. Had Jane Austen become the mistress of Manydown, the nature of the relationship between the sisters would have been changed forever. Such a change might easily have provoked rivalry, if not treachery, between them.

Whatever advice Cassandra gave her sister that December night would inevitably reflect upon this relative balance of their fortunes. However closely bound together they might be in feelings, the difference in their immediate situations must have imposed its own burden of awkwardness. Even if they were both agreed in regarding a loveless marriage as a form of generous sacrifice that might be undertaken (as Eliza Hancock had married de Feuillide) for the general good of the family, there was all the difference in the world between the outlook of the prospective victim of such a sacrifice, and that of a potential beneficiary. Another passage in *The Watsons* may be revealing. 'To be so bent on marriage,' Emma exclaims; 'to pursue a man merely for the sake of situation – is a sort of thing that shocks me. I cannot understand it. Poverty is a great evil, but to a woman of education and feeling it ought not, it cannot be the greatest.' Emma protests that she 'would rather be a teacher at a school (and I can think of nothing worse) than marry a man I did not like'. Yet if this seems hard-headed enough, her sister can be equally ruthless in evaluating the prospects for women with neither youth nor fortune to recommend them. 'I would rather do anything than be a teacher at a school,' she replies. 'I have been at school, Emma, and know what a life they lead you; you never have. I should not like marrying a disagreable man any more than yourself. But I do not think there *are* very many disagreable men; I think I could like any good-humoured man with a comfortable income.' As with Charlotte Lucas, the emphasis is on a *comfortable* home and a *comfortable* income; and Harris Bigg-Wither surely possessed both of those. Were these the terms in which the sisters' nocturnal conversation was conducted? Did they consider, with a sense of gloomy foreboding, a dismal future as school-teachers in some putrefying tenement in Bath?

That night at Manydown was one of the most terrible of Jane Austen's life, as she was forced to contemplate, with blank horror, the stupidity of what she had done in agreeing to marry Harris Bigg-Wither. She had committed the kind of reckless error which it was easy enough to remedy in the case of a fictional heroine, whose misadventures might always be brought to a felicitous conclusion by the providential contrivances of the plot. But in real life such an assent could not be withdrawn without considerable disagreeableness and shame. She, who had such an ironic talent for exposing the emotional equivocations and tender self-deceptions of her fictional heroines, had sadly failed to employ this talent in her own life. She had rationalized where she should have *felt*; she had thought to balance a nice equation of relative benefits in a situation where only her instincts mattered: 'the place & fortune which would certainly be *his*, could not alter the *man*.' This she had known, yet she had blinded herself to the knowledge. It was some comfort to know that she could acquit herself of acting selfishly. When she had given her consent it had not been from any motives of personal pride or gratification, but from a sense of familial duty. Had she allowed herself to think *selfishly* from the start, she would never have agreed to Bigg-Wither's proposal. Others no doubt might have accused her of mercenary motives, but she herself would have known the falsity of that charge. But none of that made it easier to behave selfishly *now*, and retract the word she had given. Now that she realized what a terrible mistake she had made, what could she do about it? She had given her word, and such a thing could not be easily broken. At the very least it must risk a complete rift between the families, with the loss of the friendship of Catherine and Alethea, who had always been so dear to her. How she wished she could call back the past twelve hours! How she wished that he had never asked her, and that she had not said *yes*. When Charlotte, the impetuous heroine of 'Frederic and Elfrida', found herself in a similar predicament (though she, in fact, had engaged herself to *two* men she did not love), she had thrown herself into a stream. *That* hardly seemed an appropriate solution. When Jane had written that story she had still been dreaming of marriage to the princely Henry Frederic Howard Fitzwilliam of London – but Harris Bigg-Wither was certainly no Prince Fitzwilliam.

In the end it was her sense of art, rather than her sense of prudence, which guided her to a decision. Much as she loved to mock at romanticism in her novels, she could never entirely abandon that optimism of the imagination which lay at the heart of romance. At the end of all her novels, the heroine always married the man she loved, whose comfortable income was a symbol of his frank and manly instincts, rather than a substitute for them. Only the minor characters, like Charlotte Lucas, were condemned to suffer the cynical misfortunes of an adverse providence. Even at the late age of twenty-seven, Jane Austen determined to lead the life of a heroine, come what may. Even now, she wrote 'only for fame, and without any view to pecuniary emolument', and she would marry the same way – or not at all. By dawn she had made her decision. Bitter as it was, she must acknowledge her error and confess her mistake.

Early that morning of Friday 3 December, she met her fiancé of twelve hours and told him that she had changed her mind. She no longer wished to marry him. That morning at Manydown was a dismal scene. Servants summoned at short notice to pack and carry the Austen sisters' belongings to a waiting carriage; the Bigg sisters, Catherine and Alethea, hastily summoned to cover the departure with a show of formality. Unspoken words, eyes averted, a guilty silence. And a carriage hurriedly moving away under the bare trees.

★   ★   ★

When Mary Lloyd finally heard the reason for the sudden departure of her sisters-in-law, she expressed regret and some surprise
at Jane's perverse decision. The match, she insisted, would have
been highly desirable. Her daughter Caroline affected to show
greater understanding. Harris Bigg-Wither, she noted, was 'very
plain in person – awkward & even uncouth in manner – nothing
but his size to recommend him – he was a fine big man – but one
need not look about for secret reasons to account for a young
lady's *not* loving him.' Thereafter, the story became the stuff of
family legend, and the nieces competed in offering their own
accounts. Catherine Hubback, who claimed to have read Jane
Austen's own letters on the subject, offered this version. 'I gathered
from the letters that it was in a momentary fit of self-delusion that
Aunt Jane accepted Mr Wither's proposal, and that when it was
all settled eventually, and the negative decisively given she was
much relieved. I think the affair vexed her a good deal, but I am
sure she had no attachment to him.' 'To be sure she should not
have said yes – over night,' declared Caroline. 'But I have always
respected her for the courage in cancelling that yes – the next
morning. All worldly advantage would have been to her – & she
was of an age to know *this* quite well. My aunts had very small
fortunes & on their father's death they & their mother would be,
they were aware, but poorly off. I believe most young women so
circumstanced would have taken Mr W. & trusted to love after
marriage . . .'

Harris Bigg-Wither himself seemed not unduly discouraged by
Jane Austen's refusal. Less than two years later, he consoled himself by marrying Anne Howe Frith, of Carisbrooke on the Isle of
Wight, whose father was a lieutenant-colonel in the North Hants
militia. 'Harris Wither and his wife are still at Quidhampton and
seem very happy,' Mrs Lefroy remarked, somewhat tactlessly,
shortly afterwards. 'Everyone in the neighbourhood seems pleased
with the bride.'[53] 'Everyone', in this case, did not include Harris's
father, Lovelace Bigg-Wither. The two men quarrelled once more,
and Harris took his wife to live at Wymering, near Cosham in
Hampshire, where seven of their ten children were born. He did
not return to Manydown until after his father's death in 1813.

CHAPTER 8

The Wrong Place

I proposed and pressed being sent home on Thursday, to prevent the possibility of being in the wrong place.

Jane Austen, Letter to Cassandra, August 1805

'Something like the truth'

For the Countess, the autumn of 1801 was wretched and bleak. For weeks, her son Hastings endured the most heart-rending agonies that it had ever been her misfortune to witness. His death, when it came, was 'a desirable release'. After the long series of torments which the 'dear sufferer' had undergone, she confessed herself 'most thankful' for their eventual termination. To Phylly, she expressed her humble hope that her 'dear child' might at last have exchanged 'a most painful existence' for 'a blessed immortality'.[1] Henry, too, was unwell. For five months it seemed he had never enjoyed an hour's health, and Dr Baillie remained a regular visitor to the house in Upper Berkeley Street, with his various remedies and prescriptions. That October, they proposed a visit to Godmersham that had been promised for all of four years. Perhaps the air of Kent would have a salutary effect on Henry's consumptive symptoms, though Eliza promised herself little peace or tranquillity from the visit. Edward's Elizabeth had just produced her sixth, or was it her seventh, child? Such a dedication to conjugal duties was really quite astonishing. Had she been 'in spirits', she remarked to Phylly, she would have made some observation on the handsome premium to which these prolific parents must surely be entitled 'for such an addition to the number of his Majesty's liege subjects'.[2]

It was while they were at Godmersham, as Eliza did her best to find solace in little George's habit of pulling her hair about her ears, and Lizzy's fondness for untying her sashes, that they received the first news of the peace treaty. The men were naturally sceptical. Seven years of soldiering had somewhat altered Henry's attitude towards their Gallic neighbours. He did now rather incline to regard those murdering *mounseers* as perfidious, half-starved, lousy devils. All the more reason, the Countess said, to rescue her late husband's property from their grasping hands. As his widow, she was entitled to a share of the estate at Guienne. At first, Henry hesitated. Only recently he had become implicated in an awkward financial *contretemps* with Eliza's (god)father over some other property to which she felt herself entitled. *That* episode had come close to costing him Mr Hastings's good-will and it had taken all Henry's skills in self-abasement and flattery to mollify the old man's suspicions. 'I regarded with sensations little short of horror,' he had written to him, 'the possibility of appearing to you capable of meanness or rapacity.'[3] But the Countess was insistent, and, as she always told Phylly, Henry 'has no will but mine'.[4] Eventually, they embarked on their expedition to recover what was rightfully hers. The French authorities, however, saw things rather differently. 'Mrs Austen' was informed that her late husband, the so-called 'Comte' de Feuillide, had died a confessed murderer and a thief. As such, his property was confiscated by the state. Worse, while Eliza and Henry haggled with lawyers and officials, the brief truce between England and France came to a sudden end, and war was resumed in May 1803.

Mr and Mrs Henry Austen now found themselves in danger of being captured and interned at Verdun as enemy subjects. But Eliza was not unduly dismayed by this unwelcome turn of affairs.

She had escaped from France once before, she announced, and would do so again. All it needed was for them to masquerade as a loyal French couple. They agreed that Henry should be relegated to an invalid role in the corner of their travelling carriage. No one at the posting stations could detect her nationality, and her own perfect command of French was sufficient to disarm all suspicion.[5] Their escape brought back nightmarish memories of her desperate flight eight years before; but what it also called to mind was an episode from the story 'Henry and Eliza', which Jane had written many years before. *That* Eliza had set sail for England defiantly 'in a man-of-war of 55 guns' (the sort of fighting-ship in which Captain Frank Austen might even now be patrolling the coastline off Boulogne). *This* Eliza contented herself with sneering at the tricolours that had replaced the fleur-de-lys along the quayside buildings as they boarded the ship for home.

Frank, too, was soon back on land. He was ordered to take command of a volunteer force of 'Sea-Fencibles' and charged with 'effectually preventing the landing of an enemy in this country'. These 'Sea-Fencibles' were a ramshackle corps of fishermen, old soldiers, retired navy men and civilians, and Frank's task was hardly easy. While Charles was quickly promoted to command of the sloop HMS *Indian*, Frank was ordered to protect a long coastal strip 'From Sandown exclusive to the North Foreland inclusive', with Pegwell Bay, an ideal place for enemy landings, at its centre. His orders 'required and directed' him to 'repair forthwith to Ramsgate, and take upon you the command of all such men as may from time to time enroll themselves within the said district, for the defence of the coast'.[6]

He arrived in Ramsgate in July 1803, and quickly established a reputation for piety unusual in one of his profession. Dr Johnson, when once visiting a ship-of-the-line, had felt himself compelled to rebuke the foul-mouthed commander, beseeching him 'not to use one oath more than is absolutely required for the service of his Majesty'. Frank's demeanour was very different, and he became known as 'the officer who knelt at church'.[7] His sober manner soon endeared him to Mary Gibson, the pretty eldest daughter of a respectable family with a town house in the High Street. Yet the Austens viewed his fondness for the Gibson girl with something less than enthusiasm. Ramsgate was one of those seaside towns which Jane Austen disliked. 'He talks of fixing at Ramsgate – Bad taste!' she remarked of one hypochondriac acquaintance. With its grandiose pier, dull Assembly Room and plentiful medical men, Ramsgate was one of those places which specialized in catering for the affectations of those, like Harriet Foote, who cultivated their indispositions as a way of life. 'She is a poor honey,' Jane once remarked to Frank; 'the sort of woman who gives me the idea of being determined never to be well – & who likes her spasms & nervousness & the consequences they give her, better than anything else.'[8] Her opinion of the place was not much improved when she visited Frank there that autumn, and found herself mightily patronized by Sir Egerton Brydges, who was just the sort of man who liked holding forth in the seaside card rooms. 'Cheeks a little too full' was all that Sir Egerton recalled of Jane. Author of such novels as *Mary de Clifford* and *Arthur Fitz-Albini*, Sir Egerton prided himself on his status as a man of letters, and would discourse on literary topics with an air of authority which Jane was too polite to contradict. 'I did not know that she was addicted to literary composition,' he later observed, with characteristic condescension.[9]

One person who did know of Jane's literary addiction was her brother Henry. Now that she had turned down Harris Bigg-Wither's offer of marriage, Henry thought it high time for his younger sister to exploit her literary talents. He advised Jane to make a second copy of 'Susan' with a view to publication. By the time this work was completed (with the inclusion of some topical allusions to Maria Edgeworth's new novel, *Belinda*), Henry himself was in Paris. But he had left word with Mr Seymour, his man of business in London, to arrange for the sale of the book to Richard Crosby & Co., of Stationer's Hall Court. The sum agreed for the sale – £10 – was hardly a generous amount (Mrs Radcliffe had received £500 for *The Mysteries of Udolpho*). However, Jane was greatly encouraged by the stipulation for an 'early publication'. She was even more encouraged when an advertisement for 'Susan, a Novel in Two Volumes' was included in Crosby's *Flowers of Literature* later that year.[10] It gave her a secret gratification, while condemned to endure Sir Egerton Brydges's homilies on the novelist's art, to know that she must soon be acknowledged as the authoress of a work in which the far-fetched romances which Sir Egerton approved would be ridiculed.

Ramsgate was not the only seaside town to which Jane Austen affected to take an exception. Weymouth also earned her disapproval, though chiefly, it seems, because when Cassandra, Henry and Eliza visited it in the summer of 1803, she herself was left behind at Lyme with only her parents for company. 'Weymouth is altogether a shocking place, I perceive,' she wrote archly to her sister, 'without recommendation of any kind.'[11] Not only had Cassandra been disappointed in her hopes of seeing King George and his family embark on their Royal Sovereign yacht, but she had also found the town to be entirely devoid of ice. 'No ice!' Jane exclaimed in mock-horror. 'For every other vexation I was in some measure prepared . . . But for there being no ice, what could prepare me!' Sadly, it seems that Lyme was equally deficient in this respect. On the night of 5 November, while Jane Austen was staying there, a fierce fire broke out in the centre of the town which destroyed several houses. 'The flames were considerable,' she recalled five years later, when a fire in Southampton brought back all the fears of that November night; 'they seemed about as near to us as those at Lyme.'

Jane Austen's opinions regarding such places as Ramsgate and Weymouth, however facetiously expressed, are at least a matter of record. Her attitudes to Bath itself, where the Austens had their family home for five years between 1801 and 1806, are less easy to determine. Yet most biographers are in no doubt about the matter. They have been happy to take it on the word of later family members that her time at Bath was a miserable period of virtual imprisonment. According to Fanny Lefroy, part of the appeal of Harris Bigg-Wither's proposal was that 'he would take her from the Bath she disliked and restore her to the country she loved'. Her novels have been quoted to reinforce this view. We are reminded that Anne Elliot dreaded the 'white glare' of Bath in the heat of a September day, and entered the family's rented house in Camden Place 'with a sinking heart, anticipating an imprisonment of many months, and anxiously saying to herself, "Oh! when shall I leave you again?"'[12] The temptation to regard Anne Elliot's sinking feelings as indicative of the author's own emotions has usually proved irresistible, even though *Persuasion* was not begun till nine years after Jane herself had left Bath. The novel which she was actually working on while living in Bath was 'Susan' (*Northanger Abbey*), whose heroine viewed the city with altogether different emotions: 'They arrived at Bath. Catherine was all eager delight; – her eyes were here, there, every where as they approached its fine and striking environs, and afterwards drove through those streets which conducted them to the hotel. She was come to be happy, and she felt happy already.'[13]

The truth is that we know virtually nothing about the state of Jane Austen's emotions during her years at Bath. We possess only five letters that she sent from the city during the whole of that five-year period. Of these, three were addressed to Frank in January 1805, with details of their father's death. There are only two letters, both sent to Cassandra in April 1805, which offer any real indication of Jane's true feelings about life in Bath. Two letters in five years are meagre evidence on which to base any general conclusions, *especially* when these letters actually demonstrate *not* despondency and a sinking heart, but considerable energy and buoyancy of spirits ('Here is a day for you! Did Bath or Ibthrop ever see a finer 8th of April? . . . We were out again last night . . . [and] we are engaged tomorrow evening. What request we are in!'). One later letter, it is true, would appear to lend credibility to the traditional view. In October 1808, Jane wrote to Cassandra: 'It will be two years tomorrow since we left Bath for Clifton, with what happy feelings of escape!'[14] Yet the place which she escaped *to*, we notice, was not the bucolic retreat of rural Hampshire, but Clifton, another fashionable spa. And what she was escaping *from* in 1806 was less the city of Bath itself than the humiliation of an increasingly impoverished and unsettled existence after the death of her father, and after the circulation of yet more scurrilous rumours concerning her aunt Leigh-Perrot.

In fact, there is evidence to suggest that the Austens were quite contented with their life at Bath. When the nine-year-old Anna Austen visited them at Sydney Place, she was greatly struck by how much her grandparents 'seemed to enjoy the cheerfulness of their town life ... I have always thought that this was the short holyday of their married life,' she wrote. At the age of seventy, George Austen was still a handsome man, somewhat vain of his appearance, who delighted in all the public admiration which his fine head of white hair would receive on his promenades in Sydney Gardens, or at Pump Room assemblies. 'His hair in its whiteness ... was very beautiful and glossy, with short curls above the ears,' Anna recalled. 'I can well remember ... what notice he attracted, when on any public occasion he appeared with his head uncovered.' So proud was he, that he had a miniature portrait painted which showed off his white curls to advantage. He and his wife also sat for silhouettes, and in hers, Mrs Austen was equally keen to emphasize her handsome Leigh family nose.[15]

There was indeed something of a holiday atmosphere about those first few years at Bath. With its handsome squares and elegant crescents, its splendid gardens and extensive walks, Bath was still the most fashionable of cities. Over forty thousand visitors a year came to Bath, among whom were numbered all the leading figures in society, literature and the arts. Every week, the *Bath Chronicle* proudly announced the latest arrivals; Richardson and Sterne, Cowper and Smollett, Johnson and Boswell had all visited the city. Burke and Goldsmith had lived in the North Parade; Sheridan in the Royal Crescent; and the young Horatio Nelson had a house in Pierrepont Street. Family members who came to visit the Austens at Sydney Place might be taken to the Lower Room, 'one of the pleasantest in the kingdom for a morning lounge, commanding a view of the adjacent hills, woods, the valley and the river Avon'. They might take a promenade in the Pump Room, where Beau Nash's 'Rules of Etiquette' were still posted for all to see; or they might attend the Theatre Royal to see Kemble's *Macbeth*. Shortly after the Austens' arrival, a grand picnic, ball and card party was held in Sydney Gardens to celebrate the birthday of the Duchess of York, attended by all 'the superlative belles of our fair city'.[16] There were musical parties in the Gardens, organized by the Harmonious Society of Bath, at which Jane Austen was grateful for the company of the Holders ('I cannot utterly abhor them, especially as Miss Holder owns that she has no taste for music'). Mr Wilkinson lectured on galvanism at the Lower Rooms and Mr Rauzzini arranged subscription concerts in the New Assembly Rooms. It was a city of chance encounters and sudden friendships, and Jane relished the variety of such unpredictable alliances. One year it would be Mrs Chamberlayne with whom she would be striding across Sion Hill; another year it would be Miss Irvine who would join her in a 'very pleasant walk to Twerton'. She was careful never to mistake such casual friendships for real intimacies, and was always on her guard against confidences too easily bestowed. 'She seems to like people rather too easily,' she remarked of Miss Armstrong, her walking-companion on the Cobb at Lyme.[17] Yet her novelist's imagination was always stimulated by the rich diversity of human specimens that a city like Bath afforded, and she would regard each new companion with a kind of detached fascination. 'She is a funny one,' she remarked once of Miss Irvine; 'I have answered her letter, and have endeavoured to give something like the truth with as little incivility as I could.' 'She is very conversable in a common way,' she commented on Miss Armstrong; 'I do not perceive wit or genius – but she has sense & some degree of taste, & her manners are very engaging.'[18]

A city of visitors like Bath, or a seaside resort like Lyme, were places where she might encounter, without the risk of long-term association, a far wider repertoire of characters and manners than would ever be available to her in a rural Hampshire village. On her first arrival in Bath she could not entirely extinguish, however well she might disguise it, something of the same anticipation that Catherine Morland felt, 'her eyes . . . here, there, every where'. Even four years later, some vestiges of that initial excitement remained. So many people, she boasted, were constantly demanding her company: 'I shall endeavour as much as possible to keep my intimacies in their proper place, & prevent their clashing . . . Among so many friends,' she added, 'it will be well if I do not get into a scrape.'[19]

Ill health, however, placed some constraints upon family happiness and sociability. Throughout their years at Sydney Place, Mr Austen was subject to intermittent bouts of a feverish complaint which even the most assiduous efforts of Dr Bowen – who had quite supplanted Mapleton as the physician of choice – were ineffectual to cure. At Paragon, uncle Leigh-Perrot was still a martyr to the gout, while his wife could never quite throw off a persistent cough, which she attributed to her months in Ilchester gaol. Then, in the early months of 1804, Mrs Austen was very ill, and Bowen was frequently at her bedside. For several weeks, her condition remained serious until at last, in mid-March, Fanny Austen was able to write in her diary that Grandmama Austen was now 'perfectly well'. Mrs Austen felt such grateful relief at her recovery that she was inspired to record it in some humorous verses entitled 'Dialogue between Death and Mrs A'.

> *Says Death, 'I've been trying these three weeks and more*
> *To seize on old Madam here at Number Four,*
> *Yet I still try in vain, tho' she's turned of three score;*
> *To what is my ill success owing?'*
>
> *'I'll tell you, old fellow, if you cannot guess,*
> *To what you're indebted for your ill success –*
> *To the prayers of my husband, whose love I possess;*
> *To the care of my daughters, whom Heaven will bless,*
> *To the skill and attention of Bowen.'*[20]

Shortly afterwards, Mr Austen abruptly 'threw up' the lease at Sydney Place, which still had three months to run, and took his family on a summer tour of the seaside resorts of Devon and Dorset. It was a time of general upheaval. Frank, now engaged to the Gibson girl, had ended his tour of land duties with the Fencibles and taken command of the fifty-gun HMS *Leopard*, patrolling the sea approaches to Boulogne. In London, Henry and Eliza had decided to quit their house in Upper Berkeley Street in favour of a small terraced house in Michael's Place, overlooking the fields and gardens of Brompton. Henry also moved his offices from Cleveland Court to Albany in Piccadilly. Jane was delighted when she heard that Henry and Eliza planned to accompany the Austens on their seaside trip. It was the first time she had seen Eliza since the death of poor Hastings three years earlier, and she was keen to learn how she was suited to the life of a London banker's wife. In the late summer, the little party arrived at Lyme Regis, where they stayed at Pyne House in Broad Street. Jane was anxious to know from Henry if he had heard anything from Crosby & Son concerning her novel, but he had no news for her. Publishers, they all knew, took their time about such matters, and a year was surely a short time to wait for the appearance of such a little masterpiece. Henry then took Eliza and Cassandra on to Weymouth, while Jane remained with her parents in a smaller boarding-house at Lyme.

Jane wrote to Cassandra from Lyme on Friday 14 September. The letter is significant less for what it says than for the fact that it exists at all. For this is the first letter which survives after the three-year silence. Yet it will hardly do to scrutinize her words for any signs of alteration or disillusionment in the attitudes of the twenty-eight-year-old Jane Austen from those of her twenty-five-year-old self. This letter survived Cassandra's censorship, we may surmise, precisely *because* it offers no tell-tale insights into the disturbances of those intervening years. In it we find the same ingredients as before; the same witty preoccupations with dancing and darning, the same mixture of mocking asides and literary allusions. One whimsical servant is depicted as a walking anthology of fictional parallels. His skill with boots puts Jane in mind of *Tristram Shandy*: 'James is the delight of our lives,' she writes, 'he is quite an uncle Toby's annuity to us.'[21] His desire for adventure suggests a character from *Sir Charles Grandison*: 'He has the laudable thirst I fancy for travelling, which in poor James Selby was so much reprobated.' But the man's own reading is Defoe: 'he has read the 1st vol. of *Robinson Crusoe*'. However much the distractions of Bath may have interfered with Jane Austen's love of writing, it seems that her love of reading had continued with unabated enthusiasm. Her own skill for brisk, deflationary ironies had, if anything, grown more assured with the years. 'It was absolutely necessary that I should have the little fever & indisposition which I had,' she observed; 'it has been all the fashion this week in Lyme. Miss Anna Cove was confined for a day or two, & her mother thinks she was saved only by a timely emetic (presescribed by Dr Robinson) from a serious illness.'

'Quizzing' – a kind of scornful ogling – was, she found, just as much the fashion at Lyme as at Bath. ('There was a monstrous deal of stupid quizzing, & common-place nonsense talked, but scarcely any wit,' she had once remarked of a tedious walking-party in Sydney Gardens.) At one ball in Lyme, she found herself impudently quizzed by 'an odd-looking man' who 'had been eyeing me for some time'. 'I think he must be Irish,' she concluded, probably one of the Barnwell tribe, 'bold, queer-looking people, just fit to be quality at Lyme.' Much as she affected to deplore this fashion, she was actually an accomplished 'quiz' herself. Her brisk portrait of the elusive Miss Seymer of Bath is a masterpiece of the 'quizzing' style ('her dress is not even smart, & her appearance very quiet. Miss Irvine says she is never speaking a word. Poor wretch, I am afraid she is *en Penitence*').[22] At twenty-eight she had lost none of her satirical style, and was still disposed to prefer witty vice to dull virtue. Their versatile servant James, she noted, had 'a great many more than all the cardinal virtues (for the cardinal virtues in themselves have been so. often possessed that they are no longer worth having)'.

Sea-bathing was something of a novelty, and one that she took to with great pleasure. She found it 'so delightful' to splash about in the gentle waves that she was often tempted to stay in the water too long, and as a consequence, would feel 'unreasonably tired' in the hot afternoons. 'I shall be more careful another time,' she promised, without any great conviction. The truth was that tiredness, reasonable or otherwise, was a perfect excuse for avoiding household duties. She gave a lively sketch of the genteel seediness and decay of the boarding-house, with its slatternly servants whose coarse maladies seemed to parody the fashionable indispositions of their social superiors. There was a 'general dirtiness' in 'the house & furniture, & all its inhabitants,' she complained, and 'nothing . . . can exceed the inconvenience of the offices'. It even made her think longingly of their tidy house at Sydney Place, now occupied by the pompous Coles: 'The Coles have got their infamous plate upon our door,' she noted with some impatience.

In Cassandra's absence, she affected to despair of ever equalling her sister's skill in household management. 'I endeavour as far as I can to supply your place,' she wrote, '& be useful & keep things in order.' She pictured herself battling hopelessly against a rising tide of disorder. 'I detect dirt in the water-decanter as fast as I can, and give the cook physic, which she throws off her stomach. I forget whether she used to do this, under your administration.' Even Pyne, the landlord of their previous lodging-house, was causing difficulties. 'I have written to Mr Pyne on the subject of the broken lid; it was valued . . . we are told, at five shillings, & as that appeared to us beyond the value of all the furniture in the room together, we have referred ourselves to the owner.' Little wonder that she far preferred the luxury of sea-bathing to such tiresome anxieties as these.

In the evenings there were balls at the Assembly Room near Bell Cliff and Cobb Gate. The Austens would arrive a little after 8 p.m., and Mr Austen would remain there 'very contentedly', playing at Commerce or Speculation, till half past nine. He would then walk home with 'uncle Toby' James and a lanthorn, though the lanthorn did not need to be lit when the moon was up. Jane and her mother would stay rather longer, and Jane would dance sometimes with Mr Crawford, and sometimes with the one she called *le Chevalier*. The identity of her partner scarcely mattered; what she loved was dancing itself, in that room with its three glass chandeliers hanging down from a high-arched ceiling, and its large windows looking out over the moonlit sea.[23]

The chief pleasure of Lyme was its walks, along the sinuous line of fine high cliffs to Charmouth, across the Downs to Uplyme, or along the ancient Cobb. It was at Lyme that Jane met Mrs Armstrong, a lady with engaging manners but uncouth parents and depressingly domestic habits (she spent the whole of one of Jane's visits darning a pair of stockings). 'I do not mention this at home,' Jane confided, 'lest a warning should act as an example.'

One day, the two of them 'walked together for an hour on the Cobb', that massive semi-circular pier jutting out on the far side of the harbour, with its two causeways, on different levels, known as the Upper and Lower Cobb. At one point on their walk they passed a precipitous flight of rough-hewn steps, from the Upper to the Lower Cobb, known as 'Granny's Teeth'. Unprotected, steep and treacherous these steps presented a dangerous obstacle to lady walkers in long dresses. The dizzying view downward, from the Upper to the Lower Cobb, remained in Jane Austen's mind for many years and inspired the incident of Louisa Mus-grove's fall in *Persuasion*. When the poet Tennyson visited the town, his friends were keen to show him the place where the Duke of Monmouth had landed in 1685. 'Don't talk to me of the Duke of Monmouth,' he exclaimed. 'Show me the exact spot where Louisa Musgrove fell.'[24]

'We cannot be supposed to be very rich'

The Austens returned to Bath on 25 October and rented a house in Green Park Buildings, No. 3, on the east side. Perhaps the landlord had raised the floors, as Mr Philips, the landlord of No. 12, had promised to do, but nothing more was heard about the dangers of putrefaction. The rooms there had the benefit of a fine view of Beechen Cliff across the Avon, and were deemed perfectly adequate to their needs.[25] On 16 December, Jane Austen celebrated her twenty-ninth birthday at Green Park Buildings with some niggling irritation at the continued silence from Crosby & Son. On the same day, at Ashe in Hampshire, Madam Lefroy rode out from the rectory, accompanied as usual by her servant, to go shopping in Overton. On her way she met James Austen, riding back to Steventon, and mentioned to him how the horse she was riding was so stupid and lazy that she could scarcely persuade him to canter. The next day, James was astonished to receive news of Madam Lefroy's death. As his daughter recalled: 'After getting to the top of Overton hill [her] horse seemed to be running away – it was not known whether anything had frightened him – the servant unwisely, rode up to catch the bridle rein – missed his hold and the animal darted off faster. He could not give any clear account, but it was supposed that Mrs Lefroy in her terror, threw herself off, and fell heavily on the hard ground. She never spoke afterwards, and she died in a few hours.'[26] Five days later, James buried her body in the graveyard at Steventon.

The news of Madam Lefroy's death came as a shock to Jane Austen. This was the second time a female friend had been killed in a road accident. Six years earlier, Jane Cooper (Lady Williams) had been killed by a runaway dray-horse. That had been a profound loss. About Madam Lefroy she had more ambivalent feelings, which made her death – on Jane's own birthday – especially poignant. For several years, the relationship between them had been marked as much by suspicion as by affection. Jane found it hard to forgive Madam Lefroy's intervention to frustrate the intimacy between herself and Tom Lefroy; an injury which had only been compounded by the subsequent insult of her attempt to promote the Reverend Blackall in Tom's place. Now, the fact of Madam Lefroy dying on Jane's own birthday seemed to link them in a kind of fatal coincidence. Amid the sorrow that Jane felt, some unextinguished flickerings of resentment provoked a certain sense of guilt.[27]

Only a few weeks later, she suffered an even greater loss. On Saturday 19 January, her father was seized with a sudden and violent return of the feverish complaint to which he had been often subject over the three last years. The same remedy of cupping, which had before been so successful, was immediately applied to – but without such happy effects. Towards evening, however, Mr Austen seemed to recover. He had a tolerable night, and on Sunday morning was so greatly improved as to get up and join the family at breakfast, walking about with only the aid of a stick. When Bowen called in to see him, a little after midday, he pronounced himself quite satisfied with the patient's progress and felt sure he would do 'perfectly well'. But as the day progressed Mr Austen's symptoms became more distressful; the fever grew stronger than ever, and, when Bowen visited him again at ten o'clock that night, he was compelled to revise his opinion. Mr Austen's situation he now declared to be 'most alarming'. He called early to see him the following morning, and requested the presence of his friend, the physician Dr Gibbs. Gibbs examined the patient and reported gravely that it was 'absolutely a lost case . . . Nothing but a miracle could save him.' At twenty minutes after ten o'clock Mr Austen died.[28]

It fell to Jane to inform her brothers of the sad event. That afternoon, she set to her unhappy duty with some well-practised phrases of comfort and consolation. She wrote to Frank, aboard the *Leopard* off Dungeness, telling him that their father had died 'almost as free from suffering as his children could have wished'. Even their mother, she assured him, 'bears the shock as well as possible; she was quite prepared for it, & feels all the blessing of his being spared a long illness'. 'The loss of such a parent,' she concluded, 'must be felt, or we should be brutes'; yet the heavy feelings which it brought were considerably softened by the 'thousand comforts' of knowing he had suffered 'comparatively speaking, nothing'.

Having composed, and sent, such a dignified letter it came as a considerable irritation, the following morning, to receive a letter from Frank which indicated that he was not at Dungeness at all, but at Portsmouth. So her mournful task was all to do again. Dutifully, she repeated her elegiac phrases, with just a few variations inspired by a night of watching over their father's body. 'The serenity of the corpse is most delightful!' she wrote. 'It preserves the sweet, benevolent smile which always distinguished him.'[29] By the time she wrote this second letter, James had already arrived, having posted over from Steventon as soon as he heard the news. Henry, who was paying his usual New Year visit to Godmersham, was also on his way, though Edward was unaccountably prevented from joining them. James was already urging his mother to return to Steventon as soon as the funeral was over, but she had no enthusiasm to abandon her independence and live as a house-guest of Mary Lloyd in the home that had been her own for more than thirty years. 'I do not believe she will leave Bath at present,' Jane wrote to Frank. 'We must have this house for three months longer, & here we shall probably stay till the end of that time.'

The funeral took place on 26 January in Walcot church, where Mr and Mrs Austen had been married forty years before. Frank sent apologies for his unavoidable absence, and Henry wrote to assure him that the family knew enough of his situation 'not to indulge unreasonable demands'. Mrs Austen picked out two little items from among her husband's personal property and asked Jane to send them on to Frank as keepsakes. The first was the little compass/sundial in its own black shagreen case with which Mr Austen had proudly sought to plot the voyages of his naval sons around the globe. The other was a pair of scissors. 'We hope these are articles that may be useful to you,' Jane wrote. 'We are sure they will be valuable.'[30]

The death of Mr Austen placed Mrs Austen and her daughters in a precarious financial state. The greater part of Mr Austen's income, deriving from his parish livings and small annuity, terminated with his death. But the Austen sons needed no promptings to acknowledge their obligations. 'Whilst . . . our dear parent continues to inhabit this world,' Henry wrote to Frank, measures must be taken 'to assure her a continuance of every necessary, I hope of every comfort.' He reckoned the value of Mrs Austen's own 'assured property', together with the interest on Tom Fowle's legacy to Cassandra, as producing 'about £210 per ann', hardly sufficient to support three ladies in such an expensive city as Bath. Directly after the funeral, James was the first to offer his support. 'James behaves like a man of feeling and a true son on the occasion,' Henry wrote happily to Frank: 'He has appropriated fifty pounds a year to our dear trio.' 'I shall do as much,' he promised, 'so long as my present precarious income remains.' Edward, he added, had been 'very properly written to on the occasion – I shall be more than surprised if he does not pledge himself to as much as James & I together.' Though he could not find the time to attend his father's funeral, £100 a year was surely little enough for Edward to spare from the vast wealth of Godmersham. That left only Frank and Charles, but Henry was too tactful to solicit annual payments from men whose incomes were so largely dependent on unpredictable prize monies. 'You see therefore, my dear brother,' he wrote, 'that you need not abridge yourself to any part of your own modicum – I know of what you are capable.' However, he added, with what he took for a witty flourish, if Frank should be so fortunate to capture a galleon, 'you shall keep a carriage for my mother if you choose.'[31]

Away in Portsmouth, Frank was rather nettled by the patronizing tone of Henry's letter. He did not care for the assumption that a naval officer could not support his widowed mother just as well as a banker or a clergyman. Far from possessing a mere 'modicum', Frank had just been appointed to command the eighty-gun HMS *Canopus*, and his likely revenues, as he was pleased to inform his brother, would amount to something of the order of £500 *per annum*. He also wondered at Edward's failure to attend their father's funeral. Of course the squire of Godmersham should contribute at least £100 a year to support his widowed mother, and, in a gesture to remind Edward of his filial obligations, Frank pledged himself to contribute the same amount – £100 *per annum* – to that cause. He at least knew what was, or should be, expected of a loving son. But he required Henry to keep this offer a secret from their mother; Frank was never one for ostentatious flourishes. Henry, of course, did no such thing. As soon as he received Frank's letter, he blurted its contents to his mother. 'It was so absolutely necessary that your noble offer towards my mother should be made more public than you seemed to desire,' he wrote; 'that I really cannot apologize for a partial breach of your request.'

Naturally, Mrs Austen was effusive in her gratitude. 'With the proudest exultations of maternal tenderness the excellent parent has exclaimed that never were children so good as hers. She feels the magnificence of your offer,' he wrote, 'and accepts of half.'[32] Henry, too, had his pride, and he and James were not to be outdone in displays of generosity by their gallant uniformed brother. 'I shall therefore honour her demands for £50 annually on your account.' And so it was agreed. These three brothers would each contribute £50 a year to their mother's support. James was more sensitive to Frank's desire for confidentiality than his brother, and as soon as he reached Steventon the following Wednesday, he sent Frank an apology on Henry's behalf. 'You will I am sure forgive Henry for not having entirely complied with your request,' he wrote. 'I would not upon any account have lost the pleasure I derived from such proof of your feelings of delicacy – I will not pay you so bad a compliment as to say I was in the least surprised at it . . . I knew your heart & your wishes; and I rejoiced to find that your means & your prospects are such as enable you to indulge them. You would indeed have had a high gratification could you have witnessed the pleasure which our dear mother experienced when your intention was communicated to her . . .'[33]

No word had yet been heard from Edward, but Henry continued to live in hopes. 'If Edward does the least he ought,' he wrote, 'he will certainly insist on her receiving £100 from him.' In fact, Henry was blithely optimistic about his mother's prospects. 'She will be very comfortable,' he reckoned. 'In the receipt of a clear 450 pounds per ann . . . my mother & sisters will be full as rich as ever. They will not only suffer no personal deprivation, but will be able to pay occasional visits of health and pleasure to their friends.' Yet, even if Henry's cheerful calculations of the 'dear trio's' likely income was accurate, it took no account of the irksome abridgement of their independence in being now so wholly dependent on these voluntary contributions from the Austen sons. Already, Henry and James were taking it upon themselves to decide how and where their mother and sisters should live. 'My mother [will] . . . probably reduce her establishment to one female domestic & take furnished lodgings,' Henry thought, 'as a smaller establishment will be as agreeable to them.' 'Her summers will be spent in the country amongst her relations & chiefly I trust among her children,' wrote James; 'the winters she will pass in comfortable lodgings in Bath.' Either James did not know, or else he did not care to acknowledge, how little the 'dear trio' relished the prospect of summers at Steventon as guests of his ill-humoured spouse.

In all their letters, it is noticeable that the Austen sons speak chiefly about making provision for their mother; their sisters are barely mentioned. Yet it was Jane who felt most acutely the new sense of invidious dependency. Her mother had some funds, amounting to something less than £200 a year, in her own right.

Even Cassandra had her small income from Tom Fowle's legacy. But Jane had no money at all of her own. Everything she possessed must now be received as a gratuity from her brothers. Towards Frank she felt no sense of awkwardness in accepting his open generosity; yet Frank would shortly be married, with responsibilities of his own, and every week the newspapers carried ominous reminders of the sudden deaths of naval officers killed in warfare at sea. Henry, too, she loved, but knew him to be too feckless to be relied upon. He had none of that discretion which, she had always believed, must be necessary to a successful man of business. His manner of divulging Frank's confidence was hardly the sort of thing, it seemed to her, that a conscientious banker should do. And Eliza's tastes were never inclined towards economy. On the whole, Jane thought it unwise to trust entirely to Henry's annual £50. As to James, she found rather too much complacency in his manner of expressing a 'just satisfaction' that their mother's circumstances would be 'easy', and his way of congratulating himself that she would enjoy 'all those comforts which her declining years & precarious health call for'. Recalling Anna's sad complaints of stepmotherly neglect, Jane Austen found little reassurance in the thought that, henceforward, her own 'comforts' might be enjoyed only at the discretion of the jealous Mary Lloyd, who was, as James had told them, expecting her first child.

Once again, with great reluctance, Jane's thoughts turned to the depressing prospect of school-teaching. As the little family at Green Park Buildings went about the process of reducing their 'establishment', one of the younger maids requested a reference for another post. She was intending to go into service, she said, with a Miss Colbourne, who kept a school in the Upper Crescent. When Jane met this lady, she was surprised at Miss Colbourne's evident rationality in requiring only to be assured of the girl's *tolerable* temper. 'To be rational in anything,' she remarked to Cassandra, 'is great praise, especially in the ignorant class of school-mistresses.'[34] Yet this encounter only added to her sense of foreboding. She had become so confident in her opinion that a profound ignorance was the universal characteristic of all school-mistresses, as to convince herself that the possession of a rational intelligence might safely preclude her from ever joining their ranks. It was sobering to meet a young woman who *was* rational and still kept a school.

Apart from marriage, or school-teaching, Jane Austen had one other hope for securing a modest income – her writing. In the continuing silence from Crosby & Son about 'Susan', she turned her thoughts to revising another of her novels for possible publication. Her choice was a surprising one. She did not opt for the family favourite, 'First Impressions', nor her own beloved *Sense and Sensibility*, but for *Lady Susan*, the most cynical of all her works. It was *Lady Susan* that most nearly caught the tones of artful coquetry and snobbish affectation that she was sure to hear each day in the Upper Rooms or Sydney Gardens. If she were at last to descend from her lofty resolve to write 'only for fame', and consent to aim instead at 'pecuniary emolument', she considered that *Lady Susan* might be sufficiently harsh to catch the public mood. It also included references to a splendidly incompetent school-teacher, Miss Summers of Wigmore Street, who failed even in her principal obligation – that of humiliating her pupils.

When the lease on No. 3 Green Park Buildings expired, Mrs Austen moved to lodgings at 25 Gay Street, a smaller, though more central, location halfway up the hill towards the Circus. Almost immediately, Cassandra was called away to Ibthorpe, where Martha Lloyd was tending her sick mother. Old Mrs Lloyd had 'been failing in mind and body for some time past' and it was clear the end could not be far away. The prospect of a third death in almost as many months had a strange effect on Jane. Left alone in their new lodgings with her mother, who was herself always liable to bouts of real or imagined illness, Jane made a conscious endeavour to exclude all feelings of gloom or despondency. Letters from Henry were a great help; feckless he might be, but he was always affectionate, kind and, above all, entertaining. 'There is no merit to him in *that*,' she wrote to Cassandra, 'he cannot help being amusing.'[35] Eliza wrote too, and her dry wit was a constant inspiration to Jane in her redrafting of *Lady Susan*.

The weather in Bath that April was warm and balmy and

wonderful for walking. 'Here is a day for you!' she wrote to Cassandra in defiant exultation; 'Did ever Bath or Ibthrop ever see a finer 8th of April? . . . We do nothing but walk about.' Every day she would set out on some fresh expedition, as much to banish gloomy thoughts as for exercise or company. She would walk in the Crescent with Miss Irvine; or to Lansdown with the Chamberlaynes; or in the fields, alone; or to St James Square and the Paragon with her mother; or in Sydney Gardens with the Cookes; or to Weston with Miss Armstrong; or to Twerton with Miss Irvine again. One day, she sought out Mary Cooke for a *long* walk and together they drank tea in Alfred Street. But chiefly what she sought out were the crowds, the bustle, the sense of life in the city at springtime. 'We did not walk long in the Crescent yesterday,' she told Cassandra, 'it was hot and *not crouded enough*.'[36]

In the evenings there were invitations and engagements ('What request we are in!'). One evening it would be tea with Miss Irvine at Lansdown; the next, supper with the Cookes, tea with the Chamberlaynes, or a visit to Lady Leven. There were meetings with the Bickertons and the Blachfords, the Bonhams and the Bendishes: 'Among so many friends, it will be well if I do not get into a scrape . . . I should have gone distracted if the Bullers had stayed.' Really, she was become quite a *habituée* of the Bath social scene. One morning, she went with the Chamberlaynes to Dash's riding-house in Montpellier Row to see the young Miss Chamberlayne 'look hot on horseback'. It put her in mind of a previous visit to the same establishment seven years earlier, to witness Jemima Lefroy's equestrian performance. 'What a different set we are now moving in!' she boasted to Cassandra. 'But seven years I suppose are enough to change every pore of one's skin, & every feeling of one's mind.'[37]

Indeed, she *did* feel very different from the romantic young girl of twenty-two who had once 'doated' on the handsome black eyes of Mr Taylor. Four years of Bath, in particular, had lent her tone a more worldly assurance. Even without money, she had discovered, one's significance might be maintained by assuming a confident *style*. Naturally, the company one was seen in was also of great importance, and some invitations were, in consequence, to be avoided. Miss Armstrong from Lyme was quite dismayed at the way Jane Austen seemed to ignore her in Bath '& gently upbraided me in her turn with change of manners to her'. It was, of course, very flattering to be of 'such consequence' to this 'agreeable girl', and Jane grandly condescended to maintain a 'tolerable acquaintance' with her, while carefully determining *not* to introduce her to her more fashionable friends. 'I shall endeavour as much as possible to keep my intimacies in their proper place, & prevent their clashing.'[38]

One intimacy, in particular, became the source of much embarrassment. That April, Jane heard the first alarming rumours that her aunt Leigh-Perrot had once again been charged with theft. The details were not clear, but it appeared the lady had endeavoured to steal some greenhouse plants from a commercial garden in the city. According to some accounts, she had been taken before the city magistrates. There were some scurrilous verses in circulation, said to be in the hand of the magistrate Dr Harington, which alluded to the affair.

Sub judice lis est

> *To love of plants who has the greater claim,*
> *Darwin the bard or Perrot's wily dame?*
> *Decide the cause, Judge Botany, we pray,*
> *Let him the laurel take and her the Bay.*[39]

Although Jane might admire Dr Harington's facility for ingenious word-play, his *double-entendre*, which linked her aunt's love of plants with the penal settlement at Botany Bay, was really quite alarming. The magistrate might consider it a diverting witticism to award his 'laurel' to Dr Erasmus Darwin and 'the Bay' to Mrs Leigh-Perrot, but Jane found it a joke in exceeding bad taste. Inevitably, the gossip began once again about the trial, and the lace and the rumours of bribed jurymen. Once again, her aunt was in need of family supporters, but this time Jane felt little inclination to supply it. Mrs Leigh-Perrot was most anxious to procure for Jane a ticket to a grand Sydney Garden breakfast, but 'such an offer I shall of course decline,' she wrote to Cassandra, '& all the service she will render me therefore, is to put it out of my power to go at all, whatever may occur to make it desirable.'

It was, of course, impossible to avoid all contact with her aunt. On 23 April, Jane was reluctantly obliged to tell Cassandra that 'my Uncle & Aunt drank tea with us last night, & in spite of my resolution to the contrary, I could not help putting forward to invite them again this evening'.[40] In the circumstances, she recognized that it must be 'of the first consequence to avoid anything that might seem a slight to them'. So the Leigh-Perrots were invited to dine with the Austens' other guests, as a demonstration that they had not been shunned by their family. But for Jane it was a painful business. 'I shall be glad when it is over,' she wrote, '& hope to have no necessity for having so many *dear friends* at once again.'[41]

Indeed, it was often her relatives, with their depressing ailments and unsavoury reputations, who caused Jane most irritation. Assuming her own 'Lady Susan' manner, she refused to be cast down by their misfortunes. When Cassandra wrote from Ibthorpe with solemn news of Mrs Lloyd's sickly state, her letter only inspired Jane with feelings of impatience. She hoped she would soon receive another letter, she wrote, 'to say that it is all over'. 'Poor woman!' she added quickly. 'May her end be peaceful & easy, as the exit we have witnessed.' But this brief allusion to their father's recent death was rapidly banished from her mind. 'And I dare say it will,' she concluded, with an almost casual air. Death was not a subject that she cared to dwell upon. There were no death scenes in her novels, which were filled instead with balls and *beaux* and girlish chatter. When her father died, she had written to Frank: 'The loss of such a parent must be felt, or we should all be brutes.' Yet there was something almost brutish about the style she now affected. Cassandra wrote in solemn tones of Mrs Lloyd's agonies, but Jane responded with smart chatter, sarcasm and *bons mots*. 'The nonsense I have been writing in this & in my last letter, seems out of place at such a time,' she acknowledged; 'but I will not mind it, it will do you no harm, & nobody else will be attacked by it.'[42]

Officially still in mourning, she wore black crape on formal occasions, but spoke of it rather as a fashion accessory than as a mark of respect. 'You were very right in supposing I wore my crape sleeves to the concert,' she told Cassandra. 'I had them put in on the occasion; on the head I wore my crape & flowers, but I do not think it looked particularly well.' The constant presence of so many invalids in the city depressed her, and she took a private revenge by mocking them in her letters. She remarked of the sensible Dr Buller of Colyton that 'his appearance is exactly that of a confirmed decline', and made cruel fun of the deaf Lord Leven, who had no idea who they were when they came to call. In the face of death and bodily decay, she maintained a determined and defiant tone of cheerfulness and gaiety. 'How happy they are at Godmersham now!' she wrote, envious of the carefree life of Edward's Kentish estate, where wealth made light of all misfortunes. Henry was already making plans for another seaside trip that summer, which would be 'more desirable and delightful than ever'. Making a virtue of necessity, she was determined to enjoy, not merely endure, the brotherly patronage on which she was now so utterly dependent. 'I think we are just the kind of people & party to be treated about among our relations,' she wrote; 'we cannot be supposed to be very rich.'[43]

Lady Susan relieved her feelings, with its sharp surface of malicious wit, but it also disappointed her. Rereading what she had written, Jane was forced to recognize that this satiric sketch could never be refashioned into a full-length novel. The humour was too cynical, the characters too crude, the epistolary style too old-fashioned, and the plot too slight. Turning it into a novel would require investing this brisk social satire with *humanity*, and that was, currently, a commodity in short supply with her. Instead, she amused herself by rounding off the story with some ridicule of her own epistolary style and three sharp, satiric paragraphs to dismiss her principal characters. The girl Frederica, she wrote, remained 'fixed' in her uncle's family until such time as Reginald De Courcy 'could be talked, flattered and finessed into an affection for her'. Which process, she reckoned, might 'in general' have been done in three months; but owing to Reginald having utterly abjured all future attachments and sworn his detestation of the sex, 'might be reasonably looked for in the course of a twelvemonth'. Whether Lady Susan was happy or not in her second marriage to a man she despised, she left to the world to judge: 'She had nothing against her, but her husband, and her conscience.' As to her foolish husband, Sir James, Jane recommended him 'to all the pity that anybody can give him'. *Her* only pity, she wrote, was for Miss Maynwaring, who, having put herself to an expense in clothes in order to secure Sir James for herself, was left 'impoverished . . . for two years'.

Away at Ibthorpe, Mrs Lloyd died on 16 April, and Jane promptly sent Martha some jaunty verses, in the form of an order to 'an uncivil dressmaker' for mourning clothes.

> *. . . Some yards of a black ploughman's gauze,*
> *To be made up directly, because*
> *Miss Lloyd must in mourning appear*
> *For the death of a relative dear . . .*[44]

There is little sign of grief in these verses, which again make a show of being more concerned about clothes than emotions. However, Martha was hardly likely to impoverish herself, like poor Miss Maynwaring, by the purchase of a few yards of 'black ploughman's gauze'. Ever since Mr Austen's death, it had been privately agreed amongst them all that Martha, who was now quite alone in the world, should come to live with the Austens at Bath. It was time for that understanding to be made public. 'I am quite of your opinion as to the folly of concealing any longer our intended partnership with Martha,' Jane wrote to Cassandra; '& whenever there has of late been an enquiry on the subject I have always been sincere.'[45] She had even sent word of the arrangement to Frank, at sea in the Mediterranean. Her eagerness to enjoy Martha's company accounted in part for her lack of regret at the death of old Mrs Lloyd. Offering a home to Martha appealed to the more benign side of Jane's nature; it also had the gratifying effect of allowing her to act in the agreeable role of benefactress, rather than always as the humble recipient of family charity.

In June, the Austen ladies took their leave of Gay Street and set out for Godmersham, travelling via Steventon, where Mary was expecting her new baby. It was generally agreed that Anna could be of little use at home at such a time, and she too was invited to join the trip to Kent. It was delightful to be at Godmersham again, and enjoy once more the luxurious freedom of its spacious rooms and fine parkland. Fanny was now twelve, the same age as Anna, and a lively spirited girl, forever inveigling them all into play-acting and games. She had, though, a somewhat alarming predilection for playing at 'school', and forcing her aunts, her governess, her mama, and even her grandmama, to dress up and play their parts. In one version, Cassandra was 'Mrs Teachum, the Governess'; Jane herself was 'Miss Popham, the Teacher'; and Mrs Austen was 'Betty Jones, the Pie woman'.[46] Reluctant as she was to assume the school-ma'am role, Jane was inhibited from expressing her opinion of the unconquerable ignorance of all school-mistresses by the presence in the house (and in the play) of the children's governess, Miss Sharp. Alas, like Miss Colbourne of Bath, Miss Sharp of Godmersham proved to be a most rational young woman, pleasingly animated in her conversation though sadly tormented by ill health, who expressed the most gratifying opinions of Jane Austen's own writings. The two of them quickly became firm friends and when, the following year, Miss Sharp was compelled by her illness to abandon her duties at Godmersham, they continued to visit and correspond.

Throughout June and July, the vogue for theatricals continued. After dessert one evening, as Fanny Austen recorded in her diary, 'we acted a play called *Virtue Rewarded*. Anna was Duchess St Albans, I was the fairy Serena and Fanny Cage [her cousin from Milgate] a shepherdess "Mona". We had a bowl of syllabub in the evening.' Another time, 'Aunt Cassandra and Jane, Anna, Edward, George, Henry, William and myself acted *The Spoilt Child* and *Innocence Rewarded*, afterwards we danced and had a most delightful evening.'[47] Jane loved the spontaneous exuberance of these impromptu theatricals, which brought back all the fun and excitement of plays performed in the Steventon barn all those years before.

They soon had word that Mary had given birth to a baby girl, whose name was to be Caroline Mary Craven, and, at the end of July, Mrs Austen left Godmersham, taking Anna with her. Jane and Cassandra remained in Kent for the rest of the summer, dividing their time equally, but separately, between Godmersham and Goodnestone. While Jane was with Edward's family at God-mersham, Cassandra would be with the Bridges at Goodnestone, and vice versa, as if the two of them were in such very great demand that neither house could bear to dispense with them entirely.

Jane liked the informality of Goodnestone, where everything seemed 'for use and comfort', not for show. She particularly loved the dilapidated state of Lady Bridges's bookcase and the corner shelves upstairs. 'What a treat to my mother to arrange them!' she declared. All this she found rather more appealing than the formal-ity of Eastwell, where Lady Elizabeth had 'astonishingly little to say for herself' and Miss Hatton 'not much more'. 'Her eloquence,' Jane noted, lay in her fingers; 'they were most fluently har-monious.'[48]

There were visits to the balls at Canterbury during August Race Week, when Henry made a flying visit to join them, and at Ashford; evening walks to Rowling, and hairdressing by Mr Hall of London, whose charges Jane affected to find quite excessive. 'He charged Elizabeth 5s for every time of dressing her hair,' she protested, 'allowing nothing for the pleasures of his visits here, for meat, drink & lodging, the benefit of country air.' 'Towards me,' she conceded, 'he was as considerate as I had hoped for . . . charging me only 2s 6d for cutting my hair . . . He certainly respects either our youth or our poverty.'[49] Lack of money remained a niggling concern for Jane among her wealthier relations. 'Instead of being very rich,' she told Cassandra, 'I am likely to be very poor'; she could barely afford 10s as a leaving present to Susannah Sackree, who had served her as a maid. Inevitably, her impoverished and dependent status brought with it all kinds of minor humiliations, whether in the matter of obtaining a half-price hair-cut, or in her reliance on the kindness of others for carriages to convey her back and forth. Towards the end of August, the Eastwell family and Lady Forbes were full of plans for attending a grand ball at Deal, to which Harriot Bridges was also graciously invited. This invitation caused Jane quite a flurry of anxiety 'from fear of being in the way if they do not come to give Harriot a conveyance'. Eager 'to prevent the possibility of being in the wrong place', she made immediate plans to leave Goodnestone, but Harriot 'would not hear it', being 'totally disinclined' to accept the Forbes's summons. Fortunately, for both women, the King's brother died on 25 August, forcing the cancellation of the ball as a sign of respect. 'The Duke of Gloucester's death sets my heart at ease,' Jane wrote, 'though it will cause some dozens to ache.'[50] The awkwardness of the incident was a nagging reminder of how easily her own plans and preferences could be overturned at the whim of wealthier acquaintances.

Some of her greatest pleasure came from playing with the Austen, Finch and Bridges children. At Eastwell, ten-year-old Daniel, with his 'quite bewitching' countenance, was her favourite, and the two of them were partners for two rubbers of cribbage (which they won). At Godmersham, she would often spend a morning playing battledore and shuttlecock with seven-year-old William, or talking books with his sister Fanny, 'the happiest being in the world'. Already, at twelve, the girl was well versed in literary references, and would send teasing messages to her mama full of coy allusions to the improving school-room text that Miss Sharp had recommended, *Letters from Mrs Palmerstone to her Daughters, inculcating Morality by Entertaining Narratives*. Not to be outdone in the way of solemn reading matter, Jane dutifully set herself to study Thomas Gisborne's dour *Enquiry into the Duties of the Female Sex*. In it, she learnt that play-acting was 'almost certain to prove injurious to the female sex'. Acting, Gisborne asserted, was an encourager of female vanity and a destroyer of female modesty 'by the unrestrained familiarity with the other sex, which inevitably results from being joined with them in the drama'. 'I am glad you recommended Gisborne,' she wrote mischievously to Cassandra, 'for having begun, I am pleased with it.'[51] After which, she rejoined

Fanny and Miss Sharp, and the three of them set about planning their latest theatrical venture.

At Goodnestone, the children were all grown up, and Jane's time was mainly spent with Harriot, or with her clergyman brother Edward, whose hospitable attentions towards her were quite beyond praise. 'He made a point of ordering toasted cheese for supper entirely on my account.'[52] Whether her vanity had been encouraged and her modesty destroyed by her fondness for amateur theatricals, Jane Austen soon found herself flirting with this eager young clergyman, who was curate of the local parish. Once, the poor man even made himself late for a cricket match on her account! In the evenings, after dinner, they would walk together toward Rowling, and Jane took great pleasure in the proprietary manner in which he showed her over the house and ground. Like most young men (Mr Edward Bridges was just twenty-six, four years younger than herself), he was forever wanting to be *doing* something, or *rushing* somewhere. Sometimes he would be dashing to St Albans, sometimes to Broome, sometimes to Mr Hallet's at Higham. When Jane caught word of his last proposed absence, it even persuaded her to postpone her departure from Goodnestone until after his return. Edward Bridges was a lively, impetuous man, quite in his element attempting to arouse the spirits of all the neighbouring squires to 'support their rights' against the 'evil intentions' of those uniformed poachers, the Coldstream and Grenadier Guards, to march from Deal to Chatham only two days before the start of the partridge-shooting season. It amused her to see all the energy and eloquence that he brought to this cause, and how dismally it was received by his neighbours.[53] He was equally eloquent when he proposed to her. The proposal, when it came, was hardly unexpected. Mr Bridges's attentions to her had been so marked that his intentions could hardly be in doubt. Naturally, she refused him, though this time she had at least been afforded a decent opportunity for proper reflection. Of course, it was flattering that yet another young man should desire to marry her; but there could be no question of her consenting. Mr Edward Bridges, however amiable and attentive, was altogether too young and thoughtless to be considered a suitable husband. If she were to think of it at all, it would be, as with Harris Bigg-Wither, not the *man*, but the house and living that she must be thinking of. Yet in this case there was neither enough love, nor the certainty of enough money, to assure her of a tolerable situation as a Bridges wife.

Her final letter to Cassandra from Goodnestone that summer carried no hint of emotional turmoil. 'It would be inconvenient to me to stay . . . longer than the beginning of next week,' she wrote, but gave only the blandest of reasons: 'on account of my clothes.' Of course, there were the usual difficulties about carriages and other arrangements. A letter from Elizabeth at Godmersham made her 'anxious' once again 'to hear more of what we are to do or not to do'. Henry's suggestion of a visit to London struck her as 'a point of the first expediency', though she did fear it might 'injure' their scheme for spending the autumn at Worthing. ('We shall not be at Worthing so soon as we have been used to talk of, shall we?') It was dismaying to be always so much dependent on the arrangements of others. But she allowed herself to be preoccupied with more trivial concerns. 'I suppose everybody will be black for the D[uke] of G[loucester]. Must we buy lace, or will ribbon do?'

On reflection, Jane sometimes wondered whether she had made the right decision about Mr Edward Bridges. To Mr Bigg-Wither she had said 'yes', and then regretted it; to Mr Bridges she had said 'no', and then, at times, regretted that too. It was certainly no great enhancement of her boast of independence to be so constantly in want of funds. When they met again, she warned Cassandra, 'it is as well . . . to prepare you for the sight of a sister sunk in poverty, that it may not overcome your spirits'.[54] In mid-September, she and Cassandra were reunited at Godmersham, from where they set out with Edward and his family for Worthing, to join Mrs Austen and Martha Lloyd who were already in lodgings there. As ever, Fanny Austen kept careful notes of all their doings in her diary. 'I went with G.Mama in the morning to buy fish on the beach,' she wrote on 18 September, '& afterwards with Mama & Miss Sharpe to bathe where I had a most delicious dip.'[55]

Even here at Worthing, Jane soon found that the family could not escape from disagreeable rumours concerning her aunt Leigh-

Perrot. A woman called Hind in the neighbouring village of Findon, had heard all about the theft of the greenhouse plants from her friend Mrs Rich, who lived close by Scarlets, at Sonning. Mrs Hind was inclined to tell the story to anyone who cared to listen. It appeared, she said, that Mrs Leigh-Perrot

was cheapening plants at a gardener's and wanting to buy a small one then growing which he refused to sell at the price she proposed; on his back being turned a young lady in the garden saw her stooping down to the border and appearing very busy with her hands which was to loosen it from the ground, for on rising she dropped her pocket handkerchief on the spot, and then stooped to pick up that and the plant together, and put both in her pocket. The young lady told the gardener, who taxed her with it. She positively denied the charge, but he insisted on searching her pockets where it was found; she then burst into tears, and intreated that it might not be put into the papers. The man resolved on prosecuting her, but this was put a stop to from the father of the young lady precipitately taking her from Bath to prevent her appearing in a court of justice as a witness against this infatuated woman.[56]

Ever since this shocking incident, Mrs Hind claimed, 'everybody has dropped Mrs Perrot's acquaintance' and the poor woman was now 'universally shunned'. Certainly, Jane felt little inclination to rush to her aunt's defence, nor even to acknowledge their relationship. Her cousin Edward Cooper at Hamstall went further; he was indiscreet enough to voice his suspicions, and for that his aunt never forgave him. Distasteful as it was, the Austens were compelled to wonder whether their aunt had indeed been guilty of stealing the lace from Miss Gregory's shop in Bath. In her letters, Mrs Leigh-Perrot complained constantly that the judge had prevented her counsel Mr Bond from exposing the full villainy of the shopman Filby. 'The judge acted very wrong,' she would say. She was convinced Mr Bond would 'have made that villain Filby squeak pretty loud', if the judge had not stopped him.[57] Yet despite all her protests, no charge of conspiracy, or even of perjury, had ever been laid against Filby or Gye. Why was that?

Was Mrs Leigh-Perrot guilty of larceny after all? Her counsel Mr Jekyll certainly thought so. She was like other rich ladies, he said, 'who frequent bazaars and mistake other people's property for their own'. That was 'the blunder of my client, Mrs Leigh-Perrot'. Gradually, and reluctantly, the Austen family came to a similar view. Many years later, Alexander Dyce, an Oxford friend and contemporary of Jane Austen's nephew James Edward Austen-Leigh, made some notes on Mrs Leigh-Perrot in his copy of *Northanger Abbey*. 'The lady mentioned,' he wrote, 'had an invincible propensity to stealing, and was tried at Bath for stealing lace; the printed account of her trial still exists. The family were dreadfully shocked at the disgrace which she brought upon them. For many years she lived in seclusion at Scarlets (a handsome place) where she died.' Richard Austen-Leigh expressed a similar opinion. 'Jekyll considered Mrs L.P. was a kleptomaniac,' he noted, believing that she 'did steal the material, and probably meant to'.[58] In 'Henry and Eliza', written fifteen years earlier, Jane Austen had cheerfully championed a heroine whose career began with the theft of a £50 bank-note. In real life, things were rarely so simple, and an aunt with a fondness for stealing was quite as shaming as a brother who was mad. What particularly vexed Jane about her aunt's conduct was the sheer *irrationality* of it. She, after all, had never known what it was to lack money; and yet she was the one who shamed them all by stealing. One evening, after dining at four, the family went to a raffle where, as Fanny proudly recorded, 'Aunt Jane won & it amounted to 17s.' For a woman 'sunk in poverty', but with a scruple against larceny, such unexpected riches were not to be despised.

England expects . . .

Frank Austen stood on the quarter-deck of *Canopus* and looked towards the harbour at Cadiz. His orders were to stand in close to shore; so close, in fact, that one of his escort vessels had run

JANE AUSTEN (1775–1817)
watercolour sketch by her sister Cassandra, c.1810

THE REVEREND GEORGE
AUSTEN (1731–1805)
miniature, c.1763

MRS GEORGE AUSTEN
(1739–1827)
silhouette, c.1800

CASSANDRA AUSTEN (1773–1845)
undated silhouette

Illustrations by Cassandra for Jane Austen's
History of England, *c.1790: Mary Tudor, Edward IV,*
Henry V, Mary Queen of Scots, Elizabeth I and Charles I

ELIZA HANCOCK (1761–1813)
miniature, c.1780

THOMAS LANGLOIS ('TOM') LEFROY (1776–1869)
miniature by Engleheart

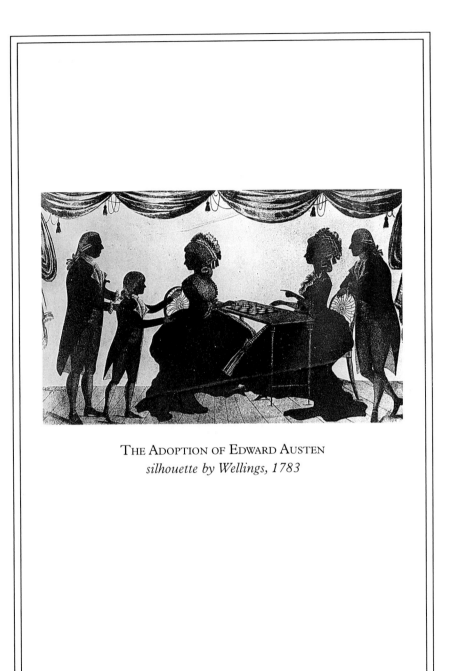

The Adoption of Edward Austen
silhouette by Wellings, 1783

EDWARD AUSTEN (1767–1852)
portrait done in Rome by unknown artist, c.1787

JANE AUSTEN
watercolour by Cassandra, c.1804

aground and had to be towed off. A position like this was full of dangers; a sudden squall might force the ship on to the rocks and wreck it, or carry it within range of the shore batteries; an unnoticed enemy frigate might slip the blockade under cover of night and rake his decks with gunfire. Admiral Collingwood had memories of the fatigue of keeping a similar station off Brest; up on deck the whole night long, and often going a full week without once changing his clothes. From his own look-out, Frank kept a close watch on the masts of the ships ranged against him. 'Stood in till all the enemy's fleet were open to the town, and had an opportunity of distinctly counting them,' he recorded in his log for 16 September. 'The whole force consisted of thirty-three sail of the line and five frigates, all apparently quite ready for sea.'[59] If this armada were suddenly to break out from the harbour and engage the British blockade, *Canopus* would be among the first ships in the firing-line. Frank sorely lacked a swift frigate able to take prizes.

Canopus itself was a prize ship, originally *Le Franklin* and captured by Nelson at the Nile. It was Nelson who had arranged for Frank to command it. 'Captain Austen . . . is an excellent young man,' he had written in March; 'he cannot be better placed than in the *Canopus*, which was once a French Admiral's ship, and struck to me.'[60] But, though handsomely built, *Canopus* was slow and heavy in the water and badly in need of repair; foretop and maintop sails were sadly tattered, and the hull bore the scars of battle. Aboard *Canopus* with Frank was the 'old Crocodile', Admiral Louis, Nelson's second-in-command. A veteran of Ushant and St Vincent, Louis was full of stories. How he had acted as Nelson's shield at the Nile, using his own ship to draw the fire from the French warships, *L'Aquilon* and *Le Spartiate*. It was Louis's action, Nelson said, which had turned the battle in their favour. Wherever there was danger, Frank knew, the old Crocodile was certain to insist on being in the thick of it.[61]

This time, they were determined Villeneuve should not escape them, as he had done in the spring. Then, the French Admiral had slipped suddenly out of Toulon harbour and made for the West Indies with a fleet of eighteen ships. Caught by surprise, Nelson had been slow to follow. *Canopus* had been part of that desperate sea-chase, pursuing Villeneuve for more than 3,000 miles across the Atlantic. Frank, leading the lee line of the fleet, had made sure to keep his own battered vessel within sight of Nelson's flag-ship; '*Victory* north one mile', he would write in his log.[62] But when at last they had reached the sugar islands, Villeneuve had eluded them again, promptly turning tail and sailing all the way back across the Atlantic. In London that summer, Nelson had been welcomed home by cheering crowds; but their Lordships of the Admiralty were rather less impressed. The *Naval Chronicle* thundered against the 'ill-judged and over-weening popularity which tends to make another demi-god of Lord Nelson at the expense of all other officers in the service'. Aboard HMS *Prince of Wales*, Calder was court-martialled for failing to engage the enemy fleet during a mist at sea. What the government required was 'an annihilation' of the French and Spanish fleets, not a reckless ocean race to the Caribbean.[63]

At home, Frank's letters were eagerly awaited, but often went astray, and his family was left to search the globe for hints of the sailor brothers' movements. Mrs Austen and Mrs Leigh-Perrot would often argue about whether Charles's vessel was a frigate bound for the East Indies, or a sloop on its way to Nova Scotia, while Jane would fret to know where letters should be directed. Henry sent on Mary Gibson's letters to Frank via General Tilson at Spithead. 'Would it be possible,' Jane wondered, 'for us to do something like it?' In August, she was angry when a letter sent to her by way of Henry's office was diverted first to Dover and then to Steventon before reaching her at Godmersham. 'He is in a great hurry to be married,' she told Cassandra, when at last the letter arrived; '& I have encouraged him in it.'[64] James, too, wished Frank well for his forthcoming marriage. 'May you have a speedy return,' he wrote, '& reap the reward which your principles & exertions deserve in the enjoyment of domestic comforts & in the society of her who can best make your home comfortable to you.'[65] Frank was pleased to receive this letter, which seemed to indicate a mellowing of the family attitude to Mary; but just at present he had more urgent matters on his mind than matrimony.

On 28 September, Nelson arrived off Cadiz and summoned

Admiral Louis to attend him on HMS *Victory*. Water and stores were urgently needed from Gibraltar, he told him, and *Canopus* must return to the Rock to fetch them. Louis protested at being sent away on such a mission when a battle was surely imminent. But Nelson assured him there was time enough for *Canopus* to reach Gibraltar and return before the enemy dared to come out. *Canopus* was his 'right hand', he said, and would be indispensable in any fight.

Frank shared Louis's dismay at these orders. A fortnight later, he wrote to Mary from *Canopus* 'at sea, off Gibraltar': 'We sailed again last night to return to the fleet, having got on board . . . 300 tons of water.' On their last night in Gibraltar he and Louis had gone to a performance of *Othello* by brother officers, but Louis had walked out after the first act. This was no time for play-acting. The heat and stuffiness of the theatre only added to frustration at being away from the action. 'Having borne our share in a tedious chase and anxious blockade,' Frank wrote, 'it would be mortifying indeed to find ourselves at last thrown out of any credit and emolument which would result from such an action. Such, I hope will not be our lot.'[66] His mind went back to the last time he had sat in a theatre, that February night in London with 'a fair young lady . . . from Ramsgate' by his side. 'Do you happen to recollect anything of that evening?' he asked her, tenderly. 'I think you do and that you will not readily forget it.' The night was sultry and Frank was tormented by the tedium of inactivity. If he could not be with Mary, he wanted to be fighting the enemy fleet, not wasting his time on this errand-boy assignment. 'I do not profess to like fighting for its own sake,' he wrote, 'but if there has been an action with the combined fleets I shall ever consider the day on which I sailed from the squadron as the most inauspicious of my life.'[67]

Even as Frank wrote these words, the French and Spanish fleets were preparing to leave harbour. On 19 October, Villeneuve led his five squadrons out of Cadiz and along the coast towards Cape Trafalgar. On the morning of 21 October, Nelson came on deck wearing the four stars of his military honours on his breast and hoisted his famous signal to the fleet: 'England expects . . .' Warned that his decorations would make him an easy target for sharp-shooters in the rigging of enemy ships, the Admiral replied that it was too late to remove them. In the light prevailing winds, the enemy force of thirty-three sails formed a six-mile curve along the horizon as the two fleets came within range of each other's guns. The captain of the French *Redoubtable* trained all the fire-power of his seventy-four guns against the *Victory*, with musketeers placed in the shrouds to cut down the British marines. As the two ships closed together, blocks, spars, sheets and sails came clattering down. In the black, acrid smoke from the gunfire, the decks of the *Victory* were soon covered with blood. Broadsides of sixteen guns at a time exploded into the enemy hull, with batteries of carronades and musket-shots from the top-men in their swivel-posts. Sailors were crushed under the avalanche of falling timbers, or trapped below deck, screaming, beneath the weight of recoiling guns. But French casualties were even heavier. Five hundred men killed on the *Redoubtable* alone; a similar number on *Achille* and the *Fougueux*. By the end of the day, as the smoke began to lift, it was clear that the entire French and Spanish fleets had been destroyed or crippled. An 'annihilation' was what the government had required; an annihilation was what had been achieved.

When Frank heard the news, he could not restrain his bitterness. 'Alas! my dearest Mary,' he wrote, 'all my fears are but too fully justified.' Of course, he rejoiced that 'a most decisive victory' had been gained, but he could not conceal his anger at being absent from the battle: 'To lose all share in the glory of a day which surpasses all which ever went before, is what I cannot think of with any degree of patience.' What made his bitterness worse was the terrible news of Nelson's death, cut down by a musket-shot from the *Redoubtable*. 'A melancholy situation,' he wrote. 'Great and important as must be the victory, it is alas! dearly purchased at the price paid for it.' Frank had no sympathy with those who had sometimes cavilled at Nelson's bold tactics. 'His memory will long be embalmed in the hearts of a grateful Nation,' he wrote. 'May those he left behind in the service strive to imitate so bright an example!!!'[68] But his own sense of disappointment overwhelmed all other feelings. 'As I cannot write upon that subject without complaining,' he told Mary, 'I will drop it for the present, till time and reflection reconcile me a little more to what I know is now inevitable.'

In England, the name 'Trafalgar' became a sudden fashion and Mary Austen of Steventon was soon embellishing her needlework with the 'Trafalgar stitch'. Jane, though, found something vulgar in all the clamour of national celebration. Naturally, she was delighted at a victory which seemed to put an end to fears of a French invasion. That summer, Buonaparte broke up the forces of his *grande armée* camped at Boulogne and sent them to be deployed along the Danube. Jane even found some amusement in all the scandalous stories surrounding Nelson's relationship with Lady Hamilton, stories which had the irresistible appeal of investing the dead Admiral with the mystique of a lost romantic hero. That January, she gave her young Steventon nephew, James Edward Austen, a copy of *The British Navigator, or a collection of voyages made in different parts of the world,* to remind the eight-year-old lad of his family's proud naval traditions.[69] In *Persuasion,* she made Admiral Croft a veteran of 'the Trafalgar action'. In *Mansfield Park,* she paid tribute to Frank's own ship. 'Whereabouts does the Thrush lay at Spithead?' William Price cries out: 'Near the Canopus?' But Devis's painting of *The Death of Nelson,* which was received with such popular acclaim, struck a more discordant note with her. Dressed all in white, his face haloed by a ship's lantern, and with the blood-stained timbers of the *Victory* rising like a crucifix behind him, the fallen hero was here canonized as the nation's redeemer and patron saint. For her, such pictorial grandiloquence mistook the true qualities of the naval profession and, by the time she embarked upon *Sanditon,* in the last year of her life, the name 'Trafalgar' had come to signify less a moment of national triumph, than an excuse for national humbug. 'One other hill,' the enterprising Mr Parker informs his visitors, 'brings us to Sanditon . . . You will not think I have made a bad exchange, when we reach Trafalgar House – which by the bye, I almost wish I had not named Trafalgar – for Waterloo is more the thing now. However, Waterloo is in reserve.' By the use of such patriotic names, Mr Parker has no doubt of attracting numerous lodgers to his new, ugly, seaside boarding-houses.

The Austen family had never been slow to exploit the financial benefits of military victories. In his letter to Mary Gibson, just before the battle, Frank made no secret of the fact that what he chiefly feared was 'to find ourselves thrown out of any credit or emolument which would result from such an action'. It would be a bitter blow, he said, to bear 'the loss of pecuniary advantage as well as of professional credit'.[70] Jane found no discredit in such a declaration. 'We are all happy to hear of [Frank's] health & safety,' she once wrote; 'he wants nothing but a good prize to be a perfect character.'[71] But she did think that the prizes and emoluments of victory should go to the heroes who had earned them, rather than to the Mr Parkers who debased the names of famous battles for their own catchpenny trade.

This blurring of boundaries between public service and private gain could bring penalties as well as prizes. Official salaries were often notional, usually paid in arrears, and might not be paid at all if the enterprising office-holder could, as expected, find some commercial means to supplement his income. As late as 1801, Frank Austen was still soliciting the directors of the East India Company for reimbursement of expenses incurred eight years earlier. When General Mathew died, the day after Christmas 1805, the wretched state of his finances bore sorry testimony to the perils of such casual procedures. Although the General had been personally appointed by George III to the Governorship of Grenada, His Majesty had never thought to ratify the General's salary with the officers of the Royal Exchequer. As a consequence, in 1792 the General had been presented with a Treasury demand for £11,000, being the sum which he had drawn as salary in Grenada. But the King had lost his memory and there was no means to rectify the error. Nothing was paid, and the Treasury continued to rack up the General's debt at compound interest. After the General's death, his family (including James and Mary at Steventon) was presented with a bill for £24,000. This, as James's granddaughter recalled, 'was a great anxiety to the Austens'.[72] The annual sum of £100 which the General had paid on Anna's behalf, was immediately forfeited, together with all but £2,000 of the money she had hoped to inherit. James himself, who had once proudly staged a performance of Sheridan's *The Rivals* in Steventon barn, was now full of recriminations against the government in which Sheridan served as Treasurer of the Navy.

Fortunately, an expedient was soon at hand. Mr Fowle of Hamstead Marshall died in February and Lord Craven, as patron, invited James to take over the living. What he had in mind, he indicated, was a strictly temporary tenure; there was a young man whom Craven eventually intended for the parish but who still lacked some years of ordination. It was a handsome enough benefice, worth £300 a year, and quite the thing for a man like James, who was suffering a temporary financial difficulty. Mary agreed. To her, Hamstead Marshall was perfect in every way and she could not understand why Austen seemed to hesitate. But James was a man who prided himself on his principles, and to him the offer of a living on such terms was highly suggestive of simony. Clerical posts were not to be trafficked in this manner, he said, and he strongly doubted whether a secular promise to vacate the living at some future time, at his patron's whim, 'did not go against the clerical statement' he would be required to make upon accepting it. Mary could not see why he strained so at these technical formulas. His Majesty had hardly been so punctilious when he had appointed Anna's grandfather to a Governor's post without the Governor's salary that should accompany it. Rather than confront his wife directly, James appealed to the arbitration of his daughter. Giving Anna the words of the clerical statement of acceptance to read, he asked her to interpret their meaning. When she did so, to her father's satisfaction, Mary was furious. 'What does it signify,' she protested, 'what a child like that thinks of the meaning? What is the sake of asking her?' 'Because,' James replied, 'being a child, it is only the most obvious and natural sense of the words which she will see, which is the sense in which they were meant to be taken.' To Mary's disgust, he refused the offer of Hamstead Marshall.[73]

Jane, Cassandra and Mrs Austen visited the family at Steventon that January and commiserated over the loss of the General's fortune. They had left the house at Gay Street and Mrs Austen, with all of £68 in hand, refused to be cast down by financial worries.

James, too, still the poet of the family, would often find a pleasing refuge among his books from the pecuniary pressures with which Mary was so constantly preoccupied. In the quiet of the library he would read his daughter lines that he had penned on 'rich and high born neighbours' who 'of all poverty, will find/The worst is Poverty of Mind'.[74]

When Mrs Austen returned to Bath, she took Anna with her and together they found temporary lodgings in Trim Street. Meanwhile, Jane and Cassandra prepared themselves for a difficult expedition – to Manydown. It was the first time Jane had returned there since that fateful visit more than three years before. Now that Harris was married and living at Wymering, there was no real cause for alarm. But Jane was still anxious about the reception she might receive from Catherine and Alethea. Mary continued to mutter about the unaccountable whims of women, no longer young enough to lay claim to foolish romantic notions, who yet preferred to depend upon the extravagant generosity of their impoverished brother than accept the honourable offer of a sensible man with a substantial fortune of his own. As far as the Biggs were concerned, Jane need not have worried. They welcomed her and Cassandra without constraint. There was orange wine to be drunk, there were stories to exchange, and Jane was struck again by the similarities between the Bigg sisters of Manydown and the Bridges sisters of Goodnestone, not the least of which, perhaps, was that they both had brothers who had proposed to her.

Returning to Bath in March, Jane and Cassandra found their mother much dissatisfied with her temporary lodgings. '*Trim Street Still*' she wrote in exasperation at the head of a letter to Mary.[75] She had entertained hopes of altogether more suitable lodgings in St James's Square, but someone else, she found, was 'in treaty for the whole house, so of course he will be prefer'd to us who want only a part'. Other places had been looked at but '[we] don't quite like the situation'. With luck, she hoped, they would have more choice a few days hence, 'as it is to be supposed many will be quitting Bath when this gay week is over'. Indeed, Bath that spring was very gay. The King's ball on Monday 'was not a very *full* one,' she told Mary, 'not more than a *thousand*'. Rauzzini's concert, at which Mrs Billington sang for the last time, 'was very full & very hot'. At the Theatre Royal, Cooke was performing *Macbeth* to packed houses; Martha insisted on attending, despite a bout of nervous fatigue. But all these festivities must surely conclude after Mr Le Bas's ball on Friday at the Lower Rooms.

After the bitter disappointment of missing the Trafalgar action, Frank found some consolation in sailing with Sir John Duckworth's squadron in pursuit of what remained of the French fleet. At first, there was more frustration. There were reports of enemy ships at Madeira, but when the English fleet arrived there in December, the French had gone. It angered Frank that *Canopus* was so slow; 'nearly the last ship' in the line, he complained to Mary. Throughout January they sailed the South Atlantic in search of enemy ships, and around the sugar islands from Barbados to St Kitts. At last, on 6 February, the engagement took place off St Domingo. 'Five minutes before seven,' Frank wrote in his log, 'Enemy's ships are of the line.' At a quarter past ten, he noted, 'the *Superb* commenced to fire on the enemy's van'. By half past ten, he was in action himself; 'opened our fire on the first ship in the enemy's line . . . with one broadside brought her masts by the board . . . ten minutes to eleven, the dismasted ship struck . . . Engaged with the three-decker . . . ten minutes to twelve, gave her a raking broadside which brought down her mizzen mast . . .'[76] The next day, he wrote to Mary to assure her he had 'escaped unhurt' from an action of which, he knew, reports would soon be flying 'like wildfire in England'. It was glorious to be able to tell her about 'giving the three-decker a tickling which knocked all *his sticks* away'. Now at last he could be proud to return to Old England. 'Oh, how my heart throbs at the idea!' he wrote.[77] As the fleet sailed home with their three captured prize ships, Frank heard still more glorious news. The captain of an American ship newly out of Trinidad reported that the French were everywhere beaten, 'their armies destroyed, and Bonaparte flying or killed'. There were votes of thanks from the President and Council of St Kitts, and the night sky echoed with gunfire salutes at the joyful news of victory.

When Frank disembarked from *Canopus* at Plymouth in early May, he was disappointed to learn that the reports of French surrender were quite false. Still, there were some personal consolations. He was presented with a silver vase, worth £100, by Lloyd's Patriotic Fund, in recognition of the St Domingo action, and also a gold medal. The family were all urgent to congratulate him, and the Coopers of Hamstall Ridware invited him and all the Austens to spend the summer with them in Staffordshire. But Frank had other plans. Though his prize money scarcely amounted to a fortune, he judged it sufficient to maintain a sensible wife who, in marrying a naval officer, would hardly anticipate riches. He quickly fixed a date for his marriage to Mary Gibson; and, since he had no doubt of being soon appointed to another command, was eager to find a home where his new bride might be among friends during his absences at sea. It occurred to him that nothing could be more satisfactory, if all other parties were in agreement, than for Mary to share a home with his mother and sisters. All other parties, it seemed, *were* in agreement; or, at least, they offered no very violent signs of disapproval at this scheme. And so it was arranged. Mrs Austen, Jane, Cassandra and Martha would leave Bath and move to Southampton, where they would all live in Frank's house with Mary Gibson. For Frank, it was the perfect arrangement; they would now be in close proximity to the great naval dockyard at Portsmouth, a place where he was bound to call from time to time, whatever ship he might command. He readily conceded that Southampton could boast few of the fashionable splendours of Bath, with Signor Rauzzini's concerts, Mr Le Bas's balls and Mr Cooke's performances of Shakespeare; yet it was a place not meanly regarded among those with a connoisseurship of the south coast towns. There were summer balls at Mr Martin's Rooms, winter assemblies at the Dolphin Inn, a fine new theatre in French Street and many handsome buildings in the Polygon and Bellevue. Altogether, Frank considered the Southampton plan as 'equally suited to his love of domestic society and the extent of his income which was somewhat restricted'.[78] On 24 July, Frank was married to Mary Gibson at Ramsgate, and the couple went to Godmersham to spend their honeymoon.

Jane was too polite, and too fond of Frank, to quarrel with such an eminently sensible arrangement; it was only a minor vexation that, as usual, her own wishes should be subordinated to practical family needs. Yet Southampton, with its stinking fish and putrid fevers, was not a place of happy memories for her. To share in Frank's domestic company again would be a considerable pleasure. But when her brother was absent, as he must often be, she was less confident that the perpetual company of Mary Gibson would be entirely delightful. Miss Gibson, in her view, belonged to that numerous class of young ladies 'considerably genteeler than her parents'. She and Cassandra did not attend the wedding in Ramsgate, since it was not their wish to strike up an intimacy with her parents, the Gibsons of Ramsgate High Street. Instead, at the start of July, the Austen ladies, together with Martha Lloyd, journeyed the short distance to Clifton, high above the river Avon. In this small and barely fashionable spa, it amused Jane to compose her own fanciful version of her brother's nuptials in a set of verses which assumed the voice of her niece, Fanny Austen of Godmersham. Even then, she did not describe the wedding ceremony itself, but celebrated the 'lovely couple's' escape from Mary's parental home to the splendours of Edward's estate.

> *See they come, post haste from Thanet,*
> *Lovely couple, side by side;*
> *They've left behind them Richard Kennet*
> *With the parents of the bride!*

Clifton was a place which inspired Jane to such idle versifying. Martha had hopes of travelling to Harrogate with her old acquaintance Mr Best and was greatly distressed when he announced he had no plans for Harrogate that year. Jane chided him in rhyme.

> *Oh! Mr Best, you're very bad*
> *And all the world shall know it;*
> *Your base behaviour shall be sung*
> *By me a tuneful poet –*

> *You used to go to Harrogate*
> *Each summer as it came,*
> *And why I pray should you refuse*
> *To go this year the same?*[79]

These new poems were all about movement. She imagined Frank and Mary careering through Canterbury, Stamford Bridge and Chilham village; she pictured Martha and her reluctant escort 'driving at full speed from Newb'ry to Speen Hill'. She often imagined herself being transported at speed in a coach by a bold man to some unknown destination. They would be strangers, of course, as men and women always were – even after they were married. She thought of her little fable of Mr Harley, riding in a stage-coach beside a beautiful woman whom he did not recognize as his wife. Would Frank, now he had married his Gibson bride, be subject to such strange losses of memory? Would he, like the forgetful Mr Harley or the bad Mr Best, be unable to recognize the woman he travelled with? 'Take her, and wonder at your luck,/ In having such a trust', she advised Mr Best.

> *But if you still refuse to go*
> *I'll never let you rest,*
> *But haunt you with reproachful song*
> *Oh! wicked Mr Best! –*

CHAPTER 9

Abuse Everybody but Me

Abuse everybody but me.

Jane Austen, Letter to Cassandra, January 1807

The Stoneleigh inheritance

At the end of July, Mrs Austen and her daughters took their leave of Clifton and journeyed on to Adlestrop rectory, where Mrs Austen's cousin the Reverend Thomas Leigh had been busily introducing all the most *à la mode* improvements to his estate. The village green was no more, but in its place an enclosed and private parterre; the village cottages, likewise, vanished and planted out to provide a more elegant perspective from the house. Repton had been hired and for a fee of five guineas a day had refashioned doors and windows, laid out flower gardens, diverted streams and merged the grounds of the rectory with those of Mr James Leigh at Adlestrop House.[1] Yet barely had the Austens had time to admire the pictur-esque beauties of the lively stream, which now led through a flower garden, over ledges of rock and, 'after a variety of interesting circumstances', fell into a lake, when they were suddenly required to leave the place. Thomas Leigh had received an urgent letter from his lawyer, Mr Hill, which made him very excited indeed. Mr Hill informed him that on 2 July the Hon. Mary Leigh of Stoneleigh Abbey had died. All the Leighs of the Stoneleigh branch had now died out and, although some curious wording in the will of the eccentric last Lord Leigh left the true line of inheritance in some dispute, Hill was in little doubt that Thomas had the best title to the Stoneleigh estate. However, to forestall the efforts of rival claimants, he advised Mr Leigh to take immediate possession, and proposed accompanying him to Stoneleigh with all speed. Accordingly, Hill and his wife arrived at Adlestrop on 4 August and Thomas Leigh set out for Warwickshire the following day. Not wishing to seem unduly inhospitable to his Austen cousins, Thomas invited them to accompany him, his sister Elizabeth and, of course, the indispensable Mr Hill to his new ancestral estate.

As they travelled, Mr Hill did his best to untangle the complexities of the situation. It all went back to the old lunatic Lord Leigh's will, he said. Lord Leigh had died unmarried and insane, leaving the estate to his sister, the deceased. Thereafter, the will provided that it should descend 'unto the first and nearest of his kindred, being male and of his blood and name'.[2] That stipulation of the *name* was very apposite, Hill thought. They all knew of descendants in the female line, like Mr Hanbury Leigh and Colonel Smith Leigh, who had pompously added *Leigh* to their names to try to establish a claim.[3] Every lawyer laughed at that idea, he said. He had not even troubled himself to write to them about it. Of course, Mr James Leigh, as the head of the Adlestrop branch, could be expected to urge his own case, but he was hardly 'the first and nearest', by which terms Hill understood the will to mean the *eldest* of the remaining Leighs. (Naturally, no one considered the claim of mad Thomas Leigh, shut up at Monk Sherborne with Jane's idiot brother George.) Lord Craven and Mr Leigh-Perrot had both greatly interested themselves in the matter, Mr Hill added. He had met Mr James Leigh and Mr Leigh-Perrot in London and explained to them his opinions.

What Mr Hill did *not* say was that the advice he had given to Mr James Leigh and to Mr Leigh-Perrot in London was rather different from that which he vouchsafed to Mr Thomas Leigh at Adlestrop. Actually, he had told Mr Leigh-Perrot that it was now 'universally allowed' that Lord Leigh's will must 'be set aside for the uncertainty of it'.[4] He had likewise told him that he had written to summon Mr Thomas Leigh to London to discuss these matters with him and was 'not a little nettled' that he had refused to do so. Mr James Leigh was more than nettled; he was 'greatly offended' by his uncle's odd behaviour. When Thomas Leigh had still not presented himself at the reading of the Hon. Mary's will on 5 July, Mr Hill had declared himself 'surprised' and 'displeased'. He also expressed surprise at a little extra codicil in the lady's will by which he himself was appointed a joint executor and residuary legatee of her estate. 'This codicil,' Hill protested, '[he] knew nothing of and [was] very much hurt at it, fearing the ill-natured world [would] call his character in question.'[5] Mr Leigh-Perrot was not at all ill-natured. At Mr Hill's home that night, he happily enjoyed a meal of mackerel, neck of venison, chicken, beans and bacon, followed by a most delicious cherry tart. But even he could not refrain from noting that the wily lawyer would 'probably get three or four thousand pounds' from his former client's generosity.

For his own part, Mr Leigh-Perrot, though professing himself 'confused' and affecting to find more pleasure in counting the steps of his London lodgings at Hatchett's (seventy-four), than in all this lawyers' talk, was by no means a disinterested spectator in these deliberations. Even now, should he (aged seventy), outlive Mr Thomas Leigh (aged seventy-two), there was every reason to suppose he might claim a life-interest in the Stoneleigh estate, and thus frustrate Mr James Leigh's hopes. As he wrote to his wife: 'Mr James Leigh was particularly attentive to me and uncommonly civil in his enquiries after you; from which I infer that he is apprehensive that I may make use of the power I have and give his uncle and him some trouble.'[6]

Stoneleigh Abbey was an enchanting place. However valiantly Jane sought to armour herself against its seductive spell, with cruel mimicry of the legalistic cant of all those Leighs, half-Leighs and would-be-Leighs now squabbling over its ownership, she found it irresistible. The Avon ran near the house amidst green meadows bounded by large and beautiful woods, full of delightful walks. It was such a pleasure to walk through these dark and ancient woods, impenetrable to the sun even in the middle of an August day. The house itself was vast, far larger than she could ever have supposed. Imagine, forty-five windows, all facing to the front! Originally an ancient abbey of the Cistercian order, the buildings had been refashioned, with more discretion than was customary in such things, and now presented a pleasing façade of mellow sandstone rising amidst the trees. Inside, there were twenty-six bedrooms, several long galleries hung with pictures, and innumerable dark corridors and ancient winding flights of stairs. Mrs Austen was so full of the place she could hardly wait to describe it all to James's Mary at Steventon. 'Everything is very grand & very fine & very large,' she boasted. 'I expected to find every thing about the place very fine and all that, but I had no idea of its being so beautiful.'[7]

Even Mr Thomas Leigh was somewhat disconcerted by the vastness of the place and almost despaired of ever finding his way among its labyrinthine corridors and staircases. Whereupon Mrs Austen, to everyone's amusement, proposed to him the expedient of setting up *directing posts* at every corner. What most appealed to her, who shared with Jane's heroine Susan an anticipation of abbeys being solemn and gloomy places, was the cheerfulness and cleanliness that was everywhere to be found. 'I had figured to myself long avenues, dark rookeries and dismal yew-trees,' she told Mary, 'but here are no such melancholy things.' Indeed, 'were you to cut your finger,' she added, 'I do not think you could find a cobweb to wrap it up in.'

Yet the place was not entirely devoid of Gothic delights. Hidden behind the old picture gallery they discovered a small drawing-room, and behind that, the state bedchamber, with its high dark crimson bed. 'An *alarming* apartment,' they all agreed, 'just fit for a heroine!'[8] And if it were ghosts they were seeking, there in the hall was a memorial to Lady Audrey Leigh, exhumed from her grave and appearing astonishingly lovely and lifelike; 'her flesh quite plump as if she were alive, her face very beautiful, her hands exceedingly small and not wasted.' The Austens returned from their exploration of the house delighted not to have been denied these small gratifications of their romantic notions, yet happy to be in a house which exhibited all the comforts of ancient wealth with none of the concomitant barbarities of medieval taste. The noble parlour, where they feasted on fish and venison and 'all manner of good things' at a late hour of the night, was hung round with family pictures. Here was the Sir Thomas Leigh who sheltered Charles I at Stoneleigh when the citizens of Coventry turned against him. In the velvet drawing-room was the Sir Thomas Leigh who was Queen Elizabeth's Lord Mayor of London; and in the silk drawing-room the resplendent first Duke of Chandos.[9]

In such surroundings it was difficult to suppress entirely some wistful fantasies about how very different life could be. Mrs Austen could not refrain from itemizing the splendours of the place, quite as if she were drawing up an inventory. 'The garden contains 5 acres and a half. The ponds supply excellent fish, the park excellent venison; there is also great plenty of pigeons, rabbits, & all sorts of poultry.' She noted the dairy, which produced 'good Warwickshire' butter, cheese and cream; the quantity ('beyond imagination') of beer casks in the cellar, and the abundance of small fruits in the kitchen, which, she told Mary, 'exceed anything you can form an idea of'. On 12 August, they were joined at dinner by a Mr Holt Leigh, the member for Wigan in Lancashire. This Mr Holt Leigh, she wished Jane to note, was *a single man*, and although 'the wrong side of forty' was 'chatty, well-bred, *and has a large estate*'.[10]

Jane was long accustomed to deflecting such hints, and yet could not pretend to an utter indifference concerning the fate of Stoneleigh. For her, the vast sums that were daily under discussion in Mr Thomas Leigh's huddled conversations with Mr Hill were almost inconceivable. She and Cassandra had recently benefited from legacies themselves. Old Mrs Lillingston of Walcot, one of aunt Leigh-Perrot's friends, had died in January, leaving small bequests to her circle of friends in Bath. Jane and Cassandra had received £50 each; a small enough sum when measured by Stoneleigh standards, but more than sufficient to meet all Jane's expenses that year.[11] Mrs Austen soon ascertained that, as far as the Austens themselves were concerned, the most fortunate outcome of the Stoneleigh business would be that which favoured her brother, Leigh-Perrot. And, having once established in her mind that such was the most desirable conclusion, it was a natural step to believe that it was also the just one. Jane herself could pretend to little real affection for her aunt and uncle, but had always been conscientious in her duties towards them, however disagreeable the circumstances. She thought of all those hours of dutiful visits to Paragon, and the unselfish offer to stay with her aunt in Ilchester gaol. Such loyalty, she was sure, could not go unrewarded if Mr Leigh-Perrot should prove successful in his ambitions for the Stoneleigh estate.

Among other Leigh family relatives who suddenly discovered an urgent wish to visit Stoneleigh that summer was Lady Saye and Sele. As the mother-in-law of Mr James Leigh, she was understandably anxious to safeguard her son-in-law's claims. Yet Lady Saye and Sele was hardly a natural diplomat. Her late husband, father of the 'adultress' Miss Twisleton, had twice attempted suicide: once, unsuccessfully, at Kensington gravel pits, and then at home in Harley Street when, in order to be sure of success, he had cut his throat with a razor while stabbing his stomach with a sword. Naturally, none of the Stoneleigh company would have been so ill-bred as to allude to such a misfortune. They were all 'disposed to be pleased,' Mrs Austen said; 'endeavour to be agreeable and I hope succeed.' Sadly, Lady Saye and Sele herself observed no such decorum. Asked one night at dinner whether she would take 'some boiled chicken', she refused, and then insisted on offering an explanation. After her lord 'destroyed himself', she said, she had eaten boiled chicken in her chamber every day for a fortnight. But ever since that time, she had not 'been able to touch it'. Another evening, she startled the clerk of the kitchen by interrogating him before the rest of the company on his recipe for macaroni.[12] 'Poor Lady Saye & Sele to be sure is rather tormenting, tho' sometimes amusing, and affords Jane many a good laugh,' Mrs Austen confided to Mary. Jane took great delight in the noble lady's lack of discretion; but for Mrs Austen, adhering to her policy of 'endeavouring to be agreeable', such aristocratic outbursts were very tiring; 'she fatigues me sadly on the whole.'[13]

Excursions were planned to sites of interest in the neighbour-hood. At Kenilworth, the Austens found 'much entertainment' in surveying the ruins of the once noble castle where Queen Eliza-beth, whose memory Jane loved to abuse, had been so extravag-antly courted by the Earl of Leicester. At Warwick Castle, they found still more to divert them; but majestic as these ancient edi-fices were, they did not compare with the splendours of Stoneleigh, where history and utility combined in such a wholesome harmony. No excursion could yield a greater pleasure than walking through Stoneleigh's beautiful woods, or watching the blackbirds and thrushes at dinner on the soft fruits in its gardens. They were reluctant to depart, but their cousin, the Reverend Cooper, was impatient to welcome them to Hamstall and eventually, on 14 August, they set out for his Staffordshire rectory. 'Staffordshire is a good way off,' Jane had once remarked. In terms of distance, Hamstall was a mere 38 miles from Stoneleigh; in terms of elegance, it belonged to a different world. The rectory was hand-some enough, backed by some pretty woods (though nothing to compare with Stoneleigh), and St Michael's church had a fine stone spire. But the eldest Cooper boy was quite insufferably pompous (fancying himself a sermon-writer at twelve years old), and all the other Cooper children had whooping cough, which they were so generous as to pass on to their aunts. The Austens spent five weeks at Hamstall, after which Jane spent a similar period recovering from her infection.[14]

Over the succeeding months, Mrs Austen affected to think no more about the Stoneleigh inheritance; or, if she did think of it, would only do so in a manner which indicated how utterly she disclaimed any personal interest in the outcome. There were 'so many legacies to pay,' she wrote to Mary, so many 'heavy fines' and 'other demands' on the estate, not to mention all the funeral expenses, that really it would not amount to such a vast fortune. 'I do not think Mr Leigh will have more money than he knows what to do with,' she declared with lofty resignation.[15] It had become quite a boast with her how thriftily she might flourish on quite a small competence. At the beginning of the year her wealth had amounted to £68; but a twelvemonth later she was worth all of £99, and that after spending £32 on a purchase of stock. Even amid all the luxury of Stoneleigh itself, she had maintained her frugal diet. Every morning the breakfast table had offered its lavish provisions of chocolate, coffee and tea, plum cake, pound cake, hot rolls, cold rolls, bread and butter, but every morning she had disdained them all, with her cheerfully modest request: '*dry toast for me*'.

Jane Austen's instincts were entirely the opposite. She was heartily tired of such virtuous frugality. Luxury was what she dreamt of. At least on visits to Godmersham she could indulge her expensive tastes. 'I shall eat Ice & drink French wine,' she boasted, '& be above vulgar economy.'[16] But in reality, vulgar economy was the order of her existence. As she prepared for life in Southampton with Martha, Mary and Frank, she thought it prudent to take a careful reckoning of her personal expenses. Her income for the year she calculated at £50 15s 0d.[17] From that, she must deduct £13 19s 3d for clothes and pocket money, £8 14s 5d for washing and as much as £3 17s 6½d for the letters and parcels without which she could not bear to survive. Her charities must not be neglected; £3 10s 3½d was little enough for those. And although 'presents' at £6 4s 4d seemed to bulk very large in these accounts, these might be prudently justified as investments in good-will. The real indulgences were more personal; but 17s 9d could hardly be reckoned a vast sum to spend on a whole year's entertainments at water-parties and plays. Indeed, it dismayed her to think it was so little. Finally, there was the pianoforte. That was an extravagance, no doubt. She looked at the figures: £2 13s 6d for the year's hire of a pianoforte. But it was an extravagance which she could not – which she *would not* – be without. Since her own instrument at the rectory had been sold, she had always been allowed the hire of a replacement. She had had a pianoforte in Bath and saw no reason why she should not have one at Southampton. To her, a pianoforte was scarcely less indispensable than her books and letters. Her playing of 'The Yellow Haired Laddie' or 'Queen Mary's Lament' of a morning hardly approached the heights of musical accomplishment, yet afforded her great satisfaction.

Martha and Mary (Frank's Mary that is; or 'Mrs F.A.', as Jane now called her) were both at their separate accounts. As a result of their various deliberations, it appeared that each party felt 'quite equal' to their present expenses. But they were all agreed that much increase in house-rent 'would not do'.[18] Frank was resolved to limit himself to £400 a year, it seemed, which was prudent enough in the circumstances. At least it was some relief that Steventon Mary ('Mrs J.A.') had ceased to pester them with talk of *her* poverty (though she did let it be known that there was 'no hope' of James buying another horse next summer). She and James were now very much set on a visit to Stoneleigh, and May was talked of as a suitable time. As to Stoneleigh itself, all sorts of rumours were heard of treaties and covenants and agreements, and Jane could not stifle her sense of resentment when she heard how many thousands Mr Leigh-Perrot was likely to gain from renouncing his claim to inherit. She was quite out of patience with a letter from their aunt Leigh-Perrot full of her constant grumbles about colds and coughs 'much worse than any she ever had before'. With the negotiations between them and their Adlestrop nephew 'so happily over', she wrote to Cassandra, 'what can have power to vex her materially?'[19]

Southampton

Their arrival in Southampton that October was hardly auspicious. Jane was still suffering the tiresome effects of the whooping cough she had contracted at Hamstall, and Frank was anxious to secure any temporary lodgings that might be quickly procured for a reasonable charge before having to resume his naval duties. The lodgings they found were anonymous enough; the sort of place that endeavoured to compensate for its lack of refinements by the generous size of its rooms. Inevitably, such capaciousness put it quite out of their power to refuse visitors. Almost as soon as they arrived there, Jane found herself reluctantly compelled to assume the role of host. Martha quickly departed to spend Christmas with the Fowles at Kintbury and Cassandra was honoured by an invitation to Godmersham. In their place, James and Mary decided to visit Jane and Mrs Austen, bringing their children with them.

It was hardly the most festive of occasions. The weather was in general too bad to allow for much walking, and James, who hated to be confined within doors, grew quickly bored and fretful. Mrs F.A., already pregnant, was subject to fainting fits; Mrs J.A. had no patience with books or reading and soon resumed her denunciations of the government's iniquitous handling of the Mathew business. It fell to Jane to supervise all the entertainment of their guests, from the food they ate to any amusements that might be devised, and to lament the deficiencies of both. The boiled leg of mutton which they ate one evening when Captain Foote was their guest was 'underdone even for James', which was sad as Captain Foote had 'a particular dislike to underdone mutton'.[20] The books she proposed for reading aloud in the evening were scarcely better received. After only twenty pages of Madame de Genlis's *Alphonsine* the company declared themselves 'disgusted' at such 'indelicacies' from a pen 'hitherto so pure'. Charlotte Lennox's *The Female Quixote* (a book which Jane much admired) was quickly substituted, and Mrs F.A. seemed to enjoy it. But Mrs J.A. had little taste for that, or any other, book. In desperation, Jane put herself to sketching out, for Mrs F.A.'s diversion, some little dialogues on 'the business of mothering'. This at least was a subject on which Mrs J.A. might claim some expertise, and, affecting to defer to her superior wisdom in such matters, Jane encouraged her to expound (in the character of 'Mrs Enfield') her own views on the dangerous temptations of plum cake.[21]

Always, it seemed, there were more guests to be entertained, who needed more than plum cake to satisfy them. Frank knew so many officers in this military neighbourhood, who could not wait to view his new home and bride. After Captain Foote there was Admiral Bertie and his daughter. And after the Berties came the Lances. 'Our acquaintance increase too fast,' Jane protested. She found her only relief from the duties of hospitality in writing to Cassandra. 'When you receive this,' she wrote on 7 January, 'our guests will be all gone or going; and I shall be left to the comfortable disposal of my own time, to ease of mind from the torments of rice puddings and apple dumplings.'[22] She envied her sister's pleasant hours of 'quiet and rational conversation' in Kent, even those spent with old Mrs Knight at Canterbury. Her only fear, she wrote, was 'of your being so agreeable, so much to her taste, as to make her wish to keep you with her forever'. Once again, she felt her old anxiety at the prospect of losing Cassandra to the seductive pleasures of Godmersham. 'If that should be the case, we must remove to Canterbury,' she wrote, but then paused. However delightful the pleasures of Godmersham, and however disagreeable the inconveniencies of Southampton, there was a greater independence in living here as joint-tenants with their brother Frank than in Kent, as poor relations of their brother Edward. On balance, she believed, 'I should not like [Canterbury] so well as Southampton.' Indeed, now that their guests were finally leaving, she even felt some pangs of guilt at the lack of warmth she had shown to them and regretted that 'I did not take more pains to please them all.' But this was only a fleeting feeling. Accompanying Frank on a return visit to the Lances, she experienced a familiar sensation of annoyance at being required to simulate pleasure at their officious civility. 'They must be acting by the orders of Mr Lance of Netherton' (a friend of the Lloyds), she concluded, 'as there seems no other reason for their coming near us.' Mrs Lance did not impress her. 'Whether she boasts any offspring besides a grand pianoforte did not appear,' she remarked. It was, though, a very *grand* pianoforte, far more handsome than the one for which Jane herself was paying £2 13s 6d a year. She concluded, with some relief, that the Lances were altogether too grand to trouble the Austens with over-familiarity. 'They will not come often, I dare say. They live in a handsome style and are rich, and she seemed to like to be rich, and we gave her to understand that we were far from being so; she will soon feel therefore that we are not worth her acquaintance.'[23] If she were condemned to being poor, she could at least be defiantly so.

Jane soon found that the departure of their guests brought little relief from her besetting mood of ill humour. She would do her very best, she wrote to Cassandra, to 'ring . . . the changes of the glads & sorrys' in her letters; but inevitably the 'sorrys' still far outnumbered the 'glads'. 'Unluckily . . . I see nothing to be glad of,' she reported, 'unless I make it a matter of joy that Mrs Wylmot has another son & that Ld Lucan has taken a mistress.' 'But to be sorry,' she wrote, 'I find many occasions.'[24] Indeed, she contrived to make quite a little essay out of her 'sorrys'. She was sorry at the difficulties in purchasing fish (even in Southampton!). She was sorry (or at least *claimed* to be so) at having affronted Cassandra with her frank opinion of Harriot Bridges's new husband, the Reverend Mr Moore. (But surely Cassandra knew that the man was 'universally hated' in Kent?) It was said that on his first appearance at church after marrying Harriot, the congregation united in singing the funeral hymn instead of the usual nuptial psalm. 'I do not mean ever to like him,' Jane boasted: 'You see I have a spirit, as well as yourself.'[25] She was sorry about Mrs Whitfield's illness; she was sorry about Marianne Bridges's sufferings; and she also supposed she might be allowed to lament the news that Mrs Deedes was to have yet another child. She was angry and sorry at Martha's prolonged 'detention' in Hampshire, where, even now, she must be enduring the Debarries' bad breath. ('I cannot help thinking she will marry Peter Debarry,' she wrote with impatience.) She was particularly sorry at the prospect of another visit from James and family. 'I am sorry & angry that his visits should not give one more pleasure,' she confessed. 'The company of so good & so clever a man ought to be gratifying in itself; but his chat seems all forced, his opinions on many points too much copied from his wife's.' She could not help remarking on the mighty contrast between these two brothers. James would spend his time fretfully, 'walking about the house & banging the doors, or ringing the bell for a glass of water'. Frank, on the other hand, even when afflicted by a 'very bad cough', would always make himself useful, and thought nothing of lending a hand with mending, stitching and even making a 'very nice fringe for the drawing-room curtains'. 'Fraternal love, sometimes almost everything,' she wrote in *Mansfield Park*, 'is at others worse than nothing.'[26]

Even reading afforded her little pleasure. They were currently attempting Sarah Burney's *Clarentine*, which she had formerly enjoyed, but was now surprised to find 'how foolish it is . . . full of unnatural conduct & forced difficulties, without striking merit of any kind'. But most of all she was sorry at Cassandra's continued absence at Godmersham. 'It is no use to lament,' she wrote bleakly. 'I never heard that even Queen Mary's Lamentation did her any good, & I could not therefore expect to benefit from mine.' At times of despondency it was still her habit to compare herself to the ill-fated Queen of Scots, whose plaintive song she had copied into her book of 'Songs & Duetts'. And yet, however ineffectual such lamentations might be, she could not refrain from making them. When the end of the month still brought no word of Cassandra's return, she could not repress her feelings of irritation. 'I confess myself much disappointed at this repeated delay of your return,' she protested.

In the meantime, Frank had fixed upon a permanent dwelling at Castle Square and, in Cassandra's absence, he and Mary found themselves left to take charge of all the domestic arrangements. 'Frank and Mary cannot at all approve of your not being at home in time to help them in their finishing purchases,' Jane wrote; '& desire me to say that, if you are not, they shall be as spiteful as possible & chuse everything in the stile most likely to vex you; knives that will not cut, glasses that will not hold, a sofa without a seat, & a bookcase without shelves.'[27] For her own part, she added, though she had 'pretty well given up all idea of your being with us before our removal, I felt sure that March would not pass quite away without bringing you.' But by now, she said, all she expected were delays and excuses: 'Before April comes, of course something else will occur to detain you.'

In this morose mood, only the most perverse events had any power to divert her. Mrs F.A. had a particular friend in Southampton, a certain Miss Fowler, who had left her calling card one day. But this Miss Fowler, as it now appeared, was also a friend of the troublesome Miss Pearson, who still harboured a quite unreasonable grudge against Henry Austen and his family. 'What a *contretemps!*' Jane wrote with some wry amusement. 'The Black gentleman has certainly employed one of his menial imps to bring about this complete tho' trifling mischief.' Household decorations at Castle Square were in hand by Mr Husket, Lord Lansdowne's painter; '*domestic* painter, I should call him,' she added, 'for he lives in the castle.' This correction prompted a sarcastic afterthought: 'Domestic chaplains have given way to this more necessary office, & I suppose whenever the walls want no touching up, he is employed about my lady's face.'[28] She took a malicious pleasure in passing on news of a foolish, unhappy young woman who had married herself to a foolish, vicious young man; 'he swears, drinks, is cross, selfish & brutal.' And she affected indignation at the 'shameless' pretensions of Lady Bridges who, on her death-bed, had had the bad taste to nominate her successor as Lord Bridges's second wife. 'It is a piece of impertinence indeed,' she wrote, 'in a woman to pretend to fix on anyone as if she supposed it cd only be ask & have.' As she wandered through the cheerless rooms of their temporary lodgings that winter, malice was her only source of pleasure. 'I am forced to be abusive,' she told Cassandra, 'for want of subject, having really nothing to say.'[29]

Of course, there *were* things to be glad of, though in her present mood she would only acknowledge them grudgingly. The new house at Castle Square was both spacious and elegant, and the garden was already 'putting in order' by an agreeable man with a 'remarkable good character', a 'very fine complexion' and, more to the point, who required 'something less' by way of payment than the others they had tried. There were to be borders of sweet-briars, roses and laburnum, raspberries, gooseberries and currants, and, at Jane's special request, some syringas. 'I could not do without a syringa,' she said, for she carried always in her head Cowper's lovely lines, '. . . laburnum, rich/In streaming gold; syringa, iv'ry pure'.[30] Already it was said that their garden was 'the best in the town'. Indoors, Mrs Day was busy with carpets and Mrs Hall with bedding, though Mrs Austen, as usual, was playing the martyr, insisting that '*she* [did] not want' any carpet in her room. All well and good, said Jane; 'it may certainly be better done without in her room than in Martha's & ours.' Their landlord, Lord Lansdowne, was another source of amusement. The King had once called him the 'best-bred man' he knew, which was more than anyone could say of his lady wife, a vulgar, overdressed Irish widow 'larger than Mrs Fitzherbert'.[31] Lansdowne had built his own Gothic folly of a castle just opposite the house that the Austens now rented from him.

Jane Austen's most amusing hours were spent in the company of little Catherine Foote, whose father continued to visit them despite the unfortunate boiled mutton. The young girl would chatter away by Jane's side, 'examining the treasures of my writing-desk drawer', as she wrote her letters to Cassandra. Or at other times, the two of them would play together at spillikins with a set donated from Godmersham. But even these moments of relaxation gave rise to feelings of regret. Little Catherine was such a 'nice, natural, open-hearted, affectionate girl . . . so unlike anything that I was myself at her age', that Jane could not help wondering at the awkward, diffident, sulky manner of her own younger years. 'I am often all astonishment & shame,' she wrote: 'What is become of all the shyness in the world?' In Catherine Foote she seemed to see a child of a new era, hopeful, confident and unafraid. 'Moral as well as natural diseases disappear in the progress of time,' she mused, '& new ones take their place. Shyness & the sweating sickness have given way to confidence and paralytic complaints.'[32] With only half of that girl's confidence, she thought, she herself might now be a successful published author, instead of still fretting with vexation at the continued silence from Crosby & Son. Nothing, not games of spillikins nor abuse, would serve to lift her spirits for long. Even the wintry weather had lost its power to charm her. In January, she had relished 'one of the pleasantest frosts I ever knew' and shared in Frank's exhilaration as he went skating on the water-meadows near the beach. But six weeks later, she had grown tired of the wet snow lying in dirty puddles in all the alley-ways and streets. They grew accustomed to the wind blowing a constant gale from the north-west; 'Castle Square weather', they called it. 'We are cold here', was her final despondent comment to Cassandra at the end of February. 'I expect a severe March, a wet April, & a sharp May.'[33]

Cassandra eventually returned to Southampton in mid-March, though even Jane's repeated lamentations did not prevent her from spending several days in London with Henry and Eliza *en route*.

Henry had recently taken another of his Oxford militia friends, a Mr James Tilson, into partnership, and had moved offices once more, from Albany to No. 10 Henrietta Street in Covent Garden. He was full of all sorts of ideas for a brewery scheme, but, like so many of Henry's ideas, it would probably come to nothing. Cassandra had barely had time to settle herself at Castle Square (where, she was relieved to find – despite Jane's threats – that the sofa was fully equipped with seats and the bookcases with shelves), when Frank was appointed to command HMS *St Albans* for convoy duty to and from South Africa, China and the East Indies. Mrs F.A. was inevitably dismayed at such a distant posting, but Frank persuaded her to see it in a better light. Despite the long absences that his duties must inevitably entail, the compensating benefits were much to be desired. Returning to the Far East would provide him with an opportunity to renew those lucrative connections which he had formerly enjoyed, and would thus serve his 'pecuniary advantage' quite as much as his 'professional credit'.

Summoned to Sheerness on 4 April for the fitting out of his ship, Frank was more determined than ever to insist upon adequate provisions. Several letters passed to and fro between himself and 'the principal Officers and Commissioners of His Majesty's Navy' concerning deficiencies in stores and men.[34] In the meantime, he quickly re-established contact with sympathetic Company men like Mr Iggulden, the Company's harbour agent at Deal. As a result of these negotiations, he was absent from Southampton for the birth of his first child on 27 April. Despite (or quite possibly on account of) Mrs J.A.'s advice to her on 'the business of mothering', poor Mrs F.A. had a sad time of it, and was 'most alarmingly ill' for some days before the delivery. Eventually, though, all was safely concluded, and the baby, named Mary-Jane, was pronounced 'a fine little girl' by all who saw her. Frank set off in the *St Albans* from Sheerness on 21 May and arrived at Spithead a few days later, just in time for the baby's christening at All Saints church on 31 May.

Though Mrs F.A. bore the prospect of Frank's lengthy absence with the fortitude expected of her as an Austen and a sailor's wife, she could not entirely suppress a certain melancholy apprehension when she considered the recent career of Frank's sailor brother Charles. It was now more than four years since Charles had last been in England. For most of that time he had been patrolling the Atlantic seaboard of America, from Nova Scotia to the Caribbean, charged with enforcing the right to search for deserters and for traders in contraband goods. This was a dangerous and unprofitable duty. British policy had imposed an embargo on all trade between France and its West Indian possessions. But it was not unknown for enterprising American shipmasters to connive at a lucrative form of evasion, rerouting West Indian cargoes by way of a New England port, where they would be transferred to a 'neutral' ship defiantly flying the Stars and Stripes.

However, it was not merely the dangers of a sailor's life which dismayed Mrs F.A. She was equally alarmed at what Jane called its *'douceurs'*. Charles Austen's time, she knew, had not been entirely confined to weathering Atlantic storms aboard the sloop *Indian*. While stationed at Bermuda he had found an opportunity to become acquainted with Fanny Palmer, the sixteen-year-old daughter of the island's former Attorney-General. The pair of them were engaged in the spring of 1806 and married a year later. Frank Austen was granted one month's shore leave to spend with Mary and his new-born daughter Mary-Jane before sailing for the Cape of Good Hope on 30 June. As they said their sad farewells, Mrs F.A. could not help wondering when, if ever, she would see her husband again; and how many pretty sixteen-year-old girls he might encounter in the meantime.

Jane herself was always passionately proud of both her sailor brothers. Where they were concerned, she would happily suspend all her sceptical tendencies, and was content to believe all the most agreeable things that were said of them. She utterly forgave Lord and Lady Leven for their social maladroitness when they spoke up with generous praise for Charles. And she quite warmed to Earle Harwood when he assured her (entirely without evidence) that Charles was 'looked up to by everybody in all America'.[35] As soon as Frank sailed from England, Mrs F.A. left the house at Castle Square. It was to be only a short absence, she said. She would take the baby down to Kent; first to Ramsgate to show her off to her grandparents, and then on to Godmersham. No sooner had she left than her place was filled by Edward Cooper and his family, who decided on a summer visit to Southampton. Jane counterfeited the appropriate degree of delight at their arrival, but was at least genuinely pleased to note that the children were now free of the whooping cough. At Godmersham, Edward Austen also had thoughts of a summer holiday. He considered it might be an agreeable enterprise to bring together all the family members who remained in England. But Godmersham was at such a distance from both Steventon and Southampton that it might hardly seem the ideal place for such an event. Twice that spring Edward had visited his Chawton estate in Hampshire, which had been recently vacated by his tenant Mr Coulthard. Although less hospitable than Godmersham, the place, he judged, was a good deal more convenient, in terms of location, for the grand family reunion he had in mind. Accordingly, it was agreed. At the end of August, the Austens travelled from Steventon, from Southampton and from Kent for a house-party at Chawton manor.

Mrs Candour

As soon as she entered the great house, Jane experienced agreeable feelings of excitement. It was not the first time that she had visited Edward's Chawton estate, but it was the first time she had stayed there. Since his elevation to Knight-hood, Edward had always chosen to live in Kent and had paid little attention to his Hampshire properties, being content to lease the house to a succession of gentlemen who, for a short term at least, relished an opportunity to assume the borrowed role of rural squire. Of course, it was not as imposing as Stoneleigh, nor even as grand as Manydown; yet the older parts of the house dated back at least to the sixteenth century, with two red-brick gabled wings that had been added in Stuart times. As Jane explored the old place, she took as her companion her young niece Fanny, who was as much in love with the romance of its curious passageways and antique rooms as any imaginative fourteen-year-old ought to be. Jane loved her open spirit and quick-witted humour. 'She is quite after one's own heart,' she told Cassandra; 'almost another sister. [I] could not have supposed that a neice would ever have been so much to me.'[36]

Fanny was under strict instructions to send as precise a description as might be given to her governess, Miss Chapman. 'This is a fine large *old* house,' she wrote, 'built long before Queen Elizabeth I believe, & here are such a number of irregular passages &c &c that it is very entertaining to explore them, & often when I think myself miles away from one part of the house I find a passage or entrance close to it.'[37] 'I don't know when I shall be quite mistress of all the intricate & different ways,' she remarked. There was something quite artless, Jane noted, about the way she spoke of being 'mistress' of the place. For Fanny, it was not a question of whether, but *when*. As the daughter of a wealthy man of property, it was quite natural for her to think of these grand houses as her natural domain. The girl took a natural pride in all the family portraits stretching back through the centuries. 'It is very curious to trace the genealogy of the Knights & all the old families that have possessed this estate, from the pictures of which there are great quantities,' she wrote, keen to demonstrate to Miss Chapman her particular attention to *history*. 'Some descriptions of them have been routed out, so that we are not at a loss for amusement.' *Natural* history was not forgotten either. There were, she noted, 'quantities of trees about the house (especially beech) which always makes a place pretty, I think'. What she did not remark upon was a small red-brick cottage, formerly the village inn, hard upon the road beyond the church and village pond. It was not the kind of place that Fanny would notice; not at all romantic, and hardly deserving the epithets either 'pretty' or 'charming'. But on their rambles through the estate, calling on neighbours or tenants in the village, Jane Austen did notice, and remember it.

In mid-September, the Austen ladies returned to Southampton, where it was now their turn to entertain Edward and his family. With her scrupulous dedication to itemizing all her pleasures, Fanny continued to record their daily diversions. On Sunday, after church, there was a stroll to the Polygon; on Monday, a trip to the theatre. Another day, there was a boat-trip to Hythe to visit Charles's new mother-in-law, Mrs Palmer, who was holidaying in Hampshire with her younger daughter Harriet; and in the evenings there were delicious walks with aunts Cassandra and Jane along the tree-planted beach with its wheeled bathing-machines. Before the Godmersham party departed, uncle Henry came down briefly from London to join them. It was he who arranged their New Forest tour and a picnic among the picturesque ruins of Netley Abbey. When she left Southampton towards the end of September, Fanny Austen had more than enough to convince her governess Miss Chapman of a holiday well spent.

That winter, while Frank mapped the anchorages of Cape Town Bay and noted the trade of its inhabitants, Jane and Cassandra paid visits to Steventon and Manydown. They were at Manydown for Christmas, where Jane took part in a Twelfth Night perform-ance of Sheridan's *School for Scandal*. Elizabeth Bigg was recently widowed and returned to Manydown with her young son William, who remembered the great spirit with which Jane Austen played the part of Mrs Candour, protesting she could 'not bear to hear a friend ill-spoken of'. ('Abuse everybody but me,' she wrote privately to Cassandra.)[38] In February, when Frank was bound for St Helena, Jane and Cassandra stayed at Kintbury with the Fowles. Of the four Fowle sons who had once been Mr Austen's pupils, only the eldest, Fulwar, was still alive. Tom had died at St Domingo, William in Egypt and Charles, whom Jane always fondly remembered for his bespoke silk stockings, had died sud-denly at home two years before. Fulwar had never risen to be Secretary of State, as the young James Austen had once confidently predicted; but he had at least received congratulations from King George as 'the best preacher, the best officer and the best rider to hounds in all my royal county of Berkshire'.[39] His son Tom was now a midshipman under Charles Austen's command aboard HMS *Indian*, and the families exchanged what news they had from Bermuda.

In May, Jane was in Brompton, staying with Henry and Eliza

in their terraced village house at 16 Michael Place. Although not in London, Brompton was quite the most fashionable place to be, Eliza always insisted. Their house had been designed by the same émigré Polish count who had rebuilt the Opera House, and they found themselves surrounded by the most brilliant and celebrated people. Miss Pope, the actress, lived at No. 17; Miss Billington, the singer, at No. 15, and Mr Liston, the comedian, at No. 21. Though now forty-six, Eliza still craved gaiety and excitement and naturally they all betook themselves to the King's birthday celebrations on 4 June. Ten days later it was off to the Bath Hotel in Arlington Street, where James and Mary had just arrived *en route* for Godmersham. With them they brought their two younger children, James and Caroline, but not Anna, who had been packed off to Mrs Austen's at Southampton. It was a pity, Jane thought, that Mrs J.A. would make so little effort to disguise her dislike of the girl. But Mrs J.A., who was never content unless she had something to cavil at, was entirely in her element grumbling at the Bath Hotel ('most uncomfortable quarters – very dirty, very noisy, and very ill-provided').[40]

Jane was delighted that for once it was she, not Cassandra, who would be enjoying the splendours of Godmersham, and was determined that not even Mrs J.A.'s constant complaints should alloy the many pleasures she anticipated from the visit. To make room for Jane in the carriage, James had gone on ahead by the five o'clock stage, leaving Henry (who seemed not at all downcast by the failure of his brewery scheme) to see the ladies off. For the first eight miles, Mrs J.A. complained that it was too hot (though the agreeable heat put Jane Austen in mind of her first journey to Kent, fourteen years earlier). Then, after Blackheath, Mrs J.A. pronounced it too cold. At the Bull Inn at Deptford she denounced the bad butter (which Jane also remembered, but this time without complaint). The more Mrs J.A. complained, the more Jane felt herself obliged to maintain a tactful silence ('I will never join in ridiculing a friend', as Mrs Candour said). In truth, she confessed to Cassandra, 'we *were* rather crowded' and little Caroline *did* fidget so. But, she added quickly, 'it does not become me to say so, as I and my boa were of the party, and it is not to be supposed but that a child of three years of age was fidgety.'[41] Even this modest protest struck her as rather too bold, and she begged Cassandra 'to keep all this to yourself, lest it should get round by Anna's means'. Just as it was Mrs J.A.'s role to fret and grumble, it was Jane's to be meek and grateful (in public at least) for the privilege of sharing her brother's carriage while he made the sacrifice of travelling by public conveyance. They reached Godmersham by six o'clock, where 'our two brothers were walking before the house as we approached, as natural as life'.

Undeniably, the presence of Mrs J.A. among the Godmersham guests cast a certain shadow over Jane's enjoyment of the place. The Godmersham family themselves were all affection. Fanny and Lizzy greeted them 'with a great deal of pleasant joy' and Marianne, Charles and Louisa gave her 'a very affectionate welcome'. Yet, as she sat writing in the Yellow Room, Jane felt distinctly out of place. 'It seems odd to me to have such a great place all to myself,' she wrote to Cassandra, 'and to be at Godmersham without you is also odd.'[42] It was strange how diffident the influence of Mrs J.A. could make her feel. Cassandra, she was sure, when she had been staying here without Jane, had never felt so isolated. 'I feel rather languid and solitary,' she wrote; 'three years ago we were more animated with you and Harriot and Miss Sharpe.'

Almost as soon as she arrived, there were tactful questions about how and when she would depart. After breakfast on the second morning, Edward called her to his room for a *tête-à-tête* about her 'plans'. Apparently, both he and James had urgent business to attend to. Naturally, they were both willing to convey her to some point near her home (Alton perhaps, or Winchester), but sadly, it would need to be rather soon. Jane, of course, signified her desire to be as little trouble as possible. 'I should have preferred a rather longer stay here certainly,' she wrote privately to Cassandra, 'but there is no prospect of any later conveyance for me.' Mrs J.A. had left her in little doubt that conveying her *away* from Godmersham would be even more inconvenient than bringing her had been. Already she and James had received an invitation from the Cookes at Bookham which they were not disinclined to accept, but 'my being with them would render it impractical'. Accordingly, Jane accepted Edward's gracious offer to carry her to Alton from whence she would 'get on' to Southampton 'somehow or other'. 'I shall at any rate be glad not to be obliged to be an incumbrance on those who have brought me here,' she wrote, 'for, as James has no horse, I must feel in their carriage that I am taking his place.'[43]

These were the minor vexations which always reminded her what a difference money made to happiness. When Louisa Bridges paid them all a visit, Jane was struck by how 'remarkably well' she looked. 'Legacies are a very wholesome diet,' she noted ruefully. Instead of sauntering in the park, like someone who belonged there, she sought to make herself useful in the house, like someone who must earn her keep. Elizabeth Austen, who was now expecting her eleventh child, must be fatigued by attendance on so many children. 'I have, of course, tendered my services,' Jane told Cassandra. Self-denial was still a powerful instinct. Feeling impoverished and dependent, she would modestly disclaim any title to the luxuries of Godmersham and affect a consuming fascination with more humdrum concerns: 'You know how interesting the purchase of a sponge-cake is to me.'[44] When her trunk arrived, she offered presents from Southampton; a rug 'which was received most gratefully' and a frock 'kindly accepted'. A letter from Southampton met with less universal admiration. Mrs J.A. expressed her 'surprise' that the Maitlands (whom she disliked as relations of James's first wife) should take tea with Cassandra, and there was general regret at the news of the cutting off of Anna's hair. When the company went on to 'regret [Anna's] not coming with her father and mother', Mrs J.A. made no reply. Jane was distressed and perplexed to witness her brother's cool disregard for his eldest daughter's concerns. 'I have tried to give James pleasure by telling him of his daughter's taste,' she wrote, 'but if he felt, he did not express it.'

Gradually, Jane came to realize that, for all her air of complacency, it was actually Mrs J.A. who felt most ill at ease at Godmersham that summer. It was her first visit to the house for more than ten years and, naturally, she made a point of exclaiming how much she was 'struck with the beauty of the place'. But the truth was that she felt rather overawed by its grandeur, and her children, too, found it rather daunting. 'I don't think I was very happy there, in a strange house,' Caroline recalled. 'I recollect the model of a ship in a passage, and my cousins' rabbits out of doors, in or near a long walk of high trees.' Jane Austen noticed the little girl's unease. 'Little Caroline looks very plain among her cousins', she noted, '& tho' she is not so headstrong or humoursome as they are, I do not think her at all more engaging.'[45] These discoveries brought a mighty relief to Jane's own anxieties. Quite suddenly, after only a week at Godmersham, and while Mrs J.A. still struggled to ingratiate herself with her wealthy relations, Jane began to feel quite at home there. It came to seem the most natural thing in the world to gossip in the Yellow Room or breakfast parlour, to saunter along the Temple Walk or read in the library. 'My languor is entirely removed,' she announced to Cassandra. When the happy news arrived of Frank's unexpected return ('in the true sailor way, just after our being told not to expect him for some weeks'), it was a delight 'to be among people who know one's connections & care about them'. It afforded her no end of amusement 'to hear John Bridges talk of "Frank"'.[46]

Now, instead of people wishing to hurry her away, she found herself 'kindly pressed to stay longer', for the whole summer, if possible, 'in consequence of an offer of Henry's to take me back some time in September'. No longer compelled to simulate gratitude for an enforced early departure, she found herself required to confess her secret reasons for being unable to stay. 'I have felt myself obliged to give Edwd & Elizth one private reason for my wishing to be at home in July,' she told Cassandra.[47] Catherine and Alethea Bigg were due to visit Southampton in August. After the embarrassing *contretemps* of their brother's proposal, Jane could not countenance an absence which might strike them as a snub. 'My honour, as well as my affection will be concerned in it,' she wrote. Edward and Elizabeth acknowledged 'the strength' of her scruple and said no more about it; 'one can rely on their secrecy,' said Jane. They were equally discreet when another former suitor, Edward Bridges, came with his mother to dine at Godmersham. Jane noted that he looked 'very well' and 'with manners as unaltered as hers'. His situation, too, was unaltered, she observed;

still single, though having added the rectorship of Bonnington to his other clerical livings, he now enjoyed a modest financial competency. Had Jane been staying longer in Kent, it would not have been impossible that they might have continued to enjoy each other's company. But no such pressing invitation was offered that might have disrupted her plans.

If Jane really must leave them in July, then Elizabeth proposed a 'very sweet' Christmas scheme in compensation. Jane and Cassandra must accompany young Edward home from school at Winchester at the end of the year, and join in the Godmersham winter festivities. It was indeed a delightful notion, but alas! Jane thought, where was the money to come from? 'A legacy might make it very feasible,' she wrote to Cassandra.[48] The more she fretted at her lack of funds, the more she dreamt of some fortuitous legacy that would put an end to these wretched privations. But where was it to come from? From Stoneleigh? From uncle Leigh-Perrot? From Mrs Knight? From some mysterious unknown benefactor? She did not care where it came from, so long as it came from *somewhere*. 'A legacy is our sovereign good,' she declared to Cassandra.

In default of a legacy, she must be happy to acknowledge smaller benefactions. She was invited to visit Mrs Knight at Canterbury, who sent a letter 'containing the usual fee, & all the usual kindness'. Once at White Friars, Jane was surprised by how much she relished the old lady's company. But clearly, she was not the only one with hopes of a legacy from that source. Mrs Knight was quite besieged by a constant stream of well-wishers. During the time that Jane was with her, troupes of Moores and Milles, Gregories and Grahams, Knatchbulls and Bridges arrived to pay their compliments. Jane was greatly impressed by the old lady's skill in discriminating between so many flattering friends. James and Mrs J.A., she gathered, were *not* favourites with her. 'I fancy Mrs K feels less interest in that branch of the family than any other,' she noted. But the Southampton Austens were a different matter. 'Mrs Knight is kindly anxious for our good, & thinks Mr L.P. [Leigh-Perrot] *must* be desirous for his *family's* sake to have everything settled.'[49] By 'everything', of course, she meant the business at Stoneleigh. But, gratifying as they were, hints like these only made for further vexations. Thomas Leigh was in London 'on business', they heard, 'which we of course think can be only *one* business'. He had posted all the way up there from Adlestrop in a single day, a feat which convinced Henry that the old man 'will live for ever'. 'I do not know where we are to get our legacy,' Jane wrote with some bitterness, 'but we will keep a sharp look-out.'[50]

Amid all the general rejoicing at Frank's safe arrival in England, there was one discordant note. Mrs F.A.'s cool reaction to her husband's sudden return gave rise to much gossip at Godmersham. It was known that she and baby Mary-Jane had been invited to spend part of the summer as Mrs Craven's guests on the Isle of Wight. This, it was generally agreed, was an 'admirable thing'. There was much amusement at Mary-Jane's delight at crossing the Solent which, they all said, showed 'the child's knowledge of her father being at sea'. Mrs Craven sent glowing reports of her guests, which only served to confirm how agreeably Mrs F.A. was now 'rising in the world' since leaving her Gibson connection behind her. 'She was thought excessively improved in her late visit,' Jane noted. It came then as something of a shock when it appeared that Mrs F.A. was in no hurry to greet her homecoming husband. At Godmersham, no one could wait to see him. Fanny was 'in hourly expectation' of his arrival there. Henry talked of rushing down from London to welcome his brother in the Downs. But Mrs F.A. seemed content to remain at her summer retreat on the island. 'Mary's not chusing to be at home occasions a general small surprise,' Jane wrote. 'When are calculations ever right?' she wondered. 'I could have sworn that Mary must have heard of the *St Albans* return, & wd have been wild to come home, or to be doing something.'[51] Mrs F.A.'s coolness towards Frank's return, like James's coolness towards his daughter, demonstrated that perversity of human nature that always fascinated her.

There could be few more striking instances of human perversity than Harriot Bridges's new husband, the Reverend George Moore, whom Jane had determined to dislike even before she met him. When she *did* meet him, she found little reason to change her opinion. 'I will not pretend in one meeting to *dislike* him,' she told

Cassandra; 'but I can honestly assure [you] that I saw nothing in him to admire.' His manners, she conceded, were 'gentlemanlike', but 'by no means winning'. Indeed, the man was a curious mixture, as one might expect from the son of an Archbishop of Canterbury and grandson of a butcher. After a second meeting, she declared that his manners to Harriot 'want tenderness' and might even incline towards violence. But after a third, she considered him 'not un-agreable'; he was, after all, 'a sensible man & tells a story well'. She hardly liked to admit that it was the man's very want of conjugal tenderness that now intrigued her; she had rather warmed to the way he ordered his wife to bed at ten o'clock, before adjourning to the dressing-room with his guests 'to eat tart & jelly'.[52]

As if inspired by such examples, Jane, too, affected a more perverse and arrogant style. Greatly fortified by the possession of Mrs Knight's 'fee', she came to assume an altogether more confident demeanour. No longer fascinated by the purchase of sponge cakes, she allowed herself to acknowledge an appetite for 'elegance & ease & luxury'. For the moment, even letters to Cassandra had lost their charm. 'I assure you I am as tired of writing long letters as you can be,' she confessed. What was the reason for her new style of writing 'without . . . effort'? She was rich, she joked; '& the rich are always respectable, whatever be their stile of writing.'[53] Instead of writing long dutiful letters, she would indulge, as the rich did, a love of gossip and scandal. ('One hears nothing else but scandal', as Mrs Candour said.) Had Cassandra read the shocking news in the *Courier* about Mrs Powlett? It was said that the man she had eloped with was a 'Viscount S', which Mr Moore was clever enough to guess at being Lord Sackville. 'I should not have suspected her of such a thing!' said Jane.[54]

There were also shocking stories about their distant relative, Fanny Austen; but at least the girl had finally contrived to get herself married. Jane was sorry the wretched young woman had 'behaved so ill' but 'there is some comfort to *us* in her misconduct,' she remarked: 'We have not a congratulatory letter to write.' In this new cavalier style she disported herself 'quite *a la* Godmersham'; strolling with the others through Bentigh woods, visiting the

Temple plantation, or watching the dragging of Buckwell pond. She even initiated Mrs J.A. into the 'mysteries of Inman-ism', taking her and the children to visit blind old widow Inman with a basket of fruit. By the end of her stay, Jane had become quite at ease with this style of life, and was even tempted to remark on how far superior her Yellow Room was to her 'Brompton quarters' with Eliza. It was a way of living that she could easily take to. 'It will be two years tomorrow,' she observed on 1 July, 'since we left Bath for Clifton, with what happy feelings of escape!' Luxury and escape were all that she dreamt of. 'I shall eat Ice & drink French wine, & be above vulgar economy,' she boasted. All it required was a legacy.[55]

Even when she returned to Castle Square, that sense of escape did not entirely forsake her. Mrs Austen promptly departed for a visit to Steventon, while Frank and Mary seemed to prefer the privacy of the Isle of Wight to shared accommodation in South-ampton. As a consequence, Jane and Cassandra had the house almost to themselves for the visit of Catherine and Alethea Bigg. Catherine was now engaged to marry the Reverend Herbert Hill, uncle of the poet Robert Southey. Mr Hill was certainly not a *young* man, Catherine conceded, though she did not think he was quite sixty. He had been many years chaplain to the British factory at Oporto, until the threat of a French invasion there had driven him back to England. That was no longer merely a threat, said Frank, visiting the house. On his voyage back from St Helena he had exchanged numbers with the *Raven*, a brig from off Lisbon. The French were now masters in Spain, and the Spanish royal family were taken prisoner. Without a doubt, he said, he too would soon be returning to Spain in support of Wellesley's troops, or Sir John Moore's.

When the ladies questioned him about his last voyage, Frank was diffident at first, then warmed to his topic. About St Helena, he told them: 'Every person who is above the rank of a common soldier is in some shape or other a trader.' And, though the inhab-itants were all English, or 'of English descent', their patriotism was scarcely evident in the extravagant prices they charged to homeward-bound English.[56] But what he most disliked was the slavery on the island. It was true that the St Helena slaves were not subjected to the same brutality and despotism as their fellows on the West India islands. But, he said: 'Slavery, however it may be modified is still slavery, and it is much to be regretted that any trace of it should be found to exist in countries dependent on England, or colonised by her subjects.'[57]

There was a refreshing sanity, Jane found, about all Frank's moral principles. Neither a zealot nor a hypocrite, he found no contradiction in profiting from the commercial opportunities of his naval command. But Frank would never tolerate the exploitation of human suffering that was so complacently countenanced by those who drew their fortunes from slave estates. While her brother talked, Jane hemstitched some cambric pocket handkerchiefs as a wedding gift for Catherine. The St Helena islanders, said Frank, charged so much to passing ships for even the simplest supplies, that a couple of acres of potatoes or a garden of cabbages there would provide a decent dowry for any daughter. Jane looked down into their beautiful Castle Square garden and thought of Edward Bridges. Would syringas do instead? she wondered

MAD

At daybreak on 19 August, a thick fog hung over the *St Albans* where she lay at anchor off the little town of Phenice on the coast of Portugal. There were twenty-three troop transports in Frank Austen's convoy and most of them were slow and heavy. It had taken all of twenty days to sail from the English Channel to Corunna, where the *Defiance* brought new orders from Sir Arthur Wellesley, who was then near Figuero. As the fog began to lift in the light morning breeze, the *St Albans* sailed closer to the shore, hoisted out all boats and began to disembark the troops. The landings went on through the night as, one after another, the transports put their soldiers ashore. By the following day, the French had found out their position on the hills of Vimiera, and the generals Kellerman and Berthier sent in their own troops to dislodge them. 'Observed an action between the English and

French armies on the heights over Merceira,' Frank wrote in his log for Sunday 21 August. The next day he wrote: 'Sent all the boats on shore to assist in taking off the wounded of our army to the hospital ships.'[58] As well as English wounded, the boats also collected numbers of French prisoners from the beaches. At noon on 24 August, the *St Albans* led its convoy of twenty-nine troop-ships back towards Oporto, and thence to Spithead, where, early in September, the prisoners were transferred into the prison-hulks anchored there. Frank Austen ferried across to the Isle of Wight, where Mary had found new lodgings at Yarmouth.

It was a pity, Jane thought, though entirely to be understood, that her brother and Mrs F.A. should continue to prefer the Isle of Wight to Castle Square for his brief periods back in England. Their Yarmouth quarters, from what she heard, were very 'nice'; and 'with fish almost for nothing, & plenty of engagements & plenty of each other', they must, of course, be 'very happy'.[59] Yet Jane could not entirely suppress her feelings of disappointment that such a well-loved brother should be living so close by, and be seen so seldom. The idea of all the ladies living together at Castle Square had perhaps been a little too utopian in its aspirations to meet with much success. Mrs F.A. had never greatly cared for a scheme which placed her so constantly under Mrs Austen's supervision, and Martha was frequently away on visits to Kintbury where Mrs Dundas was forever proclaiming that she 'could not do without her'. Mrs Austen herself, once the prime mover of the scheme, had ceased to find attractions in the constant crowds of Southampton city streets. She found dissatisfaction with the chalybeate springs, which, for all their vaunted remedial properties, had proved quite useless in her case; she had grown tired of noise and visitors. And as to rents, these were increasing at a quite alarming rate. The news that Mrs Lyell was expected to find 130 guineas' rent for her modest property in the town was spoken of with great dismay.

To Jane, it seemed that her mother's dissatisfactions with South-ampton had started on their return from Chawton the previous September. Ever since that visit, Mrs Austen had seemed to hanker after a return to the Hampshire countryside, and, from one or two remarks which he had subsequently let fall, it appeared that Edward might not be disinclined to assist her in that wish. Alton was now the place spoken of. Mrs Austen was very much in favour of Alton and talked as if she had quite made up her mind to move there. As to the inconvenience of purchasing new furniture, she was quite reconciled to that, and talked of 'the *trouble*' as the only evil.

In September, Henry was despatched to Alton, where he had some banking connections, to spy out some unexceptionable dwelling there, while James and Mrs J.A. and their children paid what was generally expected to be a final visit to Castle Square. Young James Edward Austen, now in his eleventh year, was the only one who seemed to experience regret at the prospect of the move. For him, it was a delight to look down from the windows of Castle Square at the magical 'fairy equipage' of the Marchioness of Lansdowne drawing up before the 'Gothic' castle opposite. He found it quite enchanting to watch her light phaeton, drawn by six, and sometimes by eight, little ponies, each pair decreasing in size, and becoming lighter in colour, through all the grades of dark brown, light brown, bay and chestnut.[60]

At the end of the month, Cassandra went to Godmersham to assist with Elizabeth's confinement. This was only just, since Jane had been the one chosen to enjoy the elegance and ease of Kentish life in June. Fanny Austen dutifully informed her governess, Miss Chapman, how much she appreciated her aunt's visit: 'it will be a great comfort to me to have her assistance in the lessons,' she wrote, 'as well as her company.'[61] In the event, Cassandra reached Godmersham too late to be present at the birth of Elizabeth's eleventh child, Brook-John. Jane wrote to congratulate her on having missed the great event. 'We are glad it was all over before your arrival,' she wrote. Naturally, she said how 'extremely glad' they were to hear of the birth, and expressed her hope that everything would proceed 'as well as it begins'.[62] But she had grown to dislike the flurry of these occasions and was not entirely reconciled to such extravagant fecundity. Cassandra's letter also brought news of the birth of an eighth child to Mrs Tilson, the wife of Henry's partner in his London banking business. 'Poor woman! How can she be honestly breeding again?' Jane demanded. She preferred to think of childbirth as a metaphor or conceit, and compared the duties of hospitality to a painful parturition. 'Our labour was not a great deal shorter than poor Elizabeth's,' she wrote of one evening visit by the Harrisons and Debarries; 'for it was past eleven before we were delivered.'

Even marriage might be rendered amusing when transformed into a kind of comic parlour game. Following Catherine Bigg's engagement to her elderly clerical beau, Jane diverted herself by devising yet more incongruous matches between others of her acquaintances. 'I have got a husband for each of the Miss Maitlands,' she proudly proclaimed. Colonel Powlett and his brother were the two men she had fixed on. The Colonel had acquired some local notoriety since his wife's elopement with Lord Sackville, and had won £3,000 damages against the adulterous pair. Now, there was a man who knew how to value a wife! 'If the brother shd luckily be a little sillier than the colonel,' she wrote, 'what a treasure for Eliza!'[63]

There was always a malicious pleasure to be gained from such satirical reflections; but, for the most part, Jane experienced a kind of tedium alone in the empty house with only her mother for company. A letter from Yarmouth which desired her 'to send Mary's flannels & furs &c' confirmed Frank's decision to stay away from Castle Square. Instead of her brother's company, she found herself besieged by an almost constant procession of visitors. 'Everybody who comes to Southampton finds it either their duty or pleasure to call on us,' she complained. Bricklayers and mason's men trudged through the house and hammered on the roof as they set about repairing a chimney, which 'they found in such a state as to make it wonderful that it shd have stood so long'.[64] It briefly amused her to imagine herself 'thumped with old bricks' in the next high wind, until she found herself troubled by genuine head-pains and an occasional deafness. Henry's Eliza (no one called her 'Countess' any more) obligingly scribbled down a favourite remedial concoction of her own, but Jane took little comfort from that. It rather dismayed her to think that such a wild, impulsive woman should have dwindled at last to this matronly role, sending patent remedies to her female relations. She preferred to humour the melancholy Mr Lyford by allowing him to prescribe her a balm of cotton moistened with oil of sweet almonds. 'It has done me good,' she conceded; 'I feel it a great blessing to hear again.'

It was something less of a blessing to be forced to listen to ladies who either projected, or had just returned from, foreign travels. What right had such tasteless and insensitive creatures as the Miss Ballards got, she demanded sourly, 'to go their late tour'? Miss Sharp and Miss Bailey were likewise intending to 'travel southward' unless, as Jane noted, 'anything more eligible offer'. Thoughts of eligible offers brought back memories of Edward Bridges, and she experienced a distinct unease to hear that Cassandra was now on quite such friendly terms with the family at Goodnestone. 'I wish you may be able to accept Lady Bridges's invitation,' she wrote in early October, 'tho' *I* could not her son Edward's.' But, in the absence of other eligible offers, lack of money must remain a besetting preoccupation. What was the use of taste and feeling without money to display them? What chance for her to make a 'tour' like the Miss Ballards when she dared not even venture a second pool at Commerce with the Maitlands? ('. . . The stake was three shillings, & I cannot afford to lose that, twice in an eveng.')[65] It deeply vexed her that a favourite gown, dyed black for mourning-wear, had been quite ruined in the process. 'There was four shillings thrown away; to be added to my subjects of never failing regret.' Even the pleasure of receiving a letter from little Edward Austen at Winchester was somewhat lessened by the obligation of paying postage for it.

Confined to her own narrow domestic world, she allowed her prejudices to shrink to match her straitened circumstances. In the evenings she would sometimes read aloud, by candlelight, *Dom Espriella's Letters* by Robert Southey, but only to denounce it. 'Horribly anti-English,' she exclaimed. 'The man . . . deserves to be the foreigner he assumes.'[66] Her most agreeable hours were spent in her very English garden, among the laburnums, fruit-bushes and syringas. 'I gather some currants every now & then,' she told Cassandra, 'when I want either fruit or employment.'

On the night of Tuesday 4 October, Jane was roused from her reading-desk by the ominous sight of smoke and flames billowing across the night sky. She and her mother watched in alarm from their windows as the flames leapt higher and seemed, at one point, to threaten much of the city. The fire had begun at Webb's, the pastrycook, it was said, but whether in their bakehouse or the back of their dwelling, no one could tell. A toy-shop was next engulfed by the flames, and Hibbs, whose house stood hard by, was so scared from his senses that he began giving away all his goods. The poor man in a frenzy threw his most valuable laces and all kinds of finery to the crowds that swarmed in the High Street.[67] As the engines were summoned and struggled to extinguish the flames, Jane was seized by a momentary panic. What would she do 'if it came to the worst'? What favourite manuscript or beloved object would she choose to save from the conflagration? By ten o'clock the alarm was over; the fire was put out, the crowds dispersed.

The next letter Jane received from Godmersham brought terrible news. Elizabeth, who had seemed in such a flourishing state after the birth of her new baby, had died quite suddenly. 'Oh! the miserable events of this day!' Fanny scrawled with a shaking hand in her diary for 10 October. 'My mother, my beloved mother torn from us! After eating a hearty dinner, she was taken *violently* ill and *expired* (may God have mercy upon us) in ½ an hour!!!!'[68] The shock of this unexpected blow filled Jane with grief for all the Godmersham family, but especially for Fanny. 'My dear, dear Fanny! I am so thankful she has you with her!' she wrote to Cassandra. 'You will be everything to her, you will give her all the consolation that human aid can give.' In her imagination she seemed to share in all the sorrows of this girl with whom she felt a special kinship. Her mind filled with vivid images of the melancholy household. 'I see your mournful party in my mind's eye under every varying circumstance of the day,' she told Cassandra, '& in the eveng especially, figure to myself its sad gloom – the efforts to talk – the frequent summons to melancholy orders & cares – & poor Edward restless in misery going from one room to another – & perhaps not seldom upstairs to see all that remains of his Elizabeth.'[69] She, too, shared that restless need to visualize those mortal remains upon the death-bed. 'I suppose you see the corpse,' she wrote to Cassandra, 'how does it appear?'

As she and Martha parcelled up the mourning clothes of bombasine and crape for Cassandra to wear, Jane could not resist trying them on, even trying on the shoes. Something about the ritual of death – of this death in particular – appealed to her instinct for an elegiac solemnity that was neither gloomy nor pompous. She had become, in her own imagination, a connoisseur of death, and it vexed her to the heart that others, less tactful in these affairs, might cause further pain to the bereaved by their crude and ill-judged sympathies. 'I have written to Edwd Cooper,' she told Cassandra, '& hope he will not send one of his letters of cruel comfort to my brother.'[70] She was dismayed that James and Mrs J.A. had taken charge of young Edward and George, removing them from Winchester to Steventon. 'The poor boys are perhaps more comfortable at Steventon than they could be here,' she wrote to Cassandra; 'but you will understand *my feelings* with respect to it.' Mrs J.A., on past record, was hardly the most congenial comforter for a bereaved child. 'I should have loved to have them with me at such a time,' she confessed.

Evidently, Edward agreed, and a week later Jane had her wish. The two boys arrived at Castle Square quite chilled through, having travelled by choice on top of the coach, huddled up in the coachman's own great-coat. Yet to Jane's eyes, they had never looked better. Little George, now thirteen, was quite a 'new acquaintance', she said, so grown up in appearance and, as to manners, quite as engaging as Edward. But what most impressed her was their spirit, which combined all the affecting sensibility of childhood with a becoming youthful manliness. '*They behave extremely well*, in every respect,' she told Cassandra, 'showing quite as much feeling as one wishes to see.' Reading over a letter from their father, George 'sobbed aloud' but Edward's tears, as befitted an elder brother, did not 'flow so easily'. Yet both boys, she judged, were 'very properly impressed' by what had happened.[71]

It became her endeavour so to vary her nephew's studies and

amusements that the consolation of tears was intermingled with the pleasure of boyish diversions. She found a kind of escape from her own dismal preoccupations by entering into their childhood world. They would play together at bilbocatch, spillikins, riddles, conundrums and cards; they would float paper ships on the Itchen, and watch the ebb and flow of the river as it flowed down to the Solent. Then they would sit together in church, where Edward was much affected to hear Dr Mant preach on the litany: 'All that are in danger, necessity or tribulation'. Then it would be back to the quayside, with George happily flying from one side to the other, or skipping on board a collier barge. Another day, it was a water-party, from the Itchen ferry up to Northam, with two boys rowing part of the way, and entertaining their aunt with their ceaseless questions and remarks. At Northam, they landed and surveyed the construction of a handsome new seventy-four-gun ship-of-the-line, and in the evening it was home to play at Speculation, which was 'so much approved that we hardly knew how to leave off'.[72] Their father was so touched by the reports he received of such generous behaviour that he renewed his offer to provide a new home for his mother and sisters. Instead of Alton, he suggested a house at Wye in Kent, not far from Godmersham, where they might visit his family often. All such plans must remain a secret until discussed fully with Martha and Frank, but Mrs Austen was soon talking openly of the advantages of Wye, which now, in her mind, quite outweighed the supposed benefits of Alton. When Mrs J.A. got word of this scheme, she expressed her 'fear' of them settling in Kent. Surely somewhere nearer to Steventon would be more convenient, she thought. Young George busied himself making and launching paper ships, which he then shot down with horse-chestnuts brought from Steventon for the purpose. That seemed to Jane a most appropriate metaphor.

If Wye would not serve, Edward suggested to Cassandra the little cottage at Chawton which had formerly served as a tavern. Against that, he believed, there could be no objection. Jane agreed. 'Everything you say about it,' she told Cassandra, 'will, I am sure ... make my mother consider the plan with more and more pleasure.' As usual, she herself did not venture an opinion. With Henry still searching out some unexceptionable house in Alton, her mother talking about Wye and Cassandra now urging the conveniencies of Chawton, Jane was resigned to leave the choice of her future home to those with the will, and the wherewithal, to determine it. Meanwhile, young Edward sat twisting in his chair, intent upon Miss Porter's *Lake of Killarney* and chewing at one of the apples sent in two great hampers from Kintbury, the rest of which now covered their little garret floor.

One inevitable consequence of Elizabeth's death was that Cassandra must stay at Godmersham far longer than originally intended. Edward, it seemed, could not bear to part with her at such a time, and Fanny, too, added her voice to the universal pleas for her to remain among them. 'Aunt Cassandra . . . has been the greatest comfort to us all in this time of affliction,' she told Miss Chapman, '& will not leave us yet I hope.'[73] Reluctantly, Jane resigned herself to her sister's absence. 'It is no more than I expected,' she wrote to her; 'and what must be, but you cannot suppose I like it.' Martha had returned to Castle Square the day after the fire, when the Alton scheme was still much in favour. There had been a hare and a pheasant sent from Gray's of Alton to celebrate her homecoming. 'Is this to entice us to Alton, or to keep us away?' Jane wondered.[74] But already it was clear that Martha would not be in Southampton long, whatever her own inclinations might be. Mrs Dundas was not the kind of woman to be denied. Martha '*wishes* to stay with us till Christmas if possible,' Jane noted, but the wishes of dependent relatives, they both knew, were of little consequence. Martha could no more refuse the invitation of Kintbury than Cassandra could deny the will of Godmersham.

By November, the Chawton scheme had quite replaced all others in their minds and was almost a settled matter. Frank, who visited Godmersham towards the end of the month, signified his approval. Henry ceased his house-hunting in Alton and visited the Chawton cottage to survey it on their behalf. There were six bedchambers, he reported ('just what we wanted to be assured of,' said Jane), and several garrets convenient for storeplaces. One

of these Mrs Austen immediately planned fitting up for the convenience of Edward's manservant, until Jane suggested they might
have greater need of it for a manservant of their own. 'His name
shall be Robert, if you please,' she pronounced, in a teasing aside
to Fanny. (The girl had recently denounced *Robert* in a discussion
with Miss Chapman of babies' names. 'Robert is too hideous to
be borne,' she said, 'except by my two aunts, Cassandra & Jane,
who are very fond of both *Robert* and *Susan*!! Did you ever hear
of such a depraved taste?')[75]

Their Southampton acquaintances, though much concerned at
their going, expressed a universal approval of their choice. Chawton, they agreed, was such a 'remarkably pretty village', and the
house itself, which everyone claimed to know, quite charming.
However, as Jane wryly noted, 'nobody fixes on the right [one]'.[76]
Her own expectations of Chawton were more modest. The chief
attractions of the place were financial. With Edward as their landlord they would be free at least of the fear of spiralling rents and
the consequent need for frequent removals. The sense of security
which that knowledge brought her went some way to alleviate her
bitter sense of disappointment when she heard word, later that
month, that the Stoneleigh business was at last concluded.

For some days there had been rumours of a settlement. Henry
had picked up word that Mr Leigh-Perrot had renounced all claim
to the property for the sum of £24,000, together with an annuity
of £2,000. James was still anxious for any word of the promised
help with arrears on the Mathew estate. A letter from aunt Leigh-
Perrot seemed to promise an entire explanation, but instead was
full of the usual petty complaints. Mrs Austen was quite shocked
that the wife of a brother who had just acquired a fortune of
over £20,000, could fill her letter with nothing but ill-humoured
grumbles about housemaids catching cold on the coach journey
to Bath. But Jane herself was neither shocked nor surprised by
this demonstration of selfishness. '*I* see nothing in it out of nature,'
she told Cassandra, 'tho' a sad nature.'[77] She was used to the
way that her aunt would 'look about with great diligence . . . for
inconvenience & evil'. What did dismay her was the total silence
concerning any benefits to the Austens themselves. James had

heard something 'in a *general way*' about his arrears, but nothing for certain. Henry had had some 'confidential conversation' with Mr Thomas Leigh at Stoneleigh, but the settlement that now appeared bore little relation to his expectations.

Jane herself 'did not like to own our previous information of what was intended last July' when Mrs Knight had been so encouraging in her hints. To her mind, the whole affair was a 'vile compromise', which reflected little honour on any of the parties involved and promised even less by way of advantage to themselves. Her attitude was hardly softened by a letter from Mrs J.A. which informed her that aunt and uncle Leigh-Perrot had graciously agreed to allow James the sum of £100 a year. This 'donation', they said, was intended 'as a compensation for his loss in the conscientious refusal' of the living at Hampstead Marshall. All this was accompanied by the most high-flown language of affection, fulsome hopes 'of their being much more together in future' and a great deal more to the same effect. 'My expectations for my mother do not rise with this event,' she noted grimly, then added: 'We will allow a little more time however, before we fly out.'[78]

The letter from aunt Leigh-Perrot put an end to Jane's fond hopes of a legacy. Not that she had ever allowed herself to invest too many or too solid hopes in that direction, despite the several encouragements she received from many quarters. Yet she had for once been guilty of neglecting to forearm herself against disappointment by expecting, or even *wishing for*, it; and the disappointment, when it came, was all the greater. There was to be no providential benefaction that might afford her a long-wished-for independence, and she must resign herself to continue, as before, with her life of 'vulgar economies'. Cassandra's next letter from Godmersham contained a further shock. Edward Bridges was to marry Harriet Foote. Though Jane had never seriously entertained the thought of marrying him herself, the recognition that this possibility too was now beyond her reach brought many sobering reflections. 'Your news of Edw: Bridges was *quite* news,' she replied, barely disguising her surprise. Of course, she said all the conventional things ('I wish him happy with all my heart, & hope his choice may turn out according to his own expectations'), but could not resist one sly note ('& beyond those of his family'). 'I dare say it will,' she added, assuming her most worldly tone: 'Marriage is a great improver.'[79] She recalled just how much she had once felt Mr Bridges needed to improve. One Foote sister (Eleanor) was already married to the eldest Bridges brother, and there was no reason (except money, of course) why Harriet should not be as happy as Eleanor. 'As to money, that will come, you may be sure,' she noted cynically, 'because they cannot do without it.' She, alas, was only too well accustomed to doing without it.

Doubtless, the proposed removal to Edward's Chawton cottage had much to recommend it in terms of necessary thrift. But for Jane it was a kind of retreat. At Chawton, there could be none of the excitement of theatre visits, water-parties, grand assemblies and sea-side promenades. There would be none of the chance acquaintance-ships or adventitious diversions which a bustling city afforded and which, though it was often her custom to mock at them, provided a constant distraction from less agreeable musings. Summoning up a kind of desperate energy, she determined to throw herself for a final time into the giddy social world. 'Yes, I mean to go to as many balls as possible,' she told Cassandra. 'A larger circle of acquaintance & an increase of amusements is quite in character with our approaching removal.' She was insistent that Frank must take herself and Martha to the playhouse. 'Martha ought to see the inside of the theatre once while she lives in Southampton,' she declared.

But the balls, when she attended them, produced mingled feel-ings of reminiscence and resignation. Here were the same gaggles of young women 'standing by without partners, & each of them with two ugly naked shoulders!' One particular ball, at the Dolphin Inn, brought many memories flooding back: 'It was the same room in which we danced 15 years ago!' she told Cassandra, recalling the time when the two of them had stood by among the other single ladies, with their shoulders bare and their hopes high. And, in spite of 'the shame of being so much older', she was able to claim, without undue exaggeration, that she was 'quite as happy now as then'. She even found herself a partner, a French-speaking stranger with fine dark eyes like Mr Edward Taylor's. 'I do not know his name,' she said, mightily pleased with this coquettish conquest; '& he seems so little at home in the English language that I believe his black eyes may be the best of him.'[80]

Her birthday that year was an occasion for painful self-appraisal. At the age of thirty-three she was entering that period of her life when the opportunities for fresh interests or new friendships must be expected to diminish. It must be her endeavour, with Cassandra, to consolidate those friendships they had, whose number, in the course of years, must be inevitably depleted by death, rather than look to new ones. The news of Mr Bridges's marriage was a sharp reminder of choices she had *not* made, at a time when she had still enjoyed the freedom to choose. Now she must bear the consequences of those earlier decisions. Marriage might be 'a great improver', but it was many years indeed since she had ever seriously desired that particular form of improvement for herself.

For the past four years, her birthday celebrations – such as they were – had been overshadowed by guilty memories of Madam Lefroy, the anniversary of whose death fell upon the same day. This year, Jane made a strenuous endeavour to exorcise that guilt by writing some elegiac verses 'To the Memory of Mrs Lefroy, who died Decr 16 – my Birthday'.[81] For her, the writing of such verses was most unusual. She had composed nothing of the kind for Jane Williams, nor for James's first wife, Anne, nor for Edward's wife, Elizabeth, nor even for her own father. But the ominous coincidence of this day stirred feelings which she found difficult to control.

> *The day returns again, my natal day;*
> *What mix'd emotions with the Thought arise!*
> *Beloved friend, four years have pass'd away*
> *Since thou wert snatch'd forever from our eyes –*
>
> *The day, commemorative of my birth*
> *Bestowing Life and Light and Hope on me,*
> *Bring back the hour which was thy last on earth.*
> *Oh! bitter pang of torturing Memory! –*

It was not customary for her to regard the death of a devout Christian in such terms of bitter torture. Usually, her confidence in heavenly salvation was sufficient to outweigh all but the most modest display of earthly grief. 'The Goodness which made him valuable on Earth, will make him Blessed in Heaven,' she had written to Phylly Walter on the death of her father. Even her own father's death had inspired more feelings of hope than of sorrow. 'Heavy as is the blow,' she wrote to Frank, they could feel 'a thousand comforts' in 'the consciousness of his worth & constant preparation for another World'. Why did the death of Madam Lefroy cause her such a 'bitter pang of torturing Memory'? Why could she not take 'a thousand comforts' from remembering the manifold Christian virtues of her dead friend?

> *Angelic Woman! past my power to praise*
> *In Language meet, thy Talents, Temper, mind.*
> *Thy solid worth, thy captivating grace! –*
> *Thou friend and ornament of humankind! –*

As she struggled to find a 'Language meet' to celebrate Madam Lefroy's saintly dedication (teaching the village children to read and write, vaccinating them against the smallpox), she still felt something hollow in her praise. How bitterly she regretted the cruel comments she had made about Madam Lefroy's habit of interfering. The woman now seemed to haunt her as a reproachful vision of perfection.

> *I see her here, with all her smiles benign,*
> *Her looks of eager love, her accents sweet.*
> *That voice and countenance almost divine! –*
> *Expression, harmony, alike complete . . .*
>
> *She speaks; 'tis eloquence – that grace of tongue*
> *So rare, so lovely! – never misapplied*
> *By her to palliate vice, or deck a wrong,*
> *She speaks and reasons but on virtue's side.*

And yet, even as she forced herself into this vein of rhapsodic praise, she could not entirely disguise from herself a guilty consciousness of resentment. Even as she wrote that her friend's eloquence was 'never misapplied', she felt the painful memory of the time when Madam Lefroy had used her 'grace of tongue' to persuade Tom Lefroy to abandon Jane herself. Of course, she had been speaking and reasoning 'on virtue's side'. But in her private moments, Jane was sometimes tempted to think that 'the cardinal virtues in themselves have been so often possessed that they are no longer worth having'. In her next letter to Cassandra, Jane wrote: 'I consider everybody as having a right to marry *once* in their lives for love, if they can.'[82] It was Madam Lefroy who had deprived her of that right, leaving her a life which might strain after virtue, but would never find the solace of wedded love. Jane concluded her poem with a dream of atonement between herself and the vision that haunted her every birthday.

> *Fain would I feel an union in thy fate,*
> *Fain would I seek to draw an omen fair*
> *From this connection in our earthly date.*
> *Indulge the harmless weakness – Reason, spare –*

The 'harmless weakness' for which she now begged indulgence was her superstitious instinct to find a 'union' or 'omen' in the coincidence of their natal and fatal days. She still sought to disguise, even from herself, the bitter memory of the time when Madam Lefroy had not spared her reason to confound another 'harmless weakness'; when Jane had sought a different kind of 'union', and dreamt, not of an omen, but of a man. Now all thoughts of marriage must be indulged with a due degree of self-mockery. Mrs Knight, she heard, was busily concocting a match between her and Mr Papillon, the rector at Chawton. 'I am very much obliged to Mrs Knight for such proof of the interest she takes in me,' Jane wrote back wryly. 'She may depend upon it, that I *will* marry Mr Papillon, whatever may be his reluctance or my own. I owe her much more than such a trifling sacrifice.'[83]

Once the decision for Chawton was quite settled, Jane found a certain satisfaction in applying her mind to the management of details. They must certainly be safely installed there by October at the latest, she thought, in time for Henry to visit them for some shooting. And if their removal could be accomplished by September, they might also enjoy Edward's company on his return from taking the boys back to Winchester. Her mother seemed determined to dignify the removal by the purchase of new oddments of silverware – '*a whole tablespoon*,' Jane mocked, as well as 'a whole dessert-spoon & six whole teaspoons'. Such treasure, she noted ironically, 'makes our sideboard border on the magnificent'.[84] But she, too, had her own extravagances to propose. 'Yes, yes, we *will* have a pianoforte,' she insisted; 'as good a one as can be got for 30 guineas.' Such an instrument might be used to amuse their nephews and nieces with country dances 'when we have the pleasure of their company'. Already, she heard, Mrs Digweed was looking forward 'with great satisfaction to our being her neighbours'. Jane herself took less satisfaction in the prospect of returning to the society of Digweeds, Hintons and Harwoods. 'I wd have her enjoy the idea to the utmost,' she wrote, 'as I suspect there will not be much in the reality.'

A little before Christmas, James and Mrs J.A. paid a final visit to Castle Square. They, at least, were utterly reconciled to the settlement of the Stoneleigh inheritance. James now found himself worth some £1,100 a year, after the payment of a curate. This was more than enough to provide for the keeping of a carriage and *three* horses, two of which, Mrs J.A. insisted, must be 'fit to carry women'. They were also proud to announce that their children were invited to a Child's Ball at Manydown in the New Year, and Mrs J.A. did not even appear to resent Mrs Hulbert's presenting Anna with a pair of white shoes for the occasion. Jane was delighted that Anna was about to embark upon the bare-shouldered pleasures of young womanhood, though she remarked privately to Cassandra that 'at *her* age' (fifteen), such a modest Child's Ball 'would not have done for *me*'.

After their departure on Christmas Day, the house at Castle Square seemed strangely quiet. Mrs F.A. sent a message for more clothes, which disappointed Jane by its clear implication that she and Frank did not envisage 'a very early return to us'. Snow lay on the ground for more than a week, which was most unusual for Southampton, and the occasional visitors to Castle Square seemed scarcely less frosty. One dull evening was spent 'yawning and shivering' in a silent, lugubrious company, their chairs drawn up in a wide circle around the fire. Only the widgeon and preserved ginger ('delicious') rescued the evening from being utterly wretched. Among such obstinately taciturn companions, who *would* not speak, Jane rather preferred the society of poor deaf Mr Fitzhugh, who *could* not speak. Mr Fitzhugh was so totally deaf that everyone said he could not hear a cannon, even if it were to fire directly behind him. 'Having no cannon at hand to make the experiment,' Jane remarked, 'I took it for granted.' Instead, she did her best to converse with him in remembered gestures of the queer little deaf and dumb sign language she had used as a child with her poor idiot brother George. '[I] talked to him a little with my fingers, which was funny enough,' she said.[85] It was odd to think of poor George, who must now be a man of over forty years old, but whom she had not seen or heard of for many years. But where nothing could be amended it was useless to repine, and she quickly dismissed all conscious thoughts of her idiot brother from her mind, as they had all been taught to do as children. It was more salutary to think of Charles, who, they heard, had lately captured a French schooner, but was parted from his prize in bad weather. His young wife, Fanny, was already expecting their first child.

In the absence of other diversions, she was reduced to talking politics and military strategy. It seemed that the *St Albans* must soon be despatched to Spain to bring home what remained of Sir John Moore's poor battered army from Corunna. Melancholy musings on this theme served to fill a paragraph or two of a letter to Cassandra ('we are doing nothing ourselves to write about'), but it still seemed a poor expedient. 'Unlucky, that I should have wasted so much reflection on the subject!' she wrote in apology. On the whole, she was happier disputing the relative merits of the rival card games Brag and Speculation than considering the relative strengths of opposing armies in Spain. Even now, when she had banished all thoughts of a legacy from her mind, she was still plagued by kindly well-wishers, like old Mrs Birch of Barton Lodge, who insisted that she would not be satisfied 'unless a very *handsome* present is made to us immediately from one quarter'. But from that 'quarter' itself came a very different message. Aunt Leigh-Perrot, now returned to Paragon, sent a letter which 'was much like those which had preceded it', with all its usual grumbles about dirt and damp and ungrateful servants.

It pleased Mrs Austen to be precise about details, despite all the evidence of her experience that such precision, when applied to future arrangements, must often prove illusory. Hence it was that before the middle of January, she had already determined upon an exact itinerary for their movements later in the year. They would leave Southampton on Easter Monday, 3 April, she decided, and sleep that night at Alton. From there, they would visit the Cookes at Bookham, where they would remain till the following Monday. On Tuesday 11 April, they would travel towards Godmersham by the Croydon road, staying overnight at Dartford. Once at Godmersham, they would remain for much of the summer while the necessary refurbishments were undertaken at Chawton.[86] At last, on 4 September, they would take up residence at their new home.

There was something so cheerfully utopian about such a decided scheme that Jane could not bring herself to utter a word of scepticism; yet it came as no surprise to her when, only a week later, Edward and Henry 'started a difficulty' about their proposed journey. The first of many, she suspected. She was still distressed by the quantity of snow in the streets ('everything seems to turn to snow this winter'), and her principal diversion lay in observing a curious sequence of *contretemps* between Martha and the clergyman Mr Mant. The wretched man had taken to running after Martha in the street to apologize for some earlier slight, but his extraordinary style of penitence merely aggravated the supposed offence. 'Poor Mrs Mant can stand it no longer,' Jane told Cassandra. 'She is retired to one of her married daughters.'[87]

More sermons arrived from Hamstall, where the Reverend

Cooper seemed intent upon becoming the first proselyte to his own evangelizing zeal. 'We are to like [these] better than the . . . others,' she remarked glumly; 'they are professedly *practical.*' She did not greatly care for the new fashion in ostentatious piety. 'I do not like the Evangelicals,' she declared in response to Cassandra's recommendation of Hannah More's *Coelebs in Search of a Wife.* 'Of course I shall be delighted when I read it, like other people,' she added. 'But till I do, I dislike it.' She was, though, possessed of enough sense of religious decorum to find something rather shocking in the reports she heard of the death in Spain of Sir John Moore, who had perished, as it seemed, more preoccupied by public opinion than by God. 'I wish Sir John had united something of the Christian with the hero in his death,' she remarked. It was a relief to her that Frank had still been spared from rejoining the dismal Spanish conflict, whose outcome seemed so perilous. 'Thank Heaven! we have had no one to care for particularly among the troops,' she wrote.[88]

Her own most dismal preoccupations were entirely domestic, and concerned a flooded store-closet quite ruined by the melting snows, and a nursery-room utterly drenched by torrential rains overflowing a blocked gutter. 'We hear of similar disasters from almost everybody,' she wrote, with only the merest hint of irony. 'Disasters', she knew, were inevitably relative. If aunt Leigh-Perrot, with all her riches, could find disaster in a dirty house, she herself need feel no very great compunction in finding more to lament in the sodden consequences of a blocked gutter than in the deaths of unknown soldiers at Corunna.

In the event, it was Mrs Austen's own ill health which prevented the fulfilment of her ambitious travel plans. '*One* of her old complaints,' Jane noted, acknowledging the wide repertoire of her mother's indispositions.[89] By mid-April, they had reached as far as Alton, where a renewed bout of illness enforced another lengthy delay. As a precautionary measure, Mrs Austen was moved from the inn to a nearby cottage, where Mrs F.A. had newly chosen to settle following Frank's recent despatch to China. At Godmersham, they heard that it was 'very uncertain' whether Mrs Austen would be 'well enough to continue her journey'. All thoughts of

Kent, it seemed, must be postponed, for this year at least. Yet, by the middle of the following month, Mrs Austen had rallied sufficiently to anticipate more pleasure in the prospect of a visit to Edward's family than in a continuation of her sojourn with Mrs F.A., who was imminently expecting a new baby. The Austen ladies eventually arrived at Godmersham on 15 May and remained there till the end of June.

As a final act before leaving Southampton, Jane wrote an angry letter to Richard Crosby & Co. in London. Crosby's had had possession of her manuscript of 'Susan' for six whole years, and in all that time had shown not the slightest indication of publishing it. No doubt it seemed a little foolish on her part to have left it with them for so long without enquiring after its fate. The industrious Irish lady author Miss Owenson, who claimed to have written her novel *Ida of Athens* in just three months, would never have been guilty of such dilatoriness. But Jane had never felt an urgency to receive that curt rejection which, she feared, must be the inevitable consequence of any direct solicitation.

Biographers and critics have been greatly puzzled by the strange silence which fell upon Jane Austen during her Bath and Southampton years. During her last three years at Steventon rectory she produced three full-length novels, 'First Impressions', 'Elinor and Marianne' and 'Susan'. Yet it was as if, on leaving Steventon, her imagination had run dry. No new novels were undertaken, and no serious revisions planned to those already in existence. 'First Impressions' was seldom brought out to be read aloud for the amusement of family parties. No publisher's interest was sought for 'Elinor and Marianne', even under its grand new title of *Sense and Sensibility*. To many of Jane Austen's biographers, this apparent evidence of a desiccation of her imaginative powers during the Bath and Southampton years merely confirms their sense of the feelings of unhappiness and displacement which she must have experienced in these busy cities. The true sources of her inspiration, it might appear, lay deep in the rural countryside of her native Hampshire. And it comes as little surprise to these biographers that Jane Austen's genius seemed to flourish again, as if by magic, as soon as she was established in the homely village retreat of Chawton.

While this interpretation has much to recommend it, it seems to presuppose our own conviction that novel-writing was Jane Austen's peculiar province, and the activity to which she ought most usefully to devote her life. She herself acknowledged no such settled sense of public literary ambitions or literary destiny. Her juvenile writings make great play of claims to literary fame, but, like the spoofs and parodies which they introduce, these hyperbolic claims form part of an elaborate rhetoric of self-mockery. Yet, when Thomas Cadell declined to take an interest in reading 'First Impressions' with a view to publication, she had made no attempt to have it considered by other publishers. For her, the first design of all her writings at Steventon was as a form of private amusement, shared between Cassandra and herself, or as a literary diversion for the entertainment of the wider circle of family and friends. At Steventon, all their entertainments had been of this home-made kind; Bath and Southampton, by contrast, afforded such abundance of public diversions and amusements, and presented such plentiful opportunities for new and varied acquaintances, that there was neither the time nor the inclination for private literary diversions. Nor is there any evidence that Jane Austen considered the curtailment of her former literary pastimes, in favour of visits to the Pump Room, the Assembly Rooms, Sydney Gardens or the theatre, as any form of sacrifice. Her biographers have chosen to imagine that unhappiness at her unsettled, hectic city life cast a pall over her imagination in the years between 1800 and 1809. Yet happiness may be just as destructive of literary dedication as unhappiness. And it is equally possible to suggest that it was an abundance of amusements, rather than the absence of inspiration, that prevented her from writing. Her silence might then be interpreted not as evidence of mental dejection, but as a natural consequence of alternative distractions. 'I assure you, I am as tired of writing long letters as you can be,' she wrote to Cassandra from Godmersham in the summer of 1808, at a time when her mind was filled with dreams of eating ice, drinking French wine, and indulging all the other delights of a life of 'Elegance & Ease &

Luxury'. If her life seemed frequently too full of other distractions for writing long letters to Cassandra, there should be less surprise that there was little time for writing novels.

At Chawton, things would be very different. There, once again, they would be compelled to furnish their own amusements. There could be nothing more suitable for filling the long afternoons and evenings, when they were neither visiting nor visited, or when the weather was not suitable for walking, or when her mood did not incline to playing her pianoforte, than reading and writing. In recent months, Jane's pleasure in her own compositions had been rekindled by the lively interest that young Fanny seemed to show in them. 'I am gratified by her having pleasure in what I write,' she told Cassandra, then added: 'but I wish the knowledge of my being exposed to her discerning criticism may not hurt my stile, by inducing too great a solicitude. I begin already to weigh my words & sentences more than I did, & am looking about for a sentiment, an illustration or a metaphor in every corner of the room.'[90] One corner of the room seemed to provide a particularly apt comparison for her leaky imagination. 'Could my ideas flow as fast as the rain in the store-closet, it would be charming,' she wrote. Yet Fanny's admiration, however gratifying, was not sufficient on its own to induce her to write to Richard Crosby. That decision proceeded from more rational considerations.

It was now beyond a doubt, whatever kindly hopes old Mrs Birch or Mrs Knight might yet entertain of the matter, that there was to be no legacy, no 'handsome present' to rescue her from vulgar economies. At thirty-three she was also well beyond any expectation of 'eligible offers' of another kind. Yet, without vanity, she knew she might fairly boast a certain skill in the way of novel-writing. And whilst her family might well be guilty of some partiality in their generous opinions of her work, it had long been universally acknowledged amongst them that her writings far exceeded the productions of several other literary ladies. If Mrs Grant's *American Lady* ('still the same faults'), Mrs Sykes's *Marigana* ('a very fine villain') and Miss Owenson's *Ida of Athens* ('it might be worth reading in this weather'), could all find publishers for their works, it was surely not beyond the bounds of reason to suppose that she might do likewise. It was with a lively sense of indignation that she eventually addressed herself to Messrs Crosby & Co. on 5 April, just a week before leaving Southampton for good.

Gentlemen,
In the Spring of the year 1803 a MS novel in 2 vol. entitled *Susan* was sold to you by a gentleman of the name of Seymour, & the purchase money £10 recd at the same time. Six years have since passed, & this work of which I avow myself the authoress, has never to the best of my knowledge, appeared in print, tho' an early publication was stipulated for at the time of sale. I can only account for such an extraordinary circumstance by supposing the MS by some carelessness to have been lost; & if that was the case, am willing to supply you with another copy, if you are disposed to avail yourself of it, & will engage for no further delay when it comes into your hands . . .[91]

The notion of a 'lost' manuscript was a particularly lucky hit, she thought, calculated to pre-empt what Henry had always assumed would be Crosby's most likely excuse. The threat of supplying a second copy was perhaps a little bold, but after waiting patiently for six years she felt entitled to some revenge, if only of the slightest rhetorical kind. But her real threat was in the final sentence. 'Should no notice be taken of this address,' she wrote, 'I shall feel myself at liberty to secure the publication of my work, by applying elsewhere.' For the purpose of this letter she devised herself a new pen-name, 'Mrs Ashton Dennis'. The sole purpose of this pseudonym was to enable her to sign off with the initials – MAD. Mad was how she felt, and that was how she signed herself, in bold letters at the foot of the page. She received her reply by return of post. According to Crosby, she had got it all wrong. There was 'not any time stipulated for . . . publication' of her manuscript, 'neither are we bound to publish it'. Furthermore, Crosby went on: 'Should you or anyone else [*sic*] we shall take proceedings to stop the sale.' She could have the manuscript back, he told her, 'for the same as we paid for it'.[92] To make matters worse, an anonymous two-volume novel called *Susan* was published that June, though Jane was relieved to find it had not stolen her plot.

At Godmersham, she got the advice of Edward and Henry. Henry's bank, it seemed, was doing exceedingly well – at least, according to Henry. With all those increasing profits, she told him, he must not 'work poor High-diddle so hard as he used to'. Eliza was at Godmersham too, her first visit in almost eight years. Although rarely in good health, the years did not seem to diminish her, and she was as ebullient as always, full of their latest plans for leaving Brompton for an exquisite house in Sloane Street, which was really the most handsome street leading from the charming village of Chelsea to the western, and most fashionable, side of town. It put her quite in mind of Longchamps and the *Bois*, where everyone – in happier times – used to parade in the avenue to show their fine clothes and fine equipages. She was amused to hear of Cassandra's mishap the previous week, when a gust of wind caught her white pelisse as she descended from a carriage, '& dashed it against the wheels in such a manner that she was covered with black mud'.[93] *That* reminded Eliza of the courtiers at Versailles in the time of the old king, when powder was so universally worn that the heads in general looked as if they had been dipped in meal-tubs. By the time she left, all the children were chattering in her queer little language of half-French. 'Uncle & Aunt Henry Austen went away early *ce matin. Quel horreur!!*' Fanny wrote in her diary.[94] Before they went, Henry undertook to look into the Crosby business. He and Eliza were both in agreement that it was high time for all Jane's novels to be published. Once they were back in London, and she was at Chawton, they would do what was necessary, they said.

PART IV

Chawton

―

Our Chawton home – how much we find
Already in it to our mind,
And how convinced that when complete,
It will all other Houses beat...

Jane Austen, to her brother Frank, July 1809

CHAPTER 10

One's Own Concerns

*I do think of you all I assure you, & want to know
all about everybody ... 'mais le moyen' not to
be occupied by one's own concerns?*

Jane Austen, Letter to Cassandra, April 1811

Deaths by violence

Edward brought them to Chawton in the first week of July. The
house was much as Jane remembered it from her visit two summers
before, when Seward, Edward's bailiff, had still been living there.
It was not as pretty as Rose Cottage at Alton, where Mrs F.A.
lived, but Jane liked it all the same. It was practical; it was sturdy.
She admired its honest red-brick construction and its tight tiled
roof which showed no tell-tale signs of leakages like the roof at
Castle Square. There was, too, an agreeable absence of symmetry
about its curious L-shaped structure and its six bedrooms all of
different sizes, which she particularly loved.

All through the spring, Edward's men had worked at repairs
and renovations, improving the offices with new pipe-work, painting and restoring the outbuildings. Here, at the front, they had
bricked up one window nearest to the road so that the noise of
the London coaches should not prove too troublesome. In its stead

they had made another window in the wall that looked towards
the garden. They were still at work when Jane, Cassandra and
their mother arrived, chopping firewood for the winter, and
retrenching the large kitchen garden. Looking down the columns
of Edward's estate book, Jane noted £45 for alterations and a
further £35 for pipe-work, all to make the cottage more convenient
for their use.[1] They all expressed their gratitude for the little donkey-carriage which Edward had also put at their disposal, and for
his agreement to pay the costs of corn and hay. She sent a poem
to Frank to express their general satisfaction with the place.

> *Our Chawton home – how much we find*
> *Already in it to our mind,*
> *And how convinced that when complete,*
> *It will all other Houses beat,*
> *That ever have been made or mended,*
> *With rooms concise or rooms distended.*[2]

In terms of location, the house was perhaps a little closer to the
road than might have been thought entirely desirable. It stood at
the corner of the village, where the road forked in two directions
beside the village pond. By the right-hand fork, coaches from
London passed by on their way to Winchester and Southampton;
the left-hand fork led on past the manor house and St Nicholas's
church, towards Fareham and Gosport. The front door opened
on to the road, with a narrow enclosure on either side to protect
it from runaway vehicles. Was it true, Jane wanted to know, that
the cottage had used to be a coaching inn? Not for more than
fifteen years, she was told. At that time, it was called the New Inn
and kept by William Bruce. Before that, it was known as 'Petty
Johns' and owned by John Marchant, who sold it to Mr Knight.
It was Mr Knight who put in William Bruce as inn-keeper. Then
the house was well-known as one of the best inns in the neighbourhood, with its fine new brewing copper and two vast brew-casks
which each could hold ten hogsheads of good old beer.[3] And was
it also true, as she had heard, that a man was murdered there?
Edward knew nothing about any murder and did not wish his

mother to be discomposed by any such nonsensical tales. Lurid rumours of that kind, he believed, belonged more to the realm of Mrs Radcliffe's novels, than to honest rural life. ('Could such atrocities ... be perpetrated without being known, in a country like this, where social and literary intercourse is on such a footing; where every man is surrounded by a neighbourhood of voluntary spies, and where roads and newspapers lay every thing open?')[4] Yes, Jane found; it appeared that they could. There were people in the village who remembered very well the events of that Michaelmas Night more than thirty years ago, when all the local farmers' labourers had gathered at the New Inn. Old Michaelmas Day was when the men were paid off from one employment and waited to be hired for a new one. They had money in their pockets, and drank rather too much of Mr Bruce's good old beer, she was told, and before long there was a quarrel. But the poor man was not killed in the house itself. They went out in the street to fight. The jury at the assizes brought it in as manslaughter, though it had been grisly enough for murder.

But that was not the only killing at the cottage. There was another man killed there some years later when Henry Miller fought John Gellett. Henry Miller struck Gellett such a violent blow on the head with his heavy stick tipped with iron, that the poor man never recovered. But the jury said it was John Gellett who gave the first blow and they brought in that killing as a manslaughter too.[5] After that, the inn was closed down, and Mr Knight gave the cottage to his bailiff to live in. It was a strange feeling to live in a cottage where two men had been violently killed; to Jane it brought back memories of the tales she wrote at Steventon, full of sudden murders and rural suicides.

The village seemed less dangerous now, though Maria Beckford, who was one of Edward's tenants at the great house, was cousin to the notorious William Beckford of Fonthill Abbey. During their first few days at Chawton, Jane was quickly introduced to all the leading local families. The Prowtings lived in a large house set back from the High Street. He was a magistrate and deputy lieutenant for the county and his two unmarried daughters, Catherine-Ann and Ann-Mary, seemed lively, agreeable girls. Mr Middleton was Edward's new tenant at the manor house, where he lived with his six young children and his sister-in-law, Miss Beckford. Mr Papillon, the rector, lived alone with his spinster sister Elizabeth, and Cassandra would often remind Jane of her whimsical promise to make the 'trifling sacrifice' of becoming Mr Papillon's bride. After all, the rectory, which Mr P. had recently rebuilt, was a very handsome dwelling. But could any Austen sister seriously contemplate marrying the man who had once so churlishly refused to sell Henry the right to the Chawton living?

The Hintons lived at Chawton Lodge and they, like the inevitable Digweeds of Alton, threatened to become regular visitors. 'There were a few families living in the village,' Caroline recalled; 'but no great intimacy was kept up with any of them – they were upon *friendly* but rather *distant* terms, with all.'⁶ Miss Middleton found Jane 'stiff and cold' and Cassandra '*very prim*'. Most inevitable of all their neighbours was poor Miss Benn, the impoverished sister of Mr Benn, the rector of Farringdon. With a dozen children of his own, there was little Mr Benn could do to help his sister, and the poor woman was reduced to renting a little ramshackle cottage from Old Philmore, one of the local villagers. In her ragged long fur tippet, the garrulous Miss Benn was soon established as one of the fixtures of their new world.

On the whole, Jane found surprisingly little to vex her in her new surroundings. The proximity of the main road was, at first, a little disturbing. Away in Canterbury that October, Mrs Knight was amused to receive a report 'of the Chawton party looking very comfortable at breakfast' from 'a gentleman who was travelling by their door in a post-chaise about ten days ago'.⁷ Yet even the frequent clatter of Collyer's Flying Post galloping past their windows might be construed as an advantage. Unlike Steventon, isolated and enclosed among its narrow lanes and hedgerows, Chawton was a country village with ready access to a wider world. When little Caroline came to stay there, she found it 'most delightful . . . to have the awful stillness of night so frequently broken by the noise of passing carriages, which seemed sometimes, even to shake the bed'.⁸ 'You'll find us very snug, next year;/Perhaps with Charles & Fanny near –' Jane wrote in her verses to Frank that summer. 'Snug' was the very word, she thought. '*Some* bedrooms very small,' Caroline noted; '*none* very large.'

The occasion of Jane's verses to her brother was the birth of his son, also called Frank, at Rose Cottage only days after their arrival at Chawton. 'May he a growing blessing prove,/And well deserve his parents' love!' she wrote. From what she heard, little baby Frank showed every sign of inheriting his father's spirit along with his name. But fond parents, she well knew, were much given to such flattering fantasies. Her mother had just received a letter from Charles, away in Bermuda, boasting about his own new-born daughter, 'the finest that ever was seen . . . and as fat as butter'.[9] In the case of young Francis William of Alton, however, Jane felt inclined to humour parental feelings. It pleased her to recall her brother's waywardness as an infant, and imagine how his new baby son might copy them.

> *Thy infant days may he inherit,*
> *Thy warmth, nay insolence of spirit; –*
> *We would not with one fault dispense*
> *To weaken the resemblance.*

That was how she always thought of Frank as a boy – daring, bold, defiant.

> *Fearless of danger, braving pain,*
> *And threaten'd very oft in vain,*
> *Still may one terror daunt his soul,*
> *One needful engine of controul*
> *Be found in this sublime array, –*
> *A neighbouring donkey's aweful bray!*

Away in the China seas that summer, Frank Austen had more than the braying of a neighbouring donkey to contend with. Sailing by way of Prince of Wales Island off the Malay Peninsula, he made landfall at Port Cornwallis, with its population of Malays, Chinese, Cochin-Chinese, Siamese, Birmans, Bengalees, Malabars and Chulians. Here was a mighty braying indeed! 'The languages are as various as the nations,' he noted; 'more than thirty, totally distinct from each other, are spoken in the Bazar.'[10] From Penang, the *St Albans* was sent on to China with its convoy of East Indiamen, and anchored in the Canton river. The river was infested with pirates – *ladrones* – who robbed and murdered, devastated the local countryside and even threatened the town of Canton itself. For some years, the Chinese government had engaged an English vessel, the *Mercury*, to act against the pirates, and as soon as the *St Albans* arrived, Frank was asked if he would consider offering his help too. This request was neither unforeseen nor unwelcome; but Frank insisted on receiving it in writing from the Viceroy of Canton. There was also the matter of removing all restrictions on British vessels passing through these waters. Frank signified his willingness to wait on the Viceroy to discuss these and other matters, and an appointment was made for him to meet the Viceroy at the Hoppo's house on 2 November at two o'clock. Frank presented himself at the appointed time, but after waiting nearly half an hour in a close, dirty kind of lobby, 'exposed to the stare of every blackguard who could squeeze himself into the passage' and 'having our noses assailed by a combination of villainous smells', he was informed that the Viceroy had gone away. Frank stormed out of the house in fury at such unaccountable behaviour. 'I am inclined to set it down to the score of imbecility,' he wrote in his log; 'and a struggle between pride and the conviction of his own inability to arrest the progress of the pirates, in which the former has obtained the victory.' From England he had recently received news of his son's birth, and with it a copy of Jane's verses which praised him for being 'considerate & kind;/ All gentleness to those around'. Gentleness and kindness were all very well, Frank thought, but just for once he was tempted to make an exception in the case of the Viceroy of Canton.[11]

The only viceroys that Jane was apt to meet at Chawton were confined to the pages of books, but she did not greatly repine at the absence of titled acquaintances. Her most frequent visitors were the little family from Steventon; it soon became a regular thing for her nieces Caroline and Anna, and often their brother

James Edward too, to travel the short distance from the rectory to spend days, and sometimes weeks, with their aunts Jane and Cassandra. With them she happily fell into a habit of story-telling, mingling romantic tales of unfortunate queens and peremptory viceroys with extravagant fables of a more fanciful kind. 'She would tell us the most delightful stories . . . of Fairyland,' Caroline remembered. 'And her fairies all had characters of their own.' 'Her long . . . stories [were] so delightful!' Anna agreed. Continued 'for 2 or 3 days' at a time, and 'begged for . . . at all possible or impossible occasions', they were 'woven, as she proceeded, out of nothing but her own happy talent for invention'. 'Ah!' regretted Anna, many years later, 'if but one of them could be now recovered!'[12]

The children's enthusiasm for her stories gave Jane considerable pleasure. Cassandra was more stiff and solemn with her nieces; she was the one who chided them for their ill manners or occasional sulky moods. It was Jane who loved to play with them. 'Aunt Jane was the great charm,' said Caroline. '*Every*thing she could make amusing to a child . . . She seemed to love you and you loved her naturally in return.' 'Aunt Jane was the general favourite with the children,' Anna agreed; 'her ways with them being so playful.' 'She could throw the spilikens for us, better than anyone else,' said Caroline; 'and she was wonderfully successful at cup and ball . . . As a very little girl I was always creeping up to her, and following her whenever I could.' When she was not telling them stories, or playing with them at spillikins, Jane would sometimes amuse her little nieces and nephew with favourite songs that she sang at the pianoforte. 'Aunt Jane began her day with music,' Caroline remembered; 'she practised regularly every morning . . . before breakfast, when she could have the room to herself.' 'The music,' she added, 'would now be thought disgracefully easy . . . and none of her family cared for it much.'[13] But to Jane herself it mattered little that the tunes she loved to play were simple airs and ballads. She filled her little manuscript book with her favourite songs, including 'Queen Mary's Lamentation', 'The Yellow Haired Laddie', and the little French song which began 'Que j'aime à voir les hirondelles/Volent ma fenêtre tous les jours'. Caroline confessed a special fondness for that one ('this was my favourite, & was what I asked for the oftenest'). Another song Jane loved to play was Dibdin's 'The Soldier's Lament', though, for Mrs F.A.'s amusement, she altered it in her manuscript book to 'The Sailor's Lament' instead. Often, in the evenings, it would be her pleasure to sing and play these favourite ballads for the entertainment of her nephews and nieces. Many years later, her nephew Edward recalled the haunting power of those 'simple old songs, the words and airs of which, now never heard, still linger in my memory'.[14]

Much as they loved her, the Steventon children were still often puzzled by their aunt Jane's whimsical humour, as when she solemnly assured them that 'if she ever married at all, she could fancy being Mrs Crabbe'. ('I doubt whether she cared much for poetry in *general*,' said Caroline, 'but she was a great admirer of Crabbe.') But love and literary admiration were surely two very different things? It disturbed the children greatly to hear her claim that she could happily contemplate marriage with this favourite author 'quite as an abstract idea . . . ignorant and regardless of what manner of man he might be'.[15] To Caroline, it was a settled thing that her beloved aunt Jane was 'as far as possible from being either censorious or satirical'. Aunt Jane 'never abused' friends or relations, she said, 'or *quizzed* them'. Yet Jane could not entirely resist teasing her dear ingenuous nieces with real-life fairy tales about her intention of marrying Mr Cowper on account of his poetry, or Mr Papillon on account of his sermons.

In October, Edward came to Chawton, bringing with him Fanny and little Charles. While their father busied himself attending to his estates, the children enjoyed an agreeable holiday at Chawton cottage. Fanny was always Jane's favourite niece, dearer even than Anna or Caroline ('almost another sister'). The prospect of her company was always a delight. 'Who can keep pace with the fluctuations of your fancy, the capprizios of your taste, the contradictions of your feelings?' Jane wrote to her.[16] 'You are so odd!' For the present, though, it was the capprizios of Anna's taste which most concerned the family, and Fanny's presence at Chawton was not entirely innocent of design.

Anna, now sixteen, had recently engaged herself, entirely against her parents' wishes, to the Reverend Michael Terry of Dummer. James and Mrs J.A. were naturally furious at such unaccountable behaviour. The man himself, it had to be admitted, though twice Anna's age, was in other ways unexceptionable; 'tall & good looking & well connected with the certainty of a comfortable family living'.[17] But it was the violent and imprudent haste of this attachment, coupled with the sly manner of its disclosure, which set them against it. Parental remonstrations, however, merely strengthened Anna in her obstinacy, and it was reckoned that the advice of a cousin of her own age might perhaps be more effectual in making her see reason. When this had no immediate effect, Anna was packed off to Godmersham with her cousins and her uncle Edward for a good long absence, of several months at least, during which it was hoped this impetuous attachment might naturally die away.

Alas, Anna's confinement among her Kentish cousins had no such benign effect. Thwarted in her romantic designs, she became the more moodily intense in her expression of them. People were so terrified of imagination, she declared. Why, even the Godmersham family had no real fondness for aunt Jane. The children liked her as a 'teller of stories' but that was all. A little talent went a long way with them and the Bridges of Goodnestone, she said. Wit like aunt Jane's went 'a long way too far' for such dull spirits as theirs.[18] It pleased Anna to cast herself in a martyr's role (alongside aunt Jane) as a woman cruelly mistreated for her fine sensibility.

At last, in the New Year, Mr Terry's sister Charlotte pleaded his cause with the family and Fanny wrote to Cassandra to mediate on Anna's behalf. As a result, James eventually gave his consent to the engagement and Mr Terry was allowed to visit Anna at Godmersham in March. As might easily have been predicted, this compliance on her father's part was more effective in preventing the match than any amount of threats. Anna's sudden attachment to Mr Terry had always owed more to her spirit of defiance than to any settled affection for the man himself. No sooner had her father given his consent, than she promptly withdrew hers. That April, she spent three miserable days with Mr Terry's family at Dummer and, on her return, calmly announced that she would not marry him after all. Even Fanny was astonished by such capriciousness. 'Heard from Anna,' she noted in her diary. 'She is actually wishing to break off her engagement!!!! What a girl!!!!' A little later she wrote: 'Heard from Anna, and *all* is *over*, she has no longer anything to do with Mr Michael Terry. Heavens! What will she do next!' 'As a match it would have been about as suitable as one between Lizzie Bennet & Mr Collins,' one of Anna's daughters later wrote.[19] Anna's parents took a less indulgent view of her impulsiveness, and the embarrassment that it had caused them. The girl was once again banished from Steventon, this time to Chawton cottage, where it was hoped the influence of her aunts Jane and Cassandra might exert a beneficial effect.

To Anna, aunt Jane was always something of a heroine. She remembered her as the kindly protector who had befriended her as a poor motherless three-year-old girl, and sheltered her from an unfeeling stepmother's harshness. She was full of romantic admiration for the way her aunts now worked at teaching the poor village children to read and write. For her part, Jane privately found much to envy and admire in her niece's spirited behaviour. Frank was not the only Austen blessed with a fine 'insolence of spirit' and Jane discerned something of her cousin Eliza's bold imagination in Anna's reckless defiance. While their sailor menfolk could satisfy their adventurous instincts in the conquest of new territories and the exploration of strange lands, the Austen women must be content to circumnavigate the globes of their own imagination. Jane pictured Anna's mind as a *terra incognita* of unexplored wonders.

> *In measured verse I'll now rehearse*
> *The charms of lovely Anna*
> *And, first, her mind is unconfined*
> *Like any vast savannah.*
>
> *Ontario's lake may fitly speak*
> *Her fancy's ample bound:*
> *Its circuit may, on strict survey*
> *Five hundred miles be found.*

Her wit descends on foes and friends
Like famed Niagara's Fall;
And travellers gaze in wild amaze,
And listen, one and all.[20]

'Nonsense' was the condescending verdict of Anna's half-brother Edward, when he read these verses ('all this nonsense was nearly extempore').[21] Of course, the spontaneous impulses of such an unconfined imagination must appear nonsensical to a rational male mind ('Remember the country and the age in which we live. Remember that we are English, that we are Christians. Consult your own understanding, your own sense of the probable, your own observation of what is passing around you . . .').[22] But had there not been murders in this very house? Had not Eliza's husband been sent to the guillotine? Had not aunt Leigh-Perrot been tried for a capital crime? The world was sometimes stranger, more dangerous and more full of wonders than these rational men might like to admit. Jane found in Anna's unruly wit that natural, untamed exuberance at which unwary travellers might indeed 'gaze in wild amaze'. At the bazaar on Prince of Wales Island, Frank had marvelled at the hectic polyglot commerce; but there were other mysteries, nearer to home, which were equally difficult to translate into the language of simple common sense.

Another world must be unfurled,
Another language known,
Ere tongue or sound can publish round
Her charms of flesh and bone.

Jane loved the waywardness, the recklessness of her sixteen-year-old nieces. 'You are the paragon of all that is silly & sensible, common-place & eccentric, sad & lively, provoking and interesting,' she told Fanny. She found a kind of freedom in submitting her long-forgotten manuscripts to the capprizios of Fanny's taste or to the torrents of Anna's Niagara wit. As they listened to her impromptu comic stories, her nieces constantly encouraged her to seek a wider audience for her wit. Cassandra's comments were more judicious. To her, Jane's talent was of an essentially private nature. She could imagine nothing, in the glare of public notice or the caprice of public taste, which might in the slightest degree enhance the value of her sister's humour. The nieces, though, were rather less in awe of their aunt Cassandra's judgements, and were even inclined to resent the way Jane would constantly defer to her elder sister's opinions. Aunt Cassandra's superiority in calligraphy they were all willing to concede. 'Your close written letter,' Jane once declared to her, 'makes me quite ashamed of my wide lines.' They would even grant her superior skill in folding and sealing a letter, though aunt Jane's paper, too, 'was sure to take the right folds, and *her* sealing wax to drop in the proper place'.[23] But as to the *matter* of what they wrote, there could be no comparison. It never failed to puzzle them that Jane would never acknowledge any distinction above her sister. 'I truly believe she did always *really* think of her sister as the superior to herself,' Caroline recalled.

It was Cassandra whom the nieces blamed for the fact that their aunts had 'taken to the garb of middle age unnecessarily soon'. Cassandra, as it seemed to them, had always been middle-aged. But Jane, even in her middle thirties, was still essentially youthful, playful and inventive. The house at Chawton was always a cheerful place, 'never troubled by disagreements', yet even Caroline, who described it as a place of 'perfect harmony', could not fail to note some disconcerting silences. Aunt Jane 'seldom committed herself *even* to an opinion,' she noted. Miss Middleton agreed. 'She used to sit at table at dinner parties without uttering much,' she said.[24] Silence, it seemed, was the price of domestic harmony. Jane Austen's private opinions were divulged only in the form of fairy tales and fictions, in which her love of quizzing could run no risk of causing personal offence.

Privately, Jane found new inspiration in the odd, untamed vagaries of Fanny's wit and the wildness of Anna's capricious fantasies. What these girls brought back to her with a compelling vigour was that most delicious of all subjects, 'A Young Lady's Entrance into the World'. Like Madame D'Arblay's Evelina or her own Susan, these young Austen girls were full of that impetuous animation needful to all heroines of fictional romance, and equally equipped to mock all middle-aged cautions 'against the violence of such noblemen and baronets as delight in forcing young ladies away to some remote farm-house'. That summer, Jane read *Evelina* again, taking a special pleasure in reading aloud the comical section on Mr Smith and the Brangtons to a group of guests including young Fulwar-William Fowle. The young man was most impressed, she could tell. 'It was like a play,' he said.[25]

Life at Chawton was not all diversions, however. Between them, Jane and Cassandra determined upon a division of the household duties which their mother was now too elderly to attend to and which might not be entrusted to their maid's care. Jane's own duties were chiefly confined to the mornings. After practising her music, it was her task to make breakfast at precisely nine o'clock. '*That* was *her* part of the household work; the tea and sugar and stores were under *her* charge – *and* the wine. Aunt Cassandra did all the rest.' After breakfast she might occupy herself with satin stitch or reading, and after luncheon she and Cassandra would generally walk out. 'It was a very quiet life, according to our ideas,' said Anna. Sometimes they would go to Alton for shopping, or make a visit to the great house, or stroll about the grounds to Chawton Park, a noble beech wood, just within a walk. Jane found a pleasure in these simple recreations, and often she would tell herself that a life devoted to such modest and useful pastimes was quite sufficient to her needs. She would even grow a little vexed at the frequent promptings of her nieces, forever urging her to seek a wider audience for her writings than the narrow circle of family and friends. That particular vanity was over, she would tell them. The world, in the shape of Messrs Cadell and Crosby, had delivered its opinion on her modest literary talents. She had no need or inclination to risk another such rebuff.

Yet her nieces would not be satisfied, and when Henry's voice was added to theirs, the temptation to try once more for publication was almost irresistible. Gradually, Jane allowed herself to acquiesce in their wishes, less for her own sake than in deference to opinions so consistently and vehemently expressed. Jane contrived to detach her own views from those of her well-wishing relatives. Naturally, it was highly gratifying to receive from them such lively commendations of her talents; but, while she might affect to honour their judgements, she privately suspected them of an unreasonable (and unreasoning) partiality. It was not that she did not entertain a good opinion of her own work; rather the contrary. But the pleasure which she and Cassandra had always taken in her satirical literary diversions carried with it no expectation that such writings would find favour elsewhere. And at times it even seemed to her that the promptings of her nieces bore an uncomfortable likeness to those frequent hints she had been used to receive concerning the 'legacy' that must surely be her due. On the strength of such hints, she had been foolish enough to allow herself to indulge hopes in that direction, and the bitterness of that disappointment still rankled with her. This time, she would permit herself no such romantic delusions.

As if to confirm her own prejudices, she set herself to read through the earliest and least publishable 'novels' she had written in her youth. There were passages in these comic stories which still made her laugh out loud. How she loved the character of Charlotte in 'Lesley Castle', whose mind ran constantly upon roasted beef, broiled mutton, cold pigeon pie and stewed soup! When that very rational young lady received the news that her sister's marriage was 'broke off' (on account of her intended having been 'thrown from his horse ... fractured his scull [*sic*] and ... pronounced by his surgeon to be in the most emminent [*sic*] danger'), her reaction was splendid. 'Good God! ... you don't say so? Why what in the name of Heaven will become of all the Victuals! We shall never be able to eat it while it is good.'[26] But even Henry could not imagine that such girlish amusements would delight the world at large. Perhaps that was part of their charm. Here at least there could be no danger of her own whimsical taste conforming to the requirements of an insatiable reading public. Yet it amused her to make emendations to these pieces, quite as if they were the ones she intended to present for a London publisher's edification. In 'Evelyn', she changed a date ('Augst 19th 1809') and in *Catharine*, written eighteen years before, inserted a modish reference to Miss More's pious novel *Coelebs in Search of a Wife*.

When it came to *Sense and Sensibility*, her feelings were less easy to define. This was the work which Henry was now pressing her to send him. Having abandoned, for the present, the attempt to find a publisher for 'Susan', Henry had contacted Egerton's of Whitehall on Jane's behalf. They, it seemed, had expressed interest in *Sense and Sensibility*. Nervously, Jane applied herself to revising the text. Accuracy of reference was the least that she should strive for, she believed. Hence the scrupulous new detail concerning the London twopenny post and the addition of Scott's name as a popular poet alongside Cowper and Thomson. Yet, even as she made these alterations, she allowed herself to entertain few hopes that this novel would enjoy a more fortunate reception than either 'First Impressions' or 'Susan'. Cassandra was even less sanguine about the outcome of all Henry's endeavours on Jane's behalf, and she demonstrated her lack of enthusiasm for this latest venture by a conspicuous silence. To her, the revision of the manuscript and the despatch of it to Egerton's were activities which merited less approbation than her sister's skills at needlecraft. She was relieved when the thing was sent, and they were enabled to resume their customary private diversions.

The chief pleasure of that summer should have been Frank's return from China. The Chawton family were all delighted when the *St Albans* was reported in the Downs at the end of July and made landfall at Deal on 1 August. Yet, instead of coming home to Alton, Frank chose to remain with his ship, first at Deal and afterwards at Chatham, where Mrs F.A. went to stay with him in lodgings in the town. At first, Frank's reluctance to return to Hampshire seemed quite unaccountable. But gradually, awkward rumours began to circulate about vast quantities of gold and a dead Chinaman. At a time of war, when so many men were being slaughtered in sea battles, the fate of one dead Chinaman seemed to Jane a singular matter for their Lordships of the Admiralty to concern themselves about. No doubt there must be reasons of a political nature to provoke such a punctilious inquiry.

The facts of the matter, as Frank Austen presented them, were clear enough. Relations between the crew of the *St Albans* and the local Chinese had become soured when some officers from the ship, who had gone hunting ashore, were compelled to shoot a buffalo which threatened to gore one of their number. Numerous Chinamen immediately gathered round, full of indignation at the slaughter of the beast, and attacked them in a most violent manner. The Englishmen were able to escape only by offering money. A little later, when the *St Albans* was preparing to put to sea, Frank was informed that they would not be permitted to depart. The reason given was that a Chinaman had been killed in the town by, as they claimed, an Englishman. Frank made no secret of his contempt for this accusation, and for the supposed 'evidence' that supported it. In a letter to Admiral Drury, Commander-in-Chief in India, he complained of the unreasoning 'pertinacity' with which the natives adhered to their false assertions 'in defiance of justice, equity and common sense'. One witness, Frank claimed, swore 'that there was neither noise nor fighting', while another swore 'there *was* noise and . . . fighting for ten minutes'.[27] 'One of them states it to be quite dark, and the other that it was moonlight.' Despite this, the Chinese Mandarins insisted on upholding the charge, which drove Frank into a fury. The word 'Mandarin', he suggested, 'comprises every bad quality which has disgraced human nature'. And, with something less than the 'gentleness to all' for which his sister praised him, he concluded by declaring, 'A Mandarin is not a reasoning animal, nor ought to be treated as a rational animal.'

What Frank did *not* tell Admiral Drury was the true reason for the Viceroy's reluctance to see the *St Albans* depart. Deep in the ship's hold were some one hundred chests of gold and treasure worth almost 500,000 dollars. This rich cargo had nothing to do with Frank's official duties in these waters, where he charted the China coast, the inlets of Nanka island and the mouth of the Canton river. Instead, as the Viceroy knew, it had everything to do with Frank's own private commerce as an East India Company agent. Eventually, a compromise was agreed, no doubt assisted by a 'gift' of some part of the treasure. The *St Albans* and its convoy were permitted to leave on condition that Frank held his own inquiry into the killing during the voyage home. Honour was settled when it was learnt that three armed crewmen from the *Cumberland* had indeed taken part in the fight.

On reaching England, Frank at once delivered the remaining ninety-three chests of treasure, now valued at 470,000 dollars, to Mr Iggulden, the Company's agent at Deal. Whereupon the Company signalled their satisfaction with his services by making him a reward of 500 guineas.[28] But Frank hardly considered this adequate payment for all the risks and hardships he had undergone. On 4 October, he petitioned the Company for additional moneys to cover the full costs of transporting the treasure. The Company were well used to such demands from naval officers who thus hoped to be paid twice over for their time at sea. But on this occasion they agreed to Frank's request. A warrant was prepared in his name for £1,177, with the stipulation that he must return 'any sum which may have been paid to the Admiral on account of the same'. Still, Frank was not satisfied. Two days later, he sent the Company a new petition for '£2 per cent' of the full value of the treasure, in addition to the costs of carrying it. Once again the Company acceded to his request. A week later Frank wrote to assure them that he had now 'authorized his agents' to receive the sum of £1,500.[29] Only when all this was agreed, and the money was safely lodged in Henry's hands, did he send the Company 'the results of the investigation made into the circumstances connected with the death of a native of China'.[30]

As a result of his Chinese expedition, Frank was at last enabled to enjoy a life of relative prosperity. His wealth, of course, bore no comparison with that of Edward at Godmersham, or of uncle Leigh-Perrot at Bath. But he at least stood no longer in fear of poverty for himself and his family. His first act on receiving payment from the Company was to relinquish command of the *St Albans* and join his wife and infant children. Jane was full of admiration for the boldness that had brought her brother the 'good prize' he needed to become 'a perfect character'. She envied that native 'insolence of spirit' which had carried Frank to the riches he deserved. There was something in his success which emboldened her to risk a similar piece of daring on her own behalf, in despite of all Cassandra's caution. For she, too, had her own good news to impart: Thomas Egerton of London had agreed to publish her manuscript of *Sense and Sensibility*. The only inconvenience was in the financial arrangements which the publishers proposed. They would take the book, they said, only 'upon commission' – that is, at the author's own expense. Even her excitement at the prospect of appearing in print could not dull Jane's apprehension of the risk of such a venture. As she told everyone who was kind enough to ask her about it, she was quite convinced that 'its sale would not repay the expense of publication'. Cassandra remained unconvinced of the wisdom of such an uncertain undertaking, but, having ventured thus far, Jane was not inclined to draw back. She had prudently 'made a reserve' from her slender income, she said, 'to meet the expected loss'.[31]

'I am really very shocking'

That March, Jane travelled up to London to stay with Henry and Eliza in Sloane Street while she worked at correcting the publisher's proofs of *Sense and Sensibility*. Quite suddenly, she felt the return of a sense of elation, an almost giddy, girlish excitement at the new world that awaited her. She had thought that, for her, the life of concerts and balls, theatre visits and parties was over, and had resigned herself to the modest, quiet, humdrum diversions of village life at Chawton, doing charitable works among the poor, and visiting Miss Beckford and Miss Benn. But once in London, she quite abandoned her drab middle-aged country attire, and treated herself to a handsome new wardrobe of pretty coloured muslins, silk stockings and fine pelisses. She felt quite guilty confessing to Cassandra how vain she had become. 'I am getting very extravagant & spending all my money,' she wrote. 'I am really very shocking . . . & now nothing can satisfy me but I must have a straw hat.'[32] But it was really a most delicious kind of guilt, so much more agreeable than all those vulgar economies. And Cassandra need hardly chide her, since almost half the purchases she made were intended for both of them. 'Our buttons seem expensive,' she wrote, then thrust aside such evasiveness: '*are* expensive, I might have said – for the fact is plain enough.' The fact was plain enough, too, that she was loving this opportunity to be extravagant and reckless, and if Cassandra, in her thrifty way, did not care for all the finery that she had chosen, Jane said, '[you] must not think yourself at all obliged to take it . . . I shd not in the least mind keeping the whole.' After all, she added mischievously, the fabric was 'just what we prefer'; 'we' (that is, Cassandra) had preferred a sensible green 'crewel' worsted; what Jane had bought was a bright muslin patterned with small red spots.

Dressed in her handsome new outfit, Jane was modest enough to be gratified, but vain enough to affect little surprise, at the approving notice she attracted at smart London parties. 'A pleasing young woman' was how Mr Wyndham Knatchbull described her. That was agreeable enough. Still to be thought 'young' at thirty-six was a considerable fillip to one's self-esteem. 'That must do,' she commented to Cassandra; 'one cannot pretend to anything better now – thankful to have it continued a few years longer!'[33] She had just corrected that part of *Sense and Sensibility* where Marianne expressed her horror at the thought of a man of thirty-five ('thirty-five has nothing to do with matrimony'). It was one of the abiding pleasures of authorship to be able to contradict such assertions.

Cassandra herself was at Godmersham, but for once, Jane felt no stirrings of envy at being excluded from the pleasures of Kent. Eliza was determined as ever to surround herself with gaiety, excitement and with everything that was calculated to exhibit the most fashionable mode of existence. Jane's life at Sloane Street was a perpetual round of elegant diversions. The Cookes were also in London, and on one day she was taken to Piccadilly, with Mary Cooke, to observe the exhibits in Bullock's Liverpool Museum of natural history. In *Sense and Sensibility* it was the wild beasts at Exeter Exchange that Elinor and Marianne visited, she pointed out. But that was now accounted altogether too hackneyed a spectacle. There was nothing in all Europe to compare with Bullock's collection of rarities, which included the mighty cameleopard (stuffed), thirty-two species of monkeys (from the pig-tailed baboon to the Palatine monkey), the head of a rhinoceros, a striped hyena, a termites' nest (ten feet in height) together with a rice paste model of the Death of Voltaire and a Jew Rabbi, done with hot iron on wood.[34] From there, it was on to the British Gallery in Pall Mall, where they saw, among other wonders, Mr West's vast new painting of *Christ Healing the Sick*. Yet even in these grand and august institutions, she could not think of herself as a mere *spectator*, conversing with a picture, as Mr Addison might put it, or finding an agreeable companion in a statue.

She now entered each new arena of life with the sensibility of a lady novelist; one whose business it was to study and depict the varieties of human nature. As such, it became her conscious habit to attend rather to the characteristics of those living human exhibits who walked the galleries beside her, than to the stuffed and painted specimens hanging on the walls. 'I had some amusement at each,' she wrote to Cassandra, 'tho' my preference for men & women always inclines me to attend more to the company than the sight.'[35] Theo Cooke was one prime exhibit ('nothing-meaning, harmless, heartless civility'); another was Mr Brecknell ('very religious, & has got black whiskers').

To any connoisseur of human curiosities, Eliza's circle of London acquaintances offered many splendid opportunities for the observation of rare specimens. Jane was particularly intrigued at the prospect of meeting Eliza's fashionable French friends, the D'Entraigues and Count Julien, about whom she had heard so much. But when at last the evening designated for this meeting arrived, it was marred by a misfortune which threatened to disappoint all their plans. Eliza's horses slid and slipped their collar on the newly gravelled hill that led to Hyde Park Gate, and the two ladies were reluctantly compelled to abandon their carriage and stand for several minutes in the chill evening air. As a consequence, poor Eliza took a terrible cold upon her chest, and it seemed as if they must abandon their promised entertainment. But Eliza was one for whom the obligations of sociability far outweighed any terrors for her health. They arrived at the Count's house only a little later than was fashionable, and found their French hosts as solicitous for their safety as they were accommodating to their tastes. Indeed, Jane was at a loss to find anything to dislike in these Frenchmen 'but their taking of quantities of snuff'.

Monsieur the old Count was all courtesy, and insisted on showing the ladies his collection of fine paintings. For Jane, even an exquisite miniature of Philip V of Spain was of less interest than their host himself. After considering him a good while, she pronounced him 'a very fine looking man', and even 'good enough for an Englishman'. From her, there could be no higher praise. 'If he wd but speak English,' she told Cassandra, '*I* would take to him.'[36]

Even she was a little surprised at how curiously engaging she found the people whom she met at tea-parties and supper-parties. Instead of seeking to avoid such unmeaning encounters, as had become her habit in Southampton, she now sought them out with unfeigned enthusiasm. 'I find all these little parties very pleasant,' she told her disbelieving sister. At least she was rational enough to acknowledge that it could hardly be the world that had improved, but merely her perspective upon it. The book had changed everything. In the excitement of imagining herself a published author, she found herself discarding several dowdy layers of unsociability along with her drab country clothes. And although she constantly did all in her power to forearm herself against the evils of disappointing sales and unkind reviews (both of which were to be anticipated and dreaded), she could not entirely suppress an intense feeling of satisfaction. 'No indeed,' she told Cassandra, 'I am never too busy to think of *S & S*. I can no more forget it, than a mother can forget her sucking child.'

It was quite unforgivable, she knew, to find such utter pleasure in the shallow London world of tea-parties and glee singers and émigré French aristocrats. 'I am a wretch to be so occupied with all these things,' she told Cassandra, 'as to seem to have no thoughts to give to people & circumstances which really supply a far more lasting interest – the society in which you are.' There was another 'seem'; but this time she did not boldly strike it out. Of course, she *ought* to be less selfish in her preoccupations. 'I do think of you all I assure you,' she wrote, '& want to know all about everybody . . . "*mais le moyen*" not to be occupied by one's own concerns?'[37] The little French phrase (it was borrowed from Lord Chesterfield) was deliberate. She hoped it would reassure Cassandra that she had not entirely lost her capacity for self-mockery.

The sisters had always loved to laugh at the way that literary people talked, especially the Cookes' Bookham friends, the Burneys, with their '*caro sposo*'s. Was that how she would be talking soon?

Henry was a constant delight, the more so for the way his peremptory enthusiasms were perpetually at odds with his lamentable lack of practical application. He would pop up at a *soirée* quite unexpectedly, and be the very life and wit of the party for a whole quarter of an hour, before whisking himself and her away in a hackney coach. He was forever making plans for theatre visits which had always to be cancelled at the last moment. On one occasion, she acknowledged, the cancellation had been her fault. They had been due to go to the Lyceum, but she had a cold which put an end to that design. Another time, when they were to see *King John*, the theatre managers withdrew the play and substituted *Hamlet*, which was rather less to their taste. Jane had a passion to see the celebrated Mrs Siddons in the role of Lady Macbeth, and Henry promised he would take her to the very next performance. But when he went to the theatre, the box-keeper told him that Mrs Siddons would not appear, and, as a consequence, Henry gave up their places and all thoughts of that particular play. Imagine Jane's dismay when she heard the lady *had* acted it after all. 'I should particularly have liked seeing her in Constance [in *King John*],' she told Cassandra, 'and could swear at her with little effort for disappointing me.' They *did* see a performance of *The Hypocrite* ('an old play taken from Moliere's *Tartuffe*') and were 'well entertained'. The heroine in that piece was acted by Mrs Edwin. 'Her performance is just what it used to be,' said Jane, affecting the knowing tone of a playhouse *habituée*.[38]

By far the grandest event in her busy London diary was a large party given by Eliza, at which some eighty of the most fashionable and lordly people were invited to attend. Dear Eliza never could forget the splendours of those Versailles parties that had so bewitched her in her youth, and, with whatever means she had at her disposal, she contrived to turn their Sloane Street house into a miniature of the *ancien régime*. There was music, 'very good music', with five hired professionals ('three of them glee-singers') besides amateurs and a harpist called Wiepart ('whose name seems famous, tho' new to me'). The rooms were dressed throughout with flowers, and a fine looking-glass was borrowed for the mantel-piece. 'We were all delight & cordiality of course,' said Jane, who was particularly delighted to find herself so greatly in demand among the gentlemen; 'what with Mr Hampson, Mr Seymour, Mr W. Knatchbull, Mr Guillemarde, Mr Cure, a Capt Simpson (brother to *the* Capt Simpson), besides Mr Walter & Mr Egerton . . . I had quite as much upon my hands as I could do.' However, she was not so preoccupied by all her gentlemen admirers as to neglect marking the musical airs for the amusement of her favourite niece. 'It opened (tell Fanny) with "Prike pe Parp pin praise pof Prapela" – & of the other glees I remember "In peace Love tunes", "Rosabelle", "The red cross Knight" & "Poor Insect".' She hoped pis pittle pallusion to the nonsense language she and Fanny used to share might convince Cassandra that she had not entirely forgotten those 'people & circumstances which really supply a far more lasting interest'. The party began at half past five and the house was not clear till after midnight. The following day, Eliza was gratified to find a mention of 'Mrs H Austin's [*sic*] musical party' in the *Morning Post*. This was what it was to be living in society.[39]

Above all, Jane's thoughts were now concentrated on the London literary scene. She had corrected two sheets of *Sense and Sensibility*, 'but the last only brings us to W[illoughby]'s first appearance'. Henry was doing all he could to hurry the printers, but she feared Mrs Knight would be disappointed in her hopes of seeing the book by May. 'I have scarcely a hope of its being out in June.' She was, though, 'very much gratified' by the old lady's interest in the book. 'I think she will like my Elinor,' she said (which was by way of being an oblique compliment to Cassandra), 'but I cannot build on anything else.' She had no idea that a book could take so long to be printed, and as she waited, day by day, for each new sheet to appear, she became increasingly anxious about the success of other lady novelists. Mary Brunton's *Self-Controul* was much talked of, and she attempted to obtain a copy 'but in vain'. 'I *should* like to know what her estimate is,' she confessed, 'but am always half afraid of finding a clever novel *too clever* – & of finding my own story & my own people all forestalled.'[40]

Speaking of cleverness, she was vastly diverted by a brief note from Fanny, pull pof papital Ps. 'What is there to be said on the subject? – Pery pell – or pare pey? or po.' She always loved to hear from her wayward nieces, though Anna, as it now appeared, was become quite a paragon of all the maidenly virtues. 'She is quite an Anna with variations', was Jane's comment at this news; 'but she cannot have reached her last, for that is always the most flourishing & shewey.' Was she herself, she wondered, now entered upon that final flourishing phase?

Not the least of the attractions of London was to find herself at the heart of national affairs. All round her, she heard gossip of this scandalous minister or that villainous bill. Henry was the first to bring news of Sir Edward Pellew's succeeding Lord Gambier in the Admiralty. As a consequence, she told Cassandra, Frank would give up command of the *Caledonia* in its watch on the French coast. She had also heard that Charles might be back in England by the end of the month. It was highly gratifying to find herself such an adept in political affairs, and she even turned her hand to composing some doggerel verses on the wicked Weald of Kent Canal Bill against which Edward was striving to rouse up the county. Would Edward, she wondered, have more success in his strivings than Edward Bridges in confronting the predatory manoeuvres of the Grenadier Guards?

Enjoying so much knowledge gave her an unaccustomed sensation of power. Why should she concern herself when all the usual difficulties arose about deciding which brother should escort her home, and when? If James's plans for meeting her should alter, 'I can take care of myself,' she said; 'I have explained my views here.' It all seemed a far cry from the dread of becoming a lowly school-teacher. That thought was put in her mind by Cassandra's mention of Miss Allen, the new governess at Godmersham. 'By this time I suppose she is hard at it, governessing away,' she wrote. 'Poor creature! I pity her, tho' they *are* my neices.'[41]

By the beginning of May, it became obvious that she must not look for an early appearance of *Sense and Sensibility*. She could

not disguise her dismay, and complained about the printer's endless delays. She had hoped to carry her new-born 'child' away
with her from London; but instead she returned to Chawton
empty-handed, save only for her red-spotted muslin, her fur pelisse
and new straw hat. Despite this disappointment, her spirits
remained quite buoyant. At Chawton, the garden was in glorious
bloom, with columbines, pinks and sweet williams all along the
shrubbery border, a handsome peony beneath the fir tree, and her
favourite syringas just coming out. She heard that an apricot had
been detected on one of the trees, and they were like to have a
fine crop of Orleans plums, just like the ones the Bath ladies used
to wear on their heads. Only Cassandra's plants seemed to be
wilting: 'I will not say your mulberry trees are dead,' she wrote,
'but I am afraid they are not alive.' As for Cassandra's mignonette,
she was sorry to report it made 'a very wretched appearance'.[42]

Anna was still at Chawton when she returned there and had
become quite the young belle of village society, always either
visiting or visited. She would spend several days with the Benn
girls at Farringdon, pass an afternoon with the Prowtings, learning
to make feather trimmings of Miss Anne, and then spend a most
delightful evening with the Miss Middletons – 'syllabub, tea,
coffee, singing, dancing, a hot supper, eleven o' clock, everything
that can be imagined agreable'. Thunder and lightning were nothing to her ('I never knew such a spring for thunder storms'); nor
for sore throats either. She was out every day that the weather
allowed. Which was rather lucky since it meant she was not at
home when an invitation arrived from the Digweeds to spend an
evening with Mrs and Miss Terry. Naturally, Anna was invited
too, but Jane thought it 'safest to keep her away from [that] family'.
It was in the nature of her niece's constant variations to be always
doing 'too little or too much' where the Terrys were concerned. All
things considered, Anna was much better suited to the company at
Farringdon, where she might enjoy 'plenty of the miscellaneous
unsettled sort of happiness which seems to suit her best.'

Another thunderstorm blew down the chimneys at the great
house, but this was not the only local hazard. Much to the inconvenience of his neighbours, Mr Prowting had opened up a gravel

pit before the approach to his front door. 'It looks a little as if he meant to catch all his company,' said Jane, then added wryly: 'Tolerable gravel.' With her newly sophisticated London eye, she amused herself assessing the charms of all the local ladies; Miss Harding 'elegant, pleasing, pretty looking, . . . with flowers in her head & music at her fingers ends'; Miss Webb, 'short & not quite straight, & cannot pronounce an R any better than her sisters'; and Mary Cooke, who, with *two* curates now lodging in Bookham, 'must fall in love with one or the other'.[43]

Despite its six bedrooms, the cottage was ill-equipped for accommodating many guests, and before long she was back to worrying about exactly who their summer visitors might be, and when, and for how long. The Cookes talked of making a family visit, which seemed an agreeable notion until a letter arrived from Frank and Mary, stating their intention of bringing the children to stay with them at Chawton on their way back from Steventon to Cowes. 'But supposing Martha to be at home,' wrote Jane, 'it does not seem an easy thing to accommodate so large a party.' Fortunately, the Cookes put off their visit ('they are not well enough to leave home'), but the incident reminded Jane of the narrow limits of village hospitality. There could be no thought of entertaining eighty people here – or even a dozen. When would they ever see the Cookes now, she wondered? 'Probably never, in this house.' At least their diet now demonstrated certain hints of sophistication, thanks to her gradual policy of introducing London refinements. 'We began our China tea three days ago,' she told Cassandra, '& *I* find it very good. My companions know nothing of the matter.' A hamper of port and brandy arrived from Southampton, and the chickens were all alive and 'fit for the table'. 'But we save them for something grand,' she wrote, meaning, of course, the publication of *Sense and Sensibility*. Even in Chawton, where glee-singers were unknown and China tea a rarity, she was determined there should be a feast to celebrate that grand event. But for Henry, when he paid a call in early June, a 'sumptuous provision of a neck of mutton' was deemed quite sufficient. Jane supervised the cooking of the mutton herself. Did Cassandra have any notion, she demanded, 'how many hours' it had taken her to prepare that neck of mutton?[44] Henry was accompanied by his banker partner Mr Tilson, and they had not wished Mr Tilson to suffer the same fate as poor Captain Foote in enduring a dish of underdone mutton. After dinner, they had all taken a walk to Chawton Park, where Mr Tilson revealed how much more perfectly adapted he was to the banker's profession than Henry. They had all been admiring the beech trees in the wood and Henry had said many fine things about their foliage. Mr Tilson admired them too, but then remarked how much it grieved him 'that they should not be turned into money'.

The publishers now spoke of September as a possible date for the appearance of *Sense and Sensibility*. The *Hampshire Telegraph* had reports of a terrible battle at Almeida, with lists of dreadful casualties among the Duke of Wellington's troops. 'How horrible it is to have so many people killed!' she wrote. 'And what a blessing that one cares for none of them!'[45]

'Sterne's darling maid'

Cassandra left the school-room where Miss Allen was 'governessing away' with the aid of Hannah More's *Practical Piety*, and walked upstairs to her favourite Yellow Room. Fanny, she knew, had little patience with such moralizing works. The girl could hardly wait for Jane's *Sense and Sensibility* to appear, and was forever insisting that it would entirely eclipse the vogue for Mores and Burneys and Radcliffes. It was in vain for Cassandra to tell her that she must on no account divulge aunt Jane's authorship of *Sense and Sensibility*. The girl boasted of it to everyone she met, treating it as a mighty secret which, like all the best secrets, must immediately be shared with half the world. Mrs Knight was just as bad. She could not contain her impatience at the publisher's delays, and only wondered at Henry's judgement in placing the book with such a procrastinator as this Egerton seemed to be. To her, Jane was quite a heroine; she was always hatching schemes on her behalf, to provide for her with impossible legacies, or marry her off to some rich clergyman (a contradiction in terms). Her latest plan was for Jane to spin herself into a fortune. She was determined to present her with her very own spinning-wheel, she said. Cassandra wondered how it would alter the old lady's opinion of her sister if she were to learn of Jane's annoyance at this charitable offer. 'If she persisted in giving it,' Jane had written, 'I would spin nothing with it but a rope to hang myself.'[46] Cassandra feared that all the excitement of imagining herself a published author had quite turned Jane against such humble occupations as spinning yarn. Now she was for everything that was most expensive and gaudy; red-spotted muslins, straw hats, grand London parties and China tea.

Cassandra herself was neither surprised nor even greatly dismayed at Mr Egerton's delays. Naturally, she wished the book well; but she, at least, remembered the dashed hopes that had resulted from Jane's previous efforts at publication with Messrs Cadell and Crosby. A little rational reflection, she thought, among all the fervency of exaggerated expectations, would be most salutary. *She* recognized, even if others did not, that it might be no easy matter to defray the costs of publication, let alone hope for any profit. *She* understood what Jane appeared to have forgotten, that a mere handful of unkind reviews might not only jeopardize her hopes of financial reward, but also destroy her private tranquillity of mind. It would be time enough to boast of authorship, Cassandra believed, when the book was assured of its welcome.

Cassandra's caution proceeded from an entirely rational and sisterly wish to protect Jane from disappointment. There was no shadow of jealousy in her reserve. It was true she felt a certain dismay at the frivolity of Jane's London letters, and at the way her sudden fascination with play-houses, cameleopards and French aristocrats seemed to have banished all serious thoughts from her mind. Cassandra was well aware how the nieces all loved Jane's mercurial wit. *She* was the great charm of their visits to Chawton; they would always be creeping up to her, following her about, playing at spillikins with her, pestering her to entertain them with her fanciful stories. Towards herself they were respectful, but distant. They did not *dislike* her, but neither did they warm to her. She did not tell them stories or play with them at cup and ball.

She knew it was a mystery to them why their beloved aunt Jane should so constantly tell them that it was she, Cassandra, who *knew* most, and who 'could teach everything much better than she could'.[47] What she had to teach them, they did not wish to know, for she could not, as Jane did, disguise her lessons in beguiling fairy tales. In truth, Cassandra could have wished that Jane did not so frequently insist on her superior talents for pedagogy since, knowing as she did Jane's lowly opinion of school-mistresses, it was a commendation which seemed sometimes to verge upon satire. That, at least, she thought, was how the nieces understood it. Although elder sisters themselves, neither Anna nor Fanny was yet of a maturity to comprehend the full responsibilities of an elder sister's role. No one, not even their mother, could truly comprehend the bond which existed between Jane and herself. What the others saw was a pairing of opposites; Jane, whimsical, quick-witted and bold; herself, stiff in opinions and reserved in manner. Yet, without her own steadfastness to guide her, Cassandra believed that Jane would lack half the courage to dare the things she did. If Cassandra appeared less impatient than others in the family to witness the public baptism of Jane's 'sucking child', it was because she felt an almost godmotherly apprehensiveness at the solemnity of the event. Sincerity and humility were the predominant virtues, according to Hannah More, and Cassandra felt no reason to quarrel with that judgement.

When she returned to Chawton that summer, Cassandra was distressed to find her mulberries all dead, just as Jane had warned her. But Jane was wrong in her prognostications for the Orleans plums. It was a poor year for fruit altogether; surrounded by orchards as they were, there was scarcely an apple to be had. In August, Eliza came to stay from London and was quite shocked at the absence of fruit. Why, there were more apples and apricots and plums and greengages to be had within a hundred yards of Sloane Street than here in the heart of the country.

Cassandra thought she had never seen Eliza in such good health before; nearly fifty years old and still chattering on like a giddy girl of fifteen about balls and *soirées* and parties. Best of all was when Charles arrived, with his wife and two dear pretty little girls. It was hard to believe that it was seven years since any of them had seen him, and they were all vastly relieved to find him undiminished in health and unchanged in mind. His wife, Fanny, was generally pronounced a 'very pleasing little woman', gentle in her motherly ways and amiable in her manners. She was fair and pink, with very light hair, and obviously made Charles very happy. Yet since in life there must always be something to wish for, they all agreed in wishing that Charles might have rather more money. Everything in England was so expensive now, he said, even the necessaries of life. He was rather afraid they would find themselves very, *very* poor.[48] Of course, there was much talk of *Sense and Sensibility* and how eagerly they all awaited it. Jane must make all their fortunes for them, said Charles. That was only fair, since they had all spent so many years as the victims of her whimsical wit. Did she remember the piece she had written for him when he was just a child? All about Mr Clifford and his extraordinary journeys from Dean Gate to Basingstoke and Clarkengreen and Worting? (Fanny longed to see the places all traced out on a map.)

Sadly, poor Eliza was deprived of the most whimsical item of all. Barely an hour after she had departed for London, they got the newspaper and found in it a confirmation of Phylly Walter's marriage to Mr George Whitaker of Pembury. Imagine Phylly, at the age of fifty, at last embarking upon those 'conjugal duties' which she had always regarded with such awe! In recent weeks, as she felt the happy day advancing towards her, poor Phylly had seemed to doubt the wisdom of her late conversion to matrimony. Cassandra wrote at once to rally her spirits, or at least to reconcile her to her chosen marital fate. 'Where is the situation on earth exempt from evils?' she wrote. Phylly was 'too wise and too good', she was sure, 'to dwell on the wrong side of the picture'. 'Use will reconcile you to some things which appear evils at first, and others you will bear as the necessary attendants of humanity.'[49] Jane thought it was Mr Whitaker who might be most in need of encouragements to bear the 'necessary attendants of humanity'. But she applauded Cassandra in wishing Phylly a kind of stoical bliss. 'I am determined you shall be happy,' wrote Cassandra, 'whether you will or no.' Maintaining her careful policy of silence, Cassandra said nothing about *Sense and Sensibility* in her letter. Phylly might be surprised, and even a little hurt, when she eventually discovered how much she had been deceived by a letter which only told her that Jane and Mrs Austen sent their 'good wishes'. But now that the publication was imminent, Cassandra felt particularly anxious to shield her sister from exposure. Alone in their bedroom, she looked at the sketch she had done of Jane the year before.[50] Here were the curling ringlets round her forehead, the large hazel eyes and the fine blade of a Leigh family nose. The sketch was unfinished, which was how Jane wanted it; no ostentatious folds of drapery (red-spotted or otherwise); no fancy bonnet or expensive silks. Cassandra had drawn her as she often sat, her mouth drawn tight, her arms (just glimpsed in outline) folded across her lap. It was a private face, not soft or pretty, but with an expression of secret defiance. What would become of that private face once *Sense and Sensibility* was published? There was indeed no situation on earth entirely exempt from evils. If the book were to fall a miserable victim to the reviewers' savage execrations, it would be Cassandra's duty to assuage her sister's pain. But if the book were to have a huge success, the evils might be even greater. What would happen then to the special bond between them? Would they still continue, as before, with never a thought concealed between them?

At the end of September, Cassandra wrote again to Fanny, begging her once more to tell no one that aunt Jane was the author of *Sense and Sensibility*. For as long as possible she wished to keep the secret pleasure of all the private memories that she and Jane had shared. Nothing in the book gave Cassandra greater pleasure than its final sentence: '. . . among the merits and the happiness of Elinor and Marianne, let it not be ranked as the least considerable, that though sisters, and living almost within sight of each other, they could live without disagreement between themselves, or producing coolness between their husbands.'[51] A novel in which marriage was shown not to diminish, but rather to strengthen, the bond between sisters, was one which Cassandra could be happy to admire.

Sense and Sensibility at last appeared in late October. It was published in three volumes at a price of 15s, and written, as the title-page declared, 'By A Lady'. But some of the advertisements got this wrong and printed 'By Lady A –' instead. Lady Augusta Page was highly flattered, Eliza told them, when the Duke of York assumed it must have been written by her. And though Jane was somewhat mortified to have her darling child pass thus disguised and unacknowledged in the fashionable world, it was, Cassandra thought, a blessing that her identity should be further obscured by this artless error. In late November, Jane spent some days at Steventon, where James and Mrs J.A. were let into the secret – though not Anna, who could by no means be trusted to keep it. After her return, James sent Jane an 'anonymous' note, written in a disguised hand, and containing some flattering verses 'To Miss Jane Austen the reputed Author of *Sense and Sensibility*'. The sentiments were so typical of James; generous, literary and unassuming.

> *On such subjects no wonder that she shou'd write well,*
> *In whom so united those qualities dwell;*
> *Where 'dear Sensibility', Sterne's darling maid,*
> *With Sense so attemper'd is finely pourtray'd.*
> *Fair Elinor's self in that mind is exprest,*
> *And the feelings of Marianne live in that breast.*
> *Oh then, gentle lady! continue to write,*
> *And the sense of your readers t'amuse & delight.*
>
> *A Friend.*[52]

It remained a wonder to Cassandra that James himself should have gained no wider recognition for his poems, which were universally acknowledged, within the family at least, to show such fineness of feeling. Yet in some ways she rather approved a talent which could rest content with only the applause of family and friends, and which found its highest inspiration in domestic subjects, as in his affecting lines to his son.

> *May the light woes of early youth,*
> *Teach you this salutary truth,*
> *That every sorrow will be light,*
> *When all within the breast is right.*[53]

Cassandra could have wished that all within her own breast were right as she waited apprehensively with Jane for the first reviews to appear. They spent an uneventful Christmas, with few friends or neighbours to disturb the quiet and warmth of their small fireside circle. 'But I do not mean to complain,' she told Phylly; 'if we have had little company to increase our cheerfulness, we have had no illness to diminish it.' That was rather more than Phylly could boast. Mr Whitaker was already an invalid, and her Christmas had been far from joyous. 'I hope . . . he has by this time shaken off his complaints,' Cassandra wrote to her in sympathy.[54]

In January, Henry paid one of his flying visits, bringing all the latest literary gossip. Apparently, they were full of *Sense and Sensibility* at Althorp. Lady Bessborough said it was 'a clever novel' but thought it ended stupidly.[55] In February, the first notice of the book appeared and was better than they could ever have hoped for. The *Critical Review* singled it out for 'particular commendation'. It was 'well written', it said:

> the characters are in genteel life, naturally drawn, and judiciously supported. The incidents are probable, and highly pleasing, and interesting; the conclusion such as the reader must wish it should be, and the whole is just long enough to interest without fatiguing. It reflects honour on the writer, who displays much knowledge of character, and very happily blends a great deal of sense with the lighter matter of the piece.[56]

Even so, the policy of secrecy was maintained. Cassandra said nothing of the novel when she wrote to Phylly in March; her most important piece of family news was that her 'eldest nephew' – Edward – had just kept his first term at St John's. Charles and Fanny were too busy to have much time for reading. Charles was now captain of the *Namur* and Fanny and the children were living with him on board ship. Cassandra rather doubted whether the scheme for this aquatic abode would prove entirely practicable during the winter, but it seemed they found their residence tolerably comfortable. It was by so much the cheapest home that Fanny could have hoped to find that she was ready to put up with some little inconveniences.

In April, Edward came from Godmersham with Fanny and her cousin Fanny Cage to pay one of his biannual visits to the Chawton estate; and since the Middletons were still in residence at the great house, they all stayed at the cottage. Fanny, of course, knew all about the book and would chatter on about literary topics on their walks with Miss Middleton to Farringdon and back. But, like most young girls of eighteen, Fanny had more exciting things than books on her mind. She was in the throes of a first romance with her neighbour Mr Plumptre of Kent. There were eleven Plumptre children, and Jane and Cassandra liked to debate with Fanny which of the two Miss Plumptres was the eldest. In the evenings, there was singing around the piano with Jane and sometimes even a little country dancing. Fanny felt a little awkward about the dancing, though. Mr Plumptre disliked dancing, she said, and similar amusements which, he believed, 'ought to be eschewed and avoided by Christian people'.[57] Mr Plumptre was evidently a man of strict principles and good habits, said Jane, all of which must make him a very worthy companion. All the same, she was not entirely convinced that a love of country dancing made her any the worse a Christian.

In June, Jane and Mrs Austen paid a visit to Steventon, returning, at the end of the month, with Anna. As soon as she was safely back at the cottage, Mrs Austen surprised them all by making a solemn declaration that this visit to her eldest son would be the last visit she would ever make. Jane and Cassandra were both at a loss to discover any reason for this abrupt pronouncement. Their mother had had one bad cold during the winter (as who had not?) but she seemed tolerably well in spirits and, at the age of seventy-two, contrived always to be busy and interested in her employments. Now that the fine weather was come, she talked with pleasure of all the labours that awaited her in the garden, and with positive *delight* of almost living out of doors.[58] To Jane, it seemed quite perverse that her mother should choose this moment to shut herself away from the world, just when it appeared that, for Jane herself, many new doors were opening. *She* returned from Steventon to find all kinds of good news about *Sense and Sensibility*. The *British Critic* had pronounced it 'a very pleasing and entertaining narrative',[59] and Egerton was soon informing her that all copies of the first edition had been sold. She could scarcely believe her 'great good fortune' when she learnt that the book had made her a 'prodigious recompense of over £100', 'for that which had cost her nothing'.[60] She immediately set about revising 'First Impressions' to see whether that too might enjoy a similar success.

The authorial secrecy which had begun (at Cassandra's insistence) out of motives of prudence and modesty, now became a delicious game of hide-and-seek. Anna was become a great devotee of the circulating library at Alton. She would run over all the latest novels and then relate them to Jane while she sat stitching away at her charity work. On one occasion, searching through the library volumes, Anna came across a copy of *Sense and Sensibility*. Immediately, she threw the book aside, with a little gesture of contempt, and exclaimed aloud, 'Oh that must be rubbish I am sure from the title.' Naturally, Jane, who was with her at the time, affected to enjoy much private amusement at her niece's apparent ingenuousness. Only later did it occur to her to wonder whether the joke was on her after all. In the Niagara Falls of Anna's wit, had she just received a dousing?[61]

Suddenly, all the nieces, too, were trying their skills at storytelling. The Steventon girls would bring Jane their verses and stories and pester her for her opinions. She told Caroline that writing stories was a great amusement, and *she* thought a harmless one, though many people, she was aware, thought otherwise. (It would hardly do, she thought, for Fanny to tell the strict Mr Plumptre that her aunt not only danced but *wrote novels* as well!) But at Caroline's age (she was barely eight), she thought it a mistake to be too much taken up with her own compositions. She should cease writing till she was sixteen, she told her. She herself had often wished she had *read* more and written *less* in the corresponding years of her own life.[62] But Anna was already well past sixteen, and possessed of a strong sense of the ridiculous.

Later that summer (with Jane's encouragement), Anna scribbled several chapters of a mock-heroic story with no other foundation than their having seen a neighbour passing by in the coach to an unknown destination. There must be some mighty mystery in this, they agreed, and gave the tale a gloriously Gothic title – 'The Car of Falkenstein'. When Cassandra returned from Godmersham, she grew quite fatigued at the constant repartee of literary nonsense between her sister and her niece. 'How *can* you both be so foolish?' she would protest, begging them both to leave off.[63] Anna's own literary tastes ran always towards sensibility rather than sense, and the tears of her heroine flowed without ceasing throughout 'The Car of Falkenstein'. A favourite book with her was Mrs Hunter's *Lady Maclairn, the Victim of Villainy*. This was another splendidly lachrymose piece in which all the characters, male and female alike, were given to sudden bouts of tearfulness. After returning to Steventon in September, Anna sent Jane several sketches in Mrs Hunter's vein, depicting such sepulchral spots as a gloomy abbey, a satanic mill and a lonely tomb. Replying, Jane assumed the appropriate tone of sentimental excess. 'Miss Jane Austen's tears have flowed over each sweet sketch in such a way as would do Mrs Hunter's heart good to see,' she wrote. She only hoped that Hampshire's own 'Mrs Hunter' might be provided 'with a more safe conveyance to London than Alton can now boast'.[64] If not, the tearful young lady of Steventon might suffer a similar fate to the unfortunate hero of *Love and Freindship*, overturned in his phaeton and mistaken by his wife for a leg of mutton. For, she warned, 'the Car of Falkenstein, which was the pride of that town, was overturned within the last 10 days'.

For Jane, the indulgence in such light-hearted literary diversions as these afforded both a recreation and a refuge. For years, her comic sketches and burlesque dramas had provided entertainments at home; even as her novels grew longer and more serious, she seldom failed to include such witty episodes or comic scenes as might be read aloud at family parties. Now that she had the opportunity to address herself to a vast and unknown public, she experienced a not inconsiderable anxiety. It was not exactly that she either feared or disdained the vulgarity (as some might call it) of becoming a professional lady novelist. Rather that she found it difficult to reconcile the character of 'aunt Jane', who seldom voiced a serious opinion, with the authority of a lady novelist, whose opinions must be constantly on display. There was something almost shocking about such a complete exposure. Many years ago she had written (in a novel as yet unpublished) this sentence: 'A woman especially, if she have the misfortune of knowing anything, should conceal it as well as she can.' But for a woman who set herself up as a novelist there could be no such concealment. Her opinions must be openly declared from her very first paragraph. 'It is a truth universally acknowledged, that a single man in possession of a good fortune must be in want of a wife.' There was an opinion which she would scarcely dare to utter at a private dinner-table of Digweeds, Prowtings and Benns. But soon it would be open and published, and available for all to read. The thought of it gave her a strange sensation of mingled guilt and exultation. Though her writing might be done in private, and her identity kept secret, all the brilliance and the cleverness that she delighted in would be exposed for all to see.

For practical purposes, she contrived for herself a kind of middle way between secrecy and self-display. At her little writing-table in the drawing-room she was often to be seen scribbling letters, or composing the little comic sketches which might be read aloud to family or friends. When it came to writing her novels, more privacy was required. She would write these at the same table when she was alone there in the mornings; or in the evenings, when her mother was nodding by the fireside knitting gloves and Cassandra was occupied with satin stitch. The room was luckily provided with a creaking door, to alert her to the approach of strangers. Whenever she heard its warning sound, she had time enough to conceal her notebooks before welcoming their guests.[65] Throughout that summer, while guests saw her diverting herself with 'The Car of Falkenstein', she was privately engaged in revising 'First Impressions'.

This novel, though written almost fifteen years before, still pleased her and seemed in little need of drastic alteration. It was perhaps a little more brilliant and sparkling than anything she might now attempt; but once she had 'lopt and cropt' it, she felt quite satisfied, even a little vain, at the result. There was one vexation which hindered her work. Some years before, a woman of the name of Holford had had the temerity to publish her own novel, likewise entitled *First Impressions*. For Jane, it was a constant dread that she might find her own story and her characters 'all forestalled'.[66] At the very least, another title must be found, and she discovered it in one of her favourite novels, Miss Burney's *Cecilia*. In the pages of the fifth volume of *Cecilia*, the phrase 'Pride and Prejudice' was repeated three times in quick succession, and given greater prominence by being printed in capitals. Apart from the pleasure of echoing Miss Burney, this phrase also had the happy distinction of providing a nice parallel with *Sense and Sensibility*. Henceforth, 'First Impressions' would be known as *Pride and Prejudice*.

Many of her revisions were of a purely formal kind. She changed the dates to match the calendar for the year just gone, but made few attempts to alter the manners or the style. There were, she was sure, just as many handsomely uniformed George Wickhams waiting to ruin the reputations of silly girls they met at country balls as ever there had been in 1796. And the truth 'universally acknowledged' in her opening sentence, concerning a single man, a good fortune and a wife, had lost none of its application in the intervening years. The manuscript was despatched to Egerton in the autumn, who replied with remarkable promptness. This time, there was no question of publication 'on commission', and Egerton was eager, she noticed, to secure the copyright to himself. '*P & P* is sold,' she told Martha at the end of November. 'Egerton gives £110 for it.'[67] Gratified as she was, she was also sufficiently vain to suspect that more money might have been gained by offering the work to more than one publisher. It was almost twenty years since Mrs Radcliffe had earned £500 for her *Mysteries of Udolpho*, and Jane had learnt from Frank's example that it was not always wise to accept the first offer. 'I would rather have had £150,' she told Martha, 'but we could not both be pleased, & I am not at all surprised that he should not chuse to hazard so much.' She herself might have been willing to hazard for more, but in this matter, like most others, she was not entirely a free agent. Henry was her negotiator in the business, and Henry was never the shrewdest or most determined of bargainers. 'It's being sold will I hope be a great saving of trouble to Henry,' she acknowledged, '& therefore must be welcome to me. The money is to be paid at the end of the twelvemonth.'[68]

Any rejoicing that she felt at the prospect of having a second novel in print had to be severely muted. For whilst she was in the midst of negotiations with Egerton, there came news from Kent of the sad death of Mrs Knight. The old lady left a donation of £20 to be distributed among the poor of Chawton parish, but Jane was relieved to find there was no mention of the spinning-wheel. The most obvious consequence of her death was that Edward was now obliged, by the terms of old Mr Knight's will, to give up the name of Austen and become a Knight himself. 'We have reason to suppose the change of name has taken place,' Jane wrote in her letter to Martha, 'as we have to forward a letter to Edward Knight Esqre from the lawyer who has the management of the business.' Fanny seemed quite distraught at the change. 'We are therefore all *Knights* instead of dear old *Austens*,' she wrote. 'How I hate it!!!!!!' It was affectingly perverse, Jane thought, for the girl to take so much pleasure in the material benefits of the Godmersham inheritance, and yet make such a mighty protest at the name which provided it. She preferred to register her own distaste for her brother's new designation in a less histrionic fashion; 'I must learn to make a better K,' she remarked drily to Martha. She did, though, feel a certain repugnance at this sudden obliteration of the Austen name. When Edward next appeared in Chawton, accompanied by Fanny, Lizzie and their cousin Mary Deedes, it pleased her to treat him in the style of a visiting Eastern potentate. 'Edward & his harem' was how she described them.[69]

Mischievous remarks like these, however, were rather too much in the manner of Elizabeth Bennet to be frequently admitted. Cassandra and her mother were much on the alert for any tell-tale signs of authorial vanity on her part, to say nothing of Fanny, still under the influence of the strict Mr Plumptre. Jane judged it altogether more prudent to adopt the style of her newest heroine, the modest Fanny Price, to dispel any suspicions of inflated self-esteem. 'You have obliged me to eat humble-pie indeed,' she told Martha, who, despite all her selfless and valiant labours at the bedside of poor Mrs Dundas, had yet found time to send her a lengthy letter.

Having once decided on her humble-pie diet, Jane set about it with an appropriate self-mortifying relish. Martha was 'made for doing good,' she wrote, not only 'physicking little children' but conferring a 'mental physick' on Mrs Dundas which 'bears a stamp beyond all common charity'.[70] She herself could only stand in awe of such conspicuous goodness, though she did her best to imitate Martha's virtue with careful enquiries about calico and woollens for elderly relatives and friends. She and Cassandra were much concerned for poor Miss Benn, whose long fur tippet was almost worn out. 'Something of the shawl kind to wear over her shoulders within doors in very cold weather might be useful,' she thought, though 'it must not be very handsome or she would not use it.' Yet, despite her best endeavours, something of the Bennet mockery could not be entirely subdued. She could not resist penning a wicked quatrain on Miss Wallop, who had finally caught herself a husband in the shape of an elderly curate called Wake ('Having in vain danced at many a ball,' she wrote, the lady was 'now very happy to jump at a Wake'). The lines were in poor taste perhaps (and had been refined somewhat by James); but thoughts of the belated bride Phylly Walter sitting by her new husband's sick-bed had put the idea in her mind. ('Of what a mistake were you guilty in marrying a man of his age!' as Lady Susan declared: 'just old enough to be formal, ungovernable and to have the gout – too old to be agreable, and too young to die.')[71] The most prudent expedient, she decided, was to disguise all her pleasures as *duties*. They were already planning their Christmas duties, she wrote, which were to include 'eating turkies' and 'laying out Edward's money for the poor'.

CHAPTER 11

Wild Beast

━━━

If I am a wild beast, I cannot help it. It is not my own fault.

Jane Austen, Letter to Cassandra, May 1813

'Solemn, specious nonsense'

Less than a week before *Pride and Prejudice* was due to be published, Cassandra left Chawton for a visit to Steventon. The visit had been long arranged and there seemed no solid reason to postpone it. The fact of her not being at home would not delay the appearance of Jane's book for as much as a single day, and there would be ample time to admire it in the months and years ahead. Naturally, Jane acknowledged the justice of her sister's remarks; there was no reason whatever why the family's movements should be at the mercy of Mr Egerton's schedules. All the same, she could not conceal some disappointment that Cassandra felt no desire to share with her the happy moment of her 'darling child's' first appearance. It seemed somewhat akin to the way her mother had suddenly declared her intention to shut herself up from the world. It would be too severe a reflection to suspect either her mother or her sister of envy. But there was undoubtedly an absence of that frank and open joy she had hoped for in their reactions to her success.

Now that she felt herself possessed of a modest fortune (with the hope of more to come), Jane felt some irritation at Cassandra's obstinate thriftiness, as when she delayed sending a letter from Steventon till she could make use of Mr Chute's frank. Jane was tired of all such mean economies. She disliked it when the Clements insisted on taking her to a village party in their 'tax-cart', a sorry one-horse open farm-cart, made purposely mean to avoid the duty on carriages. Inevitably, she felt compelled to accept their offer ('civility on both sides'), though 'I would rather have walked, & no doubt *they* must have wished I had'. She made sure to escape their hospitality on the return journey: 'I ran home with my own dear Thomas at night in great luxury.'[1]

Luxury was now what she longed for, but there was little of it to be found at Chawton. As a party host, Mr Papillon was anxious, fidgety and barely conversible. Try as she might, Jane could discover nothing very promising in the way of an intrigue between him and Miss Terry in his absent manner of neglecting to help Miss T. to slices of mutton. Yet she did her best to spice even this carelessness with a hint of scandal. 'There might be design in this, to be sure, on his side; – he might think an empty stomach the most favourable for love.' Miss Benn wore her new shawl all evening – nothing very scandalous there, though Mr Papillon's niece, Jane thought, had something of the air of a rejected lover. The greatest luxury was to be free of them all, and walk through the muddy lanes to Alton on a crisp winter's morning entirely alone. Her mother might be glad to be visited by Miss Beckford ('thinner than ever'), Miss Wools and Miss Harriet Benn, but Jane was 'very glad' to escape them. Nor was she greatly delighted when Miss Papillon 'invited herself very pleasantly' to be her walking companion one morning. '*I* had a very agreable walk,' she noted; 'if *she* had not, more shame for her, for I was quite as entertaining as she was.'[2]

Though she performed her village charities diligently enough, taking Mrs Garnet an old shift and promising her a set of Austen linen, Jane was too full of literary excitement to lend much serious attention to local matters. And she was quite at a loss to account for all the grumbles and grumpiness that reached her from Steventon.

Cassandra seemed in a perpetual sulk about dirty lanes and dismal weather. 'A very sloppy lane, last Friday!' Jane retorted. 'What an odd sort of country you must be in! I cannot at all understand it.' Yes, perhaps it *was* cold on Wednesday, 'but nothing terrible'; and perhaps the lanes were a little 'greasy'. But 'upon the whole, the weather for winter-weather is delightful, the walking excellent'. She could not resist taunting her sister in her self-imposed gloomy exile. 'I cannot imagine what sort of place Steventon can be!'

When she was not out walking, Jane was reading. Now, she read everything she could lay her hands on – not just novels, but works of history, politics and foreign travels. She read Carr's *Travels in Spain*, Clarkson's *Abolition of the African Slave Trade*, Buchanan's *Christian Researches in Asia* and Captain Pasley's *Essay on the Military Policy and Institutions of the British Empire*. Captain Pasley was her favourite. No longer content with fanciful, ladylike romances, she eagerly studied and endorsed Pasley's sobering argument that 'Nothing but our naval superiority has saved us from being at this moment a province of France.' Such sentiments only confirmed her belief that it was upon men like Frank that the whole liberty of the nation depended. She was almost 'in love' with Captain Pasley, she told Cassandra, 'the first soldier I ever sighed for; but he does write with extraordinary force & spirit'.[3]

Suddenly, everyone in Chawton seemed to be reading, Miss Benn, Miss Papillon and even Mrs Digweed; 'we quite run over with books.' Jane heard that the Miss Sibleys of West Meon were set upon establishing their own Book Society, 'like ours', on their side of the county. Here was another excuse for crowing. 'What can be a stronger proof of that superiority in ours over the Steventon & Manydown society, which I have always foreseen & felt,' she wrote. Cassandra, she knew, was due to visit Manydown the following week, but instead of envying her good fortune, she chose to taunt her. She imagined her sitting in her thin China crape amid the 'enormous great stupid thick quarto volumes' in the breakfast parlour there. 'Poor wretch!' she wrote, 'I can see you shivering away, with your miserable feeling feet.'[4]

At last, when the book appeared, all this taunting had to cease. 'I have got my own darling child from London,' she told Cassandra on 29 January. *Pride and Prejudice* 'by the Author of *Sense and Sensibility*' was advertised in the previous day's *Morning Chronicle*, priced at 18s. 'He shall ask £1–1s for my two next, & £1–8s for my stupidest of all,' Jane predicted. Almost at once, the *British Critic* declared *Pride and Prejudice* 'very far superior to almost all the publications of the kind which have come before us'. Yet among the family, a certain tact was required in presenting even such an acclaimed work. Henry had complicated matters in a typically Henryish way by mistaking her directions about the distribution of advance copies. He had sent one to Charles and another to Godmersham, 'just the two sets which I was least eager for the disposal of,' Jane complained. The brothers whose opinions she most wanted were Frank and James, but they had been sent no copies at all. So instead of receiving *their* congratulations, she was forced to send them *her* apologies. She begged Cassandra to apologize for her to James and Mary 'with my love'. 'I shall write to Frank,' she added, 'that he may not think himself neglected.'

It was curious how many apologies this publication seemed to entail, most especially to Cassandra. More than once, Jane felt herself compelled to hope that her sister would suffer no 'unpleasantness' as a result of the book's appearance. For Cassandra's sake, she wrote in one letter, she was almost relieved that no copy of *Pride and Prejudice* had yet been received at Steventon, 'as it might be unpleasant to you to be in the neighbourhood at the first burst of the business'. A week later, she wrote again. The caution observed at Steventon with regard to the publication of *Pride and Prejudice* was, she said, 'an agreable surprise to me, & I heartily wish it may be the means of saving you from everything unpleasant'.[5] But was it really such a terrible thing to have written a book of which the *British Critic* declared: 'the story is well told, the characters remarkably well drawn and supported, and written with great spirit as well as vigour.'[6] Even the pose of anonymity began to seem less like a prudent modesty and more like a symptom of shame. What was there for her to be ashamed of?

At Chawton, they played a trick on Miss Benn when the first copies arrived, by professing their utter ignorance of the author's identity. 'I believe it passed with her unsuspected,' said Jane. The three ladies devoted their subsequent evenings to reading the book aloud. For Jane, this was hardly an unalloyed pleasure ('I had some fits of disgust,' she told Cassandra). The principal problem was her mother's 'too rapid way of getting on', rattling through the dialogue as though impatient with it: 'tho' she perfectly understands the characters herself, she cannot speak as they ought.'[7] How greatly Jane missed Cassandra, who could have given each character the exact degree of wit and animation. Fanny's praise, sent to her in a letter that morning, was very gratifying. 'My hopes were tolerably strong of *her*,' she said, 'but nothing like a certainty. Her liking Darcy & Elizth is enough. She might hate all the others, if she would.' But Fanny was already something of a diplomat, and while her letter to Jane was 'all praise', she conveyed a more candid opinion in a letter to aunt Cassandra. This 'was not & is not less acceptable,' said Jane; even 'the more exact truth which she sends *you* is good enough'.[8] It was Cassandra's own judgement which Jane most feared and desired, and when it came, it filled her with pleasure. 'I am exceedingly pleased that you can say what you do, after having gone thro' the whole work.' All her love, all her reverence for her sister returned as she read Cassandra's remarks. If Cassandra approved of the book, there could be no higher commendation. Meanwhile, at home, the readings continued with her mother and Miss Benn. 'Still work for one evening more,' she remarked with resignation on Tuesday evening; 'it is raining furiously.'

By now, the pretence of anonymity was over. The Terrys of Dummer had passed on the secret to Mrs Digweed, who had passed it on to Miss Benn. It now seemed ill-mannered to exclude even the most indiscreet family members from sharing the secret. 'Yes, I believe I *shall* tell Anna,' she wrote to Cassandra; '& if you see her & do not dislike the commission, you may tell her for me.' However badly her mother read her lines, Miss Benn seemed constantly amused by them. 'Poor soul!' said Jane; '*that* she cd not help . . . with two such people to lead the way; but she really does seem to admire Elizabeth. I must confess that *I* think her as delightful a creature as ever appeared in print, & how I shall be able to tolerate those who do not like *her* at least, I do not know.'[9]

Even at such a distance (fifteen years since she had first written it!), she still found it quite impossible to be impartial about *Pride and Prejudice*. She allowed that it was perhaps 'rather too light & bright & sparkling', it wanted shade; 'it wants to be stretched out here & there with a long chapter – of sense if it could be had, if not of solemn specious nonsense . . .' As soon as she began to indulge herself by imagining just what this long solemn chapter might be, all her vanity, that vanity she had striven so hard to keep in check, burst forth in a gloriously insolent spirit of exultation. Why not something quite unconnected with the story? 'An Essay on Writing, a critique on Walter Scott, or the history of Buonaparte'? Or 'anything that would form a contrast & bring the reader with increased delight to the playfulness & epigrammatism of the general stile'.[10] Suddenly, in that brave moment, she felt as if there was nothing that she could not or dared not write. The *Critical Review* declared that *Pride and Prejudice* 'rises very superior to any novel we have lately met with in the delineation of domestic scenes. Nor is there one character which appears flat, or obtrudes itself upon the notice of the reader with troublesome impertinence.'[11] But Jane found herself rather in the mood for impertinence, troublesome or otherwise. She thought there could be few more impertinent things for an English spinster to write than a history of Buonaparte. Cassandra, she knew, would hardly approve of such recklessness. 'I doubt your quite agreeing with me here – I know your starched notions,' she wrote.

For the next few weeks, her mind was in a constant oscillation between exultation and apology. 'We admire your charades excessively,' she told Cassandra, anxious to assure her sister that she was not entirely taken up with her own literary concerns. There was 'so much beauty in the versification,' she said, that finding out the riddle was 'but a secondary pleasure'. 'I grant you that *this* is a cold day,' she added, as if in contrition for her earlier tauntings. She even contrived to catch cold herself, in sympathy with her poor sister shivering at Manydown, and then made it worse by her wilfulness in walking out in all weathers. As a penance, she would confine herself within doors, and punish herself by poring over all the misprints in the text of *Pride and Prejudice*. She was determined that her new novel must be as free from blunders as she could make it. From Sir John Carr's *Travels in Spain* she learnt that there was no Government House in Gibraltar ('I must alter it to the Commissioner's'), and she was anxious to know from Cassandra, or from anyone else who might furnish the information, whether Northamptonshire was indeed 'a country of hedgerows' as she designed it. *Mansfield Park*, she had decided, was to be devoted to a much more sober topic – one that Cassandra and even Mr Plumptre might wholeheartedly approve – ordination. She asked Cassandra to find out from James the length of time required for the process of ordination to be completed. This was to be a point of great importance for the *dénouement* of her plot.

Fanny Price was to be an altogether different kind of heroine from any whom Jane had yet portrayed. From the Laura of *Love and Freindship* to Lady Susan, Elinor Dashwood and Elizabeth Bennet, her heroines had habitually been lively and eloquent women, with something of the wild, defiant rebel about them. She loved the moment in *Pride and Prejudice* when Elizabeth presented herself at Netherfield with her petticoat six inches deep in mud, drawing from Miss Bingley the comment that 'she really looked almost wild'. And then the boldness of Elizabeth's retort to Mr Darcy after the man had rehearsed his definition of an accomplished woman: 'I am no longer surprised at your knowing *only* six accomplished women. I rather wonder now at your knowing *any*.' To be surrounded by all the insolence that wealth and power could bestow, and yet to be so unbowed! These were the satirical remarks and shocking sentiments that Jane herself had often longed, but seldom dared, to utter. Instead, she had placed them in the mouths of her heroines. *They* had expressed her defiance for her. She had grown to love this way of committing acts of impertinence by subterfuge. There was a kind of impromptu rebellion in the fantastical, improbable tales she invented for her nieces, and in the animated spirit with which she joined in all their childish games. She loved the power that her writing gave her to expose a Mr Collins, to humble a Lady Catherine de Bourgh, or to chasten a Mr Darcy.

Now, suddenly, it was as if all the constraints had been removed.

For the first time in her life, she had money of her own; hardly yet a fortune, but a modest competence sufficient to support an independence she could formerly only have dreamt of. Her mother and Cassandra no longer overwhelmed her with prudent advice; her mother seemingly determined upon withdrawal from the world, and Cassandra retreated to Steventon, whence her opinions seemed both diffident and distant. In their place were new voices, flattering, beguiling, full of praise.

Within weeks of its first appearance, *Pride and Prejudice* was established as the most fashionable novel of the season. According to Henry, the playwright Sheridan had told a lady he was dining with that *Pride and Prejudice* 'was one of the cleverest things he ever read'. Another literary gentleman, much celebrated for his wit, had solemnly informed Henry that it was 'much too clever to have been written by a woman'.[12] No longer a person who deferred to others, Jane Austen now found herself transformed into a person to whom others deferred. She dashed off a letter to Martha Lloyd, full of modish witticisms and fashionable French phrases. Henry was busily enquiring into the state of the hedgerows in Northamptonshire, she wrote, a commission she had been glad to give him '*sans peur et sans reproche*'. What was Martha's opinion on the Princess of Wales, she wanted to know, whose letter of grievances against her husband had just been reprinted in the *Hampshire Telegraph*? Jane was inclined to sympathize with her. 'Poor woman,' she wrote, 'I shall support her as long as I can, because she *is* a woman, & because I hate her husband.'[13] In her newly elevated self-esteem, it even occurred to her that support from the lady author of *Pride and Prejudice* might be useful to the beleaguered princess, and consequently ought not to be offered unconditionally. 'I can hardly forgive her calling herself "attached & affectionate" to a man whom she must detest,' she wrote. 'I do not know what to do about it; but if I must give up the princess, I am resolved at least always to think that she would have been respectable, if the prince had behaved only tolerably by her at first.' She affected a certain ease in talking of princes and princesses, as if they were her familiar companions, instead of Digweeds, Prowtings and Benns. Why should she not write a history of

Buonaparte? At times she felt greatly tempted to indulge the Buonaparte instinct within herself. From Manydown, Cassandra wrote
that Mrs Sclater of neighbouring Tangier Park was continuing her
fussy interventions. 'Kill poor Mrs Sclater if you like it' was her
imperious reply.[14]

Much as she loved the power and the praise that came with all
this sudden success, she was also rational enough to distrust them.
She was only half a rebel. As with her brother Frank, her own
insolence of spirit was coupled to an even stronger sense of Christian duty. Too much liberty, as events in France had surely demonstrated, was as great an evil, if not greater, than too much
submission, and must ineluctably lead to the destruction of any
liberty at all. As she felt the constraining influences of mother,
sister, family and friends begin to weaken and diminish, overwhelmed by the fashionable choruses of praise from literary
London, Jane experienced a disturbing moral dilemma. No longer
obliged to be modest and self-effacing, one part of her longed for
the notoriety, the celebrity of a Buonaparte or a Princess Caroline;
but another, and deeper, part of her strove to recreate the very
constraints she had loved to jeer at with identical, yet more powerful, constraints of her own invention.

In Fanny Price she chose a heroine whose virtues were of the
silent, rather than the eloquent, kind. Rarely invited to offer an
opinion (and even when called upon to do so, usually declining
to attempt anything so presumptuous), she was to be a heroine
who, even in her most private thoughts, must be entirely innocent
of wit. She was to be a submissive character, in everything that
bore no taint of vice; diffident and self-denying, and guilty only
of that species of self-mortifying humility which, to those with
the sensitivity to observe such things, might seem to carry the
implication of moral reproach. There was, indeed, a degree of
self-reproachfulness in the writing of this new novel, *Mansfield
Park*. When Jane read, in *Coelebs in Search of a Wife*, Hannah
More's critical remarks on 'how little justice has been done to the
clerical character in those popular works of the imagination which
are intended to exhibit a picture of living manners', she could
not but reflect on how far her own portrait of Mr Collins had

contributed to the popular ridicule of a profession for which she had the highest respect.[15] Greatly as she relished the sudden acclaim of literary London which greeted *Pride and Prejudice*, she could not entirely silence an inner voice of conscience which distrusted the values of a metropolis so dedicated to modish novelties and so easily seduced by displays of epigrammatic wit.

As a contrast to Fanny Price, she created the character of Mary Crawford, the model of the sophisticated modern woman such as was to be found everywhere in London society. Mary was a character whom it was easy to imagine. She was a character that Jane had spent her life perfecting; witty, bold and free. Her lines, wicked, clever and teasing, were (or had been) Jane's own lines. It was glorious to imagine Miss Crawford's *bon mot* on the subject of the country clergy ('A clergyman has nothing to do but to be slovenly and selfish – read the newspaper, watch the weather, and quarrel with his wife. His curate does all the work, and the business of his own life is to dine').[16] It was a delight to deliver Miss Crawford's indelicate witticism on naval men and manners ('My home ... brought me acquainted with a circle of admirals. Of *Rears*, and *Vices*, I saw enough. Now do not be suspecting me of a pun, I entreat'). What would be more difficult would be to repudiate such wit, or to make Miss Crawford's style of mental liveliness the symptom of an inner depravity. Yet that was the task which Jane now set herself to accomplish.

'Naked cupids'

In March, the Middletons left the great house, where they had been living for five years, and Edward (Edward *Knight*, as Jane must now call him) arrived to occupy it with all his family. They were dismayed at what they found. 'We are half frozen at the cold uninhabited appearance of the old house,' Fanny complained.[17] Naturally, she was used to all the comforts of Godmersham. Perhaps she should try the wretched ruin of a place Miss Benn was forced to live in, Jane thought. It had been quite terrible for her during all the storms of wind and rain. And now Old Philmore, the landlord, was even threatening to drive her out of it. Whatever would become of her?

Edward brought dismal news from London concerning Eliza's health. So dismal that Jane insisted on accompanying him back to Sloane Street the next day. Eliza's illness had been long and painful. It was a wretched thing to see that brave, defiant woman suffering as she did. The end could not be far away, said Henry, and so it proved. Eliza died just three days later; 'a release at last,' said Jane. The former countess was buried in Hampstead parish churchyard alongside her mother and son. 'A woman of brilliant, generous and cultivated mind' were the words chosen by Henry for her epitaph. It was a fitting tribute, Jane thought, if a little tame. She preferred her private memories of the irrepressible young woman who had fired her childish imagination with fabulous tales of the Queen of France adorned in sumptuous Turkish silks, of Indian princes and their costly jewels, and of daring balloonists soaring high above Paris.

Jane returned to Hampshire the following week, but was not entirely surprised when Henry soon discovered he could not do without her assistance in settling Eliza's affairs. Together they travelled back to Sloane Street in mid-May. Though the occasion that drew her to London was a melancholy one, she was not depressed in spirits. In fact, she relished the prospect of basking in her new-found fame. 'I never saw the country from the Hog's Back so advantageously,' she boasted; 'it was an excellent journey & very thoroughly enjoyed by me.'[18]

'Before I say anything else,' she wrote to Cassandra the following day, 'I claim a paper full of halfpence on the drawingroom mantelpiece; I put them there myself & forgot to bring them with me.' She rather liked that as an opening gambit. She knew how all the Chawton folks suspected her indulgence in what Phylly Walter would call the 'dissipated life' of London. She would let them know she had not become so very grand as not to know the value of a halfpenny as well as another. 'I cannot say that I have yet been in any distress for money,' she admitted, 'but I chuse to have my due as well as the devil.' Actually, she knew, there was no way to defeat such settled prejudices. If she were expensive in her tastes, they would accuse her of excessive luxury; if she were modest, then meanness would be the charge. At Guildford, she bought some gloves for just 4s; 'upon hearing which', she knew 'everybody at Chawton will be hoping & predicting that they cannot be good for anything'.[19] She loved to mock her prudent sister's solicitude on her behalf. The weather for her journey 'was delightful', she said, which made her fancy 'it might then be raining so hard at Chawton as to make you feel for us much more than we deserved'.

Once arrived in London, she felt her spirits soar with a kind of heady excitement. She was determined to be quite brilliant, polishing her every phrase into an epigram. She paid a visit to young Charlotte Craven at school, and was amused to find the drawing-room 'so totally un-school-like'. 'It was full of all the modern elegancies,' she noted, '& if it had not been for some naked cupids over the mantlepiece, which must be a fine study for girls, one should never have smelt instruction.'[20] *That* was a *bon mot* that might have done for Mary Crawford, she thought. A London school, even without its naked cupids, was hardly the place for Fanny Price.

Henry had now determined to leave Sloane Street and move to an apartment above his business premises in Henrietta Street. Jane confessed to being just a little surprised at how easily he had reconciled himself to Eliza's death. But then, she reasoned with herself, 'his mind is not a mind for affliction. He is too busy, too active, too sanguine.' Sincerely as Henry had loved Eliza, and excellently as he had behaved towards her, he was well used to being away from her at times, and consequently the loss of her was 'not felt as that of many a beloved wife might be'. In other ways he was still the old Henry, full of grand schemes for escorting Jane to all the most fashionable sights in town; schemes which, as often as not, were frustrated by unforeseen mishaps. They were to have gone to the exhibition of paintings at Somerset House, but a series of unaccountable mistakes and delays left her driving about town all day with Mr Tilson until it was 'too late for anything but home'.

They *did* go to the exhibition at Spring Gardens, where Jane allowed her vanity to run wild. So full as the world was of chatter about her heroines, she fancied she saw their likenesses in the portraits before her. A sweet-faced miniature of a lady 'dressed in a white gown, with green ornaments' must certainly be designed for Jane Bingley, she believed. It was so 'excessively like her', 'exactly herself . . . there never was a greater likeness'. The portrait convinced her, she said, 'of what I had always supposed, that green was a favourite colour with her'. 'I dare say Mrs D[arcy] will be in yellow,' she added.[21] But alas! even she could not distinguish Elizabeth Darcy's features in any of the portraits that she found there, nor at Sir Joshua Reynolds' exhibition, which she visited the next day. 'I can only imagine that Mr D prizes any picture of her too much to like it should be exposed to the public eye,' she wrote to Cassandra. 'I can imagine he wd have that sort of feeling – that mixture of love, pride & delicacy.' Actually, she knew, it was *she* who harboured these feelings. It flattered her vanity to imagine her creature, Jane Bingley, on public display; but Elizabeth was too personal, too precious a creation to be conceived by any mind but her own. Fanny endeavoured to amuse her with a letter contrived in the style of Darcy's sister Georgiana, but Jane excused herself from replying in similar vein. 'Even had I more time, I should not feel at all sure of the sort of letter that Miss D would write,' she lied. In reality, she disliked these attempts to mimic and appropriate her characters. They were *hers*, they belonged to her alone. Only she could know how they really wrote and thought and spoke.

At the Henrietta Street bank, Henry insisted on opening a new account for her ('to my great amusement,' she remarked). Money was flowing in at a most agreeable rate, and it quite shocked her to find how much she enjoyed it. 'Every copy of *S & S* is sold,' she told Frank, who was away on HMS *Elephant* in the Baltic; 'it has brought me £140 – besides the copyright, if that shd ever be of any value. I have now therefore written myself into £250 – which only makes me long for more.' On Sunday, she attended fashionable services at Belgrave chapel in the morning and at St James's in the evening. She drank tea with the Tilsons, dined with Lady Drummond Smith and drove with Henry to Windsor ('a great delight').

Everywhere she went, she seemed to meet her own creations in the shape of friends, neighbours or perfect strangers. London was one vast exhibition, and she herself, she discovered, was a prime exhibit. But was she, she wondered, a more suitable specimen to be included in Mr Bullock's Museum among the pig-tailed baboons and vampire bats, or to be admired among the handsome surroundings of Spring Gardens? 'If I *am* a wild beast, I cannot help it,' she declared. 'It is not my own fault.' Driving about town in the 'solitary elegance' of an open carriage was such a glorious sensation that she felt 'ready to laugh all the time'. But was this really *her*? 'I could not but feel that I had naturally small right to be parading about London in a barouche,' she confessed to Cassandra.[22] Undeniably, it was a far more agreeable experience than being transported around Chawton in the Clements' mean little tax-cart. But what would Cassandra think of such excessive vanity?

In the still of the evenings, alone at Sloane Street, she allowed more sober reflections to occupy her mind. Henry already spent most of his time at Henrietta Street, and she was often left to her own private thoughts. 'The quietness of it does me good,' she wrote, as if too much excitement might perhaps do her evil. 'I am very snug with the front drawing-room all to myself,' she told Cassandra, '& would not say "thank you" for any companion but you.' Cassandra was still her rock, her preserver from temptation. There was 'no change in our plan of leaving London,' she assured her. 'There is no danger of our being induced to stay longer.' In *Mansfield Park*, she depicted London as the source of all depravity. 'We do not look in great cities for our best morality,' Edmund Bertram declared. But was it really so depraved to drink claret wine and sit in a box at the theatre? Henry had never been much inclined to self-denial. When Jane returned to Hampshire, he ordered three dozen bottles of claret to be sent down to Chawton with her and placed on Edward's account.[23]

It was a happy summer of daily visits between the children at the great house and their aunts at the cottage. Following the death of Mrs Knight, Edward had given orders for Godmersham to be thoroughly redecorated. As late as July, his physician Scudamore was still quite decided in his opinion that the place was not 'fit to be inhabited' and spoke of 'two months more' being necessary 'to sweeten it'. 'My brother will probably go down & sniff at it himself & receive his rents,' Jane wrote to Frank. She was pleased to have Edward at Chawton, with all his talk of laying out new gardens and lawns. 'We like to have him proving & strengthening his attachment to the place,' she wrote, adding that Edward really seemed to be enjoying himself 'as thoroughly as any Hampshire born Austen can desire'.[24] She thought Frank might relish that sly reflection on a brother who now styled himself a Kentish Knight. Now that the secret of her authorship of *Pride and Prejudice* was a secret no more, some of the younger Austens seemed quite alarmed to think they had such a famous aunt. From Steventon, James Edward, not yet fifteen, sent her some verses.

No words can express, my dear aunt, my surprise
Or make you conceive how I opened my eyes,
Like a pig butcher Pile has just struck with a knife,
When I heard for the very first time in my life
That I had the honour to have a relation,
Whose works were dispersed through the whole of the nation.[25]

If this was intended as flattery, Jane could not help thinking the boy's choice of similes left much to be desired. As she read the rest of the poem, she rather feared she could detect a lame attempt at satire.

Now if you will take your poor nephew's advice,
Your works to Sir William pray send in a trice;
If he'll undertake to some grandees to show it,
By whose means at least the Prince Regent may know it,
For I'm sure if he did, in reward for your tale,
He'd make you a countess at least, without fail,
And indeed if the Princess should lose her dear life
You might have a good chance of becoming his wife.

Whatever her opinions of the Princess might be, Jane had certainly no desire to succeed her or supplant her. Poor James Edward! Now he had not only his sister's Niagara wit to contend with, but also his aunt's novels. It was little wonder if the boy felt somewhat overwhelmed by such daunting literary ladies. The facetious suggestion that Jane might harbour aristocratic ambitions was too absurd to be countenanced, even as a joke; but she did acknowledge an agreeable sensation of freedom in her new status as a successful authoress.

Away at Stoneleigh, Mr Thomas Leigh had finally died at the grand old age of seventy-nine, leaving 'one of the finest estates in England & . . . more worthless nephews & nieces than any other private man in the united kingdoms'.²⁶ Now at last Jane could view their squabbles with perfect equanimity, unlike some of her female relatives. 'Poor Mrs L[eigh] P[errot],' she wrote to Frank, with barely concealed amusement; she 'would now have been Mistress of Stoneleigh had there been none of that vile compromise, which in good truth has never been allowed to be of much use to them.' After all their higgling and wrangling, she thought, 'it will be a hard trial'.

Fanny was now Jane's greatest admirer. Often the two of them would spend whole mornings in private together, when the girl would pour out all her hopes and fears concerning Mr John Pemberton Plumptre. It was as if she considered Jane an authority on affairs of the heart, and Jane, while modestly disclaiming any particular expertise in such matters, offered the kind of advice that sagacious aunts were expected to dispense. The girl was much troubled by the young man's *goodness*, she said. He was so sober, so solemn and strict. As to that, Jane told her, she could admit no solid objection. No, not even if by *goodness* she meant that he inclined to become Evangelical. 'I am by no means convinced that we ought not all to be Evangelicals,' she said. She found herself more often now in a mood for such unfashionable expressions of piety, as they would soon discover from *Mansfield Park*. But the man had no *wit*, Fanny persisted. Beside her brothers, he often seemed dull and cold. 'Wisdom is better than wit,' Jane replied, '& in the long run will certainly have the laugh on her side' ('there is not the least wit in my nature,' Edmund Bertram boasted).[27] Fanny thanked her for her advice, but seemed strangely unwilling to accept it. This was not quite what she had hoped or expected to hear from the creator of Elizabeth Bennet.

After exhausting their serious conversation, they would fall to reading some favourite passages from *Pride and Prejudice*. Fanny was a fine reader, and the two of them would read with such lively animation that soon they would both be in peals of laughter. Outside the door, Fanny's sisters, Marianne and Louisa, were quite vexed to be excluded from all this merriment.[28] But when she read to them from *Mansfield Park*, they were none of them so diverted; not even Cassandra, for all her starched notions. It was Cassandra who warned Jane of the real fault in the new novel. If she designed it as a truly moral work, Cassandra said, then Fanny Price must marry Mr Crawford (a *reformed* Mr Crawford, naturally), not Edmund Bertram.[29] Jane acknowledged the justice of this observation, but was at a loss as to how bring it to effect.

The real difficulty with Fanny Price was that she was a heroine who had nothing to learn. Conceived from the start as a figure of faultless, if modest, virtue, she had none of those engaging frailties, those girlish vanities from which it must be equally the task of a conscientious authoress and upright hero to rescue her. Had it been Fanny who had longed at first for the frivolity of play-acting; had it been *she* who had fallen a helpless victim to Mr Crawford's easy charm, only to suffer the subsequent pangs of a painful disillusionment, it might have furnished the novel with that delightful sense of moral awakening which was one of the chief glories of any fictional work. But Fanny Price, *her* Fanny Price, could never be guilty of so much presumption, or deluded into such poor judgement. Her virtue was of a kind which kept itself apart. She was, as she described herself, a 'by-stander', seeing everything but saying nothing. The real challenge, Jane acknowledged, would have been to have engaged her characters of virtue (Fanny and Edmund) in an active process of change and reformation with her characters of vice (Henry and Mary Crawford). Such a scheme would have required a degree of contrivance, certainly; but a contrivance with its bias towards generosity and hope. The beginnings of this scheme, as Cassandra had noted, were already in place. They might be glimpsed in Mr Crawford's affecting reading of Shakespeare and in his solemn comments on the beauties of the liturgy. They were equally suggested by Mary Crawford's joy at Edmund's return *after* his ordination and by Fanny's pleasure at all the glee and frolic of her brother William's wit. In her concluding chapter, Jane even went so far as to acknowledge that, had Henry Crawford persevered 'and uprightly' in the process of reformation, 'Fanny must have been his reward – and a reward very voluntarily bestowed – within a reasonable period from Edmund's marrying Mary'.

It had been within her power to bestow that reward of mutual felicity upon all her characters. And yet she had drawn back from such a conclusion. It might have been easily done by bringing all her principals together for some event in which the new steadfastness of the ones and the new flexibility of the others might have combined to produce some salutary effect: the relief of a relative's distress; the rescue of a neighbour's fortunes; gallantry in the service of charity; righteousness in the cheerful disguise of hope. Yet, instead of bringing them together, she had separated and dispersed them to London, Portsmouth and Lessingby, where each might be confirmed in his or her favourite vanity; Fanny in her righteous self-denial, Edmund in his solemn self-deceit, Mary in her frivolous self-regard and Henry in his self-destroying trade of seduction. She was particularly severe in depicting the terrible consequences of play-acting. Just as Gisborne had predicted, the young ladies of Mansfield Park who vied for parts in *Lovers' Vows* were all condemned to unhappy fates, with only a difference of degree in their respective culpabilities: Maria, guilty of vice; Julia, of folly; and Mary Crawford, of a 'corrupted, vitiated mind'. The play had been like a contagion amongst them. Almost Sir Thomas Bertram's first action on returning to Mansfield Park was to burn 'every unbound copy of *Lovers' Vows* in the house'.[30]

Jane did not find it entirely easy to maintain such an austere moral view. It was not that the principles which underlay this new novel were alien to her; but they were unwarmed by any charitable vision of redemption and unrelieved by any forgiving wit. *Mans-*

field Park was an experiment in the didactic way of writing, and already she had anxieties about its likely success. 'I have something in hand,' she wrote to Frank, 'which I hope, on the credit of *P & P*, will sell well, tho' not half so entertaining.'[31] For all her new-found seriousness, Jane still had a horror of solemn piety and preachy perfectionism. It amused her greatly to read that the Reverend Blackall, that piece of 'noisy perfection', had recently married a Miss Lewis, late of Antigua. The thought of the Reverend Black-all's bride intrigued her. 'I would wish Miss Lewis to be of a silent turn & rather ignorant, but naturally intelligent & wishing to learn,' she wrote; 'fond of cold veal pies, green tea in the afternoon, & a green window blind at night.'[32] That was her Mary Crawford voice, irreverent and mocking. Fanny Price must never *preach*; though her piety might incline, at times, a little dangerously towards perfection, it could at least never be called 'noisy'. 'With you, Fanny,' as Edmund observed, 'there may be peace. You will not want to be talked to. Let us have the luxury of silence.'

'Money is dirt'

In June, Charles brought his family to stay, and when he and his wife went back to London, they left the two eldest girls, Cassy and Harriet, to remain for a month with their aunts in the country. On their return, it was most gratifying to hear how much the girls were thought to have improved – 'Harriet in health, Cassy in manners'. Harriet was a 'truly sweet-tempered little darling', Jane thought, and even Cassy '*ought* to be a very nice child'. 'Nature has done enough for her – but method has been wanting.'[33] Aunt Cassandra was very good at supplying *method*, but what would happen to the girls back in London? Cassy could be 'a very pleas-ing child', Jane thought, if Charles and Fanny would 'only exert themselves'. It was strange how, now that she had escaped the danger of being reduced to a governess's role, she could become quite governessy in her manner. Only Frank and his family were entirely absent from Chawton that summer, Frank aboard HMS *Elephant* in the Baltic and Mrs F.A. flitting from one lodging to another at Deal ('I think they must soon have lodged in every house in the town').[34]

In her letters to Frank, Jane did more than acquaint him with the latest family news; armed with opinions from Captain Pasley's *Essay on the Military Policy*, she also ventured some political thoughts of her own. 'Why are you like Queen Elizth?' she asked him. 'Because you know how to chuse wise ministers. Does not this prove you as great a captain as she was a queen?'[35] Frank might think these strange sentiments to receive from the sister who had once boldly pronounced it as Queen Elizabeth's 'peculiar misfortune . . . to have bad ministers'. 'Wicked as she was', Jane's *History of England* had declared, Queen Elizabeth 'could not have committed such extensive mischief, had not these vile and abandoned men connived at & encouraged her crimes.' But now, apparently, this 'wicked woman' had become a 'great queen', and these 'vile and abandoned men' were transformed into 'wise ministers'.

If Frank suspected his sister of satire here, he was only half correct, for the satire was directed at herself. Jane hereby formally abjured her juvenile fondness for romantic victims like the Queen of Scots. She had become, in her own mind at least, a wise politician. And politicians were well used to such changes of allegiance. Was not Frank's own mission intended to support our loyal ally Prince Bernadotte of Sweden? The same man who, just a few years before, had been our sworn enemy, Marshal Bernadotte of France. 'I have a great respect for former Sweden,' Jane declared. 'So zealous as it was for Protestantism!' She now loved to exercise the politician's talent for turning history into myth. How pleasant it must be, she thought, to voyage through such heroic lands. 'Your profession has its *douceurs*,' she wrote, 'to recompense for some of its privations; to an enquiring & observing mind like yours, such *douceurs* must be considerable. Gustavus-Vasa, & Charles 12th, & Christiana & Linnaeus, do their ghosts rise up before you?' All that rose up before Frank as he read this letter were the dark waters of the Baltic. His sister's readiness for imagining the *douceurs* of the sailor's life betrayed the charming naivety of her lady novelist's mind. Even his own ships, he now learnt, were to be immortalized in her latest fiction. 'By the bye,' she wrote, 'shall you object to my mentioning the *Elephant* in it, & two or three other of your old ships? I *have* done it, but it shall not stay to make you angry.'[36] Of course it did not make him angry. He was flattered by such a tender compliment. But it did amuse him to wonder how she might depict the *douceurs* of the lives of men who urinated and defecated on deck, who lived on salt beef and maggoty biscuits, and who were often called upon to witness floggings of fifty or a hundred lashes that tore a wretch's flesh to pulp.

Though her nieces claimed to take less pleasure in the sobriety of *Mansfield Park* than in the sparkling epigrams of *Pride and Prejudice,* Jane could not help noticing how, in real life, they all seemed determined to attach themselves to the most sober and solemn of matrimonial partners. Anna had now engaged herself to Ben Lefroy, the youngest son of that 'angelic woman' whose spirit still haunted Jane. Naturally, they were all anxious to have it 'go on well', there being 'quite as much in his favour as the chances are likely to give her in any matrimonial connection'. All the same, Jane could not entirely reconcile herself to the match. It had been done, as usual, with all Anna's customary impetuosity, and came upon them all 'without much preparation'. And although the young man was quite unexceptionable in character, being 'sensible, certainly very religious, well connected & with some independence', to say nothing of his appearance ('tall and handsome . . . [with] the charms of a very gentle voice and manner'), she still felt some 'apprehensions' about the attachment. There was, as she wrote to Frank, 'an unfortunate dissimularity of taste between them . . . He hates company & she is very fond of it; this, with some queerness of temper on his side & much unsteadiness on hers, is untoward.'[37] The proposed unions of two such volatile young women as Fanny and Anna to two such solemn young men as Mr Plumptre and Mr Lefroy would be quite as incongruous as a match between Mary Crawford and Edmund Bertram. When Anna's engagement was announced in August, there was little rejoicing at Steventon rectory. The girl was promptly packed off to Chawton, where she remained with her aunts for the next three weeks.

★　　★　　★

In mid-September, the summer house-party at Chawton finally broke up. Mr Scudamore had at last given his opinion that the family could return to Godmersham without fear of painter's colic. Edward promptly despatched an advance party of his youngest children and the household servants across country to Kent. He himself preferred to travel home in a more leisurely fashion, by way of London. He took Jane and his three eldest daughters to stay with Henry at Henrietta Street. It was only a visit of three days, but for Jane it was a gloriously hectic interlude of theatre visits, shopping trips, tea-parties, dinner-parties, card-parties, more theatre visits, invitations, compliments, new caps, new gowns, a new hairstyle and scarcely a moment to rest. 'We have not had a qr of an hour to spare,' she wrote to Cassandra in breathless excitement, enclosing a journal of her activities, scribbled in an urgent telegraph style. There was no time for elegant phrases. 'I am going to write nothing but short sentences,' she said. 'There shall be two full stops in every line.'[38] Her pen could scarcely keep up the pace. 'I must get a softer pen. This is harder. I am in agonies.' Lady Robert was delighted with *Pride and Prejudice*, and 'really *was* so', even before she knew who wrote it. And as to Mr Hastings – Jane was 'quite delighted with what such a man writes about it. Henry sent him the books after his return from Daylesford.' Oh dear, that was almost a full-length sentence. 'Let me be rational & return to my two full stops.' 'For we feel more & more how much we have to do. And how little time. This house looks very nice. It seems like Sloane St moved here.' The previous night they went to the theatre. 'We were in a private box. Mr Spencer's. Which made it much more pleasant. The box is directly on the stage. One is infinitely less fatigued than in the common way.' Did that last sentence sound too much like Lady Catherine de Bourgh? It was remarkable how a note of condescension could creep into even one's most telegraphic utterances. 'Oh, dear me, when shall I ever have done?'

She really *was* delighted at what Mr Hastings had said about *Pride and Prejudice*. 'His admiring my Elizabeth so much is particularly welcome to me.' She was only dismayed that he had not seen *Sense and Sensibility* yet. Even now, after Eliza was dead, he still kept the secret of her parentage, despite all Henry's promptings. 'Mr Hastings never *hinted* at Eliza in the smallest degree,' said Jane, who could not resist *hinting* herself.

They went to the playhouse every night, though *Don Juan* ('whom we left in Hell at ½ past 11') was their clear favourite. The girls revelled in the pantomime seducer's performance; '*my* delight was very tranquil,' Jane claimed. 'We had Scaramouch & a ghost – and were delighted.' Two nights later, having sat through *The Clandestine Marriage* ('no acting more than moderate'), *Five Hours at Brighton* ('in 3 acts, of which one was over before we arrived – none the worse'), *Midas* and *The Beehive*, it was still *Don Juan* which remained in her mind. 'I must say that I have seen nobody on the stage who has been a more interesting character than that compound of cruelty & lust,' she confessed. Fanny Price might find the language of Mrs Inchbald's *Lovers' Vows* 'unfit to be expressed by any woman of modesty'; but Jane Austen, in her London mode, rather relished the salacious boasts of this theatrical *Don Juan*. As they lay together in poor Eliza's bed that night, Jane teased Fanny by wondering what her Mr Plumptre might think of such a performance. A week later, she was able to hear the man's opinions in person when he presented himself at Godmersham Park. 'A handsome young man certainly,' was Jane's immediate opinion, 'with quiet, gentlemanlike manners'. However, she added, 'I set him down as sensible rather than brilliant. There is nobody brilliant nowadays' (apart from herself, of course!). To Frank, she complained that all the plays they had seen were mere 'sing-song and trumpery'. 'I believe the theatres are thought at a low ebb at present,' she wrote. Nobody brilliant there either.

Wealthy as she now thought herself, Jane found it touching that Edward should make her a present of £5 pocket money, just the same as he gave Fanny. 'Kind, beautiful Edward', she wrote, resolving to save up the money to share with Cassandra when she came to town. But Cassandra's movements were dependent on Henry, which meant of course that they were plagued with innumerable uncertainties and delays. 'Henry's plans are not what one could wish,' Jane wrote, as tactfully as she could. She sympathized with Cassandra's 'scruples' about leaving their mother, whose frequent headaches were being treated with leeches. Perhaps she should try the same remedy as Mrs Cooke, who had been plagued by 'the sensation of a peck loaf resting on [her] head' for several months. A quieting dose of calomel had done the trick for Mrs C. Might not the same remedy be tried by their mother?

At last, Jane grew tired of her sister's scruples and delays. 'Instead of saving my superfluous wealth for you to spend,' she wrote, 'I am going to treat myself with spending it myself.' Adorning herself like a literary heroine, she ordered a pert new cap of white satin and lace, 'and a little white flower perking out of the left ear, like Harriet Byron's feather'. Mr Hall called and set her hair all in curls. 'I thought it looked hideous . . . but my companions silenced me by their admiration.' Suddenly, she was become quite a connoisseur of all the latest fashions. Stays, she was pleased to announce, were now 'not made to force the bosom up at all; – *that* was a very unbecoming, unnatural fashion'. She bought some 'very nice plaiting lace at 3s 4d' and used the money left to buy some poplin for Cassandra. It was a present from her, she said. 'Don't say a word.'

The Godmersham girls were all in agonies with their teeth after visits to Mr Spence, the dental surgeon, who filed them and filled them, muttering all the time about their 'very bad state'. Poor Marianne had to have two teeth taken out. From outside the door, Jane and Fanny heard her screaming. But when the man began 'talking gravely' about Fanny's teeth too, Jane marked him down as a charlatan. 'The little girls' teeth I can suppose in a critical state,' she conceded, 'but I think he must be a lover of teeth & money & mischief to parade about Fanny's.' She kept her own mouth shut tight in Mr Spence's presence. 'I would not have had him look at mine for a shilling a tooth & double it.'[39] In the evenings, Henry entertained them all with accounts of his visit to Scotland. Scenes of higher beauty in Roxburghshire than anyone would have supposed. *Pride and Prejudice* warmly praised wherever he went: '& what does he do in the warmth of his brotherly vanity & love, but immediately tell them who wrote it!' Sometimes, Jane was driven to near distraction by Henry's well-meaning blunders.

Still, she found it hard not to pity him. He was in a poor state of health, and his stomach, like his plans, was 'rather deranged'. 'You must keep him in rhubarb,' she told Cassandra; '& give him plenty of port & water.'[40]

On the evening of 17 September they reached Godmersham, where they were much relieved to find all the rest of the family, who had travelled by various different means (eight of them by coach across country, two by chair and two on horseback), had arrived safely. 'It puts me in mind of the account of St Paul's shipwreck,' Jane wrote, 'where all are said by different means to reach the shore in safety.' She was rather given to such elevated comparisons at present, and wondered, in her letter to Frank, whether the King of Sweden were fully apprized of the fact that she was come to Godmersham.[41] Indeed, the place seemed worthy of a monarch's reception after its splendid redecoration. The Chintz Room, in particular, earned Jane's highest admiration. She caught a slight cold on the journey from London, which caused her some headaches, but hardly enough to depress her spirits. It was the first time in four years she had been at Godmersham, and she greatly relished the prospect of a long autumn stay – two months at least – in its spacious apartments. 'I am now alone in the library, mistress of all I survey,' she wrote, adapting Mr Cowper's lines on a poor ship-wrecked mariner to her own state of solitary splendour.

She began her letter to Cassandra with an extravagant flourish of thanks for one she had just received ('Thank you five hundred and forty times') and ended it with an even more lavish fanfare: 'Louisa's best love & a hundred thousand million kisses'. Her sense of regal splendour inspired her to such prodigal expressions of affection. ('He is a very liberal thanker, with his thousands and tens of thousands,' Mr Knightley sourly remarked of Frank Churchill.)[42] Yet no sooner had Jane tasted the delicious temptation of luxury, than she felt herself obliged to deny any lurking love of extravagance. One moment she would be asserting how absurd it was for Cassandra to make difficulties about accepting her gift of the poplin: 'Do not refuse me. I am very rich.' The next, she would be insisting that her dedication to thrift was still second to none. She was careful to send back eighteen pence that was due to her mother, together with exact accounts of all the fabrics she had bought. She also made dutiful enquiries about the precise state of Chawton provisions. Had they begun the new tea yet, or the new white wine? 'My present elegancies have not yet made me indifferent to such matters,' she insisted. 'I am still a cat if I see a mouse.' Writing to Frank the next day, she could boast of her sublime lack of concern about 'the price of bread or of meat where I am now; let me shake off vulgar cares & conform to the happy indifference of East Kent wealth'. Yet she did not fail to remind him of the 2s 3d that it had cost her to pay for the letter he sent to her ('very well worth it,' she added).[43]

It was in the elegant library at Godmersham that *Mansfield Park* was completed. This had long been one of her favourite rooms, and she was content to remain there for most of the day while the men of the house went about the grounds, shooting pheasants or netting rabbits. Sometimes Fanny would join her, and together they would pore over Bigland's *Modern History of Europe*, or recite passages aloud from Beattie's *The Hermit*. 'We live in the library except at meals,' she told Cassandra, '& have a fire every eveng.' But for the most part, she preferred to work there alone. The younger girls were greatly intrigued by her state of preoccupation. 'Aunt Jane would sit quietly working beside the fire in the library, saying nothing for a good while,' said Marianne, 'and then would suddenly burst out laughing, jump up and run across the room to a table where pens and paper were lying, write something down, and then come back to the fire and go on quietly working as before.' 'She was very absent indeed,' said Louisa. 'She would sit silent awhile, then rub her hands, laugh to herself and run up to her room.'[44] Jane enjoyed her nieces' flattering attentions, but she enjoyed it even more when they went off to amuse themselves at Goodnestone fair, leaving her entirely alone, 'mistress & miss & altogether here'.

There was to be no secrecy about *Mansfield Park*, she decided; no more evasions and lies about who the author might, or might not, be. After all, with a brother like Henry, it was impossible to hope for any real anonymity. 'The truth is that the secret has spread so far as to be scarcely the shadow of a secret now,' she wrote to Frank. 'I believe that whenever the 3d appears, I shall not even attempt to tell lies about it.' If nothing else, the mention of Frank's ships would offer a strong clue to her identity, but she was prepared for that. 'I was aware,' she assured him, 'of what I shd be laying myself open to.' If celebrity was the price of authorial success, then it was a price she was now prepared to pay in order to gain a larger financial reward. 'I shall rather try to make all the money than all the mystery I can of it,' she wrote. 'People shall pay for their knowledge if I can make them.' If that sounded brazen, then so be it. Alone, and mistress of that elegant Godmersham library, she felt equal to any eventuality. 'I am trying to harden myself,' she wrote.[45]

Her time was not entirely devoted to writing. In a house like Godmersham there was 'a constant succession of small events', someone was always 'going or coming'. One evening, she and Fanny would be 'running backwards and forwards' with young Wadham Knight's breeches in their hands, 'in the greatest of frights lest he should come upon us before we had done all'. Another evening, it would be whist and backgammon with 'Tyldens and double-Tyldens' (was there no end to families changing their names?). On Sunday, she heard Mr Sherer preach, 'a little too eager sometimes in his delivery, but that is to *me* a better extreme than the want of animation'. She even found herself quite warming towards Fanny's Mr Plumptre ('a very amiable young man, only too diffident to be so agreable as he might be'). But then, she had never wanted people to be *too* agreeable. Mr Plumptre was quite polite enough to submit himself to a rain-soaked morning in the fields out of deference to his young hosts' passion for killing things. The longer she stayed at Godmersham, the more disgust Jane felt at the way young Edward and even 'itty Dordy' now seemed addicted to hunting, shooting, drinking and all the other 'habits of luxury'. Were these the benefits of a Winchester education? she wondered. 'It is the habits of wealth that I fear,' she made Edmund declare in *Mansfield Park*. Cassandra shared her misgivings at the young men's behaviour, but what else was to be expected, she wrote, 'with so indulgent a father and so liberal a stile of living'?[46]

Although she enjoyed the privilege of privacy for her writing, Jane soon found that she did not care to be isolated quite so entirely. Where were all the grand invitations she had eagerly anticipated? 'Disastrous letters from the Plumptres & Oxendens. Refusals everywhere – a blank *partout*.' Where were her fond relations? 'Here am I in Kent, with one brother in the same county & another brother's wife, & see nothing of them.' It 'seems unnatural', she complained. She would have dearly liked it if Frank's wife and children were invited to stay for a week, but Mrs F.A., it seemed, was still not entirely *persona grata* at Godmersham – 'not a syllable of that nature is ever breathed'.[47] Meanwhile, what she heard of Mrs J.A.'s constant complaints against Ben Lefroy only increased her sense of vexation. How could she be 'so provokingly ill-judging?' Exasperated, she set herself to read Mary Brunton's *Self-Controul*, but found little comfort in it. The book might be 'excellently-meant' and even 'elegantly written', but 'without anything of nature or probability in it'. Beside Brunton's heroine, whose most 'every-day' action was a desperate voyage down an American river, even Richardson's Harriet Byron seemed a model of plausibility.

Jane briefly took to affecting the style of Harriet Byron in her letters to Cassandra, when she was not echoing the lines of *The Hermit*. But soon even books began to bore her. Her spirits sank at the prospect of Southey's *Life of Nelson*. 'I am tired of Lives of Nelson,' she wrote. She would only read this one, she said, 'if Frank is mentioned in it'. After less than a month of attempting to 'harden' herself at Godmersham, she already found herself hankering after the humdrum duties of home: 'I *knew* there was sugar in the tin ... Have you any tomatas? ... Does butcher's meat keep up at the same price? & is not bread lower than 2s 6d?'[48] These were the very 'vulgar cares' she had boasted to Frank of having 'shaken off'. But was it really such a great thing to avoid them? Was it really, she wondered, such a marvellous thing to be a celebrated author, or to ride in an open barouche through the streets of London, and be stared at like a wild beast? 'After all,' she wrote, 'what a trifle it is in all its bearings, to the really important points of one's existence in this world.' Alone in the library, she conceded that it was not Nelson, nor the King of Sweden, nor even Harriet Byron, who most inspired her, but the tender, witty, intimate letters from Cassandra at home. 'Tell me your sweet little innocent ideas,' she wrote back to her in a rush of affection, 'everything of love & kindness – proper & improper . . .'[49]

By the end of the week, the house had filled up with company, but Jane was not inclined to think this an improvement. She was of a mind to be out of humour, and could be equally so in solitude or in a crowd. She resented guests who came and went so complacently, treating the place quite like a hotel. She particularly disliked Mr Wigram ('very silent . . . *He* is certainly no addition'). 'They say his name is Henry,' she wrote, and was tempted to add an improper jest, quite in the Mary Crawford manner: 'I have seen many a John & Thomas much more agreable.' 'I cannot imagine how a man can have the impudence to come into a family party for three days, where he is quite a stranger, unless he knows himself to be agreable.' Mr Mascall was no better ('talks too much & is conceited, besides having a vulgarly shaped mouth'). She found fault with Lady Fagg and her five daughters ('I never saw so plain a family, five sisters so very plain!') and could only tolerate Mr Lushington on account of his allowing her to make use of his postal facilities. The man was the member for Canterbury, and she was prepared to play cat and mouse with him to save some coppers in postage.

Her ill humour now extended to people in Hampshire that Cassandra mentioned in her letters. 'Only think of Mrs Holder's being dead!' she exclaimed. 'Poor woman, she has done the only thing in the world she could possibly do to make one cease to abuse her.'[50] Was that an evil thought to express? 'She does not *think* evil,' she made Edmund explain in Mary Crawford's defence, 'but she speaks it, speaks it in playfulness.' Edmund went on to confess that 'though I know it to be playfulness it grieves me to the soul', but Jane's own soul was somewhat less tender than his. At least she was spared the vexation of attending a ball at Canterbury, when Fanny wisely decided against it. '*I* was very glad to be spared the trouble of dressing & going & being weary before it was half over.' The billiard-room, too, was a considerable relief. It drew all the gentlemen to it when they were indoors after dinner, 'so that my br[other], Fanny & I have the library to ourselves in delightful quiet'.[51]

Feeling oppressed by overmuch company, Jane even had misgivings about the promised visit of Charles and his family. They were sure to arrive just when the house was already full of all these other guests, which must lead to inevitable confusion. Of course she would be 'most happy to see dear Charles' if she did not know he would have 'a cross child or some other care pressing on him'. She could even be 'very happy in the idea of seeing little Cassy' if she did not strongly suspect that the girl would 'disappoint me by some immediate disagreeableness'. 'Two parties of children is the chief evil,' she wrote, with rueful foreboding. Of course, she *hoped* that the visit would pass off smoothly enough. But 'what is the use of hoping?'[52] And, of course, Charles *did* arrive just when the house was its fullest; worse than that, he arrived at such a late hour that the dinner was nearly over. So a fresh dinner had to be laid for them in the breakfast-room, with troupes of people walking back and forth from one part of the house to the other. Jane did her best to be amiable, and politely remarked how 'neat and white' his dear wife Fanny was looking. This was some strain upon her candour, for Fanny actually looked just as squat and snub-nosed as ever. It was a pity, Jane thought, that poor little Cassy seemed to have inherited her mother's looks. 'I wish she were not so very Palmery,' she wrote to Cassandra, 'but it seems stronger than ever. I never knew a wife's family-features have such undue influence.' The little girl herself was quite affectionate, though tired and bewildered and extremely thin. 'She kissed me very affectionately & has since seemed to recollect me in the same way.'

Indeed, once the Wigrams and Mascalls were cleared from the house, she began to find the atmosphere altogether more congenial. She even found herself warming towards Mr Lushington, who quite won her over with his passionate readings from Milton. 'I am rather in love with him,' she told Cassandra. How often it happened, she remarked, that 'after having much praised or much blamed anybody', one was 'generally sensible of something just the reverse soon afterwards'. However, she added, 'I dare say he is ambitious & insincere'.[53] She did not care to suggest whether such ambitious insincerity might increase or diminish her regard for Mr Lushington's charms. Perhaps Mr L. was the cat and she was the mouse? 'He has a wide smiling mouth & very good teeth.' When he left Godmersham the following day, Mr Lushington carried Jane's letter to Cassandra with him, marked 'free' and franked by parliamentary authority.

That autumn, Jane felt quite in the mood for being in love, and Mr L. was only one of her notional *beaux*. No, she told Cassandra, she had not heard of the death of Mrs Crabbe. Indeed, she had only just learnt that her poetical hero had been married at all. 'Poor woman!' she wrote, but then added, eagerly, 'I will comfort *him* as well as I can.' It was an old joke, but a good one. During her visit to London she had often expressed disappointment at 'seeing nothing of Mr Crabbe'. But a husband was one thing – stepchildren quite another. She did *not* undertake 'to be good' to poor Mrs Crabbe's children, she said, so 'she had better not leave any'.[54] She made sure to have Fanny Price include Crabbe's *Tales* among her favourite books; but how many readers, she wondered, would recognize that Fanny Price's own name was borrowed from the heroine of Crabbe's *Parish Register*? In that way, she and the poet had already conceived one literary offspring of their own. But, on second thoughts, she wondered if she might not prefer a younger husband, from a different literary dynasty. 'Perhaps,' she mused, 'I may marry young Mr D'Arblay.' It was a pleasant conceit to imagine such a union, which would bring together Fanny Burney's physical son and literary daughter.

The authoress of *Cecilia* was currently much in Jane's thoughts. She did not despair, she said, 'of having my picture in the exhibition at last – all white & red, with my head on one side'. She had in mind an affecting society portrait, done in oils, by Sir Joshua Reynolds. Or possibly (a more teasing thought) something in the manner of Fanny Burney's own portrait, done by her cousin Edward Francesco Burney.[55] She also had plans to accept Mrs

Cooke's 'two or three dozen invitations' of visiting Bookham that winter, where the Burneys had once lived. It would be pleasant to go there now that she was less afraid of invidious literary comparisons. Miss Burney had received just £30 for *Evelina*, but with the second edition of *Sense and Sensibility* now published, Jane had dreams of fabulous wealth. She hoped 'that *many* will feel themselves obliged to buy it', and confessed that she did not mind 'imagining it a disagreable duty to them, so as they do it'. Even the news that, in Cheltenham, *Sense and Sensibility* was confidently attributed to the blue-stocking Elizabeth Hamilton scarcely troubled her. 'It is pleasant to have such a respectable writer named,' she said. Meanwhile, *Pride and Prejudice* was still receiving warm acclamations wherever it was seen. 'I am read & admired in Ireland too!' she boasted.[56]

It was delicious to share these fantasies of wealth and romance with Cassandra, who was visiting Henry in London. Now that Cassandra, too, was away from maternal scrutiny, the letters between the two sisters became wildly indulgent. Cassandra must be sure 'to have something odd' happen to her in London, Jane insisted. 'See somebody that you do not expect, meet with some surprise or other . . . Do something clever in that way.' Mr Lushington and his money-saving frank were already quite forgotten. Who cared about saving coppers on postage? 'Money is dirt,' Jane loftily proclaimed. She was in a mood for recklessness. 'Whatever is, is best,' she declared, happily misquoting the 'infallible' Pope.[57] Enclosed with one letter was a note from their young niece Elizabeth, telling aunt Cassandra about old Mary Croucher, who 'gets *maderer* and *maderer* every day'. The world was full of mad people, as far as Jane could see. The Godmersham boys with their sporting 'mania', the literary world, quite mad for *Pride and Prejudice*; and Ben Lefroy, who 'must be maddish' to give up the prospect of a 'highly eligible' curacy, just because he had not 'made up his mind' to it. The foolish young man had even told James that he would 'give up Anna rather than do what he does not approve'. That was surely elevating scruple to the point of madness. Jane looked forward to meeting Ben's aunt at Goodnestone and telling her plainly her opinion of the matter. '"My dear Mrs Harrison", I shall say, "I am afraid the young man has some of your family madness – & though there often appears to be something of madness in Anna too, I think she inherits more of it from her mother's family than from ours." That is what I shall say,' she told Cassandra, '& I think she will find it difficult to answer me.'[58]

In the event, no such conversation took place. When Jane met Mrs Harrison it was not the mad aunt of a madder nephew that she saw in her features, but the sweet likeness of her dear dead sister, Madam Lefroy. 'So like her sister! I could almost have thought I was speaking to Mrs Lefroy.'[59] Other fantasies of arrogant power and fabulous wealth dwindled away in a similar fashion. Before she could enjoy any profits from the new edition of *Sense and Sensibility*, Jane must first pay the costs of production. 'I suppose in the meantime I shall owe dear Henry a great deal of money for printing &c.,' she wrote. And after all, she reflected, she was perhaps rather too advanced in years to play the part of an eager bride. There were some compensations in being middle-aged. 'By the bye,' she wrote to Cassandra, 'as I must leave off being young, I find many *douceurs* in being a sort of chaperon, for I am put on the sofa near the fire & can drink as much wine as I like.'[60]

As the relaxing effect of the claret wine and the warm fireside had their mellowing effect on her mind, she rediscovered the pleasures of simple amusements. Writing dutiful letters to her mother at Chawton had at first seemed a thankless chore ('I suppose my mother will like to have me write to her. I shall try at least'). But now, as she read through her mother's reply, full of 'little home news', she found pleasure in its simple details – a fall in the price of bread, dinners with Miss Benn. It quite shocked her to hear that Cassandra had actually taken her advice and was doing the dissipations of London with the Bigg girls. 'You & Mrs H[eathcote] & Catherine & Alethea going about together in Henry's carriage, seeing sights! I am not used to the idea of it yet.'

While Cassandra visited the sights of London, Jane made a tour of some less fashionable spots. In accordance with his duties as a visiting magistrate, Edward was called upon to inspect the local gaol and Jane was pleased to accompany him there. Her emotions on this occasion were such as she found difficult to express with any great sensitivity. 'I was gratified,' she wrote, '& went through all the feelings which people must go through, I think, in visiting such a building.'[61] Yet gratification was hardly the most obvious emotion that even casual visitors to such a grim institution would usually express. Her desire to reduce her reactions to a matter of commonplace ('all the feelings which people must go through') marked a kind of detachment, which, however cruel it might seem, she recognized as an essential part of her nature. 'Let other pens dwell on guilt and misery,' she wrote in the final chapter of *Mansfield Park*. 'I quit such odious subjects as soon as I can.'[62] The visit brought back disagreeable thoughts of the gaol at Ilchester where her aunt Leigh-Perrot had been kept. She remembered her aunt's descriptions of gaoler Scadding's filthy house; the smoke and the swearing, the constant noise of mad women and dirty children, the taste of food dressed by Mrs Scadding's knife, '*well licked to clean it from fried onions*'. But she quickly banished such unsavoury thoughts as these from her mind.

After leaving the gaol, she and Edward made no other visits that day, 'only walked about snuggly . . . & shopp'd. I bought a concert ticket & a sprig of flowers for my old age.' Feelings of mortality could not be entirely dismissed after witnessing such scenes as she had seen. A pressed flower, preserving its fragile beauty between the pages of a book, was as poignant a symbol of her own isolation as she could bring herself to admit; a concert ticket and a sprig of flowers were appropriate souvenirs for a society lady. The next day, she was restored to her splendid isolation as Edward took himself off to the woods. 'I am all alone,' she told Cassandra. 'I have five tables, eight & twenty chairs & two fires all to myself.'[63]

Then, quite as suddenly, her mood changed once more. Her last few days at Godmersham brought a renewed flurry of excitement. Once again, she could hardly find patience to set down all her multifarious activities. 'Oh! dear me!' she wrote to Cassandra, 'I have not time or paper for half that I want to say.'[64] A delightful party at Chilham Castle (Edward and Fanny pronounced it 'the pleasantest party they ever had known there') was succeeded by two glorious days 'of dissipation all through'. From morning till evening there was gossip and wine with Sir Brook Bridges, Mr

Sherer, Lady Honeywood, Mrs Harrison and all. Then it was off to a ball and a concert in Canterbury, as one of six ladies all in a row. 'We had a beautiful night for our frisks,' she reported. Fanny was less charmed by the evening. Dressed in white sarsnet and silver, with silver all in her hair, she was disappointed at the absence of dancing – 'officers idle & a scarcity of county beaux'. Jane felt no instinct to repine at the lack of young officers. What made these last days in Kent so delicious to her was the sweet sense of imminent parting. She had had her fill of elegant amusements; be the parties never so splendid, nor the companions never more agreeable, her dearest thoughts now were of Cassandra and home.

On 13 November, Edward took her to London, where poor Henry was suffering agonies of ill health ('what a thing bile is!'). She remained with him there for a fortnight, applying herself to his comfort and declining all invitations. There were to be no more literary *soirées*, despite the solicitations of a certain nobleman who confided to Henry his urgent wish that the clever Miss Austen should join a literary circle at his house. Apparently, 'the celebrated Madame de Stael' was to be of the party. But Jane had no desire for displays of literary wit, nor even for literary rambles. Cassandra had spoken of visiting the Hills at Streatham, where Dr Johnson had once had his Thralian retreat, while Jane herself had intended to call on the Cookes at Bookham, the former abode of Fanny Burney. But not any more. 'Your Streatham & my Bookham may go hang,' Jane wrote to Cassandra in a spirit of utterly unliterary exultation. Now that her book, *Mansfield Park*, was written, all she wanted was the simplicity of home. 'The prospect of being taken down to Chawton by Henry' was, for her, the most perfect plan. Before they left, Henry negotiated the sale of *Mansfield Park* to Egerton. The publisher, though he praised the new book 'for its morality' and for 'being so equal a composition' with 'no weak parts', was disappointed by its serious tone.[65] It would not, he was sure, be nearly so popular as *Pride and Prejudice*, and consequently only agreed to publish it 'on commission'. He did not offer to buy the copyright. Morality in novels might be very praiseworthy, but it did not sell well.

CHAPTER 12

A Little Disguised

Seldom, very seldom, does complete truth belong to any human disclosure; seldom can it happen that something is not a little disguised, or a little mistaken.

EMMA, III, xiii

'3 or 4 families in a country village'

By the time Jane reached Chawton, some days before her thirty-eighth birthday, the plan for her new novel had already taken shape in her mind. *Emma* was to be a novel of misapprehensions; not like *Pride and Prejudice,* in which one character misapprehends the character of another, on the basis of false first impressions; but a story whose heroine would, sometimes fortuitously and sometimes wilfully, mistake and misrepresent her own character to herself. At Godmersham, Jane had often found herself disturbed by the violent oscillations she experienced in her own disposition, constantly torn between the temptations of literary fame and the modest contentment of domestic obscurity. When she considered how, in one company or another, she would offer quite different accounts of herself, she found herself compelled to acknowledge how intimately habits of self-deception must often influence our notions of truth. 'Seldom, very seldom,' she wrote, 'does complete truth belong to any human disclosure; seldom can it happen that something is not a little disguised, or a little mistaken.'[1]

Though she did not, by any means, regret the character she had chosen as the heroine of *Mansfield Park*, the general lack of enthusiasm which the family evinced towards the book suggested that it was not an entirely happy experiment. There was, perhaps, she privately conceded, too much of the *vanity* of humility in Fanny Price's demeanour; and rather more saintliness about her than was entirely consistent with vitality. Yet those same concerns which had possessed her to write that book continued to preoccupy her thoughts. They were centred upon her own ambiguous feelings towards that dangerous and irreverent wit which she so often loved to display. How often she had tried to *will* herself into owning a more charitable and virtuous disposition. How frequently she had wished she were less ready to mock dull merit with a smart remark, or to find congenial inspiration in some scandalous repartee. In *Mansfield Park*, she had perhaps attempted too radical a piece of self-castigation. There was rather too much of the evangelical convert about it.

For her new novel, Jane determined upon a more congenial form of moral appraisal, in which self-censure might be blended with a modest degree of self-display. For her heroine she would choose a young woman whose unchecked liveliness of imagination and vanity in her own judgement might prove destructive not only to the happiness of others, but also to her own contentment. 'The real evils indeed of Emma's situation,' she wrote in her first chapter, 'were the power of having rather too much her own way, and a disposition to think a little too well of herself.' Although twice Emma's age, these were the very dangers which Jane herself now feared might alloy the many enjoyments which the life of an authoress seemed to promise her. 'I am going to take a heroine whom no one but myself will much like,' she proclaimed.[2] Yet even that declaration, she knew, was itself a form of disguise. Really, it was Fanny Price whom no one but she would care for, not Emma Woodhouse. It was the dilemma she confronted that silent virtue was always less appealing than eloquent vice.

It was a harsh winter. From the end of December till the middle of February there were heavy snowfalls, sharp frosts and thick, freezing fogs. In London, a frost fair was held on the ice-bound Thames and, for several weeks, all travel was virtually impossible. At Chawton, Jane began her new novel on 21 January, while *Mansfield Park* was away at the printers and the village lanes were too heavy with snow for walking. Beef-pudding was the favourite dish of the season (*not* one of which Mr Woodhouse would approve) and there was more than enough work for chimney-sweepers to do clearing frost-hardened soot from blocked winter flues. At last, by March, the roads were passable again, and Henry took Jane up to London on the first of the month. They travelled slowly together over the muddy, treacherous roads. Outside, a fierce snowstorm battered their coach from Cobham to Kingston, while inside, the two of them pored over the first proofs of *Mansfield Park*. Henry greatly pleased her by saying that, though it was 'very different' from her other two novels, he did not think it 'at all inferior'. But then, she remembered, he had only got as far as Mrs Rushworth's wedding. 'I am afraid he has gone through the most entertaining part,' she wrote to Cassandra. Perhaps even this modest praise might evaporate by the time he reached the end.[3]

After a winter of enforced isolation, even a snow-bound London seemed full of attractions. Kean was appearing as Shylock at Drury Lane and, having missed Mrs Siddons, Jane was very much of a mind to see this most celebrated male actor of the age. It would, she said, be 'a good play for Fanny', who was to soon join them at Henrietta Street with her father. Yet, so great was the rage to see Kean perform that Henry could only get seats in the third or fourth row. 'It is a front box, however,' said Jane; 'I hope we shall do pretty well.' While she was away in London, Charles's little Cassandra was staying at Chawton in her place. There had been much debate as to whether the sickly little girl could withstand another winter aboard the *Namur* with her parents. Charles's wife, Fanny, insisted that the ship was quite habitable. Of course, she said, they all knew 'the uncertainty of naval people', and how 'their private arrangements must yield to public duty'. But she did all she could to make their shipboard quarters quite snug, feeding pigeons, making 'tidy little spencers' and reading books from the ship's library. They even had theatricals aboard the *Namur*, and Fanny was looking forward just as eagerly to their own shipboard play as Jane anticipated Kean's performance at Drury Lane. 'Do not force Cass to stay if she hates it,' Jane wrote back to her mother; but the girl had little need of forcing to leave her cold, damp cabin for the comfort of Chawton. From the elegance of her room in Henrietta Street, where she slept 'to a miracle', Jane liked to imagine the poor bedraggled fugitive who now occupied her bed. 'Give my love to little Cassandra,' she wrote. 'I hope she found my bed comfortable last night & has not filled it with fleas.'[4]

Kean's performance did not disappoint them. 'We were quite satisfied,' Jane wrote. 'I cannot imagine better acting.' As for the rest of the cast, she was rather less enthusiastic. Miss Smith 'did not quite answer my expectation,' she wrote, and the other parts 'were ill filled & the play heavy'.[5] The whole party found themselves 'too much tired' to stay for the whole of the second play, *The Illusion, or the Trances of Nourjahad*, which boasted 'a great deal of finery & dancing ... but I think little merit'. The part of Nourjahad, she thought, was 'not at all calculated' to show off Mr Elliston's true powers. It was altogether as if Mr Yates were to find himself miscast in the role of Anhalt the clergyman, or Maria Bertram reduced to play the Cottager's Wife. 'There was nothing of the *best Elliston* about him,' she pronounced. 'I might not have known him, but for his voice.' The following night they saw *The Devil to Pay* followed by the opera *Artaxerxes* ('I was very tired'). Some nights later it was off to *The Farmer's Wife* ('a musical thing in 3 acts') at Covent Garden.[6]

Jane fancied that some more accomplished thespians might be found among Henry's London friends than on the stage at Drury Lane or Covent Garden. She had fond memories of General Tilson Chowne, the brother of Henry's banking partner, acting the role of Frederick in their own little private performance of Mrs Inchbald's *Lovers' Vows*. 'I was ready to laugh at the remembrance of Frederick,' she confided to Cassandra, thinking how it would amuse the General to see his own histrionic efforts mimicked by Mr Crawford in *Mansfield Park*. Sadly, she found the General very much subdued. 'He has not much remains of Frederick,' she complained.[7] Still, the prospect that Cassandra might join her in London filled her with pleasurable anticipations of yet more theatre visits. 'Prepare for a play the very first evening,' she announced. 'I rather think Covent Garden to see Young in *Richard* [*III*].' Failing that, she would take Cassandra to see Kean for herself. 'I shall like to see Kean again excessively,' she said, '& to see him with you too.'[8]

The weather continued fearful; the ground covered with snow, nothing but 'thickness and sleet' all day and heavy frosts at night. 'What is to become of us?' she wrote. Yet despite a heavy cold, she was still constantly surprising within herself a histrionic impulse quite as defiant as that of any stage heroine. She would venture out each evening in her most coquettish attire. Her gauze gown was rather too starched for London, she decided. 'I have lowered the bosom,' she told Cassandra, '& plaited black satin ribbon round the top. Such will be my costume of vine leaves and paste.'[9] It was the perfect London disguise.

When not out at the theatre, she was indoors reading all the latest and most fashionable books. Every volume was studied now not with the innocent pleasure of a casual reader, but with the jealous scrutiny of a professional rival. In three days, she read Mr Barrett's *The Heroine* ('a delightful burlesque'), Mr Combe's *Dr Syntax* ('I have seen nobody in London with such a long chin as Dr Syntax') and Lord Byron's *The Corsair*.[10] Meanwhile, Henry continued his own reading of *Mansfield Park*. On 3 March, he announced his admiration for Henry Crawford – 'I mean *properly*,' Jane boasted to Cassandra – 'as a clever, pleasant man'. Two days later he had reached the third volume and declared that he liked it 'better & better'. He had quite changed his mind about the book's ending, he said, and 'defied anybody to say whether H.C. would be reformed, or would forget Fanny in a fortnight'. Much encouraged, Jane was prepared to be equally generous in her praise of *The Heroine*, having 'torn through' the third volume of that novel after tea the previous day. The burlesque of the Radcliffe style was particularly well done, she thought, and did not 'fall off' at the end.

She found herself increasingly disposed to view the world through the eyes of her new heroine, Emma Woodhouse. Like Emma, she had a mind to match-making. Young Wyndham, second son to Sir Edward Knatchbull, had accepted Henry's invitation to dine. 'A nice, gentlemanlike, unaffected sort of young man,' she said; 'I think he may do for Fanny.' Yet, as she might have foretold from her own fiction, such endeavours were fraught with mishaps. The young man did not visit them after all, but only sent 'a very long & very civil note of excuse'. 'It makes one moralize upon the ups & downs of this life,' she wrote ruefully to Cassandra.[11] But instead of including such moralizings in a letter (which was otherwise quite taken up with solemn considerations as to the superiority, or otherwise, of lilac sarsnet over black China crape), she reserved them for the mind of Emma Woodhouse, in her awkward moments of reflection after Mr Elton's distressing outburst in the carriage carrying them both from Randall's ('How could she have been so deceived! ... She had taken up the idea, she supposed, and made everything bend to it ... It was most provoking'). Moreover, she was forced to acknowledge, Fanny seemed quite equal to contriving a match for herself. The attentive Mr Plumptre had followed her up to London, where he had escorted them home through the snow and ice to Henrietta Street and ate some soup with them there. Despite his professed evangelical sympathies, it was this self-same Mr Plumptre who had been so insistent on seeing *The Farmer's Wife*. He would try for a box, he declared. 'I do not particularly wish him to succeed,' Jane wrote, late on the evening of 8 March. 'I have had enough for the present.' But first thing the very next morning, before they had even done breakfast, the man was back, very pleased to announce he had secured a box for that evening.

Inevitably, Fanny and Mr Plumptre professed themselves much delighted by Miss Stephens's singing in this musical play, though Jane herself was less enthusiastic. 'Her merit in singing is I dare say very great,' she told Cassandra; 'that she gave *me* no pleasure is no reflection upon her, nor I hope upon myself, being what

Nature made me on that article.' (Like Emma, she was 'not much deceived as to her own skill either as an artist or musician'.)[12] Her own taste in singing extended little further than favourite old ballads sung around the piano, and she found little diversion in the warblings of professional singers. Miss Stephens, she said, was no doubt 'a pleasing person', but with 'no skill in acting'. Similarly, while Henry discerned a 'decided attachment' between Fanny and the attentive Mr Plumptre, Jane offered no comment. 'I have a cold,' she said.

By the time Cassandra joined her in London later that month, her enthusiasm for theatrical excursions had somewhat abated. She saw the India jugglers in Pall Mall but otherwise, as she wrote to Frank, was 'going to no parties & living very quietly'. 'I . . . care for nobody,' she declared with a mock metropolitan pout of *amour-propre* in the letter which welcomed her sister to London. With her work on the proofs of *Mansfield Park* now completed, her thoughts turned once again towards home. If little Cassy *had* filled her bed with fleas, she said, she hoped they would be so good as to confine themselves to biting only the girl herself.[13]

Not long after the sisters returned to Chawton, the whole Godmersham family descended on the village and took up their quarters in the great house. It was not merely Edward, his sons and daughters and their friends, suitors and servants that came; but also a large party of Bridges from Goodnestone, headed by the Dowager Lady Bridges, who had been declared to have only 'a good sort of gout' on her last visit to Bath the previous summer and was therefore adjudged quite equal to the expedition. This sudden arrival in such numbers of Knights, Bridges and Austens was not unconnected, Jane suspected, with the recent unpleasantness which the Hintons at Chawton Lodge had seen fit to inflict on them. The unpleasantness concerned a will, as such things usually did; in this case, a will made almost a hundred years ago, which placed an entail upon the Knight family's Chawton properties. According to this will, these properties were entailed firstly upon Mr Thomas May and his descendants, but, if their line should ever fail, thereafter upon Mr John Hinton and his. Mr May had no sooner entered into his Chawton estates (and changed his name to Knight) than he had moved to cut off this entail. At his death, his son's right to inherit the properties was undisputed; but Edward, who now held them, was not a Knight by birth, but only by adoption. No one in the village, though, would have thought to question Edward's title to the Chawton lands, had not the Hinton's nephew, Mr Baverstock, a knowing brewer from Alton, chosen to put it in dispute.[14] The entail, he contended, had never been legally terminated. There were errors in the deed of disentailment, which was, in any case, invalid for having been executed out of term-time. When the smart Mr Baverstock had first advanced his claim, at the beginning of the year, it had seemed no more than an irritation. 'Edward has a good chance of escaping his lawsuit,' Jane had written to Cassandra. Mr Baverstock, she heard, seemed likely to 'knock under', though the terms of the agreement were 'not quite settled'.[15] But instead of 'knocking under', Baverstock had redoubled his impertinent claims, and, by the summer, the situation had become quite alarming. If Edward should lose his lawsuit, he would surrender more than half his Chawton lands, and, what was worse, Mrs Austen would lose her home at Chawton cottage. Quite suddenly, there was less amusement to be derived from Mrs Bennet's plangent outcries in *Pride and Prejudice* against the odious entail upon their Longbourn house.

In such a situation, it was perhaps hardly surprising that there should be so little in the way of family rejoicing at the publication of *Mansfield Park*. Jane had been anticipating the novel's appearance daily for several weeks. 'Before the end of April,' she told Frank, it would be 'in the world'. As the great day approached, she found herself increasingly apprehensive, and, having previously told Frank there was to be no mystery about it, she now contradicted herself. 'Keep the *name* to yourself,' she begged him. 'I shd not like to have it known beforehand.'[16]

In the event, it seemed she need not have worried. The world seemed quite content to remain in blissful ignorance about both the book and its author. *Mansfield Park* was published on 9 May, when a brief notice appeared in the *Star*, which announced it as 'By the Author of *Sense and Sensibility* and *Pride and Prejudice*' and priced at 18s the three volumes. After that, there was silence. Jane sought in vain through the newspapers and magazines for reviewers' notices, but there was none to be found. Friends and relations volunteered no kind unsolicited words of praise, though Miss Papillon's friend Miss Dusautoy had taken it into her head that *she* was the real Fanny Price, if you please; or, if not her, then her younger sister, whose name was Fanny.[17] Jane began to suspect that the family shared a secret dislike of the book. Or worse still, perhaps they had merely grown tired of her writings. Now that the novelty and surprise had exhausted themselves, what was it, after all, but just another of aunt Jane's novels? Even without Baverstock's lawsuit, there were other topics to occupy their patriotic minds. In January, the Austrians, Russians and Prussians had invaded France, while Wellington's troops marched northward over the Pyrenees. In February, the French government began negotiations for peace. In March, the allies reached Paris, and on 5 April, Napoleon was forced to abdicate the throne and submit to exile on the island of Elba. These were great national events with direct consequences for the Austen family.

In May, just as *Mansfield Park* was published, Frank signed off from the *Elephant* at Spithead to join his family as a half-pay officer ashore. Charles remained aboard the *Namur* at the Nore, though Fanny hoped they, too, would soon be 'settled on shore in some way or other'.[18] Throughout the country, there were victory festivals and celebrations. At Alton, there were illuminations and a public supper for all the poorer inhabitants on 17 and 18 June. The Emperor of Russia and the King of Prussia visited London for a fortnight of festivities, during which they were mobbed and cheered wherever they went. 'Take care of yourself, & do not be trampled to death in running after the Emperor,' Jane wrote to Cassandra, who was whisked off by Henry to take part in all the celebrations.[19]

Having just been in London herself, Jane could not begrudge her sister this chance to sample the dissipations of the capital, while she remained with their mother at the home which Mr Baverstock seemed determined to snatch from them. She even indulged hopes (which she would *not* divulge to young James Edward, lest he should accuse her of hankering after a royal title) that instead of *her* travelling to London to see the King and the Emperor, *they* would travel to Chawton on their way to the Naval Review at Portsmouth. 'The report at Alton,' she wrote, 'was that they wd certainly travel this road.' All the same, it was undoubtedly tempting to think of being in London at this time, with *Mansfield Park* just published, to hear how it was talked of there. But her duty was to remain at home, with only perhaps a very brief visit to the Cookes at Bookham. Edward sought her help in drawing up his legal memoranda, and it was a peculiar sensation to walk with him through Chawton Wood, knowing that in another summer this quiet place might be no longer his. She professed herself quite content with these arrangements until Henry pressed her once more to join them in London. This time, it was more than usually difficult to contrive a decent show of reluctance. 'I certainly do not *wish* that Henry should think again of getting me to town,' she wrote to Cassandra, placing her emphasis on the *wish* rather than the *not*.

All the reports she heard made the London festivities sound so glorious. Henry had been among the two thousand guests at a magnificent White's Club ball, with the Prince Regent, the Emperor and the King. It was said that the ball had cost £10,000! The thought of it left her quite speechless. 'Henry at Whites! – Oh! what a Henry!' If he really *did* propose that she should come up to London, she mused, 'I cannot say "No" to what will be so kindly intended.' But, she added quickly, 'it could be but for a few days however, as my mother would be quite disappointed at my exceeding the fortnight which I now talk of as the outside'. At least, she said, 'we could not both remain longer away comfortably'. She left Cassandra to contemplate the significance of that *both*.[20] Meanwhile, at Portsmouth, Frank was taking part in the grand Naval Review for the benefit of their visiting majesties. 'Naval superiority', Captain Pasley had written, was the key to victory, and here it was displayed in a glorious array of ships-of-the-line: the *Sceptre* and the *St Domingo*, the *Bedford*, the *Rodney*, the *Chatham*, the *Ville de Paris*, the *Impregnable*, the *Standard*, the *Prince*, the *Magnificent*, the *Stirling Castle*, the *Andromache* and many, many more, extending in a line of battleships, frigates and sloops amounting to some seven hundred vessels. The Prince Regent in the royal barge preceded a barge carrying the Russian Imperial Standard and another bearing the Royal Standard of Prussia, as the royal visitors came alongside *Impregnable* under a cannonade of salutes from all the ships. 'We feel great difficulty', the *Hampshire Telegraph* declared, 'in attempting to describe the picturesque scene.'[21]

For Jane, such public spectacles as these bore little relation to the true strengths of the naval service which she so much admired. When she thought of naval heroism, she had in mind not only the valiant sea commanders, but also the brave women they left behind them; she thought of Mrs F.A. flitting from lodging to lodging in Deal with her swelling family; she thought of poor Fanny huddled in her tiny cabin aboard *Namur*, cheerfully resigned to the acknowledgement that 'private arrangements must yield to public duty'. In the view of Portsmouth which Jane presented in *Mansfield Park*, there were no glorious cannonades, royal barges or visiting monarchs. Instead, there was a small, cramped, overcrowded house of incessant noise and few refinements. There was the constant domestic flurry of a household striving to keep up with peremptory naval demands ('have you heard about the *Thrush*? She is gone out of harbour already, three days before we had any thought of it . . . what shall we do?'). There was a father who swore and smelled of drink, and girls who squabbled against a constant tumult of slamming doors and shouts for toasted cheese and rum and water. Such was the home of Jane's modest naval heroes, William and Sam Price; and though Fanny Price might regret to find her parents' home an abode 'of noise, disorder and impropriety', Jane Austen was happy to acknowledge it as the nursery of a certain kind of English courage. She was gratified when Frank's friend Captain Foote expressed his admiration and surprise at her power of drawing these Portsmouth scenes so well.

By the end of the month, Jane had had enough of pomp and pageantry. 'I hope Fanny has seen the Emperor,' she wrote, '& then I may fairly wish them all away.'[22] She resolved to keep to her plan of visiting Bookham, not least because the Cookes had been among the very few to offer congratulations on *Mansfield Park*. Mr Cooke called it 'the most sensible novel he ever read', and they were both delighted by her manner of treating the clergy. Bookham was also in the area of Surrey which Jane had chosen as the setting for her new novel, and she found her visit to the neighbourhood of Box Hill most useful for reviving memories of the local landscape ('English verdure, English culture, English comfort').[23] She even urged Cassandra to join her at Bookham once she had tired of metropolitan dissipations. 'Put this into your capacious head,' she wrote. A letter from Miss Sharpe, now in Yorkshire, revived her itch for match-making. The 'poor thing' was acting as governess to Lady Pilkington's children but she wrote so warmly of their uncle, Sir William, that Jane immediately suspected an *amour*. 'I do so want him to marry her!' she wrote. Imagine, to be raised up from a lowly governess to the wife of a baronet. 'Oh! Sir Wm – Sir Wm – how I will love you, if you will love Miss Sharpe!' (Sir William married Mary Swinnerton instead.)[24]

In the continuing absence of critical notices for *Mansfield Park*, Jane was reduced to the unhappy expedient of soliciting views from her friends and relations which she dutifully copied into a collection of 'Opinions of Mansfield Park'. This was not an entirely happy exercise. Everyone (or *nearly* everyone) was very tactful and judicious in their comments, but it was impossible to disguise a general air of disappointment. This book was obviously *not* another *Pride and Prejudice*, and, while the family did try to understand, and even admire, Jane's reasons for writing it, they did rather miss some of her earlier wit.[25] Cassandra said it was 'quite as clever, tho' not so brilliant as *P&P*'. Frank said that although 'we do not think it as a *whole* equal to *P&P*', it still had 'many & great beauties'. Aunt Norris, he said, was 'a great favourite' with him, and he found Fanny 'a delightful character'. He assured Jane that she need not fear the book's 'being considered as discreditable to the talents of its author'. But to her, such comments were hardly gratifying. Merely to escape being considered 'discreditable' fell some way short of being thought a triumphant success. Henry's final opinion, now he had had time to reflect upon it, was similarly judicious; the book was '*extremely interesting*' he said (much in the same polite way as Emma Woodhouse evinced a 'smiling *interest*' in a letter from Jane Fairfax to Miss Bates). At least that was by some degree preferable to the comments of Miss Bramston at Oakley Hall. *She* let it be known that she thought *Sense and Sensibility* and *Pride and Prejudice* to be 'downright nonsense', but had hoped for something rather better from this new one. Having finished the first volume, she flattered herself she 'had got through the worst'.

Yet Jane's success, it seemed, was tolerable enough to serve as an inspiration to Anna Austen, who now took it into her head that she, too, would set up as an authoress. Throughout July and August, the girl sent Jane the first eager drafts of her novel for comment and correction. In the garden at Chawton, while old Mrs Austen sat on her bench eating gooseberries, Jane would read aloud sections of the manuscript to her and Cassandra. 'We were all very much pleased,' Jane told her niece. 'The spirit does not droop at all.' In particular, the character St Julian was 'the delight of one's life', they all declared. He was indeed 'quite interesting', said Jane, remembering Henry's judicious phrase. There were, perhaps, a few minor infelicities which ought to be altered. 'As Lady H is Cecilia's superior,' Jane noted, 'it wd not be correct to talk of *her* being introduced; Cecilia must be the person introduced.' Similarly, she did not entirely care for a lover's speaking in the third person; 'it is too much like the formal part of Lord Orville [from *Evelina*],' she said, '& I think is not natural.' However, 'you need not mind me,' she assured her niece, in case the girl did not care for these fussy comments, and added, 'I am impatient for more.'[26]

Anna needed no further prompting, and more chapters of the novel quickly arrived. The girl had been mortified to discover that her choice of title – 'Enthusiasm' – had been pre-empted by Madame de Genlis, and Jane commiserated with her over this unhappy coincidence. '*Enthusiasm* was something so very superior,' she agreed, 'that every common title must appear to disadvantage.' Throughout the summer, as Jane read aloud these latest chapters to her mother and Cassandra, she found herself tempted to articulate, for Anna's benefit, certain principles of literary composition which she had never previously troubled herself to formulate. It was not enough, she told Anna, that a thing should *be* true for it to stand in a novel; it must *seem* true, or credible at least, which was sometimes a very different matter. She had 'scratched out' a scene where Anna's Sir Thomas walked out to the stables just one day after breaking his arm, 'for though I find your papa *did* walk out immediately after *his* arm was set, I think it can be so little usual as to *appear* unnatural in a book'. Similarly, certain irregularities of social conduct which might be tolerated in real life should be avoided in a novel, where the observance – or otherwise – of social proprieties must be taken as an indication of character. There was, she felt, an unintentional impropriety in Anna's clumsy contrivance for introducing her heroine's arrival in the country. 'A woman going with two girls just growing up, into a neighbourhood where she knows nobody but one man, of not very good character, is an awkwardness which so prudent a woman as Mrs F would not be likely to fall into,' Jane wrote. 'Remember, she is very prudent; you must not let her act inconsistently.' Language, too, must be consistent with character. Sir Thomas must not say 'Bless my heart' – 'it is too familiar & inelegant.' And Devereux Forester must on no account be allowed to plunge into a 'vortex of dissipation'. 'I do not object to the *thing*,' Jane assured her niece, 'but I cannot bear the expression; it is such thorough novel slang – and so old, that I dare say Adam met with it in the first novel he opened.'[27]

Jane found a distinct pleasure in thus honing her own authorial skills by means of this commentary on her niece's work. In letter after letter, she would refine Anna's style and sharpen her characters. No detail was too small for her attention. She remedied faulty topography ('Lyme will not do. Lyme is towards 40 miles distance from Dawlish & would not be talked of there. I have put Starcross indeed'). She corrected errors of etiquette ('when Mr Portman is first brought in, he wd not be introduced as *the Honble – That* distinction is never mentioned at such times'). She offered advice on settings ('You describe a sweet place, but your descriptions are often more minute than will be liked. You give too many particulars of right hand and left'). Yet she was careful always to present such advice not merely as a matter of personal opinion, but as the expression of a Chawton consensus. She always spoke of 'we' not 'I'. 'Here & there,' she wrote, 'we have thought the sense might be expressed in fewer words'; 'we think they press him [Mr Devereux Forester] too much – more than sensible women or well-bred women would do'; 'Miss Egerton does not entirely satisfy us. She is too formal & solemn, we think.'

Often, as when advising Anna against attempting any Irish scenes ('you know nothing of the manners there'), she suggested it was aunt Cassandra, not she, who was more censorious in her comments. 'Your Aunt C. does not like desultory novels,' she warned, '& is rather fearful yours will be too much so.' For herself, she said, she could find no very great objection to such a way of writing. 'I allow much more latitude than she does – & think nature and spirit cover many sins of a wandering story.' Yet she confessed herself greatly pleased when, as a result of Cassandra's criticisms, Anna restricted the wanderings of her characters and chose instead to group them in a single village. 'You are now collecting your people delightfully,' she wrote in early September, 'getting them exactly into such a spot as is the delight of my life; – 3 or 4 families in a country village is the very thing to work on.' She was also pleased that Anna had at last allowed her heroines to reach adulthood. 'One does not care for girls till they are grown up,' she declared. At last, it seemed her niece was entering upon 'the heart & beauty' of her book, and, despite some evident echoes of passages in *Mansfield Park*, she thought St Julian's comments on the madness of otherwise sensible women on the subject of their daughters' coming out was 'worth its weight in gold'. Elsewhere, she was rather severe about borrowings from her own novels. Anna would do well, she thought, to omit one particular postscript: 'to those who are acquainted with *P&P* it will seem an imitation.' She was also rather against the inclusion of a play-acting chapter, like the one in *Mansfield Park*; 'we do not thoroughly like the play,' she wrote, 'perhaps from having had too much of plays in that way lately.'

Indeed, if any confirmation were wanting of the problems posed by her own characters in *Mansfield Park*, Jane found it in reading her niece's chapters. There was something troubling about Anna's young heroine, Cecilia, 'a little too solemn and good', whose want of imagination, though 'very natural', was altogether less prepossessing than the high spirits of her sister Susan ('a very nice little animated creature'). Altogether, she decided, it was considerably more agreeable to *write* such characters than to read them, and when it came to the inevitable matrimonial debates, she found no hesitation in declaring herself very much of Susan's party. 'I like Susan as well as ever,' she told Anna at the end of September, '& begin now not to care at all about Cecilia.' She was naturally pleased to hear that Ben Lefroy had expressed approval of his future bride's literary endeavours. '*His* encouragement & approbation must be quite "beyond everything",' she wrote to Anna with just the merest tinge of irony. But she was intrigued to speculate on how such a very solemn young man would judge between these two fictional sisters. She did not at all wonder at his 'not expecting to like anybody so well as Cecilia *at first*' but, as she warned her niece, she would not be at all surprised if even he 'does not become a Susan-ite in time'.[28]

Towards the end of August, Jane went up to London, where Henry had recently removed to No. 23 Hans Place, just around the corner from his former house in Sloane Street. His partner, Tilson, lived three doors away at No. 26, and in the quiet of the evening it was possible to converse across the the intermediate back gardens. The garden at No. 23, with its pretty shrubs and flowers, was 'quite a love', she said. The house, too, she was surprised to find, was 'a delightful place', with more space and comfort in the rooms than she had supposed. Her brother James and his son Edward were expected the following day. 'Their business is about teeth & wigs,' she said. She had travelled up to London in Yalden's hot, cramped private coach. 'It put me in mind of my own coach between Edinburgh & Stirling,' she wrote, reminding Cassandra of the 'crowded and uncomfortable stage' she had described in *Love and Freindship* more than twenty years before.[29] Henry was in love, she found, or rather, in the best imitation of it he could muster. As to the passion itself he was quite decided, but had not as yet entirely fixed upon the most appropriate object of his *amour*. Sometimes he seemed to favour Miss Harriet Moore of Hanwell. 'Henry wants me to see more of his Hanwell favourite,' Jane told Cassandra, '& has written to invite her to spend a day or two here with me. His scheme is to fetch her on Saturday. I am more & more convinced that he will marry again soon, & like the idea of *her* better than of anybody else at hand.' The others 'at hand' included the Tilsons' friend Miss Burdett ('I do not know what to wish as to Miss B., so I will hold my tongue and my wishes,' said Jane), and Mrs Crutchley of Sunning Hill. Just as with Miss Pearson, many years before, Henry sought out his sister's opinion on his prospective choice of bride, and seemed determined to parade the various ladies for her approval. When they returned to Hampshire, he told her, he planned to lengthen the route of their homeward journey 'by going round by Sunning Hill'. 'His favourite, Mrs Crutchley lives there, and he wants to introduce me to her.' As with all Henry's plans, of course, there was always the chance that this latest scheme would be no sooner proposed than forgotten. 'It may never come to anything,' Jane told Cassandra, yet still felt she must 'provide for the possibility' by troubling her sister to send up her silk pelisse by Collyer's Saturday stage-coach. 'I feel it would be necessary on such an occasion.'[30]

Apart from assisting in these manoeuvres of Henry's, Jane's time in London was mainly spent quietly writing in the 'solitary coolness' of a downstairs room which opened directly upon the garden. 'Two or three *very* little dinner-parties at home, some delightful drives in the curricle, & quiet tea-drinkings with the Tilsons, has been the sum of my doings,' she wrote to Martha Lloyd at Bath.[31] Even this modest amount of social activity was, she declared, rather more than she wished for. She could happily have forgone a dinner-party with their Hampson cousins, who affected the most alarming republican sentiments, but Henry had made this invitation without consulting her. 'So I must submit to seeing George Hampson, though I had hoped to go through life without it,' she told Cassandra. 'It was one of my vanities,' she added, like Cassandra's vanity of not reading Maria Edgeworth's latest work, *Patronage*. Both sisters had fallen into the habit of affecting to resent the impertinence of other authors in publishing novels to compete with Jane's own works. 'Walter Scott has no business to write novels, especially good ones. It is not fair,' Jane wrote in a fine mock tantrum to her niece Anna. 'He has fame & profit enough as a poet, and should not be taking the bread out of other people's mouths. I do not like him, & do not mean to like *Waverley* if I can help it – but fear I must.'[32] She was, however, quite determined not to like Mrs West's historical romance *Alicia de Lacy* 'should I ever meet with it, which I hope I may not'. As to Mary Brunton's *Self-Controul*, she intended not merely to imitate, but to improve upon it. 'My heroine shall not merely be wafted down an American river in a boat by herself,' she boasted to Anna; 'she shall cross the Atlantic in the same way, & never stop till she reaches Gravesend.'

Thoughts of American rivers prompted some less cheerful reflections. The distasteful republicanism of her Hampson cousins, combined with Henry's gloomy views on the American war, provoked her into a quite uncharacteristic outburst of patriotic piety. 'If we *are* to be ruined, it cannot be helped,' she wrote to Martha Lloyd. 'But I place my hope of better things on a claim to the protection of heaven, as a religious nation, a nation inspite of much evil improving in religion, which I cannot believe the Americans to possess.'[33] She found some comfort for this hope in viewing Mr Benjamin West's huge new painting of *Christ Rejected* on exhibition at No. 125 Pall Mall. It was, she told Martha, 'the first representation of our Saviour which ever at all contented me. I want to have you & Cassandra see it.'[34] Even the latest London fashions seemed to indicate a new mood of sobriety, with long sleeves, covered bosoms and 'enormous bonnets upon the full stretch'. 'It seems to me a more marked *change* than one has lately seen,' she wrote, and she found it all 'quite entertaining'.

Her stay in London lasted for barely a fortnight, but it was long enough for her to register a new sense of distaste for a metropolitan world in which republicanism was openly spoken of, where the debaucheries of the Prince Regent and the madness of his father were the common gossip and where the most informed political intelligence was all of ruination and gloom. In such a world, it was perhaps hardly surprising that a work like *Mansfield Park* had not enjoyed a great success. She still hoped of 'getting Egerton's account' for sales of the first edition before she went away, but her mood was hardly confident. 'The language of London is flat,' she complained, already missing the good-humoured banter of Mrs Digweed and Miss Benn. The last news she heard before leaving London was that Charles's Fanny had given birth to a baby girl, aboard HMS *Namur*, a fortnight earlier than expected. It was a dangerous, painful birth, in a stinking between-decks cabin. Four days later, Fanny died, and the baby, two weeks afterwards. 'The Austin family have a great loss in the attach'd & beloved wife of Captn C: Austin; who died (by a mistake) on board a ship from whence she ought sooner to have removed,' wrote old Miss Elizabeth Leigh in her journal at Adlestrop.[35] Edward, who had suffered a similar bereavement, went to comfort his brother Charles, who promptly resigned from his command of the *Namur* and volunteered for service abroad with the thirty-six-gun HMS *Phoenix* bound for the Mediterranean, leaving his three young daughters in the care of their Palmer grandparents in Bloomsbury. Back at Chawton, Jane was relieved to find that her mother did not seem the worse for the shock of these sudden bereavements. Mrs Austen's most dismal apprehensions came in the form of Mr Baverstock's continuing manoeuvres to eject her from her home.

On 8 November, Anna Austen married Ben Lefroy. In her last letter of literary advice, sent to her niece six weeks earlier, Jane had written: 'I would not seriously recommend anything improbable', yet this match still seemed to her as improbable as anything a writer of romance might concoct. The 'maddish' young man had still not taken Holy Orders, but had at last given his promise to do so. It was said that the couple were 'so foolishly devoted' that any further delay was pointless. Yet the ceremony itself was a cheerless event.[36] 'Weddings were then usually very quiet,' Anna's sister Caroline later recalled: 'My sister's was certainly in the *extreme* of quietness.' Only the immediate family attended the service, a small group of less than a dozen people. 'The weather was dull and cloudy, but it did not actually rain.' Inside the church, there was 'no stove to give warmth, no flowers to give colour and brightness, no friends, high or low, to offer their good wishes'. All these circumstances, Caroline remembered, gave 'a gloomy air' to the proceedings. Mrs Austen seemed to catch the cheerless mood of the event by sending some wedding verses composed 'when I was on the sopha with the head-ache'.[37] After their modest wedding breakfast, the married couple departed for Hendon, in the wooded hills of Middlesex, where they were to share a house with Ben's brother Edward.

At first, Jane and her niece maintained their former literary correspondence. Anna's letters, Jane was relieved to find, were 'very sensible & satisfactory', with none of that '*parade* of happiness' which sometimes made the letters of recently married women so tiresome to receive. 'Make everybody at Hendon admire *Mansfield Park*,' she insisted, while commending the lively new scenes that Anna had added to her own narrative. The 'dog scene' in particular caught Jane's fancy. And it was, she thought, a peculiarly charming compliment for Anna to have made her dear St Julian at first in love with the aunt, before transferring his affections to Cecilia. 'I dare say Ben was in love with me once,' she replied mischievously, '& wd never have thought of *you* if he had not supposed me dead of a scarlet fever.'[38] After that, nothing more was heard of Anna's novel. Ben Lefroy's approval, it seemed, did not extend to encouraging his wife to neglect her conjugal duties in favour of literary ones. Their first child was born less than a year after the wedding, and their second eleven months later. Many years afterwards, in a fit of despondency, Anna threw the manuscript of her novel on to the fire. Her third daughter, Fanny, remembered 'sitting on the rug and watching its destruction, amused with the flames and the sparks which kept breaking out in the blackened paper'.[39] In one of her letters, Jane had ventured to criticize the hero of Anna's novel as 'too much in the common novel style – a handsome, amiable, unexceptionable young man (such as do not much abound in real life)'. As the mother of seven children, Anna Lefroy soon saw too much of real life to persist in the creation of such fantasy figures.

Anna's wedding prompted many serious reflections in the mind of her cousin and contemporary, Fanny Knight. For some years, these two lively girls had seemed to pursue parallel paths, diverting themselves with the attentions of solemn young men whose sober demeanours provided a splendid foil to their own more volatile wit. But now that Anna had taken the irrevocable step of matrimony, Fanny hesitated to follow her example. She sent her cousin a formal letter of congratulation, but to aunt Jane she wrote a long and private letter, full of painful self-doubts. Though she hesitated to be definite about it, she rather suspected she was *not* in love with Mr Plumptre after all. But how could she tell? And how could she, with honour, extract herself from an attachment which, though it fell short of a formal engagement, had been openly acknowledged for several months? 'I have no scruple in saying that you cannot be in love,' Jane replied. 'My dear Fanny, I am ready to laugh at the idea – and yet it is no laughing matter to have had you so mistaken as to your own feelings.'[40] In truth, she had never thought her niece to be quite so much in love with Mr Plumptre as Fanny herself believed. 'Oh! dear Fanny, your mistake has been one that thousands of women fall into. He was the *first* young man who attached himself to you. That was the charm, & most powerful it is.' (It was 'an old story', Emma remarks of her fascination with Frank Churchill, 'and no more than has happened to hundreds of my sex before'.) Yet Jane had never thought to caution her niece against an attachment which, even if it fell a little short of love, seemed to promise more than was necessary for tolerable happiness. Was it merely Mr Plumptre's awkward manner at the Canterbury races, she wondered, which had raised a little 'disgust' in the mind of one who now viewed him with 'rather more acuteness, penetration & taste, than love'? 'What strange creatures we are!' she exclaimed. 'It seems as if your being secure of him (as you say yourself) had made you indifferent.'

The more she wrote, the more Jane found herself imagining her niece's situation quite as if it were some nice dilemma she had contrived for one of her fictional heroines. 'My dearest Fanny,' she confessed, 'I am writing what will not be of the smallest use to you. I am feeling differently every moment, & shall not be able to suggest a single thing that can assist your mind. I could lament in one sentence & laugh in the next, but as to opinion or counsel I am sure none will [be] extracted worth having from this letter.' There was something so finely balanced about Fanny's situation that it provoked her novelist's instinct for exploring all the exquisite conflicts of sense and sensibility. When she first received Fanny's letter, it had so filled her imagination that 'I could not bear to leave off, when I had once began.' How fortunate it was that Cassandra had arranged to dine at the great house that night, leaving Jane alone to puzzle over the poignant ironies of this real-life plot. 'Poor dear Mr J.P.!' she wrote. 'What is to be done? You certainly *have* encouraged him to such a point as to make him feel almost secure of you.'

In one sense, her niece's conduct seemed almost perverse. 'You have no inclination for any other person – His situation in life, family, friends, & above all his character – his uncommonly amiable mind, strict principles, just notions, good habits – *all* that *you* know so well how to value.' In her imagination, Mr J.P. quickly began to assume the status of one of her most virtuous characters, an Edmund Bertram perhaps, or even a Mr Knightley. 'Oh! my dear Fanny, the more I write about him, the warmer my feelings become, the more strongly I feel the sterling worth of such a young man & the desirableness of your growing in love with him again. I recommend this most thoroughly.' After all, what was there to be said against him, but his modesty? 'If he were less modest, he would be more agreable, speak louder & look impudenter; and is not it a fine character, of which modesty is the only defect?' Fanny's brothers might choose to make fun of the young man's solemn *goodness* and pious evangelical manner. 'Do not be frightened from the connection by your brothers having most wit. Wisdom is better than wit, & in the long run will certainly have the laugh on her side.' 'Don't be frightened by the idea of his acting more strictly up to the precepts of the New Testament than others,' she added. 'I am by no means convinced that we ought not all to be Evangelicals, & am at least persuaded that they who are so from Reason & Feeling, must be happiest & safest.' But then, having wrought herself up to this high point of solemn religious principle, she allowed herself to descend to the more practical matter of Fanny's feelings. Of course, if Fanny *really did not like him*, she must on no account accept him. 'Anything is to be preferred or endured rather than marrying without affection.' After her several paragraphs of lofty praise for Mr J.P.'s sterling virtues, this sudden, brisk injunction might appear a little terse. But what it lacked in eloquence it made up for in sympathetic conviction.

Jane was well aware how difficult it was to make one's deepest feelings correspond with one's highest beliefs. 'I am very fond,' she had recently told Anna, 'of Sherlock's sermons', in which those very New Testament precepts that Mr J.P. threatened to 'act up' to were most eloquently expounded. Yet was it really possible, as the Gospel required, to love one's neighbours as oneself? The day before, she had watched the sad wagons which removed the possessions of their Chawton neighbours, the Webbs. The three Miss Webbs had never succeeded in pronouncing their 'R's and their mother had proved similarly unequal to managing her slender income. 'When I saw the waggons at the door, & thought of all the trouble they must have in moving, I began to reproach myself for not having liked them better,' Jane wrote to Anna, 'but since the waggons have disappeared, my conscience has been closed again – & I am excessively glad they are gone.'[41]

'The most unlearned, & uninformed female'

Jane returned to London at the end of November, when the first edition of *Mansfield Park* was all sold. Egerton had said nothing about a second edition, and it was Henry's opinion that the question should be quickly resolved. Jane agreed. 'I am very greedy & want to make the most of it,' she told Fanny, though as her niece was 'much above caring about money', she promised not to 'plague' her with 'any particulars'. 'The pleasures of vanity are more within your comprehension,' she wrote, '& you will enter into mine, at receiving the *praise*, which every now & then comes to me, through some channel or other.'[42] No books, it seemed, had ever occasioned quite so much curiosity and gossip as her three novels, and 'everybody was desirous to attribute them to some of their own friends'. Mrs Carrick, she heard, had declared that 'All who think deeply & feel much will give the preference to *Mansfield Park.*' And her nephew James Edward sent an anonymous note (from 'an Admirer') begging her to add another volume to *Mansfield Park*, 'in which the example of useful and amiable married life may be exhibited in the characters of Edmund and Fanny'. In his opinion, *Mansfield Park* had only one fault: 'it is too quickly read.'[43] Yet, while all this was very flattering, it offered less solid gratification than ready sales. 'People are more ready to borrow & praise, than to buy,' Jane noted ruefully, adding, 'tho I like praise as well as anybody, I like what Edward calls *pewter* too.'[44]

Once in London, Jane found herself expected to play host again to Henry's Hanwell beauty, Miss Harriet Moore. It was not a role she relished, 'for tho' I like Miss H.M. as much as one can at my time of life after a day's acquaintance, it is uphill work to be talking to those whom one knows so little'. She was even threatened by a coach trip with only Miss Moore's sister Eliza to accompany her. 'I rather dread it,' she told Fanny. 'We shall not have two ideas in common.'[45]

A visit to Anna at Hendon was more congenial, though when Anna repeated the invitation a few days later, Jane found an excuse to decline it, informing her niece that she had 'not a day disengaged'. Anna's Hendon arrangements were agreeable enough, Jane found, though she could not help thinking her niece's insistence on the purchase of a pianoforte an unwarrantable extravagance. 'It seems throwing money away,' she told Fanny. 'They will wish the 24 gns in the shape of sheets & towels six months hence.'[46] She was pleased when Edward brought his eldest son to town, and together they all went to the theatre to see Miss O'Neal in the title role of Garrick's *Isabella, or the Fatal Marriage.* As usual, though, Jane found something wanting in the performance. 'I took two pocket handkerchiefs, but had very little occasion for either,' she told Anna. Miss O'Neal, she acknowledged, was 'an elegant creature however & hugs Mr Younge delightfully'. But yet there was something lacking. 'I fancy I want something more than can be. Acting seldom satisfies me,' she wrote.[47] The following day, she visited Charles's daughters at Keppel Street, where little Harriot sat in her lap, Fanny talked incessantly 'with an interesting lisp and indistinctness' and the 'little puss' Cassy asked 'a thousand' impertinent questions about Anna's wedding. 'She does not shine in the tender feelings,' Jane commented. 'She will never be a Miss O'Neal; more in the Mrs Siddons line.'[48]

Whatever she found wanting in Garrick's play or Miss O'Neal's performance was more than compensated for in the continuing drama of Fanny's predicament *vis-à-vis* Mr J.P. The girl had no sooner received Jane's long letter, and acknowledged it in her diary ('A letter from . . . Aunt Jane Austen full of advice &c &c'), than she wrote again, a letter full of tremulous anxieties. In the coolness of the downstairs room at Hans Place, Jane composed herself to reply. Her niece, she noted, despite all the intensities of her emotions, retained a natural genius for comedy. The poignant little sketch in which she described her attempt to rekindle her amorous feelings for Mr J.P. by a secret visit to his room, amused Jane 'excessively'. 'The dirty shaving rag was exquisite!' she declared. 'Such a circumstance ought to be in print. Much too good to be lost.'[49] Yet the situation, she knew, was not at all a comic one, and she felt a certain dread at how much her niece seemed to rely on her views. 'You frighten me out of my wits,' she wrote, insisting that the girl 'must not let anything depend on my opinion. Your own feelings & none but your own, should determine such an important point.'[50] She would not retract what she had previously written. She still maintained that even Fanny's present feelings, 'supposing you were to marry *now*, would be sufficient for his happiness'. But *his* happiness was not the matter at issue. 'The risk is too great for *you*, unless your own sentiments prompt it.' The unpleasantness of appearing fickle was certainly not inconsiderable, she conceded; yet it was as nothing when 'compared to the misery of being bound *without* love, bound to one, & preferring another'. '*That*,' she wrote, 'is a punishment which you do *not* deserve.' Perhaps, she thought, her niece might think her perverse, since in her previous letter 'I was urging everything in his favour' but was now 'inclining the other way'. 'I cannot help it,' she confessed. 'I am at present more impressed with the possible evil that may arise to *you* from engaging yourself to him ... than with anything else.' Whatever was to be done must be resolved quickly. Mr J.P. was in London and had left his card at Hans Place the previous day. Her uncle Henry was surprised that Fanny's father had not requested that the young man should be invited to dine with them, and it was left to Fanny's brother to make excuses about not knowing his address. Even these clandestine letters between Fanny and herself bore an uncomfortable appearance of conspiracy. 'Write *something* that may do to be read or told,' she begged her. If Fanny *could* revive her past feelings for the man '& from your unbiassed self resolve to go on as before,' Jane said, she would 'be glad ... but this I do not expect'. Above all, she wrote, 'I cannot wish you to be fettered.'

Jane wrote this on the morning of 30 November, before going with Henry to see Egerton about *Mansfield Park*. It was not a happy meeting. The man refused to engage for a second edition of a book whose reception had fallen sadly below his expectations. Jane returned to Chawton the following week with her next novel almost completed, resolved upon finding a publisher for *Emma* who would be more sympathetic to what she called her 'greed'.

At Chawton that winter, the continuing lawsuit between the Austens and their Hinton neighbours threatened to sour village relations. Edward still expressed himself full of confidence about the outcome; his 'hopes ... in his cause do not lessen,' Jane wrote, though she kept her own opinion on the matter to herself. Her mother hoped, somewhat improbably, for a sensible resolution to the dispute which would not greatly distress either party. She still endeavoured to maintain civil relations with the Hintons and was gratified when Miss Hinton condescended to pass on to her some particulars of the wedding in Southampton of her goddaughter Elizabeth-Matilda Butler-Harrison to another Austen cousin, the Reverend William Austen of Horsted Keynes. At Christmas, Mrs Austen told Anna that they continued to visit the Hintons 'as heretofore and are apparently as good neighbours as we were before the tremendous law-suit threatened us'.[51]

Neighbourliness of this kind, however, did not preclude a good deal of malicious gossip. Miss Hinton took great pleasure in treating her friend, Mary Russell Mitford of Shinfield, to some acid comments on the subject of their most celebrated Austen neighbour. Miss Mitford's mother had once described Jane as the 'silliest, most affected husband-hunting butterfly'. But Miss Hinton regarded Jane as an 'old maid' ('I beg her pardon – young lady') of a very different character. 'She has stiffened into the most perpendicular, precise, taciturn piece of "single blessedness" that ever existed,' she declared. Once, Miss Hinton alleged, Jane Austen had been 'no more regarded in society than a poker or a fire screen or any other thin, upright piece of wood or iron that fills its corner in peace and quiet'. Now that she was known as a celebrated novelist, she was 'still a poker but a poker of whom everyone is afraid'. For her part, Miss Mitford had no hesitation in lamenting the 'want of elegance' in Jane Austen's work. 'It is impossible not to feel in every line of *Pride and Prejudice*, in every word of "Elizabeth", the entire want of taste which could produce so pert, so worldly a heroine as the beloved of such a man as Darcy,' she wrote.[52]

At Steventon, little Caroline, now nine years old, was the latest in the line of female Austens with ambitions to set up as an authoress. On a visit after Christmas, Jane patiently read through her niece's first literary effort, a story called 'Olivia'. She was pleased to see the girl had chosen a 'good-for-nothing father' as the villain of her tale, responsible for all the heroine's tragic sufferings.[53] 'I hope *he* hung himself,' she declared. Three days were spent at Ashe rectory with the Lefroys, whose young son Charles was soon to visit Ben and Anna at Hendon. 'A very fine boy, but terribly in want of discipline,' was Jane's comment. 'I hope he gets a wholesome thump, or two, whenever it is necessary,' she wrote to Anna in her best stiff-poker manner. She set herself to read Mrs Hawkins's sober tale *Rosanne*, a work avowedly designed to illustrate 'the inestimable advantages attendant on the practice of pure Christianity', but found it tedious, flat and filled with 'a thousand improbabilities'. The reading of such works only increased her determination to complete her own novel, *Emma*. 'I cannot flourish in this East wind,' she wrote to Anna that spring, though her industry belied this assertion.[54] Throughout February and March, while Napoleon contrived his escape from Elba, she devoted herself to events in her own fictional world of Highbury. By the end of March, when the French Emperor resumed power in Paris, she had finished the book.

Having endeavoured to write a novel in which the sins of selfishness and snobbery might receive their just rebuke, Jane had yet contrived in *Emma* to salve her instincts (at the expense, if necessary, of her conscience) by the creation of a heroine whose wilfulness was only partially redeemed by contrition. Emma must be made to feel, with all due penitence, the force of Mr Knightley's admonishment for her mockery of poor Miss Bates at Box Hill. She must be forced to endure a painful and humiliating reassessment of herself and all her social machinations: 'the blunders, the blindness of her own head and heart! . . . She was proved to have been universally mistaken . . . she had done mischief. She had brought evil on Harriet, on herself, and she too much feared, on Mr Knightley.' Yet for all that, her rehabilitation was achieved with remarkably little real discomfiture, and rewarded with the promise of 'perfect happiness'. Jane made sure to make Mr Knightley recommend, with all the noble force of his virtuous eloquence, 'the beauty of truth and sincerity in all our dealings with each other'. Yet Emma's agreement to this proposition was accompanied by 'a blush of sensibility on Harriet's account, which she could not give any *sincere* explanation of'.[55] Could not, or *would not*? Jane was content to leave it as a matter of dispute whether it were she herself, or her heroine, who gave it as her opinion that 'complete truth' very seldom belonged to any human disclosure.

What she did *not* leave as a matter of dispute was that, for all Emma's apparent assent to the doctrine of frankness and sincerity, she did not choose to inform her future husband of Harriet Smith's passion for him. Nor did Emma, chidden and then chosen by Knightley, entirely forsake her fondness for malicious wit. Jane opted to present Emma's acceptance of Mr Knightley's proposal of marriage in the oblique manner of a formula: 'What did she say? Just what she ought of course. A lady always does.' Such felicitous impersonality of phrasing allowed her, in the closing pages, to indulge herself by indicating how very *un*-ladylike her heroine might still be in continuing to say and think just what she *ought not*. There was her 'saucy conscious smile' at the thought of her nephew Henry being 'cut out' from inheriting Donwell Abbey. There was her wicked raillery at poor Harriet's expense, as when she solemnly assured her future husband that he was surely mistaken in the reason he ascribed for Mr Robert Martin's enthusiasm: 'It was not Harriet's hand,' she said, that had inspired the man's admiration, but 'the dimensions of some famous ox'. Or when she amused herself with the malicious thought that 'it really was too much to hope of even Harriet, that she could be in love with more than *three* men in one year'. Above all, it was there in the secret affinity which Emma still admitted, between herself and Frank Churchill, in their love of deception. 'I am sure it was a source of high entertainment to you, to feel you were taking us all in,' she tells him, 'because, to tell you the truth, I think it might have been some amusement to myself in the same situation'.[56] This from the woman who had recently sealed her betrothal with a pledge to 'the beauty of truth and sincerity' in all her dealings.

In *Mansfield Park*, Jane had presented wit as the enemy of truth with Edmund Bertram's solemn boast 'there is not the least wit in my nature'. But in *Emma*, she allowed herself a greater freedom. Here it was the vulgar Mrs Elton who appeared as the contemner of wit: 'I am not one of those who have witty things at everybody's service. I do not pretend to be a wit.' Emma, the wittiest and most satirical of all the characters, was also the most blessed, being, in Knightley's eyes, 'the best of all creatures, *faultless in spite of all her faults*'. Oh, for such a comforting indulgence! No wonder Jane described her heroine 'in dancing, singing, exclaiming spirits'. To be reformed, forgiven, blessed, *and yet unchanged* in all the essentials of her being, and with all her former vanities restored. 'Oh! I always deserve the best treatment,' she boasts to Mr Knightley (she still cannot call him 'George'), '*because I never put up with any other*.'[57] That was the kind of boast that Jane herself longed to make.

Frank Austen, who had now taken up residence in the great house at Chawton, was spared involvement in the renewed hostilities which followed Buonaparte's return to power in France. Instead, he spent time with his mother and sisters, offering advice to Jane on some nautical details for inclusion in any further editions of *Mansfield Park*. Even Charles, in the intervals between chasing after enemy warships in the Mediterranean, found some leisure for literary diversions. He had been praising Scott's *Waverley*, he told Jane in a letter sent from Palermo in early May, 'when a young man present observed that nothing had come out for years to be compared with *Pride and Prejudice, Sense and Sensibility* &c'. No doubt, he said, she 'must be anxious to know the name of a person of so much taste. I should tell you it is Fox, a nephew of the late Charles James Fox.'[58] To receive such high commendations from so dubious a source was, Jane felt, at best an equivocal compliment. She was hardly surprised when Charles added (lest she be 'too much elated at this morsel of praise') that Mr Fox 'did not appear to like *Mansfield Park* so well as the two first'. There, at least, the young man was true to his uncle's reprobate principles. As to her brother's high opinion of *Waverley*, Jane was reluctantly compelled to agree. Her mother, too, was vastly impressed by the book. '[It] has afforded me more entertainment than any modern production (Aunt Jane's excepted) of the novel kind that I have read for a great while,' she told her granddaughter Anna.[59]

Throughout the summer, the small cottage at Chawton was full of children; Caroline came from Steventon, little Cassy came from Keppel Street, and together they played with Frank's tribe of children, Mary, Frank, Henry, George and baby Cassandra Eliza from the great house. It pleased Jane to see this infant comradeship between her little nieces and nephews. 'I like first cousins to be first cousins, & interested about each other,' she wrote to Anna. 'They are but one remove from Br & Sr.' ('Children of the same family, the same blood, with the same first associations and habits,' she wrote in *Mansfield Park*, 'have some means of enjoyment in their power, which no subsequent connections can supply.')[60] When not playing at spillikins, or acting little plays, the children listened for news of the campaign against Buonaparte, and Frank patiently explained to them about manoeuvres and strategies. There was much rejoicing when they received word of the great victory at Waterloo in June. Old Boney would not find it quite so easy to escape from his exile on St Helena, Frank told them, enthralling the children with his reminiscences of that lonely island. Later that summer, Lord Byron wrote a poem 'in the Character of Buonaparte', reflecting on the exiled Emperor's fate, which began 'Farewell to the Land, where the gloom of my glory/Arose, & o'ershadowed the Earth with her fame . . .' Now that the danger was over, Jane found a certain appeal in this true-life fable of hubris and nemesis. Wondering again about attempting a Life of Buonaparte, she copied out Byron's lines to keep.[61]

She found herself in a rare mood for writing. Barely was one novel finished than she was sketching out the next. Partly it was the hope of *pewter* that inspired her; but more than that, it was a kind of restless mental energy. She had a conviction that she was at the height of her inventive powers. New characters would present themselves to her imagination with an irresistible urgency. Already her mind was set on a new novel, about naval men home from the wars, their friendliness, their brotherliness, their openness and uprightness. How would they fare, these poor half-pay officers, like Charles, in peace-time, which was universally allowed to be such a bad time for 'getting on'?[62] On 4 August, Mary Austen took Caroline back to Steventon and, four days later, Jane began work on her new novel. Despite this bold start, she soon found her progress interrupted by more immediate concerns. Irritated by Egerton's unhelpful attitude towards *Mansfield Park*, she and Henry had agreed to approach Byron's own publisher, John Murray, with the manuscript of *Emma*. When the two of them presented themselves at Murray's handsome Albemarle Street offices in early September, they were both agreeably impressed by his courteous manner. Delayed on their homeward journey to Hampshire, they called in unexpectedly at Steventon, where Caroline affected a professional interest in everything that related to novels and their publication, and proudly presented her aunt with yet another manuscript.[63]

Back at Chawton, little Cassy was still demanding the attention of both her aunts. At the end of August, Ben and Anna Lefroy left Hendon to settle at Wyards, a large farmhouse near Alton and within walking distance of Chawton. But it was not a walk that little Cassy greatly favoured. Given the choice between a village fair at Chawton and a visit to her cousin at Wyards, the obstinate girl opted firmly in favour of the fair, 'which we trust will not greatly affront you,' Jane wrote to Anna. 'If it does, you may hope that some little Anna hereafter may revenge the insult by a similar preference of an Alton fair to her cousin Cassy.'[64] She had not long to wait for the first part at least of this prophecy to be fulfilled. Baby Anna-Jemima Lefroy was born at Wyards just three weeks after this letter was written. Having still not felt 'quite equal' to scrutinizing young Caroline's manuscript, Jane used this excuse to mollify the girl's feelings by writing from London to congratulate her on her new status as a 'sister-Aunt'. 'Now that you are become an aunt,' she wrote, 'you are a person of some consequence & must excite great interest whatever you do. I have always maintained the importance of aunts as much as possible, & I am sure of your doing the same now.' She even consented to allow the girl to practise on her own pianoforte at Chawton, but advised her to 'try to make out some other tune besides *The Hermit*'.[65] *That* was a piece associated in Jane's mind with her own most extravagant vanities at Godmersham, and she hardly felt it wise for even so exalted a figure as a literary sister-aunt to confine herself to such lonely sublimities.

From September till the end of the year, Jane spent much of her time in London, at Hans Place, waiting for Murray to make up his mind about *Emma*. For all his charm, she soon found the man to be almost as mercenary a scoundrel as the others in his trade. William Gifford, editor of the *Quarterly Review*, which her young people at Mansfield Park had lounged over, had undertaken to read the manuscript on Murray's behalf. Gifford 'had nothing but good' to say of the book. Indeed, he told Murray, that he had been 'sure of the writer' before the publisher had even mentioned her name. There were, he said, 'some . . . little omissions, and an expression may now and then be amended in passing through the press'. But he said that he would 'readily undertake' such revisions as were necessary.[66] Jane supposed it was some sort of compliment to have one's grammar corrected by the editor of the *Quarterly Review*. All this was concluded before the end of September, and yet still Murray delayed in coming to terms. It was not until almost three weeks later that Jane was able to write to Cassandra from Hans Place with news of his proposals. 'Mr Murray's letter is come; he is a rogue of course, but a civil one. He offers £450 – but wants to have the copyright of *MP* & *SS* included.' Murray, she discovered, was another of those people far more lavish with praise than with pewter. 'He sends more praise ... than I expected,' she told Cassandra. 'It is an amusing letter.'[67]

Life at Hans Place was thrown into consternation next day, when Henry suddenly fell ill with a severe feverish attack. From Monday to Friday he lay on his bed in the back room upstairs while Mr Haden, the clever apothecary from the corner of Sloane Street, took 20 ounces of blood from his body each day. 'I am not alarmed,' Jane wrote to Cassandra. 'Henry is an excellent patient, lies quietly in bed & is ready to swallow anything.' The hot sticky weather – so unseasonable for mid-October – was enough to make anyone unwell. Mrs Tilson, from three doors away, was no help at all, 'quite a wretch, always ill'. ('Nobody is healthy in London,' Jane made Mr Woodhouse observe, 'nobody can be.')[68]

Jane quickly found herself surrounded by medicines, potions, tea, barley-water and dirty clothes. One evening, she was compelled to entertain, all alone, the Creed family from Hendon ('all strangers to me'); another, she was reduced to the 'comical consequence' of dining *tête-à-tête* with Mr Seymour, who had once professed himself her ardent admirer. At least she was spared any more of Miss Harriet Moore's relations and friends, many of whom, fortunately, were sick too, she told Cassandra. At last, by the end of the week, Henry appeared well enough to sit up in his bed and dictate a letter of reply to Murray's proposals. Whether it was his illness, or the awkwardness of expressing himself through what he termed 'an amuensis' (Latin had never been a strong subject with Henry), the letter was stiff with Henry's most pompous prose. The terms that Murray offered, he said, were 'so very inferior to what we had expected, that I am apprehensive of having made some great error in my arithmetical calculation'.[69] From what Jane knew of Henry's skill in arithmetical calculation, this did not seem an impossible conclusion, but she was grateful for her brother's valiant efforts on her behalf, even if his epistolary style left much to be desired. 'Documents in my possession,' Henry went on, 'appear to prove the sum offered by you for the copyright of *Sense & Sensibility, Mansfield Park & Emma,* is not equal to the money which my sister has actually cleared by one very moderate edition of *Mansfield Park.*' (Murray had expressed astonishment that such a very small edition – barely more than a thousand copies – 'should have been sent into the world'.) At that point, Henry's voice drifted away. Even the effort of dictating this letter proved too much for him, and he suffered a severe relapse, which necessitated the sending for Mr Haden once more to bleed him.

For several days, Henry's life seemed in danger and Jane sent urgent letters to all her brothers and sisters, summoning them to London. Edward arrived the following evening and James brought Cassandra up from Chawton two days later. Dr Baillie of Lower Grosvenor Street, who had treated Henry once before, was brought in to assist with medical preparations and by the end of the week there were signs of recovery. Amid all this uncertainty, Jane felt quite unequal to offering any formal reply to Murray's proposals, though the publisher, hearing of Henry's illness, kindly sent him a copy of Scott's *The Field of Waterloo.* 'It will end in my publishing for myself I dare say,' Jane remarked to Cassandra.

At last, by the end of October, Henry's condition had improved sufficiently for his brothers to return home, leaving Jane and Cassandra to care for him. It was now that Jane decided to take matters into her own hands. On 3 November, she wrote to Murray. Her brother's illness, she explained, had occasioned this long delay in replying, and while she still remained 'fearful of harassing' Henry 'by any business', she was nevertheless 'desirous of coming to some decision on the affair in question'. She proposed a simple expedient. 'I must beg the favour of you to call on me here any day that may suit you best, & at any hour in the eveng or any in the morng except from 11 to one.'[70] Mindful of poor Henry's formal flourishes, Jane was inclined rather to rely on her personal diplomatic skills than on his stilted banker's rhetoric. 'A short conversation,' she suggested, 'may perhaps do more than much writing.' Murray responded promptly to this invitation, and their short, courteous conversation at Hans Place resulted in her having both more to risk, and more to gain, from the publication of *Emma*. Murray agreed to publish two thousand copies of the book at the author's expense, with all profits to her after she had paid him a ten per cent commission.[71] Jane made one more stipulation. The book must be published immediately; within the month if possible, as she intended leaving London by early December. Again Murray agreed. His printer, Roworth, he assured her, was the most expeditious and exact that it was possible to find.

It so happened that Dr Baillie, who now attended on Henry's recovery, was also one of the Prince Regent's physicians and he told Jane that the Prince was a great admirer of her novels, that 'he often read them, and had a set in each of his residences'.[72] Dr Baillie had taken the liberty of informing His Royal Highness that Miss Austen herself was now in London, and the Prince, in reply, had expressed a desire that Mr Clarke, the librarian of Carlton House, should 'speedily wait on her'. Accordingly, this Mr Clarke, a clergyman who had formerly seen service as a naval chaplain, presented himself at Hans Place, where he warmly endorsed all Dr Baillie's previous compliments and invited Jane to visit Carlton House. The Prince, he told her, had charged him to show her the library there, adding 'many civilities as to the pleasure his R.H. had received from her novels'.

As a consequence, a few days later, Jane was shown over the Prince's exquisite Carlton House palace: 'A hall with walls of green and verd-antique, and Ionic columns of brown Siena marble led into ante-rooms and drawing-rooms of crimson, gold, blue and rose with flowered carpets and hangings of velvet and satin elaborately draped . . . with buhl and ormolu in every corner.'[73] There was an Ionic dining-room, a Gothic dining-room, and a splendid Gothic library. Her cicerone on this visit, Mr Clarke, was a man of excessive politeness and some complacency in the estimate of his own fine taste and literary achievements. He had written a book on Nelson and several other learned tomes, and treated Jane with great civility as a fellow author. He also liked to do watercolour sketches, chiefly of naval vessels, but also rising to a recognizable likeness of the poor Princess Caroline. That unhappy lady's daughter, the Princess Charlotte, was also, Jane learnt, an admirer of her works, and had even thought she could discern a striking likeness of disposition between herself and Marianne in *Sense and Sensibility*. Mr Clarke had a great fund of royal anecdotes, which he liked to interlard with quotations from his favourite authors, Beattie, Goldsmith and La Fontaine, to display the extent of his literary connoisseurship. Towards the end of her visit, speaking again of the Prince's admiration of her writing, he declared himself charged to say 'that if Miss Austen had any other novel forthcoming, she was quite at liberty to dedicate it to the Prince'. Perhaps, he suggested, his own efforts might serve her as a model, showing her the florid three-page panegyric to the Prince which prefaced his illustrated work, *The Progress of Maritime Discovery*.[74] This suggestion came as a considerable shock to Jane. Whilst she found it flattering to hear of the Regent's partiality for her novels, and enjoyed the vanity of this private visit to his palace, the man himself remained, above all other mortals, one whose profligate conduct and licentiousness she most deplored. 'I hate [him],' she had told Martha Lloyd, only two years before.[75] To receive praise from the nephew of that dangerous Whig libertine Charles James Fox was embarrassing enough; to think of dedicating a novel to a man whose gambling and debauchery were the subjects of every caricaturist's pen and whose profligate behaviour threatened to place the monarchy itself in jeopardy, was too much to contemplate. Her mind went back, guiltily, to her nephew's teasing lines suggesting that the Regent would make her 'a countess at least' ('And indeed, if the princess should lose her dear life,/You might have a good chance of becoming his wife'). As she stared around the ornate forty-foot library she experienced a kind of horror at the thought. She contrived to make 'all proper acknowledgements' to Mr Clarke for the Prince's gracious offer and left Carlton House in considerable consternation of feelings.

In her own mind, Jane was quite resolved upon *not* accepting the Prince's offer, but when she reached Hans Place she found that Cassandra and Henry were of quite another opinion. They advised her that what the unctuous Mr Clarke had expressed as a permission must be considered as a form of command. This advice discomposed her greatly, and she wrote back promptly to him for clarification. 'I intreat you to have the goodness to inform me how such a permission is to be understood,' she wrote; '& whether it is incumbent on me to shew my sense of the honour, by inscribing the work now in the press, to H.R.H. I shd be equally concerned to appear either presumptuous or ungrateful.' Mr Clarke's reply, she found, was not entirely helpful. 'It is certainly not *incumbent* on you to dedicate your work now in the press to His Royal Highness,' he wrote, emphasizing the word *incumbent* as if to indicate how utterly remote from the Prince's mind was any hint of such disagreeable compulsion.[76] If, however, she *wished* to do the Regent that honour, 'either now or at any future period', he was happy to assure her that it would not require 'any trouble or solicitation on your part'. *That*, Henry assured her, did indeed amount to a command. He had no doubt that the Regent would now consider it an insult if she did not avail herself of this royal 'permission'. But Mr Clarke went further. Amid all his familiar flatteries of her 'genius', her 'principles' and her 'powers of discrimination', he ventured to suggest a subject for some future novel. Why did she not 'delineate . . . the habits of life and character and enthusiasm of a clergyman', a man 'something like Beattie's Minstrel "*Silent when glad, affectionate tho' shy*"', who passed his time 'between the metropolis & the country . . . fond of, & entirely engaged in literature' and who was 'no man's enemy but his own': someone, in short (though he did not say so in as many words), rather like himself? No writer of the present day, Mr Clarke opined, had yet given the true character of the modern English clergyman, and Miss Austen, he was sure, was the very person to do so.

Jane rather thought that she *had* given the image of such a modern clergyman as Mr Clarke in the figure of Mr Collins. She thanked him graciously for his suggestion, but modestly insisted upon her own utter incapacity for drawing such a character as he proposed. 'The comic part,' she ventured, she 'might be equal to';

but not 'the good, the enthusiastic, the literary'. 'Such a man's conversation,' she wrote, 'must at times be on subjects of science & philosophy of which I know nothing.'[77] A mere woman like herself, she indicated (confident in the man's inability to discern irony where his own egregious vanity was concerned), had enjoyed none of those benefits of a classical education, and but little of that 'very extensive acquaintance with English literature, ancient & modern' which made Mr Clarke himself so formidably learned. 'I think I may boast myself to be, with all possible vanity, the most unlearned, & uninformed female who ever dared to be an authoress,' she concluded, with the same coy triumphant fleer with which she had once pronounced herself 'a partial, prejudiced and ignorant Historian'.

Awkward as she felt about accepting the Prince Regent's compliment, Jane was sufficiently rational to recognize the potential benefits, in financial terms, of such a mark of royal favour. Upon Murray its effect was quite decided, producing a sudden burst of energetic activity. Until that moment, the publisher had been somewhat dilatory about attending to *Emma*. Henry had written to him on 20 November, returning the copy of Scott's *Waterloo* and enquiring about the progress of Jane's novel. He had not then received the civility of a reply. Now, Jane wrote to Murray herself to express how 'very much disappointed & vexed' she was at the printers' delays. 'Is it likely that the printers will be influenced to greater dispatch & punctuality,' she enquired, in her most insinuating manner, 'by knowing that the work is to be dedicated, by permission, to the Prince Regent?'[78] Even before her letter was sent, she received her answer in an avalanche of proof-sheets together with profuse apologies from Roworth the printer. Murray had evidently heard the news from another source and was now anxious to propitiate her. But Jane sent her letter anyway, and received such an ingratiating reply from Murray that it was 'quite overcoming'. The printers had been waiting for paper – the blame was thrown upon the stationer – but Murray gave his word that she should have 'no further cause for dissatisfaction'. 'He has lent us *Miss Williams* & *Scott*, & says that any book of his will always be at *my* service,' Jane told Cassandra who had now returned to Chawton. 'In short,' she concluded wryly, 'I am soothed & complimented into tolerable comfort.'[79] Such, it seemed, were the benefits of royal favour.

Others were less impressed. A disapproving note from Martha accused her of being influenced by 'the most mercenary motives'. Once again Jane felt herself obliged to assume a kind of secrecy, begging Cassandra's compliance in 'letting nobody know that I *might* dedicate &c – for fear of being obliged to do it'. As if to mitigate the offence of the dedication, she strove to affect a distinct hard-headedness about the terms and extent of her obligation. 'It strikes me that I have no business to give the P.R. a binding, but we will take counsel upon the question.'[80]

Gradually, Henry's health began to recover, though it was a slow process. On Thursday the 23rd, he took his first step outdoors for several weeks, venturing as far as the balcony; the following day, he managed a visit to his fellow invalid, Mrs Tilson at No. 26. Now that she was reassured her brother's life no longer lay in any imminent danger, Jane was not entirely unhappy at the slow progress of his cure, which necessitated the frequent visits of the amiable Mr Haden. Dr Baillie might have his grand connections among the Prince Regent's circle, but it was the quick-witted Mr Haden who most delighted her. 'Tomorrow Mr Haden is to dine with us,' she told Cassandra on the 24th. 'There's happiness! We really grow so fond of Mr Haden that I do not know what to expect.' Mr Haden, Mr Tilson and Mr Philips had made up their little 'circle of wits' the previous night, together with Fanny, visiting from Kent to avoid the attentions of Mr J.P., who played to them most delightfully on the harp she had hired from Chappells in Bond Street. Jane was really most aggrieved when Mrs Latouche and Miss East presented themselves as additional dinner-guests the following evening, which quite destroyed her plans for an agreeable *tête-à-tête* with the charming medical man. 'I am heartily sorry they are coming!' she confessed to Cassandra. 'It will be an eveng spoilt to Fanny & me.'[81]

Yet she contrived to find a quiet moment for some literary banter with this lively young man (not yet thirty!) who quite overwhelmed her with his enthusiasm for notions which might have seemed dangerously radical had he not urged them with such a becoming good humour. She told him of her axiom that 'one did not care for girls' – in fiction, at least – 'till they were quite grown up'. Mr Haden begged to disagree. This view of hers, he said, was founded upon a false notion of infancy. 'Infants should be treated like rational beings,' he contended; 'be spoken the truth to and be never deceived.' He held a low opinion of nurses, and was full of ideas for improving the health of infants and their mothers. Nothing could be more deleterious for the nation's health, he said, than the present woeful state of female education. 'If young women were educated more with a reference to health, and less to personal accomplishments,' he maintained, 'the number of inefficient mothers would be greatly reduced.'[82] Despite this, Mr Haden did not fail to tease her about her own apparent lack of accomplishments in the musical sphere. The man even had the impudence to cite Shakespeare on his side:

> *The man that hath no music in himself,*
> *Nor is not moved with concord of sweet sounds,*
> *Is fit for treasons, stratagems, and spoils . . .*

'I have been listening to dreadful insanity,' she wrote to Cassandra in a postscript late that night, full of excitement at the young man's beguiling conversation. 'It is Mr Haden's firm belief that a person *not* musical is fit for every sort of wickedness. I ventured to assert a little on the other side, but wished the cause in abler hands.'[83] It was not often that she felt herself thus outmanoeuvred in argument. Even when she challenged Mr Haden to make good his own assertions by singing to them, he found means to outwit her. 'He will not sing without a p.forte accompaniment.'

The next evening, Mr Haden dined with them again, and was full of praise for *Mansfield Park*, even preferring it to *Pride and Prejudice*. He also seemed full of admiration for Fanny, and listened to her play upon the harp for a full hour. Jane could not help dwelling upon the awkward seating arrangements, which had poor Henry and herself 'making the best of it' on the sofa-side, with their two unwelcome guests, Mrs Latouche and Miss East, while Fanny and Mr Haden were placed side by side on two adjacent chairs ('I *believe* at least they had *two* chairs'), talking together in the most intimate manner. 'Fancy the scene!' she wrote to Cassandra. 'And what is to be fancied next? – Why that Mr H dines here again tomorrow.' In the company of Mr Haden, Fanny seemed to forget all about Mr J.P. 'Mr Haden, a delightful clever musical "Haden" comes every evening & is agreable,' she recorded in her diary.[84] Of course, Fanny had all the advantages of the best music-masters for *her* accomplishments. Even here at Hans Place, the egregious Mr Meyers was calling to give her three lessons a week, altering his days and hours just as he chose, never punctual and never giving good measure. 'I have not Fanny's fondness for music masters,' Jane remarked sourly to Cassandra. 'They are . . . made of too much consequence & allowed to take too many liberties with their scholar's time.' If Mr Haden must find fault with her on account of her own incapacity with the harp, well so be it. It was too late for her to learn new tricks like these. Yet she hoped he would *not* find fault with her.

It was strange how much her thoughts seemed to dwell upon this energetic young man, so full of all his doings at his little low-roofed Brompton Dispensary. She tried to convince herself that her enthusiasm for this young man was all on Fanny's behalf, yet could not disguise from herself how fretful she became when Mr Haden's attentions were devoted exclusively to her niece and not at all to her. When Cassandra wrote with sly enquiries after this apothecary who seemed to figure so largely in her sister's correspondence, Jane affected to resent this slight to her new hero's status. 'You seem to be under a mistake as to Mr H.,' she wrote. 'You call him an apothecary; he is no apothecary, he has never been an apothecary, there is not an apothecary in this neighbourhood.'[85] It suited her to forget that it was she herself who had first described Mr Haden as an apothecary in a letter to Cassandra six weeks earlier. Now, the man had so risen in her estimation that he defied all such categories. 'He is a Haden, nothing but a Haden, a sort of wonderful nondescript creature on two legs, something between a man & an angel – but without the least spice of an apothecary.'

She felt a little guilty at the excitement she experienced in this young man's company when, in sober truth, she ought to be giving more attention to the sombre plight of those around her. Henry was still not well, and Mr Haden prudently forbade him to venture out in a carriage for fear of the uncertain November weather. Yet Henry's physical ailments were only part of his misfortunes. For some weeks, it had been an open secret that his Alton bank was on the verge of failing. 'I wonder that with such business to worry him, he can be getting better,' Jane wrote to Cassandra as the financial crisis loomed in the final week of November. In some ways, it seemed almost as if Henry's illness were a kind of refuge from outside pressures. When Mr Seymour called, a few days later, to tell him the worst was over and 'there was not the least ocasion for his absenting himself any longer', it came as a kind of relief. That Saturday, Henry, bound in stiff white strengthening plaster, took the Chelsea coach to sign bonds in Henrietta Street.[86] There was still a chance that the failure of the Alton branch of Austen, Gay and Vincent might not entail the complete collapse of the London bank of Austen, Maunde and Tilson, and for some days Henry strove as best he could to avert that possible catastrophe. The Austen family fortunes had seldom stood in such danger of calamity. In addition to the threat from Mr Baverstock's lawsuit, Edward now stood to lose the £20,000 surety he had pledged when Henry had been made Receiver-General for Taxes in Oxfordshire two years before. Uncle James Leigh-Perrot had similarly pledged £10,000, and that sum, too, was now at risk. 'When a man has once got his name in a banking house,' Jane had written twenty years before, 'he rolls in money.' That confident maxim seemed more than a little ill-conceived in their present plight.

Though Jane had never seen her brother as entirely fitted for a banker, she did not believe his present misfortunes to be of his own making. His extensive loan, to Lord Moira, amounting to some £6,000, were perhaps a little ill-advised (the money was never repaid); but they had been made with the best interests of the family in mind. His Lordship had been most assiduous in promoting Frank's claims to command of the *St Albans* and, as

Governor-General of Bengal, he was a man whose favour was at least as well worth cultivating, on behalf of Frank and Charles, as the Prince Regent's was, for her. Small wonder, though, that Jane's mother at Chawton should feel unwell at the prospect of seeing two of her sons, in their prime of life, reduced to ruin. It was more surprising how little unease Jane herself felt in the present crisis. Whether it were simply the invigorating company of Mr Haden, or the Regent's condescending flattery, she could not disguise a distinct sensation of elation. 'I am sorry my mother has been suffering,' she wrote to Cassandra, '& am afraid this exquisite weather is too good to agree with her.' As for herself, she could seldom remember better weather in her life. She luxuriated in it. '*I* enjoy it all over me, from top to toe, from right to left, longitudinally, perpendicularly, diagonally; – and I cannot but selfishly hope we are to have it last till Christmas; – nice, unwholesome, unseasonable, relaxing, close, muggy weather! Oh!'[87] All her hopes at present were exquisitely selfish and unwholesome.

She dashed off a letter to Murray dictating the terms of the title-page, '*Emma*, Dedicated by Permission to H.R.H. The Prince Regent'. She would leave all the 'trade' arrangements to Murray's judgements, she said, only stipulating that he should do everything 'most likely to clear off the edition rapidly'. She also sent a corrected copy of *Mansfield Park* ready for a second edition, which Murray had now undertaken to produce on the same basis as *Emma*. Meanwhile, friends and relations seemed determined to overwhelm the little household at Hans Place with their presents. A brace of pheasants from Mr Mascall on Thursday; another brace of pheasants from Mr Fowle the following day. 'We shall live upon pheasants,' Jane boasted to Cassandra. 'No bad life!'[88] The next day, it was a hare and four rabbits from Godmersham. 'We are stocked for nearly a week.' Whatever the state of poor Henry's finances, Jane herself felt quite rich and even sent Cassandra 'five one pound notes, for fear you should be distressed for little money'. She offered commiserations for Frank's cold in much the same insouciant manner: 'Sweet amiable Frank! why does *he* have a cold too? Like Capt Mirvan to Mde Duval, "I wish it were well over with him."' She offered thanks for *dearest* Charles's *perfect* letter – 'Poor dear Fellow! Not a present!' Why, she had a good mind to send him all twelve presentation copies of *Emma,* that 'were to have been dispersed among my near connections' – which 'near connections' she grandly described as 'beginning with the P.R. & ending with Countess Morley'.[89] As she sat in the cool downstairs room at Hans Place, surrounded by proofs, she had seldom felt more contented. 'A *sheet* come in this moment,' she reported excitedly; '1st & 3d vol. are now at 144 – 2d at 48. – I am sure you will like particulars.' Nor was there any more trouble about returning corrected sheets to the publisher; 'the printer's boys bring & carry'.

It was a sad fact but a true one that, as Henry's health improved, Jane found her own contentment decline correspondingly. Now, alas! there was no more excuse for Mr Haden to continue paying his daily visits. Henry spent a pleasant weekend with the Moores at Hanwell, where 'he met with the utmost care & attention', while Jane contrived to pass a whole quarter of an hour with Charles's children at Keppel Street, making strenuous efforts to regard them, as Mr Haden decreed, as little rational beings. On Henry's return, Jane arranged a 'gala' evening, with Mr Haden 'secured for dinner'. Her arrangements were briefly threatened when the impertinent Malings endeavoured to impose themselves on the party; but 'by manoeuvring & good luck we foiled all [their] attempts upon us'. She hardly needed to tell Cassandra that the resulting evening gathering was altogether delightful, since it included 'our precious' Mr Haden, and no unwelcome interlopers. But it was the last such evening she was to enjoy. A week later, Edward took Fanny back to Kent. Henry was already talking of travelling to Oxford by the middle of the month, by which time Jane herself would be returning to Chawton. She received a disagreeable note from Murray, pointing out, in the most courteous terms, how she had failed to understand the etiquette of a royal dedication. It pained her to be required to resume an abject manner. Her error, as to the form of the title-page, was, she said, 'arising from my ignorance only', and she thanked Murray for putting her right. 'Any deviation from what is usually done in such cases,' she said, 'is the last thing I should wish for.' She felt happy, she said, 'in having a friend to save me from the ill effect of my own blunder'.[90]

A more embarrassing blunder had been the foolish way she had allowed her emotions to be flattered by the companionship of young Mr Haden. Naturally, she had allowed nothing to be said or done which might betray her feelings or disgust his; but for a woman in her fortieth year who could write long letters of moral advice on such matters to her niece Fanny, it was a foolishness scarcely to be countenanced to have written as she did to Cassandra of her fondness for the young apothecary. What made it worse was the remembrance of those sharp moments of jealousy she had experienced, watching that same niece sitting so close beside Mr Haden, playing for him on her harp, and attending so eagerly to his every word. It brought to mind those feelings of mortification which Emma Woodhouse had endured on hearing Harriet boast of supposed encouragements from Mr Knightley. But such parallels as might exist between this fact and that fiction only occasioned further emotions of regret. For her, unlike Emma, there would be, she knew, no happy final chapter.

Two days before leaving town, she wrote a brief note to Mr Haden. It was no more than a scribble to accompany the books that he had kindly lent her – lent *them* she should say – during their stay in London. To her irritation, *Emma* was still not published, despite an advertisement in the *Morning Post* a fortnight earlier, and so she was denied the opportunity to send him a copy. *That* at least was an accomplishment he might have appreciated. On the whole, she decided, fewest words were best. She restricted herself to four brisk sentences, concluding: 'I leave town early on Saturday, & must say "Good bye" to you.'[91] Mr Haden would go back to his projected 'women's paper' full of good advice on motherhood and child-rearing, while she would resume her latest novel about a woman who, having once been unwisely persuaded to give up the man she loved, was offered, by the benignity of authorial providence, a second chance of happiness. She left London on 16 December, her fortieth birthday. She would never return there again.

CHAPTER 13

My Own Style

I must keep to my own style & go on in my own way.

Jane Austen, Letter to James Stanier Clarke,
April 1816

A doctrine of selfishness

Jane was greatly vexed at Murray's failure to bring out *Emma* before she left London. The book was twice announced in issues of the *Morning Post* during the first week of December, and in the Sunday *Observer* for 10 December it was clearly promised for 'Saturday next', the very day she had appointed for her departure. But Saturday came and went with no sign of her novel. At last, on 23 December – barely in time for Christmas – the *Morning Post* announced her book as 'published this day . . . by the Author of *Pride and Prejudice*'. The price was one guinea. Murray had devoted a whole page to her grand royal dedication, and each three volume set, she must agree, had a fine, handsome appearance. The set for the Prince of Wales was elegantly bound and delivered, as promised, a few days before publication, to Carlton House, where Mr Clarke accepted it on the Regent's behalf. She received his flattering letter shortly after her return to Chawton. Though Mr

Clarke had only peeped into the first few pages, he was full of admiration for what he read: 'so much nature . . . and excellent description of character . . .' Mr Clarke, it seemed, was now chiefly preoccupied with apprehensions for his own new book, a Life of James II, and steeling himself, he said, 'to stand the sharp knives which many a Shylock is wetting [*sic*] to cut more than a pound of flesh from my heart'.[1] Yet not so preoccupied that he neglected to encumber her with more of his literary advice. By all means, he wrote, 'let us have an English clergyman after *your* own fancy' (though he rather contradicted this grand permission by indicating how much his own 'fancy' was still at work on the project). 'Describe him burying his own mother,' he begged her, 'as I did.' Or why not 'carry your clergyman to sea' (as he had been)? When not fondly imagining himself as the hero of the next novel by Miss Austen, Mr Clarke was much given to maudlin self-description in the guise of Beattie's *Hermit*, and extended her an invitation to share his 'cell' in Golden Square. Jane thanked him for his many kindnesses, and noted his generous offer of a copy of *James II* 'when it reaches a second Ed'.

That Christmas, Jane busied herself despatching presentation sets of *Emma* to selected friends and relations. She sent one set to the Countess of Morley, a new friend, to whom she had been introduced by Henry earlier that year. Lady Morley had once been widely rumoured to be the true author of *Pride and Prejudice*, but Jane did not begrudge her this moment of borrowed fame. It was something of a compliment, she thought, to have her own brain-child attributed to such a spirited lady whose other celebrated achievement – this time a genuine one – was to have cured her erring husband of his addiction to young mistresses. She was, as she confessed to Lady M., still greatly fearful about the success of this latest work and filled with apprehensions that she might, 'as almost every writer of fancy does sooner or later', have already 'overwritten herself'. The Countess did not disappoint her. She expressed her 'infinite obligations' for this new novel, whose characters, she was sure, would interest and amuse her quite as much as 'the Bennets, Bertrams, Norriss & all their admirable predecessors – I can give them no higher praise'. Jane was delighted with this response, which was not, in truth, entirely candid; privately, the Countess told her sister-in-law that she ranked this new novel somewhere below both *Mansfield Park* and *Pride and Prejudice*.[2] Much emboldened, Jane even ventured to send a copy of *Emma* to Maria Edgeworth, but this grand literary lady did not even deign to acknowledge the gift, contenting herself instead with private expressions of distaste for Miss Austen's domestic scenes and descriptions of '*thin water-gruel*'. Other copies of the book were sent to members of the family. To Anna Lefroy Jane *lent*, but did not *give*, a copy, with a brief note to say that as she herself greatly wished to see Anna's Jemima, she was sure that Anna would be equally keen to see her *Emma*.[3]

Once the family had read the book, Jane solicited their opinions, which she drew up in a careful list, as she had done for *Mansfield Park*. Frank's comments stood at the head of the list. 'Captn Austen. – liked it extremely, observing that though there might be more wit in *P & P* – & an higher morality in *MP* – yet altogether, on account of its peculiar air of Nature throughout, he preferred it to either.' ('So much nature . . .' as Mr Clarke had said.) Cassandra liked it 'better than *P & P* – but not so well as *MP*'.[4] Jane was not greatly surprised at that, nor at her mother taking an exactly opposite view. (Mrs Austen 'thought it more interesting than *MP* – but not so interesting as *P & P* – No characters in it equal to Ly Catherine & Mr Collins'.) Edward took a landowner's privilege to tease his sister about a slip in her celebrated observations of nature. 'Jane,' he wrote, 'I wish you would tell me where you get those apple-trees of yours that come into bloom in July.' Anna Lefroy thought the book 'not so *brilliant* as *P & P* – nor so *equal* as *MP*' though she 'preferred Emma herself to all the heroines'. *That* preference was reckoned hardly surprising, since it was rumoured in the neighbourhood (though Jane herself denied it) that Anna was the model for Miss Woodhouse. When Anna's husband caught that rumour, it provoked a spirit of contradiction. He 'did not like the heroine so well as any of the others,' he roundly declared. Poor dear Fanny did her best to like the book, but really she could not *bear* Emma herself. She thought she *might* like Jane Fairfax 'if she knew more of her'. But Charles was always reliable.

Though far away in the Mediterranean, he was quickly writing home to express his admiration. '*Emma* arrived in time to a moment,' he wrote. 'I am delighted with her, more so I think than even with my favourite *Pride & Prejudice*, & have read it three times in the passage.'

Even the Shylocks of the literary reviews were quite kind to her. Throughout the spring and summer, a steady stream of politely gratifying notices appeared in print. 'Whoever is fond of an amusing, inoffensive and well-principled novel, will be well pleased with the perusal of *Emma*,' opined the *British Critic*. The *Monthly Review* agreed: 'the work will probably become a favourite with all those who seek for harmless amusement,' it declared, 'rather than deep pathos or appalling horrors in works of fiction.' 'The story is not ill-conceived,' observed the *Literary Panorama*; 'it is not romantic, but domestic.' 'Amusing, if not instructive,' was the judgement of the *Gentleman's Magazine*, which noted that the novel had 'no tendency to deteriorate the heart'. The *British Critic* was particularly relieved that the book did not 'dabble in religion; of fanatical novels and fanatical authoresses,' it declared, 'we are already sick'.[5]

Although all such notices inclined to be favourable, Jane could not help observing how their tone of grudging approbation was elicited less for her novel's positive virtues than for its avoidance of obvious vices. To be thought 'harmless' and 'inoffensive' was, no doubt, a kind of praise, though it fell somewhat short of what she had hoped for. The *Augustan Review* found 'a remarkable sameness' in all her novels, and complained of the tediousness of Miss Bates's gossip. The *British Lady's Magazine* also disliked Miss Bates, though the *Champion* liked the novel's 'lively sketches of comfortable home-scenes' and even complimented the author as 'a woman of good sense, knowledge of the world, discriminating perception and acute observation'.[6]

The most important notice appeared in the *Quarterly Review*. Since Murray was the *Quarterly*'s proprietor, Jane trusted she would not be disappointed by that journal's sagacious observations. What she did not know was that Murray himself had reservations about *Emma* which he had thought prudent to withhold from her. In a Christmas letter to Walter Scott, Murray asked if Scott would care to 'dash off an article on *Emma*'. The book, he conceded, 'wants incident and romance', but 'none of the author's novels have been noticed and surely *Pride and Prejudice* merits high commendation'.[7] Scott's review was quickly finished and appeared, unsigned, in the *Quarterly*'s March issue. Murray promptly sent a copy of it down to Chawton. When Jane read the review, she experienced a strange mixture of contradictory emotions. The first, of course, was gratitude, with a queer trembling of secret pride to find her writings treated to such serious and extensive commentary (the piece was *very* long). But she also felt a kind of irritation and impatience; the piece was not only long, but leisurely, written with that ostentation of literary connoisseurship which the *Quarterly* often affected.[8] The reviewer (whose identity she could only guess at) indulged himself by taking a grand survey of the history of the novel, and she twirled over the first dozen or so paragraphs without finding more than a passing allusion to her own works. Such references as occurred were gratifying enough. The present work, the reviewer wrote, proclaimed 'a knowledge of the human heart, with the power and resolution to bring that knowledge to the service of honour and virtue'. Yet there was still a lingering hint of condescension in the manner of identifying her chief talent as a kind of copyist's skill. 'Instead of the splendid scenes of an imaginary world,' he wrote, what she offered was 'a correct and striking representation' of 'such common occurrences as may have fallen under the observation of most folks'. And it was hardly the highest form of commendation, she thought, to have her works compared to 'the Flemish school of painting'. 'Precision' was the word which the reviewer most frequently employed, as if her characters were little more than careful copies of real-life originals. *That* was an accusation which she had always found peculiarly painful. It had once been confidently asserted that the character of Mr Collins was drawn from life, and no amount of denial on her part, she discovered, could remove such a settled conviction. Though it was certainly her practice to note peculiarities of manner, of style or even phrasing in the delineation of her characters, she would never be guilty of such an invasion of social proprieties as to fill her novels with mere living caricatures. As she told her friend Mrs Barrett, 'I am much too proud of my own gentlemen ever to admit that they are merely Mr A or Major C.'[9] It vexed her, too, that the reviewer, whilst including brief remarks on *Sense and Sensibility* and *Pride and Prejudice*, seemed utterly oblivious to the existence of *Mansfield Park*. And was it really necessary for him to conclude his remarks with the airy comment that 'the youth of this realm need not at present be taught the doctrine of selfishness'? Her novels had, it seemed, depressed him by appearing to 'couple Cupid indivisibly with calculating prudence' and by their tendency 'to substitute more mean, more sordid and more selfish motives, for the romantic feelings . . . of love'.

Yet the more she read the review, the more she found reason to modify her initial sense of dismay. The reviewer acquitted her of producing a 'mere sign-post likeness'. Although 'keeping close to common incidents, and to such characters as occupy the ordinary walks of life', he praised her for producing 'sketches of such spirit and originality, that we never miss the excitation which depends upon a narrative of uncommon events'. Originality was the word most often coupled with precision; her country gentlemen and ladies were sketched 'with most originality and precision'; Mr Collins was drawn 'with force and precision'. The 'original' Mr Bennet, he acknowledged, was her own fictional creation, though many others, quite unknown to her, had subsequently borne the nickname. Her characters, he concluded, were 'finished up to nature, and with a precision which delights the reader'. It gave her special pleasure that the reviewer should choose, as evidence for this assertion, a passage of dialogue between Mr Woodhouse and Isabella from chapter twelve of *Emma*. 'Well, that *is* pleasant!' she observed. 'Those are the very characters I took most pains with, and the writer has found me out.'[10]

Her feelings of indignation had not entirely abated when she wrote back to Murray to thank him for loaning her the copy of the *Quarterly Review*. Though she acknowledged that 'the authoress of *Emma*' had 'no reason . . . to complain of her treatment in it', she still protested at the 'total omission of *Mansfield Park*' in the review.

She could not but be sorry, she wrote, that 'so clever a man as the reviewer of *Emma*' should consider her earlier novel 'as unworthy of being noticed'.[11] Murray would no doubt be pleased to hear that she had received the Prince's thanks for 'the *handsome* copy I sent him of *Emma*', she added, laying ironic stress upon the adjective, which seemed to indicate the Regent's greater fondness for elegant appearances than moral content. 'Whatever he may think of *my* share of the work, *yours* seems to have been quite right.'

Throughout the following months, she returned often in her mind to the grudging terms in which the reviewers of *Emma* had so frequently implied a criticism of the narrowness of her perspective. Was it really true that in her avoidance of grand, romantic themes, and 'the splendid scenes of an imaginary world', she was guilty of inculcating a 'doctrine of selfishness'? Suddenly she found herself besieged by well-meaning friends and relations all urging her to seek some grander subjects for her pen. The irrepressible Mr Clarke wrote to her from the Brighton Pavilion to suggest that 'any Historical Romance illustrative of the History of the august house of Cobourg would just now be very interesting'.[12] Her niece Caroline, still producing stories at a great rate, found inspiration in the tales of Madame de Genlis, however much she might affect to disapprove of them. But that indelicate style of romance was precisely the kind of writing which Jane could not bring herself to contemplate. 'Even now, at my sedate time of life,' she told Caroline, she could not bear to read *Olympe et Theophile* 'without being in a rage. It really is too bad! . . . Don't talk of it, pray.'[13] And now she found that even Caroline's brother, James Edward, had ambitions to be a novelist. One week, Caroline would send her latest story for approval ('it made me laugh heartily,' said Jane). The next, it would be James Edward, requiring her opinion of his own literary endeavours. 'Tell Caroline that I think it is hardly fair upon her & myself,' Jane wrote to Cassandra, 'to have him take up the novel line.'[14] Yet her nephew's work intrigued her. It was 'extremely clever,' she said, 'written with great ease & spirit' and, what struck her most about it, 'in a style, I think, to be popular'. She could well understand the young man's utter mortification when two and a half chapters of his precious work suddenly went missing. 'It is well that *I* have not been at Steventon lately,' she wrote to him, '& therefore cannot be suspected of purloining them; two strong twigs & a half towards a nest of my own, would have been something.' However, she protested, 'any theft of that sort' would not, in reality, be very useful to her. 'What should I do with your strong, manly, spirited sketches, full of variety & glow?'[15] She wrote that last phrase to flatter her nephew's vanity, yet it contained an important truth. However popular her nephew's style of writing might prove to be, it was not a style that she would ever attempt.

Having now had time to reflect seriously upon the reviewers' comments on *Emma*, she was more than ever resolved on keeping to her own familiar way of depicting the common incidents of daily life. Once, she had imagined herself equal to writing a Life of Buonaparte, but now she modestly declined all temptations to aspire to such heroic themes. Accordingly, she wrote to Mr Clarke to thank him for his most recent literary suggestion. 'I am fully sensible,' she wrote, 'that an historical Romance, founded on the house of Saxe Cobourg might be much more to the purpose of profit or popularity, than such pictures of domestic life in country villages as I deal in.' But, she assured him, 'I could no more write a romance than an epic poem.'

What followed was the nearest thing to that grand abstraction – a literary manifesto – that she ever could, or ever would, be guilty of; and it was only possible for her to write it because of the amusement she felt towards the man whose well-meaning but absurd suggestion had provoked it. 'I could not sit seriously down to write a serious Romance,' she declared, 'under any other motive than to save my life, & if it were indispensable for me to keep it up & never relax into laughing at myself or other people, I am sure I should be hung before I had finished the first chapter. No – I must keep to my own style & go on in my own way; and though I may never succeed again in that, I am convinced that I should totally fail in any other.' Similarly, she assured her nephew that his glowing, manly chapters, however spirited and clever, could be of no service to her miniaturist's style. 'How could I possibly join them on to the little bit (two inches wide) of ivory on which I work with so fine a brush, as produces little effect after much labour?'[16]

As if to confirm her instinct for laughing at herself, she spent some time that May composing a burlesque 'Plan of a Novel' made up of the many ludicrous hints (and some criticisms) she had received over the preceding months.[17] Here were jumbled together Mr Clarke's suggestions for a clergyman 'going to sea as a chaplain to a distinguished naval character' alongside Mr Sherer's request for a portrait of 'an exemplary parish priest'. From Mr Clarke again came the melancholy detail of the priest 'having buried his own mother', placed beside Mary Cooke's hint that 'all the good people [must] be unexceptionable in every respect'. From Mary Brunton's *Self-Controul* came the pathetic episode of a heroine 'reduced . . . to work for her bread . . . worn down to a skeleton, and now and then starved to death', while Anna Lefroy's ill-fated novel provoked the idea of continually shifting the scene 'from one set of people to another'. Fanny, who was visiting, suggested details of the starving heroine's elegant accomplishments, while Jane contrived to compensate for the lamentable absence of improbable incidents in her previous novels by having this latest heroine endure 'at least 20 narrow escapes'. There; if such a preposterous novel as that did not satisfy the critics, Jane quite despaired of the popular taste.

Had her mind been truly as much preoccupied with sordid motives of calculating prudence as the *Quarterly* reviewer pretended, Jane felt she might at least claim the extenuation of circumstances. She could never recall a time when the family's fortunes had appeared in greater jeopardy. The occasional vexation of an ill-disposed critic's displeasure was as nothing to the overwhelming danger of financial ruin which threatened her brothers, Henry and Edward. At last, in the first week of March, came the long-expected blow. Henry's banking business collapsed. It was Gray, the grocer partner in Alton, who had precipitated this crisis, being the first to feel the effects of a sudden post-war reduction in government orders for victuals, clothing and other stores. His failure, at the end of December, brought down Austen, Gray and Vincent of Alton, which in turn caused the collapse of Austen, Blunt and Louch at Petersfield. As Henry's several merchant creditors rushed to redeem their worthless bank-notes for gold at his London bank in Henrietta Street, that too collapsed. On 6 March, an order of bankruptcy was issued against the house of Austen, Maunde and Tilson.

Theirs was not the only bank to fail in this period of economic turbulence, and, as Caroline recalled, 'no blame of personal extravagance' was ever imputed against her uncle Henry.[18] Yet, in the catastrophe of sudden poverty, this thought brought little consolation. To Henry, the bankruptcy 'was ruin, and he saw the world before him to begin again'. Charles lost 'hundreds' in the bank's collapse, while Edward, still fighting to maintain his Chawton properties, stood liable to lose the whole of his £20,000 surety. However, even in this time of crisis, Jane was relieved to find how little sign of bitterness, or recrimination, there was within the family. Abandoning his own house at Hans Place, Henry became a welcome guest in the homes of all his brothers and sisters. And, as after the death of Eliza, three years earlier, it was remarkable how quickly his 'sanguine elastic nature' recovered its customary cheerfulness. At the end of March, he visited Steventon, '*apparently*', as Caroline recalled, 'in unbroken spirits'. Shortly afterwards, he went to Godmersham, where Edward welcomed him with no hint of reproachfulness. 'No doubt it will have done him good,' Jane wrote to Caroline. 'Tell your mama that he came back from Steventon much pleased with his visit to her.'[19]

Jane herself had suffered hardly at all from the collapse of Henry's bank. The £600 she had already received as profits on her novels was safely invested in Navy 5% stock, and she had only lost £13 7s of profits on *Mansfield Park*, which remained in her Henrietta Street account. For her mother, the situation was less cheerful. Frank and Henry now found themselves unable to continue sending her their annual payments of £50 apiece, a sum which poor Charles had never managed to match even before the present disaster. Mrs Austen was now wholly dependent on the support of James and Edward, together with whatever sums Jane was able to contribute to the household budget from her literary earnings. Jane promptly redoubled her efforts to complete her latest novel, to which she gave the provisional title 'The Elliots'.

As the heroine of this new novel, she had chosen, for the first time, a woman who was no longer young. Anne Elliot, in her twenty-eighth year, was not as old as Jane herself; yet there was nothing of the giddy girl about her. She was a woman who had not only loved and lost, but who had the sober capacity for reflection and resignation that came with maturity. Jane could not deny that there were many elements of her own character in Anne Elliot; the same habits of self-denial and self-effacement struggling against a conviction of greater insight than was vouchsafed to those about her; the same restless desire (forever curbed) to show others the errors of their ways ('Anne longed for the power of representing to them all what they were about, and of pointing out some of the evils they were exposing themselves to'). Confided in by everyone (as Jane was), Anne's voice, like Jane's, was seldom allowed to be decisive, even on her own behalf; and she was frequently required to support the pretence of family agreement by which many individual pleasures must be sacrificed to the appearance of general gratification ('Anne . . . admired again the sort of necessity which the family-habit seemed to produce, of every thing being to be communicated, and every thing being to be done together, however undesired and inconvenient').[20] Yet, even as she compared Anne Elliot's character with her own, she must admit some differences. There was something rather more saintly and forbearing about her heroine than she herself could ever aspire to. Though she could admire, sincerely admire, such patient selflessness, she could not entirely depend upon herself to emulate it. Everything that 'revolts other people', Anne's pompous father declared (such as 'low company, paltry rooms, foul air, disgusting associations'), was 'inviting' to his daughter, who was seldom more contented than when nursing some ailing relative or friend. Jane could hardly pretend to share such a love of sick-rooms. And in the most pertinent point of all – Anne's refusal of the man she loved – there was an important difference. Anne's acquiescence to persuasion in rejecting Frederick Wentworth had been the effect of 'weakness and timidity'; 'forced into prudence in her youth', she had 'learned romance as she grew older'. But Jane had always been happily *imprudent* in her youth. It had not been *she* who had first yielded to persuasion, but Tom Lefroy. Yet, as she described Anne's feelings after meeting Wentworth again ('Once so much to each other! Now nothing! . . . Now they were as strangers; nay, worse than strangers, for they could never become acquainted'), it was hard not to imagine herself in a similar predicament, and to share all her heroine's agitation of emotions.[21]

In this novel, however, it was not Tom Lefroy who served as the model for her hero, Wentworth, but Jane's valiant brother Frank. Like Frank, Captain Wentworth had achieved glory in the St Domingo action; his naval anecdotes were borrowed from Frank; his upright manners and easy style were all Frank's. In *Mansfield Park*, she had written of that 'strengthener of love, in which even the conjugal tie is beneath the fraternal'. In this new novel, she contrived to bind these ties together.

No sooner had Henry's bankruptcy been declared than the Austens suffered another blow, with the news of Charles's shipwreck off the coast of Asia Minor, near Smyrna. His ship, the *Phoenix*, sent to harry pirates in the Greek Archipelago, had foundered during a hurricane, owing to the ignorance of the local pilot. Happily, the crew were saved, and Charles himself acquitted of all blame; yet such misfortunes, as Caroline noted, were 'always a disparagement; and the war being over, he knew he was likely to wait long for another ship'. ('These are bad times for getting on,' Admiral Croft observed in 'The Elliots').[22] Having lost all his money in the collapse of Henry's bank, it was a dismal homecoming for Charles, whose birthday, on 23 June, Jane dutifully noted.

Even the weather was unseasonably bleak that summer; 'much worse than anybody *can* bear,' Jane wrote to James Edward in July; 'I begin to think it will never be fine again.' The pond in front of the house was brimful with rainwater, the roads were dirty, and the walls of the cottage damp with the constant rain, and with the splash and spatter of countless post-chaises rumbling through the puddles outside their windows. She imagined these post-chaises filled with Winchester boys, their future 'heroes, legislators, fools, & villains'.[23] She worried about finding a way to contrive a final reconciliation between Anne Elliot and Wentworth. It could be laid at Admiral Croft's lodgings, she thought. Anne's mind would be full of perplexity; 'altogether a confusion of images and doubts . . . an agitation which she could not see the end of'.[24]

But the real agitation was in her own mind, she knew, not her heroine's. She stared out at the rain still falling. 'Oh! it rains again; it beats against the window,' she wrote to her nephew. 'Mary Jane & I have been wet through once already today, we set off in the donkey carriage for Farringdon . . . but were obliged to turn back before we got there, but not soon enough to avoid a pelter all the way home.'[25] Normally, a soaking in the summer rain would hardly have concerned her, but the pains in her back were become increasingly troublesome, and had not let her alone for several weeks. Her visit with Cassandra to Cheltenham spa had done little to lessen them. Cheltenham in May was very charming, of course, even in such a damp May as this one; but a whole fortnight of taking the waters had proved ineffectual in removing the aches she endured. Their persistence put her in mind of Mrs Sclater, who, she heard, had still not quit Tangier Park. Irritating woman. How would it be, she wondered, to contrive an overheard conversation between the Admiral and Captain Wentworth? Anne hearing her own name often repeated – much distressed – not knowing what to do or what to expect. She began to scribble the words down. 'Phoo, phoo,' answered the Admiral, 'Now is the time. If *you* will not speak, I will stop & speak myself.' (She rather liked that 'Phoo, phoo' – it was just how Admiral Croft must speak.) 'Very well sir, very well sir,' said Captain Wentworth. But then what? Jane paused. The next scene must bring Anne and her beloved Captain together. She could see the characters clearly in her mind, and feel all their awkwardness and uncertainty. Yet the words would not come to her. 'A silent, but a very powerful dialogue,' she noted. 'On his side, supplication, on her's acceptance. – Still a little nearer – and a hand taken and pressed –' She stopped again.[26] The images misted over – 'a confusion of images & doubts'. Altogether, it was much easier to comment on her niece's writing than continue with her own. The girl had such a droll way of expressing things; Jane could never for the life of her discover if it was deliberate or quite by chance. As when Caroline had written of 'finding' her little cousin Fanny. 'I suppose you had worn her in your stays without knowing it,' Jane wrote back in reply; '& if she tickled you, thought it only a flea.' She twirled over once again the pages of Caroline's latest story. 'I am particularly glad to find you so much alive upon any topic of such absurdity, as the usual description of a heroine's father,' she wrote to her. 'You have done it full justice.'[27] That was rather more than James Edward had done her for the cheese she had sent him the previous week. Why had he not thanked her for it? 'I cannot bear not to be thanked,' she warned him.

Jane was almost alone in the cottage now, with only her mother and Frank's daughter Mary-Jane for company. Cassandra had gone to London the previous day with Frank about some business of Henry's. Jane did not entirely know whether to laugh or cry at Henry's latest scheme, which was nothing less than to travel to France in hopes of reclaiming some of Eliza's property, now that order and the monarchy had been restored in that country. At least, she thought, such an expedition must demonstrate that her brother had not entirely abandoned his sense of optimism; though whether that optimism were entirely well founded, she would not incline to say. Edward's sons, Henry and William, had offered to accompany him on his quest. It was not merely the rain, nor even the pains in her back, which prevented her from completing the pages of the manuscript which lay open on her writing-table before her. No other heroine she had yet attempted had come so close to her own sensibility as Anne Elliot. Previously, it had always been her practice to fracture and diffuse her thoughts and feelings among several different characters, giving to Elizabeth Bennet her wit, to Fanny Price her solemnity, and to Emma Woodhouse her pride. With Anne Elliot there was less disguise, less *brilliance* perhaps, but more feeling. And the chapter she was now embarked upon was perhaps more full of painful feelings than any other. The persuasion of Lady Russell, to which Anne had succumbed in refusing the man she loved, must recall, however obliquely, the family persuasions that had put an end to any hopes of marriage between Tom Lefroy and Jane herself. Jane was careful to insist that Anne felt the same respect for Lady Russell that she had always felt for Madam Lefroy; yet still she could not suppress her inner conviction that on that most intimate of subjects her friend had been wrong. How to represent that conviction without conveying a hint of resentment? And how to manage that final reversal of fortunes without suggesting a moment of revenge?

As so often in the past, she found herself compelled to juggle an apparent conflict between morality and wit. Wentworth was witty ('bewitching in [his] wit'); but, she wrote, 'Lady Russell had little taste for wit'. In this case, she decided, wit must be the test of character. She took up her pen. 'Bad morality again,' she wrote. 'A young woman proved to have had more discrimination of character than her elder – to have seen in two instances more clearly what a man was than her godmother!' She paused. Was it Anne she was writing of now? Or herself? 'But on the point of morality,' she went on, 'I confess myself almost in despair after understanding myself to have already given a mother offence – having already appeared weak in the point where I thought myself most strong and shall leave it to the mercy of mothers & chaperons & middle-aged ladies in general.'[28] She stopped there. That would never do, she knew. 'I' was not a pronoun she easily admitted, except in the mouth of a character. As an author, she almost never said 'I'. She might *think* 'I', as she did now, remembering how she *had* given offence to her mother, not only over Tom Lefroy but also over Harris Bigg-Wither. But this was not the time for confessions. She took her pen and crossed through the last paragraph she had written, before walking down to see if her mother had any last requests to make of her before retiring to bed.

That night, as she lay on her bed, listening to the sound of the rain on the window-pane, and feeling still the dull ache in her back, Jane allowed herself to imagine how it might have been. It was, at least, a kind of vicarious gratification to confer on her heroine the consummation that had always been denied to her. She sat up, lit a candle, and wrote. 'It was necessary to sit up half the night & lie awake the remainder to comprehend with composure her present state, & pay for the overplus of bliss, by headake

& fatigue.'[29] There. Was that too much? The headache and fatigue she knew well enough – she felt them even now, as she pored over her notebook. But what of the 'overplus of bliss'? What did she know of that? In her own experience, all bliss had indeed to be paid for. She thought of riding triumphantly through London in an open carriage after the success of *Pride and Prejudice*, and declaring grandly to Cassandra that 'Money is dirt!' But money was not dirt, as Henry had found, and Edward too. 'Perfect happiness,' as she had written in *Emma*, 'even in memory, is not common.'[30]

Somewhere between the momentary triumph of a vain self-conceit and the penance of self-mortification, there was a place – in fiction at least – for justice. Somewhere, amid all the confusion of images and doubts, she must find a space for hope and for the rational expression of deeply cherished truths. Turning back the leaf of her notebook she began to write again, picking her way carefully between the obliterated lines of the paragraph she had crossed out. 'There *is* a quickness of perception in some,' she wrote; 'a nicety in the discernment of character – a natural penetration in short which no experience in others can equal – and Lady R had been less gifted in this part of understanding than her young friend; – but she was a very good woman; & if her second object was to be sensible & well judging, her first was to see Anne happy.' That was more generous, she thought, and more honest.

She wrote more rapidly now. Anne and her Captain were reconciled and the final paragraphs were quickly done. She ended, as she had intended, with a tribute to naval men as having 'more worth and warmth than any other set of men in England'. Anne 'gloried in being a sailor's wife,' Jane wrote, though 'she must pay the tax of quick alarm for belonging to that profession which is – if possible – more distinguished in it's [*sic*] Domestic Virtues than in it's National Importance'.[31] No doubt the reviewers would pride themselves on identifying her words 'pay' and 'tax' as further proof of her mean, sordid calculations. That was always the way with reviewers.

When Cassandra returned at the end of the month, Jane read

her the final chapters of 'The Elliots'. Cassandra said she liked them, but Jane did not believe her. She did not like them herself, she said. They were still too tame and flat; she knew she could produce something better. But could she? She felt a terrible weariness through all her limbs, brought on by the pains in her back and the dampness that seemed to pervade the whole cottage. It had become her custom to lie down after dinner, not on the sofa, which was reserved for her mother, but on three chairs which she arranged for herself, with sometimes a pillow behind her back. Little Caroline could never understand why she did not lie down on the sofa. 'Aunt Jane, you look so uncomfortable,' she would say. If the sofa was vacant, why would she not use it? She could not possibly like the chairs best. So often the girl tormented her with her well-meaning questions that at last Jane admitted to her that, if she ever used the sofa, 'Grandmama would be leaving it for her, and would not lie down, as she did now, whenever she felt inclined'.[32] The pains in her back would soon pass, she said. It was only the damp weather and the stooping over her writing-desk which caused them.

That night, after reading the end of 'The Elliots' to Cassandra, she felt particularly weary. She retired to her bed more depressed in spirits than she could ever recall. Nothing about the novel satisfied her, not even the title. She lay awake in the darkness, searching in her mind for ways to improve those final chapters while Cassandra slept by her side. Mrs Smith's narrative was too long, she knew, and too much depended on it; the attachment between Louisa and Captain Benwick was scarcely credible; and that between Mr Elliot and Mrs Clay was the merest contrivance. But even these things might be made acceptable if the reconciliation scene between Anne and the Captain were stronger. That was where the real weakness lay. Admiral Croft's lodgings would not do; it must be a place which was both public and private, somewhere where the pressures of social obligations must continue to inhibit the open expression of personal feelings. Overhearing was a good idea, but it must be the Captain who overheard Anne, not the other way round. Anne must say something, as Jane herself was accustomed to do, in a public manner which would be understood, in its private and proper application, by this one special individual only.

Suddenly, it all came to her. She could hear Anne's voice speaking, ostensibly to Captain Harville, but actually to Captain Wentworth, of female constancy and male inconstancy. 'We certainly do not forget you, so soon as you forget us. It is, perhaps, our fate rather than our merit.' Captain Wentworth's reply must be similarly oblique – oblique but intense – not spoken, but written in a letter, a letter he would be writing to Anne even as he listened to her voice. 'I can listen no longer in silence. I must speak to you by such means as are within my reach. You pierce my soul. I am half agony, half hope. Tell me not that I am too late, that such precious feelings are gone for ever . . .'[33]

In the morning she wrote it, her spirits greatly revived. Cassandra remarked on the cheerful change in her manner, and hoped for 'brighter inspirations' to guide her pen.[34] The chapter in Admiral Croft's lodgings was quite abandoned and this new chapter substituted in its place. Yet one phrase she was reluctant to lose; the Admiral's 'Phoo, phoo' gave her much foolish pleasure. But could it really be only the Admiral who said it? Charles was a man of lively interjections, too. She changed it accordingly. '"Phoo! phoo!" replied Charles, "what's an evening party? Never worth remembering . . ."' It also afforded her a small but particular pleasure to have her heroine, who had dreaded the 'white glare' of Bath and who had felt a dismal, silent horror at her first dim view of its extensive buildings, 'smoking in rain', find her supreme happiness ('senseless joy') in those same, hectic, crowded streets. Away from meddling family and friends, amid Bath's 'sauntering politicians, bustling house-keepers, flirting girls . . . nursery maids and children', her hero and her heroine were now 'exquisitely happy'. She completed the novel with few other alterations (she changed the very last words – about the navy – to 'national importance' rather than 'national renown') and read it again to her sister. Cassandra was kind enough to approve all her revisions and noted, in her careful way, the date on which the novel was finished, 6 August 1816. She even liked the new title, *Persuasion*.[35]

Jane was not the only one afflicted by the miserable weather.

Away at Steventon, Mrs J.A. was frequently unwell and was advised that a visit to Cheltenham might prove beneficial. She had hopes of persuading one of the Austen sisters to accompany her there, but Jane had no inclination for another remedial visit, and it fell to Cassandra to comply with this request. Even as Cassandra was preparing to leave, Jane herself suffered another painful attack, but she insisted that her sister must not disappoint Mary on her account. Accordingly, Cassandra and Mrs J.A. went to stay at Mrs Potter's cold, noisy house in Cheltenham High Street, for which they were charged the exorbitant sum of three guineas a week. 'Three guineas a week for such lodgings!' Jane protested. 'I am quite angry . . . Mrs Potter charges you for the *name* of the High Street.' She was shocked, though hardly surprised, to learn that the mean Mrs P. had not even provided her guests with a fire in their room. 'So glad that you have your pelisse!' she exclaimed. Surely, if they 'looked about well', they could find other, more suitable lodgings in 'some odd corner' of the town.[36]

For her part, Cassandra was most anxious for news of her sister's health, but Jane, as usual, made light of her sufferings. Her back, she said, 'has given me scarcely any pain for many days'. 'Agitation', she believed, caused it as much harm as fatigue, and she was inclined to believe that she was ill 'at the time of your going, from the very circumstance of your going'. And yes, she said; she saw quite as much company as she could desire, visiting the 'Alton 4' at Wyards where they are all very pleasant ('venison quite right – children well-behaved – & Mr & Mrs Digweed taking kindly to our charades and other games') and receiving calls from Frank, Mary and the children. Henry and the Knight boys were back from France, and she was pleased to hear Edward speaking of the French 'as one cd wish, disappointed in everything'. From what she heard, the whole country there was 'a scene of general poverty & misery – no money, no trade – nothing to be got but by the innkeepers'.[37] No wonder that Henry had met with little success in his enquiries after Eliza's estate.

Henry's latest scheme was to try for the church, as he had always intended before Eliza dissuaded him. Jane offered no opinion about that. Privately, she acknowledged, there might be a scruple against entering the church merely as a livelihood, but Henry, she was sure, though by no means of an evangelical disposition, had quite as much of a vocation for the life as James. She recalled the words of Edmund expressed in *Mansfield Park*: 'I see no reason why a man should make a worse clergyman for knowing that he will have a competence early in life.'[38] For Henry, this was scarcely a decision made 'early in life', and even now, he was not assured of 'a competence'. The height of his ambition was merely to become Mr Papillon's curate here at Chawton; hardly a vain or selfish aspiration for a man who, only two years before, had been revelling with emperors and princes at White's Club.

Jane's favourite companion, during her sister's absence, was her nephew James Edward. This handsome young man was full of hopes of completing his novel before going up to Oxford later that year, and together the two of them would converse, author to author, on the technicalities of the novel-writing trade. He loved to tease her with questions about 'what happened' to her characters, and she would invent details to amuse him. Kitty Bennet, she told him, was satisfactorily married to a clergyman near Pemberley, while Mary obtained nothing higher than one of her uncle Philips's clerks. Mr Woodhouse would probably have prevented Emma and Mr Knightley from settling at Donwell for about two years, she believed, and the word contained in the letters which Frank Churchill placed before Jane Fairfax and which she swept away unread, was 'pardon'.[39] It gave her much pleasure to talk, in this informal way, of characters who were almost as real to her – if not more so – than Mrs Digweed or Miss Benn, Mr Papillon or Miss Gibson. She scarcely noticed how weary she was, while Edward was constantly amusing her with his lively quips and anecdotes. But once he had gone, the fatigue returned. 'I enjoyed Edward's company very much,' she told Cassandra, '& yet I was not sorry when Friday came.' It had been a busy week, and now all she wanted was 'a few days' quiet, & exemption from the thought & contrivances which any sort of company gives'.

In Cassandra's absence, Jane found herself once again compelled to assume responsibility for the daily domestic arrangements. How she dreaded the numbing effect of all those mundane chores.

'Composition seems to me impossible,' she protested, 'with a head full of joints of mutton & doses of rhubarb.' How 'good Mrs West' could possibly have written such excellent books as *Advantages of Education, A Gossip's Story* and *A Tale of the Times*, beset as she was with all sorts of family cares, was, Jane thought, 'a matter of astonishment!' Charles and his family threatened a visit to Chawton at the end of September and, much as she wished to see them all, Jane earnestly hoped that Cassandra would be safely returned before their arrival. 'When you have once left Cheltenham,' she wrote, 'I shall grudge every half day wasted on the road.'[40]

Huddled in her long pelisse in Mrs Potter's dark, unheated rooms, Cassandra read through Jane's letters with a melancholy heart. She knew her sister too well to be deceived by her efforts at cheerful insouciance, as when she boasted of her 'beautiful walk home by moonlight' from Alton. All Cassandra's anxious enquiries after Jane's health were deflected with a rather too ready air of casualness. She was 'nursing herself up into as beautiful state as can be,' she wrote. There was really no need, she insisted, for Dr White to be troubling himself about her. It was typical of Jane that, rather than dwell on her own illness, she would remark on the ailments of everyone else. In one letter, she wrote that Fanny 'does not seem any better', and that Anna was 'not equal to the fatigue' of travelling from Alton; in another, she reported that Mrs F.A 'seldom either looks or appears quite well – little embryo is troublesome, I suppose'. Thoughts of mortality seemed to preoccupy her, though she affected to make light of them. When old Mrs Leigh died in the spring, Jane refused to grieve for her. 'The death of a person at her advanced age, so fit to die, & by her own feelings so *ready* to die, is not to be regretted,' she declared. Jane often liked to joke about death: 'I treat you with a dead baronet in almost every letter,' she wrote to Cassandra, noting the recent demise of Sir Thomas Miller. She was quite *mortified*, she wrote, at Cassandra's refusal to cultivate new acquaintances among the fashionable company at Cheltenham. 'Do pray meet with *somebody*,' she insisted: 'I am quite weary of your knowing nobody.'[41] But there was something strangely hollow, Cassandra thought, about her sister's style of worldly banter. From a neighbouring room came the din of a pianoforte being pounded by another inexpert pupil. Cassandra folded away Jane's letter and stared down at the wet pavements of the High Street outside. She had no desire for new acquaintances here at Cheltenham. Her thoughts were all with her sister at home.

When Cassandra returned to Chawton, she found, much as she had feared, that Jane's condition was worse than her letters acknowledged. She was easily tired, often snappish, and would spend longer each evening reclining uncomfortably across her three chairs. Throughout the autumn, Jane continued to compile her list of 'Opinions' on *Emma*. It hardly seemed to matter to her whether the opinions received were positive or hostile; she recorded them all with the same weary dedication. Sometimes, it almost seemed to Cassandra that the hostile comments were the ones that Jane sought out most eagerly, whether it was Mr Sherer complaining about her pictures of clergymen, or Mr Fowle boasting that he had read only the first and last chapter of *Emma* 'because he had heard it was not interesting'.[42]

A distressing letter arrived from Miss Sharp, who was very ill; only surviving, she wrote, thanks to the care of an elderly physician, who treated her 'from pure love & benevolence'. At least *Emma* had brought some moments of pleasure into a life that was otherwise filled with pain. Miss Sharp thought it better than *Mansfield Park*, was delighted with Mr Knightley, and called Mrs Elton 'beyond praise'. It was perhaps hardly surprising that she should be less satisfied with Jane Fairfax. She herself had suffered too much in the governess trade to find much comfort in such a portrait.

Henry was a frequent visitor to the cottage, and would often treat them both to extempore disquisitions on scriptural texts as he set about preparing himself for his new clerical role. Jane was impressed by his diligence. 'Uncle Henry writes very superior sermons,' she wrote to James Edward at Steventon. 'You & I must try to get hold of one or two, & put them into our novels; – it would be a fine help to a volume; & we could make our heroine read it aloud of a Sunday evening.' Henry's sermons, they all

agreed, were vastly superior to those of the Reverend Cooper, full
of zealous Bible Society cant of Regeneration and Conversion.
The only zealousness of which Henry might stand accused was in
his enthusiasm for getting up his Greek New Testament. The
Bishop of Winchester was quite disconcerted, when he came to
examine him, at Henry's eagerness to quote from the Greek text.
Despite such erudition, Henry was ordained, before Christmas, at
Salisbury and appointed as curate at Chawton. The reward for
his duties, he told them, would be the princely stipend of fifty-two
guineas a year.[43]

Quietly, Cassandra did all in her power to ease her sister's discomforts. There was no reason for Jane to be anxious about the
visit of Charles and his family, since the great house was unoccu-
pied and had ample space to accommodate all the children. In the
event, it was a real delight to have so many of the family gathered
together, and to see both Charles and Henry so much improved in
health and spirits. Jane's own health continued to be troublesome,
though, as usual, she did her best to conceal it. But she could not
entirely conceal her disappointment at being compelled to decline
a birthday dinner in her honour at Wyards. Anna Lefroy had just
given birth to a second daughter and the dinner was to have been
a joint celebration. At least Jane was candid enough to write to
James Edward that 'the walk is beyond my strength' and that the
winter was 'not a season for donkey carriages' (though she insisted
on adding that she was 'otherwise very well'). Her letter was written
to congratulate the young man on having finally left Winchester,
and Cassandra noted how Jane contrived to maintain a fine pose
of appropriate worldliness and high spirits. 'Now you may own,
how miserable you were there,' she wrote. 'Now, it will gradually
all come out – your crimes & your miseries – how often you went
up by the mail to London & threw away fifty guineas at a tavern,
& how often you were on the point of hanging yourself – restrained
only . . . by the want of a tree within some miles of the city.' Jane
even revived the old joke about Mr Papillon wanting to marry her.
The man would soon make his offer, she said, 'probably next
Monday . . . his *intention* can be no longer doubtful in the smallest
degree'.[44] But Monday came and went with no offer, only the gift

of a turkey from Anna at Wyards. 'Such highmindedness!' their mother protested as they set about carving the beast on Christmas Day. She said she could not help grieving that the Lefroys had not kept such a fine turkey to themselves, while helping herself to the very best portion.

'It is a vile world'

Jane had always found illness a terrible *bore*. It was neither agreeable to endure nor interesting to write about. She had never been one of those ladies who derived consequence for themselves from their various indispositions. She began the New Year with a settled determination to be well again. 'We are all in good health,' she wrote to Alethea Bigg, '& I have certainly gained strength through the winter.' She sent the same message to her niece Caroline at Steventon. '*I* feel myself getting stronger than I was half a year ago,' she told her, '& can so perfectly well walk to Alton, *or* back again, without the slightest fatigue that I hope to be able to do both when summer comes.'[45] *Thinking* herself well, she decided, was the first step to *being* so, and she set about maintaining a style of buoyant high spirits as an effectual remedy against any tendency to depression. What she relished, in particular, was a perverse, contradictory kind of playfulness. She marked the birthday of Frank's daughter Cassy by sending, not to her, but to Charles's Cassy instead, a form of backwards greeting contrived in a style of mirror-writing: 'Ym raed Yssac,' it began, 'Siht si elttil Yssac's yadhtrib, dna ehs si eerht sraey dlo.'[46]

With Caroline she played a different kind of word-game, swapping English phrases for French ones, and teasing the girl for her modish style. 'Your Anne is dreadful!' she wrote in mock exasperation at her niece's latest literary offering. Imagine the absurdity of a heroine who could not bring herself 'to pronounce the word *shift*!' 'I could forgive her any follies in English,' Jane told her, 'rather than the mock modesty of that French word.' Affecting to hate foreigners, and the French in particular, had become rather a habit with her, especially after poor Henry's failed attempt to gain satisfaction in the matter of Eliza's French properties. When she heard of friends, like the Williams family, who insisted on travelling abroad, she could only lament their foolhardiness. Letters from such people, she told Alethea Bigg, 'would not be satisfactory to *me* . . . unless they breathed a strong spirit of regret for not being in England'. Irritated that the winter weather deprived her of even a donkey-carriage ride to Alton, she pretended to find the idea of English ladies rambling about the Continent too painful to contemplate with patience. It was one of the most damning comments on Frank Churchill's character that he should declare himself 'sick of England'.[47]

James Edward was a constant source of amusement. One evening in January, he read them his two latest chapters – 'both good, especially the last'. But Jane's chief delight was Fanny. Her letters were like rays of sunshine in these gloomy winter days. 'You are inimitable, irresistible,' she wrote to her. 'You are the delight of my life. Such letters, such entertaining letters as you have lately sent! Such a description of your queer little heart! . . . You are worth your weight in gold, or even in the new silver coinage.' The girl now believed herself to be in love with Mr James Wildman of Chilham Castle; or maybe it was he who was in love with her. Or both; or neither. Really, it seemed, she couldn't be sure, but the uncertainty of it all was clearly delicious and provoked her to send her aunt Jane page after page of confused, hectic, witty, emotional scrawl. To Jane, 'sweet, perverse Fanny' was like a whole volume of characters bound up in one. 'You can hardly think what a pleasure it is to me,' she wrote, 'to have such thorough pictures of your heart.' 'You are the paragon of all that is silly & sensible,' she told her; 'common-place & eccentric, sad & lively, provoking & interesting . . . You are so odd! – & all the time, so perfectly natural – so peculiar in yourself, & yet so like everybody else!'[48] It was painful to think of this queer, eccentric, bewitching creature ('quite after one's own heart', as she had once described her) dwindling into matrimony with *anyone*, even with young, handsome and rich Mr Wildman. 'Oh what a loss it will be, to me, when you are married,' she wrote; then crossed out 'to me'. It would be a loss to everyone, she decided, most of all, perhaps, to

Fanny herself. 'I shall hate you when your delicious play of mind is all settled down into conjugal & maternal affections. Mr J.W. frightens me. – He will have you. – I see you at the altar.' What would become of all her beguiling wickedness then? She thought of Anna Lefroy, who had paid a visit the previous Saturday with her husband, Ben. Anna looked 'so young & so blooming & so innocent, as if she had never had a wicked thought in her life'. Which, said Jane, even laying aside the doctrine of Original Sin, was rather a difficult notion to accept, 'if we remember the events of her girlish days'. If even Anna's Niagara wit could find itself becalmed in the still waters of motherhood, what hope could there be for the capprizios of Fanny's imagination, once she too suc-cumbed to matrimony?

Fortunately, Jane detected no real signs of a settled attachment. Why, the girl was still evidently jealous of Mr John Plumptre's new female friends. 'Why should you be living in dread of his marrying somebody else?' she teased her. 'You did not chuse to have him yourself; why not allow him to take comfort where he can?' And why this monstrous display of pique that the coquettish Miss Clewes had made herself the belle of the Godmersham ball? That was 'pretty well,' she thought, 'for a lady irrecoverably attached to one person!' 'Sweet Fanny,' she concluded, 'believe no such thing of yourself. Spread no such malicious slander upon your understanding, within the precincts of your imagination. Do not speak ill of your sense, merely for the gratification of your fancy.' The truth, she said, was clear enough: 'You are *not* in love with him.'

The influence of Fanny's lively wit had an invigorating effect on her own, and within days of sending this letter, she felt the itch to start a new novel. She was not yet satisfied with *Persuasion*, but had not the patience at present for the kind of delicate work of revision that such a serious novel must entail. The heroine's character, she thought, was 'almost too good for me'. She did not find herself in a sufficient state of composure to deal adequately with such goodness. She was in a mood for oddness and eccen-tricity. 'Pictures of perfection, as you know, make me sick & wicked,' she wrote to Fanny.[49]

The new novel, to be called 'The Brothers', would be quite different, more satirical and modern – a picture of *im*perfection, set among the new south coast villas, with their pompous names (Trafalgar House, Waterloo Crescent), their vulgar terraces, verandas and Venetian windows.[50] In the evenings, she would sit with Cassandra, dreaming up dialogue for the dreadful Diana Parker ('Activity run mad!') and for the 'downright silly' Sir Edward Denham, who must spout all the latest 'hard words' culled from the literary reviews ('It were hyper-criticism, it were pseudo-philosophy to expect from the soul of high-toned genius, the grovellings of a common mind'). 'The Brothers' must be like a caricature of modern England turned upside-down by the mania for speculation. It would begin, as a caricaturist might draw it, with an overturned coach, with the first line of speech to be like a caption: 'There is something wrong here.' All the principals must speak the language of the newspaper advertisements from which they drew their sole inspiration and solace (for people like these could find no sort of comfort in anything of a more spiritual nature).

It made for an agreeable hour's amusement to practise the egregious Mr Parker's lines with Cassandra. 'Such a place as Sanditon sir, I may say was wanted, was called for. Nature had marked it out – had spoken in most intelligible characters. The finest, purest sea breeze on the coast – acknowledged to be so – excellent bathing – fine hard sand – deep water ten yards from the shore – no mud – no weeds – no slimey rocks. Never was there a place more palpably designed by nature for the resort of the invalid – the very spot which thousands seemed in need of. The most desirable distance from London! One complete, measured mile nearer than Eastbourne. Only conceive, sir, the advantage of saving a whole mile, in a long journey!'[51]

At other times, they talked of *The Watsons*, abandoned so many years ago. It was not, Jane said, that she had forgotten that book; nor that she was without ideas on how to continue with it. The outline was clear in her mind; Mr Watson would die; Emma would become dependent upon her brother and his narrow-minded wife; she would decline an offer of marriage from Lord Osborne, but would eventually marry Mr Howard.[52] It was the *feeling* of the book which discontented her; she was too distant from its characters and the thoughts that once inspired them. 'Catherine', the novel she had once called 'Susan' (until Mr John Booth published a two-volume novel of that name), was quite different. That was a book she had always loved, her first book, and full of a youthful wit. She still smarted over Crosby's refusal, but was nervous of risking another rebuff. Murray had recently sent his detailed accounts, which made for dismal reading. *Emma* was selling well enough and had already earned her over £220. But *Mansfield Park* remained a disappointing failure, and she had lost over £180 on the second edition. A year before, following the success of *Pride and Prejudice*, she had allowed herself to indulge hopes of gaining financial security and independence from her writing. The reality was far less comforting. Her total profits that spring amounted to just £38 18s; hardly the sort of sum to inspire her to risk publishing a book that was almost twenty years old.

The new novel began well enough, and through February she managed to write several chapters. But her health still caused her difficulties and she found herself easily tired. She had little patience, or inclination, to give her characters depth or subtlety of feeling. She was determined, though, to make light of her indisposition. 'Sickness is a dangerous indulgence at my time of life,' she told Fanny. At least, she now thought that she understood her own case. 'I am more & more convinced that *bile* is at the bottom of all I have suffered,' she wrote to Alethea Bigg, 'which makes it easy to know how to treat myself.'[53] She was particularly anxious to be well enough to attend Henry's first service in St Nicholas's church. 'It will be a nervous hour for our pew,' she wrote, 'though we hear that he acquits himself with as much ease & collectedness, as if he had been used to it all his life.'

At the end of February, she fell ill again, and, by the middle of March, even she was forced to concede she was 'very poorly' with 'a good deal of fever' and 'indifferent nights'. Though she rarely acknowledged any great vanity concerning her looks, it was the alarming effects of her illness on her facial appearance which she found most distressing. Her skin became mottled, 'black & white

& every wrong colour,' she told Fanny. 'I must not depend upon ever being blooming again.'[54] Yet she continued to express her greatest concern for the ailments of others, rather than her own. There was poor Charles, suffering from rheumatism, who now had 'a great eruption in his face & neck'; and his little daughter Harriet, who had water on her brain, though the surgeons did not despair of drawing it off with mercury. Anna Lefroy had a bad cold '& we fear something worse'; and Fanny's brother William was 'bilious'. Conversation was reduced to an exchange of reported opinions by their various eminent medical men, Mr Curtis and Dr White, Sir Everard Home and Mr Lyford. Jane wrote to Caroline in mid-March to applaud her 'improvements in the gentleman quack' in one of her stories. Her own new novel (to be called perhaps *Sanditon* rather than 'The Brothers') would contain injuries and ailments, imaginary as well as real, on almost every page. The Parkers, she decided, were to be a family of imaginary invalids, forever suffering from the latest and most fashionable indispositions. Diana would lay claim to the 'spasmodic bile', being 'hardly able to crawl' from her bed to her sofa; Susan would endure nervous headaches, scarcely relieved by the operation of six leeches a day and the drawing of three teeth; while Arthur, 'too sickly for any profession', would boast an extensive repertoire of ailments, rheumatic, nervous or bilious, as the mood might take him.

One consequence of Jane's illness was an undisguised increase in irritability. She found young children particularly troublesome. Her visit to Frank's family at Alton in January had been quite spoilt by the antics of so many children, 'very noisy & not under such order as they ought,' she complained. Everywhere she looked there seemed to be more and more children, and women determined to produce them at a quite alarming rate. Mrs Deedes, she heard, had just given birth to her *eighteenth* child. 'I wd recommend to her & Mr D. the simple regimen of separate rooms,' she wrote sharply to Fanny. At Alton, Mrs F.A. was pregnant again, though 'by no means remarkably large for *her*,' Jane noted. And Anna's 'cold', as she feared, was a sign that she too was breeding again, barely six months after giving birth to her last. 'Poor animal,' wrote

Jane, 'she will be worn out before she is thirty – I am very sorry for her.' She was sorry, too, for Mrs Clements, who was also 'in that way again', and for all the other procreative female animals. 'I am quite tired of so many children,' she protested.[55] The characters of children were so unaccountable – they seemed to defy all the best hopes of heredity. 'How soon, the difference of temper appears!' she wrote to Fanny. Among Anna's brood, Jemima already displayed 'a very irritable bad temper', though Julia was quite sweet, 'always pleased & happy'. One might happily be rid of the duties of marriage and motherhood altogether, she thought, if the alternative were not quite so dismal. 'Single women,' she wrote to Fanny, 'have a dreadful propensity for being poor – which is one very strong argument in favour of matrimony.' The *Quarterly* reviewer would no doubt consider that a mean, sordid motive; but as she reflected on the £38 18s she had earned from more than two years of literary labours, it seemed a very reasonable motive to her. 'But I need not dwell on such arguments with *you*, pretty dear,' she resumed in her letter to Fanny. 'You do not want inclination.'[56] If matrimony could not be entirely avoided, it could at least be prudently postponed. And 'by not beginning the business of mothering quite so early in life' Fanny might hope to remain 'young in constitution, spirits, figure & countenance' while her friend Mrs Hammond grew old with her constant confinements and nursing. If that were a 'doctrine of selfishness', well, so be it. 'It is a vile world,' she wrote to Caroline, 'we are all for self & I expected no better from any of us.'

She found the newspapers filled with 'scandal & gossip'. So the young Earl of March was to marry Lady Caroline Paget. What a family they were, with their duels, elopements and adulteries! 'What can be expected from a Paget,' she demanded; 'born & brought up in the centre of conjugal infidelity & divorces?' She would *not* be interested about Lady Caroline, she declared: 'I abhor all the race of Pagets.'[57] Weak and irritable, she was troubled in her conscience about the public support she had been persuaded to offer to that even more celebrated adulterer – and bigamist – the Prince of Wales. She felt as if the world were slipping beyond her powers of control or comprehension. So many things seemed quite unaccountable. What did it mean, Fanny wanted to know, when Miss Branfill danced with 'her' Mr J. Wildman? But Jane was at a loss to provide an explanation. 'Who can understand a young lady?' she replied hopelessly, though once she might have claimed an especial understanding of the ways of young ladies at balls. Why had the Moores parted with their governess, just when their daughters had most need of one? 'They have some good reason, I dare say,' Jane wrote, but preferred to amuse herself by inventing a bad one. Such tiny gestures of malicious comedy were her sole consolation now. It was 'absolutely impossible,' she wrote, for her to match the wit of Fanny's brilliant letters. 'If I were to labour at it all the rest of my life & live to the age of Methusalah, I could never accomplish anything so long & so perfect.'

That phrase, the 'rest of her life' had a melancholy cadence. As she wrote it, she wondered how long it might be. Nothing like Methuselah's span, that was certain; perhaps even less than the life of one of those poor female animals, worn out by constant child-bearing. Her letter to Fanny had the tone of a solemn valediction, and she included an inventory of works yet unborn. 'Miss Catherine is put upon the shelve for the present,' she wrote, 'and I do not know that she will ever come out; but I have a something ready for publication, which may perhaps appear about a twelvemonth hence.' This information, she insisted, 'is for yourself alone'. Even now, she still found herself addicted to secrecy, and did not wish even such a splendid gentleman as Mr Wildman to know of her hopes. 'Adieu my dearest Fanny,' she wrote at the end of her letter, as if bidding farewell for the last time. 'Good bye & God bless you.'[58]

Privately, she wondered to herself how it might be that with 'so much imagination, so much flight of mind, such unbounded fancies', Fanny could still display such excellence of judgement. 'Religious principle,' she concluded, 'must explain it.' Religious principle was much on her mind at present. Forced by her failing health to abandon *Sanditon*, she devoted her wakeful hours to the composition of prayers.[59] 'Teach us to understand the sinfulness of our own hearts,' she prayed, 'and bring to our knowledge every fault of temper and every evil habit in which we have indulged to the discomfort of our fellow-creatures, and the danger of our own souls.' Would God forgive her, she wondered, for those outbursts of malicious wit which even now compelled her to acknowledge that 'pictures of perfection' made her 'sick & wicked'? ('There are so many', as Mrs Smith said in *Persuasion*, 'who forget to think seriously till it is almost too late.') 'Give us grace,' she prayed, 'to endeavour after a truly Christian spirit to seek to attain that temper of forbearance and patience of which our blessed Saviour has set us the highest example.' Christ had said: 'Suffer the little children to come unto me, and forbid them not: for such is the kingdom of God.' It was one of His principal commands, included in all the Gospels. Did that make it a sin for her to write, as she had done, only days before, that she was 'tired of so many children'? She prayed to be purged of all unworthy selfishness. 'Incline us oh God! to think humbly of ourselves, to be severe only in the examination of our own conduct, to consider our fellow-creatures with kindness, and to judge all they say or do with that charity which we would desire from them ourselves.'

While she commended herself to God's protection, she had not abandoned hope of finding an effectual remedy for the pains and fevers which had so lowered her strength. Exercise, she believed, might be as beneficial as rest, and as the weather grew more spring-like she hit upon a scheme that might allow her to take the air. The donkey-carriage was inconvenient and uncomfortable, but donkey-*riding* might be altogether more agreeable. It would be 'more independent & less troublesome' than the carriage, she said, and would enable her to join Cassandra on her walks to Wyards and Alton.[60] (She banished from her mind the thought that in *Emma* it was Mrs Elton who affected a delight in donkey-riding.) Cassandra was less sanguine about this scheme but was reluctant to say anything that might depress her sister's spirits further. Accordingly, on 24 March, when she judged Jane's strength to be equal to the effort, she and James Edward led her out, seated astride the cottage's most peaceable donkey, and took her for a short ride up Mounter's Lane, where the new cottages were to be. Jane was greatly encouraged by this triumph of equestrianism and wrote immediately to the family at Steventon to boast of it. Her brother James was very happy to receive such a 'good account' of her success 'written by her own hand' but was sceptical of its continuance. 'All who know her must be anxious on her account,' he wrote to Anna at Wyards.[61] For the moment, though, Jane determined to be rid of all anxieties. Another letter from Murray had arrived, enclosing almost £20 of profits from the new edition of *Sense and Sensibility*. That was the best kind of inspiration, she told Caroline, and it had filled her with a 'fine flow of literary ardour'. She congratulated Caroline on her own latest literary offering, particularly the character of Julia, 'a warm-hearted, ingenuous, natural girl'. But perhaps Caroline, with her Frenchified tastes, would not take that as praise. 'I know the word *natural* is no recommendation to you.'[62]

Writing to Fanny, she again boasted of her donkey-ride ('the exercise & everything very pleasant') and expressed impatience that her saddle was yet to be completed. She affected to be vexed that Fanny had been subjecting poor Mr Wildman to an enforced course of reading her aunt's novels. 'You are the oddest creature!' she declared. 'Do not oblige him to read any more. Have mercy on him . . . he deserves better treatment than to be obliged to read any more of my works.' Fanny, of course, insisted on teasing her with questions about the mysterious new novel. 'You will not like it,' Jane assured her, 'so you need not be impatient.'[63] The girl was evidently surprised that, having been told the book was such a mighty secret, her uncle Henry seemed to know all about it. 'Do not be surprised,' Jane wrote to her. When Henry had directly asked if she had anything ready for publication, 'I could not say no . . . But he knows nothing more about it.' Henry was a regular visitor. He and Frank had dined at the cottage a few nights before on a splendid ham sent from the family at Steventon. But now Henry must leave Hampshire for a visit to the capital. 'London is become a hateful place to him,' Jane wrote, '& he is always depressed by the idea of it.'

Jane herself had no time for depressing ideas. After the burial of Old Philmore in the parish churchyard the previous day, she was determined to be cheerful. 'A very handsome funeral,' she remarked to Triggs the gamekeeper, who walked behind the coffin in his smart green coat. Triggs, though, was less inclined to cheer-fulness, and 'his manner of reply made me suppose that it was not generally esteemed so'. Mrs Philmore, as chief mourner, was indeed a melancholy figure, walking through the village wreathed in her black bombasine with heavy black crape flounces. The sight of her filled Mrs Austen with dismal forebodings. They were all in daily apprehension of mournful tidings from Scarlets, where old Mr Leigh-Perrot was very ill, until Jane became impatient with the sense of gloom. 'I shall be very glad when the event at Scarlets is over,' she wrote to Fanny; 'the expectation of it keeps us in a worry, your grandmother especially; – she sits brooding over evils which cannot be remedied.'[64] The real evils which her mother feared lay somewhat closer to home, but it pleased Jane to pretend that uncle Leigh-Perrot's condition was the only cause. There were other, equally rational, motives (the *Quarterly* reviewer might call them 'sordid') for Jane's impatience. The Leigh-Perrots had often signified their intention to deal favourably by their Austen relations. Now, what with Henry's bankruptcy and Mr Baver-stock's lawsuit, there could hardly be a more opportune moment for such favour to be shown.

The sad event took place on 28 March, and Cassandra promptly set off for Scarlets to comfort the grieving widow, closely followed by James, as Mr L.P.'s sole trustee. Jane regretted the absence of Cassandra, who had done so much to soothe and help her during the past painful weeks; 'such an excellent nurse,' she wrote to Fanny, 'so assiduous & unwearied'. But she approved heartily of the reasons for her sister's embassy, and was tolerably satisfied that the worst of her own illness was behind her. 'I . . . am consider-ably better now,' she told Fanny, '& recovering my looks a little.'

How much Jane's hopes of recovery were founded upon her expectations of Leigh-Perrot's generosity was cruelly exposed the following week, when the terms of their uncle's will were made known. Cassandra's journey was all in vain. Leigh-Perrot had left everything – the house at Scarlets, the house at Bath, together with all their contents and the sum of £10,000 – to his wife Jane '& her heirs'. It was true that he bequeathed some other properties 'in trust' to James, but Jane Leigh-Perrot was to have all the income from them for the rest of her life. The Austen nephews and nieces were likewise promised £1,000 apiece, but *only* after the death of their aunt, Jane Leigh-Perrot.[65] For the present, there was nothing for any of them; and nothing at all, either now or in the future, for Leigh-Perrot's only surviving sister, Mrs Austen at Chawton, for his brother Thomas, in confinement at Monk Sherborne, or for his nephew, Richard Cooper at Hamstall Ridware. The wife whom Leigh-Perrot had once likened to the soft breeze and radiant sunshine of a summer's day was to have it all. The shock of this sudden disappointment was too much for Jane to bear. She suffered a violent bilious attack, with frequent bouts of fever. For more than a week she lay confined to her bed, unable to write, scarcely able to think.

At last, on 6 April, she found strength to write to her brother Charles, but could not disguise her feelings of dismay and despondency. 'I am ashamed to say that the shock of my uncle's Will brought on a relapse,' she confessed.[66] On the day before Leigh-Perrot's funeral, she had been so ill that she had pressed for Cassandra to return home with Frank immediately after the ceremony – 'which she of course did'. Now, whether it was on account of Cassandra's presence, or of Mr Curtis's care, her disorder was somewhat abated. 'I live upstairs however for the present,' she told him, '& am coddled.' Her mother, she said, had 'borne the forgetfulness of *her* extremely well', assuring everyone that 'her expectations for herself were never beyond the extreme of moderation.' 'I am the only one of the legatees who has been so silly,' she added, 'but a weak body must excuse weak nerves.' She was, however, by no means the only one of the potential legatees who felt shocked and dismayed by their uncle's neglect. The following day, she received an embittered letter from her cousin Cooper at Hamstall. 'Being thus disowned by him at last does hurt me a good deal,' he wrote. 'I never suspected him to harbour those unfavourable dispositions towards me of which he has left behind him so marked & convincing a proof.' The Reverend Cooper begged to enquire what period of mourning the family at Chawton intended to keep in honour of the uncle who had so conspicuously failed to honour them, 'as we would wish to do the same as you do'. As far as his own little boys were concerned, he said, he was inclined to think that 'one suit of black' would be quite sufficient.[67]

Jane herself contrived to appear calm, even magnanimous, despite her disappointment. 'Poor woman!' she remarked of her widowed aunt (resisting the temptation to write 'rich woman'), 'so miserable at present . . . we feel more regard for her than ever we did before.' Only after she had written these brave, forgiving sentiments did she realize that she had neglected to inscribe them on the appropriate black-edged paper. It was an effort beyond even her Christian magnanimity to copy them out again.[68]

Jane had heard that her niece Caroline had expressed a wish to visit her, and it was accordingly decided that the girl should spend some days at Chawton cottage while her parents were away at Scarlets arranging the late Mr Leigh-Perrot's affairs. But when the day came for the visit to begin, Jane suffered another feverish attack. Literary conversation was clearly out of the question, and it was generally agreed that Caroline would be better accommodated at Wyards, with her sister Anna. The following day, Anna and Caroline walked over to Chawton to make enquiries after their aunt Jane. She was keeping to her room, they were told, but would be happy to see them. Slowly, they made their way upstairs. Many years afterwards, Caroline could still vividly recall the poignant scene that greeted them.[69]

'She was in her dressing gown and was sitting quite like an invalid in an arm chair – but she got up and kindly greeted us – and then pointing to seats which had been arranged for us by the fire, she said, "There's a chair for the married lady, and a little stool for you, Caroline."' Strange how those few trifling words should lodge themselves so firmly in Caroline's memory. They were the last words of Jane's that she ever remembered. Whatever conversation followed – and there must have been *some* – was utterly lost and forgotten. It was as though Caroline had been in a trance, for she retained no recollection of anything else that was said. All she remembered was the sad, frail image of her aunt, seated in her chair. How she had altered! 'She was pale – her voice was weak and low and there was about her a general appearance of debility and suffering.' The visit was a short one. Jane was not equal to the exertion of talking, and Cassandra soon appeared to conduct them both downstairs. 'I do not suppose we stayed a quarter of an hour,' said Caroline, though the memory of that quarter of an hour, and the echo of those words, 'and a little stool for you, Caroline', remained with her for the rest of her life. 'I never saw Aunt Jane again.'

Other visitors were dissuaded from calling, though Mr Curtis, the apothecary from Alton, was in regular attendance, and Cassandra rarely left her sister's side. Henry, Frank and James offered what help they could, debating amongst themselves whether exercise or rest might seem to offer the best hope of recovery. There was talk of Jane removing to Winchester, where she might be attended by Lyford; not the Lyford who once pleased them all with his praise for Mr Austen's mutton, but his nephew, Giles-King Lyford, now Surgeon-in-Ordinary at the County Hospital. This Lyford had produced a quite remarkable improvement in Jane's condition during her previous bout of illness, when Curtis had been at a loss to help her. But then Curtis was merely an apothecary – not a Haden.

One evening, after keeping to her bed for a full fortnight of fevers, bile and violent pains, Jane drew up her last will and testament. 'To my dearest sister Cassandra Elizth,' she wrote, 'I bequeath . . . every thing of which I may die possessed, or which may be hereafter due to me . . .'[70] The sums were so little that she could make no great parade of generosity to the rest of the family, but she made one tiny exception, in favour of Henry, who stood in need of every penny he could find. 'A legacy of £50 to my brother Henry,' and then added, as an afterthought, '& £50 to Mde Bigeon.' That last bequest might seem a little eccentric, she realized; to give £50 from her meagre stock to a woman she hardly knew. But Madame Bigeon, who had been Henry's housekeeper in London for so many years, had suffered as greatly as anyone from the bankruptcy and the loss of Hans Place. The kindly little Frenchwoman, despite the pains of frequent asthmatic attacks, had helped Henry after the death of Eliza and through all his subsequent financial troubles. Jane remembered sitting with her in the kitchen at Henrietta Street, as the poor woman fretted herself over the lack of Henry's favourite raspberry jam. People like Madame Bigeon were so often the innocent casualties of others' misfortunes. They ought not to be forgotten. 'May the comforts of every day be thankfully felt by us', she wrote in a prayer; 'may they prompt a willing obedience of thy commandments and a benevolent spirit toward every fellow creature.'

She told no one about her will, and did not even ask Cassandra to sign as a witness. It would only distress them to think that her thoughts had turned to such melancholy offices. It occurred to her to wonder if a will without witnesses was an entirely legal document, but she contented herself by reflecting that it was such a simple statement, so brief in its directions and modest in the bequests, that no one would find an interest in disputing it.

For three more weeks she lay confined to her bed with more feverish nights, weakness and languor. She felt quite embarrassed to be the subject of so much unfailing attention by the rest of the family. 'Every dear brother so affectionate & so anxious!' she wrote to Anne Sharp when at last she felt well enough to sit up in bed with a pen and paper. 'And as for my sister! – Words must fail me in any attempt to describe what a nurse she has been to me. Thank God! she does not seem the worse for it *yet*.'[71] Martha Lloyd, too, was 'all kindness'. 'In short,' she said, 'if I live to be an old woman I must expect to wish I had died now, blessed in the tenderness of such a family.' So much enforced idleness, though, was very irksome to her. Why, even Frank's wife had had 'a much shorter confinement than I have,' she joked, 'with a baby to produce into the bargain!' *Really*, she insisted, she was quite equal to being out of bed now, but rest was thought to be good for her. The family wondered that she should exert so much effort writing to such a distant acquaintance as Miss Sharp. But it was exactly such poor unfortunate friends as Anne Sharp and Madame Bigeon that Jane now most wished to remember. 'I have so many alleviations & comforts to bless the Almighty for!' she wrote to her, trying to drive from her mind all sordid reflections on such things as Mr L.P.'s will. Her prayers aspired to the same spirit of thankfulness. 'We feel we have been blessed far beyond any thing that we have deserved,' she prayed, imploring God 'to pardon the presumption of our desires'.

On Saturday 24 May, James and Mary sent their carriage from Steventon to convey Jane to Winchester, where she might be treated by Lyford. 'I am now really a very genteel, portable sort of invalid,' she joked. It rained hard all day, and the carriage wheels squelched in the mud as it drew up outside the cottage. It was really very kind and charitable of Mrs J.A. to send the carriage for her, Jane said, though she could not help observing that it was also somewhat out of character. In the main, Mary was '*not* a liberal-minded woman'. Nor did Jane expect any change in Mary's character from the promise of wealth when Mrs Leigh-Perrot finally died. It was 'too late, too late in the day,' she said, to hope for any decrease of presumption in Mrs J.A.'s desires.[72] Particularly as old Mrs L.P. might well survive for another ten years! The journey to Winchester was sixteen miles, all in the rain, but nothing Jane could say would prevent Henry from accompanying the carriage on horseback, together with young William Knight. It distressed her to see the two of them picking their way through the puddles and drenched in the constant downpour. She herself was quite comfortable, she assured them when at last they arrived; 'very little fatigue'. The lodgings in College Street were very comfortable too – a neat little drawing-room with a bow-window overlooking Dr Gabell's garden. Here at last, she believed, she would make a proper recovery. Lyford thought so, too. 'Mr Lyford says he will cure me,' she wrote to James Edward, '& if he fails,' she joked, 'I shall draw up a memorial & lay it before the Dean & Chapter, & have no doubt of redress from that pious, learned & disinterested body.'[73] But she was determined that he should not fail. 'I am gaining strength very fast,' she told her nephew after only three days in her new lodgings. She could not yet boast that her face had entirely recovered its 'proper beauty', but she was out of bed from nine in the morning till ten at night – 'upon the sopha t'is true', and eating her meals 'in a rational way' with Cassandra. It was a relief to be away from her mother, who worried and fretted constantly at witnessing her feverish attacks. Happily,

Jane believed, all such attacks were now things of the past. 'The Providence of God has restored me,' she wrote; '& may I be more fit to appear before him when I *am* summoned, than I shd have been now!'

The conviction that she was *not* fit yet to appear before her Maker was something which both sustained and alarmed her. Try as she might to subdue her wicked wit and strive after a truly Christian spirit of forbearance, she could not entirely suppress some less benign reflections. Though James himself was all kindness to her, she could not entirely resist a few malicious asides on his wife's vanity and presumption. And, whilst she endeavoured to put from her mind all worldly repining at the cruel disappointment of Mr L.P.'s will, she could not avoid the bitter reflection that it was her uncle's narrow parsimony that had brought on her latest bout of fever. She wrote as much in a letter to Mrs Tilson in London, then checked herself. 'But I am getting too near complaint.' She resigned herself to accepting that her illness was 'the appointment of God, however secondary causes may have operated'.[74]

For her first week at College Street, she lived chiefly on the sofa of Mrs David's drawing-room and was happy to receive a succession of well-wishing friends, relations and handsome young men. One day, it would be Henry bringing young William Knight; another day, it would be William's younger brother Charles, now a boy at the school. Mrs Heathcote (the former Elizabeth Bigg) called every day, but not her sister Alethea, she being 'frisked off' (like half England, it seemed) into Switzerland. 'I have been out once in a sedan-chair,' she told Frances Tilson, 'and am to repeat it, and be promoted to a wheel-chair as the weather serves.' But the approach of summer weather brought no improvement in her condition. On 6 June, Mrs J.A. came to Winchester and was shocked at what she found. Lyford, who was always encouraging to Jane herself (he 'talks of making me quite well,' she wrote), was more candid to her sister-in-law, telling her that 'the end was near at hand'. Mrs J.A. promptly resolved to remain with the Austen sisters at College Street, 'to make it more cheerful for them' and to take her share in the burdens of attendance.[75] Cassandra was grateful for Mary's help. The nurse they had employed 'could not be trusted,' she found, 'having been more than once found asleep'. Between them, Mary and Cassandra took turns in watching over Jane throughout the night. James came to visit them the following Tuesday, when he found Jane 'much altered, but composed and cheerful'. In a letter to his son James Edward, he wrote: 'I must tell you that we can no longer flatter ourselves with the least hope of having your dear valuable Aunt Jane restored to us ... Mr Lyford has candidly told us that her case is desperate. I need not say what a melancholy gloom this has cast over us all.'[76] Charles, already depressed at his daughter Harriet's illness, arrived in Winchester on Friday 13 June and noted in his diary that his sister was 'very ill'.[77] James and Henry were frequent visitors, and Jane took Holy Communion from them while she was still strong enough to attend fully to the service. Frank did not visit her, which was a disappointment, though Jane did her best not to show it.

However, contrary to all expectations, Jane's condition now showed some signs of improvement. When Charles returned to College Street five days later, he found that 'Dear Jane' was 'rather better'. The next morning, she was 'a little better' still. Charles and Henry lost no time in conveying this heartening news to their mother at Chawton, who was 'very poorly' herself from her constant anxieties. She was delighted at this tiny gleam of hope and immediately passed the good news to Anna at Wyards. 'You will be happy to know that our accounts from Winchester are very good,' she wrote. 'Mr Lyford says he thinks better of her than he has ever done, tho' must still consider her in a precarious state.'[78] The improvement was sufficient for Mary to return to Steventon, and, throughout the following fortnight, Cassandra contrived to send more hopeful messages to all the family. 'I had a very comfortable account of your Aunt Jane this morning,' Mrs Austen told Anna on 14 July; 'she now sits up a little. Charles Knight ... saw her yesterday and says she looks better and seemed very cheerful.'

The following day – St Swithin's day – Jane even felt well enough to dictate a set of comic verses on the subject of the Winchester races. Angry that such 'races & revels & dissolute measures' should take place on his own holy day, the saint promises his blight on their pleasures by drenching the races with rain. The proximity of the races, and the nearby saint's shrine, provided Jane with her comic material; but the real themes of this curious six-stanza poem are death and immortality. She pictures the saint leaping from his Cathedral shrine to curse the 'depraved' subjects of Winchester. 'When once we are buried you think we are dead/But behold me Immortal!' he cries.[79] Even now, as she strove to attain a serene state of forbearance, Jane could not refrain from celebrating immortality in the form of a satiric curse. Almost immediately, her complaint returned; 'there was a visible change,' wrote Cassandra, as Jane drifted into a heavy sleep. Mrs J.A. had been summoned back to Winchester the previous day, and together she and Cassandra again took turns in watching over the sleeping invalid. A last letter arrived from Fanny and, when Jane awoke, Cassandra cut the seal and gave it to her. 'She opened it & read it herself,' Cassandra told Fanny, '& then talked to me a little & not unchearfully of its contents, but there was then a languor about her which prevented her taking the same interest in any thing, she had been used to do.'[80]

For two more days, Jane lay in her bed, 'more asleep than awake'. 'Her looks altered,' wrote Cassandra, '& she fell away, but I perceived no material diminution of strength.' The end, when it came, was sudden, though not unexpected. It was to Fanny alone that Cassandra felt herself bound to impart her solemn description of those final hours.

> She felt herself to be dying about half an hour before she became tranquil & apparently unconscious. During that half hour was her struggle, poor soul! she said she could not tell us what she suffered, tho she complained of little fixed pain. When I asked her if there was any thing she wanted, her answer was she wanted nothing but death & some of her words were 'God grant me patience, Pray for me, Oh Pray for me'. Her voice was affected but as long as she spoke she was intelligible. I hope I do not break your heart my dearest Fanny by these particulars, I mean to afford you gratification whilst I am relieving my own feelings. I could not write so to

any body else, indeed you are the only person I have written to at all excepting your Grandmama, it was to her not your Uncle Charles I wrote on Friday. Immediately after dinner on Thursday I went into the town to do an errand which your dear aunt was anxious about. I returned about a quarter before six & found her recovering from faintness & oppression, she got so well as to be able to give me a minute account of her seisure & when the clock struck 6 she was talking quietly to me. I cannot say how soon afterwards she was seized again with the same faintness, which was followed by the sufferings she could not describe, but Mr Lyford had been sent for, had applied something to give her ease & she was in a state of quiet insensibility by seven o clock at the latest. From that time till half past four when she ceased to breathe, she scarcely moved a limb, so that we have every reason to think, with gratitude to the Almighty, that her sufferings were over. A slight motion of the head with every breath remained till almost the last. I sat close to her with a pillow in my lap to assist in supporting her head, which was almost off the bed, for six hours, – fatigue made me then resign my place to Mrs J.A. for two hours & a half when I took it again & in about one hour more she breathed her last. I was able to close her eyes myself & it was a great gratification to me to render her these last services. There was nothing convulsed or which gave the idea of pain in her look, on the contrary, but for the continual motion of the head, she gave me the idea of a beautiful statue, & even now in her coffin, there is such a sweet serene air over her countenance as is quite pleasant to contemplate.[81]

CHAPTER 14

Pictures of Perfection

―――

Pictures of perfection as you know make me sick
& wicked.

Jane Austen, Letter to Fanny Knight, March 1817

It was as a beautiful statue, benign in life, serene in death, that the Austens chose to remember their departed aunt and sister. The process of beatification began immediately after her death. Cassandra retrieved Jane's final poem and underlined the phrase 'When once we are buried you think we are dead/But behold me Immortal!', conveniently forgetting that these words – the last that Jane Austen ever wrote – were expressed in the form of a curse, not a blessing. The word 'dead' though was too much for her to bear and, at the expense of a rhyme, she softened it to 'gone'. Mrs J.A. claimed to remember how, during her lonely night-time vigils by the bedside, Jane had whispered a last grateful tribute: 'You have always been a kind sister to me, Mary.' How very different from the last words that we know Jane to have written about Mary ('*not* a liberal-minded woman'). Within days of Jane's death, Cassandra had taken to describing her as a 'dear angel'. 'If I think of her less as on earth, God grant that I may never cease to reflect on her as inhabiting Heaven & never cease my humble endeavours (when it shall please God) to join her there.'[1]

The funeral took place on the morning of Thursday 24 July at Winchester Cathedral. 'It is a satisfaction to me,' Cassandra wrote to Fanny, that her sister's dear remains were 'to lie in a building she admired so much – her precious soul I presume to hope reposes in a far superior mansion.' Only three of the brothers – Edward, Henry and Frank – were present at this 'last sad ceremony'. Charles, at Eastbourne, was too far away to attend; James, too, stayed away. 'In the sad state of his own health and nerves,' he said, 'the trial would be too much for him.' Women were not expected to attend such melancholy ceremonies; their grief, it was thought, might overcome them. The funeral was held in the early morning; it 'must be over before ten o'clock,' Cassandra told Fanny, 'as the Cathedral service begins at that hour'. Before the coffin was closed, she cut off several locks of Jane's hair as family mementoes. 'Everything was conducted with the greatest tranquillity,' she wrote. She and Martha Lloyd 'watched the little mournful procession the length of the street & when it turned from my sight I had lost her for ever'. Even then, she said, 'I was not overpowered . . . Never was human being more sincerely mourned . . . than was this dear creature. May the sorrow with which she is parted from on earth be a prognostic of the joy with which she is hailed in Heaven!'[2]

Late on the sunny afternoon of 21 July 1817, Francis Cullum made his way back home over the fields from the parish church of All Saints in Monk Sherborne. He had just witnessed the wedding of Charles Munday to Sarah Woods. Neither bride nor groom could read or write, but both had made their cross in the parish register with the church pen gripped tightly in their fists. Francis had added his own name underneath, as he always did, in his office of parish clerk. The Woods girl was already six months pregnant, just as his own wife, Elizabeth, had been, more than thirty years before. Elizabeth, too, unable to read or write, had marked her name with a cross. Francis's family had considered it a foolhardiness on his part to have become involved with one of the Bye girls (Elizabeth's sister Martha had already had two bastard children by different fathers). But he had loved her and she had borne him eight healthy children. Over more than twenty years as parish clerk, Francis had witnessed many a less hopeful marriage than that of the young pair who had embarked on holy matrimony that sunny afternoon. Having no money to start with, they might at least escape the delusion, so frequent among the families of the gentry, of believing that money was the principal ingredient of marital felicity. And if their children should prove slow to learn, or (as God forbid) betray symptoms of idiocy, they would not take it as a sign of shame, and cast the poor infant out to be cared for among strangers.[3]

Francis's own children were all grown now, save only Elizabeth, just seventeen. Charles had set up as a thatcher and the other boys found no lack of work on the neighbouring farms. But there were still two wretched souls remaining in his house – infants in mind, though not in body – for Francis and Elizabeth to care for. Mr Thomas Leigh was seventy years of age, and had been with the Cullums for nearly all his life. The Leighs were very rich, and, as Francis heard, owned vast estates, with a castle in Warwickshire as well as several other handsome properties. But Mr Thomas Leigh had known nothing of such riches. For more than sixty years his entire world had been confined to a small room in the Cullums' farmhouse at Monk Sherborne. He was old now, and in poor health, but for him, each day was alike; with only the change of the seasons to add or subtract some small variation to his daily routine, as the weather might encourage or prohibit a walk in the yard or surrounding fields. His companion for more than forty years had been his nephew George Austen, brother to the celebrated lady novelist, and, like Mr Leigh, consigned in infancy to the care of the Cullum family when he first demonstrated distressing signs of idiocy. Neither the Austens nor the Leighs cared to be reminded of the existence of these imbecile relatives. There were no fond enquiries after their welfare, no cheerful visits to relieve the monotony of their daily routine. From time to time, Mr James Austen, George's elder brother and vicar of the adjoining parish, called in with money to meet the costs of his brother's board and lodging. But Mr Austen did not linger for conversation, preferring to pass his time with Mr Chute at the Vyne, or Lord

Dorchester at Kempshott Park, where there was always fine hunting to be had or some witty companion to dine with.

Over the years, the money from the Leighs and the Austens had been adequate (but scarcely generous) to meet the needs of Mr Thomas and Mr George. There had never been any danger of Francis himself growing rich from the discreet service he provided to these two proud families in sheltering their unfortunate relations from public view. As he crossed the open field opposite his house, Francis reflected with a degree of bitterness on his treatment some years earlier when he had sought to fence in this land for his own use. He had been presented before the Court Baron of the manor for his pains, and threatened with a fine of 40s if he did not throw open the field again to common grazing. The following year, he had been accused of taking away dung and manure from the common land. For that, he had been fined 10s.[4] It was against the dignity of a parish clerk to be presented before the Court Baron in such a humiliating manner. If either the Austens or the Leighs would deal with him as, in conscience, they were obliged to do, he would not find himself compelled to such wretched shifts as these.

Only the previous week, Mr James Austen had made one of his infrequent visits to the house, on his way back from officiating at the christening of the latest Dibley boy at Sherborne St John. His sister Jane, Mr Austen said, was very ill at Winchester and like to die. He added that he, too, was ill. If his sister should die that week, as he greatly feared she might, he would hardly have the strength to attend her funeral. Francis never saw Mr Austen again. It was some weeks before Francis came to learn that Miss Austen had indeed died at Winchester that very week in July. Mr James Austen himself died less than two years later, in the bleak winter of 1819.

Though he *could* read, Francis Cullum was no great reader, yet he had, for the sake of curiosity rather than in any hope of edification or amusement, ventured to sample the writings of George Austen's famous sister. What he read did not greatly impress him. He found that a great emphasis was placed, in all her writings, on the shared love of brothers and sisters. In one novel, he read of such an intensity of family affection that 'even the conjugal tie is beneath the fraternal'.[5] That was hardly the kind of family sentiment that Francis had witnessed in the conduct of the Austens towards their poor brother George. After Miss Austen's death, her brother Henry had published two more of her novels, with a prefatory notice which said much about her Christian virtues and her great love for all her fellow creatures. But Francis was more struck by a small incident, unnoticed, as he imagined, by many of Miss Austen's admirers, in one of these last novels, *Persuasion*. There was a family mentioned in it, the Musgroves, who had the ill fortune to have a 'troublesome', 'thick-headed', 'hopeless' son, who went by the name of 'poor Richard'. But, so it said, the Musgroves had 'the good fortune to lose him before he reached his twentieth year'. This thick-headed, 'unprofitable' son, she wrote, 'had been sent to sea, because he was stupid and unmanageable on shore; . . . he had been very little cared for at any time by his family, though quite as much as he deserved; seldom heard of, and scarcely at all regretted.'[6] When he read that, Francis put down the book and looked over towards poor George Austen, sitting motionless as he often would, staring out of the window at the rain falling gently in the yard outside.

Jane Austen's will was proved on 10 December 1817. After the payment of the legacies to Henry and Madame Bigeon, and the funeral expenses (£92), Cassandra received the residue of £561 2s 0d. She also became the owner of all her sister's manuscripts and personal effects. 'In looking at a few of the precious papers which are now my property,' she wrote to Fanny, 'I have found some memorandums, amongst which she desires that one of her gold chains may be given to her god-daughter Louisa & a lock of hair be set for you.' Vowing that 'every request of your beloved aunt will be sacred with me', Cassandra begged Fanny to say whether she would prefer a brooch or a ring as a setting for the precious lock of hair. Fanny opted for the hair to be set in an oval brooch, bearing Jane's name and the date of her death. For herself, Cassandra had a lock of hair set in pearls and fashioned into a ring which she wore constantly. A third lock was sent to

Miss Sharp, together with a pair of clasps which Jane had sometimes worn and a small bodkin. 'I know how these articles, trifling
as they are, will be valued by you,' Cassandra wrote. Other locks
of hair were sent to each of the brothers and also to Harriet Palmer.
Martha Lloyd received Jane's topaz ring, which she treasured for
the rest of her life.[7]

After Jane's death, the Austens' family life quickly resumed its
familiar pattern of local triumphs and defeats. That spring, Edward
was at last obliged to buy off Mr Baverstock's lawsuit with a
settlement of £15,000; a vast tract of timber was felled from Chawton wood to raise the money. Henry became a 'zealous preacher
of the gospel' and married Miss Jackson, niece to the Chawton
vicar, Mr Papillon. Charles remarried the same year, though his
choice of bride – his sister-in-law Harriet Palmer – was hardly to
his mother's taste ('one must pity her,' she wrote, 'tho one can't
much like her').[8] Mrs Austen herself remained at Chawton cottage,
with Cassandra and Martha Lloyd, until her death at the grand
old age of eighty-seven, in 1827. Whereupon Martha, now aged
sixty-three, agreed to marry Frank, whose first wife, Mary, had
died four years before. Frank eventually rose to the rank of Admiral
of the Fleet and lived on his own estate at Portsdown Lodge, near
Portsmouth. Charles, too, became an Admiral and was appointed
Commander-in-Chief of the East India and China station. He died
of cholera in 1852 while on active service up the Irrawaddy river
in Burma.

When Francis Cullum died, aged seventy-eight, in the spring
of 1834, his son George assumed the care of George Austen. At
the time of Mrs Austen's death at Chawton, the money from her
South Sea Annuities had been divided equally among the surviving
Austen children, Cassandra, Henry, Frank, Edward and Charles.
But for George, there was nothing. He, as usual, was excluded
and forgotten. It was Edward Knight who, as an act of kindness,
made over his share of the money 'for the use of my brother
George, being his full share of the £3,350 Old South Sea
Annuities'.[9]

George Austen died of dropsy at Monk Sherborne on 17 January

1838, at the age of seventy-two, and was buried five days later. In Winchester Cathedral, the tomb of his sister Jane was inscribed with a loving tribute from her family. 'The benevolence of her heart, the sweetness of her temper, and the extraordinary endowments of her mind obtained the regard of all who knew her, and the warmest love of her intimate connections.' Less than twenty miles away, Jane's brother George was laid to rest in an unnamed grave in the churchyard of All Saints church, Monk Sherborne. In death, as in life, he was to be forgotten, his remains unmarked by any stone. Only George Cullum was in attendance at George Austen's death. It was he who noted for the death certificate that George Austen was 'a gentleman'.

'Pictures of perfection as you know make me sick & wicked,' Jane Austen had written in one of her last letters to Fanny Knight; but it was as a picture of perfection that her family determined to remember her. 'She was a humble, believing Christian,' declared her nephew James Edward: 'Her life had been passed in the performance of home duties, and the cultivation of domestic affections, without any self-seeking or craving after applause.' 'Her needlework . . . was excellent,' he added, 'and might almost have put a sewing-machine to shame.' Caroline Austen agreed. Her aunt, she said, was 'a great adept at overcast and satin stitch'. Nothing was said, in the inscription on Jane Austen's tomb, about the fact that she also wrote novels.[10]

Living alone at Chawton cottage after her mother's death, Cassandra contrived to turn the house into a kind of shrine to her dead sister. She carefully preserved every scrap of manuscript which might do honour to dear Jane's memory, while burning anything that might tend to suggest a less perfect picture. She copied out Jane's prayers but destroyed her more malicious letters. In her own copy of *Persuasion*, Cassandra marked this passage:

How eloquent could Anne Elliot have been, – how eloquent, at least were her wishes on the side of an early attachment, and a cheerful confidence in futurity, against that over-anxious caution which seems to insult exertion and distrust Providence! – She had been forced into prudence in her youth, she learned romance as she grew older – the natural sequel of an unnatural beginning.

Against this passage, in the margin of the book, Cassandra wrote: 'Dear, dear Jane! This deserves to be written in letters of gold.'[11] For Cassandra, Jane's writings became a kind of sacred text, and her beloved image almost a holy icon. When she thought of Jane, she thought in terms of ritual objects of veneration: letters of gold, a beautiful statue, or a precious lock of hair, set in a ring of pearls. 'She was the sun of my life,' she wrote, 'the gilder of every pleasure, the soother of every sorrow.' Twenty years after Jane's death, when her great-niece Fanny Caroline visited the cottage at Chawton, she was greatly struck by the way Cassandra spoke of her dead sister, 'There was such an accent of *living* love in her voice.'[12] But though the love was living, the object of all that sisterly affection had been transformed into a myth of perfection. There was little, among all these precious relics of her sister so carefully preserved, to record the restless spirit of the woman who said of herself: 'If I *am* a wild beast, I cannot help it. It is not my own fault.'

Notes

―――

Abbreviations

Works which are frequently cited in the notes are abbreviated as follows:

Manuscript sources

Manuscript material is in the Austen-Leigh Collection, Hampshire Record Office, unless otherwise indicated.

Fanny Knight's Diary	The Diaries of Fanny Knight (later Lady Knatchbull), 1804–72, Centre for Kentish Studies, Maidstone (MSU951 F24/1–69)
Hubback MS	Notes towards a family history, compiled by Mrs John Hubback (*née* Catherine-Anne Austen); contained in the family archive of Frank Austen
James Austen, 'Verses'	Collected Verses of James Austen, copied out by his son, James Edward Austen-Leigh
Lefroy Family History	Family History, written *c.* 1880–85 by Fanny-Caroline Lefroy
Lefroy MS	Notes towards a family history, compiled by Mrs Anna Lefroy (*née* Austen)
Stoneleigh Papers	Shakespeare Birthplace Trust, Stratford-upon-Avon (MSSDR/18/)

Published sources

Austen Papers	*Austen Papers 1704–1856*, ed. R.A. Austen-Leigh, with a new introduction by David Gilson, London, 1995

Catharine and Other Writings	*Catharine and Other Writings*, ed. M.A. Doody and Douglas Murray, Oxford, 1993
Critical Heritage	*Jane Austen: The Critical Heritage*, vol. I, ed. B.C. Southam, London, 1968
Facts and Problems	R.W. Chapman, *Jane Austen – Facts and Problems*, Oxford, 1948
Family Record	*Jane Austen: A Family Record*, William Austen-Leigh and Richard Arthur Austen-Leigh, revised and enlarged by Deirdre Le Faye, British Library, London, 1989
Gilson	David John Gilson, *A Bibliography of Jane Austen*, The Soho Bibliographies, Oxford, 1982
Honan	Park Honan, *Jane Austen: Her Life*, London, 1987
Letters	*Jane Austen's Letters*, 3rd edn, ed. Deirdre Le Faye, Oxford, 1995
Life and Letters	*Jane Austen: Her Life and Letters*, W. and R.A. Austen-Leigh, London, 1913
Memoir	J.E. Austen-Leigh, *A Memoir of Jane Austen by Her Nephew*, London, 1870, revised 1871; London, 1989
Minor Works	*The Works of Jane Austen*, vol. VI: *Minor Works*, ed. R.W. Chapman, Oxford, 1954; with revisions by B.C. Southam, Oxford, 1987
My Aunt Jane Austen	Caroline Mary Craven Austen, *My Aunt Jane Austen: A Memoir*, published by the Jane Austen Society, Winchester, 1952; new edn, for the Jane Austen Society, Winchester, 1991
Reminiscences	Caroline Mary Craven Austen, *Reminiscences*, ed. Deirdre Le Faye, Jane Austen Society, Winchester, 1986
Sailor Brothers	J.H. and E.C. Hubback, *Jane Austen's Sailor Brothers*, London, 1906; reprinted by Ian Hodgkins, London, 1986
Tucker	G.H. Tucker, *A Goodly Heritage: A History of Jane Austen's Family*, Manchester, 1983

CHAPTER 1: *Family Secrets*

1 Letterbook of Tysoe Saul Hancock, British Library, Add. MS 29236, fols 1–27
2 Deane parish records, Hampshire Public Record Office, MS 66M83PR1
3 Deane parish records
4 'Pedigree of Austen' privately printed, London, 1940; reprinted with *Austen Papers*
5 Edward Hasted, *The History and Topographical Survey of the County of Kent, etc.* (Canterbury, 1778–99), III, 48
6 'Memorandum [*sic*] of Elizabeth Austen, 1706–7', *Austen Papers*, 3–19
7 William Austen's Will, PROB 11/686
8 *Life and Letters*, 3
9 Lefroy MS, quoted in *Family Record*, 3
10 Hubback MS, quoted in *Family Record*, 3
11 'Nothing is known of Leonora's life except that she was still alive in 1769 and apparently then largely dependent upon the charity of family connections' (*Family Record*, 3)
12 Mrs Austen's portrait is mentioned in Cassandra Austen's testamentary letter, 9 May 1843, Ray Collection, Pierpont Morgan Library
13 Tucker, 66–7
14 Lefroy Family History
15 Mary-Augusta Austen-Leigh, *James Edward Austen-Leigh* (privately printed, 1911), 15
16 *Memoir*, 18
17 George Austen's account at Hoare's Bank, London
18 Lefroy MS
19 *Sailor Brothers*, plate facing p. 8
20 *Austen Papers*, 18
21 Joan Johnson, *Excellent Cassandra: The Life and Times of the Duchess of Chandos* (Gloucester, 1981), 12
22 Lefroy Family History
23 Lefroy MS
24 Hubback MS
25 Hancock Letterbook, BL Add. MS 29236, fol. 17
26 *Austen Papers*, 34–6
27 A. Mervyn Davies, *Clive of Plassey* (London, 1939), 121; Mark Bence-Jones, *Clive of India* (London, 1974), 68, 316
28 Hancock Letterbook, fols 1–2
29 Hancock Letterbook, fol. 4
30 Hancock Letterbook, fol. 14
31 Hastings Letterbook, British Library, Add. MS 29094, fol. 161
32 Bence-Jones, *Clive of India*, 220, 342
33 Hancock Letterbook, fol. 21

34 Hancock Letterbook, fol. 1

35 British Library, Add. MS 29132, fol. 159

36 British Library, Add. MS 29126, fols 98–9

37 Hancock Letterbook, fol. 17

38 Hancock Letterbook, fol. 14

39 *Memoir*, 8

40 Tucker, 18–19

41 Deane parish records, 1765

42 *Memoir*, 6–7

43 *Memoir*, 38

44 *Austen Papers*, 333; Susanna (Kelk) Austen's Will, PROB 11/942; Mrs Jane Leigh's Will, PROB 11/943

45 *Memoir*, 7; *Family Record*, 17, 258

46 *Austen Papers*, 22

47 *Austen Papers*, 22–3

48 *Austen Papers*, 23

49 *Austen Papers*, 23

50 *Memoir*, 38

51 *Austen Papers*, 24

52 *Austen Papers*, 25

53 *Austen Papers*, 27

54 *Family Record*, 21–2

55 *Austen Papers*, 28

56 *Austen Papers*, 27

57 Hancock Letterbook, fol. 14

58 Hancock Letterbook, fol. 20

59 George Austen's account at Hoare's Bank

60 Hancock Letterbook, fol. 22

61 *Austen Papers*, 29

62 Lefroy MS, quoted in *Family Record*, 10

63 *Austen Papers*, 30

64 Hancock Letterbook, fols 4–5

65 Hancock Letterbook, fol. 16

66 Hancock Letterbook, fol. 9

67 Hancock Letterbook, fols 5–6

68 Hancock Letterbook, fol. 22

69 Hancock Letterbook, fol. 9

70 Hastings Papers, British Library, Add. MS 29232, fols 83–4

71 Hastings Papers, fols 81–2

72 Hancock Letterbook, fol. 26

73 Hancock Letterbook, fol. 25

74 *Austen Papers*, 31

75 *Austen Papers*, 32–3

CHAPTER 2: *Noisy and Wild*

1 *Hampshire Chronicle*, 1 January 1776, 12 May 1777
2 *Letters*, 275
3 *Memoir*, 17–19
4 Anna Lefroy to James Edward Austen-Leigh, 20 July 1869, *Family Record*, 18
5 MS poems by James Austen and *Family Record*, 13
6 *Memoir*, 20
7 *Letters*, 28
8 *Letters*, 56
9 *Memoir*, 18
10 *Hampshire Chronicle*, 9 March 1782
11 *Hampshire Chronicle*, 25 January and 31 July 1773
12 *Hampshire Chronicle*, 27 July 1776
13 *Memoir*, 6
14 *Austen Papers*, 89–90
15 George Austen's account at Hoare's Bank
16 Austen-Leigh Collection, Hampshire Record Office, 23M93/M/50/1/1
17 Emma Austen-Leigh, *Jane Austen and Steventon* (London, 1937), 23; Tucker, 70–1
18 Austen-Leigh Collection, Hampshire Record Office, 23M93/M/50/1/1; 58/1
19 *Hampshire Chronicle*, 5 November 1774, 5 July 1777
20 *Austen Papers*, 89–90
21 *Austen Papers*, 92
22 *Correspondence of George III*, ed. Sir J. Fortescue (London, 1927), vol. IV, no. 2773
23 *Austen Papers*, 91
24 *Austen Papers*, 93–4
25 *Austen Papers*, 86–8
26 *Austen Papers*, 91
27 *Austen Papers*, 95
28 Abbé Michel Devert, 'Le Marais de Gabarret et de Barbotan', *Bulletin de la Société de Bordas* (1970), no. 340, 331–50
29 *Austen Papers*, 97–8
30 *Austen Papers*, 98
31 *Austen Papers*, 99–105
32 *Austen Papers*, 125
33 Stoneleigh Papers, DR/18/31/859–61
34 *Austen Papers*, 17
35 Lefroy MS
36 *Austen Papers*, 31
37 *Memoir*, 35

38 Lefroy MS

39 *Memoir*, plate facing p. 11. The original portrait remains in the possession of the Knight family

40 Edward Austen's portrait is reproduced in David Cecil's *A Portrait of Jane Austen* (London, 1978), facing p. 176

41 *Letters*, 196; Fanny Knight's Diary; *Emma*, I, xi

42 See 'The adventures of Mr Harley' and 'Henry and Eliza', in *Catharine and Other Writings*, 37, 31–6; also Jane Austen's inscriptions in the specimen marriage banns of Steventon parish register, Hampshire Record Office

43 Deirdre Le Faye, 'Anna Lefroy's original memories of Jane Austen', *Review of English Studies*, NS XXXIX: 155 (1988), 417–21

44 Austen-Leigh Collection, Hampshire Record Office, 23M93/60/3/2

45 Dr Thomas Franklin, *Matilda: A Tragedy* (1775)

46 Manuscript volume, now known as *Volume the Second*, vii, 2. The texts of most of Jane Austen's juvenile writings are contained in three manuscript notebooks known as *Volume the First*, *Volume the Second* and *Volume the Third*. The MS of *Volume the First* is in the Bodleian Library, Oxford; the MSS of *Volume the Second* and *Volume the Third* are in the British Library. For a discussion of these manuscripts see Brian Southam, *Jane Austen's Literary Manuscripts* (Oxford, 1966)

47 *The History of Goody Two Shoes* (edn *c.* 1780). Jane Austen later presented her copy to her niece Anna Austen (Gilson, 442)

48 *The Loiterer*, no. 9, 28 March 1789

49 M.L. South, 'Epidemic diseases, soldiers and prisoners of war in Southampton, 1550–1800', *Proceedings of the Hants Field Club and Archaeology Society*, 43 (August 1987), 185–96

50 George Austen's account with Hoare's Bank shows payments to Mrs Cawley of £50 in April 1783 and £10 in September 1783

51 Thomas Phillips, *Monumental Inscriptions in the County of Wilton*, 274

52 *Letters*, 54

53 *Hampshire Chronicle*, 22 November 1783

54 Frank Austen to Anna Lefroy, 9 October 1855

55 'Jack and Alice', in *Catharine and Other Writings*, 20

56 George Austen's account with Hoare's Bank

57 'Biographical Notice' 1818, *Critical Heritage*, 73–8

58 *Northanger Abbey*, I, i

59 Le Faye, 'Anna Lefroy's original memories of Jane Austen', 417–21

60 *The History of England from the reign of Henry the 4th to the death of Charles the 1st*, facsimile edition, with an introduction by Deirdre Le Faye, published by the British Library (London, 1993)

61 George Austen's bank account shows the following payments for his daughters' school fees:

S. La Tournelle	Aug 20th, 1785	£37 19 0
	Feb 13th, 1786	£36 2 6
	Jan 2nd, 1787	£16 10 0

62 See C. Tomkins, *Eight Views of Reading Abbey* (1791); W. Dugdale, *Monasticon Anglicanum*, new edn (London, 1846), vol. 4; Leslie Cram, *Reading Abbey* (Reading, 1988)

63 Details of life at the Abbey School are taken from F.J. Harvey Darton (ed.), *Life and Times of Mrs Sherwood* (London, 1910), 121–34 and 142–51. See also *Gentleman's Magazine* (1797), 983

64 *Emma*, I, iii

65 *Letters*, 5

66 Lefroy Family History.

CHAPTER 3: *Growing Up*

1 Deirdre Le Faye, 'Three Austen family letters', *Notes & Queries*, 32: 3 (1985), 335–6

2 *Austen Papers*, 111–12

3 James Austen, 'Collected Verses', MS volume at Jane Austen's house, Chawton

4 Lord Brabourne (ed.), *Letters of Jane Austen* (1884), 1, 35–6

5 Verses sent to Frank Austen, 26 July 1809; *Letters*, 175–8

6 Frank Austen's Memoir, contained in family archive; quoted in *Family Record*, 53

7 Christopher Lloyd, 'The Royal Naval Colleges at Portsmouth and Greenwich', *Mariner's Mirror*, 52 (1966), 145

8 See *Mariner's Mirror* (1977), 317, 324

9 *Austen Papers*, 88–113

10 Le Faye, 'Three Austen family letters', 333–4

11 'The Leigh Pedigree', verses written by Mary Leigh of Adlestrop, 31 December 1777, Austen-Leigh Collection, Hampshire Record Office, 23M93/50/1/1

12 *Austen Papers*, 123

13 *Austen Papers*, 123–6

14 *Austen Papers*, 126

15 *Austen Papers*, 127–8

16 Le Faye, 'Three Austen family letters', 331

17 *The Wonder: A Woman Keeps a Secret*, Act 1

18 Austen-Leigh Collection, Hampshire Record Office, 23M93/60/3/2

19 See Prologue to *The Tragedy of Tom Thumb*, 'Acted in a small circle of select friends', 22 March 1788

20 The entries on the specimen page of the Steventon marriage register in Hampshire Record Office read as follows:

The banns of marriage between *Henry Frederic Howard Fitzwilliam* of *London* and *Jane Austen* of *Steventon*

Edmund Arthur William Mortimer of *Liverpool* and *Jane Austen* of *Steventon* were married in this church

This marriage was solemnized between us, *Jack Smith & Jane Smith late Austen*, in the presence of *Jack Smith, Jane Smith.*

21 *Mansfield Park*, II, iv
22 *Persuasion*, II, v
23 Keith Feiling, *Warren Hastings* (London, 1954), 343–66
24 *Austen Papers*, 129–30
25 *Austen Papers*, 130
26 *Austen Papers*, 132
27 *Austen Papers*, 131
28 *Austen Papers*, 132–4
29 *The Loiterer*, no. 9, 28 March 1789
30 *Austen Papers*, 133
31 *Northanger Abbey*, I, xiv
32 *Letters*, 26
33 Reading List (1807) in *Lord Byron, The Complete Miscellaneous Prose*, ed. Andrew Nicholson (Oxford, 1991), 1–7
34 *Letters*, 306
35 *The Loiterer*, no. 9, 28 March 1789. It cannot be asserted as a certainty that Jane Austen was the 'Sophia Sentiment' who offered her opinions to *The Loiterer*. However, most recent authorities agree in attributing the letter to her, and the tone of the piece is consistent with her many juvenile essays in the style of literary parody.
36 'Biographical Notice' 1818, *Critical Heritage*, 73–8
37 Leslie A. Fiedler, *Love and Death in the American Novel* (London, 1970), 122
38 *Letters*, 22
39 *Northanger Abbey*, I, v
40 *The Loiterer*, no. 9; *Northanger Abbey*, I, xiv
41 *The Loiterer*, nos 1, 2, 5, 11, 20
42 *The Loiterer*, no. 21, 20 June 1789
43 *Letters*, 5
44 *Northanger Abbey*, I, xiv
45 *Memoir*, 79
46 David Gilson, 'Jane Austen's books', *Book Collector* (Spring 1974), 27–39
47 Lord David Cecil, Foreword to *Jane Austen's 'Sir Charles Grandison'*, transcribed and ed. Brian Southam (Oxford, 1980), ix.

48 For the best discussion of Jane Austen's 'Grandison' sketches see Brian Southam's edition of *Jane Austen's 'Sir Charles Grandison'*

49 *Catharine and Other Writings*, 17, 10

50 Austen-Leigh Collection, Hampshire Record Office, 23M93/60/3/2

51 *Austen Papers*, 136–8

52 *Austen Papers*, 134–6

53 Frank Austen archive, quoted in *Family Record*, 61

54 *Sailor Brothers*, 16–20

55 *The Loiterer*, no. 4, 21 February 1789

56 Court Book of the East India Company, India Office MSS B/128 (1798–9), fol. 680 and B/132 (1800–1), fol. 1020. See also Honan, 68

57 *The Loiterer*, no. 24, 11 July 1789

58 *The Sultan; Or a Peep into the Seraglio*, a farce in two acts by Isaac Bickerstaff, Act 1

59 *High Life Below Stairs*, a farce of two acts by the Reverend James Townley, 1759

60 *Hampshire Chronicle*, 7 July 1787

61 Marginalia in the Austen family copy of Goldsmith's *History of England*, now kept in the Austen-Leigh Collection

62 *Hampshire Chronicle*, 2 January 1790

63 *The Loiterer*, no. 10, 4 April 1789

64 *Hampshire Chronicle*, 23 May, 11 July 1789; 20 February 1790

65 *The Loiterer*, no. 9

CHAPTER 4: *Partial, Prejudiced & Ignorant*

1 *Austen Papers*, 138–40

2 *The Loiterer*, no. 27, 1 August 1789

3 *Austen Papers*, 138–40

4 *Austen Papers*, 140–1

5 *Austen Papers*, 142, 144

6 *Austen Papers*, 142–3

7 *Northanger Abbey*, I, v

8 *The Loiterer*, no. 7, 14 March 1789

9 *Northanger Abbey*, I, xiv

10 Marginalia in the Austen family copy of Goldsmith's *History of England*. Some later Austen has added 'Bravo Aunt Jane' after her remarks on the Stuarts.

11 *Letters*, 121

12 See the fully illustrated facsimile edition of Jane Austen's *The History of England* with an introduction by Deirdre Le Faye, published by the British Library (London, 1993)

13 My italics

14 Caroline Austen to James Edward Austen-Leigh, 1 April 1868 or 1869, published in *Family Record*, 249–50

15 *Letters*, 335

16 *The Loiterer*, no. 7

17 The manuscript notebook known as *Volume the Third*

18 *Austen Papers*, 143–4

19 *Austen Papers*, 142, 145

20 *Austen Papers*, 147–8

21 *Sense and Sensibility*, I, vi

22 Lefroy MS, quoted in *Family Record*, 69

23 *Austen Papers*, 146

24 *Hampshire Chronicle*, 25 June 1791

25 *Austen Papers*, 148

26 British Library, Add. MS 42170, fol. 2

27 *Austen Papers*, 148–9

28 *Sense and Sensibility*, I, x

29 *Austen Papers*, 150; *Letters*, 61

30 *Austen Papers*, 149–50

31 Stoneleigh Papers, DR/18/31/861; *Austen Papers*, 149

32 In 1780 Jane Austen dedicated a poem to him entitled 'An Epistle to Fulwar Craven Fowle, Esqr. supposed Secretary of State in the reign of Geo. 4th, by J. Austen as a Country Curate'

33 British Library, Add. MS 42160; 11 August 1793

34 Hubback MS, quoted in *Family Record*, 77

35 Lefroy family history, quoted in *Family Record*, 77

36 James Austen to Anna Lefroy, 19 June 1818

37 R. Cannon, *Historical Record of the 86th Regiment of Foot* (London, 1842), 10–13; James Edward Austen-Leigh's Diary, 30 November 1849

38 *Recollections of the Early Days of the Vine Hunt*, by 'A Sexagenarian' (James Edward Austen-Leigh) (London, 1865; reprinted London, 1995), 8–9, 20–2; *Hampshire Chronicle*, 19 January 1793

39 Court Book of the East India Company, 1800–1, India Office MSS B/132, fols 1020, 1125

40 Butler-Harrison MS family history, quoted in *Family Record*, 79; *Sense and Sensibility*, I, xxi

41 Lefroy MS, quoted in *Family Record*, 79–80

42 *Hampshire Chronicle*, 7 April 1792, 23 May 1798

43 *Austen Papers*, 321–3

44 *Austen Papers*, 152–3

45 *Letters*, 82

46 *Northanger Abbey*, I, i

47 *Letters*, 12

48 *Letters*, 10

49 Vera Watson, *Mary Russell Mitford* (London, 1949), 119–20

50 Mr Thomas Knight's Will, PROB 11/1252

51 *Hampshire Chronicle*, 22 October 1785

52 See Honan, 1–7, and John Masefield, *Sea Life in Nelson's Time* (London, 1920)

53 British Library, Add. MS 29173, fol. 281, and *Austen Papers*, 226–7

54 For details of the Princess's distressing manners and inadequate hygiene, see *Diaries and Correspondence of James Harris, First Earl of Malmesbury*, 4 vols (London, 1844), III, 153–211.

55 George Austen's account with Messrs Ring of Basingstoke.

56 *Life and Letters*, 81

57 *Reminiscences*, 7–9

58 *Austen Papers*, 170

59 *Letters*, 17, 20

CHAPTER 5: *Profligate and Shocking*

1 Keith Feiling, *Warren Hastings* (London, 1954), 352–60

2 *Austen Papers*, 153–4

3 *Austen Papers*, 227

4 *Austen Papers*, 330

5 *Letters*, 4

6 *Letters*, 3

7 *Letters*, 1–4

8 *Letters*, 1

9 *Letters*, 2

10 *Letters*, 3–4

11 *Letters*, 4

12 *Letters*, 19

13 Deirdre Le Faye, 'Tom Lefroy and Jane Austen', *Jane Austen Society Report* (1985), 8–10

14 *Austen Papers*, 162

15 *Austen Papers*, 155

16 *Austen Papers*, 155

17 *Letters*, 5

18 *Austen Papers*, 155

19 *Letters*, 12

20 *Letters*, 5–12

21 *Letters*, 9

22 *Letters*, 10

23 *Letters*, 5

24 *Letters*, 6, 9

25 *Letters*, 43

26 *Letters*, 47

27 *Letters*, 12
28 *Letters*, 12
29 *Austen Papers*, 155
30 *Austen Papers*, 156
31 *Austen Papers*, 156–7
32 *Letters*, 8
33 *Austen Papers*, 228
34 *Austen Papers*, 157
35 Verses, 'To Mary on her Wedding Day, Jany 17th 1812'
36 Mary-Augusta Austen-Leigh, *James Edward Austen-Leigh* (privately printed, 1911), 17–18
37 Lefroy Family History, quoted in *Family Record*, 93
38 *Reminiscences*, 17
39 *Letters*, 13
40 *Austen Papers*, 159
41 *Austen Papers*, 161
42 *Austen Papers*, 167
43 Lefroy Family History, quoted in *Family Record*, 94
44 Deirdre Le Faye, 'Anna Lefroy's original memories of Jane Austen', *Review of English Studies*, NS XXXIX: 155 (1988), 418
45 *Memoir*, 122; MS at St John's College, Oxford (MS 279)
46 *Letters*, 40; *Austen Papers*, 167; Gilson, 442, K14
47 *Austen Papers*, 160
48 *Austen Papers*, 160–1
49 *Austen Papers*, 162
50 *Austen Papers*, 164–6
51 *Austen Papers*, 164; *Letters*, 138
52 *Austen Papers*, 167
53 *Austen Papers*, 168–9
54 *Austen Papers*, 170–1
55 *Austen Papers*, 171
56 Lefroy MS, quoted in *Family Record*, 96
57 Lefroy Family History
58 Le Faye, 'Anna Lefroy's original memories of Jane Austen', 418
59 'Jack and Alice', in *Catharine and Other Writings*, 23; *Letters*, 216
60 *Letters*, 19
61 *Austen Papers*, 229
62 *Austen Papers*, 230–1
63 The house and grounds are described in *Tour through the Isle of Thanet* (1790) by Zachariah Cozens and in Nicola R. Bannister, *Godmersham Park: An Historic Landscape Survey* (English Heritage, 1995). See also Nigel Nicolson, *Godmersham Park, Kent* (Jane Austen Society, Alton, 1996)

64 *Pride and Prejudice*, III, i
65 *Letters*, 14
66 *Letters*, 15–18
67 *Letters*, 20
68 *Letters*, 21
69 *Letters*, 17, 20
70 *Letters*, 24
71 *Letters*, 20, 25
72 *Letters*, 18
73 *Letters*, 23
74 *Letters*, 27–8
75 *Letters*, 25
76 *Letters*, 26
77 *Letters*, 26
78 *Letters*, 27

CHAPTER 6: *I Say Nothing*

1 *Letters*, 28–31, 35
2 *Sailor Brothers*, 49
3 *Letters*, 32
4 *Letters*, 34
5 *Letters*, 35
6 *Letters*, 34
7 *Letters*, 30
8 *Letters*, 33
9 *Letters*, 38
10 *Letters*, 40–1
11 *Bath Chronicle*, 22 May 1799
12 *Northanger Abbey*, I, ii. In the published version the heroine is called Catherine, not Susan, and other changes may have been made in the transition from first draft to posthumously published novel.
13 *Letters*, 43
14 *Bath Chronicle*, 6 May 1799
15 *Letters*, 42
16 *Letters*, 48
17 *Letters*, 44
18 *Letters*, 43
19 *Letters*, 48–9
20 *Letters*, 37
21 *Letters*, 35, 44
22 Jane Leigh-Perrot's recollections of these events are taken from her letter to her cousin Montagu Cholmeley, 11 September 1799, *Austen Papers*, 182–6

23 *Austen Papers*, 186–9
24 *Austen Papers*, 197–8
25 *Austen Papers*, 186
26 *Austen Papers*, 192–7
27 Frank Douglas MacKinnon, *Grand Larceny* (London, 1937; reprinted London, 1995), 25–7
28 Jack Ayres (ed.), *Paupers and Pig-Killers: The Diary of William Holland, a Somerset Parson, 1799–1818* (Gloucester, 1984), 29
29 *Austen Papers*, 199
30 Austen-Leigh Collection, quoted in *Family Record*, 108
31 *Austen Papers*, 205–6
32 The most detailed account of the trial is contained in MacKinnon's *Grand Larceny*, 51–117. This includes the full (42-page) trial transcript taken by John Pinchard.
33 *Austen Papers*, 209
34 *Austen Papers*, 209
35 *Austen Papers*, 207, 211
36 *Austen Papers*, 209
37 *Grand Larceny*, 123–6
38 *Austen Papers*, 214
39 *Austen Papers*, 219
40 *Letters*, 49
41 *Letters*, 50
42 *Letters*, 52
43 *Letters*, 51
44 *Letters*, 53
45 *Letters*, 61–2
46 *Letters*, 56, and letter from Mrs Charles Powlett to Miss Peters, 20 June 1799, Powlett archive, quoted in *Family Record*, 114
47 *Letters*, 55–6, 59
48 *Letters*, 58
49 *Letters*, 62
50 *Letters*, 56
51 *Letters*, 60
52 *Letters*, 59
53 Caroline Austen, 1 April 1869, quoted in *Facts and Problems*, 46
54 *Life and Letters*, 156–7; Elizabeth Jenkins, *Jane Austen: A Biography* (London, 1938; revised edn, London, 1986), 86; David Cecil, *A Portrait of Jane Austen* (London, 1978), 90; Honan, 155
55 *Family Record*, 114; Honan, 156; *Facts and Problems*, 47
56 *Family Record*, 113
57 *Letters*, 68–9
58 *Austen Papers*, 208

59 *Letters*, 212–13
60 *Letters*, 69
61 *Letters*, 67
62 *Letters*, 67, 76
63 *Letters*, 66, 68
64 *Letters*, 73; galinies are domestic hens, from the Latin, *gallina*, a hen
65 *Letters*, 67
66 *Letters*, 71
67 *Letters*, 70
68 *Letters*, 74
69 *Letters*, 78
70 *Letters*, 68
71 *Letters*, 90
72 *Letters*, 76
73 *Letters*, 70–1
74 *Letters*, 78
75 *Letters*, 79

CHAPTER 7: *Conspiracy*
1 *Austen Papers*, 172–4
2 *Austen Papers*, 174
3 *Letters*, 79
4 *Letters*, 71
5 *Austen Papers*, 172–5
6 *Austen Papers*, 176
7 *Austen Papers*, 170
8 *Sailor Brothers*, 81–90
9 *Sailor Brothers*, 90; *Letters*, 80
10 Deane and Steventon parish registers, Hampshire Record Office
11 *Letters*, 80
12 *Letters*, 81
13 *Letters*, 82
14 *Letters*, 85
15 *Letters*, 87
16 *Letters*, 88
17 *Austen Papers*, 175
18 *Letters*, 88, 91
19 *Letters*, 87
20 *Letters*, 90
21 *Letters*, 85
22 *Letters*, 90–1
23 *Letters*, 92
24 Testimonies to Jane Austen's appearance from the following: Henry

Austen, 'Biographical Notice' 1818; Fulwar-William Fowle, quoted by Kathleen Tillotson in 'Jane Austen', *Times Literary Supplement*, 17 September 1954, 591; Charlotte-Maria Middleton, quoted by Deirdre Le Faye in 'Recollections of Chawton', *Times Literary Supplement*, 3 May 1985, 495; Anna Lefroy, quoted by Deirdre Le Faye, 'Anna Lefroy's original memories of Jane Austen', *Review of English Studies*, NS XXXIX: 155 (1988), 417–21; Sir Egerton Brydges in *The Autobiography, Times, Opinions and Contemporaries of Sir Egerton Brydges* (London, 1834), II, 39–41; Caroline Austen, *My Aunt Jane Austen*, 5; Louisa Knight, quoted by Elizabeth Jenkins in 'Some notes on background', in *Jane Austen Society Collected Reports*, vol. III: *1976–85* (Alton, 1989), 152–68

25 Testimonies to Jane Austen's character from the following: Henry Austen, 'Biographical Notice' 1818; Caroline Austen, *My Aunt Jane Austen*, 8; James Edward Austen-Leigh, *Memoir*, 155, 184

26 *Letters*, 124

27 *Austen Papers*, 175

28 Caroline Austen's account is in an undated letter to her brother for the expanded (1871) edition of his *Memoir*, quoted in *Family Record*, 126–7

29 Marginal note by Louisa Lefroy, later Mrs Bellas, in her copy of Brabourne's edition of *Letters of Jane Austen*, quoted in *Facts and Problems*, 67–8

30 Chapman (*Facts and Problems*, 64–5) prints this as an extract from a letter from Caroline Austen to Mary Leigh; Le Faye (*Family Record*, 126–7) presents it as part of the letter to James Edward Austen-Leigh. For a discussion of variations and inconsistencies between different accounts of this episode in Jane Austen's life see *Facts and Problems*, 63–9

31 Lefroy Family History, quoted in Honan, 186

32 *Family Record*, 127

33 Honan, 185

34 Extracts made by Austen-Leighs from Madam Lefroy's diary, 1801; *Austen Papers*, 175

35 *Bath Chronicle*, January 1802

36 *Letters*, 267

37 Anna Lefroy, Monk Sherborne, 8 August 1862; Austen-Leigh Collection, quoted in Honan, 187

38 These journeys were recorded in Mary Lloyd's diary for 1802, now lost, though the information was transcribed by the Austen-Leighs. See *Family Record*, 121.

39 Principal sources of information about Harris Bigg-Wither's proposal are Caroline Austen's account to Amy Austen-Leigh, 17 June 1870, Catherine Hubback's letter, 1 March 1870 (*Facts and Problems*, 62) and

Fanny Lefroy's comments (Lefroy Family History) quoted in Honan, 194

40 From *Fair Virtue, the Mistress of Philarete* (1622)

41 See Reginald F. Bigg-Wither, *Materials for a History of the Wither Family* (Winchester, 1907)

42 *Letters*, 206

43 *Letters*, 206

44 *Letters*, 83

45 *Letters*, 46

46 Bigg-Wither, *Materials for a History of the Wither Family*, 59

47 *Pride and Prejudice*, I, xxii

48 *Persuasion*, II, xi

49 *Emma*, I, x

50 *Persuasion*, II, xi

51 *My Aunt Jane Austen*, 11

52 *Persuasion*, I, vi; *Mansfield Park*, I, xvii

53 Quoted in Honan, 198

CHAPTER 8: *The Wrong Place*

1 *Austen Papers*, 174–5

2 *Austen Papers*, 175–6

3 *Austen Papers*, 177

4 *Austen Papers*, 169

5 *Memoir*, 23

6 *Family Record*, 123; *Sailor Brothers*, 113–14

7 Autobiography of Miss Cornelia Knight (1861), I, 15–16; *Sailor Brothers*, 114

8 *Letters*, 239, 231

9 Sir Egerton Brydges, *The Autobiography, Times, Opinions and Contemporaries of Sir Egerton Brydges* (London, 1834), II, 38–41

10 *Flowers of Literature*, vol. I (for 1801–2), 1803

11 *Letters*, 92

12 *Persuasion*, II, iii

13 *Northanger Abbey*, I, xiii

14 *Letters*, 138

15 Lefroy MS, quoted in *Family Record*, 120. The portrait of Mr Austen was bequeathed to Anna Lefroy by Cassandra Austen in her letter of 9 May 1843 (MS Ray Collection, Pierpont Morgan Library).

16 See *Bath Chronicle*, 12 May 1802; *Letters* (Topographical Index), 592–4; Jean Freeman, *Jane Austen in Bath* (Jane Austen Society, Alton, 1969); Honan, 167–70

17 *Letters*, 94

18 *Letters*, 115, 94

19 *Letters*, 104

20 Lefroy MS; Lefroy Family History, quoted in *Family Record*, 125

21 *Letters*, 92–5; 'Have I not a hundred and twenty pounds a year, besides my half pay? cried my uncle Toby' (*Tristram Shandy*, III, xx)

22 *Letters*, 99

23 *Letters*, 92–5; *History and Antiquities of Lyme Regis* (1834), 234

24 John Vaughan in *Monthly Packet* (1893), 271–9

25 *Bath Chronicle*, 25 October 1804; *Letters*, 95–8

26 *Reminiscences*, 6

27 See verses 'To the Memory of Mrs Lefroy who died Decr 16 – my Birthday', *Catharine and Other Writings*, 238–40. The poem is discussed on, pp. 343–5

28 *Letters*, 95–7

29 *Letters*, 97–8

30 *Austen Papers*, 232–4; *Letters*, 98

31 *Austen Papers*, 232–4

32 *Austen Papers*, 234–5

33 *Austen Papers*, 235–6

34 *Letters*, 101

35 *Letters*, 102

36 *Letters*, 99–106; my italics

37 *Letters*, 99

38 *Letters*, 104

39 See Sarah Markham, *A Testimony of Her Times: Based on Penelope Hind's Diaries and Correspondence 1787–1838* (Salisbury, 1990); Sarah Markham, 'A gardener's question for Mrs Leigh-Perrot', *Annual Report of the Jane Austen Society* (1991), 11–12; G.H. Tucker, *Jane Austen the Woman* (London, 1994), 157–60

40 *Letters*, 103–6

41 *Letters*, 106; my italics

42 *Letters*, 100

43 *Letters*, 101

44 *Catharine and Other Writings*, 234

45 *Letters*, 105

46 Fanny Knight's Diary, 26 June 1805

47 Fanny Knight's Diary, 30 July 1805

48 *Letters*, 107

49 *Letters*, 108

50 *Letters*, 110

51 Thomas Gisborne, *Enquiry into the Duties of the Female Sex* (1797); *Letters*, 112

52 *Letters*, 110

53 *Letters*, 112

54 *Letters*, 108

55 Fanny Knight's Diary, 18 September 1805

56 Markham, 'A gardener's question for Mrs Leigh-Perrot', 11–12; Tucker, *Jane Austen the Woman*, 159

57 *Austen Papers*, 216

58 See Gilson, 89; Tucker, *Jane Austen the Woman*, 160; Austen-Leigh Collection, note by R.A. Austen-Leigh, and *Notes & Queries* (1947), quoting Jekyll to Lady Gertrude Sloane Stanley, 29 November 1832

59 *Sailor Brothers*, 147–8

60 John Marshall, *Royal Naval Biography* (London, 1824–35), II, 278

61 Honan, 208–9

62 *Sailor Brothers*, 136

63 *Sailor Brothers*, 144–5

64 *Letters*, 102, 108

65 *Austen Papers*, 236

66 *Sailor Brothers*, 150

67 *Sailor Brothers*, 151–5

68 F.W. Austen MS, National Maritime Museum, Greenwich, MS Aus/7-/9; *Sailor Brothers*, 155–6

69 Gilson, 433

70 *Sailor Brothers*, 154–5

71 *Letters*, 132–3

72 Lefroy Family History

73 Austen-Leigh Collection, quoted by Honan, 233; *Reminiscences*, 18–19

74 James Austen, 'Morning – to Edward', 1814

75 *Austen Papers*, 237

76 *Sailor Brothers*, 170–1

77 *Sailor Brothers*, 174–6

78 Frank Austen Memoir, quoted in *Family Record*, 137

79 *Catharine and Other Writings*, 235–6

CHAPTER 9: *Abuse Everybody but Me*

1 Humphry Repton, *Observations on the Theory and Practice of Landscape Gardening* (London, 1803), 36; see also Mavis Batey, 'Jane Austen at Stoneleigh Abbey', *Country Life*, 30 December 1976, and 'In quest of Jane Austen's "Mr Repton"', *Gardening History*, v: i (1977), 19–29

2 *Life and Letters*, 194–5

3 Lefroy MS; Stoneleigh Papers, DR/18/17/32; *Austen Papers*, 327

4 *Austen Papers*, 239

5 *Austen Papers*, 241–4

6 *Austen Papers*, 242

7 *Austen Papers*, 244–7

8 *Austen Papers*, 246

9 *Stoneleigh Abbey Pictures* (privately printed, 1921), 30

10 *Austen Papers*, 247

11 Austen-Leigh Collection, Hampshire Record Office, 23M93/51/1

12 Anna Lefroy, quoted in Honan, 226

13 *Austen Papers*, 247

14 British Library, Add. MS 42171, and Edward Cooper's letter to Thomas Leigh, August/September 1806, Stoneleigh Papers, DR/18/17/32

15 *Austen Papers*, 247

16 *Letters*, 139

17 Jane Austen's pocket diary for 1807, Pierpont Morgan Library, MS MA 2911; printed in Honan, 244–5

18 *Letters*, 116

19 *Letters*, 122

20 *Letters*, 115–16

21 Deirdre Le Faye, 'The business of mothering: two Austenian dialogues', *Book Collector* (Autumn 1983), 296–314

22 *Letters*, 114

23 *Letters*, 117

24 *Letters*, 118

25 *Letters*, 119, 556

26 *Letters*, 121, 123; *Mansfield Park*, II, vi

27 *Letters*, 119

28 *Letters*, 119–20

29 *Letters*, 124

30 *Letters*, 119; Cowper, *The Task*, 'The Winter Walk at Noon', vi, lines 149–50

31 R.A. Austen-Leigh, *Jane Austen and Southampton* (London, 1949), 16

32 *Letters*, 119

33 *Letters*, 117, 124

34 *Sailor Brothers*, 186

35 *Letters*, 161

36 *Letters*, 144

37 Fanny Knight to Miss Chapman, 30 August 1807, Centre for Kentish Studies, MS C 106/7

38 Charlotte M. Yonge, *John Keble's Parishes* (London, 1898), 92; *Letters*, 116

39 George Sawtell, 'Four Manly Boys', in *Jane Austen Society Collected Reports*, vol. III: *1976–85* (Alton, 1989), 222–8

40 *Letters*, 125

41 *School for Scandal*, II, ii; *Letters*, 126

42 *Letters*, 125

43 *Letters*, 126

44 *Letters*, 128

45 *Reminiscences*, 20; *Letters*, 132
46 *Letters*, 137–8
47 *Letters*, 133
48 *Letters*, 133
49 *Letters*, 132, 138
50 *Letters*, 138
51 *Letters*, 137–8
52 *Letters*, 129, 130, 133–6
53 *Letters*, 130
54 *School for Scandal*, I, i; *Letters*, 131
55 *Letters*, 138–9
56 *Sailor Brothers*, 191–3
57 *Sailor Brothers*, 192
58 *Sailor Brothers*, 200
59 *Letters*, 141
60 *Memoir*, 73
61 Fanny Knight to Miss Chapman, 24 September 1808, Centre for Kentish Studies, MS C 108/9
62 *Letters*, 139
63 *Letters*, 140
64 *Letters*, 143
65 *Letters*, 145, 143
66 *Letters*, 141
67 *Letters*, 143–4
68 Fanny Knight's Diary, 10 October 1808
69 *Letters*, 147–9
70 *Letters*, 148
71 *Letters*, 149–50
72 *Letters*, 151–2
73 Fanny Knight to Miss Chapman, 23 November 1808, Centre for Kentish Studies, MS C 108/13
74 *Letters*, 151, 144
75 *Letters*, 153; Fanny Knight to Miss Chapman, 17 June 1809, Centre for Kentish Studies, MS C 107/7
76 *Letters*, 156
77 *Letters*, 154
78 *Letters*, 158
79 *Letters*, 153
80 *Letters*, 156–7
81 *Catharine and Other Writings*, 238–40
82 *Letters*, 159; see *Emma*, II, xiii: '. . . for they say everybody is in love once in their lives'
83 *Letters*, 156

84 *Letters*, 161
85 *Letters*, 160
86 *Letters*, 163
87 *Letters*, 166
88 *Letters*, 173. It was widely reported that, on his death-bed, Sir John Moore had 'said nothing about God and the other world, but a good deal about public opinion in England, and his hope that it would acquit him' (Notes to *Letters*, 400).
89 *Letters*, 167
90 *Letters*, 169
91 *Letters*, 174
92 *Letters*, 175
93 Fanny Knight to Miss Chapman, 17 June 1809, Centre for Kentish Studies, MS C 107/7
94 Fanny Knight's Diary, 15 July 1809

CHAPTER 10: *One's Own Concerns*
1 *My Aunt Jane Austen*, 2–4; Chawton Estate account book 1808–19, quoted in *Family Record*, 155
2 *Letters*, 175–8
3 Hampshire Record Office, MS 18M61/BOX/A/14/1; *Reading Mercury*, 3 September 1787. See Robin Vick, 'Jane Austen's house at Chawton', *Jane Austen Society Report* (1995), 18–21
4 *Northanger Abbey*, II, ix
5 *Hampshire Chronicle*, 16 October 1775, 20 February 1790
6 *My Aunt Jane Austen*, 7–8
7 Deirdre Le Faye, 'Recollections of Chawton', *Times Literary Supplement*, 3 May 1985, 495
8 *Life and Letters*, 242; *My Aunt Jane Austen*, 4
9 *Sailor Brothers*, 209–10; MS in Ray Collection, Pierpont Morgan Library
10 *Sailor Brothers*, 218
11 *Sailor Brothers*, 220–1
12 *My Aunt Jane Austen*, 5; Deirdre Le Faye, 'Anna Lefroy's original memories of Jane Austen', *Review of English Studies*, NS XXXIX: 155 (1988), 418
13 *My Aunt Jane Austen*, 6–7
14 Caroline Austen to James Edward Austen-Leigh, early 1870; *My Aunt Jane Austen*, 7–8; *Memoir*, 78
15 *My Aunt Jane Austen*, 8; *Memoir*, 79
16 *Letters*, 328–9
17 Lefroy Family History, quoted in *Family Record*, 161
18 Le Faye, 'Anna Lefroy's original memories of Jane Austen', 419
19 Fanny Knight's Diary, 1809; Lefroy Family History

20 *Catharine and Other Writings*, 244–5
21 *Memoir*, 85
22 *Northanger Abbey*, II, ix
23 *My Aunt Jane Austen*, 7
24 Le Faye, 'Recollections of Chawton', 495
25 *My Aunt Jane Austen*, 10–11
26 'Lesley Castle', in *Catharine and Other Writings*, 110
27 *Sailor Brothers*, 221–4
28 East India Company Court Book, April–September 1810, India Office MS B/151, fols 535, 538, 655
29 East India Company Court Book, October 1810–April 1811, India Office MS B/152 fols 777, 780, 786–7, 809
30 East India Company Court Book, October 1810–April 1811, India Office MS B/152, fol. 829
31 'Biographical Notice' 1818, *Critical Heritage*, 73–8
32 *Letters*, 179–80
33 *Letters*, 186
34 William Bullock, FLS, *A Companion to the Liverpool Museum* (1810); *Letters*, 179
35 *Spectator*, no. 411; *Letters*, 179
36 *Letters*, 184–5
37 *Letters*, 182, 180–1
38 *Letters*, 184
39 *Letters*, 182–5
40 *Letters*, 186
41 *Letters*, 186
42 *Letters*, 187–8
43 *Letters*, 189, 191
44 *Letters*, 193
45 *Letters*, 191
46 *Letters*, 190
47 *My Aunt Jane Austen*, 11
48 *Austen Papers*, 249
49 *Austen Papers*, 248–9
50 Watercolour sketch, *c.* 1810, now in the National Portrait Gallery
51 *Sense and Sensibility*, III, xiv
52 Mary Lloyd's diary for 1811; R.W. Chapman, *Jane Austen: A Critical Bibliography*, 2nd edn (Oxford, 1955), 19; Gilson, 9
53 Verses, 'To Edward', 30 January 1811
54 *Austen Papers*, 250–3
55 Gilson, 6–12
56 *Critical Review*, February 1812; *Critical Heritage*, 35–9
57 Lord Brabourne (ed.), *Letter of Jane Austen* (1884), II, 269–72

58 *Reminiscences*, 26; Mary Lloyd's Diary for 1812; *Austen Papers*, 251
59 *British Critic*, May 1812, xxxix, 527; *Critical Heritage*, 40
60 Henry Austen, 'Biographical Notice' 1818; *Critical Heritage*, 76
61 Lefroy Family History, quoted in *Family Record*, 171
62 *My Aunt Jane Austen*, 10
63 *My Aunt Jane Austen*, 8; Le Faye, 'Anna Lefroy's original memories of Jane Austen', 419
64 *Letters*, 195
65 *Memoir*, 91
66 *Letters*, 202; Margaret Holford, *First Impressions* (London, 1800)
67 *Letters*, 197
68 *Letters*, 197
69 *Letters*, 196; Fanny Knight's Diary, October 1812
70 *Letters*, 195–6
71 *Catharine and Other Writings*, 244; *Lady Susan*, letter 29

CHAPTER 11: *Wild Beast*

1 *Letters*, 198
2 *Letters*, 200
3 C.W. Pasley, *Essay on the Military Policy and Institutions of the British Empire* (1810), I, 1–2; *Letters*, 198
4 *Letters*, 202
5 *Letters*, 201–3
6 *British Critic*, February 1813; *Critical Heritage*, 41–2
7 *Letters*, 201–3
8 *Letters*, 205
9 *Letters*, 205, 201
10 *Letters*, 203
11 *Critical Review*, March 1813; *Critical Heritage*, 43–7
12 British Library, Add. MS 41253, fol. 17; 'Biographical Notice' revised version, 1832, for Bentley's edition of *Sense and Sensibility*, 1833
13 *Letters*, 207–8
14 *Letters*, 206
15 Hannah More, *Coelebs in Search of a Wife*, vol. II (1809)
16 *Mansfield Park*, I, xi
17 Fanny Knight's Diary, 21 April 1813
18 *Letters*, 210
19 *Letters*, 209–10
20 *Letters*, 211
21 *Letters*, 212
22 *Letters*, 212–14
23 *Mansfield Park*, I, ix; *Letters*, 213–14
24 *Letters*, 214–17

25 M.A. Austen-Leigh, *Personal Aspects of Jane Austen* (London, 1920), 149–51

26 *Letters*, 216

27 *Letters*, 280; *Mansfield Park*, I, ix

28 Constance Hill, *Jane Austen, Her Homes and Her Friends*, new edn (London, 1904), 202

29 Elizabeth Jenkins, 'Some notes on background', in *Jane Austen Society Collected Reports*, vol. III: *1976–85* (Alton, 1989), 152–68

30 *Mansfield Park*, II, ii

31 *Letters*, 217

32 *Letters*, 216

33 *Letters*, 216

34 *Letters*, 207

35 *Letters*, 214–15

36 *Letters*, 217

37 Lefroy Family History, quoted in *Family Record*, 182; *Letters*, 231–2

38 *Letters*, 217–22

39 *Letters*, 228, 220, 223–4

40 *Letters*, 223

41 *Letters*, 229

42 *Letters*, 224–8; *Emma*, III, xv

43 *Letters*, 225–9

44 Hill, *Jane Austen, Her Homes and Her Friends*, 202; Jenkins, 'Some notes on background', 26

45 *Letters*, 231

46 *Austen Papers*, 252

47 *Letters*, 235

48 *Letters*, 235, 239

49 *Letters*, 236

50 *Letters*, 236–8

51 *Mansfield Park*, II, ix; *Letters*, 239

52 *Letters*, 238

53 *Letters*, 240

54 *Letters*, 243

55 *Letters*, 250

56 *Letters*, 252

57 *Letters*, 245–6

58 *Letters*, 242, 249

59 *Letters*, 251–2

60 *Letters*, 251

61 *Letters*, 248

62 *Mansfield Park*, III, xvii

63 *Letters*, 249

64 *Letters*, 251–4
65 'Opinions of *Mansfield Park*' collected and transcribed by Jane Austen; *Minor Works*, 431–3; *Critical Heritage*, 48–51

CHAPTER 12: *A Little Disguised*

1 *Emma*, III, xiii
2 *Memoir*, 140
3 *Letters*, 255
4 MS in Ray Collection, Pierpont Morgan Library, 16 February 1814; *Letters*, 256
5 *Letters*, 257–8
6 *Letters*, 260–1
7 *Letters*, 262, 258
8 *Letters*, 261, 258
9 *Letters*, 261
10 *Letters*, 256–7
11 *Letters*, 256–8
12 *Letters*, 260–1; *Emma*, I, vi
13 *Letters*, 261–2
14 *Reminiscences*, 39
15 *Letters*, 260
16 *Letters*, 262
17 *Letters*, 265
18 Fanny Palmer Austen to Mrs Esten, 8 March 1814, MS in Ray Collection, Pierpont Morgan Library
19 *Letters*, 263
20 *Letters*, 264–5
21 *Hampshire Telegraph*, 24 June 1814; see also William Gates, *History of Portsmouth – A Naval Chronology* (1931), 204–6
22 *Letters*, 264
23 *Emma*, III, vi
24 *Letters*, 265
25 'Opinions of *Mansfield Park*'; *Critical Heritage*, 48–51
26 *Letters*, 266–7
27 *Letters*, 266–9; 274–8
28 *Letters*, 277
29 *Letters*, 270–2
30 *Letters*, 271
31 *Letters*, 272–4
32 *Letters*, 277
33 *Letters*, 273–4
34 It seems ironic that Jane Austen should praise West's Christian iconography in a letter which accuses the Americans of lacking religion. She

may not have known that West was an American, or she may perhaps have regarded his decision to settle in London as a demonstration of his desire to reside in a nation 'improving in religion'.

35 *Letters*, 274; Elizabeth Leigh's MS journal, 20 September 1814, Jane Austen's house, Chawton
36 *Letters*, 278; Lefroy Family History, quoted in *Family Record*, 195
37 *Reminiscences*, 39; Lefroy Family History; MS in Robert H. Taylor Collection, Princeton University Library
38 *Letters*, 282–5
39 Lefroy Family History, quoted in *Family Record*, 193
40 *Letters*, 278–82
41 *Letters*, 278
42 *Letters*, 281
43 'Opinions of *Mansfield Park*'; *Critical Heritage*, 48–51; R.W. Chapman, *Jane Austen: A Critical Bibliography*, 2nd edn (Oxford, 1955), 43
44 *Letters*, 287
45 *Letters*, 287
46 *Letters*, 283, 285
47 *Letters*, 283
48 *Letters*, 287
49 Fanny Knight's Diary, 22 November 1814; *Letters*, 282
50 *Letters*, 285–7
51 *Letters*, 283; Mrs Austen to Anna Lefroy, 24 December 1814, MS in Taylor Collection, Princeton University Library
52 Reverend A.G. L'Estrange (ed.), *A Life of Mary Russell Mitford, related in a selection from her letters to her friends* (London, 1870), I, 300, 305
53 *Letters*, 288
54 *Letters*, 289
55 *Emma*, III, xv
56 *Emma*, III, xv, xviii
57 *Emma*, III, vii, xiii, xxviii; my italics
58 British Library, Add. MS 41253, fol. 19; *Sailor Brothers*, 270
59 Mrs Austen to Anna Lefroy, 24 December 1814, MS in Taylor Collection, Princeton University Library
60 *Letters*, 283; *Mansfield Park*, II, vi
61 D.J. Gilson, 'Jane Austen's verses', *Book Collector*, 33: 1 (Spring 1984), 25–37
62 *Persuasion*, II, vi
63 Mary Lloyd's Diary, 3 September 1815
64 *Letters*, 290
65 *Letters*, 294
66 Gilson, 66–7
67 *Letters*, 291

68 *Letters*, 291–3; *Emma*, I, xii
69 *Letters*, 293–4
70 *Letters*, 295
71 Gilson, 59–60 and 66–9
72 *My Aunt Jane Austen*, 12
73 *My Aunt Jane Austen*, 12; John Steegman, *The Rule of Taste, from George I to George IV* (London, 1986), 161–2
74 *My Aunt Jane Austen*, 12; Reverend James Stanier Clarke, *The Progress of Maritime Discovery* (1803)
75 *Letters*, 208
76 *Letters*, 296–7
77 *Letters*, 305–6
78 *Letters*, 297–8
79 *Letters*, 298
80 *Letters*, 300, 304
81 *Letters*, 298–300
82 Charles Thomas Haden, *Practical Observations on the Management and Diseases of Children*, published by Dr Alcock (London, 1827). See Winifred Watson, 'The Austens' London doctor', in *Jane Austen Society Collected Reports*, vol. I: *1949–65* (Alton, 1967; reprinted Alton, 1990), 194–7
83 *Letters*, 300; *The Merchant of Venice*, v, i
84 *Letters*, 301; Fanny Knight's Diary, 20 November 1815
85 *Letters*, 303
86 *Letters*, 209, 302–3
87 *Letters*, 303
88 *Letters*, 299
89 *Letters*, 302
90 *Letters*, 305
91 *Letters*, 308

CHAPTER 13: *My Own Style*

1 *Letters*, 306–7
2 *Letters*, 308; W.A.W. Jarvis, 'Jane Austen and the Countess of Morley', *Jane Austen Society Report* (1986), 9–16
3 Gilson, 71; *Letters*, 310
4 'Opinions of *Emma*, collected and transcribed by Jane Austen', *Critical Heritage*, 55–7
5 *Critical Heritage*, 70–2
6 Reprinted by William S. Ward in 'Three hitherto unnoted contemporary reviews of Jane Austen', *Nineteenth Century Fiction*, 26: 4 (March 1972), 469–77
7 Samual Smiles (ed.), *A Publisher and his Friends* (1891), I, 288

8 *Quarterly Review*, March 1816, xiv, 188–201; *Critical Heritage*, 58–69

9 R.W. Chapman, 'Jane Austen's friend Mrs Barrett', *Nineteenth Century Fiction*, 4: 3 (December 1949), 171–4

10 Ibid.

11 *Letters*, 313

12 *Letters*, 311

13 *Letters*, 310

14 *Letters*, 319

15 *Letters*, 323

16 *Letters*, 312, 323

17 'Plan of a Novel', *Catharine and Other Writings*, 230–2

18 *Reminiscences*, 48

19 *Letters*, 314

20 *Persuasion*, I, x

21 *Persuasion*, I, viii

22 *Reminiscences*, 47; *Persuasion*, II, vi

23 *Letters*, 311, 315–16

24 R.W. Chapman (ed.), *The Manuscript Chapters of Persuasion* (Oxford, 1926; reprinted London, 1985), 3–4

25 *Letters*, 316

26 Chapman, *The Manuscript Chapters of Persuasion*, 10–16

27 *Letters*, 317

28 Chapman, *The Manuscript Chapters of Persuasion*, notes to p. 32

29 Chapman, *The Manuscript Chapters of Persuasion*, 27

30 *Emma*, II, ix

31 Chapman, *The Manuscript Chapters of Persuasion*, 32–9

32 *My Aunt Jane Austen*, 13

33 *Persuasion*, II, xi

34 *Memoir*, 147

35 Cassandra's note: 'Persuasion begun Augt 8th 1815 finished Augt 6th 1816', *Minor Works*, plate facing p. 242

36 *Letters*, 319–22

37 *Letters*, 321

38 *Mansfield Park*, I, xi

39 *Memoir*, 139–40

40 *Letters*, 321–2

41 *Letters*, 318–22

42 *Critical Heritage*, 55–7

43 *Letters*, 322–3; *Life and Letters*, 333

44 *Letters*, 322–4

45 *Letters*, 326

46 *Letters*, 324: 'This is little Cassy's birthday, and she is three years old'

47 *Letters*, 328; *Emma*, III, vi

48 *Letters*, 328–31
49 *Letters*, 335
50 'The Brothers', later published as the unfinished novel *Sanditon*
51 *Sanditon*, ch. 1
52 *Memoir*, 4th edn (London, 1879), 364
53 *Letters*, 336, 326–7
54 From the evidence of Jane Austen's declared symptoms, it has generally been concluded that she was a victim of the then unrecognized Addison's Disease. See Sir Zachary Cope, 'Jane Austen's last illness', in *Jane Austen Society Collected Reports*, vol. 1: *1949–65* (Alton, 1967; reprinted Alton, 1990), 267–72
55 *Letters*, 330, 336
56 *Letters*, 332
57 *Letters*, 325, 333
58 *Letters*, 333–4
59 *Minor Works*, 453–7
60 *Letters*, 333
61 MS in Austen-Leigh Collection, quoted in *Family Record*, 221
62 *Letters*, 334, 338
63 *Letters*, 335–7
64 *Letters*, 336
65 Mr Leigh-Perrot's Will, PROB 11/1591; *Austen Papers*, 332–3
66 *Letters*, 338–9
67 *Austen Papers*, 253–4
68 *Letters*, 338–9
69 *My Aunt Jane Austen*, 14–15
70 *Letters*, 339
71 *Letters*, 340–1
72 *Letters*, 340–1
73 *Letters*, 342
74 *Letters*, 343
75 *My Aunt Jane Austen*, 15–16
76 *Life and Letters*, 392–3
77 Charles Austen's Diary, 1817, National Maritime Museum, Greenwich, MS AUS/109
78 Lefroy Family History; MS in Taylor Collection, Princeton University Library, quoted in *Family Record*, 225–6
79 *Catharine and Other Writings*, 246 and xxi–iii; *Minor Works*, 450–2. See Introduction for a discussion of these verses
80 *Letters*, 343–4
81 *Letters*, 344–5

CHAPTER 14: *Pictures of Perfection*

1 *Letters*, 347–8

2 *Letters*, 345–8; letter from Caroline Austen to James Edward Austen-Leigh, quoted in *Family Record*, 231

3 Monk Sherborne parish registers, Hampshire Record Office

4 Manor Court Book, Monk Sherborne, 1769–1830, Hampshire Record Office, MS 10M57/M6. The Courts Baron at which Francis Cullum was presented were held on 26 May 1809 and 24 June 1810

5 *Mansfield Park*, II, vi

6 *Persuasion*, I, vi

7 *Austen Papers*, 332; *Jane Austen Society Collected Reports*, vol. II (1966–75), 38–9; *Letters*, 346–8

8 Mrs Austen to Anna Lefroy, MS in Taylor Collection, Princeton University Library

9 Tucker, 117

10 It was not until 1872 that a brass tablet was erected in the north wall of the Cathedral nave which noted that Jane Austen was 'known to many by her writings'. The text chosen for this tablet was Proverbs 31, xxvi: 'She opened her mouth with wisdom and in her tongue is the law of kindness'

11 *Family Record*, 241

12 *Letters*, 344; Constance Hill, *Jane Austen; Her Homes and Her Friends*, new edn (London, 1904), 258; *Family Record*, 241

Index

'JA' indicates Jane Austen

Index

Rev. Thomas Leigh (d.1764)
Rector of Harpsden

Thomas Leigh
(1747–1821)
*mentally handicapped
and kept away from
the rest of the family*

James Leigh
(1735–1817)
*(later called James
Leigh-Perrot);
m.
Jane Cholmeley,
tried for grand
larceny in 1800,
d.1836*

Jane Leigh
(1736–1783)
*m.
Dr Edward Cooper,
and had two
children, Edward
and Janet*

1. James Austen
(1765–1819)
*Rector of Steventon
m.
(1) Anne Mathew,
and had one
daughter, Anna;
(2) Mary Lloyd,
and had one son,
James Edward, and
one daughter,
Caroline Mary
Craven*

2. George Austen
(1766–1838)
*mentally
handicapped and
kept away from the
rest of the family*

5. Cassandra-
Elizabeth Austen
(1773–1845)
did not marry

6. Francis-William
Austen
(1774–1865)
*known as 'Frank'
m.
(1) Mary Gibson, and
had eleven children;
(2) Martha Lloyd, and
had no further children*

7. Jane Austen
(1775–1817)

8. Charles-John
Austen
(1779–1852)
*m.
(1) Frances Palmer,
and had four
children;
(2) Harriet Palmer
(Frances's sister),
and had four more
children*